The Gun Digest® Book of

The 1911

PATRICK SWEENEY

Published by

Gun Digest Books
An imprint of F+W Publications
700 East State Street • Iola, WI 54990-0001
715-445-2214 • 888-457-2873
www.gunlistonline.com

Please call or write for our free catalog of publications.
Our toll-free number to place an order or obtain a free catalog is 800-258-0929
or please use our regular business telephone 715-445-2214.

Library of Congress Control Number: 2001091075
ISBN 13-digit: 978-0-87349-281-2
ISBN 10-digit: 0-87349-281-1

Printed in the United States of America

About The Covers

Front Cover

Back in service: These 1911 pistols were exquisitely restored by Doug Turnbull Restoration Inc. of Bloomfield, NY. using the same techniques and methods employed at the time they were manufactured.

Doug Turnbull, president of the company, says, "We strive to accurately recreate the look and feel of classic firearms through diligent research and painstaking work during every step of the process. We give our customers the chance to see and hold a gun that appears just as it did when it left the factory."

While Turnbull and his craftsmen can work on just about any type of firearm, they do have their specialties, among them is the Colt Model 1911 pistol. Work on a 1911 can include anything from complete metal preparation to the original specifications, re-roll marking and applying the appropriate finish as dictated by the serial number of the pistol.

"The 1911 is one of the most popular pistols out there. There are plenty of people who have a war era pistol that is not only a valuable collector piece, but also a family heirloom. We can make those pistols look like new. By the time we get done, everything will be just as it was originally produced," said Turnbull.

Write to Turnbull at: Doug Turnbull Restoration Inc., P.O. Box 471, Dept. 1911, Bloomfield, NY 14469. Phone 585-657-6338. On the worldwide web at www.turnbullrestoration.com, or contact him via email at turnbullrest@mindspring.com.

Back Cover

Ready for anything: Creating custom guns for the price of stock models Dan Wesson Firearms offers their Pointman Major and Pointman Seven with standard features for which shooters used to pay extra.

"Quality and performance are the two things we offer in the Pointman series," says Bill Jeffery. "Top shooters demand accuracy and reliability and that's what we provide in a very reasonably priced pistol."

The out-of-the-box quality of the Pointman Seven was driven home at the 2000 New York State IDPA championships when Gary Hellmers borrowed a pistol from the Dan Wesson display booth and used it to win the title.

"His other pistol was not working and he asked if he could use a Pointman Seven," said Jeffery. "He sighted in the pistol and proceeded to dominate the competition."

The list of standard features on the Pointman pistols would make a custom gunsmith see nothing but dollar signs. From the match-grade components to the beveled magazine well and the lowered and relieved ejection port, every Pointman pistol comes out of the box looking as if it just came from a custom shop.

"Using a Ransom rest we are getting sub-3/4-inch groups at 25 yards," said Jeffery. "That's accuracy you can't get even from most custom guns costing thousands of dollars and our retail prices start at $799. Soon we'll be coming out with more models and more calibers. We have something for everyone."

Dan Wesson looks to be the new name in accuracy and reliability on the 1911 frame. If the work of the Pointman series is any indication Dan Wesson Firearms will be taking production pistols to a new level of performance.

Contact Dan Wesson Firearms at 119 Kemper Lane, Dept. 1911, Norwich, New York 13815. Phone 607-336-1174.

Foreword

Is there any other pistol like the 1911? Sure, there are variations. There are pistols built along the same lines. Some have minor modifications, some have major modifications and all seem to borrow something from the original. But the 1911-A1 stands as an icon, above all the rest. Indeed, to inject a bit of Eastern philosophical rhetoric here: All others are merely shadows, while the 1911 is the sun.

But that's the kind of power this pistol has. I'm not talking about velocity, energy or an IPSC power factor. I'm talking about kind of power it takes to have some 30 pages of the Brownells catalog devoted just to one model of pistol. I'm talking about the power to have one model of pistol grace the cover of more popular shooting magazines that another weapon currently in production. On top of stopping power, the 1911 has staying power and popular appeal. Think of all the fads that have come and gone in the 90 years since John Browning designed what many call his masterwork.

Can you think of any other pistol that could serve as long as the 1911? Here is a firearm that was adopted by the U.S. military when the cavalry charge was still an accepted and effective means of warfare. Two World Wars and couple of police actions later, the same pistol was still so popular that it became the basis of several different classes of firearms competition. It has been modified for super-accurate target shooting, high-speed, run-and-gun events and ultra-reliable self-defense use. And now, when police agencies go looking for the perfect pistol for their elite units, the 1911 is being recalled to active duty.

The 1911 pistol is simple, rugged and reliable. It is a masterpiece. Yet it is a masterpiece that takes very kindly to further adornment and even experimentation. It is the one pistol that will do everything you could ever reasonably ask a pistol to do. And it will even pull off some of those unreasonable requests.

Here, Patrick Sweeney presents an in-depth look at the 1911. This book cannot be complete, because this pistol is as dynamic as the people who use it, modify it and adore it. There will always be something new for the 1911 and no one who has ever felt the heft of this American classic could ever doubt that this pistol will be up to the task.

Kevin Michalowski
Firearms Book Editor
Krause Publications

Acknowledgments

I would like to thank the firearms manufacturers for the loan of their pistols. Without handguns to test, this would have been a slim book indeed. As usual, the folks at Springfield, Caspian, STI, Les Baer and Ed Brown were very helpful. The staff of Wilson's Combat were beyond helpful, repeatedly sending more gear than I asked for, and sending it the moment I raised a question.

Bruce Gray of Oregon Trail Bullet Co. had bullets on my doorstep almost before I had hung up my phone, and sent me reams of loading data for every application. Just as my delivery driver was recovering from unloading the Oregon Trail boxes, Eric Hampton of Rainier Bullets had more boxes for him to bring.

Many others were quick to offer assistance and knowledge, and held nothing back, and I would like to mention Reid Coffield of Brownells, Jack Weigand, Joe Cominolli and Bill Laughridge. Bill Wilson and I spent quite a few electrons e-mailing to nail down details he has spent years discovering.

Please take the time when you talk to any of the manufacturers represented in this book, to thank them for their assistance. It brightens their day, and lets them know that the readers pay attention and care.

In the course of learning to write (some would say I'm still learning) I had the good fortune to meet and fall in love with a master wordsmith. As with my previous books, without the encouragement of Felicia, this book would have been more roughly written, less informative, poorly photographed and late. As much as I owe thanks to everyone else in the project, I owe her much, much more.

Table of Contents

Introduction

Mature Technology. The very phrase makes a venture capitalist's head spin. Mature technology is one that has reached the balance of tool to the job for greatest efficiency, and the only improvements that can be made are cosmetic. Some equate "mature" with obsolete, but that is a mistake.

Within its realm, a mature technology is still very efficient. The Romans perfected infantry unit combat with edged weapons, and for that combat developed perfected tools. A Roman Gladius is a short sword that looks like a straight-edged machete. It is in a properly-made example, a terrifyingly efficient killing tool. The Roman Legions worked as large teams, and each legionnaire was the others' back-up. It did no good for a valiant and dashing barbarian to crash through the front lines swinging a battle ax, as the second and third lines would simply envelop him and chop him down. As a tool for a team, the Gladius was great, and a battle ax isn't. (I know from experience, having used a battle ax in SCA competition.) Faced with a French aristocrat of the 18th Century and his lightweight rapier, a Gladius would be outmatched. The rapier by the Age of Enlightenment had evolved into a tool for individual combat, light, fast and intended for thrusting. Within its use, it is another terrifyingly efficient tool. Modern fencing, with a foil or epee is a sport derived from the court rapier.

Taken out of context, any tool or technology is inefficient. Within every context, there are some tools that are more efficient than others. And in any field, one stands out.

In the field of handguns, a firearm designed by John Moses Browning is usually more durable and reliable than other designs. It is also heavier, but he designed for durability and long service life. In the area of handguns, the Model 1911 stands out. Now nearly a century after its unveiling, the Model 1911 is still unsurpassed in many regards. Newer designs can do as well, some at less cost or with less weight. Some are "safer" only if you intend a handgun to be used by someone with little or no training, and desire fewer accidents even at the expense of operational efficiency. Few, if any will equal the longevity and durability of the Model 1911.

The Model 1911 was mature technology in...1911. To give you an example of just how advanced it was, consider a few other items that were new and exciting technology at the time. A camera would hold either one piece of film, for one shot, or you could use a Brownie, with many shots. Shutter speeds were not adjustable, except by close approximation. Film speed? If you use today's standard, where a common film has a speed of 400, a fast film of the time would have a speed of...6. A "high-speed" film of 12 would be an exotic film used by a professional. The reason so many of your snapshots of grandparents in the album show them standing still, was with a film speed equivalent of 6, on a bright day the shutter speed would have to be a full second.

Well, how about a typewriter? A manual, upright, using-a-ribbon, typewriter? The last radio station I was at had an ancient manual that took a lot of force to use. I joked then about my typing style being not so much hunt and peck as search and destroy. And the machine was only 50 years old. We used ribbons from the teletype machine to keep it going because, even by 1980, typewriter ribbons were hard to come by.

Well, lets consider cars. A car of 1911 would have to be crank-started, require constant maintenance and adjustments, had no radio (come on, a

We weren't done with the testing when this photo was taken. Could I ever wear out this much brass?

It took a lot of ammo and film to test and record the information for this book. The ammo, film and the pistols have come a long way since 1911.

radio receiver in 1911 was not much smaller than the car was!) no heater, no hard top, probably not any doors, and you would be hard-pressed to find a paved road outside of the city. The electric starter motor system was patented in 1911, and first appeared on the 1912 Cadillac line.

In 1911, radio transmitters and receivers were either experimental or military. The first commercial radio stations popped up in the 1920s. No television, no penicillin, horses were still leaving tons of manure in city streets each day, and you don't want to know what the state of dental technology was. (Do you recall Dustin Hoffman in "The Marathon Man"?)

The fastest and most modern luxury ship ever made was coming off the slips when the 1911 was tested. The Titanic was made with low-grade mild steel (by today's standards) it was riveted (it would be another 20 years before a ship near its size would be welded) and it used coal. And in a year's time it would be at the bottom of the Atlantic.

But before The War to End All Wars you could buy a pistol that would not be improved in design for the rest of the century. That is, as soon as commercial production began, after all, the government paid for the testing, they wanted the first ones off the line.

In the course of working on this book, I was in hog heaven. I've always had a fondness for the 1911. My second handgun was an Ithaca-manufactured 1911A1, made in 1943. I own more 1911-pattern handguns than any other, and have done most of my handgun competition shooting with a Model 1911. To inspect, test-fire and compare the best guns of the best makers, with ammunition supplied by ammunition companies and components makers is an opportunity not to be turned down. Obviously I have fallen in with the wrong crowd, as every member of my gun club who heard of the book wanted to know if I needed any help with all that shooting?

There were several pistols loaned to me that I hated to have to send back. The fit, finish and function of the modern-production 1911 pistol is fantastic. If you have any experience with or affinity for precision machinery, you'll find a top-end 1911A1 to be a marvel. Unfortunately, there are also the ones that don't make it. Some pistols arrived so roughly-machined and ill-fitted that I was reluctant to fire them. And a couple did not function. Rather than damn them for all time (or at least until the 2nd Edition of this book, when we look at the progress made in five or 10 years) I left them out. Not all pistols are represented. Some manufacturers could not supply a sample pistol within the time constraints of my delivering the book to my editors. Do not assume exclusion from the book is a negative mark.

I hope you'll take the information here and use it to make a prudent decision about the 1911 you will be purchasing, and the competitive, defensive or hunting application to which you'll apply it. While in the course of test-firing these pistols I filled a 30-gallon drum to overflowing with empty brass. I am of the firm conviction, based on decades of shooting various 1911 pistols, that I could have put all that ammo through the best of the pistols tested, and never had a failure. While I had to send back the pistols (gun writers do not get free guns!) I still have that brass, a lifetime supply.

You might think that after months and months of being chained to a computer keyboard, and trip after trip to the range for work and no fun, that I would be sick and tired of working with and writing about the 1911. First of all, it was never work, even when it was hard work. Second, I could never get tired of the 1911. And finally, with the manuscript in, I will be playing with several of the pistols on long-term loan, forming the basis of the second edition of this book. I hope you enjoy reading as much as I enjoyed producing this book.

Patrick Sweeney

CHAPTER ONE

A Brief History Of Perfection

A century ago, the world had just gone through a revolution. Until the 1880s, firearms used gunpowder. We now call it black powder. Touching off a round loaded with black powder created large amounts of smoke. Black powder is not an efficiently-burning compound, and high percentage of the charge is turned into ash. The black powder burned at a low pressure, limiting muzzle velocity. The smoke obscured targets. The residue was not only created in large volumes, but was hygroscopic. That is, it attracted water. The large amounts of residue impeded mechanical functions, so to work at all, a firearm had to be manually-operated. For handguns, this meant the single-action revolver was king. Because of the low velocity, large calibers ruled. I won't say that a cowboy using a .32-20 was considered a "sissy boy", but he sure would have felt more confident with a larger caliber.

When smokeless powder came along, everything changed. Smokeless powder burned with, well, a whole lot less smoke. The powder residue didn't attract water even though the early priming mixtures were corrosive. The corrosive primers meant pistols still had to be cleaned after firing, but the greatly reduced powder residue meant self-loading mechanisms could work. And the higher operating pressures of smokeless meant higher velocities for bullets.

When John Browning turned to the problem of self-loading pistols, there were already two working competitors. The Mauser company had the 1896 Mauser, known ever since as the "Broomhandle Mauser" because of the shape of its grip. Georg Luger had his improvement of the Borchardt design, recently (in 1900) adopted by the Swiss Army. Both were chambered in small-caliber high-velocity cartridges. Both

used .30 caliber jacketed bullets of 86 to 90 grains. The Luger started its bullet at 1,100 fps, while the Mauser started at a spectacular 1,300 fps. Why? Because they could. The mild recoil made it easier to shoot, and the flat trajectory meant it was easier to hit at moderate ranges. All the early self-loading pistol designers had to design new cartridges to go with their pistol designs. For his first two self-loading pistols, John Browning designed the 7.62 Browning (known in the U.S. as the .32 Auto) and the .38 Auto. The .38 Auto was shown to the U.S. Army Ordnance Office in 1898, who found some of the features of the pistol wanting, but who were impressed enough to encourage more submissions. Soon after, Browning offered a pocket pistol to Fabrique National, with its own new cartridge, the 7.65 Browning. The .32 Auto managed to launch a 71-grain bullet into the robust velocities of the mid-900 fps range. Why were shooters of the time willing to put up with such modest ballistic? Because his pistol design was flat, compact, robust and reliable. In 12 years, Fabrique National sold a million of them. The production of Mausers and Lugers combined didn't approach that figure until the production increased to meet the needs of WW I. The American revolver cartridges most popular a century ago were the .45 Colt, .44-40 and .38 Colt, all firing lead bullets of 200 to 250 grains in the 800 fps range.

As soon as the flat trajectory of the new .30-caliber bullets was noticed, shooters insisted, and manufacturers started making, shoulder stocks for them. Particularly popular in China, a Mauser with a shoulder stock was considered a useful weapon that filled the same niche for which the U.S. Army later invented the M-1 Carbine.

When Browning turned to the autoloading pistol, two pistols and their calibers already existed. Left to right, .30 Luger, 7.62 Mauser, 9mm Luger, .45 ACP

Left to right, .45 Colt, .45 ACP, 9mm Luger, .38 Colt, .30 Luger, .32 ACP

When the U.S. Army wanted an autoloader, they were already using the SAA, in .45 Colt. They didn't want to give up the power just to get a self-loading pistol.

However, in the U.S. handguns were not impromptu carbines, they were the weapon of the Cavalry. All tactical doctrine, training and design came from the influence and desires of the Cavalry. The Luger was causing quite a stir, and had just been adopted by the Swiss Army, so the U.S. Cavalry naturally tested the Luger. In the spring of 1901, the Army purchased 1,000 Lugers for test. They were chambered in .30 Luger, and were distributed among the Cavalry units for field testing and evaluation. The reports came back, and the results were tabulated. A pistol for Cavalry use had to be simpler. It had to be capable of one-handed use. It had to be more rugged, and it had to be in a bigger caliber. The 1,000 test pistols were used hard, and after the test they were sold on the surplus market. Today, a Luger collector would consider a U.S. Test Luger in any condition as a feather in his collector's cap.

The Thompson-LaGarde tests of 1904 turned out to be pivotal for the selection of a new Cavalry weapon. The two Army officers tested the effectiveness of various handgun calibers by the simple method of taking a box of pistols to a slaughterhouse and shooting various cattle about to be butchered. By today's standards, it was messy, unscientific, poorly tabulated and had far too small of a data base. But it was enough for the times, and the new Cavalry weapon had to be in .45 caliber.

John Browning had been working on automatic pistols for a few years by then. He started with the Model 1900 he provided to Fabrique National. That pistol, along with the Auto-5 shotgun, pulled that company from bankruptcy. He then proceeded to make larger pistols for Colt.

Original cartridges dating from before WWI. The 9mm Parabellum wasn't good enough for the U.S. Cavalry, they had to have a .45.

The beginning of the line was the Colt Model 1900. At first glance it looks much like the 1911, but then you see the differences. The 1900 grip is straighter. Inside, the 1900 uses two links, at the front and rear of the barrel, to lower and unlock the barrel from the slide. One noticeable detail is the feed ramp. The 1900 has a feed ramp integral to the barrel. If only he had kept that going on from the 1900/1903 series into the 1905 and then 1911. One big difference and weakness of the 1900 is the design of the front of the slide. Unlike the 1911, the front of the slide on the 1900 and 1905 is open. There is a cross wedge that keeps the slide on the frame. Should the wedge fall out, or the slide break at the wedge, the rear half of the slide could come off the frame straight at the shooter. The old .38 Auto cartridge is a mild cartridge. A .38 Super load could prove too much. Despite the fact that Browning and Colt felt the method was strong enough to withstand the .45 cartridge of the Model 1905, steel does not get stronger with age. Keep the Supers out of any 1900 pistol! If you have a 1905 pistol, keep it as a family heirloom or collector's piece and do not shoot it!

One can hardly avoid comparisons to the brief episode of the U.S. Armed Forces in the late 1980's and the Beretta M-92 (Its military designation is M-9). It seems that some slides, for a then-unknown reason, were cracking. A few slides broke and launched their rear halves off the frame. When Browning faced this problem in 1900, he designed the slide so it couldn't break. When the Armed Forces faced this problem in the 1980s, Beretta re-designed the M-92 so the broken half couldn't leave the frame.

One aspect of the introduction of the Colt 1900 should not be overlooked: its modernity. Compared to a bulky revolver, or the complex designs of the Mauser or Luger, the Colt was flat, sleek, smooth and clean. It was 20th Century! If you watch movies from the 1930s, you'll see that the country bumpkin sheriff carries a great big revolver, while the 1930s equivalent of our modern "high-speed, low-drag"

As much of a revolution as the Model 1911 pistol was, John Browning had created another revolution behind the scenes. At this distance in time it is not obvious to us, but for many shooters then the 1911 was just another Browning. In the 11 years between the appearance of the FN Model 1900 and the adoption of the 1911, Browning designed and his associated manufacturing partners made six different models of automatic pistols, with two more variations of the main six. (Browning also worked on as many prototypes) All of the six were blowback designs, not using a locked-breech system. They were flat, light, compact and reliable. For daily carry, who wanted a revolver when you could have a Browning? Around the world, Brownings and copies of Browning designs, sold like hotcakes.

In the first decade of the 20th Century, a grown man would not leave the house unless he was dressed in a suit and tie. Even factory workers would wear a coat to work, and then work in shirtsleeves. The clothing was not the lightweight fabrics we are accustomed to. A small pistol could be carried in a pocket, the smallest in a vest pocket. The Browning designs were perfect. (I might add that in that decade there were few restrictions on concealed carry, and prudent people carried pistols when traveling any distance.)

The 1911 may be Browning's crowning achievement, but the other pistols made him more money. (He was already rich from his 15-year association with Winchester) By the time the 1911 went into production, he had probably already sold a couple million of his pocket pistols, and the 1911 would not dampen their sales. The basic Browning designs for the pocket pistols are so simple, easy to manufacture and reliable, that small workshops around the world have made them. A blacksmith who can work on small parts can repair anything on a Browning pocket pistol. A patient craftsman can make one from scratch without power tools. Interested collectors have noted Browning designs made in all corners of the world, sometimes with odd local variations of the name Browning on them.

In WW I, the French decided (wisely) that they needed more pistols for their troops than the pre-war tables of equipment called for. Every French factory was busy producing other war material, so the French turned to Spanish manufacturers. The Spanish turned out millions of .32 and .380 (mostly .32) Browning-style pistols. I don't know about other parts of the country, but here in the Midwest these pistols are common. Until the manufacture of Davis pistols (a Browning derivative!), if someone brought a .32 pistol in for repair, it was probably a Spanish WW I Browning knock-off. If you're at a gun show and you see a medium-sized, all steel, blocky looking .32 with Spanish proofs, you're looking at a WW I-era pistol, and Browning's design genius made it possible for someone to create the guns in back rooms in little villages in Spain. Barring a trip to the smelter, that pistol will work for centuries to come, and its design is so simple that anyone could repair it except for the magazine. The magazine alone requires expert repair if it becomes damaged.

The Browning designs have proved so useful and durable, that a standard description of almost every pistol being made could start out "Basic Browning tilting-barrel mechanism...." The Browning designs were so popular that other designs didn't have a chance. Oh, the Luger continued to be made, but it had been adopted by the Germans, and they were damned if they were going to adopt a non-German design for their pistols. And due to its capacity and ability to use a shoulder stock, Mauser had a near-religious following in China for the broomhandle Model 1896. But anywhere else you went, you could find, borrow, buy or have made, a Browning design. Most of them the blowback design. If you think of the 1911 pistol as the longest-lasting weapon? You may be surprised to find a little Browning pocket pistol has been around longer.

The Browning blow-backs (this is a Colt .32) have been copied for a century, with no sign of stopping. Even a century ago, the little Colt was easier to carry than the big one.

For reliability, it is hard to beat the 1911. Some insist others work as well, but let's look in on them after 90 years have passed.

guys carried sleek pistols. You should not discount the effect of style on sales volume.

The Colt Model 1905 is a recognizable predecessor to the 1911. It is chambered in a Colt .45 caliber round, but the grip is still at a sharp angle and there is no grip safety. The early Colt round used a case .895 inches long, and a 200-grain bullet.

For the pistol trials of 1906, the Ordnance Department had Frankford Arsenal design and manufacture a .45 cartridge. It was very close to what we know as the .45 ACP. The case was slightly longer, and the bullet a fraction heavier. (The Frankford cartridge used a case .910 inches long, and a 234-grain bullet.) Frankford made it in two versions, rimmed and rimless. The idea was to test the subject pistols against a baseline revolver chambered for the same cartridge. Ten years later U.S. Ordnance would be chambering revolvers in a pistol cartridge, but for a much different reason.

All of the test pistols of the 1906-7 trials showed some weaknesses, but the idea of a self-loading pistol showed so much promise that it couldn't be dropped. All entrants were instructed to improve their design and prepare for the trials of 1910. While John Browning went back to iron out the bugs, the other entrants faced large problems. Of the seven contenders, only three had a chance of making their designs work well enough for the board. In addition to the Colt/Browning design, Savage had a new design and Luger had a scaled-up model of their 9mm that had just been adopted by the German Army. The Savage used an inefficient locking

mechanism and recoil was sharp and heavy. The Luger didn't seem to want to work with the American ammunition, and Georg Luger sought permission to use ammunition brought from Germany in the next trials.

In the end, Savage dropped out. Even with a delay in the tests, they could not afford the time or money to make 200 trial pistols. They were busy making rifles, and there was no assurance that a military contract for a handgun would do them any good. Luger, faced with eager buyers around the world, a plant running at full capacity, and the stubborn American insistence in .45 caliber, dropped out. (Collectors: Luger made five trial guns in .45. The location of one is known. There are four more of these million-dollar pistols out there!)

The rest is history. Colt submitted their improved pistol, and in the endurance course of the trials it fired 6,000 rounds without a failure. Were they happy? A Trooper might serve a full career in the Cavalry and never fire that many rounds! Many past and current owners of a 1911 pistol might never fire that many rounds in their lifetime. Of course they were happy. Further testing proved the Colt to be reliable, durable, and fast-firing. In one test, a shooter fired 1,000 rounds in 38 minutes. Remember, in 1911, the idea of an expeditionary force needing to deal with large numbers of natives in an uprising was still fresh in the minds of many military officers. The ability to shoot eight charging opponents in as many seconds, and reload with seven more in a second or two, was very comforting.

Skill matters more than equipment, but the right tools certainly help. Two shots, both "A" hits, both 230-grain JHP'S. Can you improve on having both empties in the air at once?

The Moros And The Thompson-LaGarde Tests.

Popular myth holds that it was the recent experience (1898 to early 1900s) of the U.S. Army with the Moros in the Philippines that kept the service pistol chambered in a .45 cartridge. Tough, wiry little opponents who used drugs and body bindings to desensitize themselves to pain, the Moros proved tough to stop using smaller calibers. This information, combined with the Thompson-LaGarde tests of 1904 (The ones where the officers shot cattle with various caliber pistols) and it was determined that the new service pistol would be .45.

Actually, the truth is a little less spectacular. Given that bullets of the time were solid lead or copper-jacketed lead and would not expand even driven through a railroad tie sideways, bigger was better. When the British switched to the .303 rifle cartridge, there were complaints that the "new service round does not stop native adversaries with the same success as the old .45 cartridge had." There are always complaints with the new, and struggles to keep the old.

And the cavalry was not thinking in terms of men. Even if the new 9mm Parabellum was a good a fight-stopper as a .45 when used against soldiers, the cavalry was thinking in terms of stopping the mount. Against horses, the 9mm was viewed with little enthusiasm.

A century-old attitude, built by centuries of experience, is hard to shake. Even today, many feel the .45 is better than the 9mm, and have constructed "stopping power" measurement methods that prove their point. (And fans of the 9mm construct methods that prove theirs is superior.) The important thing to do if you are ever considering one caliber over another is to compare like to like. Don't compare apples and oranges, or apples and cinderblocks. If you are going to use a 9mm +P with 115-grain bullets at 1,250 fps as a standard, you should not be comparing it with a 230-grain JRN .45 ACP standard load. Compare that 9mm to a 165-grain .45 +P load. All things being equal, bigger is better. Not always by much, but it is.

If you are ever in a fight, the reliability of the pistol, and your ability to hit what you're aiming at, are far more important than its caliber. As much of a fan as I am of the .45, I'd rather have a reliable and accurate 9mm when I need a pistol, than an unreliable and inaccurate .45. And vice versa. Skill matters more than equipment.

The 1911 pistol was adopted in March of 1911, along with its cartridge. The cartridge was simply the Colt 1905 case, now a nominal .898 inches long, with the Frankford bullet, weight rounded off to 230 grains. The desired muzzle velocity was just over 800 fps, giving a modern Power Factor of 185. By the time the "War To End All Wars" came along, the 1911 was the best cavalry pistol on the planet. Too bad cavalry only had a few months to go. In the early weeks of WW I combat was fluid. Units maneuvered to engage, and cavalry sought advantage. As soon as the lines were fixed, the long and glorious history of cavalry was finished. No amount of dash and enthusiasm could prevail against dug-in Maxim machineguns. Even without machineguns, no cavalry troop could maneuver and charge against a force of infantry using repeating rifles and hope to survive. What could prevail was an infantryman sneaking and crawling through the mud with a pistol and grenades, to toss a high-explosive cocktail into the gun crew's position or trenches. When it came to working in mud, the 1911 prevailed.

The 1911 was dimensioned to work no matter how dirty, and still deliver sufficient accuracy. Bathed in mud, it might rust but it would not fail to work. The Luger depended on the velocity and travel of its upper assembly hitting the frame knuckles to unlock and finish its cycle. The Mauser likewise required a precisely-machined and tightly-fitted upper assembly cycling as designed in order to work. While reasonably reliable, neither design came close to the reliability of the 1911. (It wasn't bad enough

War production means volume, and volume means not changing. The British stuck with the .455, the French with the 7.62 Long, and the eastern Europeans with the 9x18 because they already had them in production.

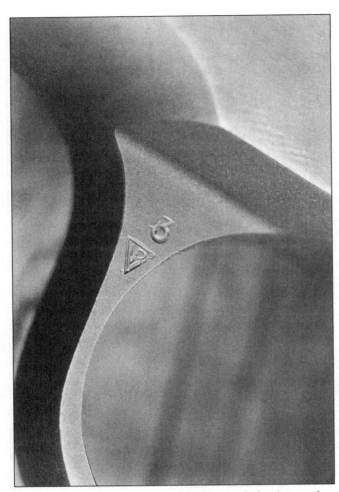

The "VP" on this Colt means visible proof, that it passed its inspection and could be sold commercially.

improvements could be manufactured and that they worked, it wasn't until 1926 that the 1911A1 came along.

The 1911A1 addressed some of the shooters' problems observed with the 1911. One change was to lengthen the spur of the grip safety and shorten the spur of the hammer. Even with the thumb-down one handed shooting style of the time, the hammer of the 1911 was known to bite some shooters. Also, some shooters with small hands found it awkward to reach the trigger. The 1911A1 had the rear of the triggerguard scalloped to provide a clearer reach for the trigger finger, and the trigger was made shorter. The mainspring housing was changed from flat to arched to improve the pointing qualities of the pistol. One change that may have seemed a large improvement at the time but made no difference by modern standards was the upgrade of the sights. The original 1911 sights had been miserable. The cavalry fired by pointing (hey, galloping horse, range of a few feet, horse and rider your target, how much aiming do you have to do?) and sights were almost an afterthought. It wouldn't surprise me to unearth a letter from a cavalry officer in 1911 suggesting that sights be done away with entirely in the newly-adopted pistol, to encourage speed and snap-shooting and prevent the time-wasting exercise of aiming. Anyway, in the 1920s the front sight got bumped up in size. The 1911 sight had been .058 inches at its base, tapering up to .038 inches. The new sights were .058 inches wide at top and bottom. Neither were more than .100 inches high. Compared to a modern front sight at .125 inches wide and .185 to .200 inches high, the old sights were not much more than speed bumps.

The next change in the 1911A1 came in 1929, when the .38 Super was adopted. The new cartridge was simply the old .38 Auto cartridge of the Model 1900, but loaded to the pressure potential that the 1911A1 design allowed. The old .38 Auto pushed a 130-grain bullet between 1,000 and 1,100 fps. The .38 Super launched bullets at nearly 1,300 fps. If it had been brought out while the 1911 was being developed, it might have swayed the Ordnance Department away from the .45. It had the weight of the medium bores, .38's and the like, with the velocity of the small calibers, the .30 Luger and .30 Mauser. If in 1911 Colt had unveiled a Model 1911, and chambered it in a .38 Super loaded to 1,300 fps, things might have been different. But they didn't, and the history of Colt is one rife with missed opportunities. As it was, the Super was somewhat popular with law enforcement, as it could penetrate car bodies much better than any other pistol cartridge did. It was also popular in Mexico, where ownership of military-caliber cartridges or firearms was forbidden.

War production creates weapons and ammunition on a vast scale. A few examples will give you an idea of the volume: The M-1 Carbine was created, tested and went into production, starting in 1941. By the war's end, the U.S. had produced nearly 6 million of them. And that was with production contracts being quickly dropped when the production committee realized the war was going to end, and they wouldn't need the several million more planned and scheduled. A week's production of .50 caliber machinegun ammo from just one plant would fill every boxcar in a long cargo train. The government had multiple plants producing 1911A1 pistols, magazines, parts and tools. There were so many made that after the war's end, the War Department (later re-named the Defense Department) did not purchase a

that when they arrived, the Doughboys brought lots of 1911s with them. They also slipped out of their trenches for night patrols with Winchester shotguns loaded with buckshot. (Pistols, grenades and buckshot, the transition to modern warfare was complete.) The most stirring example of the use of a sidearm in WW I was provided by Sgt. Alvin York, a Medal of Honor winner later immortalized on the silver screen. During his flanking of the German trenches, and his murderously effective rifle fire, a German officer figured out that one man was the problem. The officer gathered a squad, and with a shout they jumped up to charge York, bayonets first. Snatching up his pistol, York shot them down, starting with the farthest man first and working towards himself. Why? "If I shot one in front, they'd see him fall, stop and fire on me. This way they didn't know what was happening until it was too late." Some have suggested that York used a captured Luger, but we all know it was a 1911, right?

After a decade of use and serious action in wartime conditions, some improvements were suggested. By 1920, a list of desired improvement had been drawn up. Pistol production was high during the war. Following the armistice, soldiers were discharged and the Army had large amounts of perfectly-good pistols on hand, so the desired improvements had to wait. Despite a test-run contract in 1923 to see if the

This Doug Turnbull restoration is as gorgeous as the original factory finish was, maybe even better.

new 1911 until the 1980s. And then, only because Special Operations units needed upgraded 1911's, and it was cheaper and easier to buy new commercial ones than rebuild pistols in storage.

From 1929 to the late 1960s, despite another World War, a Police Action and a Counter-Insurgency effort, the 1911A1, its use and expected results stayed the same. The handgun was a security blanket in a pocket, a companion that could be with a soldier through trips to the chow line and visits to the latrine. It was handy while unloading cargo, and in close quarters inside buildings. It was also the symbol of authority. My father, during one of the few breaks his unit had from combat, was left in charge when the lieutenant had to go to the rear for a few days. Lt. Campbell left my father his .45, the visible proof of vested authority. When the lieutenant came back, my father gave him "The .45" back, transferring authority.

While the government didn't need new pistols, Colt made new pistols for the commercial market. Buyers who couldn't afford a new one bought a surplus pistol, or a "surplus" one smuggled back in soldier's gear. (The appropriation of small arms as souvenirs by American troops was so pervasive that the government issued a general amnesty. All non-automatic weapons that had "left" government service were written off the inventory, and none would be declared stolen.) In competition and in real-life use, handguns were fired using one hand, and accurate ones were picky and sometimes unreliable. Reliable ones were not always accurate. The reputation for unreliability of the 1911 came about partly because of all

those surplus pistols. Anyone with the skill to change a light bulb could swap parts on a 1911. However, due to wartime production tolerances, not all parts were drop-in fits. A pistol assembled of slightly out of tolerance parts could (and usually would) malfunction. Reliability and accuracy were not always considered opposite. In preparing for the national matches of the late 1920s and early 1930s, Hatcher reports that the service ammunition and pistols were delivering groups under 3 inches at 50 yards.

The only two bullets available were hardball, a 230-grain jacketed roundnose, and target wadcutter, a short-nosed 185-grain semi-wadcutter. There were softpoints and hollowpoints, but they didn't expand. Colt did come out with some improvements. They unveiled the Lightweight Commander right after WW II. With a barrel and slide three-quarters of an inch shorter than the Government model, it was handier to carry. And with its aluminum alloy frame, it was lighter. Light enough for daily carry without feeling like a pack mule. Then came the Combat Commander, a steel-framed Commander. For the target shooters, the Gold Cup had adjustable sights, a better trigger, and a barrel hood not compatible with the Government model.

There was one change after the war, and it was one every shooter and writer of the time commented on. The fit and finish wasn't what it had been. If you haven't seen a pristine 1930s-era pistol, you don't know what you're missing. Colt, in their Centennial commemorative book of 1936, goes into great detail about the finish. The finished and polished pistols were de-greased by dipping racks of them into vats of boiling gasoline (could I make this up?) and then immediately taken to the ovens. The gas ovens heated the pistols just enough for atmospheric oxygen to react with the steel, producing the Colt fire blue. This all happened after polishers with decades of experience had buffed them. If you want your 1911 to look like that, you have to either buy a like-new 1930s Colt, or have Doug Turnbull (his work appears on the front cover) refinish yours.

And through the post-war years, to get an accurate and reliable pistol you had to send it to a gunsmith. Actually, before the mid-1970s, you could have one or the other. It wasn't until the new shooting sport/game/training of IPSC came about that shooters insisted on, and gunsmiths had to deliver, both accuracy and reliability in the same pistol.

And still Colt was not picking up the signals. How far had their product slipped? In 1981, I won a Colt as a prize at the TargetWorld Indoor Nationals. A blued Government model, out of the box it would not feed, extract or eject hardball with any reliability. (I promptly sent it off for the obligatory reliability work.) But changes were coming.

The Eighties: Dawn Of A New Era

In the early 1980s, a bunch of gunsmiths started working in this new game, and producing a new pistol: a reliable target gun. In IPSC and other competitions like bowling pin shooting, the shooter could not stop because of a malfunction and do a stage over. He had to fix it. Rather than spend time in a match correcting problems, shooters were willing to pay to have it done right the first time. Bill Wilson was one such gunsmith (and competitor). He started working for a living as a repairing watches. Gun parts to him were huge. But still shooters were tied to the unreliable Colts, guns that had to be reworked. What was the point in buying a new pis-

You can ask Caspian to leave their name off, but why would you?

If you see the logo, you know it's good.

As a simulated real-world sport, IPSC demanded reliable pistols. What is the point in carrying an unreliable handgun into harm's way?

Springfield used to make rough-looking pistols. Now they make really good looking ones. Then and now, they're dependable and tough.

IPSC and Bowling Pin shooting consumes a lot of ammo. Even enough practice to make it to the Master level won't wear out a 1911.

tol, only to have half the parts immediately re-worked or replaced?

Enter Springfield Armory. In the early 1980s, they began offering basic guns. While Colt was making Gold Cups, polished blue Government models, and nickel plated pistols, Springfield was making basic Parkerized pistols. Oh, gunsmiths complained that they were a bit rough, and the Parkerized finish didn't polish out easily. But you could buy a

Springfield and a batch of new parts, and drop it on your gunsmith's bench for less than the cost of a Colt. For a while, Springfield even offered assembly kits. You buy the kit, and assemble it yourself.

In the background, Caspian kept working away. While they had been making parts for others for some years, in the 1980s Caspian decided to make their own name a desired product. Two problems gunsmiths had then (and now) are

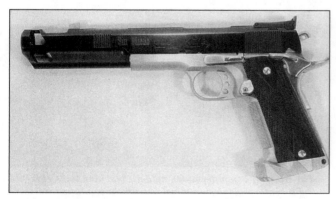

If you're serious about shooting, you need a reliable pistol (the 1911) and a good gunsmith. This Ned Christiansen comp gun is ready to win, and would never let you down.

For daily carry, the compact 1911 (this is an Officer's by Michigun) is flat, compact, powerful and reliable.

the sight slots and the fit of slide to frame. You could order a Caspian slide with the sight slots already milled. Rather than pay a gunsmith $125 to mill the dovetail and flats for a Bo-Mar rear, just order it from Caspian and get the sight milling done by them for an extra $50. (We're talking 1980s prices, here.) And Caspian's slide rails were full-sized, guaranteed to deliver a tight or gunsmith-fit slide-to-frame fit. And if all that wasn't enough, Caspian slides are hard. Many slides made through the WW II production batches were soft. For war-time production, soft slides were faster to machine and worked just as well. Until IPSC shooting came along, high-volume shooting might be something like 5,000 rounds a year. A bull's eye shooter who shot more than that was a real ammo hog. Come the IPSC and bowling pin shooters, and ammo consumption took a jump up. Even club-level shooters loading their ammo on a Star machine could burn up 20,000 rounds a year. I remember the 1982 Nationals, where Ross Seyfried was asking if anyone knew how to treat a chewed-up web of the shooting hand. Ross was sponsored by Federal that year, and had been practicing a lot. One of the other shooters suggested that the solution lay in more shooting, and his skin would toughen up. Ross turned to the rest of us and asked "Fifty thousand a year isn't enough?"

Then came Dillon progressive reloaders, and every shooter in a club could easily load and shoot 10,000 rounds a year. The serious ones went zooming past 20,000 rounds per annum. The soft slides couldn't keep up. I wore out the original slide on my Ithaca 1911A1. I replaced the slide with another military surplus one, and the chewed-up barrel promptly ate the new slide. I switched to a Caspian slide and Bar-Sto barrel, and the result is a pistol that has lasted for 15 years of high-volume shooting.

When IPSC switched from .45 ACP to .38 Super, slide hardness became even more important. Combined with Caspian's frames, you could build a durable and accurate .38 Super that would stand the wear of thousands of rounds a year of practice and competition.

In the rest of the shooting world, police departments and shooters were going ga-ga over capacity. With new bullet designs that expanded, and powders to drive them at higher velocities without exceeding design pressures, the 9mm was more attractive than ever. Combined with a high-capacity magazine, a police officer could have 15 rounds in a pistol with soft recoil, and 15 more in a couple of seconds of reloading. Each of those 9mm rounds offered better terminal performance than the .38 Special of old. Capacity was everything. Well, almost everything. There was the fiasco of the L.E.S. Rogak P-18. A double-action stainless steel 9mm pistol that held (you guessed it) 18 rounds, it was going to be the next big thing. That is until Soldier of Fortune magazine tested one and broke the unwritten rule of "say nothing bad about advertisers" and wrote what they found. It didn't work.

Still high capacity was fun, it offered advantages in a match and real life, and even "wonder-nines" worked.

Then the confluence of grass roots CCW laws and government intervention combined. In the early 1990s, states began changing their CCW laws from a "prove you need it" basis to a "shall issue" one. Under shall issue, if you apply, the state or police department you are applying through, has to prove why you can't carry. Typically, the reasons are simple: you've been convicted of crimes in the past. Suddenly people were carrying in states they hadn't before. While a high-capacity wonder-nine is fun on the range, and bearable in a duty holster, trying to carry one concealed can be a major hassle.

Then, in 1994, the Crime Bill became the Crime Law. Part of it banned the production of high-capacity magazines. The maximum capacity was 10 rounds. All of a sudden, carrying a Beretta M-92 or a S&W Model 59 became a whole lot less attractive. For the size, the Beretta or Smith is OK when it holds 15 to 17 rounds of 9mm. Limit it to 10, and it is entirely too big.

Shooters all over began deciding that if they could only have 10 rounds, they wanted 10 big ones. If they could only have 10, they wanted them in a single-stack magazine. What was old was new again, and the 1911 was once again popular. (It never stopped being so, in some parts.)

Light guns, small guns, full-size and all steel, if you made a 1911 you couldn't keep them on the shelves. While there had been those trying to steal some of Colt's market share (and even Colt tried to expand the pie) now the floodgates were opened. And even close copies of the 1911 counted, at least long enough for some manufacturers to create rare "collector" guns.

The 1911 has been copied and cloned, even by Colt. The top is a Wyoming Arms 10MM, the bottom a Colt .380 Government.

The irony of computer-aided modern machine tools making a century-old design is not lost on the manufacturers. These are machining centers at Fabrique National in Liege, Belgium. They can be switched from one model firearm to another over a lunch break.

I have three such pistols in the shop, one of which is a Colt. Colt made a scaled-down 1911 (with some design modifications) in .380 Auto. For someone used to the 1911, it made a great backup gun, or a smaller practice gun. One change Colt made was to remove the upper plate of the safety that locked the slide in place when the safety was on. Colt wanted people to load or unload it with the safety on. A friend of mine, Bart Ugguccioni, an Embassy Guard when he was in the Marines, objected to the change so much he had me notch the slide and weld the safety plate so it was just like his full-size Springfield. Another is a strange knock-off made by the Wyoming Gun Company. The one I have is a 10mm that uses a slide-mounted safety that blocks the firing pin. Putting the safety on does not drop the hammer. It does not use a Browning-style linked barrel, but it does use standard 10mm magazines. I guess no idea is too good to be re-invented.

And when it came to re-inventing the wheel, the SOCOM M-23 takes the cake. The government wanted a dependable, accurate pistol in 45 ACP. It had to hold 10 rounds, and stand up to hard use. Oh, and it had to be able to take a silencer. Instead of taking top of the line 1911's and solving the "problems" with its unreliable, undependable and inaccurate nature (tongue firmly in cheek here!) they insisted on a new pistol. They ended up with a larger, heavier, more expensive pistol that does the job just as well as....the 1911A1.

And still shooters flock to buy the 1911. Oh, it may not be entirely recognizable to a shooter a near-century ago, but he or she would still know how to use it. They might marvel at the accuracy and features, but the reliability would be known to them.

Ladies and gentlemen, I present to you, the current and future champion, the 1911 pistol.

CHAPTER TWO

How A 1911 Works - The Nickel Tour

The big questions for designers trying to come up with a self-loading pistol was, how to convert the energy of firing into a mechanical action? The obvious solution was to turn the energy of recoil into a mechanical action by moving some part of the pistol. (Of course, the obvious didn't keep Browning from experimenting with gas-operated pistols.)

Within a few years from the start of inquiries into self-loading pistols, Browning would invent a few new cartridges, cartridges that let him use the blowback principle. A blowback pistol is one where the cartridge case is kept in place during firing by the mass of the slide and the strength of the spring. The time delay for the inertia of the slide to be overcome, and the spring pressure to be overcome, keeps the slide closed to the breech until the bullet has left the muzzle and pressure has dropped. To make such designs work, Browning designed the .25 Auto, the .32 Auto and the .380 Auto. To go larger, he had to lock the mechanism. A blowback design isn't strong enough to safely contain a cartridge larger than .380 Auto. The lure of the simplicity of the blowback design has not kept experimenters and manufacturers from trying. The largest reasonably successful design to use a blowback mechanism is the Spanish Astra, the Models 400 and 600. Chambered in 9mm Largo, a cartridge equal to the .38 Auto in power, the Astra 400 has a recoil spring so stout it takes a grown man to rack the slide and chamber a round. The recoil is quite sharp. The Model 600 was chambered in 9mm Parabellum, and while I haven't fired one, with some loads it has to be downright harsh in recoil. Browning also tried larger pistols, probably because customers insisted. He designed the Model 1903

If this shooter was actually going to fire (no glasses, no muffs, no shooting) he would be starting the firing cycle. The Kimber would finish in about .04 seconds

Browning didn't design it, but he probably would have tipped his hat to Marshal Williams, who did. The .22 conversion isn't locked, and is an accelerated blowback.

To fully appreciate the genius of Browning, you need to watch a 1911 cutaway cycling (Photo courtesy King's.)

Military for Sweden, chambered in 9mm Browning Long. The 9mm Long cartridge is a .38 Auto in a different rim configuration, and for the size and recoil of the pistol, the extra power over a .380 Auto isn't worth it.

For larger cartridges, some sort of locking mechanism had to be incorporated in the design, to preclude the need for a heavy slide and strong spring. The solution for other designers was to lock some sort of breechblock to the barrel, and then unlock and cycle the breechblock. The Luger has its barrel and bolt assembly recoiling together a short distance before the bolt is unlocked and then cycles on its own. The Mauser also has its barrel assembly and bolt moving a short distance before the bolt unlocks and continues. Both designs required precise machining. The light weight of the bolt meant mud, dirt or rust could impede its travel, and cause malfunctions. An old mechanic's saying is "if it doesn't move, get a bigger hammer" that is, rather than use a higher-speed swing, get more mass involved. Browning decided to reverse the design, and rather than have the bolt in the action, he wrapped the bolt, in the shape of the slide, around the mechanism. He now had all the mass he needed. Rather than have a complicated locking mechanism, he locked the barrel to the slide with cross slots, where the interleaved slots secured the two parts together. To unlock, he first started by tipping the whole barrel down like a parallel ruler. Never liking unnecessary complexity, Browning deleted the front link from the Model 1900 series Colts, and went with a rear link only in the 1905.

The rest was refinement.

Eight Steps To Success

There are eight steps to the function of a 1911, and we will come in the middle. They are: Fire, Unlock, Extract, Eject, Cock, Feed, Chamber, Lock.

In the beginning, your pistol is cocked with a chambered round, thumb safety on, and resting in your holster. If you have a standard 1911 firing mechanism, there are three and a half obstacles to the round being fired. (Series 80 pistols have four and a half.) The three are the inertia firing pin, the thumb safety and the grip safety. The half is the half-cock notch on the hammer. The fourth, on Series 80 pistols, is the firing pin block, that keeps the firing pin locked back until the trigger is pulled.

The inertial firing pin is too short to reach the primer on its own. It has to be launched forward with enough force to overcome the tension of its return spring, and still have enough energy left to strike the primer. The hammer has that job, but the hammer isn't going anywhere right now. Theoretically, the firing pin could strike the primer. If the pistol is dropped from a great enough height, strikes a hard surface, and strikes it directly along the axis of the barrel, then, theoretically, the firing pin would have enough energy to overcome the spring and fire. The theoretical nature of the problem was not considered a difficulty until Colt considered its exposure to liability lawyers and made the Series 80 pistols. Already in a tough financial position, Colt felt the small expense of engineering was worth the diminished exposure. Not that the other manufacturers didn't care about their customers, they do. It's that the problem is so theoretical that I have never heard of a situation where it happened.

Back to our holstered pistol. The firing pin is held back by its spring. The thumb safety blocks movement of the sear. The sear holds the hammer back in full cock, and if the sear doesn't move then the hammer stays put. A thumb safety with a gap between it and the sear can allow some small amount of sear movement. One of the checks in buying a used pistol is to see if there is sear movement with the safety on. A pistol with movement must be tended to by a competent gunsmith. The grip safety prevents movement of the trigger. The trigger moves the sear, and the weight of the trigger bouncing back and forth in its slot has been known for a long time to be a source of wear and premature sear movement.

Resting it its holster, cocked, loaded and with the safety on, that pistol would never fire on its own. No, they don't "just go off." You also don't have to worry about the hammer spring taking a set. Leaving it cocked isn't going to hurt it. This cocked and safety on state of the 1911 is known as Condition One. It is perfectly safe and will never fire, but it gives some shooters the willies.

Fire

When you draw the pistol, your hand grabs and depresses the grip safety, pushing it out of the way so as to allow trigger movement. Once the sights are on the target, your thumb pushes the thumb safety off. The pistol still won't fire, for your trigger finger must push the trigger and hold it back. The trigger pushes the disconnector, which is the link between the trigger and the sear. The hammer, released from the sear, pivots forward and strikes the firing pin. The pin leaps forward and delivers its kinetic energy to the primer. The primer, being sensitive to shock, ignites and blasts the powder charge. The bullet begins its brief life as a moving object, to strike the target if your aim is good. Why can't the pistol fire if you don't pull the trigger? The hammer has a half-cock notch. If the hammer is jarred or bounced out of engagement with the sear, and your finger is not holding the trigger back, the sear will catch in the half-cock notch and prevent the hammer from falling. Doing so is very hard on the sear, but it beats the alternative.

In the Colt Series 80 pistols, there are a pair of pivot arms next to the hammer. One is pushed directly by the trigger. The first lever then engages another lever. The second lever pushes up on a spring-loaded plunger in the slide, a plunger that usually blocks the firing pin. The plunger is pushed up and moves out of the way of the firing pin. If the firing pin plunger has not been pushed out of the way by the linkage, the firing pin cannot move forward and strike the primer. Feelings can run high when discussing the firing pin safety of the Series 80 pistols. some sneer at it, feeling that if Browning himself didn't feel the need to invent it, why put up with it? Others, seeing what liability lawyers have done to other industries, feel it is the firearms equivalent of garlic and holy water.

Once firing is initiated, the bullet races down the bore, and leaves for parts unknown to it. Hopefully, those parts are known to you.

Unlock

The bullet has left, and the residual chamber pressure has dropped to nothing. I had the opportunity to view high-speed film of the cycle of a pistol, where the full hammer fall to hammer fall took nearly a minute. The firing cycle took a few seconds, and the bullet was never seen on film. The bullet is long-gone before the unlocking cycle starts.

The inertia of the bullet's launch pushes the rest of the pistol rearward. The push is generated from the base of the case. The base pushes the slide back, and the slide, locked to the barrel, hauls the barrel with it. For a short distance the two weights work against the recoil spring, and then the link gets involved. Once the slide has moved a short distance the link begins pulling the barrel down out of engagement with the locking lugs of the slide.

A compensator works two ways to dampen felt recoil in the inertia phase. One, the extra weight of the comp slows the rearward speed of the slide/barrel assembly. Two, the gases striking the rear faces of the expansion chambers create a forward force that the rearward motion of the slide/barrel assembly must overcome. The comp pulls the barrel forward.

Once the barrel lugs release from the slide, unlocking is done.

Extract

While the barrel pivots down and stops, the slide continues to move to the rear. The empty case is trapped against the breechface by the extractor. When the barrel stops, the case must continue, pulled by the extractor. If the hook is worn, or improperly shaped, or the extractor lacks sufficient tension, then extraction may not be the reliable act we expect and desire. Many small pistols were designed without an extractor, depending on residual gas pressure to blow the empty out of the chamber. The 1911 remains locked too long for that. Excessive pressure, or a rough chamber, can reduce extraction efficiency. Inspect your brass for signs of tool marks or heavy extractor hook marking to see if your loads are too heavy or your recoil spring too light.

The 1911 cycles quickly enough that it is hard to see, and hard to photograph. Most attempts are like this, muzzle up and brass nearby.

Look closely, and you'll see the slide going forward to chamber a round, with two empties in the air. The gun will be done in about .01 seconds, but the shooter won't fire again for .15. Who is waiting for who?

Eject

The empty, held by the extractor, travels back with the slide until the ejector deals it a smack. The ejector rests on the left rear of the top deck of the frame. The slide has a slot cut through it, and the ejector fits in this slot. Ejection direction and force depends on the proper location of the pivot tip of the ejector. It is fashionable to have an extended ejector, to strike the empty sooner, when the slide velocity is higher. Extension can be overdone.

If you were to install a 9mm ejector, which is very long, in a .45, you would be hurling the brass out at high velocity. Higher than needed. You would also be preventing "live eject", which is the ability to eject a loaded round through the ejection port.

The ejected brass must make it out of the slide through the ejection port. The extended ejector also hits the brass higher, lowering its angle out. If you install an extended ejector in an old slide with a high sidewall, you actually make ejection less certain.

Cock

As the slide moves back from Fire, it initially starts cocking the hammer. However, since your finger is holding the trigger down, simply cocking the hammer won't do any good. Unless the trigger is removed from the linkage, the hammer won't stay cocked. Underneath the slide is a small semicircular notch. The top of the disconnector rests in that notch.

The disconnector acts as the link between the trigger and the sear. As the slide move back, beginning unlocking, and cocking the hammer, it is also doing one more job. As the slide rides back, the semicircular notch for disconnector clearance moves back. The tip of the disconnector is depressed, and its bottom end is pushed out of linkage between the trigger and sear.

With the trigger no longer pushing on it, the sear can now pivot back into the hammer's path, and catch it at full cock.

When you later let go of the trigger, it is pushed forward by the same spring that pushes the disconnector up and back into the path between the trigger and sear.

Taking the disconnector out of a 1911 will not turn it into a machinegun. What it does is make the pistol pretty much useless.

Feed

After it has gone to the rear, extracted and ejected the empty, and cocked the hammer, the slide still has work to do. Going forward under the impulse of the compressed recoil spring, the slide strikes the top round in the magazine. With nothing blocking its path, the round strips forward out of the magazine. The 1911 is a controlled-feed mechanism. That is, the rim of the cartridge goes under the extractor hook before the cartridge goes into the chamber. Feeding in the 1911 is a hard path for the cartridge. It bangs against the feed ramp, it snaps up against the top of the chamber, it pivots over the cam edge, and all the while the slide is pushing it forward.

Chamber

Once the round is stripped off and rudely shoved up the ramp, it gets inserted into the chamber. The chamber is the cartridge-shaped opening in the rear of the barrel, and the round has to be pressed all the way into it in order for the pistol to work. If it doesn't go forward far enough, due to dirt, powder fouling, lead scrapings or a too-small or rough chamber, the pistol won't fire.

Browning designed it so the disconnector can't get back in line with the trigger and sear unless the slide is fully forward. He wanted to keep shooters from being injured by an unlocked pistol. Your chamber must be large enough to take the ammo you are feeding it. But, it must not be any larger than necessary. Too small and it won't be reliable, too large and your brass won't last very long.

Lock

Once chambered, the last operation is locking. The fully-chambered cartridge offers no resistance, and the slide now pushes the barrel itself forward. The barrel rides up the curve of the bottom lug, and nestles into the locking slots of the slide. When the feet of the bottom lugs stop against the shaft of the slide stop pin, the cycle is complete.

How Fast Is Fast?

The best shooters can shoot a 1911 amazingly fast. A good competitor can get pairs on a target with splits (time between shots measured with an electronic sound-sensitive timer) of .18 second. The really fast shooters, using compensated guns on a large target at close range shooting at warp speed, can get splits down to .12 second. Seem fast? That equates to a machinegun rate of 500 rounds per minute, and 500 rpm is sedate for a machinegun. From the experience of having heard a bunch of different machineguns being fired, and firing a few myself, I have a bit of feel for cyclic rates. (What can I say, a mis-spent adulthood?) I have been nearby on three different occasions when a 1911 "ran away." That is, something went wrong and it emptied its magazine in one burst. The sound is faster than the fastest machinegun I've heard, at 1,200 rpm.

Even with the fastest shooters, the 1911 is spending most of its time waiting for you to get your trigger finger in gear, and shoot the next shot.

CHAPTER THREE

What Is The 1911 Good For?

That is, what uses can you put it to? The 1911 is merely a tool, one that hurls a large metal projectile in the direction you indicate. Whether that projectile is then compelled to produce a hole through paper or through flesh is a decision selected by the operator. One obvious use, and no doubt the one for which John Browning built the pistol, is defense. In this world, as evolved or designed, the larger and stronger species in an ecological niche displaced the smaller and weaker ones. The same process happens on a personal level. I just watched a documentary about wolves being re-introduced to Yellowstone National Park. There had always been coyotes there, but the wolves were now displacing the coyotes. With the previous demise of the wolves, the coyotes had been top dogs for a long time. The current coyotes had a lot to learn. Since the wolves averaged three times the size of a coyote, and traveled in packs vs. the loner coyotes, the coyotes had to learn to look over their shoulder. Constantly.

Early man had much the same problem. Lacking claws, fangs, armor or fleetness of foot, he had to be wary. Early humans had to learn to make tools. In the documentary, the wolf pack in question catches a coyote stealing a meal from their elk, and rushes in with amazing silence, speed and efficiency. In a couple of seconds, there was no coyote. A wolf pack doing the same to an early man, armed with spear and stone ax, may have prevailed, but the lesson would be memorable. They would be more cautious and less enthusiastic the next time.

Today, the wolves are two-legged, and less likely to travel in packs, but the stakes are much the same. Many states have provisions for carrying a concealed weapon, and many people have gone through the process of acquiring a CCW permit. (I know of some people who have gone through the process in several states. Since many allow out-of-state applications, these aspiring shooters have filled out the paperwork for several states. The record so far I've heard was 22. Yes, licensed to carry in 22 States. And that doesn't include reciprocity, where one state recognizes another state's carry permit.) When it comes to a useful carry pistol, you are hard-pressed to do better than a 1911.

But not everyone who owns a handgun does so with the intention of carrying it and using it defensively. For some, the competition it offers is the reason to own. Just as early man used tools to create and defend, I'm sure there was competition. Maybe when clans got together at the end of the warm season, before migrating (or not) or in celebration after a big kill, there would be competitions. Foot races, stone throwing and weapons prowess would all be logical competitions. Indeed, you could make a case for the definition of man not being solely the tool-making animal, but the competitive tool-using animal.

In order to have a grasp of the competitions currently available, you have to know how they came about, and what limitations any competition operates under. When the 1911 was invented, handgun competition was already an organized activity in the United States. The U.S. Revolver Association had been holding organized matches for many years, and the new National Matches had been moved to Camp Perry a few years before. The influence of the cavalry in training and competition was inescapable. All competition was fired standing, one handed, at stationary bull's eye targets. Each string was five rounds. Why five? The Colt Single Action Army, despite its nickname of "six-shooter" is

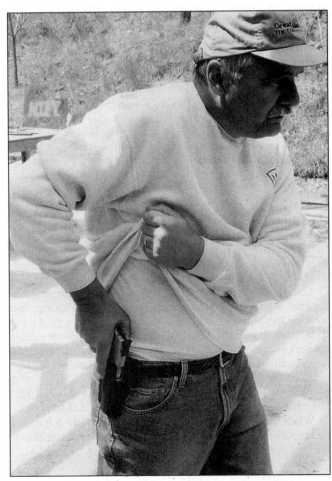

If you're going to carry concealed, you really should practice concealed. At least some of the time.

If winning means hitting, then to win you have to use both hands and the sights, too.

only a five-shot revolver. Five shots if you want to be safe, that is. You cannot leave the hammer at rest with six rounds in it, as the firing pin would rest directly on a primer. Later revolvers were safe to carry with six rounds, and the then-new 1911 was obviously safe with eight in it. Still, each string of fire remained five rounds.

Bull's eye competition has remained the same for more than a century. For much of that time there was no alternative. After WW II, a young U.S. Marine officer by the name of John Dean Cooper (Jeff to those who know him) thought there had to be a better way. Even then, it was nothing new to have a trained police officer empty his revolver at a criminal, sometimes from a range of a few feet, to no effect. The officer had proven his ability to hit a target on the range, so what was the problem? Stress management. In the 1950s, the U.S. was in the grip of the Western movie. Fast-draw and Quick-draw competitions were held all over the country. Cooper wanted something different than the then-current training or competition. Holding his matches at Big Bear, California, he modified the format of one of the types of western competitions, the "Walk and Draw." In such a competition, the two competitors are side by side, walking towards their targets. On the signal to fire, they stop, draw and fire. The first one to hit wins. What Cooper did, and what started practical shooting on its course, was ask, "What are we trying to do here?" Simply a variation of the military statement of the Purpose of the Exercise, it was a question no one in competition had asked to that point. In competition, you fired the number of shots in the time allotted, in the position required. Period. Now known as The Cooper Question, "What are we trying to do here?" requires the honest questioner/respondent to study the result of a training or competition program.

Some decades later, an aspiring competitor who was handed the position of club president defined a basic principle of competition. I modestly call it the "Sweeney Competition Rules Axis" and it is very simple: Clarity and fairness are antagonistic. I had a club to run, and I found out quickly that many shooters felt they were being disadvantaged in the matches. You (or I) can make a rule very simple, but then the competition becomes unfair. Or, you can strive to make the competition as fair as possible, and the rules become very complex. Tax law is one example. (You don't think its a competition? You aren't looking at it correctly.) A law is written, and found to be unfair. In order to make the law as fair as possible, it has to be interpreted, exceptions granted, definitions refined. The church is simple, "Give us ten percent" but the tax code runs to tens of thousands of pages. Another example is, what is a stock car? If you want to race, you'd better have that definition nailed down, or the rules will get you. Can you change the tires? How much stuff can you take off to lighten the car? What about shocks and springs? These things matter.

At Big Bear, Jeff Cooper went for simplicity. In the Walk and Draw, anyone could use any handgun. Shooters could fire it in any manner they wished. The Cowboy purists were, no doubt, outraged. Letting people shoot double-action revolvers and pistols? Unfair! But who cares, everyone "knows" the single action points most naturally of all handguns from the hip, so we'll still beat them, right?

A Deputy Sheriff by the name of Jack Weaver figured out that hits win, and fast misses from the hip don't. He developed a method of shooting two handed, using the sights at eye level. Everyone knew that shooting from the hip was faster, but Jack kept winning. "I was determined to prove Jack wrong" (Jeff Cooper in 1987) "And so I kept hip-shooting and losing. For two years. Then I switched to aimed fire and Jack never beat me after that."

If shooting fast was the purpose of the exercise, then hip-shooting was the best method. But, by re-defining it to hit-

Sheila Brey at the World Shoot 1999 in the Philippines, proving you don't have to be big, strong or a man to shoot well, even with a scuba tank on.

ting the target by any means possible, and being first, competition became a method of testing technique. But any competition, in order to test, must be relevant. Sweeney's Second Axis of Competition: Relevancy and ease of scoring are antagonistic. At the beginning of bull's eye the organizers opted for ease of scoring, and came up with a form far from relevant to the real world.

Let's back up a few years and look at another approach. In the early 1930s, the U.S. was in the grips of the Great Depression. Armed gangs roved the country, robbing banks. With lots of firepower they could overwhelm the police departments of small towns. With powerful automobiles they could quickly flee the local jurisdiction. (John Dillinger favored Fords because of their durability and V-8 engines. He even wrote Henry Ford a letter explaining why he always stole Fords if he could.) The newly-armed Federal Bureau of Investigation needed proper training, and they quickly developed the PPC. The Police Pistol Course was a marvel of the time. When everyone else was thumb-cocking their revolvers, the FBI was shooting double-action. When everyone else was practicing at 25 and 50 yards, the FBI insisted on training closer, much closer. And, they used all six shots in a revolver. It was amazing and revolutionary. And as soon as it was accepted as THE training program, it was cast in concrete and not changed one iota. I was reading articles in the 1980s of FBI training, showing agents firing from a crouch, without using the sights, and with their left arm clasped across their chest. In 1935, PPC was relevant, by 1985 it wasn't. It hadn't been since 1965, but those in charge weren't paying attention. It took a lawsuit to change the FBI, but more on that later.

The Walk and Draw in Big Bear was fun, but had limited relevancy. It was also boring after a while. To expand, the competitors began constructing scenarios, stages with a particular problem in mind. Some have gone on to become famous and embedded in the lexicon. Others faded. Everyone who has gone to a practical match and listens long enough will hear about "El Presidente" but only old-timers know of the "Guatemalan Exercise."

The stage conduct was simple. A stage was constructed, the targets positioned, and the predicament explained to the shooters. Each shooter was then free to solve the problem in his own manner. But how to score the attempts? A simple point total wouldn't do, because in real life time was of the essence. Fast shooting with misses doesn't get the job done in real life. And who is to say what the "correct" time was in which to solve any particular problem? The solution was a scoring method called "Comstock." The points earned by shooting would be divided by the time it took to shoot. Faster was better, until dropped points or misses started piling up. The stage was set, and the many eager readers of Jeff Cooper's magazine articles and books wanted to try this new shooting.

Meanwhile, bull's eye shooters kept on doing what they had been doing the whole 20th century. The times, distances and targets did not change. The FBI PPC had gone from an innovative training program to a qualification course and a competition. In the late 1960s, the organizers of PPC were at an impasse. The shooting times for each string had been laid out at a time when real men shot real (i.e. full-power) loads, and reloaded from their pockets or loops on their belt. The invention of speed loaders threw all the times out the window. The center ring, the "V" or 5-point ring on the target, was 8 inches across. As an example of the predicament organizers faced, one string of fire calls for the shooter to fire six shots, reload and fire six more, at 7 yards. This is to be done in 25 seconds! Loading from a pocket or belt loops (this is with a revolver, no one shot PPC with an automatic back then) 25 seconds was just enough time. With a speed loader, 25 seconds was interminable.

The solution? Rather than decrease the times, the organizers shrank the scoring rings. The "V" ring went from five points to 10, and from 8 inches to the size of a playing card.

It is a demonstration of Sweeney's Second Axis at work in rule changes; by making it easier to score, they made it less relevant. In their defense, timers that worked from the sound of the shot would not be invented for many years. But the primary problem was insistence on being able to run a whole line full of shooters at once. If they are all shooting at the same time, they have to face the targets for the same amount of time. The only way to separate the top shooters was to make the center so small it was difficult to hit.

In 1976, a collection of competitors and trainers in the new practical shooting movement gathered in Columbia, Missouri, to organize. What came out was IPSC, the International Practical Shooting Association. The idea was to codify the burgeoning practical shooting movement, and keep it from fragmenting into a hundred splinter clubs. From that, everything else sprang. Unlike PPC or bull's eye, each course would be different. Also, the target was fixed in size, and each shooter took however much time it took him or her to solve the problem.

Modern Competition

So, why compete? After all, ammunition is expensive enough, why add to the cost of shooting by paying someone for the privilege?

Because it is fun, and you will learn things in competition that no amount of solitary practice will ever teach you.

In many forms of competition, the biggest guy, the one most inured to pain, is likely to be the victor. Shooting, on the other hand, requires good hand-eye coordination and the ability to concentrate and focus. A small shooter can be a good shooter, and even a winning shooter. Women are not handicapped because of their size. Don't think so? Two women practical shooters who come quickly to my mind are Lisa Munson and Kay Clark-Miculek. Lisa might be 5 feet tall, and could run over a hundred pounds in a driving rain storm if she was wearing her competition gear, and all the magazines were loaded. Kay is not much taller and just as slim. Both will do well in any competition they enter, besting most of the men present. Small size is not a handicap, and large size is not necessarily an advantage.

An added bonus to competition (at least in the practical shooting sports, I haven't shot at enough other kinds of clubs to get a good read so far) is that the members of a club, and competitors in a match are very egalitarian. As my girlfriend, and several other women friends I have taken to the range have all said "It was the most non-sexist environment I've ever been in." Now, I would like to think that it was due solely to my sterling character and that of the shooters I hang out with, but I can't take all the credit. Competition does. It would be very hard for a knuckle-dragger to persist in his sexist attitudes and opinions when he is being

After the match, but before the scores are posted, everyone relaxes and chats. No bragging, no whining, just a sense of accomplishment.

regularly beaten at the range by the women who shoot in the matches. There are men shooters who do hold unsavory opinions. However, you are not likely to see them at matches. I guess the beating their self-image has to take is too much, when being bested by a "slip of a girl."

Competition builds character. Since the scores are posted, it is hard to brag about how well you are doing if you aren't really doing so well. Many shooters view whining about the bad breaks of a stage or match as being close to unsportsman-like conduct. Your fellow shooters will help you commiserate over a bad shot, or the steel that didn't fall, but if you are perceived as whining about it, you can count on having lots of elbow room. The others will avoid you.

As for lessons learned, every experienced shooter can tell you many tales of new shooters who had been "practicing" on their own before they shot a match. (Probably themselves.) In many cases, the new shooter found magazines that wouldn't work, ammunition that was balky, belt gear that couldn't stand up to the hard use of a match, and practice that wouldn't stand up to the pressure of competition. If you have tested your gear in a match, you can depend on it elsewhere.

And there is the "Loot and Glory" aspect of competition. Many big matches have prize tables, with money, equipment and even guns being given away as prizes. I have won many guns, much ammunition, holsters, parts, accessories, reloading gear and components, and two years at Second Chance came "that close" to winning a Mercedes. Not everyone gets the loot and glory, but striving for it is fun, even if you don't get it.

So, what kind of competition should you consider? For that, you have to know a little about each kind. Competition with the 1911 can be divided into three broad categories, and in each the competitions differ sometimes in nuance and sometimes in large matters. In many of these matches, the 1911 is not the only, or even the primary handgun being used. But, if you show up at any of these with a 1911, you can enter and play.

The first group includes the competitions that teach (or require) marksmanship, but not additional skills.

The second group teaches marksmanship and other skills, like drawing from the holster, reloading, working under tight or self-selected time limits and dealing with increased stress.

This Caspian, built as an IPSC/Bowling pin gun, is plenty accurate enough for Bull's eye, PPC or The Bianchi Cup (a 25-yard group.)

The third type teaches all of the above, but adds the use of tactics, cover, movement and decision making.

While an entire book can be (and in many cases has been) written on each, I am providing a summary and discussion of each. The idea is give you a flavor of the match, so you can decide which ones to seek out and try.

For those who insist, I have arranged the various types of competitions in which you are likely to see 1911 pistols. These are in order from least to most relevant to those who are concerned about carrying for defensive purposes.

In the first group, we have Bull's eye, PPC and the Bianchi Cup.

Bull's Eye

The NRA has been organizing competitions ever since its founding in 1875. Bull's eye shooting is done at many old-line gun clubs, and for many shooters it is the only kind of competition there is. In outdoor matches, the distances are 25 and 50 yards. For indoor matches, the common distance is 50 feet, using reduced size targets.

You'll be assigned a flight, or group of competitors who shoot the targets at the same time. You are all shooting the same course, or string of fire, starting and stopping at the same time. Once you are done, you clear your gear out and relinquish your spot to the next shooter. The next time your name is called, you'll be shooting a different string of fire.

All shooting is done standing, with the pistol held in one hand. There is no holster work, no reloading, and a competitor is allowed to re-shoot a string for an "alibi" or malfunction.

The time frames are "Slow", "Timed" and "Rapid" fire, the fastest of which is slow by many other competitions'

measurements. The equipment used is divided into three calibers, with the largest having another separation. The times and distances are the same, and each competitor has to use a .22 rimfire handgun, an any-centerfire handgun, and a .45 pistol. The .45 was also sub-divided into the Service Pistol category. Many competitors are now using the Beretta, as it is now the service pistol, but a very-plain looking 1911 in .45 still qualifies. (The definitions are exacting, and you should write the NRA to make sure your guns fit the specifications.)

A full course involves 90 shots fired with each of the three, 270 rounds fired, and with 10 points for the center, a potential total of 2,700 points, and for obvious reasons called the "2,700 course."

In .22, few shooters use a 1911. Most conversion kits just aren't accurate enough and points matter. Those conversion kits that are accurate are closely held and never loaned. However, since rimfire ammunition presents essentially no wear to a barrel, even a 50-year-old target pistol is competitive. The ammunition is whatever is the most accurate .22 long rifle ammunition in your particular handgun.

In Any Centerfire, the selection for a pistol has been a puzzling one for many shooters. Select a .38 wadcutter pistol, for lower recoil, and put up with the occasional need to shoot alibis? Or use a .45, and use reduced-power (although not as soft as the .38) ammunition? The improvement in technology brought about by the IPSC shooters poses a third way. A .38 Super. The built and tuned 1911 will cost the same, whether it is built as a wadcutter or Super. The Super can be just as accurate. The Super will be absolutely reliable, in a way that the wadcutter gun could never be, and magazines cost less. A .38 wadcutter magazine can run $60 to $75, and still have to be tested for reliability. A .38 Super magazine can be had for $25, with no questions as to its reliability.

The one drawback to the Super is the need for reloading equipment. There is no off the shelf match ammo in .38 Super. But, the savvy shooter will be reloading anyway, for cost and to tune the ammunition to the gun, so it is only a small problem. In the Any Centerfire category, shooters will use the softest loads that will cycle, and those that shoot as accurately as possible.

IPSC shooters have brought another boon to the Bull's eye shooters besides accurate and ultra-reliable pistol. Red-dot sights. With aging eyes, some middle-aged Bull's eye shooters cannot shoot as well as they used to. The red dot sight makes aiming less tiring and focusing easier.

While red-dot sights are popular in the other categories, they are not allowed in the Service Pistol category. In .45, you can use the softest load that cycles accurately, but for Service Pistol you have to use full weight and full-power hardball. (The service pistol category handgun of many competitors was also known as a "Hardball gun", to differentiate it from the lightly-sprung .45 used in the .45 portion of the match.) Scoring of a full match is the total of .22, Any Centerfire and .45. The Service match is a separate match.

Bull's eye matches will not always be all three categories. Some indoor matches will be .22 only, and others will forego the Service pistol category. A Bull's eye match is what the organizers want it to be, within the stated time and distance limits.

Of the matches in the first group, Bull's eye is the only one that offers nothing but marksmanship. Not only do you not need a holster, using one will brand you weird. And you will not be allowed to draw from it during the conduct of the match. Bull's eye shooters bring their pistols to the range in a luggage-like hard case. Bull's eye isn't easy. It takes a large amount of practice, discipline and work to start seeing results. It just isn't relevant to concealed carry

PPC

First the bad news. The organized PPC matches held under the auspices of the NRA are limited to law enforcement personnel only. If it is an NRA-sanctioned match, you can't shoot in it without a badge, even if you are an NRA member. (I have written to the NRA many times, and they will not budge on this matter. "Law enforcement training is not for the civilians," they say.)

The good news is that many PPC leagues don't care where you're from. Many matches also don't care. Do you own that gun legally? Can you follow instructions and stay safe? Then the sign-up line forms on the right. Not a police officer? Not a problem.

I shot PPC with the local sheriff's department Wednesday night indoor league for a number of years. Back then, I was not only the only one shooting the course with a .45 auto, I was the only one shooting with a pistol. Now, many more shooters are using pistols. The first thing to keep in mind is that you cannot have a .45 load that is too soft, provided it works your pistol reliably. Load the softest-shooting .45 load that you can get to reliably cycle your pistol, and provide good accuracy. A good choice is a 185-grain semi-wadcutter loaded with enough TiteGroup to get you 600 fps. You'll probably have to use a lighter recoil spring.

As with Bull's eye, the indoor and outdoor courses differ in distance and target size, but not times. The outdoor target uses the "B-27" target, which is the black silhouette you may be familiar with. The outdoor target seems the size of a bed sheet compared to other targets, but the only part that matters are the inner rings. Indoors, you shoot on the reduced B-27, or "B-27R".

Unlike Bull's eye, PPC invariably uses turning targets. Your time starts when the targets face you, and ends when they turn away. You will have to draw from a holster, and reload against the clock. However, you do not do much moving.

You will be on the line, as in Bull's eye, with a group of competitors who are all shooting the same string of fire. The targets all turn out and back together. You shoot one target and, depending on the range layout, either move back to the farther distance or move to the next range, one set up for the farther distance. The indoor course requires 60 rounds to fire, while the outdoor course takes 150. The outdoor course has the same strings and time limits, but repeats at different distances.

Indoor PPC

The first string starts at 7 yards. When the target turns, you have 20 seconds to fire six rounds, reload and fire six more. The time used to be 25 seconds, but that was too slow even for PPC.

Indoors, you'll do the rest of your shooting at 50 feet. The second string is 18 rounds, fired in 90 seconds. Six shots kneeling, six shots left-hand barricade and six shots right-hand barricade. Unlike other competitions, when you shoot around the left side of a barricade in PPC, you must hold your handgun in your left hand. You can support it with the right, but you must change hands. Visa-versa for lefties.

At the end of the first 30 rounds, you pull the first target down and replace it.

The second target has two strings of fire, both shot at 50 feet. The first string is six shots in 12 seconds. This is a difficult string, mostly because the 10-ring is so small at the farther distance. When I shot PPC with a .45 Auto, I carried a 596 average, and this string was where I dropped points.

The second string is the final 24 rounds. On the same target, you fire six shots sitting, six shots prone, six shots right-hand barricade, and six shots left-hand barricade. The time for this is two minutes and 45 seconds. Basically forever.

The indoor PPC course is always fired for the full course of two targets, 60 shots, 600 points. Since it is done in a relatively short time period, many competitors will re-enter the match, shooting in the Open Revolver class, Pistol class, Service Pistol class, and any others that are offered. The best definition I heard of PPC, back when it was shot only with revolvers was "Double action, position Bull's eye." It isn't double-action only any more, but it is still Bull's eye fired from different positions.

The outdoor PPC course uses many of the same time limits and strings of fire, but repeats at different and longer distances. For instance, the first stage of indoor is fired at 7 yards, while outdoors the same strings are fired in the same time limit at 7 and then 15 yards. Then it is done twice again at 25 yards, with a 35-second time limit.

The shooting strategy differs slightly from the indoor to the outdoor course. Indoors, you try to punch the center out of the first target at seven yards, so you can use the hole as your aiming point for the next 18 shots. Outdoors, once the shooters get back to 50 yards, they use their sights to change their aiming point. Instead of locking the sights in the middle of the black, they use what is called the "neck hold." Sights such as an Aristocrat rib use a sliding adjustment, or knurled wheel, and for the longer range settings they have set up the sights so shooting at the head, holding at the base of the neck, drops their shots into the X-ring. Relevant to the real world? No, but it gets you more points and more X's.

It's also fun, and shooting indoors in the winter means PPC in the minds of a large number of shooters. After all, you don't have to worry about losing brass and magazines in the snow.

While the course calls for drawing from a holster, the time limits are not so short that the draw is difficult. The time limits are stated and generous. You will learn some position shooting and reloading, but mostly PPC is marksmanship.

Bianchi Cup

The Bianchi Cup came about from the efforts of John Bianchi of Bianchi holster fame, and Ray Chapman. As the newly-formed practical shooting efforts diverged further and further from the traditional shooting sports, they sought a bridge between the old and the new. The idea of a match that blended the requirements of all the shooting disciplines,

While you don't need blinding speed on the draw in The Bianchi Cup, a fast holster is a comfort. This Hogue Power-Speed holster is plenty fast enough for any game.

but was approachable to them, had appeal. The match was designed not as a tactical or technique testing ground, but as a meeting ground for all competitors.

The Bianchi Cup sometimes differs in format from the other precision matches, in that you may be organized into squads. Each squad moves as a group from course to course. Once on a course, the members of the squad then shoot the course. If the course is set up to accommodate two or four shooters at once, then you shoot in pairs or fours. If a club only has one falling plate rack (common) then you go through singly.

The Bianchi Cup consists of four stages of fire, The Practical, The Mover, The Falling Plates and The Barricades. Each stage is requires 48 rounds. The total is 192 rounds, with a maximum score of 1920.

The Bianchi Cup uses a different target than the other precision competitions. While it has circular scoring rings, they are pressed into a buff cardboard target, and not easily seen from a short distance. Again, the target was intended to be a blend of the old and new, approachable by both.

The Bianchi Cup followed the path of unrestricted IPSC competition, with equipment becoming more and more specialized and refined. The ultimate Bianchi Cup gun ended up being a multi-thousand dollar revolver or pistol, that had its only use in a Bianchi Cup match.

In the last years of the 1990s, the Bianchi Cup organizers decided that to attract more shooters and offer a safe haven from the equipment race, they would have a Stock category. (Sound familiar?) To completely shut down the equipment race, they even went so far as to prohibit the use of the barricades for support. (More of the clarity vs. fairness at work, this time in favor of clarity.) The Bianchi Cup stock is very strict, but an accurate and stock 1911 is perfect for use in the stock class. (Unless you are a dedicated revolver shooter, where for you a box-stock revolver will work nicely.)

The choices for a Stock Bianchi Cup 1911 revolve first around caliber. The .45 offers a bigger hole in the target. Before you snicker, the Open division has been won each year with a perfect score for over a decade now. The Stock division will too, someday. Points matter. The use of a 9mm or .38 Super (a .38 wadcutter gun is out from lack of reliability and magazine capacity: no alibis, and six-shot strings.) offers lighter recoil, and by using a faster bullet you need less lead on the mover. The shorter your lead the less your score is hurt by a small mistake.

The Bianchi Cup also differs from the precision matches in having a threshold of power. Your ammunition must exceed the Power Factor of 135,000, or your score is zero. In Bull's eye or PPC, so long as your bullet fully penetrates the target and its cardboard backer, it is powerful enough.

The specialized equipment kept attendance down, but the new Stock category should change that. In USPSA/IPSC competition, the Limited category soon overtook Open, and many clubs report that the ratio of entries is two-to-one, Limited to Open. The Stock category in the Bianchi Cup should do the same.

In the Second group, we have Bowling pins, The Steel Challenge, and the Handgunner Shoot-off.

Bowling pins don't seem so tough. All you've got to do is hit them, right? Wrong.

Bowling Pins

To describe the essence of bowling pin shooting is very simple. You place a set of bowling pins on a table (preferably steel) and stand back 25 feet. Start with the loaded handgun in your hands, resting on a three-foot high rail. On the start buzzer lift your handgun and shoot them off as quickly as possible. The fastest time wins. Sound silly? You bet it does. Is it fun? So much so that shooters will travel long distances to shoot a match. An indoor range an hour's drive from me has matches in the winter, and competitors will stay later than the staff wants to on a Sunday night, shooting pins.

With bowling pins we begin our look at competitions that require reactive targets. In earlier competitions, the target does not react other than to be perforated. A bowling pin moves, and that adds complexity to the problem. The moving pin draws your eyes away from the sights. Since the pin must leave the table, you must be sure it gets off, but you must also shoot the next pin. Competitors who watch the pins shoot poorly. Targets that fall, or clank, add complexity in other matches, too.

Your load must be accurate enough to place every shot on a playing card-sized target at 25 feet. Even an out of the box 1911 can do that. Lest you think bowling pin shooting is some inaccurate hosing match, it is far from it. Unlike other targets that have scoring rings, bowling pins are an all-or-nothing target. While the "sweet spot" is that playing card, the rest of the pin scores you zero. A pin hit a glancing blow only spins and topples over, and still must be knocked off the table with a follow-up shot.

Where can you shoot pins? Any gun club that can find a backstop for the tables, and 25 feet of firing room. The big show has been Second Chance, held each summer near Traverse City, Michigan. Second Chance is currently on hiatus, but club and regional matches are held throughout the Midwest in the good weather months. Pin shooting seems to be concentrated in a belt of activity from Pennsylvania through the Midwest and into Iowa. There are hot spots of pin activity in New England and the Pacific Northwest, but the warm states in the South don't seem to do much. I think snow is a factor. Pin shooting is a stationary sport. Who wants to slip and slide over ice and snow while shooting? My own club practices even through the cold months, although we switch to shotguns in the depth of winter. (Easier to find empties in the snow.) As I write this, there is 36 inches of snow on the ground outside. If our club was not right in the middle of excavating a new pin range, I'm sure someone would be out there practicing. One of the attractions of pin shooting is that you can do a lot of shooting.

At pin shoots, there are no squads, or flights. You come to the line when your name is called, and set up your gear to shoot your event. The pin setters set up your tables for the event you are shooting, and you shoot along with the rest of the line when the start signal goes off. At Second Chance, there was room on the line for 10 competitors or teams at once. You could be out there with nine to 29 other shooters.

Most pin matches will have both the Main Event and Optionals. The Main Event is Five Pin. Five pins set on a table, three on the table and two on an upper shelf. The pins are set 3 feet from the back of the table. The Main Event is six tables fired each for a time. The total of the five fastest tables is your score.

The 3-foot setting in the Main Event (and some Optionals) requires a healthy smack of the pins to move them off the table. Most pin shooters use a load that has a Power Fac-

Pin shooting doesn't require running, jumping or crawling. Just fast and accurate shooting with full-power loads.

tor of 195, or a bit more. Some use a lot more. Top pin shooter Ned Christiansen shoots a five-pin load that has a PF of 220. Opinions vary as to whether to reach the desired PF with mass or velocity. Many shooters use the 1911, and most of them use one in .45. The majority seem to go with a full-weight bullet or one close to it. One popular choice is the Speer 200-grain jacketed hollow point launched at just under 1,000 fps. The load is 6.3 grains of WW-231. It is so identifiable as a pin load that many shooters use shorthand to describe it: "Six-three and a Speer." On the top end of weight, a common load features a 230-grain jacketed hollow point at 850 fps. On the bottom end, loading a 165-grain bullet, you have to push it 1,180 fps to make the power.

The Main Event is divided into three equipment categories and two groups of ability. Depending on the handguns you use in the Main Event, you can enter one, two or all three of Space Gun, Pin Gun and Stock Gun categories. In all three categories you are limited to eight shots in the gun. A Space Gun is one with a compensator and a red dot sight. A Pin Gun may have a comp but no red dot sight. A Stock Gun must be no larger than a Government Model, and cannot have a compensator. However, it may be ported through the slide and barrel. A Stock Gun (for five-pin) can be ported, or have a hybrid barrel, provided it is not longer than a 5-inch government model.

Why these categories? Pin shooting is first and foremost a sport (although it is very instructive in some aspects of defensive shooting) and the originators wanted to keep the

Only in pin shooting would this beautiful 1911 be a Stock pistol. Ned Christiansen (Michiguns) built this Hybrid-ported .45 for Master Blaster Jeff Chudwin.

equipment race under control. The Space Gun category is for those who want to shoot their IPSC race guns. Yes, most race guns are .38 Super, but we have found a curious thing: velocity works. While an old IPSC load would have a PF of 175 to 180, the light bullet (115- or 124-grain) would be going as fast as 1,565 fps. Even though the numbers indicate the load is light, pins hustle off the tables when hit with such a load. The Pin Gun category is for the old single-stack

This old and semi-obsolete IPSC race gun gets a new lease on life as a pin Space gun.

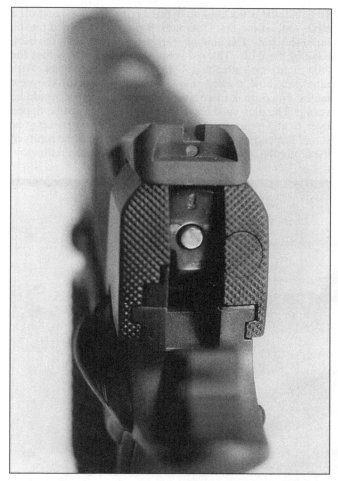

As a carry gun and a pin gun, this Michiguns .45 excels.

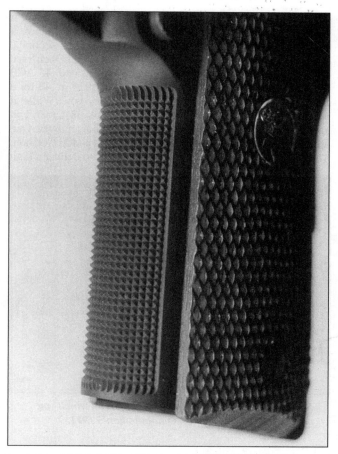

Pin shooters do not neglect checkering, as found on this Michiguns 1911.

compensated handguns. With the need for magazine capacity, optics and a compensator in IPSC competition, the old comp guns languished in gun safes across America, except for pin shooting. The Stock Gun category is, well, stock. With the newer generation of 1911s currently available, you wouldn't even have to change the sights to have a competitive gun. In the old days we would fuss and tune a "stock" gun to get the best performance. Now, I'd just use one of a host of 1911's right out of the box. Most of the guns we test in this book would be capable of shooting stock and winning, in the right hands. Yes, the hard-core competitor will add porting, but some people will do anything to win.

Not everyone uses a 1911 to shoot pins, but if you show up with a 1911 you will be in good (and fast) company. The trick is to hit each pin on its "sweet spot," an area about the size of a playing card, with the first shot. "One shot, one pin" is the mantra of the successful bowling pin shooter.

How fast is fast? That depends on which category you shoot. At Second Chance, the competitors were divided by their track record. Successful pin shooters, those who had won an Optional, or placed high enough in Five-Pin, were elevated to the status of Master Blaster. Those not elevated were termed Ordinary Standard Shooters. (Lest you think the term derogatory, there are some really fine shooters who are successful OSS, and wish to stay there.)

The speed varies depending at which club you shoot, and how many Master Blasters shoot there. At a competitive club, the winning time for a MB in Five-Pin will be 20 seconds for five tables. For the OSS, it will be under 25. Generally, the winning times with a Space Gun will be a second or two faster than those of shooters in the Pin Gun category, and Pin Gun a second or so faster than Stock. But not always.

If you enter a pin match and shoot all three categories, you have a minimum of 90 rounds to fire. Many will fire more, as it is common to fire a second time on the last pin, even when hit, in order to speed its exit from the table. If you miss, you need more shots. If you run dry on a table, it is your responsibility to reload and continue. If you leave a pin on the table you get a maximum time run of 15 seconds.

A typical Five-Pin battery would be an IPSC Open race gun in .38 Super for the Space Gun, a compensated .45 ACP for a Pin Gun, and a slightly modified plain 1911 in .45 for a Stock Gun. The choice of calibers is up to you. While it would be a rare race gun built in anything but .38 Super, you can use any caliber that generates enough horsepower. One approach is that used by Ken Tapp. He shoots a .400 Cor-bon. The .400 Cor-bon uses a heavy enough bullet to deliver a high

Second Chance had a submachinegun event, which you could also enter with your (semi-automatic) 1911.

power factor, but with plenty of velocity. The large powder charge feeds a compensator and keeps the muzzle down.

Optionals

Once your Main Event entries are done, you can re-enter the Optionals. (Every pin shoot will insist you shoot your Five-Pin entries before shooting any Optionals.) It is a rare pin shoot that doesn't have Optionals of one kind or another. At Second Chance, Optionals also included events specifically for revolvers, rifles, shotguns and submachineguns, as well as team events. I'll only cover the ones you can shoot with a 1911, and ones that you are likely to encounter at any pin match you might enter. There are also local variants, depending on the tables a club might have, or tradition.

9-Pin

While pin shooting when it started was very popular, it was not friendly to 9mm handguns. The 3-foot setting was too much for any 9mm load to overcome. Even today, a 9mm +P+ load is hard-pressed to deliver a PF higher than 160, and that is not enough to reliably push a pin 3 feet off a table. One of the first Optionals, 9-pin was designed for the 9mm shooters. The nine pins are set one foot from the back edge of the table. The old setting was nine pins across the "flat eight" tables, each a 4- by 8-foot sheet of steel. With nine pins now packed into a five-foot space of the new tables, you'd think there was no way to miss. You would be wrong. The pins must leave the table, and not just be tipped over. In all Optionals, the fastest single time you post is your score. Depending on the size of your wallet and the limits of the club rules, you could shoot it a couple of dozen times.

A pair of Nine-pin guns, a Colt 1911 and a S&W M-59. The Colt has been in the winner's circle. The S&W?

The intent was to give the 9mm high-capacity shooters a place to shine. However, by using 10-shot magazines and light loads for a .45, many pin shooters simply shoot 9-pin with their Pin Gun. While compensators are allowed, optics aren't, so a Space Gun isn't kosher. All the high-cap IPSC Limited guns would be competitive, as a light .40 load does the job. Starting as a Browning Hi-Power event, 9-pin is wide open to any gun you can get nine or more shots stuffed into. One limit is that the caliber must be .380 Auto or larger. No shooting pins with .32 Autos.

A typical 9-pin gun (of the 1911 persuasion) would be either a single-stack or hi-cap frame. The single-stack would probably be a .38 Super or a .45. The 9mm, .40 and 10mm single stack guns would lack capacity. The Super and .45 can be loaded with 10-round magazines, plus one in the chamber. Just enough. The 9mm, .40 and 10mm are, at best, nine-plus-one in the capacity column. A hi-cap frame could be any caliber, as they will come with standard 10-shot magazines, and you can buy higher capacity magazines. (It would probably be in .40, an IPSC Limited gun shooting pins.) While you don't need a compensator, most serious competitors have one, and even with the light 9-pin loads a compensator helps a bit. The best 9-pin load is a round with a PF of 130 to 140, as long as you can keep the bullet moving at over 800 fps, using a flat-point or hollow-point bullet. If you let the velocity get too low, you do not get complete penetration into the pin. Bullets sticking out of pins can cause bounce-backs. Keep the velocity up past 800 fps and you'll be happier.

A typical load for 9-pin is any flat-point or jacketed hollow-point in 9mm, factory or reload. In .38 Super, you'll have to load your own to 9mm specs, which is not a problem. For the .40 caliber and 10mm rounds, a popular load is a 135-grain jacketed hollow-point loaded to right around 1,000 fps. In .45, you have a few options. If you load a 185-grain bullet (a very common cast semi wadcutter weight) and keep your velocity at 800 fps, your PF is in the high end of the range, 148. If you use a 165-grain jacketed hollow-point, you can load to the 800 fps threshold and have a PF of 132. If you can find 165-grain JHP's, this is a nice load. The third choice is a cast 155-grain bullet, loaded at 875 fps. Some barrels do not like the 155 cast bullets, so you will have to do some experimenting to see what your gun likes.

Using a .45 with light loads as a 9-pin gun requires that you switch the regular recoil spring for a lighter one. While a 5-pin load in .45 requires an 18-pound spring, a 9-pin load might need a 12-pound spring.

What are the times? The records set at Second Chance have Master Blasters clearing a table in times near three seconds, flat. A hot OSS will do his or her table in the upper threes. At a club match, the winning time may be four to five seconds, depending on how hot the competition is.

9-Pin .22

Simply the 9-pin optional using .22 rimfire handguns. Some clubs use pins, others use the sawed-off tops of pins, others use pin-like falling plates. To shoot this with a 1911, use your conversion kit, if you have an accurate load. Those clubs with a falling plate rack where the plates tip over to rimfire hits find they have long lines to shoot 9-pin .22.

9-pin .22 times run in the same spans as regular 9-pin. You'd think a .22 would be a lot faster, but compared to the time needed to click to the next pin, aim and shoot, the recoil recovery time is not much at all.

Space Optional

The Space Optional uses the same gun as the Space Gun in the five-pin events, but a different pin set. The table has eight pins, four up and four down, set three feet from the back. Unlike the 5-pin, there is no magazine limit. The Space Optional needs full-power loads to broom the pins off. The eight-pin set is also used for other Optionals, not open to 1911 shooters: 8-pin revolver, shotgun pump and shotgun auto.

Space Optional times run at the top speed in just over four seconds, and at a club match might be in the just over five seconds.

10-Pin Auto

Five pins up and five pins down, on the 3-foot set. Your pistol is limited to eight rounds total as in a Five-Pin event, so in the course of shooting your 10 pins you'll have to reload. Again, full-power loads are needed. This optional is the pistol equivalent of the 8-pin revolver optional, in that it forces each shooter to reload against the clock.

A fast 10-pin auto time would be under six seconds, and club matches might have a winning time at seven.

Two-Man

At Second Chance, the tables are built as three, 5-foot boxes. Your entry is arranged in groups of three tables, so you'll spend your time shooting at pins on a single Supertable, one run for each of the three boxes.

In Two-Man, the two of you face a Supertable stuffed with 22 pins, arranged in all three boxes. You are limited to eight shots in the gun, so you'll both have to reload. All the pins are at the 3-foot set, so you need full-power loads to cleared the table.

I have seen local variations, using the 10-pin setting and adjacent single-box tables, for 20 pins for the two-man team.

Team events add a further complication, in that many pin shoots restrict who can be on a team. When a team is restricted, only one of the two can be a Master Blaster. If you are an OSS and are having a good day at a pin match, you can find Master Blasters hunting you down to offer their services as a team-mate. It can be heady stuff to be asked to shoot with Jerry Barnhart or Brian Enos.

The winning times for Two-Man vary greatly, with winning times at Second Chance changing by a full second or more from one year to the next. One year Gary Britt and I clear the table in 7.4 seconds and placed fourth. The next year we shot a time of seven flat and didn't make the top 10.

Three-Man

In this team event, your two teammates are equipped with shotguns, one pump and one auto. The third shooter has a handgun. Facing the same 22 pins of the Two-Man event, you have to clean them off. Where a winning time for the two-man would be in the mid to low sixes, the winning times for three-man have been in the low fours.

Handgun PEE

The Handgun PEE came about because the submachineguns were overheating. The PE Event used submachineguns at Second Chance, with falling plastic plates that used compressed air to re-set. The event ran so fast that even with four buzzguns to rotate through, they were getting smoking-hot.

To ease the wear and tear on the full-auto guns, we started shooting the eight-plate course with handguns. It

The Handgun PEE used falling plastic plates. The author used this gun in 1994 to win the event and set the (still standing) record of 2.78 seconds. A time that even beat the submachine guns.

proved so popular that it was added as an additional optional. It is basically falling plate shooting, with the gun starting on the rail, and falling plastic instead of steel plates. (The bullet passes through the plate, but tugs on it hard enough to tip it over.)

It happened only at Second Chance. I don't know of any other pin shoot that did or does it. I only mention it because

I was good at it. I won loot in it every year but one, and set the record of 2.78 seconds, faster than the record with submachineguns, of 3.12.

Man-On-Man

The Man-on-Man matches are the ones that shooters either love or hate. While you can get pin shooters who are lukewarm about Optionals ("I like 9-pin but I'm not good enough to spend money shooting it"), not so Man-on-Man. You are on the line either against one or two other shooters, depending on the table structure. If a club has individual 5-foot tables, you'll shoot against one shooter. If a club has three-box, 15-foot supertables, there will be three of you, one firing into each box.

You have to clean your table faster than the other shooters. If you lose, then your entry card is marked with a loss. Two losses and you sit down. The winner is the one left with no losses or, at best, one loss.

Part of Man-on-Man is the luck of the draw. You never know who you're up against, as the entry cards are always shuffled before tables are assigned. I offer an experience of mine as example: Mas Ayoob is a well-known gunwriter and firearms instructor. He is also a good shot. He was a lot better before he started his own school, and had time to practice, but he is still good. One year we drew adjacent slots but on different tables for Man-on-Man. I forget who we each had to shoot against, but we faced competitors of comparable skill. Mas cleared the table in 3.6 seconds and 3.4 seconds but lost both bouts and had to sit down. I shot a

Any man-on-man event is a pressure-cooker. Second Chance was no exception.

5.2 and a 4.8 on my table, won both, and kept going. You never know until you shoot the bouts.

The prize for Man-on-Man is usually the entry fees, split between the top two or three shooters, with the club getting a percentage.

And when it comes to pressure, women don't shrink away. Julie Nowlin is on her way to winning, using a (what else?) Nowlin 1911.

While you can use a spare gun in some few categories, most bowling pin shooting doesn't require a holster. However, a holster is a convenient way to carry a handgun.

Shooting Volume

How much you shoot depends on how many times you enter. At a minimum, if you enter the Main Event in a club match, in a couple of categories, and then shoot a few tables of Optionals, you can use up 200 rounds of ammo. If you go to a larger pin shoot and enter all three Main Event categories, and hammer a couple of Optionals a dozen runs each, you're easily past 300 rounds.

When Second Chance was running (I'm sorry to wax so nostalgic, but it was a lot of fun, and I came home with a lot of loot over the years) you could easily use up thousands of rounds of ammo. My record was an estimated 2,800 rounds of rifle, handgun and shotgun ammunition. And I didn't shoot the subgun event.

Gunsmithing For Pins

Bowling pin shooting is very popular with gunsmiths and experimenters, as it requires many different guns to be competitive in all events. Unlike many other matches, where you show up with your gun and maybe a spare, pins require lots of iron. It was not unusual for serious shooters to show up at Second Chance with as many as half a dozen different pistols (not to mention revolvers, rifles and shotguns) and differently-loaded ammunition for each event. A bare-bones battery would be two: a Pin Gun and a Stock Gun. You'd use the Pin Gun in Space, Nine-pin, Space Optional and all the team and Man-on-Man events. You'd use the stock gun in Stock Five-pin and as a back-up in case the Pin Gun broke.

A four-gun battery was a more likely one; Space, Pin, Stock and 9-pin, with the Pin Gun used in team events and Man-on-Man, and the Nine-pin gun as a Handgun PEE and the required handgun in the back range rifle and shotgun events.

The Steel Challenge

The Steel Challenge is an attempt at discovering just how fast competitors could shoot. Started by Mike Dalton and Mike Fichman in the late 1970s, the format is simple, even if the events have shifted over the years. The competitors travel from stage to stage in groups known as squads. At each stage, each competitor faces five steel plates. Each stage has different size plates, arrayed in a different pattern. One plate is designated the stop plate. On the buzzer, the

At the Steel Challenge, the steel doesn't fall. The plates are painted after each competitor, and you score by time

shooter draws and hits each plate with one shot. Each stage requires five runs, the four fastest of which are totaled for score. Fastest total time for the seven stages wins the match. The plates are re-painted between each competitor, so every shooter faces clean plates to start their runs.

The total for a match is 175 rounds.

You do not have to knock the plates over. Hinged plates have to be re-set, and that would slow down the conduct of the match. All you have to do is make a mark on the plate. Why a stop plate? In the beginning years, the Range Officers used stop watches to determine time. By making one

Some plates are small and far, and others are close and big. You just have to hit them faster than anyone else does.

plate the final plate, the RO only had to concentrate on that plate to stop time, average the three different stopwatches, and record the score. Now, with sound-sensitive electronic timers, having a designated stop plate isn't needed. In the interests of tradition and continuity of the match, there are still stop plates.

The Steel Challenge offers a new mix; you have to draw, you have to engage the targets, sometimes in a specified order, and you can't miss one. Misses have to be picked up, otherwise the miss penalty is worse than the extra time spent picking it up. If you have to make up too many misses, you'll have to reload. Once the start buzzer goes, you are on your own. There are no alibi re-shoots. There are a couple of stages that require movement, from one box to another. The boxes are close, a few steps apart, so it isn't like a run and gun IPSC course.

Steel Challenge shooting requires follow-through, to be sure you hit the plate, but you can't dwell on it, as time is ticking. The problem is similar to that of bowling pins, where you must hit, but having hit, you must get immediately to the next target.

As there is no need to knock the plates over, power factor is not a problem. Some of the problems include: light recoil vs. reliable function, accuracy, time-lag of the bullet strike and holster speed.

There are many categories in which you can shoot The Steel Challenge, and some of them have holster restrictions as well as handgun equipment restrictions. The 1911 is active in many categories, from Open and Stock to the IDPA pistol categories.

And when they're not shooting, they're watching.

Each year there is a contingent known as the Japanese Squad, even when there are enough of them to be two squads. These hardy souls store their guns here in the U.S. and wait each year for their vacations, so they can travel to California and shoot the Steel Challenge. They commonly shoot revolvers, and use ultra-light loads. Some will have loads (or did in the past) with a PF as low as 90. You simply cannot get a 1911 to work reliably with a centerfire cartridge and run it at a 90 PF. (I know, I've tried.) The standard Steel load is right around a 9-pin or IPSC Minor load, that is a 125 PF. You must have an absolutely reliable load and pistol. This was a trick in the old days but is a cinch today.

Your load must be accurate. The far plates will be 10-inch and 12-inch circular plates at 25 yards. Yes, you are thinking "Ten inches at 25 yards? Piece of cake." Try it against the clock, knowing that the next guy up will know just how fast you shot it and how fast he has to go to beat you.

The signal for many shooters, and confirmation of success for others, is the sound of the bullet striking steel. If the bullet is too slow, you waste time waiting to hear it. If it goes too fast, your load is going to be too loud, and you can't hear the strike at all. I shot the Steel Challenge one year where a competitor on my squad was using his regular IPSC loads, a 200 grain lead bullet at 900 fps. The gun was so loud he couldn't hear the strike of the plate. He had to look after each shot, confirm there was a fresh hit, and then move on.

The best setup for the Steel Challenge is a 1911 in 9mm or .38 Super. Many shooters feel the Super feeds a bit more reliably, and opt for it over the 9mm. I have found a properly set-up 9mm feeds 100 percent, and since I have access to once-fired 9mm brass by the literal five-gallon bucketful, I built my second and subsequent steel guns as 9mms. Can you use other calibers? Sure. The .40 offers light bullets and accurate shooting, and .40 brass is almost as common and cheap as is 9mm. Building a 10mm steel gun would not be wise due to the high cost of 10mm brass. Better to put a .40 barrel in it and scrounge cheap .40 brass. The .45 started out as THE steel gun, but Jerry Barnhart was the last one to win The Steel Challenge using a .45, and that was in the end of the 1980s. You can turn a .45 into a steel gun, by loading your ammo with 155-grain lead bullets running at about 900 fps. You may have to experiment to find a suitably accurate load, but that is

mere detail. The other path is to use a 185-grain bullet, and load it down around 750 fps. While there might be a bit of time lag, you will have an easier reloading test series finding an accurate load for the 185's. If you want to get the most out of your time and gun, start using the first accurate 185 load as a practice load, and keep shooting steel while you experiment with powders to find an accurate 155 load.

In the course of a Steel Challenge match, you'll draw 35 times, 28 of them for score. A good holster, and good technique, matters greatly. If your holster (or lack of practice) slows your draw by a tenth of second each time, you will have added 2.8 seconds to your total time. As the match has been won or lost by less than half a second, you can see the importance of a good holster. In many divisions, the holster is left up to you, but in the IDPA divisions you can only use an IDPA-approved holster.

If you are shooting Open or IPSC Limited, then a holster like the Hogue PowerSpeed would be a good choice. You have to have fast and consistent draws in The Steel Challenge, both to keep your times short, and to get you hitting steel right from the holster. I spent one of my trips to the Steel Challenge following the Super Squad and recording the time for their draws and first shot. I found two amazing things. The first was that even the Super Squad didn't have blazing fast times. There were only two shooters who had draws under 1.20 seconds each and every time, and they were Jerry Barnhart and Jethro Dionisio. The second was that they didn't miss the first shot. A dozen shooters, with five runs and seven stages means 420 recorded first shot times. There were less than a dozen times someone missed the plate on the first shot and had to make it up.

You need a fast and consistent holster to do that.

Handgunner Shoot-Off

The "Shoot-off" as many know it by, happens each year outside of Montrose, CO. Originated, organized and run by Paul Miller at his San Juan Range, what Paul figured out was that for many shooters the culmination of a match was the best part. At the end of many matches, the top eight or 16 shooters face off in an elimination ladder of one-on-one shoot-offs. He figured, why not go right for the icing on the cake, and design a match that is nothing but shoot-offs?

To do that at the Shoot-Off requires a large number of stages, 15 in all. Each stage has a squad on it, and the

Jerry Barnhart and Jerry Miculek in the Finals. Note the amounts of brass on the tarps. The Shoot-Off requires large amounts of ammo.

In the Shoot-Off, you compete against other shooters with the same skill level and equipment, until the Finals.

squads rotate through the match. Unlike other matches, where the competitors are spread out among the squads, in the Shoot-Off a squad is composed of all the competitors in the match who are in the same category. For instance, the last time I shot, I was in the "A-class Stock Auto" squad. All eight of us were there, competing directly against each other. The "B Class Stock Auto" had 14 shooters, the "C Class Stock Auto" had 27, and D had 32. The maximum squad size is 32 shooters, as that number of shooters works out perfectly in an elimination ladder. Any more and the number of points awarded in "byes" distorts the scoring, and the time needed to go through the squad takes too long. If you want to shoot, and you're in "C" or "D" class, sign up early or be left out.

At each stage, the shooters run themselves through the match. The computer has randomly assigned each shooter a place on the elimination ladder, and over the course of the match you will at one time or another (and probably several times in a small squad) shoot against everyone in your squad.

The shooting is simple. Downrange on each stage are two falling plate racks, with identical plates in each rack. Or, there is an array of poppers in two different colors. Between the racks (or in the center of the range if the stage is a popper stage) are two pepper poppers, angled towards each other slightly, so they overlap when they fall. All the steel has been adjusted to fall to a fair hit with a 130 PF load. What caliber and PF you use is entirely up to you, but there are limits, typically 115-grain minimum weight and 1,200 fps maximum velocity. Two shooters stand in their boxes. On the start signal, they each mow down their plate rack and knock down the popper on their side. The first popper down wins. If you down your stop popper but leave a

plate standing in the rack, you lose the bout, even if you're done first. The shooters switch sides, their squad mates pull the ropes to re-set the steel, and they have at it again. First one to win two bouts of the three wins the engagement. The loser sits down. The squad goes through all the first-run bouts, then starts on the second runs. In the second runs, every shooter got there by winning. Each shooter again has to win two bouts. The squad walks down the steps of the ladder until there is one shooter left. The winning position is decided by the first one to win three of the five runs.

Your score for that stage is the total number of bouts you won. Your score for the match is the total of all your winning bouts on all the stages. Your score is compared only to those in your category.

The shooting is intense. You are competing, for those bouts, directly against the shooter standing next to you, in computer parlance, in "real time." You are also competing in the overall against the other shooter in your squad who is closest to you in winning bout totals. You consume large amounts of ammunition. If all you do is step into the box, shoot your magazine dry and lose your first two bouts in every stage and then sit down, you will end up shooting at least 270 rounds. (.45 ACP and 8-shot magazines.) If you win any bouts at all, your ammo count goes up in nine- and 18-shot increments. (Or 10 and 20, if that is what your magazine holds.) Paul Miller advises that you need at least 600 rounds to shoot the match. And then there are the finals.

In the finals the Stock gun classes are paired off against each other, as are the classes in Open, Stock Revolver, Open Revolver, etc, etc. Each winner is then paired off against yet another winner. When each category is completed, then cross-category bouts are arranged until there is one man standing.

In speed shooting, the draw is vital. The fastest holster is open to debate, and serious shooters will try them all.

To shoot requires eye-hand coordination and determination. The Shoot-Off is particularly accessible to the handicapped, with no movement required.

A trip to Montrose can win you loot, and burn up over 1,000 rounds of ammunition. For the experience you, will return to your home club tested in fire (and the heat of a July in Colorado) and ready to make your fellow club members work even harder.

The Handgunner Shoot-Off does not teach tactics, movement or reloading (unless you and your squadmates make a habit of missing). What it does teach is the importance of the draw, and shooting under pressure. Not to blow my horn, but I'm a Second Chance Master Blaster, a USPSA A class shooter, and I have been competing, teaching and learning for more than 20 years. At times on the line, at the Handgunner Shoot-Off, I've had my legs shaking so badly from nerves and tension that I was sure the rest of the squad would notice. After you have shot this match, falling plates will no longer be a mystery. You will draw at the Shoot-Off not less than 30 times. And that is if you don't win a bout. Your theoretical maximum would depend on your squad size, but you could be drawing 250 times just in the match, not counting the finals.

Another useful aspect of the Shoot-Off is the length. You can learn as you go. You can start out badly, learn, adapt, and catch up to the others. You can figure things out on the range. At many other matches, a bad stage dims your chances of winning, and two bad stages dooms you. At the Shoot-Off, if the first-place guy loses his first bout on a stage, you (or the stage winner) can catch up by many points. In my squad of eight, the difference between sitting down first, or finishing, could be as many as five points (where the winner might have a score of around 75). In a large squad, you could close the gap (or open it) by nine points.

To set up something like the Shoot-Off at your home club doesn't take much more space than a bowling pin table would. At the club level you can run a lot of shooters through a one-range set-up with two racks and two poppers.

And as if all that wasn't enough, there is more shooting, still. As a warm-up match and introduction to the stages, they hold the World Challenge match. You simply shoot the same stages, but for time. Also, there are long gun side matches held the two days before the Shoot-Off. You could travel to Montrose and stay for a week, and end up shooting more than 2,000 rounds in various calibers. With Second

Chance on hiatus, this is the new high-volume winner in matches.

In the Third group are IPSC/USPSA, the Single Stack Classic, and IDPA.

IPSC/USPSA

A few years after the international organization was formed, the shooters in the United States felt the need for a local organization. The United States Practical Shooting Association is the organizing body for IPSC shooting in the U.S. As with all the other countries that join, the U.S. has slight local modifications of the international rules.

The USPSA is built around unfettered competition, within equipment divisions. You can select what kind of gear with which you want to compete, and then go out and try your skills against other shooters. The "typical" IPSC/USPSA course is a field course, where you have to deal with targets from several different shooting boxes and reload when and if necessary. Each target must have two hits, or be scored as a miss (or two). Each stage of a match will be a separately scored run at a course. Some will be short, eight or 10 rounds, and some will be long, 30 rounds or more. Some will be close, a few yards, and others will be far, out to 40 or 50. Some will mix everything in, from 2 yards to 50, with windows, doorways, doors, vehicles and walls. And there will almost always be steel. Hinged to fall, the steel must be knocked down or it is scored as a miss. A club

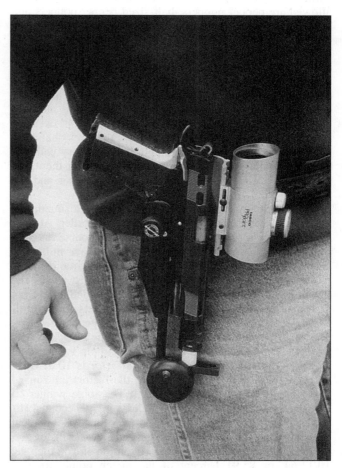

For IPSC/USPSA Open competition, almost anything goes. Comps, dots, GPS units, the only question is: "Does it help?"

In an IPSC course, you'll have to negotiate doors, windows, corners and walls.

The World Body has a slightly different target. It is smaller, with smaller scoring rings, and no head.

match might have four to six stages, with a total of 100 rounds for the day. Some clubs might even run up to eight stages, and have as many as 200 rounds fired. By the time you get to the U.S. Nationals, a match is a dozen stages or more, and 400 rounds. The World Shoot, held every three years, is 35 stages, and 400 to 500 rounds.

The targets allowed in IPSC/USPSA competition are few. There is the current cardboard target, fine-tuned from earlier designs, but still a silhouette. The steel targets allowed are pepper poppers, half-sized pepper poppers and round and square plates. The poppers and plates must be hinged to fall.

The world body, the IPSC, has slightly different rules on some guns, and differing rules on course design. The rules of the world body are adjusted by many local associations to accommodate the laws of the country of residence. (For example, in England, since there are no handguns allowed, competitors have to use borrowed guns for overseas matches.) Some countries don't allow their residents/citizens to own handguns or ammunition in military calibers. 9mm Parabellum and .45ACP are off the list for them, but since you can shoot quite nicely with .38 Super and .40 S&W, no problem.

In an IPSC match you will be assigned to a squad, and your squad will rotate through the stages in order. At each stage, members of your squad will fire the course one at a time. Scoring is rather involved. Once you have finished a stage, your time is recorded. Then your point total is calculated. You have to hit each paper target at least twice, and knock down all the steel. Your penalties are deducted from the point total. Misses, hitting no-shoot targets and not following the procedure as described are all penalties. Then, your final point total is divided by the time it took you to shoot the course. This is your Factor. (Example 1: You shoot 100 points in 10 seconds. Your stage factor is 10.0) Once everyone has shot on a stage, all of the factors are ranked from highest to lowest. (Example 2: The stage winner on this stage shot it for 92 points, but did it in 7.9 seconds. His stage factor was 11.64) The highest factor gets 100 percent of the match points for that stage, and each lesser factor gets a percentage of the match points. (Example 3: You then get 10/11.64, or 85.91 percent of the match points for that stage.) Once all the stages are fired, the aggregate of your match points for each stage is totaled, and that is your match

standing. Complex? Positively Byzantine. The match isn't done until the computer has digested the scores.

To make matters worse, the targets are not all scored the same for each caliber. In Bianchi, PPC or Bull's Eye competition, the hole you make scores the same regardless of the caliber you used. Not so in IPSC. Caliber power is divided by Major and Minor. The Major loads must post a Power Factor of at least 165, sometimes higher in a category at international matches. Minor must make at least 125. On the steel, down is down. On cardboard, the two score differently. The targets are divided into four zones, A,B,C and D. An A hit scores five points regardless of PF. The B and C zones are scored four points for a Major load, and two points for a Minor load. The D zone is scored two points for Major, and one for Minor. The end result is that if you are going to shoot a handgun in Minor, you have to either shoot it faster, or shoot as fast, but record more hits in the A zone than the other competitors in order to keep your score up. Complicated? You bet. Has anyone come up with a better method? Not one that satisfies the competitors yet.

However, because of the complicated scoring system, no one really knows who the winner is until the computer is done crunching the numbers. After big matches, all the serious competitors will hang around until the scores are posted, and the result is a great time of camaraderie at the end of the match.

The fastest shooting is found in IPSC/USPSA matches, using an Open gun. Here Jerry Barnhart is showing a class how it's done.

And to add to the noise of an Open gun, the barricades, walls and other props bounce the noise around. You simply must wear hearing protection to shoot or watch.

The Gear

Open

An Open gun is just that, open to just about anything you can find that is useful. There are limits. You can't shoot a 9mm Parabellum and declare Major. (A 165 PF.) The 9X19 case has to be pumped up to too high a pressure to make Major, and thus it is lined out. A "typical" Open gun is chambered in 9X21, 9X23, .38 Super or one of the other derivatives. There is an almost-mandatory compensator, and an Open gun would not be complete without a red-dot sight. The magazine is limited in length to 170mm, including the baseplate. Thus, most have a capacity of around 28 rounds of .38 Super.

An Open gun is loud. An efficient compensator strips the combustion gases off the muzzle and diverts them, and Open competitors use slower powders to increase the gas flow at the muzzle. An Open gun is expensive to buy and run. A poorly-built Open gun is a waste of money, so an Open gun will have a match barrel, precisely-fit to the slide, with the slide-to-frame fit as tight as possible. The scope and mount require fitting and tuning, and the magazines can cost $150 each.

The ammunition for an Open gun uses 115- or 125-grain jacketed bullets, and large amounts of slow-burning powder. You can reload 1,200 to 1,500 rounds of .45 ACP per pound of a fast-burning powder, where an Open gun will use more-expensive powder at a rate that gets you 700 reloads per pound of powder.

Why, then? Because an Open gun is like a top-fuel dragster. You can't go faster without wings. A good competitor using an Open gun will go through some courses in half the time he or she would with a stock gun. A common Open gun is an STI or Caspian high-capacity frame built as a .38 Super of some kind. The world body and the U.S. view Open guns the same.

Limited

A Limited gun isn't very limited today. It started out as a Stock gun class, but competitors and gunsmiths being as clever as they are, "stock" soon wasn't very stock. A USPSA Limited gun means three things today; no compensators or red-dots sights, a .40 caliber minimum bore to declare Major, and a magazine limited to 140mm in length. A typical Limited gun is an STI, Para Ordnance or Enterprise built in .40 S&W. There aren't many Caspian Limited guns built for an odd reason: the frame is too comfortable. The Caspian was designed and built as a dedicated .38 Super, where the other pistols were built to be .45's. The slightly slimmer Caspian magazine ends up a round or two short of the capacity of the others. At the end of a large field course, that round can matter, so many competitors opt for a larger magazine, and then figure out how to make the grip comfortable.

The World body calls this class Standard, and the pistol must fit the world box. It must do it with the magazine inserted, so magazines in Standard are 126mm long.

Limited 10

Not 10 millimeter, but 10-shot capacity. When the Crime Bill was signed into law, production of high-capacity magazines ended until the law expires. (Any bets on its being allowed to expire?) Limited 10 serves a dual purpose: it allows new shooters to compete without having to go bidding on expensive hi-cap magazines, and it brings back all the single-stack stock guns built in the old days. An out-of-

One of the restrictions on a Limited gun is the prohibition on ports or comps. While this is a Stock pin gun, the Magna-Porting removes it from IPSC/USPSA Limited or Limited 10. With an unported barrel, it becomes acceptable.

In IPSC Standard and Modified, the pistol has to fit the "IPSC box" with a magazine in place.

The Wilson KZ-45 was tailor-made for Limited 10 competition.

the-box gun like most of those we test in this book is ready to go, in Limited 10, when fed with 10-shot mags. The only thing some of them would need would be a magazine funnel. The Limited 10 is a U.S.-only division. Remember what I said about local variations of the IPSC rules? This is one of them. Limited 10 will never be an International Division for a simple reason: Minister of Sport. As one representative to the IPSC body explained to me; "If my Minister of Sport found out we could compete with 10-shot magazines, he would order all the hi-caps be turned in."

Modified

Modified is an International-only category. It has not caught on in the U.S. yet. Modified is basically an Open gun that fits in the Standard gun measuring box. You can use ports or compensators, red-dot sights, but the gun (with its magazine inserted) has to fit the box. To declare Major you have to be .40 cal or larger.

My STI set-up for the IPSC Modified division.

Holsters for competition

Actually, holsters are for schlepping a handgun around. The competition only determines which holster is appropriate. As with the competitions themselves, there are several groups. The first one is concealment/concealment competition. One of the best holsters for concealment is made by many holster makers, and is called a "Summer Special." Originally designed by Milt Sparks, it proved to be so good that many other makers produce a copy. Mine was made by Gordon Davis, and is still capable of doing its job nearly 20 years later, a time period that includes a dozen years of daily wear, two trips to Gunsite and a hit-and-run accident. I was walking across the street when a driver made a left turn and bounced me off the hood and windshield of her Taurus. While the spare change and Swiss Army knife were knocked out of my pockets, the lightweight Commander and spare magazine stayed put.

For competition that requires concealed carry like IDPA, the Wilson Tactical Assault is fast and easily concealed. To get the speed, you have to forego passing the piñata test that my Summer Special and I survived. Like many new designs, the Tactical Assault features a suede lining bonded to a shell of synthetic called Kydex. The Kydex is tough, durable, washable and holds its shape.

For all-out speed competition, like USPSA/IPSC shooting, the Steel Challenge or the Handgunner Shoot-off, the Hogue Powerspeed holster is blindingly fast. The design has a locking lever that keeps the pistol securely in the holster when you aren't on the line. The need for speed defines the design and purpose of a competition holster. While you could shoot an IPSC match with a concealment rig (your times would be slower, but you would be more relevant) you can't use a competition rig in an IDPA match.

For tactical training, and carrying large amounts of gear along with a handgun, the tactical thigh holster seems to be the current solution. Why on the thigh? Not because its cool, or the draw is any faster, but that is often the only place left. When a soldier is loaded down with all the gear he needs to carry, his waist is already packed. That leaves the thigh open. The Blackhawk holster is one element of tactical nylon designed by Mike Noell, a former Navy SEAL. Not only is it the toughest gear I've seen, but it is warranted against any damage. If you break it, send it back and they'll repair it, up to and including bullet holes!

A Milt Sparks Summer Special on the bottom, and my Gordon Davis clone on the top.

Hogue PowerSpeed.

Wilson Tactical Assault.

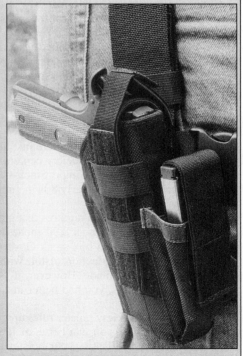

The Blackhawk Tactical, with the extra velcro closure pressed into place.

In IPSC and other speed events, this holster is allowed. In IDPA, it isn't. (The pistol wouldn't be allowed in IDPA, either.)

This Michiguns-done Officer's model would be a grand carry and Single Stack Classic pistol. Everything you need.

As accurate and reliable as this Caspian is, the coned barrel removes it from use as a Single Stack Classic pistol. Too bad, but the rules are the rules.

The 1911 Society and The Single Stack Classic

In 1994, before the USPSA added the Limited 10 division, the Single Stack Classic match was formed to bring those single-stack guns back out of the gun safes where they had languished for so long. It proved so popular that in 1996, the 1911 Society was formed to run the match and keep the records and rules. The equipment rules are simple: single stack guns with no comps or dots, no outrageous safeties, magazine funnels or cone-barrels. The gun has to use a barrel bushing, and it has to fit into a particular box. If you have a box-stock gun like many in this book, it passes muster.

The courses of fire and scoring are just like those fired in USPSA matches. The 1911 Society centers around a match held each year called The Single Stack Classic. It is like IPSC in the old days, in the early 80s in guns, but up to date in technique and holsters.

The Single Stack Classic requires that guns fit into a size box. The 1911 Society box is 8.90 inches x 6.00 inches x 1.81 inches. If you have a box-stock Government model, it will fit. It must be a production pistol, with a minimum of 500 units having been made. However, if you add some of the allowed accessories, you had better make sure your gun fits.

While the 1911 Society holster rules are not as restrictive as those of the IDPA, you can't use an IPSC race holster. For the Single Stack Classic, your holster has to rest at or behind the centerline of the side of the body. The holster and magazine pouches must be attached to your trouser belt, which must go through the belt loops of said trousers. You can use any secure holster (there isn't an approved list, as in IDPA), but the idea is to use "holsters designed for continuous daily carry and should be reasonably concealable."

The Single Stack Classic has Major and Minor Power Factors, with Minor at or about 120, and Major at or above 165. A cartridge has to be .40 or larger to be a Major load.

IDPA

The IDPA (International Defensive Pistol Association) is another splinter group from IPSC/USPSA. The organizers felt that IPSC had strayed too far from its roots, that of defensive training with a handgun. Yes, an Open gun is a marvelous tool to complete the course with, but you can't carry it in a concealable holster. Even if you could, who could shoot it in a real-life encounter without being deafened by the comp?

To shoot in an IDPA match you will be organized in squads that rotate through the stages of a match.

While it is much like IPSC, IDPA differs from all the other competitions in several aspects. First, there are holster restrictions. A holster (and the handgun that goes in it) is considered an article of daily wear, and must be comfortable and concealable. Not just any holster will do, and to shoot in an approved match you have to be using a holster that is on

IDPA rules do not prohibit improvements like checkering. The perfectly-done checkering on this Michiguns carry gun aids the grip and control.

A Summer Special, a lightweight pistol like the Kimber Ultra CDP, and you're ready to shoot IDPA.

Does he or doesn't he? Proof a concealed holster can be comfortable, fast and secure.

IDPA prohibits competition gear, so speed holsters are out. Even if you could conceal it, leave this one home and consult the IDPA-approved holster list.

the approved holster list. Holster manufacturers have to submit one of their models to the IDPA test panel in order to have it posted on the approved list.

Where IPSC courses in the U.S. can run long, going to 30 or even 40 rounds, IDPA courses are limited to 18 rounds. Some IDPA courses will require concealed carry to start a stage. You are limited as to how many magazines you can carry. A single-stack shooter can have two spares; a shooter with high-capacity magazines can have only one.

And IDPA matches feature a penalty that is unique, the "Failure to do right" penalty. If you lean out from a barricade too far to get a comfortable shooting position, or fail to engage the targets in a specified order, you can get assessed an FTDR.

IDPA is meant to be testing, training and scoring shooters ability to handle a potential defensive encounter. As such, excessive attention to gear is prohibited.

The Four Divisions

Guns are divided into four equipment divisions, Stock Service Pistol, Enhanced Service Pistol, Custom Defensive Pistol, and Stock Service Revolver. Stock Service is the

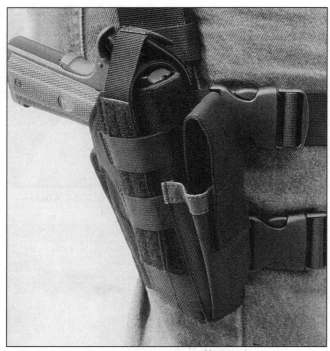

While this Wilson CQB would be approved as a Custom Defensive Pistol, the Blackhawk holster would not pass as an IDPA holster. Leave it home and go with the Wilson Tactical Assault holster.

division for double-action 9mm pistols, like S&W's, Glock, etc. Revolver is just that, wheelguns.

The Enhanced Service is for single-action pistols in 9mm, 38 Super and .40 S&W, and the threshold power factor is 125. Custom Defensive is for single-action 10mm and .45 pistols, with a threshold power factor of 165.

The modifications allowed are few. And if you are caught using equipment that is not practical for self-defense use, concealable and suitable for all day continuous wear, (and the MD is convinced you did it to gain an advantage) the Match Director can disqualify you from the match.

The Enhanced Service Pistol must fit in a box 8-3/4 inches x 6 inches x 1-5/8 inches, and have a maximum unloaded weight of 43 ounces. Magazine capacity is limited to 10 rounds. You can do cosmetic work, change the finish and checker or stipple it. You can improve accuracy and add a magazine funnel. You can't change the barrel to a coned barrel, port the barrel, comp it, add weight (tungsten guide rods and extended dust covers are out) or make the magazine button larger.

The Custom Defensive Pistol must be in 10mm, 400 Corbon or .45 ACP. I'm sure if you show up with some other big boomer (.40 Super. .45 Super, .460 Rowland) you'd be allowed to shoot, at least at the club level. The Custom has

to fit the same size box as the Enhanced, weight is limited to 41 ounces, and magazines are limited to eight rounds. The hi-cap magazine I mentioned earlier? That is for those Glocks, Berettas, etc. If you're shooting a 1911, you can have no more than eight- or 10-shot mags, depending on caliber.

The allowed modifications in Custom are similar to Enhanced, in that you can do cosmetic work, change the finish, add magazine wells and improve the trigger pull. One difference is that coned barrels are allowed, provided the barrel is 4.2 inches or less in length. (Officers Model pistols and the like.) The modifications not allowed are the same as in Enhanced Pistol.

All sights (in all divisions) must be of the notch and post design, no ghost ring sights allowed.

IDPA Scoring

The scoring method in IDPA is known as the "Vickers" method. The shooter must engage all targets in a stage with the specified number of hits. (Usually two, but not always.) For each point off of a perfect score they shoot, a half a second is added to the time it took to shoot the stage. A stage score is converted into time, and the match score is the total of all the stage times.

The penalties are quite severe. A procedural error is three seconds per infraction, hitting a non-threat target is five seconds, and a failure to neutralize (less than four points scored on a target, even if it has two hits) is five seconds. Failure to do right? That one is twenty seconds.

IDPA Matches

Since each stage is limited to 18 rounds, a match total depends on how many stages there are. A five-stage match will not exceed 100 rounds. IDPA competitors are more concerned with learning and reinforcing proper tactics than burning up lots of ammo.

Which One?

The match for you depends on many things. What equipment do you have? What level of complexity are you comfortable with? Are you more interested in competition and fun, or learning useful skills for defensive use? How much shooting do you want to do? And, what clubs near to you shoot what kinds of competitions? Unless you are willing to drive long distances, the common competitions in your area may be your only choices.

Whatever the competition, you will be a better shooter for having entered. And you'll meet a bunch of nice people.

CHAPTER FOUR

The Calibers Of The 1911

For many, the chapter title would suggest a very short chapter. To many shooters, the 1911 caliber is .45. I have had gunsmithing customers show surprise when I mentioned other calibers than the .45, although none of them tried to make .45 ammunition work in pistols chambered for other calibers. If so, they didn't tell me. Using the wrong ammunition is not a mistake you can take lightly. I once had a customer bring in a Marlin lever-action rifle, complaining of terrible accuracy. I inspected and cleaned it, and then test-fired it at the range. It plopped five 200-grain soft-point bullets from my test box of .35 Remington ammo into a nice group at 50 yards. I gave it back to him on a Saturday morning, and he was back in a few hours. You guessed it, he had grown up using a .30-30 lever-action rifle, and had no idea there were other calibers available. As you can imagine, his accuracy with .30-30 ammunition in a rifle chambered in .35 Remington was miserable.

In the 1911 in particular, the .38 Super chambering was reamed to very casual dimensions in the past. The chamber dimensions were a holdover from the days of the .38 Auto. The Model 1900s used the semi-rim of the case to control headspace. In the 1911, the semi-rim wasn't enough to adequately control headspace, but Colt made no effort to improve the accuracy of the Super, because the only caliber anyone wanted in the U.S. was .45. (Colt sold plenty of Supers, but never paid any attention to the accuracy problem except for some Match Supers made during the 1930s). Some shooters are of the opinion that the .38 Super is some sort of grab-bag chambering, and that you can fire any one of a dozen different .38 autos or 9mms out of a Colt in .38 Super. Not true. Well, not true if you want to shoot safely. My brother once owned a Colt .38 Super that had a chamber cut so oversized you might have thought it was reamed using a die sinker. That pistol would fire 9mm Parabellum, but the cases weren't happy about it. (And pardon my French, but accuracy sucked.) Instead of being tapered as 9mm's are supposed to be, the empties came out of that Super a straight cylinder with no taper. Alas, he sold that pistol. We now know that with the proper barrel plugged into it, accuracy could be stellar.

You must make sure you are using the correct ammunition/case that your pistol is chambered for.

The Beginning

The 1911 was designed around the .45 ACP, a cartridge with a nominal .473" diameter base, and a loaded overall length of 1.270". Theoretically, you could chamber it for any cartridge that would fit within those maximum sizes.

The L.A.R. Grizzly people went one better, as did the old AMT corporation, making a stretched-frame 1911 that could accommodate the .45 Winchester Magnum in the Grizzly, and the 10mm Magnum in the AMT.

But there is a limiting factor in caliber considerations in the 1911. It is the breechface. The interior face of the slide where the cartridge rim rests has to be proportioned to the rim of the cartridge being used. The ejector and its slot through the slide on one side, and the extractor and its tunnel on the other side, have to be the correct distance from the centerline, or the pistol won't work. (As an aside, dimensional instability, not a science-fiction term, but a manufacturing problem, is the cause of many malfunctions in poor-quality pistols)

For example, if you have a slide made for the .45 ACP, the breechface slot will be cut to accommodate a cartridge with a rim diameter of .473". If you throw a 9mm cartridge in there, with its rim of .406", the extractor won't even come close to grabbing the rim. Having given you this information, I must point out that I have seen pistols work with mismatched breechface-to-caliber dimensions. One was a Colt .38 Super that the late Jim Clark Sr. had converted to .38 Special. To convert it, Mr. Clark had reamed the chamber to .38 Special and opened the breechface to accommodate the much-larger rim of the .38 Special, .433" vs. the Super's .405". The owner loved the accuracy in .38, but the five-shot magazines were very expensive, and he wanted to shoot in a league that had six-shot strings. As an experiment, I

The 1911 was designed around a cartridge of a certain size, launching a bullet of a certain weight and velocity. We can stretch the limits, such as with this 265-grain lead pin load, but we can only do so much.

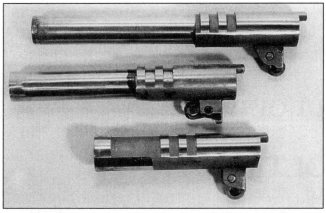

When changing calibers, you need to get all the changes correct. Note the different bottom lug configurations between the Government barrel on top, and the Commander and Officer's barrels below. Install a Government barrel in your Commander or Officers and you could damage both barrel and slide.

installed a Bar-Sto barrel in .38 Super, and a new Super extractor. It worked fine, even though the breechface was some .030" over-sized.

Later, I worked on a Springfield 10mm, on which the owner wanted a compensator installed. When the Ed Brown 10mm compensated barrel showed up, it wouldn't fit. As it turned out, the Springfield "10" was a .45 with a 10mm chamber and bore. The breechface dimensions and slide hood dimensions were .45! I sent the barrel back to Ed in exchange for a .45 ACP comped barrel, which fit perfectly. The disparity between the 10mm breechface (.425") and the .45 ACP (.480") was even greater than that earlier Super, and the Springfield worked perfectly as a 10.

Do these examples prove you can mix and match calibers in slides? No. The barrel hood and rear of the chamber wall locations preclude doing so. If you were to try and make your .45 into a .40 or 10mm, or a Super, the hoods would not come close to matching. Filing to fit would only result in a ruined barrel. If you want a different caliber across case family sizes, you have to invest in a new slide and barrel, not just a barrel.

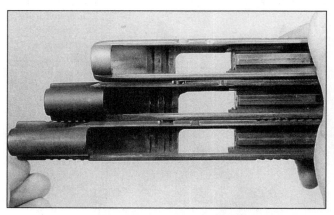

At first glance, they're similar, but not interchangeable. Notice the different length to the rear of the recoil spring housing. (L: Gov't, C: Commander, R: Officer's) And these are three different calibers, too.

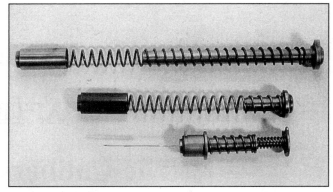

And different barrels need different recoil springs. Top: Government, middle: Commander, bottom: Officer's model.

1911 breechface sizes come in five flavors, each of which can be used for many case sizes that use a base of the appropriate diameter:

Rimfire

The rimfire breechface is cut to accept a .22 lr cartridge. The .22 lr rim is around .272" in diameter.

.38 Super

The 1911, by then the 1911A1, added the .38 Super chambering in 1929. A higher-pressure loading of the old .38 Auto, the breechface of Colt Supers was cut to accommodate the .403"-.405" rim of the Super case. The same breechface will work with the 9mm, even though the Parabellum has a rim only .390" in diameter. When setting up a slide to work with a 9mm barrel, the gunsmith (or you) only has to increase extractor tension to grab the 9mm rim.

.40S&W/10mm

The metric breechface is set up for a rim of .420" to .425" diameter. Unless you are looking to chamber your 1911 in an obsolete exotic like the 8mm Nambu, the usual cartridges for this breechface are the .357 Sig, 40S&W and the 10mm.

Could you turn a .40 cal 1911 into an 8mm Nambu? Dimensionally, yes. But why would you want to?

38 Special

A 1911 that will chamber a revolver cartridge? Yes, for bull's eye shooters. The breechface is .435", but that is not the only thing different about a wadcutter gun. The only loading that will work is full wadcutters, and only at the lightest loads. You see, that particular Colt is a blow-back pistol, and is not locked when closed. The idea was to make the softest-shooting, most accurate pistol possible for target shooting.

You can now get as soft a pistol in recoil and as accurate too, by using the .38 Super.

.45 ACP

The first, and some say the best. The breechface is set up for a .473-.475" diameter case.

While the 1911 spent most of the century chambered for .45, other cartridges are claiming a place for utility and competition. While some claim the .45 can do it all, if that were true, there wouldn't be so much effort spent on new cartridges and subtle variations of old ones. And, we wouldn't have as much fun testing, evaluating, and going to the range.

The Calibers of the 1911

The Rimfire

The smallest is the .22 lr. The long rifle began as the short, when Smith & Wesson chambered revolvers for it during the Civil War. S&W had the Rollin White patents on bored-through cylinders, so it was not until the patents expired that Colt could offer a revolver for self-contained cartridges in 1873. From the beginning, the rimfire was viewed as a small game, vermin and practice round. The 1911 did not get chambered for a .22 lr until the 1930s, when Colt made some Service Ace pistols for practice and competition. The slides were steel, with internal lightening cuts, and the very light recoil spring only worked the slide a fraction of the distance the .45 slides moved. Inside, the slide stopped against a stack of leather washers.

After the war, Colt then came out with the Ace Conversion kit, which was another lightened slide, but this design used a short-stroke floating chamber to work the slide. The chamber held the cartridge, and the chamber and empty cartridge would bear against the slide on firing. The floating chamber was stopped by an extension of the barrel, but the slide cycled full stroke. While it worked, the conversions had only average accuracy, and the floating chamber would get dirty with powder residue and gradually stop working.

Another conversion, the Kart, clamped the barrel tightly to the frame, and had a separate breechblock that cycled. The sights stayed securely fastened to the barrel, and the lightweight breechblock extracted, ejected and fed the new cartridge.

The latest conversions use slides made of aluminum, like the EAA and Ciener. The lighter weight of the aluminum slide does not require a floating chamber, and the aluminum-slide conversions are much more reliable than the old Colt conversions. The Marvel increases accuracy by having a separate breechblock, with the barrel tightly secured to the frame.

The 9mm breechface

.30 Luger, And The Point Is?

The .30 Luger is the predecessor to the 9mm Parabellum, and uses essentially the same case. At least, that's what you read. The nominal 9mm Parabellum case is .754" long. The specs for the .30 Luger call for a case .850" long. You can't make the .30 from the ubiquitous 9's, not without leaving the neck short. Not often seen in the U.S., the .30 Luger has some popularity overseas. Some countries do not allow their citizens to own military-caliber pistols, and the .30 Luger is a way around this restriction. (In which case making .30 brass from 9mm's would not be a legal option for them.) You can convert a 9mm or .38 Super to .30 Luger simply by fitting a replacement barrel. I made my own barrel by boring out a pitted .45 barrel to be a locking-lug containing sleeve, and then press-fitting a five-inch section of .30 caliber rifle barrel into it. Fitted and chambered, it works fine and was a useful learning experience.

If you are looking for a soft-recoiling centerfire cartridge, it is far easier to develop a soft load for the 9mm or .38 Super than to find and fit a .30 Luger barrel. But, they do exist. The last one I saw listed as a Colt manufactured .30 Luger pistol was a Commander made for an overseas contract in 1971. Apparently, after the contract was satisfied, Colt sold the extras, something they have done regularly. That particular pistol, one of five known in the U.S., was

The Colt conversion units are reasonably reliable, and marginally accurate. Their advantage is dirt-cheap .22 lr ammo.

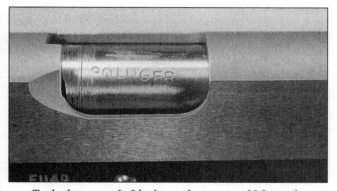

To do the research, I had to make my own .30 Luger barrel. Bar-Sto keeps promising to make some, but there are so many calibers competing for their attention the little Luger keeps slipping back.

.30 Luger Chronograph Results

Brand, Caliber, weight & style	Average	Sd.	Es.	PF.
Remington 93 gr. FMJ	1190	28.2	65.3	111

listed for sale at $7,500! In year 2000 dollars. You can load and shoot an awful lot of really soft-recoiling 9mm or .38 Super for that kind of money. A barrel would cost more in .30 Luger than in 9/38, so again, what is the point?

You would think the .30 Luger would be loaded to the same pressure specs as the 9mm Parabellum, but the loads I've tested were milder. Winchester load data shows a single load, as 25,500 cup. Loaded to 9mm pressures (34,000 psi) the .30 can be a snappy little round.

9mm, And Why?

To make a 1911 work in a 9mm Parabellum, you need to have the correct slide, with a 9mm/.38 Super breechface. You also need magazines with internal spacers. The 9x19 case is .394" or so wide at the base, and .380" at the mouth. The case taper is great for submachineguns, allowing proper function regardless of climate and cleanliness. In a handgun, especially the 1911, it can be a problem. If you use 9mm ammo in a .38 Super magazine, the cartridge has too much elbow room. During feeding the cartridge nosedives when

the slide hits it, and the tip of the cartridge can hit the front of the magazine, or the frame under the feed ramp.

With the proper magazines, a 1911 will work perfectly with 9mm ammo. The recoil can be soft, with the right bar-

Some might ask, if the Browning is available in 9mm, why a 9mm 1911? Try finding a new beavertail for your P-35, a new thumb safety, or new sights. The aftermarket parts volume is there to serve the 1911.

The 9mm Luger is a very efficient cartridge, and can be accurate if properly loaded.

9X19 Parabellum Chronograph Results

Brand, Caliber, weight & style	Average	Sd.	Es.	PF.
PMC Starfire 124 JHP	1094	6.4	17.5	136
Rem Golden Saber 124 +P	1108	33.1	85.0	137
Black Hills 124 JHP	1164	15.1	34.6	144
Federal 115 JHP +P+	1273	14.7	36.1	146
Cor-Bon 115 JHP +P	1342	6.3	15.1	154
Federal 147 Hydra Shok	945	6.9	17.3	139
W-W 115 JHP +P+ LE-Only	1348	12.0	30.8	155
Texas Ammunition Co 115 JHP	1283	16.4	38.5	147

This beautifully-done pistol by King's on a Para frame was going to be the world-ruler, until the rules were changed. High capacity, accurate, but as a 356 TSW, it could only be Minor in Limited. (Photo courtesy King's)

rel it will be accurate and with modern dies reloading the brass is a snap. So why have a 9mm 1911? With a supply of cheap or free ammo, why not? Also, if you have a carbine chambered in 9mm, you can reload ammunition for both, and practice at indoor ranges in the winter. In the northern climes, indoor shooting is sometimes the only shooting you can do. Even if you can take the cold, losing your brass in the snow is no fun. By using a 9mm carbine you can shoot on any indoor range that allows use of your 9mm 1911. Ammunition commonality is very useful.

The standard loadings of the 9mm Parabellum run at a maximum of 34,000 psi. The various factory loadings of +P and +P+ ammo operate at higher, but not defined pressures. On some 9mm cases, you will see a strange mark in the headstamp, a cross in a circle. It is the NATO acceptance mark, and indicates that that ammunition met NATO performance and manufacturing standards. NATO-spec ammo is usually good stuff, and definitely full-power ammo.

.38 Super, My Head Is Spinning

In the last 20 years, a bewildering variety of chamberings have been used in the 1911 pistol, all for competition reasons. In 1929, the .38 Super saw the light of day. After WWII, Colt came out with models in 9mm Parabellum. Until the late 1970s, the medium-recoil choice was simple:

9mm or .38 Super, neither accurate and not of much use. Then Bar-Sto began to offer match-grade barrels chambered in .38 Super, barrels that were accurate both because they were well made, and because the chamber was properly shaped.

A new kind of competition had sprung up, IPSC. Instead of standard strings of "x" numbers of shots in "y" seconds, each competitor had to solve the course himself and was timed doing it. To aid in recoil recovery, some competitors began putting muzzle brakes on their pistols. A brake, or compensator, works better when the gases going through it are high pressure rather than low. A .38 Super operates at higher pressure than a .45 does. The stage was set.

Later, magazine capacity became an issue. If a stage has 30 shots in it, a higher magazine capacity gives a competitor an advantage over someone else with a lower capacity. You can stuff more .38 Supers into a magazine than you can .45's.

So why the variety? Match rules and physics. Some shooters were loading their ammo in 9mm cases, to make the Major power factor. While a .38 Super is only slightly over the maximum pressures while making Major, a 9mm is greatly over the limit. The rule makers forbade 9mm Major ammunition. To get around the rule, some shooters began to use 9x21 cases. The 9x21 is a Parabellum case made 2mm

.38 Super Chronograph Results				
Brand, Caliber, weight & style	Average	Sd.	Es.	PF.
W-W 130 FMJ	1156	17.3	40.6	150
Cor-bon, 115 JHP	1439	13.9	32.2	165

longer, to get around that pesky rule we discussed about civilians in some countries and military calibers.

While the 9x21 had to work at the same excessive pressures as the 9x19 to make Major, it got around the rule because there were no SAAMI specs to define and restrict it.

Meanwhile, other experimenters were working on real or perceived shortcomings of the .38 Super. After 20 years of experimenting, brass fabricating and testing, we have a fistful of cartridges that are built around three minor variations of the 9mm/.38 Super case. While the dimensions are minor, getting the wrong ammo into your gun can keep it from working, or blow a case and trash a magazine. If you use a 1911 chambered in any of these, and reload your ammo, you must sort cases to make sure you don't mix them up!

The Basics

The three cases are: 9mm derivative, .38 Super derivative, and wide-base .38 Super derivative.

The 9mm Parabellum tapers from base to mouth. The base is approximately .388"-.391", while the case tapers down to .378"-.380" at the mouth. The derivative cases all use the same base diameter, and then taper down to the mouth diameter either at the datum line of the 9x19 case, or at their own, longer length. The 9X21 is a derivative, as is the Winchester 9x23. (But the 9x23 is listed with the Super derivatives because of its longer overall length (OAL))

A cartridge that was unveiled with much fanfare in competition circles, and promptly died due to rule changes, was the .356 TSW. The "three-five-six Team Smith & Wesson" was a lengthened 9mm, to get around the "no-9mm Major" rule. Its case is 22.5mm long, with an overall length the same as 9x19 ammo. The rule change that did it in was the insistence on IPSC Major ammo being a caliber larger than 9mm.

The difference between the 9mm derivatives and the Super derivatives is the loaded OAL. The 9mm derivatives stay within the OAL of a 9x19, while the Super derivatives are longer, out to the .45ACP OAL of 1.250"

The Super (L) doesn't taper, while others (9x21, R) do. If you don't sort, you'll find out the hard way when the case hits your sizing die.

The .38 Super does not taper. The case is a straight cylinder from mouth to extractor groove, .380" in diameter. The rim is actually a semi-rim, and sticks out from the case diameter. While the nominal spec for it is supposed to be .406", I have measured quite a few and most are in the .399" to .402" range. Cases derived from the Super use the straight walls, and vary the rims. Some, like the .38 Super Comp, use a thick front-to-back rim that is .385". Some shooters feel that the rims on the Super cause feeding problems, and will use special brass without the extra rim diameter. My Supers feed both, and I have had no problems with the semi-rimmed original design. However, there must be at least a few out there who have had problems, or brass makers wouldn't be making the newer designs.

The wide-base Super derivatives use a different approach. Rather than make the rims smaller, they prefer to split the difference and have the base match the rim. A large-base Super derivative like the 9mm Super Comp,

All these cases are interchangeable, although you wouldn't want to load the "38 Auto" case up to IPSC Major.

The 9x21 and the 356 TSW are derived from, and replacements for, the 9x19.

The length difference between the Super and the 9x21 is small, and you can't sort them unless you look at the headstamp. This 9x21 slipped through the inspection and got hammered by the sizing die.

Not all pistols could use these cases interchangeably. Sort your brass and know what your 1911 likes and dislikes. My Caspian will have none of these, the Colt will use all of them. Your mileage may vary.

An early attempt at a medium-diameter bullet in a 9mm package. Note the smaller-diameter rim.

9x23, and the Hornady 38 TJ (named after Todd Jarrett) will have both rim and base diameters in the .385" area. The thicker walls aid in pressure control, and the flush rim aids feeding. What it does to a pistol chambered for the regular Super is bind it up on feeding when the taper of the wide base hits the back of the regular chamber. If you are reloading .38 Super, you'll know when you run across a 9mm Super Comp, because you can't get it into the sizing die. Again, you must sort your brass before getting to resizing.

If you are using a 1911 single-stack chambered in .38 Super, you'll find that your Chip McCormick magazines may not hold 10 rounds if you use the .38 Super derivative wide-base brass. The rim of each upper cartridge nestles in the extractor groove of the one below it. The wide-base brass can't nestle, and the fat bases stack up without overlap.

Which caliber for you? If you are building a racegun for IPSC competition, your gunsmith can tell you what he prefers. If you're building a 9-pin, Bianchi, PPC or steel gun, stick with standard 38 Super. Your pistol will be marked on the chamber what it is made for. Use the brass it was made for. Yes, you can get your 9x23 gun to run using standard .38 Super brass, but the brass is being fired in an over-sized chamber (compared to what the brass was intended for) and you will find that your brass life is much shorter than it would otherwise be. If you use 38 Super brass in a pistol chambered for 9mm Super Comp, you could blow out a case and trash a magazine.

In which case having saved a few pennies on range brass, you just damaged an expensive high-cap magazine. Sort your brass, use the right stuff, and spare the $150 high-cap.

The standard pressure ceiling for the .38 Super is around 35,000 psi. In order to make Major, many competitors trade brass life for velocity, and run their cases higher. The 9x23 Winchester has a maximum ceiling of 46,000 psi. The tougher 9x23 brass does not give up useful life for velocity.

Winchester's attempt at introducing the 9X23 as a safe to use .38 Super +P+ that could make competition Major velocities didn't do as well as they had hoped. The competitive shooters liked it, as the brass is tough and durable. However, it would only fit in a 1911-sized platform, and not any of the pistols considered by Law Enforcement. When Colt ran into economic difficulties, Winchester quietly stopped production.

.41 AE, A Solution Without A Problem

The .41 Action Express is a neither fish nor fowl cartridge. The idea was to use the larger .410" diameter bullets and cases to fit, with a rebated, or smaller diameter rim. The cartridge could then be fit to a 9mm package, offering the smaller grip diameter of a 9mm, with the high capacity of the nine and a larger bullet than the nine. All this by simply switching barrels and recoils springs from 9mm to .41 AE.

10mm Chronograph Results				
Brand, Caliber, weight & style	**Average**	**Sd.**	**Es.**	**PF.**
W-W Silvertip 175 JHP	1242	13.7	28.0	217
Norma 170 JHP	1227	12.4	32.3	208
Hornady 180 XTP-JHP	1191	21.9	51.3	214
Cor-bon, 135 JHP	1467	15.5	33.3	198
Federal 155 JHP	1367	11.7	30.7	212

The rim was sized to fit 9mm breechfaces. The problem was, with the rim down out of the way, feeding problems could easily happen. When the .40 S&W came along, the .41 AE disappeared. And in a 1911, magazine capacity was not materially changed.

The .41 AE used the same pressure ceiling as the 9mm.

10 millimeter breechface

10mm

I'm covering the 10mm before the 40 because the 10mm came first. The 10mm, or .40 caliber, had been around as a revolver cartridge for a long time. The .38-40 is not a "38" any more than the .38 Special is. While the .38 Spl uses a .357" bullet the .38-40 uses a .400". The .38-40 was very popular with users of the Colt Single Action Army revolver, and it was the third most-popular cartridge chambered during the initial production run of Colt SAA's. While experimenters kept trying to come up with a medium-caliber revolver round to overcome the drawbacks of the .38-40, the pistol field was left alone. John Browning made a prototype in 1910 of a pistol that was a scaled-down 1911, chambered for a cartridge called the 9.8 mm, for field trials in Bucharest. Besides the fact that it was an actual .38, using .380" bullets, it appears to have been a Commander length pistol. Colt didn't get around to making a Commander until after WWII.

However, it wasn't until the mid 1970s that any serious and lasting work began on a medium-bore pistol cartridge. The staff at Guns & Ammo magazine went to a lot of trouble to make something new. They used cut-down .30 Remington rifle cases, and the bullets intended for use in .38-40 cartridges. Instead of working with a 1911, they opened the breechface of a Browning High Power and used special barrels bored out for .400" diameter bullets. (Why? Because there were no high-capacity magazines for the 1911, and by building the new .40 G&A in a Browning, they could have a ten or eleven-shot pistol.) The result was an efficient little cartridge, but neither gun makers nor ammunition makers were interested.

In the early 1980's, Jeff Cooper wanted to improve on the 1911 and its cartridge, and the result was a new pistol and a new round for it. Called the BREN Ten, the pistol had many desirable and useful features. The thumb safety could be switched from one side to the other. The magazines, when you could get them, were high-capacity. However, while the makers turned out guns, they were dependent on a magazine fabricator to make magazines for them, and the tubes were not forthcoming. It may seem almost reasonable to pay $125 each for high-cap mags today, but in 1985, when surplus 1911 mags went for $5-10 each, it was highway robbery.

The Ten part of the Bren was its cartridge. A true 10mm, it uses .400" jacketed bullets and .401" lead bullets. The first ammo was loaded by Norma, and their specs called for a 200-grain bullet at 1,200 fps. But with the demise of the BREN Ten, what good was a cartridge without a pistol for it? Without magazines for the few Bren Tens, the 10mm was dying, and then Colt arrived. They chambered their Delta Elite in 10mm, and now shooters were interested. The 10mm required a different breechface than the .45, a slightly relocated feed ramp on the frame, and a slightly altered magazine. By using a heavier than normal recoil spring the Colt was fully up to the task of the 200/1200 Norma equation. In 1986, three cars full of FBI agents tried to arrest two armed robbers in Miami. When the dust settled, the two robbers were dead, almost all of the FBI agents were shot, and the FBI was very unhappy with the performance of the 9mm ammunition their agents used.

The FBI quickly decided that the 10mm was what they wanted. By going to the 10mm, the FBI neatly sidestepped all the arguments that had raged for decades between the

A 10mm breechface, a 10mm magazine, and an...8mm Nambu? It can be done, but not until I've exhausted all the other questions I have on the R&D schedule.

9mm and the .45. There were only two problems: qualification and daily wear. The 10mm was a powerful round, and S&W would not make a 10mm in an alloy framed pistol. Getting agents to carry the full-size and all steel pistol was not easy. The recoil of 10mm ammo was another, larger, problem. At 200 grains and 1,200 fps, only the most dedicated agent could qualify, and no one enjoyed the experience. The FBI was already in court over training procedures that disproportionately disqualified otherwise suitable women trainees, and this cartridge made it worse.

The FBI asked for a load that some disparagingly called "FBI Lite", with a 180-grain bullet loaded to 1,050 fps. While in the process of making this new light load work, the engineers at Winchester and S&W figured out that if they could eliminate the air space the new load created in the capacious 10mm case, they could shorten the cartridge and fit it into a 9mm sized frame. Thus the .40 S&W was born.

The 10mm, as do all the 10mm case derivatives, runs right up there with the .38 Super, at 35,000 psi.

9X25, Turning Fun Into Work

The 9x25 was a brief and unsatisfying experiment with the parent 10mm case. Basically, take a 10mm case and neck it down to 9mm. Used only for IPSC competition by a few shooters for a couple of years, the advantage was singular: more gas flow for a compensator. To get a larger case to deliver the same velocity as a smaller case, you need more powder. While a .38 Super might need 10 or 12 grains of powder to get a 115-grain bullet up to Major, the 9x25 or 9x25 Dillon would use 18 grains of a slower powder to generate the same velocity.

More powder means more gas, and a slower-burning powder retains a higher pressure at the compensator. The disadvantages of the 9X25 were many. It is impressively loud, even on a range full of .38 Super shooters. The recoil, while lacking muzzle flip due to the compensator, drives straight back at the shooter. Wrist, elbow and shoulder complaints were reported by some shooters. And the impressive volumes of gas eroded barrels and comps at an alarming rate. Even for serious IPSC shooters, wearing a barrel out in 3,000 rounds gets expensive, and getting 3,000 rounds out of a 9x25 barrel was a good average.

Rarely seen any more, the supposed advantages of the 9X25 proved to be too costly and not worth the effort.

A .400-inch bullet, 180 grains, going 1,000 fps is new? On the left, a .40 S&W, 1990, center is a .38-40, circa 1890, and right a .45 ACP, 1968. OK, the .45 isn't a .400" bullet, but so what?

40 S&W

Coming out of the 10mm FBI experience, the .40 S&W was a wild card at the 1990 SHOT Show. Would it work? Would anyone want it? Were you kidding? In 10 years, the .40 has taken over the pistol market. If there is a manufacturer of 9mm pistols who doesn't offer their product in .40, shooters aren't interested. Police Departments, right in the middle of switching to 9mm pistols from .38 revolvers, started dumping the 9mms as fast as they could get their hands on .40s. In IPSC competition, the new .40 combined nicely with the brand-new high-capacity 1911 frames, and a new category came about. Suddenly, the Limited, or Stock, category at a practical match didn't mean your crusty old .45, it meant a high-capacity .40. Competitors went from eight shots to 18 in a leap.

In less than 10 years the .40 went from new to common. Commercial reloaders view 9mm brass as little more than scrap weight brass. There is so much of it some won't even

.40 S&W Chronograph Results				
Brand, Caliber, weight & style	**Average**	**Sd.**	**Es.**	**PF.**
W-W 180 FMJ White box	899	12.0	25.7	161
Remington Golden Saber 180 JHP	918	6.7	18.7	165
Cor-Bon 180 JHP	1060	9.3	23.2	191
Cor-Bon 165 JHP	1164	14.1	36.1	192
Cor-Bon135 JHP	1310	12.9	24.2	177
W-W Silvertip 155 JHP	1153	21.1	56.2	179

These .40 loads didn't blow up from being over-pressure, but from being shot in a 10mm chamber. DO NOT use .40s in a 10! (L: 10mm, R: .45 ACP)

pay for it, and will load it only from traded-in brass. The .40 has become so accepted by so many Police Departments, it is nearly as common as 9mm brass. One trip to the right police range can net you a five gallon bucket of .40 brass for little or no cost.

The .40 S&W (or .40 Auto as Ruger pistols are marked) comes in one flavor commercially loaded, and two flavors from reloaders. The standard load is a short round, meant to fit into a 9mm package. The standard load is 1.120" long, and fits inside a 9mm magazine tube. Of course, the magazine feed lips have to be altered to work with the .40, but the whole idea was to fit it into a 9mm-sized pistol, rather than needing a .45-sized pistol. But switching calibers is an engineering exercise, not simply a matter of changing barrels. I have an EAA pistol in the safe that is a switch-top gun, with slide and barrel assemblies in 9mm and .40. Two of the magazines I have will feed either 9mm or 40, while the rest feed one or the other. A .40 will not fit into a single-stack 9mm mag. While it will fit into a high-cap mag, the tighter dimensions of the 9mm feed lips will cause feeding problems with .40 caliber rounds.

When Colt made 40s, they discovered that like the 9mm, they had to put a spacer in the back of the magazine in order to get the round to feed properly. Reloaders quickly found that if they loaded their rounds longer, out to 1.200" the 40 would feed easier, and they could use 10mm magazines. (10mm magazines were/are more common and cheaper than dedicated .40 mags.)

The longer length also eased pressure problems. The .40 is a high-pressure cartridge, operating at 35,000 psi. In the 1911, the pressure is not much of a problem, but in a pistol originally designed for the 9mm, there is not as much extra steel for a safety margin. Some .40s have blown cases from firing reloads. Excess pressure in the 1911 usually expresses itself by blowing out the case base and trashing a magazine, embarrassing, but not hazardous, so long as you have safety glasses on. In other pistols, a blown case can mean a cracked frame and an expensive repair.

One additional solution to the .40 blowup problem is to use a ramped barrel. The integral ramp of the barrel allows the chamber walls on the bottom to extend back farther on the case. More of the case is thus supported by steel. You will find many IPSC competitors who shoot a .40 do so in pistols with integral ramps. The ramp also helps in controlling the brass when you are on the range with Glock shooters. Glocks tend to have larger chambers than do many 1911 barrels. The original Glock, the G-17, was built as a military pistol in 9mm Parabellum. Reloading is rare in Europe, and the use of new ammo, not reloads, common. As long as the pistol works reliably, shooters in Europe usually don't care how the brass is treated. If you pick up Glock-hammered .40 brass that has been expanded too much, shooting it in a supported-chamber 1911 is much safer than in an unsupported chamber. (Better to look for the distinctive Glock firing pin imprint, and discard any such brass rather than run the risk.)

How does loading the round to a longer length ease the pressure problem? By moving the bullet forward you increase available case capacity. The extra room allows the use of slightly slower-burning powders (powders that would otherwise take up too much room) that let you gain the velocity you seek without running pressures through the roof.

.357 Sig

The Sig is a derivative of a derivative. Basically the .40 case necked down to 9mm, velocity is its reason for existence. In the circles devoted to stopping power inquiry, the .357 Magnum loaded with a 125-grain bullet is legendary. By some calculations it has a single-shot stopping power efficiency of 96 percent. But the .357 Magnum is available only in a revolver, and revolvers are passé. The 9mm does not come close, and the difference is due to velocity. Even with special loads for law enforcement only, marked "9mm+P+" and greatly over accepted pressures, the 9mm can't muster the velocity needed for such performance. Why not a .38 Super? Because it still can't make it without going over pressure, and it is too long to fit into a 9mm-sized pistol.

.357 Sig Chronograph Results				
Brand, Caliber, weight & style	**Average**	**Sd.**	**Es.**	**PF.**
15 JHP Cor-bon	1488	5.6	12.1	171
125 JHP Cor-bon	1470	15.2	37.9	184
125 FMJ Georgia Arms	1458	18.8	45.1	182
125 JHP Federal	1393	14.1	34.3	173

.38 Special Chronograph Results

Brand, Caliber, weight & style	Average	Sd.	Es.	PF.
Federal 148 WC Match	630	8.8	25.2	93

The .357 Sig is the biggest case that will fit in a 9mm magazine tube, and work. It delivers the .357 Magnum performance, for those who want it. One such department is the Chicago Transit Police, who tested and accepted it in part because it was the only round that would penetrate the seats on trains. Such penetration is not a minor consideration if your workplace is full of train seats, as theirs is.

As a competition round, it has no advantages. The .38 Super works as well as the .357 Sig to feed in the chamber and feed gas to a compensator, and you can fit more of them in a magazine. If you reduce the load to cut down on recoil, you might as well use a 9mm, and you guessed it, get more in a magazine. As a defensive round, it is great, but only if you follow the school of light bullets at hyper velocities.

While it is a bottlenecked cartridge, it headspaces on the case mouth and not the shoulder. You cannot make .357 SIG ammo from .40 brass, (it is too short); you must use .357 SIG brass.

.224 Boz

The .224 Boz is another derivative of a derivative. Taking the .357 Sig idea to the extreme, it is a 10mm case necked down to, you guessed, .224" It launches a .224" bullet of 50 grains at 2,100 fps velocity. When I first read of this cartridge, I had to sit down. My efforts at making a .30 Luger barrel paled in comparison. But what could it be for? It couldn't make Major for IPSC, and would damage any steel targets being used. It wasn't any use for Bull's eye, because the .22 pistol has to be a rimfire, and the Any Centerfire pistol has to be at least a .32.

And, did I mention, it would damage steel...wait a minute. NATO has been on a kick lately for what they term a Personal Defense Weapon. Something better than a handgun, that is light and handy for military crews and those whose jobs are not directly combat-related, but might find a surprise around the next corner. (Forget for the moment that it was invented more than 50 years ago, and is called the M1 Carbine. Forget also, that you can do just about everything

The .357 Sig is an easy change. This 10mm went to .357 Sig in 30 seconds, including magazine loading time.

.45 ACP Chronograph Results

Brand, Caliber, weight & style	Average	Sd.	Es.	PF.
Magtech, 230 JRN	781	22.2	49.6	179
PMP, 220 JRN	873	18.3	45.4	192
PMC, 230 JRN	809	7.6	19.6	186
Black Hills Blue, 230 JRN	809	12.7	35.5	186
Black Hills Red, 230 JRN	813	12.5	27.9	187
Zero, 185 JHP	891	17.2	33.9	165
West Coast, 200 JRN	844	13.7	32.5	169
Montana Gold, 185 JHP	948	11.3	28.5	175
Rainier, 230 JRN	747	13.9	37.4	172
Sierra, 230 JHP	781	15.1	35.2	179
Texas Ammo Co., 230 JRN	828	19.2	46.4	190
Texas Ammo Co., 185 JHP	953	11.8	28.8	176
Hornady 200 JHP-XTP	878	17.5	45.6	176
Oregon Trail 200 L-SWC	869	16.8	45.8	173

.45 ACP+P Chronograph Results

Brand, Caliber, weight & style	Average	Sd.	Es.	PF.
Cor-Bon, 165 JHP	1256	36.6	89.2	207
Cor-Bon, 185 JHP	1157	24.0	51.6	214
Cor-Bon, 200 JHP	1040	18.2	40.3	208
Cor-bon, 230 JHP	942	14.3	29.5	216
Triton, 185 JHP-Hi Vel	1086	27.8	53.4	201
Triton, 230 JHP-Hi Vel	921	5.2	11.2	212
Triton, 165 JHP-Quik Shok	1202	13.9	34.9	198
Triton, 203 JHP-Quik Shok	915	10.5	26.5	210
Texas Ammo Co. 185 JHP	952	9.9	26.3	176
Texas Ammo Co. 230 JHP	821	14.9	42.0	189

While the round fits the tube, the magazine lips have to be extensively modified to feed a .38 wadcutter round.

the Boz does, by loading steel-cored bullets in a 9mm or a .30 Luger.)

The .224 Boz could fit the NATO bill. Other than that, I can't see much use for it. And the initial reports indicated that the pressure of the cartridge, and its cycling dynamics, could be damaging to the slide. For the performance, who wants a peened breechface and chipped or rounded locking lugs?

Wadcutters for targets

.38 Special, Talk About Specialized

The 1911 using a revolver cartridge? Yes, for target shooting. The Colt Wadcutter Gun is a straight blow-back pistol lacking locking lugs on the barrel and slide. It also has a spiral groove machined into the chamber, to slow down the extraction of the empty case. The idea was to make as accurate and soft-shooting a pistol as possible for the "Any Centerfire" portion of a Bull's eye match.

Jim Clark Sr. made his reputation as a gunsmith (he had already done so as a competitor), in the early 1960s by converting .38 Super pistols to work with .38 special ammunition. Both the Colt and the Clark used full wadcutter ammunition, the only ammo that would fit in a 1911 magazine. This required highly modified standard magazines. I had a customer in the late 1980s who had a Clark conversion, and wanted to shoot it. The pistol league we were in used six-shot strings, and the five-shot capacity of the .38 magazines was a real hindrance to his score.

The obstacle to any change was the breechface. The Clark (or any) conversion involved opening the breechface up to the .38 size, .435" from the 38 Super size, .405". I speculated that moving the extractor tunnel would have been too expensive for Clark, so it had to be where Colt made it. I replaced the extractor, ejector, recoil spring, and installed a Bar-Sto .38 Super barrel. The pistol worked perfectly.

Should you look into a .38 Wadcutter gun to shoot targets? Probably not. Many competitors use a .45. The .45 pistol can be just as accurate and nearly as soft in recoil as a .38 wadcutter gun. Personally, I would build an Any Center-

fire pistol in .38 Super. It will feed more reliably, the magazines are cheaper, and any good IPSC gunsmith can build a Super to be as accurate as a wadcutter gun.

The .38 Special wadcutter pressure runs at about 12,000 psi.

The First Breechface

.45 ACP

This is the original, and most common design. The .45 ACP came out of the pistol trials of 1907, and was the standard cartridge applicants had to use for the trials of 1911. The .45 used to have a reputation as a hard-kicking cartridge that was difficult to control. That was all before the .44 Magnum. Now, it is considered by most to be a soft-recoiling big bore that can be as accurate as you want it to be.

The standard and defining measurements are a bullet weight in round nose configuration of 230 grains, an overall length of 1.270" and a rim diameter of .475-.478".

The brass is common, large and easy to handle, and has a long reloading life. In reloading, the .45 operates at a low pressure, in the 16,000 to 17,000 psi range as a maximum, and is very forgiving of many reloading errors. (Many common loads in reloading manuals don't exceed 12,000 psi). The .45 is so forgiving that it is difficult to find a load that won't shoot reasonably accurately. When you refine your loading, and find a load the pistol likes, accuracy can be spectacular.

.45 ACP+P

Brass and steel are stronger now than in 1911. Powders offer more options for a desirable pressure curve. By using slower powders than were available in 1911 and, adding the extra safety margins of the tougher brass and steel, the .45 can be pumped up a step. While the standard .45 ACP load, running at 16,000 psi, can only push a 185-grain bullet at 900 fps, a +P load can achieve 1,050 to 1,100 fps. The cost is greater pressure, but the 1911 can handle it. The .45ACP+P ceiling is 23,000 psi.

If you are going to seek such velocities, you should step up in recoil spring strength, and go to an 18- or 19-pound spring. If you reload to this level, and use tired old brass, you'll find it cracking at a greater rate than the softer loads.

.38-45

A necked-down .45 in an attempt to make a softer-shooting target gun without the gunsmithing difficulties of the .38 wadcutter. Rather than heavily-modify a pistol to use .38 Special wadcutters, the .38-45 used a barrel made with a .38 bore, using necked-down .45 cases. Ultimately unsuccessful, due to accuracy and reliability problems.

.38 Casull

Instead of trying to duplicate a .38 Special wadcutter in a 1911, the Casull uses better brass and powders to reach unheard of velocities. A 125-grain jacketed bullet can be pushed to 1,800 fps. What is it good for? I don't know yet, but it may have some promise for the long-range event of the Masters. The .38 Casull has a slightly rebated rim (smaller than the case body) to provide smoother feeding, and the shoulder dimensions are different than the old .38-45.

This Bar-Sto 400 Cor-bon barrel is accurate, and the round is powerful. As a bonus, you can make practice ammo from .45 ACP cases.

41 Avenger

An early attempt at a powerful necked-down .45 case, the Avenger was necked down to, yes, .41 caliber by J.D. Jones in the early 1980s. While it delivered the power promised, the lack of suitable bullets doomed it. The short neck and overall length limitations meant it had to use relatively short bullets. At the time, the only .41 caliber bullets available were meant to be used in the .41 Magnum, and most were too long. Sierra had and has a 170-grain jacketed bullet, but that isn't much lighter than what's available for the .45.

As a handloading-only proposition, the pressure limits of the .41 Avenger were whatever the loader wanted. Many went beyond the limits of the .45 ACP case, or the .45 ACP+P loads, to achieve the performance they desired.

400 Cor-Bon

This round was created in the 1990s as a medium necked-down .45 case, with better luck than the .41 Avenger. Using .40 caliber bullets, of which there are many made for the .40 S&W and 10mm, the .400 Cor-Bon has impressive amounts of power, while delivering excellent accuracy. The .400 Cor-Bon operates in the .45ACP+P pressure range, around 23,000 to 24,000 psi. The extra power is available only in the lighter bullet weights. By the time you

.38 Casull Chronograph Results				
Brand, Caliber, weight & style	**Average**	**Sd.**	**Es.**	**PF.**
124 JHP	1842	14.1	33.8	226
147 JHP	1718	10.9	24.0	252

.400 Cor-Bon Chronograph Results				
Brand, Caliber, weight & style	**Average**	**Sd.**	**Es.**	**PF.**
135 JHP	1442	12.3	39.2	195
150 JHP	1362	16.1	44.5	204
155 FMJ	1226	9.2	21.4	190
165 JHP	1310	7.9	19.4	216

load a .400 Cor-Bon with 180-grain bullets, you have slipped down into the loading parameters of the parent .45 case. If you were to load a 400 Cor-Bon with 180-grain bullets, you would be hard-pressed to exceed the velocities possible from a straight .45 using 180-or 185-grain bullets.

Where velocity helps, the 400 Cor-Bon shines. As a bowling pin gun, it excels. Ken Tapp has used the .400 Cor-Bon to set records shooting bowling pins. The high velocity blows pins off, and the gas flow keeps a comp down.

If you are going to run your .400 Cor-bon right at the redline, use brass marked ".400 Cor-Bon" and not necked-down .45 ACP brass. The Cor-Bon marked brass has heavier case walls at the web, for more strength. For softer loads, use .45 ACP brass. Then, you can be sure your full-power ammo and soft ammo can be told apart at a glance.

45 Super

The Super derived from the old .45 Winchester Magnum. The Win Mag cases are/were trimmed to standard .45 ACP length, and the thicker case walls can withstand the higher pressures of the .45 Super. Developed by Dean Grennell, the Super delivers velocity, but you must be careful to keep the loaded ammo out of a standard 1911. The higher pressures will hammer a slide and frame using the standard recoil spring of a regular .45. In the interests of safety, I would run a 1911 as a .45 Super only with a ramped barrel. The ramp would allow full case support, taking full advantage of the tougher brass.

Loaded by Texas Ammo, and run in an Ace Custom conversion, a .45 Super runs at 37,000 psi. A 185-grain bullet leaves a .45 Super at 1,240 fps, and a 230-grain bullet travels at just under 1,100. For those hunting with handguns in areas that have foot-pound requirements, Texas Ammo loads the .45 Super Express, which keeps the 100 yard delivery of energy over 500 foot-pounds. In it, the 230-grain JHP goes 1,169 fps.

.450 SMC

The .450 SMC is another improved-brass .45 ACP-length case, designed to safely run at higher pressures. Made by Triton, to increase the strength of the case, the pocket for a large pistol primer was redesigned (easy to do with CAD/CAM equipment) to be a small rifle primer pocket.

.40 Super

The .40 Super started out as a .45 Super necked down, to gain more velocity than the .400 Cor-Bon. During testing the large pistol primer was swapped for a small pistol

.45 Super Chronograph Results				
Brand, Caliber, weight & style	Average	Sd.	Es.	PF.
Texas Ammo Co. 185 JHP-XTP (Tactical Load)	1174	15.6	39.9	217
Texas Ammo Co. 230 JHP-XTP (Tactical Load)	938	18.1	48.7	216
Texas Ammo Co. 200 JHP	1185	14.1	28.3	2378
Texas Ammo Co. 230 JHP	1074	41.7	107.2	247
Texas Ammo Co. 230 JRN	1083	10.0	23.8	249
Texas Ammo Co. JHP Express	1169	14.5	37.9	269
Texas Ammo Co. 230 JTC	1156	8.3	20.2	266

.40 Super Chronograph Results				
Brand, Caliber, weight & style	Average	Sd.	Es.	PF.
Trinton 135 JHP Hi Vel	1749	16.6	44.2	236
Trinton 135 JHP Quik Shok	1224	30.6	77.5	165
Trinton 155 JHP Quik Shok	1447	19.3	49.9	224
Trinton 165 JHP Hi Vel	1579	13.5	34.5	260
Trinton 200 JHP Hi Vel	1288	7.4	18.9	258

.460 Rowland Chronograph Results

Brand, Caliber, weight & style	Average	Sd.	Es.	PF.
Georgia Arms 185 JHP-Defense	1362	14.6	32.2	251
Georgia Arms 185 Nosler JHP	1447	15.6	38.5	267
Georgia Arms 230 Gold Dot	1347	15.7	40.6	309

primer. The .40 Super operates at 37,000 psi, and gains at least several hundred feet per second of velocity for any given bullet weight over the .400 Cor-Bon. Unlike the .400 Cor-Bon, the higher operating pressure and slightly greater capacity allows the .40 Super to use heavier bullets, and exceed the parent case velocity while using them. The .40 Super can launch a 135-grain bullet at 1,750 fps, and a 200-grain bullet up to 1,275 fps.

As with the .45 Super and .450 SMC, it would be best to build a .40 Super starting with a ramped barrel for full case support. Unlike the .400 Cor-bon, the Super cannot be loaded with .45 ACP cases. If you load soft-recoiling ammo for your .40 Super, be sure you don't mix up the loads.

.460 Rowland

The .460 Rowland avoids the problem of the .45 Super fitting in standard pistols by using a longer case. The overall length is the same as the standard .45 ACP, but the longer case won't chamber in standard pistols. While the .45 Super goes beyond a .45 +P, the Rowland moves the 1911 into .44 Magnum territory. While the Clark conversion barrel is a standard barrel without an integral feed ramp, were I building a gun from the start to shoot the .460 Rowland, I'd make it a ramped barrel gun. Not because I think there is anything weak about the barrel or brass, but because I like to have as much of a safety margin as I can get.

The .460 Rowland delivers legitimate .44 Magnum ballistics in a 1911 pistol. A 230-grain JHP at 1,350 should be plenty for hunting. If you feel the need for a handgun in bear country, then a 230-grain FMJ going at 1,350 should offer all the penetration you're going to get from a handgun. It also offers eight shots, fast, with more on the way. Not that dropping a bear with a handgun is something you can do with firepower, but if you're in for a penny you might as well be in for several magazine's worth.

More?

Larger cartridges, like the .45 Winchester Magnum, or the 10mm Magnum, can't fit into a standard 1911 magazine. To make those cartridges work in their guns, LAR Grizzly and AMT, respectively, had to make frames and magazines with more room front to back. The larger frames are harder to hold, and the increased recoil more difficult to deal with.

What caliber should your 1911 be? We'd need at least several more chapters for that question. The short and quick answer is: Buy your first one in .45, then add the others later.

CHAPTER FIVE

Disassembly

I once heard a shooter at a gun show explain that the 1911 was simple to disassemble because "...not many people could read back then." I don't know what illiteracy has to do with firearms maintenance, but my grandfather's report card indicates that even the poor school district that immigrant kids went to had semesters in Greek and Latin before high school. (He posted A's, by the way.)

No, the 1911 is easy to take apart because John Browning designed it that way. He believed that simple was strong, and in making the 1911 he simplified his earlier ideas. A basic disassembly is simple, doesn't take any tools, can be

Before you even get this far, is it loaded?

Even this full-house Michiguns Pin gun is easy to take apart, once you figure out what kind of recoil spring guide rod it has.

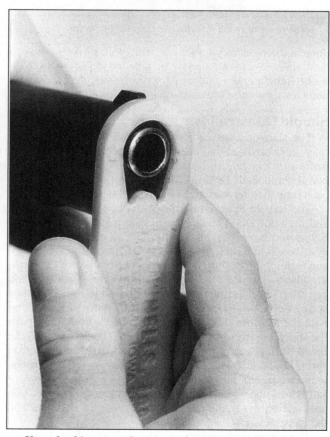

Use a bushing wrench to press the plunger back and turn the bushing.

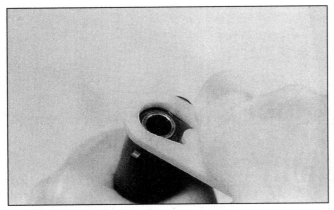

The wrench keeps the plunger in...

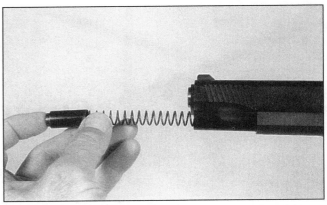

By the old method, the spring comes out forward, and can do so with authority. Don't have your face in its path.

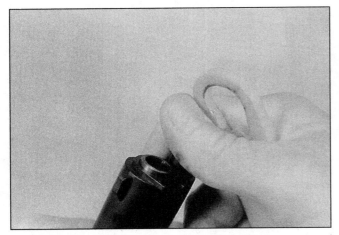

until you can catch it with your fingers, you hope.

Then line the slide notch up with the slide stop lever.

done in the field, in your lap, or using your pockets, and can be done in less than a minute. A detailed disassembly takes a drift punch and a couple of screwdrivers, and should be done on a smooth clean surface.

Simple Disassembly

The start of disassembly requires an unloaded pistol. It may seem obvious, and even silly to keep harping on it, but make sure the gun isn't loaded. I have been handed a number of "unloaded" firearms for my gunsmithing perusal, and each time disaster was averted by checking.

The start of disassembly involves the slide, the bushing, and the slide stop. The old-fashioned method of disassembly would have you resting the butt of the pistol against your bench, depressing the recoil spring retainer (or plug), and turning the bushing clockwise. The bottom of the bushing pivots out of the way of the recoil spring retainer. You can then ease the retainer out of the slide, then pull the spring out. Once the spring is out, line up the slide stop end with the shallower notch on the side of the slide, and push the slide stop free. Push the slide off the frame and catch the recoil spring guide rod. The drawback to this method is spring tension. If your fingers slip, the spring retainer can be launched free of the slide. It might strike you in the face, or sail across the room to strike something fragile. Also, you are rotating the bushing at the point where it is tightest on the barrel, increasing wear.

The newer method removes the slide stop first. Ease the slide back until you have the rear of the slide stop lined up

with the shallower notch. Wrap your hand around the slide and frame, trapping the slide in place. (Left hand clutching the slide, with your thumb through the trigger guard.) Push the slide stop through with your other hand. With the slide stop out, slide the frame backwards off the slide, keeping your fingers wrapped around the bottom of the slide as the frame comes off. You now have the slide off, with the recoil spring trapped underneath. Lift your index finger and pull the recoil spring guide out, and the spring with it. The disadvantage of this method is the need for hand strength in trapping the recoil spring. However, if you lose control of the spring, it is not pointed at or near your face.

With the slide off the frame, push the barrel slightly forward and turn the bushing counterclockwise until you see the bushing lug appear. With the lug out of its slot in the slide, you can pull the bushing free. In a 1911, with a tight fitting bushing, you may have to use the barrel as a sliding hammer to free the bushing. To do this, unlock the barrel and slide it forward. Grab the muzzle of the barrel and jerk it out of the slide, taking the bushing with it.

Thus ends the simple disassembly. At this point you can clean everything that needs cleaning to keep going during a match. Many times I have seen shooters at a match working in a Safe Area with the slide off, scrubbing gunk off or cleaning sand or grit out of their 1911s. With practice, you can have a 1911 stripped this far in a few seconds, wiped clean, and back together in less than a minute, and all while discussing the possibility of Jerry beating Robbie, or vice versa.

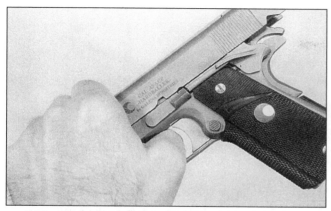

In the newer method, clamp the slide in your finger and push it back until the notch lines up.

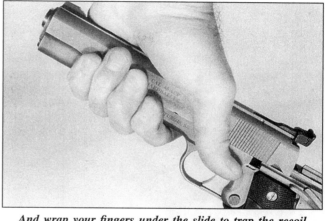

And wrap your fingers under the slide to trap the recoil spring.

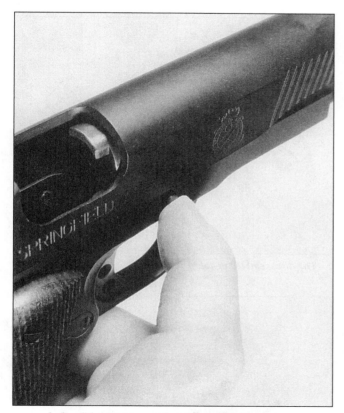

push the slide stop pin out from the right side.

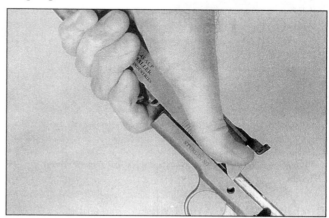

Once the slide clears the frame...

After you push the slide stop out, ease the slide forward...

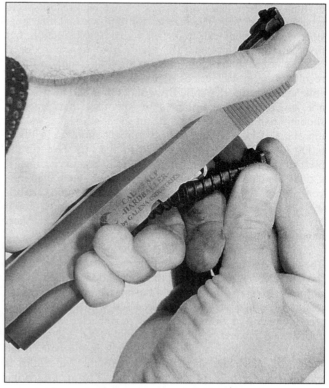

ease the spring out. If you slip, the spring is launched away from you, not towards you.

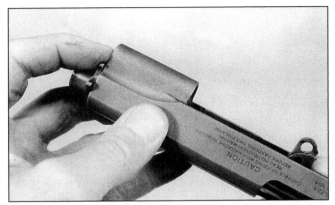

Turn the bushing clockwise to remove the recoil spring retainer.

Turn the bushing counterclockwise to free it from the slide.

The disassembled pistol.

If your 1911 has a guide rod, look at the end.

Bushings, Rods, And Caps

What do you do if your 1911 has been customized, and differs from the vanilla-plain model? What if there is no bushing? If there is a guide rod? Or a reversed recoil spring retainer? Never fear. The reasons for their use and their possible combinations can make for a messy explanation, but first, some background. The guide rod was introduced because some shooters felt that by providing support to the recoil spring, it was less likely to kink, would be more reliable, and last longer. While Browning left it out, he was also not anticipating the volumes of shooting that practical shooters had quickly worked themselves up to. The test firing of the 1911 prototype for government adoption involved 6,000 rounds, fired without a fault by the way. Even in the prehistoric days of 1978, when I started shooting seriously, a dedicated competitor would shoot more than that in a year's time. Anything that increased reliability and durability was to be considered. Do you need a guide rod? Probably not, even for high-volume shooters. Do they hurt anything? Not when properly fitted.

Guide rods come in two flavors, one-piece and two-piece. The two-piece are simple. You'll see a slot or hex socket on the end. Loosen and unscrew the end, and then disassemble normally. Even a gun without a bushing, a two-piece comes apart the regular way. A one-piece rod will usually have a small hole drilled through it an inch or so back of the muzzle end. Take a paper clip and bend one end of it to a short hook. Lock the slide open and place the hook in the hole in the guide rod. Ease the slide forward until the paper clip is trapped in the hole in the guide rod. The recoil spring retainer is now caught behind its usual location. Move the slide forward or back and line up the slide stop with its disassembly notch. Once you have removed the slide you can extract the recoil spring assembly from the rear.

There are some one-piece guide rods that do not have any holes drilled in them. Some are merely steel rods, but the Harrts is a mercury-filled steel rod. Drilling a hole in it would allow the mercury to run out. To remove a non-

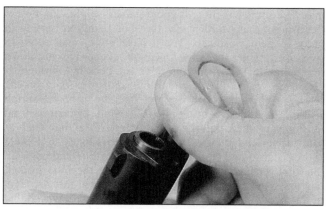

The traditional method of disassembly depends on you keeping the recoil spring retaining plug under control with your thumb.

One-piece rods require a paper clip with the tip bent.

On bull-barrel guns there isn't a lot of room.

Work the tip of the paper clip into the hole in the guide rod.

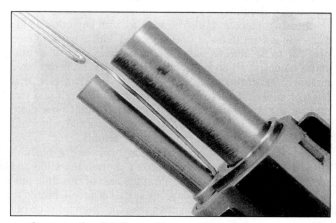

then ease the slide forward to trap the spring pin out from the right side.

Push the recoil spring assembly rearwards...

drilled one-piece rod, first look at the muzzle. On a gun with a bushing, does the end of the rod come flush with the retainer lip? If it does, you'll have to take the slide off to gain clearance. Remove the slide stop and let the rear of the guide rod shift. You'll gain enough clearance at the front that you can use your bushing wrench to turn the bushing, remove the retainer, and slide the spring off the rod. With the spring off, the rod will clear the slide when you pull it to the rear and out.

If the rod does not come flush with the retainer lip, simply use the bushing wrench to disassemble the old-fashioned way.

What if there is no bushing? The bushing is an extra part between the slide and barrel. By making the barrel large enough to fit the slide without the bushing, a gunsmith can get a tighter and more repeatable fit. He (or she) can also put more weight into the barrel, which delays unlocking without making the slide shuttle the extra weight back and forth on each shot. A bushing-free 1911 will always have a reverse recoil spring plug. Instead of the recoil spring retainer being kept in place by the bushing, on a reverse plug the retainer has a shoulder on its back end. The shoulder rests against the rear of the slide's recoil spring tunnel. It isn't as simple as sliding a reverse plug in place. The slide tunnel has a capture shoulder on its inside for the standard retainer. The gunsmith has to mill the rear of the slide tunnel to accommodate the reverse retainers shoulder (the slide can't be any longer with the new part installed) and then remove the vestiges of the capture shoulder.

On a two-piece rod, disassemble as with any other 1911. The only reason to use a one-piece rod with a bushing-free pistol is to be able to use a Harrts mercury rod. If a gunsmith built you a gun with this combination, he better have included the disassembly tool. The tool is a half-pipe that lets you press the retainer back out of the slide so you can remove the rod from the rear. Without the half-pipe there isn't any clearance between the recoil spring/guide rod assembly and the slide to remove the assembly.

Can you turn a bushing-free gun back into a bushing gun? As long as the gunsmith didn't shorten the slide and remove the bushing slot, yes. With the rear of the slide tunnel machined off, you'll have to install a recoil buffer to keep the slide from over-traveling in recoil, but that is no big deal.

Detailed Disassembly

Now you'll need tools. I once overheard another shooter at a gun show (there are a lot of people with a lot of myths about the 1911) say that "the 1911 didn't need any tools to come apart." I don't know about his, but all mine need at least some. The tools you'll need are a drift punch for the mainspring housing pin, a screwdriver for the grip screws, and a small eyeglass screwdriver.

Let's start at the slide, in the basic disassembly. The rear of the slide has the firing pin and extractor. To remove them, you must take the drift punch and press the firing pin into the slide. While holding the firing pin in, pivot the punch down to slide the retainer down. A tightly-fitted retainer

may take some wiggling. If your retainer is tight, don't press the firing pin any farther into the slide than you have to in order to gain clearance. You'll have more pivot room to work the retainer that way. Once the retainer has slid down far enough that the firing pin can't pop back out through its clearance hole, pull the punch out and press only on the retainer. When the retainer comes free, the firing pin spring will try to launch the firing pin. Restrain it. Once the spring tension is relaxed, pull the firing pin out. Take the punch or screwdriver and pry the extractor up. It is likely to come a short distance and stop. If the extractor stops, the hook on the front is caught on the breechface. Turn the slide around, and using the punch or screwdriver as a lever, flex the front of the extractor into the extractor shaft. (I am convinced that for some shooters, extractor tension problems stem from prying the extractor free, and muscling the hook off the breechface instead of easing it clear.) Pull the extractor out of the shaft. You now have your slide free of all parts but the sights. Leave them alone.

Frame Disassembly

Detailed disassembly of the frame requires all three of those tools, and you'll end up with at least 15, and, up to 23 parts, resting on your bench when you're done.

Start with the grips. Use a properly fitting screwdriver and unscrew the grip screws. Time out for minor gunsmith-

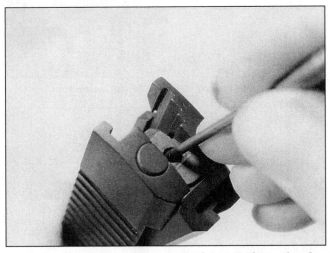

To disassemble the slide, press the firing pin forward and slide the retaining plate down.

The extractor may require some gentle prying to slide it out.

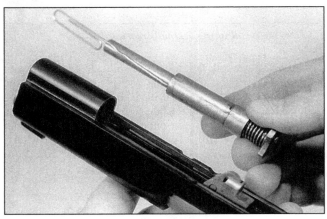

and extract it out over the barrel lugs.

Then line the slide notch up with the slide stop lever.

Ease the safety to the middle...

and push from the other side to ease it out. Don't let the spring and plunger launch themselves.

The mainspring housing is held on by a cross pin, secured by the mainspring's tension.

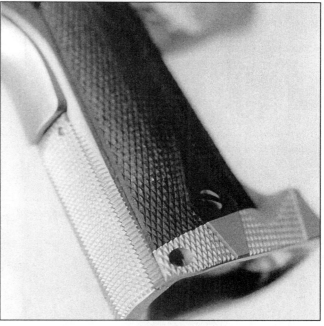

The soldered-on magazine funnel makes it very clear where the mainspring housing retaining pin is

ing. The grip screws screw into bushings that are in turn screwed into the frame. If when you unscrew the screws the bushing comes free, stop. Place a large drop of a thread locking compound on a card, and use a straw to transfer a controlled drop to the bushing screw thread in the frame. Tighten the bushing back in place and let the compound set. Then unscrew the grip screw.

With the grips off, cock the hammer if it has been lowered. When the slide is off the frame, do not dry fire a 1911. You can peen the leading edge of the hammer slot. With the hammer cocked, grasp the thumb safety and pivot it halfway

between on and off. The front shoulder of the safety will be in line with the plunger that controls it. Lift the safety straight out of the frame. In a pistol with a snug-fitting safety you may have to use the eyeglass screwdriver as a lever to pry the safety up. The plunger is spring-loaded, and may try to launch itself. The plunger assembly is supposed to be three parts that stay together, with two plungers and a spring. On many parts guns, they are not, and the rear plunger can be shot free of the frame.

While it looks like it might, the grip safety won't come free at this point. There is a modified safety that does, but most will not.

With the safety off and the plungers out, ease the hammer down. Use the drift punch to press the mainspring housing pin out of the frame. One end of the pin is cupped to make it easier to keep the drift punch in place. The pin can go in or out in either direction. With the pin out, slide the mainspring housing off. Now you can remove the grip safety. Lift the

hammer strut out of the way and pull the three-leaf spring out of the frame. Use the small screwdriver to press the hammer pivot pin out of the frame. It and the sear pivot pin have tiny heads, and can only come out from, and be inserted from, the left side. With the pin out, pull the hammer free. Repeat the process with the sear pivot pin and sear. On the right side of the frame and behind the trigger you'll find the rear of the magazine catch. The slotted head is not a screw, but the head of a tabbed retainer. If your pistol has an over-sized magazine catch, remove the large-diameter head before you try to remove the magazine catch. If your catch is longer

Slide the mainspring housing down and lift the grip safety clear.

The magazine catch retainer has to be turned. Some use Allen-head retainers.

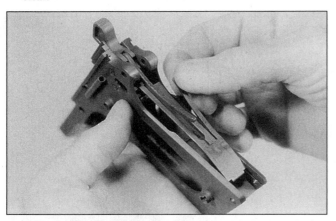

With the rear of the frame open, you can lift the three-leaf spring out.

Press the catch in from the left, then turn the retainer counterclockwise.

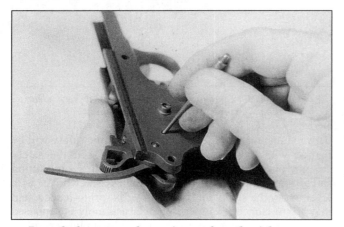

Press the hammer and sear pins out from the right.

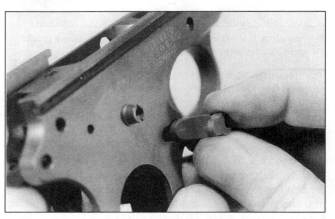

Once the retainer is trapped, lift the catch out.

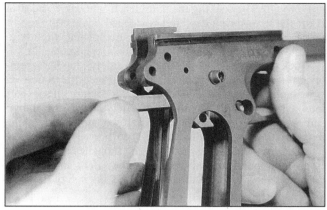

The trigger slides out the back of the frame.

but not wider than standard size, proceed. Push the magazine catch part of the way in from the left side, while you turn the retainer counterclockwise with the small screwdriver. When the retainer tab lines up with the mag catch internal slot, the retainer will move, and you can then lift the magazine catch out of the frame. With the magazine catch out, the trigger comes out of the rear of the slide.

The only things left are the mainspring assembly and the magazine catch assembly. The magazine catch is obvious. With the small screwdriver, turn the retainer out of its slot, and the spring will push the retainer out of the catch. The mainspring is a strong one. Clamp the mainspring housing in a padded vise. Use the drift punch to depress the mainspring by pushing down on the mainspring cap. Use the small screwdriver or a small-diameter drift punch to press the retainer clear of the housing. Ease the mainspring cap up. As with the thumb safety plungers and spring, the mainspring and its plungers are supposed to be an assembly, but on some pistols will not be. If you snatch the drift punch clear, you may launch the mainspring cap into the ceiling.

At this point, tend to all the cleaning or parts swapping that you had planned. Then reassemble.

Those extra parts

On some models, you'll have extra parts. On the Colt Series 80 models, there will be an extra set of levers in the frame. These levers transfer the force of the trigger pull to the firing pin plunger. The plunger blocks the travel of the firing pin unless the trigger is pulled.

If you have a Series 80, disassembly is slightly complicated. On the slide, start with the slide upside down. Press the plunger into the slide with the drift punch, and press the firing pin forward. Press the firing pin far enough that when you release the plunger, the firing pin is trapped in front of it.

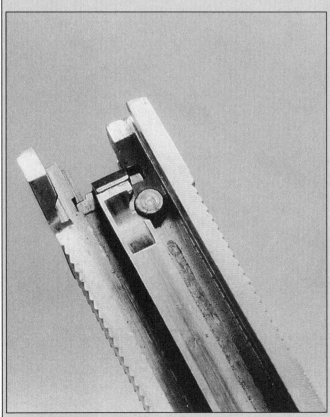

The Colt Series 80 firing pin safety plunger. You must depress this before pressing the firing pin into the slide for disassembly.

Now, press the firing pin retainer out. Put your hand or a cloth over the end of the slide. Press the safety plunger down, and the firing pin will shoot out. Remove the firing pin and spring. The extractor has a shoulder on it, keeping the plunger in the slide. Press the extractor out slightly, and the plunger will come free. Remove the plunger and spring, then the extractor.

On the frame when you pull out the pivot pins holding the hammer and sear in, the levers will be freed. You have to keep them, for without them the hammer and sear can drift on the pivot pins and not properly engage.

On older, Gold Cup Models, the sear has a small spring-loaded plunger to give it extra tension. The Gold Cup was designed with a larger trigger, and the extra mass bouncing in the trigger slot can trip the sear, dropping the hammer to half cock during firing. The spring loaded plunger prevents this. (Wouldn't a lighter trigger have done so? You bet. Why wasn't it used? You got me.)

To reassemble a Gold Cup with this pesky little plunger and spring, you have to make a slave pin. The slave pin keeps the sear and disconnector (and that lever) together while you insert the sear pivot pin.

To assemble the Series 80 frame, you have to do all the assembly while the frame lies on its right side. With the trigger in place, slide the two levers into their recess in the frame, and make sure they are properly aligned. Then install the rest of the parts as usual. To check for proper lever function once assembled, watch the lever when you carefully dry fire. (Use your thumb to capture the hammer and keep it from crashing into the frame.) If the lever lifts when you pull the trigger, you've done it. If it doesn't, then the two levers are out of position. Disassemble and start over.

Slide Reassembly

The firing pin and extractor is easy. Push the extractor in and line the notch in it up with the slot milled into the slide. Check the fit with the firing pin retainer.

Remove the retainer, insert the firing pin and spring, and compress the spring. Slide the retainer in until the firing pin pops up. On Series 80 pistols, push the extractor in. Line the extractor clearance cut up with the plunger hole. Insert the plunger and spring, then press the extractor to capture the plunger. Then, compress the plunger and insert the firing pin and spring. Press the firing pin deeper than usual and release the plunger to capture the firing pin. Install the plate, then press and release the firing pin plunger, releasing the firing pin.

For the barrel and bushing, slide the bushing over the barrel, then insert the barrel into the front of the slide. Turn the bushing to lock it into the slide. If you haven't disassembled the frame, jump to the final step. If you have, set the slide aside and reassemble the frame.

Frame Reassembly

With everything clean, start with the trigger. Slide it into the frame, and push it all the way forward. Reassemble the magazine catch, and press it into the frame from the right side. Hold the button so the right side is slightly above the frame. Turn the retainer clockwise and the spring will push the catch fully into the frame. Take the sear and disconnector and place the sear over the disconnector. The sear curve should be towards the rear, as should the bevel of the bottom of the disconnector. Push the tip of the disconnector up into the top tunnel, and place the bottom against the trigger bow. With one hand, poke the small screwdriver through the right hand side of the frame, through the sear pin hole. Use the tip of the screwdriver to line up the pivot holes of the sear and disconnector. Push the sear pivot pin in from the left side, using it to push the small screwdriver out of the frame.

Slide the hammer into place and press the hammer pivot pin into place. Lift the hammer strut. Take the three-leaf spring and place the top end under the hammer. Slide the small tab into its slot in the rear of the frame and press the spring forward to engage the sear, disconnector, and trigger. The left leaf of the spring must rest on the sear, with the spring tab outboard of the sear leg. The center leaf rides on the disconnector bevel. The right leaf works the grip safety. Clark Custom makes a four-leaf spring. On it, the center leaf is split, and one leg works the disconnector while the other puts tension on the trigger bow directly.

If you have to reassemble it, clamp the mainspring housing in a padded vise. Clamp it so you have clearance for the retaining pin. Drop the mainspring assembly in, pointy end first. Use the drift punch to compress the spring, and while holding it in place, use your other hand to press the retaining pin in from the rear side of the housing.

The next step takes a little juggling. You have to flip the hammer strut down, and place the grip safety on the frame. While keeping the grip safety in place with one hand, slide the mainspring housing in with your other. The mainspring housing traps the grip safety in place. If you put the housing on first, you can't get the safety in. Use the grip safety to keep the hammer strut centered, for if the safety doesn't keep the strut in line, the housing won't fit, or you can't cock the hammer once things are in place. With the housing on and the grip safety in place, press the mainspring housing

pin through. Try cocking the hammer. If you can't, the strut is off the mainspring cap, and is trapped against the top of the housing. Press the pin out, move the housing slightly to free the trapped strut, and press the housing home again.

Cock the hammer. Slide the thumb safety plunger assembly into its housing, smaller tip first. Place the frame on your bench right side down. Insert the thumb safety shaft into the frame and line the grip safety up so the thumb safety presses through. With it halfway down, pivot the thumb safety so the front corner is in line with the safety plunger. Press the safety down until it touches the plunger. Insert your small screwdriver under the safety and use it to compress the plunger and spring. Press the safety home in the frame.

Frame And Slide

With the slide together and the frame assembled, you need to marry the two. The old-fashioned way is to have the slide with the barrel in it, the recoil spring plug and the recoil spring, but to leave the bushing turned and the recoil spring retainer out. Slide the slide in place, line up the link with the slide stop hole, and press the slide stop in. Once the link is captured, position the slide so the clearance cut lets the slide stop run home. Run the slide forward and put the safety on. Place the recoil spring retainer on the spring and compress the spring. Once the retainer is pressed in enough, turn the bushing to capture the retainer.

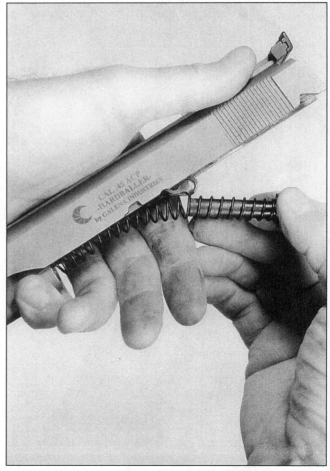

To reassemble, wrap your fingers around the slide as you compress the recoil spring.

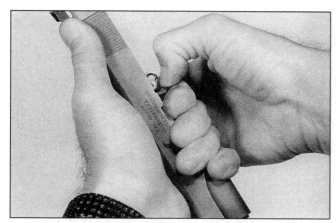

Be sure you get the recoil spring guide head in front of the bottom lugs.

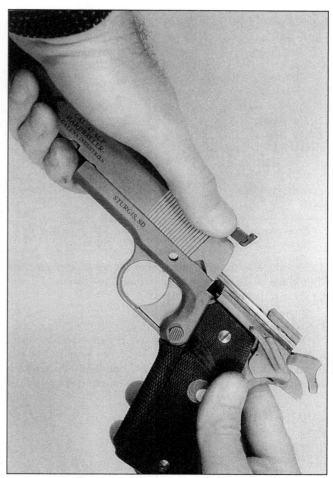

Install the slide, letting the frame push your fingers out of the way one at a time.

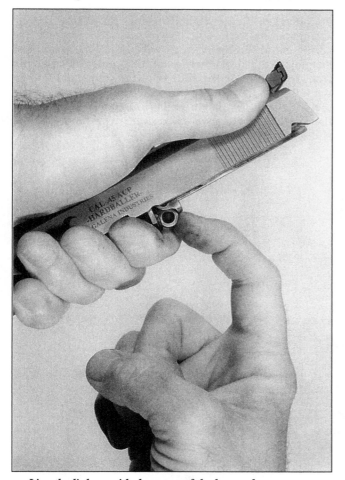

Line the link up with the curve of the bottom lug.

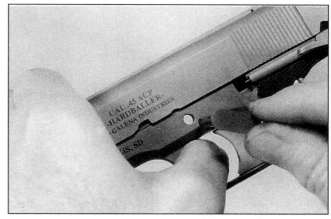

Hook your thumb in the trigger guard and push the slide back.

Safe, dependable, and if you slip you launch the retainer right past your face. Also, if you have a tightly-fitted bushing, turning it while holding the retainer down against the force of the recoil spring tension can be a difficult job.

The newer method starts with the barrel in the slide and the bushing and recoil spring retainer in place. Hold the slide with the front sight in the palm of your left hand. Stuff the recoil spring up into the slide, trapping it with the fingers of your left hand. Once you have the guide plug in place, trap the spring and guide plug under the slide. Take the frame in your right hand, and slide it onto the slide. As the dust cover moves forward, slide your fingers off the spring and onto the dust cover. Once the frame and slide are together, line the link up with the slide stop hole. Press the slide stop through to capture the link, and then press the slide to position the clearance notch for the slide stop. Press the slide stop into the frame.

The advantage of the new method is that it keeps the spring under control without pointing it at your head. The

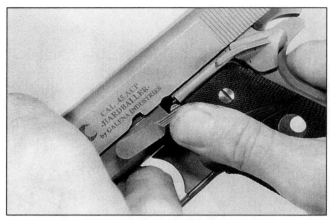

Press the slide stop home through the link, then line up the notch and slide stop. Press the slide stop home.

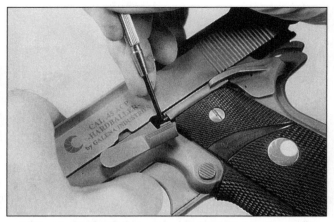

If the plunger is a little too long to cam out of the way, use a small screwdriver to press it back.

disadvantage is the risk of marring the slide. If your hand slips while pushing the slide stop home, you can put a circular scratch on the frame and slide.

Guide Rods

A two-piece guide rod is simple, assemble it by either method, and then insert the front half of the rod through the hole in the spring retainer. Tighten it with a screwdriver or Allen wrench. For a one-piece rod, if you've taken the spring and retainer off of it, place the spring on the rod. Use the retainer to compress the spring and insert the capture wire. Install the barrel and bushing in the slide, then install the guide rod assembly from behind. Slide the slide onto the frame and line up the link with the slide stop hole. Proceed as usual. Once the slide stop has captured the link and is secure, lock the slide back. Remove the capture wire, and ease the slide forward.

CHAPTER SIX

Cleaning

So there you are. You have every part that is supposed to come off lying on your bench. Your hands are dirty, as is the towel or paper towel you just wiped them on. What to clean, and how to get it clean? It, of course, is your pride and joy, your 1911.

What to clean depends on how much you've shot it, what you've done with it, and how long it will be until you shoot it again. If you have only put a couple of magazines through it, then it gets a couple of passes with a paper towel, a few patches down the bore, some lubrication and you reassemble it. If it and you just took a dunking during an amphibious landing, then you may not have the time or bench space to do a complete strip and cleaning. All you'll be able to do is remove the ammo, dunk the pistol in solvent or oil to displace the salt water, and get back to your job.

Ideally, to clean your 1911 you would have an ultrasonic tank, or at least a parts washer with solvent. However, since few readers do, and those that do are already gunsmiths, we'll talk of cleaning as a process you do either at the range or at your bench with basic tools. For a basic cleaning, those tools will be your disassembly tools, a small bottle of bore solvent, a brush, cotton swabs, a small screwdriver or brass scraper, a modified .30 Carbine case, and a cleaning rod with bore brush and patches. For a detailed cleaning, add the extra disassembly tools for detailed disassembly, a large-volume solvent, a piece of wire screen or a drain plug, a small, fine mesh wire basket, a heat gun and a stainless steel dish or pan.

For both you'll need a lubricant.

On the matter of solvents, cleaning and bore, and lubricants, many brands will do. I have found that bore solvents from the big makers work just fine. I have run into the occasional shooter who mixes his own solvent or lubricant, and

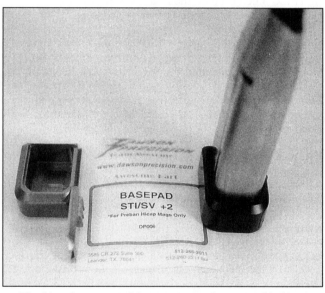

The big advantage to hi-cap mags is the removable baseplate (like this Dawson), making cleaning easier.

Even soft-recoiling pistols will need cleaning. Just because it isn't loud doesn't mean it runs clean.

Don't forget to clean your magazines, too.

Here is Brian Enos, who developed "Slide Glide", racing through a stage at the 1999 World Shoot.

For a basic cleaning, you simply need to get the slide off the frame. You can then reach everything you need to.

The frame bridge gets very dirty from powder residue dumped out of the chamber. Wipe and brush it clean before reassembling it.

all I can conclude from the experience is that they have either too much time on their hands or they really are more interested in scientific inquiry than in shooting.

For bore cleaning, I've been using Birchwood Casey Nitro Bore and Remington's Rem Clean. For extreme dry and dusty applications, I use Krunch Products Pistol Pro Mag Slick. It is intended for magazines, but keeps pistols working, too. For 1911 lubrication I use FP-10, Break Free, Chip McCormicks Trigger Job or Brian Enos' Slide Glide.

Let us consider the two usual levels of cleaning, with some extra options.

Basic Cleaning

The basic cleaning is done at the field-strip level of disassembly. While you might take the slide apart (and you might not) the frame does not get disassembled at all. You would use the basic cleaning halfway through a big match, or after a day's practice when you will be practicing again in a day or two.

On the frame, use a solvent-soaked patch or a paper towel to wipe the caked-on residue off the receiver bridge. On a stainless or plated receiver you'll see the spot immediately. The bridge, or barrel seat, is where the barrel comes down to rest during the slide's cycling. When the empty brass is extracted, the loose powder residue from it is deposited around the barrel. With enough shooting you'll get a heavy buildup on the frame, barrel and slide. The buildup may get so heavy that you need to scrape it off the frame. If you don't clean your 1911 until some time after, the buildup can become hard and crusty.

Wipe the bridge clean. Wipe the feed ramp clean. Put a drop of solvent on a cotton-tipped swab and wipe out the barrel lug clearance slot. Wipe the sludgy oil out of the rail slots and wipe the top deck of the frame behind the magazine opening clean. Thus ends your basic cleaning of the frame. As you reassemble, place a drop of oil on each rail slot, on the disconnector tip, and across the barrel seat. Now, on to the slide.

If you remove the barrel from the slide you can do a much more thorough job of cleaning. Some shooters in a hurry don't, and content themselves with scrubbing the bore and hosing the slide assembly with an aerosol cleaner. While it helps, this level of cleaning (hosing the assembly) doesn't get the gunk out of the nooks and crannies where it resides.

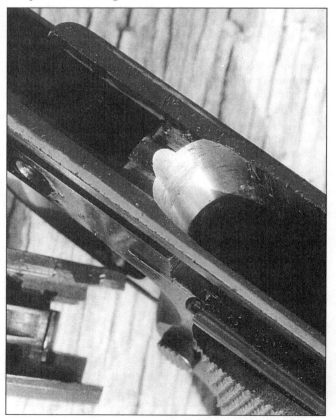

A shiny feed ramp is a nice start to your shooting session.

With the barrel and slide separated, wipe the slide rails clean. Stick the cloth or paper towel into the muzzle end of the slide with your finger and wipe the bushing seat clean. Wipe the rear underside of the slide clean. Well, as clean as you can with the cloth. Remember that powder residue that you wiped off the frame? It also resides in the slide, in the locking lugs. To do a thorough job, use either a small eyeglass screwdriver, or a brass scraper made for the job. Scrape the gunk out of the locking lugs. Take another cotton swab and put some solvent on it and wipe the lugs clean. Repeat the process in the clearance slots on the rear of the slide. The clearance slots are for the ejector, and for the lips of the magazine. The slots get packed with gunk, as most shooters never consider them, and those that do consider them don't go to the effort of getting them clean. Scrape and swab, and you'll be surprised at how much stuff is in there.

The important area to clean is the breechface. Scrub the breechface with a brush, not just a towel and swabs. Then wipe it with the towel. Look in the corner of the breechface away from the extractor. Despite the scrubbing and wiping, there will still be some gunk packed in that corner. Use the small scraper to clean it out. Brush the extractor clean. Once a year, or every few thousand rounds, remove the extractor and push a solvent-wet cotton swab through the extractor tunnel. Follow with a dry one, then an oiled one. Put the extractor back in.

When you reassemble, put a drop of oil on the locking lugs, the rails, the bushing seat and in each clearance slot.

The outside of the barrel, the bushing and recoil spring and guide rod are easy. Wipe them clean. Brush the bottom lugs of the barrel and the link clean. Make sure there isn't any gunk packed in the upper lugs. Then clean the chamber and bore.

The chamber will be packed with powder residue, and the bore will be plated with bullet material. First off, do not use a stainless brush. When they first came out, we all thought they were a wonder, stripping the lead out of a bore right away. Well, they are fast, but they are harsh. Use a bronze or plastic brush. Brush the bore. Apply a bore solvent with a patch and let it set. (The sequence of any cleaning should be brush and wet the bore, let it soak while you go on to other cleaning. Keep coming back to the bore while doing the rest of the pistol, and finish with the bore.)

The bore will require several applications of bore solvent, brushing and swabbing with a patch before it comes clean. If you have done a very large amount of shooting, or it has been a while since you thoroughly cleaned the bore, you might consider the Outers Foul-Out. It is an electro-chemical cleaning process, where you reverse plate the lead or copper off the bore and onto the sacrificial rod.

The chamber can pose a problem. The powder residue can be thick, and each round that chambered and fired added to compacting the residue into a tough sheet. The powder residue can be built up and compacted such that it interferes with proper chambering. Once it becomes a full sheet and gets packed in hard, a bore brush hardly has an effect on it. After trying a couple of different methods, I hit on using an extra .30 Carbine empty modified as a cleaning tool. You should be able to scare one up, as there are lots of .30 Carbine shooters, and hardly any of them reload their empties.

It may seem impossibly grubby, but this barrel will come clean easily and quickly. It is as dirty inside as out, so be liberal with bore solvent and patches.

An active gunsmith's work room is a dusty place. You don't want this level of dust in the house, so clean your 1911 some place easy to clean up after yourself.

Take the case and scrub it clean. Then, use a chamfering tool on the inside of the case mouth, and instead of simply breaking the edge, keep cutting until you have turned the inside of the case to a sharp-edged bevel. Now use the case as a scraper to get the packed-on residue off the chamber walls of your pistol. A .30 Carbine case works for all calibers, from .38 Super up to .45 ACP.

On reassembly, put a drop of oil on the link, the inside and outside of the bushing, and on the recoil spring guide rod.

Once you have your pistol back together, wipe the excess oil off, and add a drop of oil to the hood of the barrel, over the chamber. Cycle the slide a couple of times to distribute this extra drop, and you are done.

If all this seems a little bit much for a "basic" cleaning, perhaps you aren't shooting enough. If you go to the range once or twice a year and put a box or two through your pistol on these trips, then your pistol might need cleaning (because of the shooting, and not the weather) every leap year. However, there are times when this basic cleaning is barely enough to keep up. If you find yourself at Gunsite, or Thunder Ranch, you'll do this basic cleaning at the end of each day. You can easily consume between 1,000 and 2,000 rounds during your week at either school. If you don't clean daily at this level, you'll find yourself dealing with malfunctions in a couple of days.

The outdoors, daily cleaning you need at a match or class can be done with aerosol cleaners. However, the volatile organic solvents used to get the surface clean are too smelly to be used indoors. For home use, you have to take a different tack.

Detailed Cleaning

For the thorough cleaning that the occasional shooter might do once a year, or the serious competitor would do

This is a multi-year supply of Slide Glide. Not only is it a good lubricant, but it eases the "ca-chunk" of cycling in many pistols.

every few thousand rounds, you need more room, solvents, splash area, lubricant and a source of heat. The room and splash area can be your laundry tub or sinks. The solvent should be Brownell's d'Solve and a bore solvent. The lubricant should be an aggressive lube like Break Free, FP-10 or Rem Oil. The heat should be a blow dryer or heat gun. Add a pair of hemostats, or smooth-faced or rubber-coated needlenose pliers to your gear. Completely strip your pistol and place the parts in the stainless pan. (Unless you've been out in a soaking rain, taken a spill into a body of water, or just want to clean it, leave the mainspring housing out of the pan. It is well-sealed and does not need to be cleaned very often.) Take the pan to the laundry tub. Pour Brownell's d'Solve concentrate into a plastic jug and mix with water to working strength. Pour the d'Solve into the pan and let the parts soak. (Stop screaming in the back. Yes, I know, "Water, your pistol, the devil's work." Trust me.)

Scrub the parts clean. In the frame, concentrate on the hammer clearance slot, the trigger slot and the magazine well. In the slide, concentrate on the locking lugs and the slide clearance slots on the rear of the slide.

If you have a stainless or hard chromed pistol, finding the gunk is easy. If your 1911 is blued, you'll have to scrub and wipe everything until they are all clean. The hammer and sear will need scrubbing, as will the trigger. The firing pin tunnel and the extractor tunnel on the slide will need scrubbing, as will the firing pin and extractor.

The barrel is the one part that can be spared the aqueous ordeal. Wipe the outside clean, brush the link free of gunk, and use your bore brush to scrub the loose gunk out. Apply bore solvent by applying it to a patch that you run through the bore. Let it set for a few minutes, then brush the bore and swab clean with dry patches. Repeat. When the dry patches come out clean and without color, your bore is clean. Oil the barrel and set it aside.

Once everything is scrubbed, make sure you have your screen over the drain, and turn on the hot water. You don't need a heavy, splashing stream, just enough to rinse the parts. Let the water pour into the stainless pan and displace the d'Solve that is in there. (You can pour off the d'Solve, strain it or let the gunk settle out, and re-use it. But it is not expensive, and I prefer the ease of disposing of it to the hassle of saving it. I used to be a terrible pack rat, and saved everything. I feel much better now.) When you turn the water on, turn on only the hot water, hotter than you can put

your hands in. Once the d'Solve is washed away, pick up the small parts one at a time with the needlenose pliers and hit them with a blast of air from the blow dryer or heat gun. As you dry each one, oil it and set it aside.

You want to evaporate the water and protect the surface as quickly as possible. The hot water evaporates more quickly than cold water, and the heat gun makes sure there is no water in any out-of-the-way nooks or crannies.

If you have plastic inserts in or paint on your front sight, be careful with the heat gun as it may overheat them. Also, take it easy if you have glow-in-the-dark sights. Except for those items, you cannot produce enough heat with a blow dryer or heat gun to harm your pistol.

Once the small parts are dry, heat the slide and frame. Once they are dry, you must be thorough in oiling every surface. The cleaning and heating has made it bone dry, and unless you protect the surface with oil, oxidation can take hold. For the interior surfaces, an aerosol spray and cotton swabs are very useful in getting lubricant into every location.

Lubrication

How to get just enough in the right places is a question many shooters have. When you reassemble, there are a few places that need extra attention. Starting in the frame, the mainspring housing needs more lube, if you took it apart

If you are carrying your gun for defense, a test-fire trap is comforting. If you don't have one (they're expensive to buy and dirty to use) then clean at the range, and test before you leave.

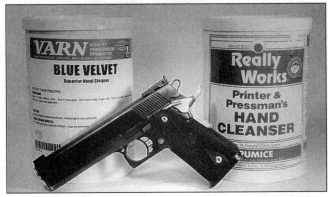

Once you've cleaned the gun, clean yourself. Printers use ink, and cleaning it can be a chore. Printer's hand cleaner makes very short work of gun grease, powder residue and oil.

When your hands are sweaty, or you need lube to keep your pistol running, you need friction in your grip. Checkering is one way to get it.

and scrubbed it. Use a light grease, like Lubriplate, or Brian Enos' Slide Glide, to lubricate, protect and seal the inside of the mainspring housing until you get to it in another five years. Coat the spring and two plungers. Put a drop of oil on the mainspring housing assembly pin hole before you assemble it. Wipe dry before installing the mainspring housing in the frame.

Use your standard lubricant on the trigger, magazine catch assembly, grip screw bushing and grip safety. Wipe the hammer, sear and disconnector with an oiled patch, and place a high-pressure grease on the sear tip and hammer hooks. I have tried both Chip McCormicks Trigger Job and Brian Enos' Slide Glide, and both have worked well. The pivot pins, thumb safety shaft and three-leaf spring all get the standard lube.

In the slide, put some oil on a cotton swab and run the swab into and out of the firing pin tunnel. Run the swab through the extractor tunnel. Wipe the rest of the slide, inside and out, with an oily cloth or patch. Put a drop of oil on the firing pin spring when you assemble, and leave the extractor wet with oil when you install it. Wipe the retaining plate with an oily patch, but do not leave it wet. If you leave too much oil on the retaining plate or firing pin, it will get jolted off when you fire, spraying oil on your shooting glasses.

Wipe the bushing with your oily patch, and assemble the barrel and slide. The recoil spring should get wet with oil, and if you use a guide rod, wipe it down like all the other parts. Apply a drop of oil to each rail slot before you install the slide to the frame, and then wipe the excess off the back of the slide afterwards.

If you lube and assemble your pistol by this method, when it is back together it will ooze oil slightly. If you will be wearing it, wrap it in a paper towel and let it sit muzzle down for half an hour or so. The oil will run out (as much as is going to) and the towel will collect it.

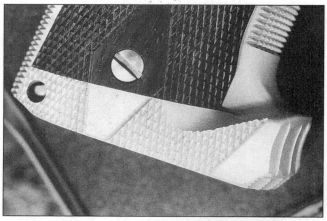

Ned Christiansen, the Master, follows the checkering of the grips down onto the magazine funnel he added to this 1911.

Clean Yourself

OK, you've cleaned your 1911, and now your hands are grubby. Now what? After all the scrubbing, scraping, solvents, lubricants and assembly, you have to clean you, and the sink you cleaned your 1911 in. If you live the happy bachelor life, and your only contact each day is with the postal delivery person and the local newscaster on television, maybe you don't have to clean up. But the rest of us do. The powder residue and the solvents and lubricants can be persistent staining compounds. Regular soap will not always clean your hands. Two occupations that have even greater exposure to grease and stains are auto mechanics and printers. Both have hand cleaning products that get the gunk off your hands without stripping the skin off. If the nearest store of these two is an auto parts store, great. If a printer's supply store is closer, a small bottle or jar of hand cleaner will last you for years. If you go to the range a lot, or travel to big matches, you might want to pick up some single-use packages of hand cleaner. With a small packet of hand cleaner and a few paper towels in your range bag, you can do an emergency strip and clean of your pistol between stages, and then clean your hands so you aren't shooting the next stage with oily hands.

"Warning! Danger, Will Robinson!!!" The State of California has deemed lead to be a toxic substance, with a lethality somewhere in between that of Plutonium and the poisons used by the Borgias. Every package associated with your firearm will warn of its potential damage to your fetus. (Exercise caution, guys. If you are pregnant, the baby you are carrying....) Ok, ok, I'm being just a bit snarky. However, I handled stuff in lab getting my Chemistry degree that was actually lethal, so I tend to view the warnings of officious bureaucrats as annoyances. Don't get me wrong, lead can be bad stuff. However, getting lead on your hands from picking up brass or loading your own ammo is not like popping lead-filled paint chips as if they were snacks during a football game. The first thing we learned about exposure to potentially lethal chemicals was: "Dose makes the poison." While some things are lethal at any level of exposure, most are not. Stay below the health-risk dose, and it's like you weren't exposed.

Here's the straight scoop on dealing with lead: I've been shooting, cleaning, reloading and handling firearms and empty brass for more than three decades. I have in my peak years fired in excess of 30,000 rounds per year (most of which I handloaded), and kept that pace for nearly two decades. Last year I had to go in for a complete (every test known to man but one) physical for a contract. Even though they were not going to test for lead (I'm a shooter, and they weren't going to test for lead, but they were going to test for every psychoactive substance they knew about, go figure.) I insisted. The results? The lead level was so low the Doctor wasn't sure it could be attributed to my shooting.

Here is the secret: I wash my hands, and I'm careful about eating. At the range, after picking up brass, even if I have to break the sheet of ice on the wash barrel I scrub before driving home. And again, once I get home. And after each reloading session, and after I clean any firearm. Don't eat on the range. Don't drink, except from a covered container. If you do have lunch at the range, scrub your hands before handling food. You aren't going to absorb lead through your skin. Very few substances go through skin, and they are either volatile solvents like acetone, or really nasty

heavy metals like mercury. If you get a dose of lead, it will be by ingesting it. Wash your hands and you won't eat the lead that is (temporarily) on them. At the range, use paper towels to wipe your hands, and toss the towels away.

With basic precautions you don't have to worry except at extremely high and persistent exposure, like weekly trips to indoor ranges with lead bullets being used. If your job exposes you to that much lead, you use oil-driller's precautions: Wash your clothes and shower on site, change to clean clothes, and have your vehicle detailed and the upholstery shampooed twice a year.

There are shooters who have had their health compromised by lead, but they weren't casual shooters. They have all been range officers or instructors, on indoor ranges. They ingested lead by breathing the smoke, eating food dusted by their lead-powdered clothes, and not washing well or often enough. Some of them even smoked cigarettes at the range, an act akin to licking bullets. You can avoid such exposure by frequenting only indoor ranges with good ventilation, washing your hands and clothes, and not eating or drinking on the range.

As for the sink, a stiff-bristle scrub brush and a scouring powder will get any and all dirt, oil and stains off. I prefer Bon-Ami, simply because it is guaranteed not to scratch. Even if I clean in a fiberglass tub, it will come clean.

Extreme Climate Conditions

Not everyone uses the 1911 just on the range in good weather. If you are going to be someplace unpleasant, what can you do? The first thing is to see about getting it plated. A hard chrome job from Accurate Plating, or an NP3 coating from Robar will go a long way to protecting your 1911, and keeping it running. Then, you adjust your lubrication. If bright white is not your thing, look into an epoxy finish like Spradlin's Tech-Cote or Wilson's Armor Tuff.

There are two variables, in four combinations, that you have to account for, and these are outside of the normal weather you would see.

Hot And Dry

As exemplified by much of Arizona, and the entire Middle East. When it looked like my brother's artillery unit was going to end up in Desert Shield /Desert Storm, I quickly looked into the subject of hot and dry lubrications. Basically, there were none. Any lubricants would attract grit, form a paste, and grind up parts. When going to a shooting school like Gunsite, in the high plateau of Arizona, you can use regular lubes because you'll be using and cleaning your pistol constantly. For training or competition, most shooters in the desert use a free-running lube like Break Free or FP-10. Some prefer to use a more persistent lube, and depend on the body of the lube to keep grit out. For such an application, the Brian Enos Slide Glide will keep your 1911 running. But in a situation where it is your daily-wear insurance, your 1911 will be subjected to large amounts of dust, and you may not be able to clean it as often as you would like, you must not use traditional oils or lubes.

The traditional method of dealing with the desert is to eschew lubricant. Leave it bare. However, since Desert Storm, there has been progress in dry lubes. One method is to use a dry spray-on lube. One is Rem Dry. Another is TW-25. While it has a lubricant carrier, you apply the lubricant paste to the rail slots, locking lugs and hammer and sear.

Then rub vigorously with a clean cloth until the surface appears dry. You now have lubricant that won't attract grit. One method I've been trying is to use Krunch Products' Pistol Pro Mag Slick as a pistol lubricant. While intended for use inside magazines, I've been using it on the rails and barrel of a pistol used in the desert. As a dry lube it won't attract grit, and so far the results have been positive.

Cold And Dry

The Arctic is nasty, but you don't have to be in the arctic to be cold and dry. Again, the traditional approach has been to leave the firearm (in this case a 1911, in the case of my father in Germany in 1944-1945 a Garand, an M-3 Grease gun, a BAR, you get the idea) dry again. The purpose of leaving it dry is not to prevent the attraction of grit, but to keep the oil/lubricant from getting gummy and hard from the cold. As with the hot and dry conditions, a spray-on dry lube like the Mag Slick, or the TW-25 works nicely.

Hot And Wet

In the cold climates, you needn't worry about rust, but the climate would keep your pistol from working. In hot and wet, speedy rust is the enemy. You can help by starting with a stainless pistol. Better yet, get a stainless pistol, and once it has all the bugs worked out and you have it just the way you like it, get it hard chromed. As an extra measure, use a black baking lacquer or epoxy finish to top things off.

In hot and wet, you need a persistent lube that won't run out from the heat, and won't wash off from the water. One place you need the protection would be the Florida Everglades. One place you might have needed such protection was Vietnam. (In the dry season, some locations in Vietnam came close to the Hot and Dry conditions.) For this climate, light oil won't do. A persistent grease like Brian Enos' Slide Glide is what you need. Treat the rails, locking lugs and hammer and sear to a light coating of grease. Wipe the outside with an oily cloth every day if you can.

Cold And Wet

The worst of the combinations, both for you and for your 1911. Bad for you due to the risk of hypothermia. A cold steady rain, and air temperatures in the 40s, and you could die without knowing you are at risk. Hypothermia is sneaky. So is cold-weather rust. For daily wear you need a persistent lubricant for oxidation protection. Inside, use the Brian Enos Slide Glide. Outside, keep your 1911 wiped down with a cloth and lube, something like Break Free or FP-10.

A Minor Addendum

Some shooters, and advocates of the 1911, suggest that a smooth pistol is preferred to a pistol with checkering, stippling or skateboard tape. The idea is that if you draw and get a bad hold, you can adjust your grip with a smooth pistol. However, consider how much lube we're using in extreme climates. In a hot and wet climate, your hands will be wet. Even if it hasn't rained lately or isn't raining at the moment, your hands will be sweaty from the heat and humidity. Your 1911 will be oozing lube. (Or if not, then quietly rusting.) When you need it, you need it, and a smooth pistol under such circumstances can be like trying to grab a bar of soap.

My pistols have checkering, stippling or skateboard tape. When I grab them, they aren't going to go anywhere except where I want them to.

CHAPTER SEVEN

Testing for Reliability and Performance

You've got your pistol, and you want to make sure it works. What to do? Testing involves two different courses of action, testing for reliability and testing for performance.

In the case of a brand-new pistol, or one just back from being built up by a gunsmith, you first want to make sure it works 100 percent. Why shoot a brand new pistol that is going to go straight to a 'smith? If anything breaks, it will likely break right away. Better to test-fire it and break things while it is still under warranty. Once the gunsmith has swapped parts, the manufacturer will no longer do a warranty repair. And, if it turns out there is some minor fix the gunsmith has to do, you can tell him what it is, having shot your 1911. I have, a few times, fired brand new pistols that threw the brass right back at my face. An easy fix, once it is known. Or, on other occa-

sions, I've test-fired a pistol that, out of the box, would not work with some particular brand or style of ammunition.

Some gunsmiths say they prefer a new in-the-box gun to one that has been fired. However, firing a 1911 before shipping it won't hurt anything.

As for the 1911 fresh back from the gunsmith, you want to break it in. There are very few gunsmiths who will shoot a pistol enough to break it in before they ship it back to you. It takes time, it costs money, and it slows down the schedule. No 'smith can spare the time, but some do anyway, and every gunsmith will have customers who want their 1911's back sooner. So, most do the work, fire a magazine or two through it and ship it back. It is up to you to break in the freshly worked-on pistol.

It isn't unusual for a brand-new or just-returned from the gunsmith pistol to stumble in the first few magazines. Just so it doesn't happen after the first box of ammo.

Your accuracy testing is a separate test from reliability testing. Check function first, then test for accuracy or lack thereof.

For the break-in you need at least 200 rounds of good ammo. Some gunsmiths recommend as much as 300 or 400 rounds as a break-in period. My experience has been that if you have some feeding problems with a 1911 back from the gunsmith, they will happen in the first few full magazines, and then never be seen again. If you are still having occasional feeding glitches at the 200 round mark, they probably won't go away at the 400-round mark, and you'll be shipping the pistol back. You should use factory ammunition or commercial reloads, using 230-grain jacketed round nose bullets. (230 JRN in .45 ACP. Use the equivalent in other calibers.) You also need at least a pair of top-quality magazines. There are not many things more frustrating than trying to de-bug a pistol that may or may not be reliable, when you can't depend on the ammunition or the magazines. Now is not the time to start reloading, or begin using your brother-in-law's reloads. Bite the bullet (so to speak) and use the good stuff. If you will be using hollow points, or ammunition other than plain, old jacketed round-nose, then you'll want to have a box of the ones you will be using as part of your test ammo. Most hollow points feed as well as ball, with the exception of the 200-grain hollowpoint from Speer, the "Flying Ashtray."

To test for reliability, you travel to the range with your ammunition, the pistol, targets and your shooting gear. If you are going to check accuracy as well, then you will need either some sandbags or a shooting rest, or better yet, a Ransom Rest with correct inserts for your pistol.

You should have inspected your pistol as soon as you got it home, either from the gun shop or the shipping package, and performed the safety inspection to check the function of the thumb and grip safety.

At the range, begin by loading your magazines with a single round. Keeping the muzzle pointed at the target, lock the slide back, insert the first magazine and depress the slide stop, chambering the round. Did the hammer stay cocked? Good. Fire the round. Check the point of impact and look to see that the slide stop fully engaged the slide and locked it open. Drop out that magazine and repeat with your other magazines.

What if the hammer fell to half-cock? Did it do it only the once? If so, be suspicious and keep an eye on the hammer during the rest of your testing. If it follows again, you should send it back. (In the case of a new pistol, you won't get to do much testing before you ship it off. Always mention that the hammer is following in your letter to the gunsmith.)

Repeat the process with two rounds in each magazine. The reason for all this folderol is to prevent the annoying and dangerous full-magazine-burst problem. Only once have I had a 1911 run away on me, and that was due to a chipped hammer hook. The experience was so exciting that when testing a new trigger job I want to avoid repeating it. By loading with one round you test feed and slide lock. Going to two rounds, you test feed, slide lock and the ability of the hammer to stay cocked. If you really feel cautious you can repeat again with three rounds, but you don't have

Many high-volume shooters have a cracked 1911. This one has even been welded a couple of times to try to make the crack go away, to no avail. It is still accurate and reliable, so the owner has left it alone.

to. If the hammer is going to stay back, it will, and if it isn't, you'll find out right away.

With the preliminaries out of the way, load your magazines and spend the afternoon shooting. Load and shoot the hardball first. If your 1911 needs a little breaking in, it is best to do it with the relatively inexpensive ammo, and with the ammo that will likely be the most reliable. You are not just blasting away, or you should not be. Pay attention to the point of impact and group size. Is it hitting to the sights? Does the group seem decently small? Does your new prize feel smooth in feeding, or do you feel occasional "chunks" as the slide goes forward? Are the empties all ejected, and do they go to the same area? Does it lock open when each magazine is empty? Do the empty magazines drop smoothly and cleanly when the magazine button is pressed?

If the answer to all these questions is yes, then you are in the catbird seat. If some are no, then you will have to return it to the gunsmith who worked on it, or will mention the problems in your letter to the gunsmith for its first trip away from home. You may also have to invest in better ammo, or magazines, or both.

It's Working

Let us assume that it works just fine. (Most do, right out of the box, either from the factory or returning from the gunsmith.) What next? Why, now we test it with your reloads. Why would it function any differently with your reloads than with the factory ammunition? How can I say

this politely? Your ammo might not be up to snuff. At the local club where I shoot practical competition, new shooters go through a several step process to reliable shooting. You can shorten the process by going through the steps in practice, and not during matches. First, they show up with new guns and factory ammo, and their gun works fine. Then they begin reloading, and have to debug their reloaded ammo. They work the larger problems out, and their pistol (not always a 1911) works reliably again. Next, they get some work done, or have a match barrel installed, and have feeding or reliability problems again. The last step is to fine-tune their reloading to remove the minor problems, and they once again have reliable pistols.

What are the problems with reloaded ammunition? Briefly (I go into much greater detail in Chapter Eleven) new reloaders have problems with getting the correct case bell and then crimp, in sizing cases, in seating primers and in overall length. Why would a worked-on pistol be less reliable with reloads than it had been before the work? As just one example, we can compare a new match barrel faced with improper and proper crimp. The crimping die presses the case mouth down to the proper diameter once the bullet has been seated. If the crimp is not enough, the case can be very slightly belled even though it looks OK. In a factory chamber, which may be reamed to the maximum allowed diameter, the excessively belled round may still feed fine. In the tighter match chamber (in the new match barrel) the very slightly over-size crimp of a reloaded round can create

Without a rest to shoot from, you are testing yourself more than you're testing the pistol. This Nowlin is much better than I am, but if you didn't know the "out" hit was a called flyer, you might think otherwise.

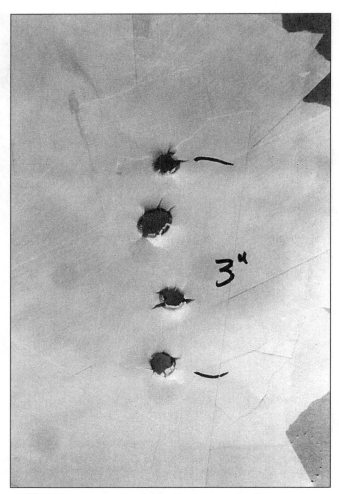

If you get a group like this in the first couple of magazines, the pistol isn't settled into the inserts. If it delivers groups like this even after being settled, your gunsmith has some explaining to do, as the barrel lockup is not right.

enough drag to keep the slide from fully closing. Especially if it has to plow through a coating of powder residue on the chamber walls. The pistol would work fine with factory ammo, but not with your reloads.

A wise investment to make when you are going to be feeding a high-performance match pistol with reloads is a check gauge. A check gauge is an aluminum cylinder reamed to the minimum allowed chamber dimensions. Once you have loaded a batch of ammunition, you drop each round into the gauge and see if it smoothly drops in and then out when you turn the gauge over. Any rounds that stick or do not drop cleanly into the gauge should be kept separate, and fired only as practice ammunition, and the fired brass they create kept separate for later study.

So, repeat the testing process, without the single and double-loaded magazines, with your reloads. If you can take a newly worked on 1911 just back from the gunsmith and feed it several hundred rounds of your reloads without a problem, you are a good reloader. If, on the other hand, the pistol that just went 200 rounds cleanly with factory ammo chokes on your reloads, you have some tuning to do. Tuning of the ammo, not the gun. If that's the case, jump to Chapter Eleven.

Decisions, Decisions

With a working 1911 on the range bench, you have a decision to make. Clean or not clean? The question comes from every shooter, competitor or new owner of a custom 1911, how long can I go between cleanings.

Some turn it into a contest. "I haven't cleaned my gun for 1,000 rounds."

"I haven't cleaned it for two thousand."

"I haven't cleaned mine since Johnson was President."

When should you clean your 1911? The simple answer is: A basic cleaning after each range trip, and a detailed cleaning every fourth or fifth trip. If your range sessions use up about 200 rounds, your pistol won't be expected to plow through too much gunk. Why are we concerned about cleaning in this chapter? Because cleanliness is next to reliability. A clean pistol (1911 or other) works better. And is less likely to spray oily gunk into your face.

You can, if you want, slack off on the cleaning for the first few range trips, and see if your pistol works fine during the first 1,000 rounds. If it does, great, keep it clean and it will not fail you. If it gets cranky when it gets dirty, then keep it clean and write or call your gunsmith. He may want to work on it some more, and he may just tell you to shoot it some more to finish the break-in process. If he tells you to shoot it some more he isn't being lazy. Most pistols take a while to get settled in and once the first 1,000 rounds are through them, they work like champs. This may seem appalling to shooters used to a low volume of shooting. "A thousand rounds! I'll be years shooting that!" Yes, but gunsmiths make pistols for competitors, for whom 1,000 rounds are nothing. Jerry Barnhart once picked up a pistol from his gunsmith in the morning and that afternoon called back with a list of changes he wanted made. "Jerry, maybe you should shoot it before changing it." His reply; "I have, 3,400 rounds so far."

How Much Reliability?

What number of malfunctions should you be willing to accept? How about none? The old standard used to be less than one per 1,000 rounds, for a 99.90 percent reliability. Today, many shooters don't know how many malfunctions their 1911 has had, because it hasn't had any since the break-in period. That Kimber I refused to send back? It failed to lock open six times, and all were found to be caused by a particular magazine. I replaced the tired spring in that magazine, and it hasn't happened since. Other malfunctions? There haven't been any.

How Long Is A 1911 Good For?

The 1911 is designed as a high-volume shooting machine. The government acceptance testing in the spring of 1911 called for each trial pistol to shoot 6,000 rounds. The test Colt did this without a single failure. While you may have to replace the recoil springs every 5,000 or 10,000 rounds, and the shock buffer if you use one, the pistol itself is designed to last as long as you do. With proper care, just how long is that? I wish I had hard data for dozens or hundreds of pistols, but I'm not the government. However, I do have some data points. One "reason" the government decided to switch from the 1911 to the Beretta 92 was that the 1911 was only good for an average service life of 15,000 rounds. Before you snicker at this, you must know that the armed services were scrapping many more 1911's for abuse than use. Each low-round-count 1911 that was lost during an airborne operation or run over by a tank pulled down the average. Each pistol issued to a guard post, and disassembled at the start of each watch but never fired, pulled down the average. And, those 1911s were old. The newest one had been bought on contract during WWII.

1911s that are shot and maintained have a different story. Practical shooters and bowling pin shooters consume large amounts of ammunition. I have a couple of pistols, and I know several other bowling pin shooters who have pistols, that have each fired more than 50,000 rounds. I started competing with my first 1911A1 in IPSC in 1978, and put large amounts of IPSC and bowling pin ammunition through it until 1993. After that it saw only bowling pin ammo until 1998. It is closing in on 100,000 rounds, and I bought it used. For my first book, Gunsmithing: Pistols and Revolvers, I obtained a loaner Kimber. The first group I shot with it, using Black Hills ammunition, was a single-hole group. Needless to say, I refused to send it back, and still have it. It now has more than 20,000 rounds through it, is on its third recoil spring and has used up half a dozen shock buffs, and it still shoots one-hole groups.

Jerry Barnhart has a Springfield Armory pistol that beats any of mine for ammo consumption. He started shooting with it in the early 1980s, and had it built by Steve Nastoff. With it he won National Championships and The Steel Challenge. He won The Steel Challenge a second time with that .45, even after it was clear the future was with the .38 Super. When he went to shoot on the Colt Team, he reluctantly sold his Springfield. Later, he came to his senses and was able to buy it back from the shooter he had rashly sold it to, and sent it back to Steve for a checkup. Jerry shot at my club when he owned that pistol, and his practice sessions for The Steel Challenge would consume a 5-gallon bucket of ammo. He would stand up the plates, spread a tarp, and shoot. And shoot, and shoot, and shoot. (I know, I watched.) That pistol has seen over 300,000 rounds, and is still accurate after its last inspection.

If you take care of your 1911, you can afford enough ammunition to wear it out only by winning the lottery.

Accuracy Testing

To test your 1911 for accuracy, you need more than a target stand and some ammunition. If all you do is stand and shoot, you are testing yourself more than you are testing that pistol. Unless it is a worn-out pistol that saw military use for decades, or has a junk barrel in it, and you are a High Master Bull's-eye shooter, you will not be able to out-shoot any 1911. Group size will reflect your skill, and not the capability of the pistol.

At a minimum, you need a solid bench with a shooting rest or sandbags, and a solid chair to sit in while you shoot. An experienced shooter can get by with just a sandbag, and shoot over the sandbag while prone, but most shooters need the bench, and will have a lot more fun at the bench. The best solution is to use a machine rest, the best of which is the Ransom Rest.

For those using the bench, proper bench technique with a pistol is markedly different than that with a rifle. With a rifle you sit up straight and you let the sandbags support the rifle while you aim and squeeze the trigger. With a handgun, unless it is a hard-recoiling one (and the 1911 isn't) your position can best be described as "bench prone." Your arms should be on the bench as much as possible. The sandbag should support the frame of the 1911, while the bench keeps your arms stationary. Rest your head against your right bicep (for right-handers, left for the southpaws in the group) to keep your head steady. Squirm around until you find a comfortable position, and one that puts your sights on the target. Move the target frame to accommodate your position, as the more natural your position, the less aiming error you will introduce.

When it comes to the shooting, focus on the front sight. Do not rest the butt or magazine on the bench, and keep the front sight centered in the rear notch as you gently squeeze. Breath naturally between shots, and put the pistol down if you have to. The best position is still not comfortable, and you are working hard. If you go slow you will not introduce fatigue into the equation. To minimize fatigue as a factor, plan your accuracy testing. Warm up by shooting some soft-recoiling ammo offhand and then from the bench. Get used to the pistol. Then shoot for accuracy before you consume large amounts of practice ammunition.

Shooting for accuracy from the bench is so hard many shooters are willing to invest in a machine rest. Back in the early 1980s, the rumor started to spread at our club that 185-grain lead bullets were not as accurate as 200-grain bullets. This was when everyone shot a .45, and compensators were just starting to appear. In a couple of years everyone who was a serious competitor would be switching to .38 Super, but at the time the .45 was King. (Still is, and always will be, but that is a different story). 185's were thought to give a slightly softer recoil, and many shooters used them. However, to give up accuracy for softer recoil was not seen as a good trade, then or now. The research group of shooters I was in (we called ourselves "The Gang of Four") decided that we could swing the cost of a Ransom Rest to find out if the rumors were true. We bought the machine, learned to use it, and found out the rumors were false. Of the variables that went into accuracy, bullet weight had almost nothing to do with it. We later tracked down the source of the rumor, and found that the two shooters who started it had determined this little tidbit of mis-information from having fired a couple of groups over sandbags at the end of a practice session, and concluded the difference in group sizes was because of the bullet weight.

In the years since, I have discovered many useful things about pistols in general and 1911's in particular from having that Ransom Rest to use.

How does the Ransom Rest work? The pistol fits in the inserts. The inserts are rubber-lined plates that are formed to fit the frame of the pistol. The plates clamp in the swinging arm that is friction and spring dampened. The adjustment screw on the front stops the swinging arm at the same place each time you press it back down into firing position. On the right side there is a trigger link, that lets you press the trigger without touching the pistol. The friction and spring offer a repeatable rate and amount of resistance to the pistol, while the swinging arm moves to the same location and points the pistol at the same spot each time.

First, the Ransom Rest has to be securely attached to a solid support. You can't just stand it on a wobbly picnic bench and expect accurate results. One neat method that I've read about was built by Dean Grennell, who wrote many books and articles on gunsmithing and reloading. He shot at an unimproved range, and could not depend on having a bench available. He built his Ransom Rest stand as a box with an extension off the back of it. The box rested on the ground, and he would simply park his truck or car with a tire on the extension. I shoot at a range with many benches and a rule against vehicles on the range, so I use the benches. I attached my Ransom Rest to a mounting board. I built a special bench out of planks, with a sheet of plywood glued and screwed to the top. I bored one-inch holes through the bench top, and 5/8-inch holes through the mounting board. To clamp the rest to the bench I simply stick half-inch bolts through the holes with washers to keep them in place. I line up the rest to the target frame and tighten the bolts. The holes are larger than the bolts so I can

wiggle the rest for final alignment on the target frame. It is easier than nudging the table over in order to move the point of impact a few inches.

Chasing The Best Group

There is great temptation to save time, ammo and effort, and depend on a group or two for each load. Statistically, it is not valid to use such a small sample. You should use the average of three groups of at least five shots to determine if a load is more accurate than another. A pistol will vary in the size of the groups it shoots, and that variance may differ between loads. I have seen too many shooters who carry a single tattered target with a tiny cluster of holes on it. They are proud of the group, but unaware that statistically it is an

What you want is a 1911 that delivers small groups consistently. Yes, this group is "only" a 2-inch group, but it is average for this Springfield, and fired at 50 yards.

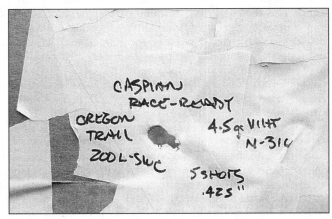

Sometimes a tight group is an anomaly, and sometimes it isn't. The Caspian Race-Ready built for the book delivers lots of groups an inch in size, so half an inch isn't a statistical oddity.

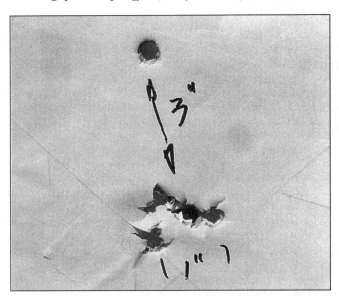

One flyer out of the group; is it you, the pistol or the ammo? You'll need a Ransom Rest and factory ammo to find out.

anomaly. Theoretically, if you took a loose and inaccurate 1911 and fired nothing but groups with it, you would eventually have shot the smallest group it will ever produce. Is that the average? No.

If you want to shoot the most accurate ammunition that you can out of your pistol, you need to know the average group size for each load.

When testing a new powder or bullets, you can use single groups to weed out poor combinations. After all, if a particular combination shoots a 5-inch group at 25 yards when you know the pistol is capable of 2 inches, who cares what the average will be for that combination? But if a different weight of that powder delivers a 2-1/2-inch group, it bears further investigation. You may be disappointed, as that single group may simply have been the smallest of the average that would have included another 5-inch group, but at least you narrowed down the combinations that had to be investigated.

But don't become obsessed by group size. Even an "average" gun that only shoots a 3-inch group at 25 yards will keep every shot in the "A" zone of an IPSC target at 50 yards. And 50 yards is a long way off.

CHAPTER EIGHT

Magazines

Without magazines, the 1911 (or any pistol for that matter) is a clumsy single-shot handgun. The 1911, in particular, is awkward to use without magazines due to the extractor design and the relatively small ejection port. The extractor is intended to slide over the rim as the round feeds out of the magazine. If you lock the slide back, weasel a round through the ejection port and in the chamber, and then close the slide, you are flexing the extractor in a direction it was not designed for. Do that enough times and your extractor will lose its tension and quit on you.

Without reliable magazines, the 1911 is like any other self-loading pistol, a headache to use. Who needs the hassle of always watching to see if it has malfunctioned again? Not me, and not you.

In the old days, we would sweat over magazines. (My first published article was on the proper care and treatment of 1911 magazines.) We would inspect them carefully (for all the good it did us) treat them gently and clean them often. Dropped magazines were wiped clean and closely inspected for any damage. And all this effort was expended on those "two-for-$10-at-the-gun-show" surplus magazines. Anyone who had a batch of reliable magazines would never loan them out to anyone. I kept my magazines sorted into three boxes, the ones that worked in the Ithaca, the ones that worked in the Colt, and the ones that didn't work.

Bill Wilson changed all that starting in 1980. The heart of a magazine is the tube, and the working parts are the feed lips. He made (or had made for him) a tube that was seamless, stainless steel, thick and tough. The feed lips, instead of the taper of the old style, were controlled feed. Bull's-eye shooters had for years been modifying magazines so the feed lips, instead of being a taper front to back, ended in an abrupt shoulder. The shoulder released the rim of every cartridge at the same point in the feed cycle. Wilson magazines were the standard. Everyone used them. My friend, Paul Askew, even gave them out to those who stood up in his wedding, engraved with the date. (I've still got mine.) As with all initial monopolies, those outside and looking in planned to get some. And they did.

Now, buying reliable magazines for a single-stack 1911 is as easy as falling off a log. You only have to make sure you buy yours from one or more of a bunch of reliable brands, and you're home free: Bill Wilson, Chip McCormick, Ed Brown, Clark Custom, Mec-Gar, Mag Pack, Pachmayr and Millett all make good mags. I'm sure there are others, but even I can't get my hands on every brand made. In high-capacity magazines, all the pistols were designed after quality magazines were taken as a given, and so you will be hard-pressed to find bad ones. Not that you can't (some shooters have a gift for finding the cheapest equipment, and wondering why it doesn't work) but it will be hard.

1911s were made to work with magazines. If John Browning had had other ideas, he would not have left the large hole in the bottom of the frame. Custom magwell by Ned Christiansen of Michiguns.

High-Capacity Feeding Devices

Otherwise known as magazines (leave it to the government to come up with such an unwieldy name), hi-caps are expensive. The original high-capacity pistol magazines were 20-round mags for the Mauser Broomhandle, and 32-round snail drums for Lugers in WWI. Later, the Browning Hi-Power became the first reliable high-capacity magazine, with its 13 rounds of 9mm. When IPSC took off, it was neck-and-neck for a while between the 1911 and the Hi-Power. As shooting technique quickly improved, the scoring advantage of shooting Major over Minor meant shooters had to use .45, and thus the 1911. The Hi-Power faded from the scene. When courses became larger and shooting ability between competitors tightened, increased capacity was a tantalizing dream. What held everyone back was the need to design and fabricate magazines from scratch. The first reliable hi-cap mag and frame for it was the Para Ordnance, in .45ACP, in 1987.

Next, competitors attempted to turn the CZ-75 and its various models into an IPSC gun. While the grip is very comfortable, the CZ had problems with 9x21 at Major. (The grip on the early models was not large enough to contain a .45 magazine.) Para Ordnance soon had a .38 super model, using pressed flutes into the body of the magazine to proportion it down from its .45 dimensions.

The Caspian frame is smaller than the Para or the later McCormick/STI/SV frames, making it perfect in size for the .38 Super. It is crowded for a .45 mag, and the capacity is limited, but if you have smaller hands and want a hi-cap frame in .38 Super, the Caspian is a good one. Just a bit heavy.

The big technological leap came with the McCormick frame. Now built as the STI and the Infinity frames and guns, the trick was simple: the rails have to be steel or aluminum, the rest can be plastic.

Current competition rules recognize three magazine sizes. For Open division in USPSA/IPSC competition, a magazine can be 170mm long. In .38 Super (most Open guns are Supers) this means a double-stack magazine capacity of around 28 rounds. For Limited division, a magazine can be a maximum of 140mm long. Most Limited pistols are .40, and thus a 140mm tube ends up with a capacity of around 18 rounds. If you were to build a Limited gun in 9mm or .38 Super (you'd have to shoot it as a Minor gun) the capacity would be about 22 rounds. In Limited 10, the magazine can be any length you want, but you can only load 10 rounds in it.

Finding the 10-shot magazines is easy; its finding the hi-caps that is hard.

In 1994, the federal government threw a wrench into the works. Because of the supposed evil nature of high-capacity magazines, further production was halted. While you can purchase replacement tubes to keep a damaged or worn-out magazine going, you can't use the tubes to build new magazines. To do so is a felony. You can use, sell or purchase existing hi-cap magazines. Only the military and law enforcement officers can purchase newly-made hi-caps, and the mags can't go with the officers when they retire. (Newly-made magazines are marked as such.) You can still buy or assemble pistols that would use the existing high-capacity magazines. Market dynamics being what they are, you can buy a new top-quality single-stack magazine for less than $30. To buy one of the existing hi-cap mags, you may have to spend over $100. The feeding frenzy was worst in Glock magazines, where for a while I saw magazines priced in the $150 range.

The law is supposed to expire (the euphemism is "sunset provision") in 2004. What do you want to bet that in 2004, some new crisis will "require" the continuance of the law?

The form of the Para hi-cap magazine is obvious, a double column of .45's coming up to an internal funnel that feeds one round at a time.

On the left a new post-ban magazine for a hi-cap frame. On the right a pre-ban 140mm magazine. Post ban cost: $20, Pre-ban: $120. Isn't an artificially-altered market wonderful?

Short Vs. Long Bullets

9mm and .40 magazines are slightly different from .38 Super and 10mm mags. While the 9mm/.38 Super and .40/10mm magazines have ribs pressed the length of the sidewalls to narrow the internal space, the 9mm and .40 cartridges are short, leaving extra space in the back of the tube. For proper feeding, the magazines have a filler in the rear of the tube. Without the filler you'd be faced with rounds that nosedive into the frame and won't lift, or rounds that porpoise out of the magazine and hit the chamber sideways. On single-stack magazines the fillers are permanently installed, and your magazine is caliber specific. Dave Skinner at STI had a better idea. He makes a plastic filler and properly-sized follower that slide into his magazines. If you're shooting .38 Super and want to use 9mms, or shooting .40 and want to switch to factory-length cartridges, you can do so. (You also have to change barrels for the .38S/9mm switch.) Disassemble your magazine and set the regular follower aside. Slide the spacer into the back of the tube. Install the new follower on your magazine spring, and reassemble the magazine.

Great, but why would you? As an example, I'll use my early experience with 9mm/.38 Super. At the time, I was

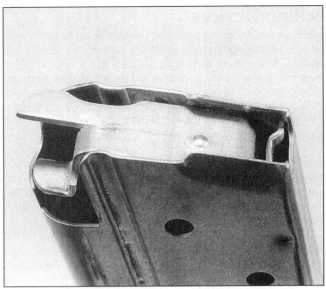

To make a .40 feed out of a 10mm tube, or a 9mm out of a 38 Super tube, the makers have to fill the back. Note the sheet metal filler at the back of this magazine.

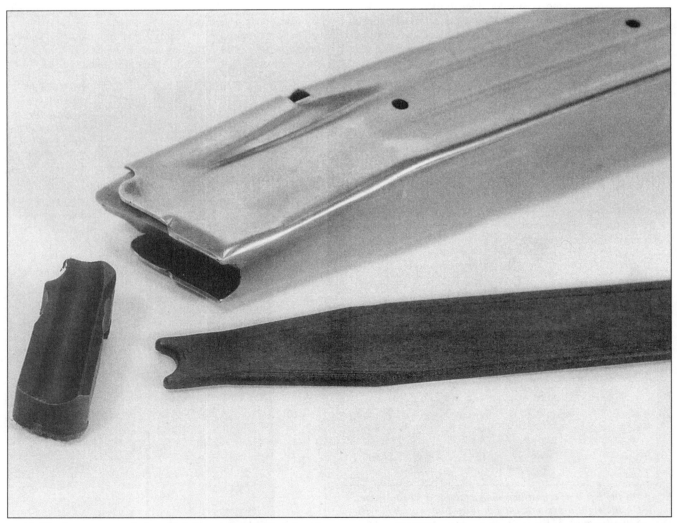

Unlike the permanently installed sheet metal filler of the other magazines, the STI can be adapted to a 9mm or .40 by installing their special short follower and plastic backer.

The removable baseplate on this McCormick magazine does double duty as a bumper pad.

Here are 10-shot .45 magazines from (l-r) Wilson, McCormick, Pachmayr and Mec-Gar. Notice the different approaches to stopping the upward travel of the magazine in the frame.

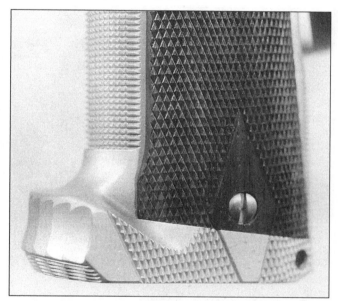

While this Michigun mag funnel only adds a small amount of extra height to the frame, you'll need magazine pads to be sure of seating a mag during the heat of a match.

shooting PPC with the local Sheriff's Department league. The only revolvers I had were single-action, snubbie or large caliber, so I shot the league with a 1911 in .45 ACP. Even the lightest .45 load I could get to cycle (a 200-grain lead semi wadcutter at about 650 fps) was deemed "a magnum" by many of the deputies, who were shooting .38 wadcutter ammo. (By the way, I carried a 596 out of 600 point average with that "magnum" for several leagues)

The boss at the gunshop where I was working then decided he would get into commercial reloading. I had just picked up a .38 Super to build as a competition gun, so I fitted a pair of Bar-Sto barrels to it. One was in .38 Super and the other in 9mm. I loaded ammo for the Super while waiting for the commercial reloading operation to go on line. My earlier experience loading 9mm had not been encouraging (it had been prior to carbide dies) so I wanted the low-hassle Super loading. Once we were loading buckets of 9mm, my plan was to switch and not do my own reloading. Unfortunately the commercial reloading never got off the

ground, but I learned a great deal about feeding 9mms in Super mags. It doesn't work, so I stocked up on 9mm mags. Switching to the Super also removed me from the status of range pariah, and lifted my average to 599.

If you have a ready supply of cheap factory-length 9mm or 40, being able to switch your magazines over is a useful option.

Bumper Pads

At any match, there are so many magazines floating around you want to make sure you can identify yours. The easiest way is to use a distinctive magazine bumper pad. Many shooters still think the pad is a cushion to soften the impact on a dropped magazine. Not so. Bumpers on mags are not like butter on bread. Each side and end of the magazine hits the ground in its full statistical compliment of times. The bumper is for you, to ease seating a magazine. In the pressure of a match, it is easy to not push a magazine all the way into the frame. On a standard frame, you have to worry about getting pinched by the magazine well opening. If you have a magazine funnel installed, then your magazine is shorter than the frame and funnel, and you need an extension. In an IPSC field course, you might shoot 25 or 30 rounds. In some huge courses I've heard of, you might need 40 rounds. If you're shooting an 8-shot .45 ACP, that means at least two, and up to five or six reloads. In a multi-stage match, you could be reloading (and loading to start a stage) 15 or 20 times. If you miss one, your score will suffer.

Most current magazines come with the baseplate already drilled for the screws to hold on a bumper pad. The pads come with "self-tapping" screws. Yes, they will work with only a screwdriver, but save yourself some hassle. If you will be installing a pad on more than one magazine, go out and buy (or call Brownell's) and get a 4x40 tap and wrench. Tap the holes, then install the pads.

You may see a positively huge magazine pad at matches, which looks like it was machined out of a chunk of aluminum. It was. The high-capacity magazine tubes need a large baseplate/pad, and to ease cleaning the larger pad can have large pins or sliding doors to ease disassembly.

Wilson Mid-cap

Bill Wilson decided that if the magazine capacity was going to be restricted to 10 rounds, there was no point in making a high-capacity frame proportioned for magazines that could hold more. While the hi-cap frames are well-proportioned, they are larger than the single-stacks. Too large for some shooters. Concealing a 10-shot single-stack magazine is something only Jabba the Hut could do. Bill designed a magazine that held 10 rounds of .45 ammo, was the same length as a standard magazine, and had as little extra width as possible.

He then put it in a polymer-framed 1911, to keep the extra width down to as little as possible. The result is a 10-shot pistol that doesn't have an extended magazine, and has nearly the same narrow girth as a standard 1911. (Can you get extended magazines for it? Someone out there is missing the point. No, because only 10-shot magazines can be manufactured.)

What you get is a 10-shot pistol that is as small as you can make without going to a short, fat grip, and without using an extended single-stack magazine. For carry, or use in IDPA, the mid-cap is great.

One type of magazine won't need a base pad or bumper pad. When the law was signed in 1994, Bill Wilson figured that if the maximum size was 10 rounds, then that was what he would make. Called the "Bureaucrat" magazine, it is a single-stack,10-shot .45 magazine. There had been longer magazines for the 1911 in the past, but most weren't reliable. In the mid-1980s we began to see some reliable Italian magazines that held 11 rounds. Their popularity in IPSC was dampened by rule changes, but bowling pin shooters loved them. With a fistful of these magazines, a shooter could shoot the 9-pin event without having to build a 9mm or .38 Super pistol. Indeed, many prizes were won in 9-pin, a game designed to let the 9mm shooters have fun away from those pesky big bore shooters, by guys packing .45s. Ned Christiansen and Jerry Miculek both won the event using .45's and extended magazines.

Quick on the ball, both Chip McCormick and Ed Brown make 10-shot magazines in .45 ACP. The McCormick magazine comes with a rubber wrap on the bottom of the tube. Rather than use a bumper pad and make a long magazine even longer, Chip made a wraparound pad that aids handling. It also acts as the magazine stop. On standard magazines the lip of the baseplate stops the magazine. Without it, the longer magazines could move too high in the frame during a reload, causing a malfunction. The Wilson and Ed brown magazine have stops welded to the magazine tube. The McCormick uses the rubber grabber/pad as a stop. You can also get 10-

shot .45 mags from King's and Mec-Gar. I have tried them all, and they work. To have more fun, and more shooting, without spending the big bucks for a wide-body frame, the 10-shot mags are just what the doctor ordered.

A close-up of the magazine butchery manufacturers have to go through to comply with the law. Try to alter this magazine and it will fall apart.

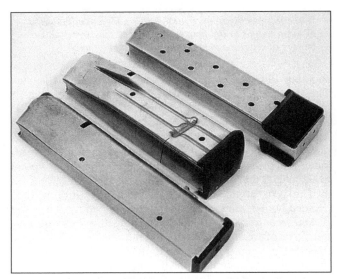

You can add capacity to a hi-cap magazine by installing an extended baseplate. The Dawson Precision basepad has the neater-than-neat sliding latch. Depending on caliber and model, it can add two or three more rounds to a magazine's capacity.

You can shoot the USPSA Limited 10 Division with a single stack, using a Wilson or McCormick magazine. Or, you can shoot your hi-cap pistol and save wear and tear on the expensive pre-ban magazines by using a crimped-tube mag.

Magazines And Capacity

The frame you are using is dependent on using the correct magazines. Even good magazines won't work if they are for a different frame than the one you are using. Single-stack mags won't work in a hi-cap frame and Paras won't work in an STI. Despite their common origins, I have heard some shooters say their STI and SV mags won't work in the other brand pistol, but the ones I've had (all STI mags) did work in several SVs I tried. Capacity doesn't depend on the particular frame you're using, but the length of the magazine. You can have the following capacities:

.45 ACP

Seven shots: The standard. Eight: The McCormick Shooting Star follower in a standard tube. Ten: With the extended single-stack tubes. Twelve: A hi-cap tube flush (126mm) with the frame. Sixteen: A 140mm tube hi-cap. Twenty: A 170mm tube hi-cap.

.40 S&W/10mm

Eight shots: Standard. Nine: The McCormick Shooting Star follower in a standard tube. There are no extended tube single-stack magazines. Fourteen: A hi-cap tube flush with the frame. Eighteen: A 140 mm tube. Twenty four rounds: A 170 mm tube.

9mm/.38 Super

Nine shots: Standard. Ten: Only in McCormick Shooting Star followers in a standard tube, and only with .38 Super brass. There are no extended tube single-stack magazines. Eighteen: A hi-cap tube flush with the frame. Twenty two: A 140 mm tube. Twenty eight: A 170 mm tube.

In addition, there are magazines for high-capacity frames that will hold only 10 rounds. These are newly-manufactured mags, and thus restricted to 10 rounds under the law. The magazine tube is dented to restrict the passage of the follower. The tubes are also crimped through except at the dents, so anyone who tries to grind out the dents will end up with two halves of a the tube.

Now capacity is a variable thing in the hi-cap tubes. You can sometimes get one more than the maximum in a mag by shortening the spring, but you often give up the option of having the slide lock open when empty, and the magazine spring will expire quickly from the extra work. (While preparing for the 1999 World Shoot, I experimented with my International Standard magazines, that reliably hold 14 rounds. I was able to get two of them to hold 17 rounds, but the springs tired quickly, and after an afternoon of practice they wouldn't feed reliably. I went back to the original springs and had no problems during the match.) There are competitors who simply must have the extra round or two, and routinely purchase extra springs to replace the shortened and soon-to-expire springs currently in their magazines. The same competitors often buy new followers, as they love to carve on the plastic, attempting to make the pistol "feed better" or hold one more round. Spring and follower makers do a brisk business with these shooters.

Some competitions are silent about capacity. The Bianchi Cup, for instance, only has six-shot strings, and doesn't allow extra shots to be fired. How many rounds your magazine could hold doesn't matter. However, where capacity matters, rules have been adjusted to reflect the impact of the 1994 law. The USPSA has instituted a new division, Limited 10. The rules are simple, the pistol has to meet the equipment restrictions for Limited (basically no comps and no dots) and you can only load 10 rounds in a magazine.

With this one change, all those retired IPSC guns that were state of the art Stock guns in the 1980s can come out of the gun safe and play again. Most of the guns we're testing in this book would fit right in place in Limited 10, and in the course of testing them I shot quite a few in our club matches in Limited 10 Division. As a matter of fact, my first Limited 10 USPSA classification was set with the Les Baer Heavyweight Monolith, a pistol I very much regretted having to send back.

Care And Maintenance

The modern magazine is a marvel of durability and reliability. The old magazines were often tinny, fragile and easily cracked. A magazine that worked perfectly might start giving feeding problems after shooting indoors, and having been dropped on a concrete floor. New designs are much more durable, and while you could damage the tube, I haven't seen one yet damaged by more-or-less normal use.

Serious competitors will have a host of magazines. It isn't unusual for a shooter using a single-stack 1911 to take a dozen magazines to a match. If they don't break, why so many? Mud and sand. Many outdoor ranges are basically sandpits. My local club has ranges that are all sand, sand and fine gravel, or dirt floors. A magazine that takes a dive into a sandbank will come out gritty. Mud is worse. At one match we held in the rain (we don't stop for weather) Andy

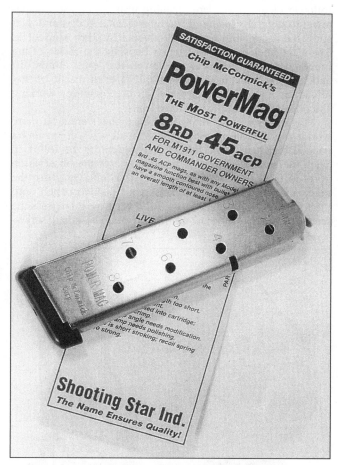

Even this ultra-durable and reliable McCormick Power-Mag needs TLC. Keep it clean and replace the spring every other Presidential election, and it will outlast you. Don't, and it will quit on you sooner than you think.

Carpenter lost a magazine in the mud. We ended up raking the range (the mud was ankle deep, and very soupy) until we found his magazine. Andy's reaction to finding it was, "I'm glad its stainless."

There may not be time in a match to strip and clean magazines, so competitors would simply stuff the now-gritty magazine in a side pocket of their shooting bag and clean it later.

Cleaning a magazine is simple. Magazines come apart two ways, with a removable baseplate, or not. The removable baseplate mags are easy. Press the retainer button in, slide the retainer off.

Well, it's supposed to be easy. If the mag has been dropped the bottom may be very slightly bent, not enough to keep it from working, but enough to make wrestling the pad off a chore. Control the spring as you remove it and the follower. One method of making it easier is to use a Dawson magazine bottom. The Dawson "pad" is a machined aluminum base with a side latch that slides to secure the magazine. Slide the latch forward and the base comes off. Press it on and close the latch, and the mag is assembled. Neat, slick and colorful. The only drawback is that the Dawson only works on hi-cap tubes, due to the need for bottom tabs that are bent outwards. (And on type-specific tubes.) On single-stacks (where the tabs are bent inwards) you can have longer pads, but nothing like the sliding tab, nor any increase in capacity.

To clean a magazine, brush it out, wipe the spring and follower clean. If you are cleaning it at home, use a paper towel to wipe the inside of the tube clean and dry, and then spray the inside with Krunch Products Pistol Pro Mag Slick. The Mag Slick decreases friction between the inside of the tube and the cartridges and follower. It doesn't attract dirt and grit like silicone sprays or oil. (I even use it on my reloading press, to keep the primer shuttle working smoothly.) Reassemble and have fun.

Magazines without removable base plates are a bit more work. You'll need a pusher rod, a small screwdriver and a padded bench. Use the pusher rod to depress the follower. Stick the small screwdriver through one of the observation ports to capture the spring but not the follower. Turn the magazine over and tap it against your padded bench until the follower drops out. Pull the follower free, then press the feed lips against the pad while you pull the small screw-

driver out, releasing the spring. Pull the spring out. Brush the interior, wipe it clean, spray it, and reassemble.

In all magazines, you have to get the spring back in correctly. Observe the spring as you take it out. It has a definite front-and-back, and a top and bottom. On single-stack mags, the bottom coil will be perpendicular to the stack of coils, and the top will be angled. The top front is the higher end of the angle. Double-stack mags are easier. The wide end is the bottom and the higher end of the top is the front.

If the magazine has a removable baseplate, that's the place to start when cleaning.

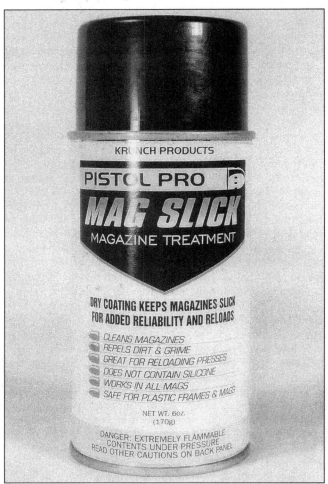

Serious shooters take care of their equipment, and taking care of magazines means Krunch Products Mag Slick.

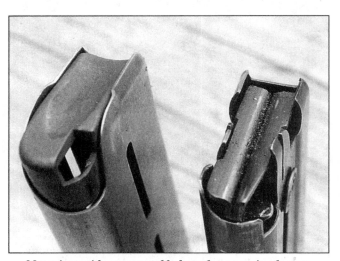

Magazines without removable baseplates require depressing the follower to clean them.

To reassemble the non-base plate mags, feed the spring in and hold it in place with a thumb. Work the rear of the follower in under the feed lips, and press it back until it is in. Use the small screwdriver to catch the top coil of the spring and make sure it is pressed flat against the underside of the follower.

If the follower is one with front and rear legs, you'll have to compress and capture the spring, then work the follower in and release the spring. Again, make sure the top coil is flush against the follower when you are done.

Spring Life

How long are springs good for? It depends on how hard you use them. A compressed spring, left that way, will last a lot longer than a spring that is used every day. At the gun shop, we once bought all the leftover gear from the widow of a Marine. They had both been career Marine NCO's, and after putting up with his (and her) gear lying around the house, she sold it to us. It almost filled two vans. (He had been dead for 18 years. Why it took that long to part with so much stuff, I don't know.)

In the gear were steel ammo cans filled with loaded magazines, 1911, Browning Hi-Power and M1 Carbine. They had been loaded at least 18 years before, and probably a lot more. Every single one of those magazines worked just fine.

Does this prove magazines last forever? No. In the mid-1980s, I bought a bunch of Chip McCormick .38 super magazines. I used them extensively for 10 years. I shot indoor league matches and PPC matches, I used those magazines in the 9-pin event at bowling pin matches, and I shot my single-stack IPSC Super using those magazines. During that time period I made up to 150 trips to the range a year, with those magazines being used more than half the time. In the early 1990s, I switched to a hi-cap Caspian for my IPSC match gun. In the late 1990s, as I was switching to a hi-cap STI in .40 as my Limited and 9-pin gun, I noticed that the McCormick magazines were not always locking the slide open. (I was testing the new .40 against the old .38 Super as a 9-pin gun.) I replaced the springs with new ones and the problem went away. Does this mean Chip makes bad mag springs? Far from it. But those other magazines were loaded for over eighteen years! Yes, and they were stressed once. The McCormick magazines had been loaded and unloaded in firing up to 1,000 times each. The least-worked one had gone through several hundred cycles.

Springs do not last forever, and even the best are inexpensive. If you find your pistol is giving you feeding problems, the magazine may be the fault. Try your ammo in a brand-new right out of the wrapper magazine. If the problems go away, invest in a new set of springs.

For good magazine springs, try Wolff, Wilson, McCormick or ISMI. I have some of each in one magazine or another, and they all work just fine.

How Many Do You Need?

At least one. Beyond that, it depends. I just checked my equipment stores, and not counting the magazines that came with the test pistols, I have 79 magazines on hand for 1911 pistols. (I'm probably overlooking a few.) Why so many? Because a good magazine is valuable enough that I haven't let any get away. (I admit I might be over-reacting to the poor magazines of my earlier shooting days.) If the magazine worked, and the price was good, I bought it. If a new

Springs last longer when used less. The .38 wadcutter mags are 30 years old and work fine. The .45 mag is less than 10 years old and has had the spring changed already. And which one has been loaded and shot more? Obviously the .45.

One reason the wadcutter gun doesn't get shot as much is obvious. It hurts to load the darned thing.

gun came with a couple of magazines, I added them to the total. I now have mags in 9mm, .38 Super, .40S&W, 10mm & .45. Their capacities range from seven rounds to 24. If I loaded them all up, I'd have 805 rounds ready to go. Perhaps I've been a little too eager to hang on to good magazines, but I know I'm not any kind of a record-setter in this regard. And besides, I needed enough magazines in each caliber to be able to compete in a match with it.

How many should you have? If all you're going to do is go to the range and plink now and then, one to three magazines will work for you. (I'll start the discussion speaking of single-stack mags, and add a few thoughts on hi-caps at the end.) With three loaded magazines you can do some good practicing without spending all your time stuffing magazines. If you are going to compete, you'll need more.

For active IPSC shooters and those aspiring to bowling pin shooting, seven is a good number. It would be a gargantuan field course that you couldn't complete with those 56 to 70 rounds. For bowling pin shooting, the Main Event is six tables, with a spare if you need to reload to finish a table. If you drop a magazine in the mud, or at a pin match it falls too far forward to retrieve right away, you still have enough mags to finish. Seven is also a good number for those using their 1911 as a carry gun. You'll carry one in the gun and one or two as spares. You can put the shooting and dropping practice wear and tear on the other four or five, and leave your carry mags undropped.

The serious shooter will have a dozen. Even a dozen costs less than another gun, and you can always keep four or five of them clean and sealed in a bag in your gear. If you hit a stage where all your mags go into sand, mud or water, you have fresh mags to finish the match. You can also leave the bagged mags fresh (once you've tested them) so the springs are not tired.

One drawback to adding a caliber to your inventory is the cost of magazines. A serious shooter adding a .40 to his or her .45 will have to duplicate the magazine investment. Such is life.

High-capacity magazines are different, in that they cost a lot more. At only $100 per, a hi-cap costs as much as three or four single-stack mags. Many competitors consider themselves well-equipped with only three or four hi-caps. What about mud, sand or water? At the cost of hi-cap mags, a dropped mag will get stripped, wiped, sprayed with Mag Slick, and reassembled before the next stage. Heavy-duty practice is done on the 10-shot versions of the hi-cap magazines to minimize wear and tear on the expensive ones. If a particular model of hi-cap runs $150 each, you could have bought all you needed of a single-stack model magazine for the cost of one or two hi-caps. Cost is the driving force behind the popularity of Limited 10 Division competition in the USPSA.

When Good Mags Go Bad

What goes wrong when a magazine stops feeding properly? If you have one of the new magazines, about all that can be wrong is it is full of grit or the spring has gotten weak. Disassemble the magazine, brush it out and spray it with Mag Slick. If the spring is weak, replace it. The new magazines are made of thicker and harder steel, and do not have any sharp corners to act as stress risers. (At least the good ones do.)

Older magazines, the ones we had to struggle with in the early days, commonly failed from cracked lips. The slot in the rear of the magazine, that the disconnector/feed shoulder of the slide passed through, was made square, with sharp corners. The rear of the lip would crack, from the corner out, and the lip would spread. Inspect your magazines. If you see that crack, ditch the mag. I tried repairing such cracks in the old days, and it was barely worth the effort back then. Now welding such cracks is a complete waste of time.

What about dents, bent magazines, misaligned feed lips, and other maladies? If your magazine is tinny enough to dent or bend, ditch it and buy a better one. If you dropped it in rocky terrain and the lips got bent, you can try bending them back. As for having someone work on them, why bother? At $30 for a brand new single stack, how much labor and test-fire ammo are you willing to do? For a high-cap, you can buy a replacement tube and transfer the guts into the new tube for less money that repairing the old one would cost.

CHAPTER NINE

Classes

You may be a new owner of a 1911, or you may have owned one for quite a few years, but the question is the same, "Why take a class?" A lot of shooters have no interest in competition, and never plan to carry their firearms for defense. They go to the range a few times a year to punch holes in paper, knock down falling plates, or plink at tin cans. I was in that group myself for a long time. My brother and I would spend our summer vacations at the cabin up north, plinking on the 100-yard range with our handguns. We became quite good at rolling tin cans. So much so that when I went to my first handgun metallic silhouette match, I was not at all impressed by the 200 yard rams. (I should have been.)

But to improve your shooting you have to develop new techniques, drop bad ones and refine the good ones. Doing that by yourself is hard. If you take a class of some kind, you can benefit from the experience of others, and be exposed to new techniques. You may not like what you learn, and it may not work for you. But as my martial arts instructor was happy to point out, even learning what doesn't work improves what does.

It is not possible in one chapter to cover (or even mention) all the instructors who are teaching shooting, even those who focus on the 1911. I do recall a book having been written by someone who went to every school in existence back then (mid 1980s), but it is probably out of print, and certainly out of date by now. To duplicate the effort now would more than fill this book, and my publisher would faint at seeing the receipts for tuition, lodging and ammunition. (But it would be so much fun!) In good conscience, I can only mention those instructors whom I have been through classes under, know personally, or who I have talked at length about with shooters whose opinions I trust, concerning the classes they took. I do not leave anyone out except for the reason that I don't know enough about them.

But if you are seeking instruction, what kind? Instruction can be divided into four broad categories, with a lot of overlap between them. The categories are Technique, Technique and Tactics, Legal/Tactical, and Competition.

Technique

A technique-based class would be what most shooters used to think of as shooting instruction. It would be exemplified by instruction you would get from the NRA, or your old Boy Scout classes, when the Scouts taught marksmanship. The classes would be devoted solely to proper form, sight alignment and follow-through. Unless you were in an NRA Home Defense course, an instructor in a technique-based class would have an attack of the vapors if you asked what the proper sight picture was on a person. You can find such instruction through the NRA or any old-line gun club devoted to Bull's eye shooting.

Technique and tactics

Gunsite

The improved instruction came out of the then-new practical shooting, and burst onto the world when Jeff Cooper opened Gunsite in 1977. The idea is to teach both the technique of using a handgun, (later he added rifle and shotgun classes, and now Gunsite teaches just about everything) using it effectively based on physical ability, not bound by artificial rules of competitions, and also teaching its use in a defensive setting.

Gunsite is located in the high plateau of Arizona, near a small resort town called Prescott. When Gunsite was founded, Prescott was nowheresville. The city and surrounding area have grown, and there are a number of firearms and equipment companies there, including the Sturm, Ruger plant. The remote location aided proper instruction (it takes elbow room to build multiple ranges, especially if they are more than just "square range" instruction boxes), but getting there and going to a class was a bit of work in the early years. Now there are plenty of hotels in which to stay, and the road is more than just a rutted two-track trail into the hills.

In the T&T schools like Gunsite, you will often find that the instructors are retired military personnel, with active-duty SWAT officers also leading classes. The last class I was in at Gunsite, the instructors were two active-duty SWAT officers and a retired Navy SEAL. Besides me, the class was mostly active-duty military (including three SEALS and one Delta operator) and sworn law enforcement officers. "The firearm as a fighting tool" is what you will find at a T&T school. In the 1970s, training with firearms as a fighting tool and IPSC competition were the same, only later did a divergence between tactics and competition arise. Legal aspects are not overlooked, but it is assumed that each student already has a grasp of the legal restrictions of using a handgun defensively. The tactics taught fit a properly legal emphasis, but the focus of instruction is to improve the shooter's skill.

Gunsite expanded marksmanship training to include tactical lessons by use of "simulators." The simulators were partial buildings, ravines or trails with targets placed in them. Each student has to go through the simulators and find

The author at Gunsite in 1987, beating Jim Fawcett in the shoot-offs. I didn't gloat, as I had to ride 2,000 miles back home with him.

Even a simple little wash like this can add amazing amounts of complexity to a simple task.

The advantage of being out in the middle of nowhere is the elbow room to set up courses like this, taking advantage of natural terrain.

A chance to rest and drink fluids before going out into a course, and reflect on the usefulness of sights.

and deal with the targets, sorting the dangerous and violent from the innocent bystanders, and dealing with each appropriately.

In the early years, Jeff Cooper taught many of the classes at Gunsite. Age has slowed him down, and he does not teach nearly as much as he used to, but the current owner (the ownership changed hands in 1993, the instruction quality trended downwards in the opinion of many, and changed hands again in 1998, surging back to and now past its old quality) and instructors teach under the watchful eye of the Master.

Gunsite started it, and many of the instructors who opened their own schools taught or trained at Gunsite.

Thunder Ranch

Located in Mountain Home, Texas, Thunder Ranch is the home base for Clint Smith. Clint was Operations Manager at Gunsite for a number of years, then opened his own school in Texas. Why Texas? It is closer to the population centers in the East, offers lots of open land, and has "good" weather. By good, that means a short cold spell with little snow. Many schools are located in the southern tier of states for the simple reason it is easier to run a class in the heat than in the snow.

Where Gunsite is more laid back, Thunder Ranch reflects the personality of Clint, and is a higher-intensity workout.

Shooters who like a fast pace have come back from Thunder Ranch positively glowing. (That and the ammunition consumption is higher at TR than many other schools.) Clint Smith built on the lessons learned and taught at Gunsite, and at Thunder Ranch added new twists. He built a new indoor simulator with moveable walls so the same building could be set up in hundreds of different configurations. He built a street to be used as a training range, engaging targets from room to room and across the street. He built a tower to be used as a multi-story simulator. (You can see why a full-time school with all the needed ranges takes up hundreds of acres at a minimum.)

Front Sight

Started by Dr. Ignatius Piazza, a multiple graduate of classes from Gunsite, Front Sight began in Bakersfield, California. While it was a convenient place to locate a range, the location in Bakersfield was not entirely suited to Front Sight, and California was rapidly becoming a most gun-unfriendly state. The Doctor moved Front Sight to a location just outside of Las Vegas.

Legal/Tactical

The thrust of the Legal/Tactical instructors is that the shooting challenge of a defensive situation is not the end of the problem. While it is imperative to survive the shooting, you must also survive the aftermath. Called "Problem Two" (the shooting incident is "Problem One") you could find yourself surviving an assault only to end up impoverished or imprisoned if you didn't know the law or its procedures. I know, it sounds grim, but I don't make the rules, I just write about them.

While the students in a T&T class are usually high-speed competitors and "high-speed, low-drag" military types, the students in an L/T class are more often store owners, instructors of other classes, and plain old ordinary homeowners who live in a bad part of town. You don't go to a Legal/Tactical class to burn up lots of ammunition. You may only go through a couple of hundred rounds. The emphasis is not on building shooting skills (although your skills will be tested, assessed and improved), but building court-proof tactical skills.

John Farnam

John Farnam is a retired U.S. Army major with combat experience in Vietnam, and an active law enforcement officer. He travels the country teaching classes. My first class taught by an outside expert was one of John's classes. John teaches classes heavy on tactics, problem-solving, stress and the legal aftermath. He views the technical problem of getting hits on a target at the range as an easy one. The hard part comes in living in the real world. (Many shooters have been exposed to John's old-lady voice "He's got a gun!" when they have gone to draw their pistol before the simulated situation would be warranted.)

As a traveling instructor, John is dependent on the facilities of the range he is at. The advantage to traveling is that he is exposed to a larger number of organizations and groups than instructors who have a home range.

Massad Ayoob

Mas is perhaps the gun writer with the longest active career (he's been at it for more than 20 years, and at any time during those years you could go to a newsstand and find a magazine with his byline.) And he has more pages to his background than you'd find anywhere else. He has been an active police officer all that time. (Last I heard he was promoted to Captain of his department, maybe Chief by now). He has worked patrols, and arrested suspects at gunpoint.

He is a court-recognized expert witness on the subject of lethal force and testifies in many cases each year. He has

The whole point of a Legal/Tactical class is to solve both problems, and that means keeping concealed guns concealed. Can you see the Kimber Ultra CDP? And the spare magazine? Are you sure?

Go for your draw early in a John Farnam class, and you'll be corrected.

Determine what you want before you select a school. If you want to win matches, great.

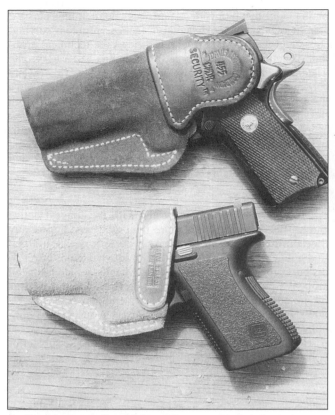

You don't need a high-speed competition holster in a Legal/Tactical class. Indeed, it would be a handicap.

If you are going to be in harm's way, learn from those who have done so, and be sure your gear is up to it. This student has the secondary Velcro latch on the Blackhawk holster secured. Great for an airborne operation, but not if you're expecting to draw momentarily.

written a shelf-full of books on firearms, tactics and the legal aspects of the defensive use of a firearm.

He was a top-flight competitor in the early days, placing high in the standings of the US IPSC Nationals, Bianchi Cup, Second Chance and many other matches. He is still a good shot. Perhaps the only strike against his being the uber-shooter is that he wasn't in the military. (Who needs to jump out of perfectly good airplanes, anyway?) Yes, I like the guy.

Mas opened Lethal Force Institute in New Hampshire in the early 1980s. At LFI, you will go through a class based on the law, a class that is more thorough on this subject than that you would get from many Law schools. At times it may seem as if you are being overwhelmed by the law, but you will be well-served to pay attention and not just daydream until you get to go to the range.

Yes, you will get to shoot. As a matter of fact, you'll do a decent amount of shooting. However, the class would be well worth the time, effort and cost even if you never fired a shot.

Competition

Competition instruction is designed to improve your performance in a particular match or types of matches. The instructors are almost all successful competitors, National and World Champions. While some will also teach high-speed classes for special operations groups and law enforcement, mostly they teach you how to win matches.

Do not discount the tactical utility of being able to win a match. My friend Gina Rappaport, who teaches in the Pacific Northwest, showed up at Second Chance one year while visiting family members in Michigan and delivering guns and

ammo to friends at Second Chance. She also planned to write about the match for "Women and Guns" magazine. When Richard Davis found out she was writing about the match, he signed her up, and all her friends loaned her their guns and ammo. Afterwards she recounted to me "I've been through lots of instruction and tactical simulations, and I never felt the tension like I did up there on the line. My hands were shaking so badly I thought I would never hit a thing." She went on to win loot in several categories.

Stress is stress, and learning to be a good shot under the stress of competition is a skill that can be useful in many things in life.

Jerry Barnhart

In a sport of nice guys, Jerry is one of the nicest guys you could ever meet. He is also a blazingly fast shooter and an implacable competitor. He has won National and World titles, shooting IPSC, The Steel Challenge, The Masters, and Second Chance. While he teaches classes for law enforcement and military organizations, you can't get into those classes unless you are already in those organizations. His open classes are devoted to competition shooting. He travels to client ranges and also teaches at his home range in Michigan.

Jerry Barnhart will teach you how to shoot, and whack large amounts of time off your runs. If you don't shoot better after his class, you must have been sleeping.

And you'll get hands-on teaching from Jerry.

Jerry Miculek

The "Other Jerry" is the nicest guy you could meet. While many might know of Jerry Miculek as the fastest revolver shooter alive today (and perhaps ever) he also shoots other firearms quickly. So quickly he has been the USPSA 3-Gun National Champion several times. One year at Second Chance he won every event he entered (handgun, rifle, team, shotgun) but one, and went home with nine AR-15 rifles from DPMS as prizes. He placed well enough in that other event to win some other firearm.

Based from his home range in Princeton, Louisiana, called The Shootout, which is also the location of Clark Custom, Jerry teaches every aspect of competition shooting.

The ranges at The Shootout are large and numerous enough to have hosted the USPSA 3-Gun nationals for several years.

Mike Voigt

Mike has been winning the USPSA 3-Gun Nationals title when Jerry Miculek and Jim Clark, Jr. haven't been hogging it. Mike was also the 1999 World Shoot Standard Champion, shooting the match right after having been elected to the office of President of the USPSA. While he may not be teaching as much for the years he is in office (he will be too busy to do much shooting, less teaching) he will do some, and will get back in the swing of things once he is out of office.

Mike's home range is in Florida (more warm-state shooting facilities) with many ranges set up for specialized instruction.

Class Equipment And Ammunition

What should you take to your class? How much ammunition should you bring, and what kind? The basic equipment for any class would be your pistol and a spare if there is not an on-site gunsmith, half a dozen reliable magazines, a holster and magazine pouches. (Of course you'll bring eye and ear protection, right? I don't have to remind you, do I?) Why a spare gun and not extra parts? You can be sure the spare gun will work. You can't be sure you brought the right parts, and even if you do you'll spend a few turns on the line testing the fixed pistol, rather than tending to the lesson plan. If you are using a standard 1911 at Gunsite, you can use a school loaner while yours is being fixed in the on-site gunsmithy. (If you like the loaner, you can even buy it.) Your belt, holster and mag pouches should be sturdy and top-quality, designed for hard, full-time use. If you don't have such gear, you can quite often buy it at the school you've gone to. After the first day, you'll know if your gear is up to the class, and if not, the gear worn by your instructors and the other students can act as a guide. Why so many mags? If you are in a small class at a high-shooting-volume school, you can shoot as much as you want. A class will usually be divided into two firing lines, and each line takes a turn shooting while the other line is reloading magazines and drinking water. Having more loaded magazines in your pockets keeps you on the line longer.

You'll want to have a basic first aid kit with the usual minor "ouchie" type stuff like band-aids, ointment, sunscreen, insect repellent, tweezers, etc. You needn't bring a full EMS kit unless you are an EMS tech and can't leave home without it. (At my shotgun class at Gunsite, one of the students ended up with an elbow full of gravel from diving prone in a drill. As the EMS tech who was in the class was trying to dig the bits out with a sharp knife, he asked one of the other students to get out of his light. The other student, an Emergency Room Board Certified Physician, said he simply wanted to watch and learn. Such are the students you can run into, but bring your own first aid stuff just in case.)

Wear sturdy clothing, clothing you aren't afraid to get dirty and risk tearing, solid shoes or boots that are broken in, and a baseball hat. Even if you are accustomed to wearing tee shirts, wear shirts with collars. On a firing line, you may find yourself being pelted by your neighbor's brass. The collar protects your neck from the sun, and by buttoning up you can keep that pesky brass from squirming down into your shirt.

Ammunition

After selecting the "right gun", the question of how much ammo to bring is probably the most controversial subject. Some schools will tell you right up front not to bring personal reloads. They have had too many hassles and too much down-time from unreliable reloads brought by students. Other schools don't have a hard and fast policy, and will let you shoot whatever you've brought. However, should your ammunition prove to be so unreliable that dealing with constant malfunctions is interfering with the instruction, your instructors may suggest you invest in a case of school ammo.

A case in point, my experience at a Gunsite class. I was going through the .223 class, using my own reloads. I had shot a year's worth of club rifle matches, and gone through Second Chance using that batch of ammo without a single fault. (What can I say, when I load, I load in large batches.) At the Gunsite .223 class I had three case separations in one afternoon. Luckily I had brought a broken case extractor (and had it in my pocket!) and was able to finish each drill, but it was not fun.

Case separations in .45 ACP are unheard of, but you had better make sure all the bugs are out of your reloading process (and use brass that has already been loaded once) before you show up with your own reloads.

For a class, you'll need glasses and muffs, a 1911, magazines and ammo, and a holster. What kind of holster depends on what kind of class. A tactical rig like this Blackhawk is great for a class of SWAT cops, but a mite slow for a class on The Steel Challenge.

What if you want to use reliable ammo, but not break the bank? Find out how much ammo your class will require, and call one of the commercial reloaders. Black Hills or Zero can ship your ammo for you. Have it shipped right to the school, in your name. (You might have them ship you a couple of boxes direct, so you can make sure your 1911 is sighted in for the load you're using.) And what load? I would use a full-weight jacketed round nose or flat point. In .45, I'd shoot 230 JRN, in .40 S&W or 10mm I'd use 180-grain flat points, and in 9mm I'd use a 125 JRN. What about factory new ammunition? If you can afford the stiff expense, go for it. However, plain ball ammo can cost an appreciable fraction of the class tuition, and high-tech hollowpoints can actually cost you more for ammo than the class fees do.

A moment for class etiquette: All schools run a clean range. You are expected to pick up as much as you shot, except in the simulators. (The maid will get those later.) If you are using school ammo, they need the brass to turn back in to their commercial reloader. If you are using your own reloads, pick up as much as you shot, but not much more. Poaching on the school brass is not good form. If you are using a special caliber or batch of brass, let the other members of your class know so they can sort yours out of each handful. I was once in a class taught by Jerry Barnhart where three of the students were using the same batch of ammo, loaded with brand new Winchester 9x23 brass. We sorted through every handful so they could get their brass back. (I was happy to do so, as my Super won't chamber 9X23 brass, and even if I waited until I got home to sort it out, I still couldn't use it.)

If you must use the cheapest possible ammo, use CCI Blazer. The non-reloadable aluminum cases are easy to identify and throw away. If you use some berdan-primed surplus ammo, every reloader who uses brass picked up at that class (and for a couple of classes on that range after) will curse you. Berdan brass breaks decapping pins unless it is sorted out of the batch before reloading.

And how much should you bring? Lots. Every school or instructor has a good idea of how much ammunition it takes to get through their class. Always bring more. If a class is smaller than expected, you'll be able to get more time on the line, and will shoot more. If a class happens to be composed of already good shooters, the lesson plan will go quickly, and you'll have more time to work on each detail. If the class runs ahead of the expected ammunition consumption, and you have more, you can shoot more. If you only have enough for the class, you'll have to stop when you run out. I've had an instructor tell me "I can teach a new shooter all he or she is going to learn, in less than 400 rounds. Even in a week-long course." So why higher round counts? "Shooters like to shoot ammo. More is better." And so it is. After all, you've waited a year, traveled several thousand miles and have spent a couple of thousand dollars so far. You're standing on the range, why not do some shooting?

A typical basic class will use at least 200 rounds per day of instruction, some more. A competition class for experienced competitors taught by Jerry Barnhart could do much more than that per day. At the top end, if you were to go to an advanced class at Thunder Ranch for a week, and be in a small class of experienced shooters, you could easily exceed 1,500 rounds for your week's stay. Compared to the rest of the expedition, the cost of ammo is cheap. Take lots.

A Package

If you want to be absolutely sure you have a reliable gun, the ammo will work, and have an at-your-shoulder warranty while you try it, you can do the Gunsite package. For a modest fee you can sign up for a class at Gunsite, and have the rental pistol and factory ammunition provided. If the pistol breaks, they'll hand you another one and take the first one back to the gunsmithy for the necessary repairs. You can even buy the gun you've used in the class, or buy it and have them add upgrades and ship it to you once they are done. For your week's vacation you get instruction, a reliable pistol, sunburn and great memories. And the skill to use your new tool.

Not all schools will offer loaners, and many will not have an on-site gunsmith. Be sure you read their brochure carefully when you make up your packing list.

CHAPTER TEN

Gunsmithing the 1911

If you're going to perform at your best you'll need a reliable pistol. With a reliable 1911 you can go to the World Shoot and see how you stack up. Is your buddy the "machinist/gunsmith" up to it?

There is no lack of books and manuals on the subject of gunsmithing the 1911. I won't try to distill a full book (a future project) into one chapter, but rather give you vital information on what gunsmithing to consider, how to get it done or do it yourself, and what to expect from the newly worked-on pistol. The woods are full of "gunsmiths" and "armorers" and "my buddy the machinist" who think they can do the work, but can only do it if there aren't any problems. If you are lucky enough to have a pistol that doesn't present any problems when being worked on, they could do well for you. But if they get in over their heads, you could end up with a custom pistol that doesn't work, and more expenses ahead to fix it.

Gunsmithing operations fall into two categories: What you need and What you desire. For a basic gun that you can

use in any competition, what you need are, "Sights you can see, a trigger you can manage, and absolute reliability." (Jeff Cooper's reply to my question of what pistol to bring to my first Gunsite class.) When it comes to pistols that satisfy those requirements, the times have never been better for buyers nor worse for gunsmiths. Most of the guns tested here would do. Some would need a little tweaking, while others needed nothing but checking to make sure the ammo hits to the sights. It is when you move into the category of Desire that you have to start making difficult decisions.

The decision-making tree is simple. One, what do you want done? Two, Can you do it yourself? If yes, buy the parts and get to work. If not, then Three, Who can do the work? Four, The two of you settle on a time and cost for the

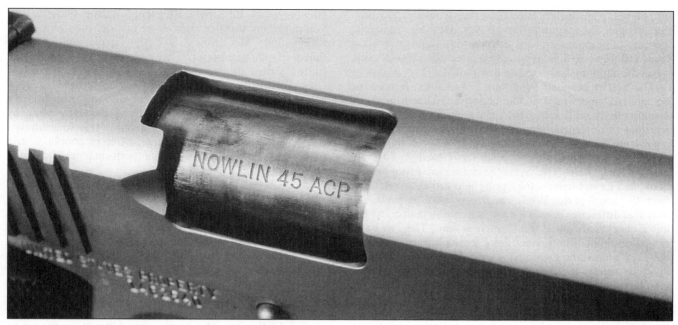

One improvement is to install a match barrel like this Nowlin.

work you want done. And then Five, You wait. (I don't consider testing and shooting it on its return a step, but rather a lifetime vocation.)

What do you want done? The various gunsmithing jobs on a 1911 can be broken into four categories: Reliability, a Basics package, Competition, and Bespoke.

Reliability work on a 1911 involves making sure it works 100 percent of the time. A pistol that has had a reliability package performed will not shoot any more accurately than it did before, and the trigger may not even be nicer, but it will work all the time. When I started gunsmithing, I chased the elusive Symptoms of Malfunction. I tried to determine just what the problem my customer's pistol was having, and then fix it. After struggling over minor problems, I decided I had to find another way. I looked over all the work I had done, and determined that there were "A" problems and "B" problems. When someone came in with a malfunctioning 1911, I first determined that it was worth working on. I wrote down the particular problem for that gun, and then I did all the "A" list work. I then took it to the range and test-fired it. More than 95 percent of the pistols worked just fine after the "A" list work. Those few that didn't, well, I had just been to the range and seen the malfunction, I could easily track the problem down. (And a number of those previous problems had not been the pistol's fault, but ammunition or magazine-related. I always used known ammo and known mags.)

What did it matter that the previous problem might have been a burred breechface, an un-tensioned extractor or loose ejector? It was easier to check and fix them all than try to determine which one it had been.

When you take (or send) your 1911 to a gunsmith for reliability, tell him what particular problem you are having, and tell him that you want your pistol to be reliable. Do not try to diagnose the problem for him. Gunsmiths get cranky when they receive a package and a note reading, "I've determined that the problem is a tight chamber. Ream the chamber and return and my reliability problems will go away."

That's because they know if the chamber is not the problem, they'll get the gun back with a nastier note. And the shooter is likely to tell everyone at his club that "Gunsmith Bob" couldn't fix a simple problem. While the details of the list might differ slightly, every good 'smith has his own version of the A and B lists.

If you have an heirloom, or collector's piece (but not an unfired 1930s Colt, or something like that) a good gunsmith can do a reliability package and leave no traces. You can fire grandad's 1911 brought back from the war, knowing it is reliable, but not make any alterations.

The line between Basic and Competition work can be very blurry, but the difference is intent. A Basic level of work would be getting your sights changed, say to night sights or larger fixed sights. Or having a larger thumb safety installed, or the slide and frame fit tightened or a match barrel fitted. The basic work improves the pistol, but doesn't make it so specialized for a particular match that it becomes a "one-use" gun. Also, basic work is like getting your kitchen cabinets refaced in that the cost is regained on sale, at least most of time. If you have a plain pistol with a Bar-Sto or Kart barrel fitted, you can easily get the cost of the barrel back in resale. If you have the sharp edges removed, called "de-horning", you can recover that cost. However, de-horning also requires a new blue job (or whatever finish you have) and you aren't going to be able to recover the cost of the new finish.

Reliability packages and Basic work used to provide a number of gunsmiths with a steady income. However, a convergence of factors has put a crimp in that situation, and pushed much work up to the Competition level. First, even Colt improved the quality and features of their pistols. If a Colt worked reliably, why pay for a reliability package? Second, the competition for the market improved all offerings. If you could buy a Springfield Loaded, or Kimber Custom, why buy a pistol with an unknown track record and then invest in work to bring it up to the same level? Third, UPS decided that since they couldn't keep their own employees from stealing handguns, they would require any-one shipping a handgun to send it Next Day Air. Suddenly, the cost of shipping a pistol to and from a gunsmith went from $10-12 up to $60. Why send a pistol for $100 in work, when the shipping is more than half that?

The border between Basic and Competition is now the hot ground, and where all the action is. What it all boils down to is, the difference between a Basic, even a loaded one, and a Competition gun, is the intent. If a gun is built for a particular match or organization, then it is a Competition gun, even if basic. I hope I haven't confused you all. An example may help. The Springfield Loaded pistol in this book, and its stablemate, the Springfield Professional, came from the same place. While the Pro is more accurate, the only real difference between them is in refinements. The Pro has a checkered frame, the Loaded is bare. The Pro has a magazine funnel, the Loaded has a beveled frame. The Pro has night sights, the Loaded does not. The Pro has an ambi-dextrous safety, the Loaded does not. If all these matter, then buy the Pro. If they don't, buy the Loaded and use the money you've saved to buy practice ammo.

A TEB gun would have a better barrel installed in order to improve accuracy. A Competition gun will have a Match barrel with a pre-determined performance level required. A Bianchi gun that can't shoot groups smaller than the X ring is not a useful competition gun. Better isn't enough, if it doesn't exceed the match requirements.

What goes into a Top-End Basic (TEB) or Competition gun? (Many 1911's sold as "Tactical" guns fit the definition of a TEB.) First, you'll be fitting a match barrel to it. While many out of the box pistols shoot accurately, a lot more don't. The fastest way to improve a pistol's performance is with a match barrel. You can have your choice of a number of premium barrels by big-name makers, like Bar-Sto, Kart,

Nowlin, Clark, Ed Brown, Kings, and Wilson. Other barrels you might not think of right away that deliver stellar accu-racy include McCormick, STI (they make guns, so who thinks of getting a barrel? Theirs are very good.), Les Baer (ditto), Briley (they don't just work on shotguns), KKM (tack-driving barrels), and Storm Lake Machine. A good barrel is a good barrel, regardless of who makes it. I have a 9mm barrel for bowling pin shooting that was made by Olympic Arms. (Yes, the AR-15 people.) It is so accurate I could sell it to any one of three different people with a phone call, based solely on its performance at Second Chance.

A TEB will have a large safety, or an ambidextrous safety installed. Something low-profile like a Wilson Com-bat Ambi, or larger like the Ed Brown. A TEB that is also a competition gun might get the King's gas pedal, so large you could get two thumbs on it.

The TEB might be tightly fitted, while the competition gun almost certainly will be. Fitting the slide to the frame takes work, skill and money. Whether you make the fit tight by peening and lapping the rails, fitting a new oversized slide, or installing the Accu-Rail system, you improve accu-racy and reliability. The drawback is that you are far out on the cost-benefit curve by the time you have tightening work done, and you won't recoup your costs. You can get the cost of a new barrel out of the person you're selling your pistol to, but you can't get the cost of peening, or Accu-rails. The improvements come at the top of the curve. If your pistol is already 99.999 percent reliable, the fitting will add another 9 to the end. Peening or rails might tighten groups a quarter-inch at 25 or 50 yards. Both are small improvement for a large cost. If you are competing, both are worth it. If the buyer of your pistol isn't competing, then the costs aren't worth it to him.

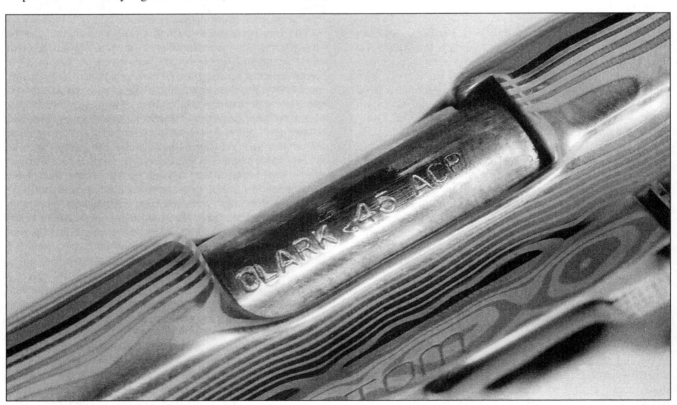

Clark also makes first-rate barrels.

Visiting a barrel maker is like going to Santa's factory, toys everywhere. (Photo courtesy of Bar-Sto Precision)

A match barrel is no good unless fitted properly. Here Irv Stone of Bar-sto fits a barrel. (Photo courtesy of Bar-Sto Precision)

It takes precision machinery to make precision barrels. Bar-sto has both. (Photo courtesy of Bar-Sto Precision)

King's makes a safety so large you might even get both thumbs on it.

A TEB will often have adjustable, or night sights. Or, fixed sights of the Novak pattern.

A TEB will have a beavertail grip safety of some brand, often with a "speed bump" on it to make sure your hand always depresses the grip safety. I have installed and used the Wilson, Safari Arms (now Olympic Arms offers the design), and the Ed Brown. I have gotten fond of the McCormick design wedge speed bump for always making sure the grip safety is down. On the .40 Super pistol I built

for the book I went with the STI grip safety. A good grip safety makes shooting more comfortable, and keeps your grip locked to the pistol.

A TEB will often have a recoil spring guide rod, often with some sort of buffer installed.

You're probably scratching your head at this point, having sneaked a peek ahead at the guns that were test-fired, wondering why so many pistols out of the box had many of

The STI grip safety being fitted to the .40 Super test gun.

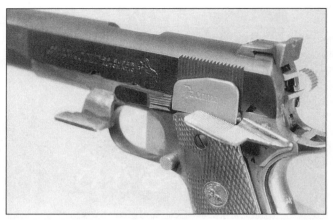

A competition gun for sure. In this case a Nine-pin gun for pins. The large safety and extra thumb rest help keep the muzzle down under recoil.

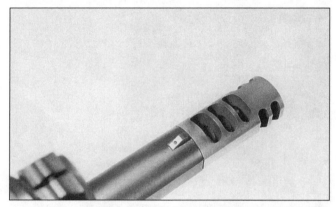

A compensator definitely takes a gun into the Competition category.

the "custom" features mentioned. Market dynamics. If people want grip safeties, just to pick one part, the savvy manufacturer offers it on his pistol as a regular feature. For a little more money to the manufacturer, the new owner doesn't have to spend a lot on shipping, a new part, and fitting, to a gunsmith for the same grip safety.

The TEB is a versatile pistol. With the right balance of features, and performance to meet the need, a TEB could compete in almost any match. With the right gun, you could shoot Bull's eye, IPSC/USPSA Limited, the Single Stack Classic, the Steel Challenge, Stock in Bowling Pins, IDPA, Handgunner Shoot-off, the Bianchi Cup and your local club matches. With one gun, you could shoot a match every single weekend (and some weekdays) of the warm-weather months. It's no wonder the gunsmiths and manufacturers have been working hard to sell you one, and you can take it anywhere except New York City. And who holds matches there?

So, how does a pistol make it out of TEB into Competition? Well, there are a few ways, but the basic method is through specialization. At the just-over-the-line end, a competition gun would be a 9mm or .38 Super built as an otherwise Stock gun for Bianchi Cup, Steel Challenge, or the "any centerfire" portion of Bull's eye. The same gun would work in the Single Stack Classic. To make a specialized "rule-beater" gun would be something like building a tack-driving 9mm or .38 Super on a lightweight Commander frame for IDPA competition.

A full-size 9mm or .38 Super, but with the frame and slide lightened for faster shooting, would be a Steel Challenge gun moving up the scale of competition guns.

The easiest way to go from TEB to Competition is to install a compensator. The compensator works one or both of two ways. It diverts the gases upwards, reducing muzzle lift, and if fitted tightly and machined properly, the gases striking the front face in the expansion chambers push the barrel and comp forward. You don't get something for nothing. To "work" a comp, you need lighter bullets and slower-burning powders than customary for a given caliber. The noise can be fierce. A .38 Super with light bullets making Major is as loud as some rifles. The pistol is being worked harder, and the barrel and comp wear faster than normal. You will also be pushed out of Stock and into Open by installing a comp.

You can have both guns in one. If you already have a TEB, then a drop-in or pre fitted comped barrel will give you the option of using either or both. Particularly popular with pin shooters, the spare barrel rides in your bag until you need or desire it. At a pin match, it is common to shoot in both Pin Gun and Stock Gun class. In the five minutes between shooting one and the other, you can have the other barrel in, ready to go. Something like the Clark drop-in comp barrel would be just the ticket. As with anything, there are those who go overboard. A few pin shooters have built their competition guns with two top ends, one stock and one comped.

Competition guns also often have some sort of permanent magazine funnel installed. On a TEB the cost isn't worth it, especially when some of the competitions don't allow them. For maximum versatility of the TEB, a bolt-on or otherwise added funnel is needed. For a purpose-built competition gun, welding on a funnel is a small thing to improve match standings.

The biggest difference that pushes a pistol into Competition status is optics. You don't go and put a red-dot sight on a 1911 unless you're going to go out and try to win a match or two. Even the least-expensive (and still pricey) method adds nearly the whole cost of building a TEB to your pistol. Add in the match barrel, fitting, magazine funnel, compensator (with optics you're shooting in Open, you might as well have the comp) and the other odds and ends, and a top-end competition gun can easily run three grand.

Bespoke

I use the word in the British sense, that being a firearm made for a particular person for a particular reason, and on which everything is either specified or custom. One such gun is the Ned Christiansen gun he sent me for testing, his personal gun. The compensator is the most efficient I have tried. With Cor-Bon 165-grain .45 ACP ammo, the front sight has negative muzzle lift. The magazine funnel is a work of art. The sights are large, bright and easy to see at speed. The thumb safety? A standard small size series 70

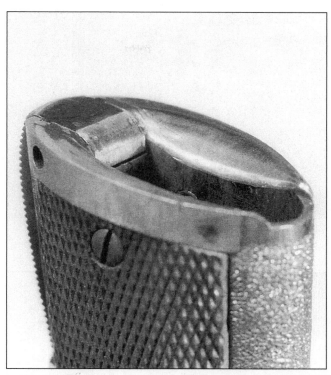

A magazine funnel attached with high-temperature silver solder.

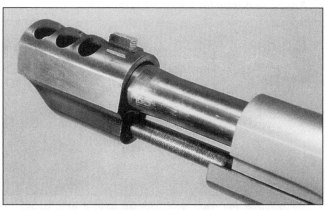

A 1911 with a comp and a cone instead of a bushing. This is a competition gun for sure.

A red-dot sight is a sure sign of a competition gun.

This STI competition gun was built with a Stock upper for IPSC/USPSA Limited matches, and a Modified upper for International IPSC competition.

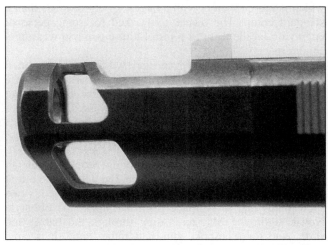

If you want an efficient compensator, you have to have precise fitting and attention to detail.

The front of the magazine funnel on the Michigun/Christiansen 1911 locks tightly to the small finger and keeps your hand in place.

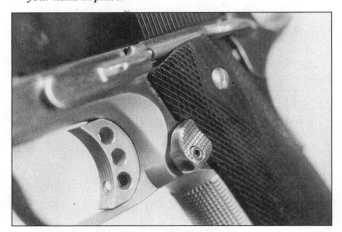

A bespoke pistol means new designs, like this magazine button extension.

safety. Why? This 1911 is built as a bowling pin gun, and Ned doesn't use the safety as a thumb lever. You don't have to worry about getting the safety off on the draw, since in bowling pin shooting you start with the gun in your hands.

His other custom gun he sent has a large safety, since the owner plans to carry it as a working gun. As it is a defensive pistol, the owner has opted for the Hybricomp system, which is more efficient with a larger variety of loads than a standard comp. The owner also asked for some personal engraving, in the form of a pistol-toting gunman wearing a sombrero.

A bespoke gun can be even more wild. I had a Modified upper built, and my STI Limited gun modified, to compete in World Shoot XII. Since it had to fit the box, we had to cut some corners. Literally. And, since I wanted a comp of some kind, but there wasn't room in the box, we used a Hybrid barrel. For sights, it got a Tasco Optima installed on the slide.

Another bespoke gun in my safe is my Stock pin gun. At first glance it looks like a TEB. Then, the details pop out at you. The soldered-on magazine funnel (crafted back when such things had to be made from bar stock) the old-style Novak sight, the Mag-na-Porting through the barrel and slide. And for a bespoke gun, it is rather tame. It is tame partly due to age. When it was built there were fewer options. Also, by swapping the Mag-na-Ported barrel for

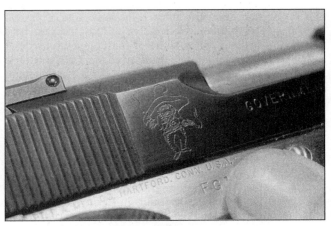

A bespoke pistol can also be personalized.

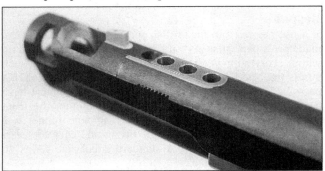

Ned not only fitted the Hybrid rib to the slide...

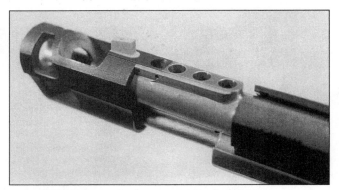

He replaced the front port with an angled one, so the exhaust doesn't scorch the front sight.

another, fitted barrel that isn't ported, it becomes a Stock pistol in many categories of shooting.

Unless you are shooting on the U.S. Army Marksmanship Team, an IPSC race gun is going to be a bespoke gun. You can't tell a gunsmith to just "build a race gun" for the simple reason that there are too many variables. As an example, the first question the gunsmith will ask you is, do you want it built on an STI, Para Ordnance or Caspian high-capacity frame? Then he'll ask what optics you want on it, and what brand of brass you'll be loading to shoot through it. All these and more, matter a great deal.

The Parts Of A 1911

When gunsmiths began building IPSC guns in the late 1970s and early 1980s, there were few parts to improve the pistols. Oh, there were "match" slides and "match" barrels

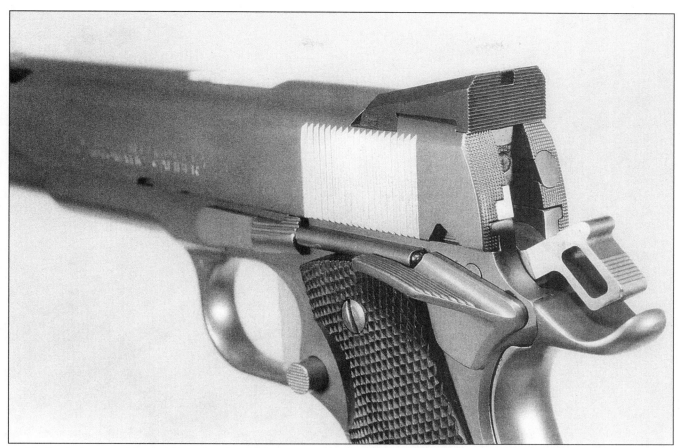

My Stock pin gun, with an old Novak sight, checkering, beavertail and Robar NP3 finish.

and oversized bushings, but they weren't much. A pre-IPSC match slide was one that was oversized on the rails, so it could be filed, stoned and lapped to a tight fit. Were the dimensions better than a standard slide? Maybe. Ditto with match barrels. The hood and lugs were oversized, but otherwise it was just as much of a crap shoot as a factory barrel. You could go to the expense of fitting a barrel, and find out it wasn't any better than the one you took out.

I still have the Ransom Rest targets I shot after having my Colt prize gun tightened, and the original barrel welded and fitted. Disappointing comes to mind.

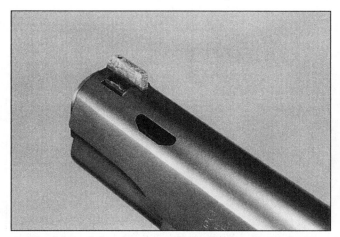

The front of the pin gun, with the Mag-na-Port exhaust slots, and the low-tech orange paint on the front sight

Oversized safeties? You made them yourself. I still remember filing and fitting a plate to be silver-soldered as an oversized thumb safety. The desire for such parts, and the lack of them, drove Bill Wilson to start making the things shooters wanted. Wilson Combat is now one of the largest suppliers of 1911 parts and accessories out there. Claudio Salassa of Briley was a gunsmith in his home country of South Africa, who was making "new" parts by welding the old ones and then machining and filing them to shape. As much work as soldering that thumb safety was, I can't imagine having to file one out of a blob of welded steel. Jim Clark, Sr. took the same route as Bill Wilson even though he started in Bull's eye. When IPSC became the shooting sport of choice, he began making the goodies we needed and wanted.

Now, the difficulty is in choosing. Many parts will serve you well. Most are well-designed and crafted, and once fitted to your 1911 will work the way they were intended. While I will show you many designs, I'm not going to advocate one over the others. (I don't want to get the primo parts makers mad at me.) One thing you should keep in mind: Quality costs. Yes, you can save a few dollars selecting one slightly less expensive part over another. But if you buy something that costs significantly less than the market average, there is likely a reason. If (as an example) top-quality match barrels seem to cost between $125 and $175, you can be well-served by buying the $125 barrel. If someone tells you of a "bargain" match barrel that is "just as good" for only $75, be suspicious. Unless the maker went out of business and the inventory was sold at a bargain price (another reason to be suspicious, why did he go under?) you have to

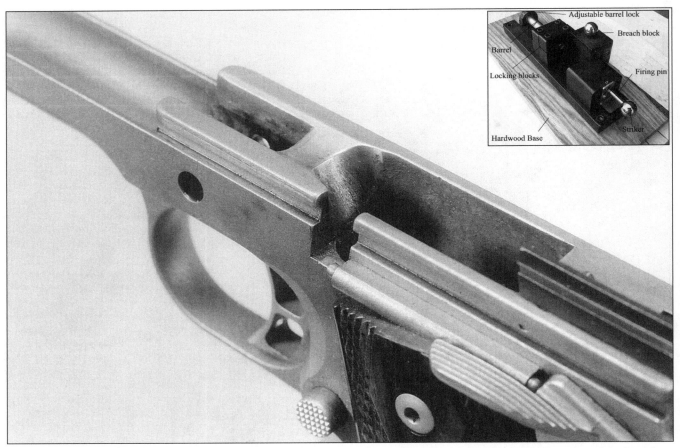

Today, a stainless frame is as tough as a carbon steel frame. Don't worry about the missing section of rail, many makers leave it out.

ask yourself "what corners did the maker cut to produce it for less money?"

Lets go over the parts that go into a re-built or custom 1911.

Slide And Frame

If you have a pistol to start with, then you already have a slide and frame. However, a seriously worn pistol may require a new slide. Or, you may want to build a pistol from the ground up. There is no lack of extra parts makers. You can order your slide with all the machine cuts already made, or bare. A fully-machined slide would have sight dovetails front and back, cocking serrations front and back, the ejec-tion ports lowered and flared. and the machine work may cost as much as the slide did.

While slides may need to be replaced, frames rarely do. Frames don't wear out like slides (and slides rarely do) but rather frames lack essential features. Or, you just want to build another gun. Frames can be had already checkered, already radiused for a grip safety, already drilled and tapped for a scope mount. If you're ordering a Caspian frame, you can have it with a magazine funnel as an integral part of the frame.

One way to have a fully-featured slide and frame set is with a Caspian Race-ready kit. The only drawback (if there is such a thing as a drawback with Caspian parts, I haven't seen it) is the need to fit the parts. Out of the box, the slide

Barrel welding and testing

In the old days, we welded barrels to fit them tightly. It was not always successful. After all, if the source of the inaccuracy was the barrel being kinked from heat-treatment, fitting it tightly won't make any difference. Or, if the bore dimensions are off, a tight lockup will make no difference in accuracy.

Welding barrels is a waste of time and effort. For the cost of welding, fitting and testing, you could have bought and fitted a new barrel.

Some barrels are better than others, even from the top makers. For those who have to have the absolute best, a barrel that is tested before it is installed is best. But how to do it? Gunsmiths through the decades have made various holding fixtures, usually starting with a scrapped slide. Joe Cominolli built one (and builds them as other gunsmiths ask for them) from the ground up. His fixture holds the barrel firmly but without stressing it, and each barrel can be accuracy tested before it goes into a gun. Cost? If you have to ask..... Were I to find myself in contention with Jerry Barnhart, Todd Jarrett and Robbie Leatham for the World Championship, I would make sure my pistol had a Cominolli-tested barrel in it.

won't go on the frame, and the barrel won't fit in the slide. You'll need a gunsmith to fit them for you. (My Caspian Race kit went off to Doug Jones, who quickly fit it together for me.) If immediately sending it off to someone else is too nerve-wracking for you, then STI has just the thing. Called their Short Block Kit, it is a frame, slide and barrel that have been fitted together by their resident gunsmith. You can order it with your choice of caliber, slide length and machined options. All you have to do is install and tune the action parts, and you're ready to go.

One choice that seems to come up again and again is: blue or stainless? In the old days, it was simple, blue. Early stainless guns were softer than carbon steel, and wouldn't wear as well. Today, stainless alloys are much improved and you will be well-served by a stainless gun. The only application I would insist on a carbon steel part is the slide for an IPSC racegun. Running .38 Super at Major is hard work, and I would want all the odds in my favor.

Barrels

The heart of the accurate 1911 is the barrel. A good barrel is so desirable, that in the old days I knew shooters who bought guns to get their hands on the barrel it contained. Now, you can buy a barrel guaranteed to deliver. Barrels come in two sizes, "drop-in" and gunsmith fit. Depending on the dimensions your pistol has been machined to, a drop-in may be a tight or loose fit. The gunsmith-fit barrel is oversized on its locking lugs and hood. If a gunsmith fit barrel drops into your pistol, there is something wrong, and you should have it inspected.

A good-fitting drop-in barrel that is accurate can be accurate indeed in your pistol. The same barrel in the gunsmith-fit that is properly fitted will be more accurate, but only a bit more. After all, you've increased most of the potential accuracy by buying the better barrel. A gunsmith-fit barrel must be properly fitted. You can't just hack away with a file until the barrel goes into place. An improperly fitted barrel will not only not be accurate, it can break or wear the slide.

Many of the makers of top-end barrels will fit their barrel to your gun. Irv Stone at Bar-Sto will fit up one of his barrels to your gun, and you can be sure it fits properly. Assuming the slide and frame you sent aren't out of spec. Then, you might get a phone call one evening giving you the bad news.

Barrels are not just barrels, they are specific to a particular model of the 1911 pistol. The starting point is the Government Model 1911. The Government Model uses a 5-inch barrel with a wide hood, full-size bottom lugs and three top lugs. The shorter Commander is 4-1/4 inches long, has the same hood, but shorter bottom lugs and two locking lugs. The shorter lugs are for clearance on the barrel as it cycles. If you install a Government Model barrel into a Commander-sized gun, you'll have a barrel that sticks out, and a hidden problem. The longer bottom lugs of the Government Model barrel will bear against the recoil spring plunger. The spring tension of the plunger will pre-load the barrel, making it easier to unlock. You can damage the locking lugs on the barrel, the slide or both if you fire such a combination too many times. If you want the long barrel look on a Commander, you have to re-cut the bottom lugs of a Government barrel to the Commander configuration as part of the installation.

Shorter still is the Officer's Model and the really short guns like the Kimber Ultra CDP. As the barrel gets shorter, the slide shrinks, and the manufacturer has to work harder to

fit all the parts in place. In addition to changing the barrel, the slide and frame also are modified. As a result, you can't simply swap parts back and forth between models. In some cases, much machine work is involved. Gunsmiths used to charge large amounts of money to chop 1911's down to very small sizes. Now, they buy the size they need and add the refinements the customer wants.

As if length wasn't complication enough, everything else can change too. Colt, when they wanted to come out with a target 1911 after the war, designed the Gold Cup. The trigger was wider, and had a stop screw installed. The trigger pull was better, accuracy was better, and they changed the hood dimensions of the barrel. The Gold Cup hood is smaller than the Government model hood. The good news is that since it is smaller, you can have your gunsmith file or machine a Government barrel so the hood fits. The bad news is, once its done, there is no going back. If you decide later you want to have that barrel installed in another gun, you can only put it in another Gold Cup. (Only gunsmiths, inveterate tinkerers that they are, would do such a thing.)

One change in barrels brought about by IPSC are ramps. The original Model 1900 used a ramped barrel, but the 1911 did not. To gain more support for the case when chambered, IPSC shooters designed and fabricated ramped barrels. (The ramp gives the case more support, preventing blow-outs and extending the useful life of the case.) The ramps come in three dimensions, which are not interchangeable. They are Wilson/Nowlin, Clark/Para Ordnance, and Bar-Sto. When ramps were new, Bar-Sto was in the forefront. When the factories started making ramped guns, they selected a different design. Bar-Sto now makes barrels with the other ramps, but if you buy an old competition gun with a Bar-Sto barrel it may have the older ramp design. In order to fit your ramped barrel to your 1911, your gunsmith will have to know which ramp your barrel uses, and have a large milling machine. He will mill the frame to accept the ramp, then fit the barrel as he normally would. Once a frame has been milled for a ramp, it used to be there was no going back. However, you can now buy a filler block that takes the place of the ramp and is held in place by your slide stop pin. It allows you to use a standard barrel in a frame that was cut for a ramp.

As if that wasn't enough, the muzzle also gets modified. Some barrels do away with the need for a bushing. Instead

Now barrels come with ramps, too. On the right is a standard barrel, in the middle a Wilson/Nowlin, and on the left a Para/Clark.

Once a frame has been milled for a ramp, that's it. You can't go back, and your choices for other ramps are very limited.

A coned barrel doesn't need a bushing, except for the Colt Officer's Model, which has both. Why? Who knows?

of machining the barrel straight on its outside, the barrel-maker turns the barrel into a cone flaring to the muzzle. The end of the barrel has a short cylindrical section that is the same (or larger, in a gunsmith fit version) diameter as the inside of the slide. When the slide goes forward, it slides up the cone to the muzzle, and securely locks onto the barrel. The lack of a bushing adds complications. Without a bushing to hold it in, the regular recoil spring plug won't work. When he fits a coned barrel, your gunsmith (this is not a home operation) will have to fit a "reverse plug" of some kind. The reverse plug can add further complications. If you select (or the gunsmith installs) a shouldered plug, he has to mill part of the slide back to accommodate the plug's shoulder. If he uses a cylindrical plug, he has to machine and then ream the recoil spring tunnel on the slide, and modify the barrel for plug clearance.

You can end up paying more for the extra machining to accommodate the barrel, than you paid for both the barrel and its fitting combined. As an example, if you were to buy a premium barrel for, say $175 out of Brownell's (2001 dollars, adjust for inflation if any) and it was a standard gunsmith fit barrel, it could cost another $50 to $75 to have it fitted. If, however, you bought a ramped and coned barrel, the extra cost of a reverse plug and the additional machining needed could turn that $50 gunsmith charge to $200.

Compensators

The origination of muzzle brakes is not an IPSC invention. The idea of using some of the muzzle gases to reduce movement was something that came from artillery. In handguns, the first modern use came about when Jim Clark, Sr. made a 1911 with an extended barrel. He threaded the barrel and screwed a slide-profiled weight on it. Called a Pingun, the weight was to reduce felt recoil. J. Michael Plaxco took the design, hollowed out the weight and put exhaust ports on top. He was unbeatable. (One might argue he was unbeatable at that time whether he had a compensator or not, but the argument would be short.) Soon, you had to have a compensator or you were not a serious competitor. I shot the 1982, 3 & 4 Nationals, and after that I went to a National competition with a compensated pistol until the Stock category was created. Why? By 1984 I was practically the only one at the match without a comped 1911.

Left, this is a slide milled for a reverse plug for the recoil spring.

The adoption of compensators led inexorably down a predictable path. The serious competitor went from .45 to .38 Super, and bullets went from 200 grains to 115 grains. (Not in one fell swoop, mind you, but over the course of almost 10 years.) The more gas you feed the comp, the better it works for you. Smaller cartridges give a magazine more capacity. The smallest high-pressure cartridge that the rules allowed was .38 Super.

Comps now range from single-port "Carry comps" to multi-port comps a couple of inches long. An IPSC gun does not have to be concealed, and competitors want to scavenge all the gas they can. It is not unusual for the comp on an Open gun to be 2 inches long and have seven ports in it. And, some will even go with a Hybricomp barrel, with ports in the barrel itself. All these ports make noise. A comped Super running light bullets (115-grain) at Major (1,521 fps at old PF, 1434 fps at new PF) is as loud as some rifles. Many competitors wear both ear plugs and muffs to protect their hearing.

The change in irrational laws has meant some equipment changes. One of the evil accouterments on firearms (so decreed by lawmakers) are threaded muzzles. The threads on your comped pistol barrel don't bother the Feds, who are only concerned about people trying to put flash hiders and grenade launchers on their AR-15s. However, the less-ratio-

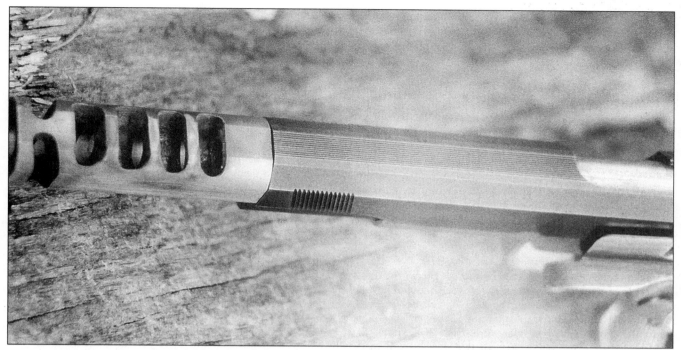

An efficient compensator for competition use is long. This one adds more than 2 inches to the gun

nal law makers of California have decreed that even a comp that is soldered or secured with Loctite is threaded and therefore evil. (Lawmakers as a group are almost all attorneys, and as such, are amazingly ignorant of things mechanical in general, and firearms in particular. But they craft and pass the laws. Don't get me wrong, we need both lawyers and lawmakers. I just wish they would expend some effort learning more than the laws concerning fund raising.) To avoid the California hassle, Dave Skinner of STI makes his Trubore barrels. The barrel and comp are made of one piece, with no nasty, evil threads lurking underneath to suddenly seize control of your mind.

Guide Rods

Many shooters feel the need for a recoil spring guide rod. John Browning didn't, but then he didn't think the barrel ramp was needed, either. The rod supports the recoil spring and keeps it from kinking and bunching under the slide. Rods come three ways, one-piece, one-piece with mercury in them, and two-piece. Some come made of Tungsten, a heavier metal than steel. The extra weight, forward and under the muzzle, helps control muzzle lift and felt recoil.

Single-piece rods are easier to make, but harder to disassemble. Some rods come drilled, but most don't. The small hole drilled in the rod allows you to disassemble the 1911 by placing a bent paperclip into the hole, trapping the spring and plug. Without the hole, you have to disassemble by using a bushing wrench and turning the bushing, then pulling the spring out the front. If you have a coned barrel, the plug won't come out the front, and you must have a drilled rod.

The two-piece rods simply unscrew to come apart. Unfortunately, they can unscrew under the vibration of shooting, so some shooters don't like them.

The mercury-filled rods, made by Harrts, are designed as small dead-blow hammers. The tube is not completely

The guide rod on this Nine-pin gun extends through the bottom of the compensator, and has an extra weight out front of the muzzle.

Early on, compensators were not super-efficient. This Nine-pin gun was built with dual Mag-na-Porting and a guide rod to keep things in line.

filled, and the mercury sloshing back and forth dampens felt recoil. Since you can't drill the rod (the mercury would leak out) you can't use a Harrts on a cone gun, or many comped guns.

Many guide rods come with shock buffers. The shock buffer is intended to cushion the impact of the slide against the frame. Some shooters love them, some hate them, and some don't care. Shock buffers are not without their drawbacks. Some guns can lock open before they are empty when a shock buffer is installed. If the edges of the slide are sharp, the shock buffer can be rapidly chewed into pieces by the slide's impact, and those pieces can gum up the pistol, creating malfunctions. If your pistol begins to manifest mysterious malfunctions after installing a shock buffer, you have two choices: leave out the buffer, or drop the gun with a brief explanation off with your gunsmith for attention.

Sights

After barrels, and sometimes before trigger work, sights are a common question. Many shooters feel that with just the right sights, they will be able to shoot much better. Well, they're partly right. Under most circumstances, a set of large and rectangular sights would work best. Known as the patridge design, they work so well that every pistol made now comes with that design sight. But there are times when they aren't enough. Two times would be: Shooting at night, and the Handgunner Shootoff. Yes, you can accurately shoot at night, as any graduate of Gunsite can tell you. Seeing your sights helps, and that is why many sights now come with Tritium inserts for glowing "three-dot" sights. (Some are two dots, know as the "figure eight", or a dot and a bar, but most are three dots.) With the night sights, seeing your sights is much easier, and shooting in darkness less stressful.

At the Handgunner Shoot-off, you are shooting in a high-altitude valley in Colorado. Usually the sky is clear and bright blue. As if the conditions weren't tough enough, the falling plates (that's all you shoot in the Shoot-off) are painted a gloss dark blue. (I occasionally wonder if Paul Miller got a deal on surplus Navy paint.) Black sights can disappear against the plate rack. Many shooters use three-dot sights, or paint their sights. One approach is to use the Middlebrook's dot-and-ring sight. While not all competitions classify it as a Stock sight, many do.

When I was new to IPSC (and IPSC was new, period) we all wanted adjustable sights. Those who could afford it went with a Bo-mar sight. The less expensive choice was a S&W rear sight installed on your 1911. Today, the only people I know who install the S&W are King's. The two choices today, for adjustable sights, are Bo-mar and Novak/MMC. Each has a different and non-interchangeable milling pattern for the sight dovetail. Once you have one installed, you can't easily go to the other.

The Bo-mar is slightly more compact, but has a more complicated pattern of machine cuts. (There are other sights

The Millett sights, inserted in a slot milled in the rear of the slide, as done by Galena Industries on their Hardballer.

A beautiful carry gun, using Novak front and rear sights.

The Bo-mar, is the original hot setup for carry and competition. Many shooters still love it.

The Novak front, with a glow-in-the-dark insert.

besides the Bo-mar, but the slide is machined much the same even though the dimensions are slightly different. The installing gunsmith doesn't care, since he or she will take the measurements from the particular sight being installed.) The Novak dovetail is simple, and the MMC sight to fit it is adjustable. Novaks sights are not adjustable. For Bull's eye competition, you can install on some pistols a sight rib such as the Aristocrat. The rib adds weight, and contains the front and rear sights. While the rib is OK in Bull's eye, it is not a Stock item in any other competition.

With iron sights, you need two, one in front and one in back. It is customary to mill the front sight in place. Again called the Novak pattern, the reasons are twofold: First, customers (you) expect it. A custom gun isn't a custom gun until the front sight is installed in its dovetail. Second, the Novak is more secure than the original method of staking the sight on. A gunsmith wants his work to work and last. While the incidence of staked-on sights coming loose is very low, there is no chance a dovetailed front sight will come out.

Optics

The next step up from iron sights are optics. The impetus for optics came from Jerry Barnhart, who in the early 1990s showed up at the USPSA Nationals with a pistol that had an early red-dot sight on it. He crushed everyone. A few months later, Doug Koenig had mounted a red-dot on his

The advantage of optics is the "head up display" view of the target and the aiming dot.

Optics are now compact, reliable, and tough enough to be mounted on the slide, as with this Tasco Optima.

pistol and won the World Shoot. The scramble was on. Early sights were fragile, and early light-bullet loads were harsh in recoil. At one Nationals I was in during the early 1990's, one of the competitors on my squad had to change his sight once a day from breakage.

Optics are now accepted, compact, inexpensive and very useful. And just when you thought the matter was settled, Jerry proves us wrong. He shot the 2000 Open USPSA Nationals with an iron-sighted gun. He placed 4th.

The two methods of attaching a scope are to the frame and to the slide. The frame method is easier on the scope, but makes for a heavier and bulkier gun. Mounting the scope on the slide saves weight and bulk, but the stress on the sight is much greater.

Frame Modifications-Grip Safety

Early on, IPSC competitors learned that they had to get a smooth grip safety with no sharp edges. (I don't mean to keep IPSC shooters in the limelight, but many, if not most of the advancements came from the lessons learned in IPSC, beginning in the mid-1970s) While a Bull's eye shooter might practice 5,000 rounds in a year, the IPSC shooters by the early 1980s could easily do 20,000. In a Bull's eye match you fire 270 rounds, but 180 are .22 or soft-recoiling "any centerfire" rounds. An IPSC shooter (and Bowling pin shooters of the same period) would shoot that much at a club match, and more in a regional or area match. Many IPSC clubs now have monthly club matches with 120-150 rounds fired, not including side matches. Under such a trial, any sharp edge can draw blood.

Once the edges were smoothed, evolution dictated that we step down the path of soldering and welding, then new designs, until we are at the end. The back end of a frame on a modern gun is shaped one of two ways. Either it has the traditional tapered tangs, or the tangs are machined to a .250" radius. The tapered tangs are for the traditional grip safety, or a slightly modified traditional safety. The modification allows the use of a Commander hammer. The radiused tang is cut to fit a beavertail grip safety, either of the Wilson pattern or of the Ed Brown pattern. The difference between those two is simple: the Wilson uses the existing curves of the frame as the path of its grip safety exterior. The Ed Brown grip safety is the highest and tightest curve the internal parts allow. If you fit an Ed brown (or, have your gunsmith fit it) you or he will have to grind, file and then

polish the rear of the frame to match the curve of the grip safety. Then, a new finish.

Both designs work, and work well. The difference? One or the other may or may not feel better in your hand. I think I shoot a little better with the Ed Brown, but I can switch back and forth and not notice which one I'm using.

Thumb Safety & Slide Stop

The thumb safety and slide stop have been the subjects of much experimentation over the decades. At first we made them bigger, then we made them ambidextrous. I even saw a pistol that had been fitted with ambidextrous and extended slide stops. An interesting technical challenge, it served no purpose and didn't work very well. (I have seen one of John Moses Browning's prototypes of the 1911, in the Browning Museum in Ogden, Utah. He originally installed the slide stop on the right side of the frame. You had to remove your finger from the trigger guard to lower the slide.)

First: Should you have an ambidextrous safety? Yes and no. Yes, if you are a left-handed shooter, or the 1911 is a competition gun or your daily carry gun. No, if you are a right-handed shooter. You can learn to manipulate the standard safety even in a stage in a match that requires "weak-hand only" shooting. You can train to shoot and manipulate

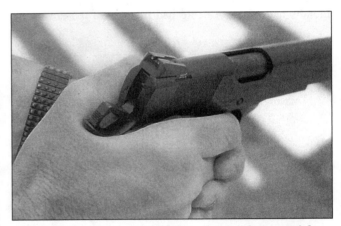

My grip on the Springfield Pro, showing how my right knuckle usually presses against the off safety lever. (The Pro offers clearance. That's good.)

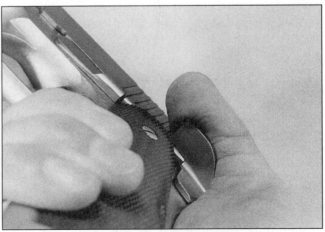

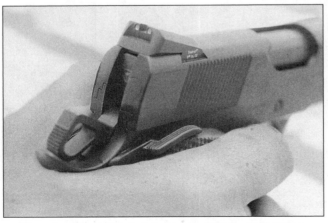

The grip of one of my test shooters, on the Springfield Professional.

The underneath view of a right-hand grip. Notice the thumb riding hard on the safety, and the unobtrusive slide stop lever.

This Open pistol built on an Entreprise frame is instructive for the slide stop and magazine catch. The slide stop is built up as an extra thumb rest, and the magazine catch is built up so the owner can get his thumb around the frame to reload.

A custom-crafted magazine catch like this one from Michiguns is neat, cool, and tuned to work 100 percent despite your fumbling.

the gun left-handed only in a defensive situation. I am somewhat biased against ambidextrous safeties due to my grip. My hand gets high enough on the gun that the main knuckle of my right forefinger interferes with the movement of the ambidextrous safety. The problem is partly due to the size of my hands, and partly from enlarged knuckles from

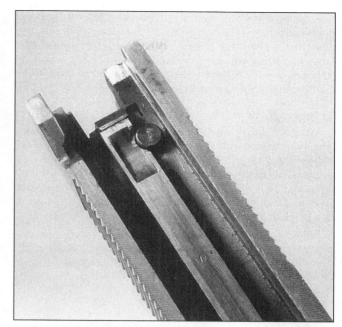

When the Colt Series 80 came out everyone complained that the trigger pull would suffer. Gunsmiths now know how to get a good trigger pull on an 80 and still leave the parts in.

years of martial arts. With some ambi safeties I have to shift my grip or the gun won't fire.

On my own competition guns, I have slimmed down the offhand safety tab so it doesn't interfere with my grip. As such, it is barely useful as an ambidextrous safety, but it is there. You should try a few guns with ambidextrous safeties on them to see if your grip poses a problem.

The slide stop should be unobtrusive, and you shouldn't know it is there until the pistol is empty. If it locks the slide back with ammunition still in the magazine, it must be tended to. It isn't going to "wear in" or learn to behave. You don't need an extended slide stop, or an ambidextrous one.

Magazine Catch

The magazine catch holds the magazine in place. Many competitors use a larger or longer (or both) magazine catch to make magazine changes easier. For a carry gun, leave it the standard size. One little detail on making the catch longer: You can trap the magazine. The catch is "C" shaped, with the magazine riding in the opening of the C. If you make your catch longer, you can now push the catch far enough that the catch binds against the magazine. Once you let go of the button the magazine will drop free. It is a minor thing, and easy to fix.

Trigger And Trigger Pull

First of all, the trigger itself has almost nothing to do with the trigger pull. The weight and feel of the pull is determined by the sear and hammer hooks. The trigger is just the lever you pull. As with their barrels, when Colt came up with the Gold Cup they changed the trigger. The Gold Cup trigger is wider than a Government trigger, and the two are not interchangeable. A match trigger is precisely fitted to its slot in the frame, and will not move up or down when you try to wiggle it. It will have a small set screw installed, to stop the rearward travel of the trigger once the sear has been tripped. And, it will probably have three holes in it. The holes serve two purposes, both marginally useful: One, they lighten the trigger. Two, they let everyone who looks know that you have a custom trigger.

If you want a better trigger pull, you need to change the relationship of the sear and hammer.

Trigger Jobs

After the fit of the slide and barrel, most shooters concern themselves with the feel of the trigger. If the trigger pull is heavy or gritty feeling, it will be difficult to use the potential accuracy of the pistol. However, if the pull is too light, you will occasionally miss from pressing the trigger too soon. In a match, you can sometimes correct that error. In a defensive situation, it may cost you dearly.

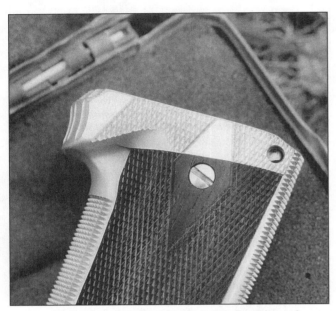

A welded-on integral magazine funnel is the ultimate luxury item. That is, until you need a super-fast reload and then it is a necessity. Gorgeous funnel by Michiguns.

A beveled magazine opening is plenty for a carry gun, even if it is lacking in a competition gun. Or is it? Practice makes up for equipment.

How light is "light enough?" For a defensive pistol, the lightest you'll want to go is between 4-1/2 and 5-1/2 pounds. In a highly-stressful shooting situation, you'll have plenty of adrenaline to increase your muscular efforts. You don't need less. Indeed, more might be good, provided the trigger pull is clean and crisp.

For a competition gun, you can go lighter, sometimes. For a Bull's eye gun, some categories require that your trigger pull be not less than 4-1/2 pounds. For a while in IPSC competition, shooters were tuning their guns to trigger pulls down under 2 pounds. While a trigger pull of 1-1/2 pounds made it very easy to accurately shoot a pistol off the bench, it didn't help shoot it any faster in a match. And when shooters found out that such light trigger pulls required constant maintenance or they would quit working, they gave up. Most now don't go under 3 pounds, simply because it is light enough to shoot well in competition, and a 3-pound trigger pull lasts forever.

How does your gunsmith make your trigger pull get lighter? By making the engagement surfaces of the sear and hammer match in geometry and by polishing their surfaces. The old way still works, and that is to lock the parts in a stoning fixture like the Power fixture, and stone the surface. The stoning corrects any errors in the geometry, and by using finer and finer stones he will polish the surfaces so they have less drag. By stoning you retain the old parts, which in some cases may be desirable or required.

If you are willing to swap parts, the new way to get a trigger job is easier, and something you can do at home, although it is more expensive. Buy a Chip McCormick sear and hammer and install them. Chip pioneered the wire EDM process of making small parts in the gun industry. Prior to Chip, hammers and sears were made from forged lumps of steel that were held in fixtures and machined. For the wire EDM process, the parts are cut from already hardened and precision-ground steel plates. The wire burns the outline of the part, controlled by computer. The parts are cut to precise dimensions, and do not require heat-treatment.

You do not stone such parts. If you get the McCormick hammer and sear, or the same parts from Wilson, Cylinder & Slide, Ed Brown or one of the many other top-end parts suppliers, do not stone them. The hammer and sear are already cut to the exact geometry, and the wire left a smoother surface than you can stone. Leave them alone!

Magazine Funnel

For some competitions, reloading is critical. A slow reload can turn a fast shooting time into an average match time. By opening and beveling the opening of the magazine slot, you increase your ability to reload quickly. On the high-capacity guns like the STI and Entreprise, the tapered top of the magazine makes a standard magazine opening into a funneled one. That doesn't stop shooters from adding a funnel to the frame anyway. Funnels attach one of three ways. First, by using a longer mainspring housing pin and extra metal or plastic on the funnel, like the STI or Clark funnels. Second, by attaching the funnel to the mainspring housing itself. The attachment can be permanent, like the S&A, or bolted on like the Wilson. Third, the funnel can be a part of the frame. The funnel can be soldered or welded to the frame, and the beveled portion filed and ground, shaped and polished, contoured and blended, (do you get the idea some are a lot of work? Good.) until they are done. I built a

Skateboard tape. Tough, cheap, grips like and looks like a bad cold.

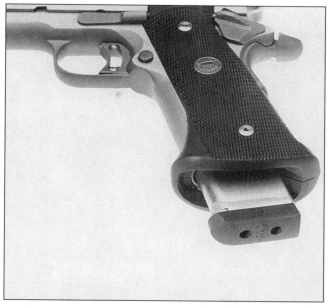

King's makes grips that offer a secure hold and act as a magazine funnel. And you thought sliced bread was trick. (Photo courtesy King's)

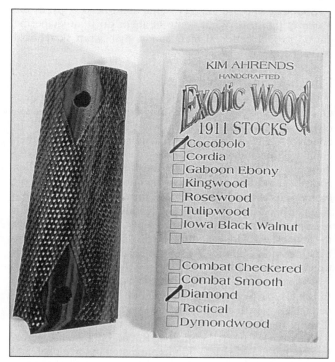

Kim Ahrends offers grips in a bunch of attractive woods, and in several checkering patterns.

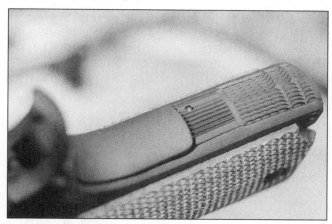

The scallops on this mainspring housing give a secure hold, but don't grab your jacket when you're carrying concealed.

few for myself and customers, and Ned Christiansen does beautiful work on mambo magazine wells.

Gripping The Frame

When you grab onto a pistol, you are holding the frame and the grips that cover the frame. What is under your hands can be important. The most elegant method of making the frame a more secure surface is by checkering. In the old days, we would file the grooves of the checkered pattern by hand. Now, many gunsmiths use programmable milling machines, and finish the job by hand. Even so, checkering is expensive. Less expensive, but still effective, is stippling. By using a pointed punch and a ball peen hammer, the gunsmith creates a randomly roughened surface on the front of

the frame. On the mainspring housing, you can get yours checkered, or buy one already checkered. As many replacement mainspring housings are cast (being cast is not a problem, there is no real stress on the part), the mouldmaker can incorporate the checkering into the mould, and viola; checkered mainspring housings.

Last, least expensive, and not exactly pretty is skateboard tape. Many competitive shooters opt for skateboard tape. It is cheap, it can be applied where it is needed, and some like having an aggressively ugly gun.

Adding to your grip are the grips. When selecting grips, you can get them of wood, synthetics, rubber, plastic or metal. Some grips are thicker than usual, for shooters with large hands. Some are slimmer than usual. Even though I have large hands, I prefer slim grips. I find that large grips reduce the "rectangular" feel of the frame, and I lose my feeling of indexing the gun by the feel of the frame. In wood, I am particularly fond of Ahrend grips by Kim Ahrends. He makes them in a number of exotic woods, as well

Some shooters don't bother with a finish. The owner of this compensator hasn't bothered to get it to match the slide in either contour or color.

Once completed, this carry gun was re-parkerized for a durable finish.

Stainless doesn't need a finish, but that doesn't stop some owners.

as laminates. He also makes half-checkered grips, where the checkering is only on the part of the grips your hand grasps.

Two other thin and sculpted grip sources are Chip McCormick and Navidrex. The McCormicks are figured wood, while the Navidrex are a jet-black ebony wood.

In rubber or rubber-like grips, I find the Pearce grips retain the slimmer profile I prefer in grips. Many other rubber grips like the Hogue add thickness. If you want the rounder feel, or have large hands, you may find the Hogues are just the grips for you.

For added weight in my pin gun, I used Ajax pewter grips. While light for a metal, pewter is much more dense than wood. The added weight helps dampen the felt recoil of hot pin loads.

If you feel that checkered wood grips just don't offer enough friction for a solid grip, then you need to order your grips from Jerry Barnhart. Jerry takes contoured grip pieces and coats them with an abrasive-impregnated epoxy. Unlike skateboard tape, as the surface wears down it exposes more abrasive-impregnated epoxy, so you don't lose the friction.

Shooters who use the STI frame don't need grips, as the frame is the grip. What some of them do is re-shape the plastic to feel better in their hands, then wrap skateboard tape for friction.

Finish-What People See

The last thing you should do is get a finish applied. Once you have your 1911 anything but blued (carbon steel, obviously, stainless need not worry) consider it cast in concrete. If you have another finish applied and then change your mind about some feature that your pistol "must have" you will incur the finishing expense, and then some, again. The old finish will have to be stripped off (some finishes will have to have the whole slide or frame stripped) and then once the new feature is added, the finish re-applied. I once hard-chromed a pistol three times before the owner was done adding extras. Yes, he paid for the blasting and re-application of the hard chrome finish each time.

Industrial hard chrome in all its variants is a desirable finish, if you like the white look. For hard chrome, I have been happy with the plating by Accurate Weaponry and Plating, in Florida. A different finish that is as durable as hard chrome is the NP3 finish of Robar. NP3 is an Electroless Nickel finish with Teflon impregnated in the nickel, and offers lubricity along with protection. For a hard-chrome that can be applied to aluminum, go with Armoloy of Dallas-Ft. Worth.

The current trend is towards durable resin finishes, like Spradlin's Tef-Cote, Wilson's Armor-Tuff or Rambear's Bearskin. The advantages to the resin finishes are several: It comes in colors (never underestimate the marketability of fashion, even in firearms) so you can have a two-tone pistol, it is durable, and it can be touched-up.

For traditionalists who can have nothing but, a rich, deep blue like that applied by Doug Turnbull is sure to attract attention. And if you want what no one else is likely to have, you can have Doug do your 1911 in a color case hardened finish, like the frames of Colt single action revolvers.

If you need the durability, you can use multiple layers. Start with a stainless 1911. Once it is in final form, have it hard chromed. Test again, then get it coated with a resin finish in a matte black or OD Green. Why do all this? For a

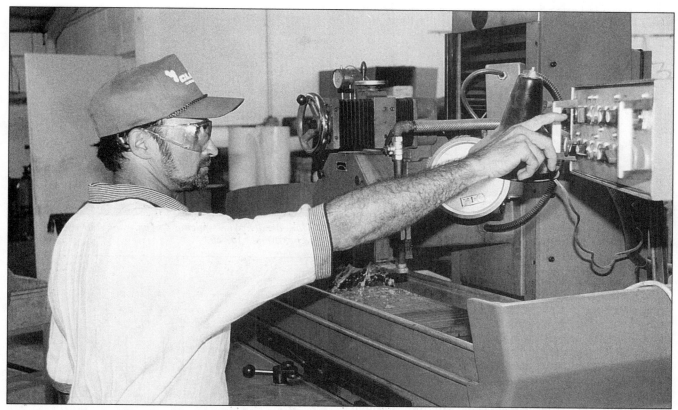

Gunsmiths try to keep busy working on your guns, so a letter is easier than a phone call. Jim Clark, Jr., would really rather sit down and read letters than be called away from the surface grinder every five minutes.

1911 that will reside on a boat, or be worn while taking your vessel along a highly-humid coast (Alaska comes to mind) you can't have too much protection for your protection.

Finding And Dealing With A Gunsmith

First, you need to find someone who will do the work you need. You can scan the list of the American Pistolsmiths Guild, but you may pass over a very good 'smith in your area, as not everyone is a member. Another method is to ask the competitors of your gun club. The serious shooters know who works on what kinds of guns, and what competitions they make guns for. After all, you don't want to go to a Bull's eye specialist for an IPSC race gun, or a carry gun specialist for an Open-class Steel Challenge gun. Ask what gunsmiths they have had work on their guns, and what they were satisfied with. Also ask what they weren't satisfied with.

Once you have a few names, sit down and write a letter. You could call, but most gunsmiths are so busy that answering the phone is something they do only when they absolutely must, and not something they look forward to. With your letter you will enclose a stamped, self-addressed envelope. Briefly describe what you want done, what match or kind of shooting it will be for, and ask three questions: Can they do it, roughly how long will it take, and roughly how much will it cost? The enclosed envelope? The gunsmith will (hopefully) quickly write his answers down, seal the letter back up in your envelope, and send it back. If you make the task easy for him, you are more likely to get an answer. Using this method, I once sent inquiries to a dozen custom stock makers about a rifle I wanted stock work on. I received eleven responses, even some from stock makers

who only worked in synthetics, and couldn't help me with the wood stock I had.

You have a gunsmith, who will do what you want and deliver in a promised time. Now you write another letter. Take your time on it. Detail every aspect that you want him to work on. Do you want the barrel replaced, and if so, by what brand? Do you want the slide and frame tightened? Trigger work? What weight of pull, and do you care whose parts are used? Specify the scope mount, if any, grip safety, the finish everything is coated or plated with, checkering, etc, etc, etc.

The letter must have your return address on it. It should have your phone number on it. You can add your e-mail address, pager, fax and cell phone number if you want. The idea is to make it easy for him to get in touch with you if he needs to.

Do not tell him how to do his job, tell him what you want done. Once the letter is done to your satisfaction, then describe the pistol itself. Add a sheet detailing the pistol and its current features, a packing invoice if you will. For example: "Colt Series 70 LW Commander, Blue, .45ACP, Bar-Sto barrel, Wilson grip safety, Ed Brown single safety stainless, Ser # 70LW12345."

Then add to the second sheet a list of the extra parts sent: "Enclosed: Videki long trigger."

Finally, add the work to be done, delivery time and cost, and reference the original letter: "Install Videcki trigger, adjust trigger pull to 4.5# clean and crisp, epoxy coat slide and sights flat black. Turnaround time two months from delivery. Quoted cost $175. As estimated in your letter dated 29 March 2001."

When you write your letter, be specific. Which grip safety? Do you provide it or does he?

More details. What spacing do you want your checkeirng to be? 20 lpi? 30? 40?

Testing your new 1911 requires 200 rounds of good ammo, known magazines, and a trip to the range

Why all the detail? Gunsmiths forget. In my nearly 20 years of commercial gunsmithing I averaged 1,500 guns a year coming through for repairs. That total didn't include the guns looked at over the counter, or guns that I fixed in five or 10 minutes during the pre-hunting season rush. By the end of the day during the rush, I couldn't remember my name or where I lived without looking at my driver's license.

A month after your phone call, will the gunsmith remember which trigger you specified? He will with the letter you wrote tucked in the work bin alongside your 1911.

You also make his work easier in a way he will remember. Rather than having to make his own notes during the phone call as to what you wanted, he has your own description, signed by you.

Box the pistol and letters up, and send them off. Send them quickly, and insured. Don't be cheap. And then you wait. You can call in a week to make sure the package arrived, and ask if he has any additional questions. He may find some aspect of your desires unclear, or a part not suited to your desire. Make notes of the phone call on the back of your copy of your letter. (You did make a copy, right?)

If the work is to take a few weeks or a month or two, call in a month and see how things are going. If the job is to take six months, wait four months before you call. Don't be surprised if the schedule has slipped a little bit. Gunsmiths of all types tend to be very optimistic about how much work they can do and how few interruptions they will face. Some deliver like clockwork, others are always a few weeks late, and a few seem to be wedded to your pistol. And all will have the occasional pistol from hell that has every problem known, or customers difficult to locate. I once took in a 1911 for work, obtained the parts the customer specified, and was ready to assemble it, but had a question. I found out he had moved, left no forwarding address, his friends didn't know where to find him, and he hadn't signed up to shoot the big match I was building the pistol for. Ten years, four BATF audits (the gun was a running joke with the Agents, "So, you still have it, eh? Perhaps you should check the obituaries?" (I had.) And one move on my part, I get a phone call out of the blue. He hadn't died after all.

The risk of late delivery is a good reason to send only a deposit with your 1911, and pay the balance upon delivery. Knowing there is a check waiting will keep many gunsmiths on schedule.

As soon as you get it back, pull it out and compare it to your list of desired work and shipped parts. If anything is amiss, call immediately and ask. It may be that the part you sent (trigger, grip safety, hammer, etc.) would not fit or work with the other parts, and he had to substitute. If so, he should either have swapped it with one of like cost, or sent the part you sent back, along with the installed one. If the appearance is correct, and the parts are there, then take it to the range and test it.

Once it is broken in and works as you expect, you can relax and enjoy your new toy.

Learning More

There are plenty of gunsmithing courses you can take if you want to learn how to do the work yourself, but not everyone does. How can you learn how the work is done, without the cost and effort of a class? Books and videos. There are several reference books on the 1911 that will go into detail, and lay out the work so you can intelligently discuss it with your gunsmith. You can get the Ed Brown 1911

Learn to speak the gunsmith lingo by watching a video, then specify what you want done to your 1911.

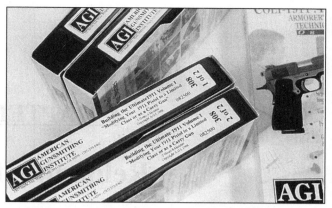

Or just the subjects you are interested in for your particular pistol.

You can get a full library...

manual, or Bill Wilsons' The Combat Auto. The American Gunsmithing Institute has a series of videos that you can look at, and Bill Wilson is thorough in offering a multi-tape video on 1911's. You can either get an overview of the custom 1911 field, or get detailed instructions on how to do the various 1911 custom jobs.

Armed with knowledge, you can specify details that matter to you, like bushing and trigger work; "The bushing should be finger-tight, and the trigger pull must hold four and a half pounds." or grip safety work; "My grip does not always properly depress a standard grip safety. I want the grip safety to work and do its job properly, but be set 'sensi-

tive' so it is disengaged as soon as possible in its arc of travel."

The purpose of learning more is not to learn to do the work yourself (although some shooters do aspire to that end) but to let you communicate clearly with your gunsmith. In any endeavor unclear communications can lead to friction, lost time, increased cost and disappointing results. In a carry gun, it can lead to an inadvertent discharge or malfunction, landing you in the courts, hospital or morgue.

And, the more you learn, the better you can weigh-in at the after match round table talks at your club. After all, a good score is one thing, but status and image count, too.

CHAPTER ELEVEN

Reloading for the 1911

Considering the cost of new ammunition, it's a wonder that all shooters don't reload. But not a wonder when you consider the initial costs. The cost-benefit analysis and time-line expenditure history to determine if reloading is for you is simple. To reload your own ammo, you need at a minimum a brass tumbler, a press with dies, a scale and compo-nents. I'm using as a comparison Dillon equipment not because they gave me any of it free, but because it is what I have. Most practical shooters use Dillon. At the 2000 USPSA Limited Nationals, almost 94 percent of those who loaded their own ammunition loaded it on a Dillon press. And in that group, 85 percent loaded their own. (In 1999, the figure was 93 percent using reloads. The increased par-ticipation in Production class, where many use factory 9mm, pulled the stats down.) Looking at the handy-dandy Dillon Blue Press (their catalog/magazine) it is currently possible to begin loading with the investment of only $450. The example setup would be a Square Deal B (it comes with dies) brass tumbler, scale and case gauge. By moving all the equipment up in scale (Dillon 550B, electronic scale, larger brass tumbler) you would increase reloading volume and ease of caliber change, but the cost would move up to $550 initially, with the ability to change calibers for only an extra $100 for each caliber. To change calibers on a Square Deal, buy a new Square Deal. Yes, you can swap dies on your present frame, but it is a hassle. I did it only once, then ordered a new Square Deal in the second caliber I wanted to load. The break-even point between the Square Deal and a 550B is three calibers. If you are only going to load three pistol calibers or less, three Square Deal B's cost the same

The Dillon Square Deal B, the best bargain for the begin-ning loader wanting a progressive press. (Photo courtesy Dillon)

Primers must be seated flush or below flush and tight. High primers cause malfunctions.

If you're going to load three or more calibers, or add a rifle caliber, it is more cost-effective to buy a 550 than three SDBs.

With labeled bins and a progressive loader, you can load your practice ammo in one partial-evening session.

or less than a 550B and three caliber setups. If you are going to load more than three calibers, or load rifle calibers, start your considerations at the 550B.

Currently, components cost about $65 per thousand rounds of .45 ACP to reload empty cases. The latest ammo catalog I just received in the mail has imported ball or commercially-reloaded ammunition at $165 per thousand. At $100 per thousand rounds difference, you would have to reload 4,500 rounds of your own to pay off the investment in equipment, 5,500 if you started larger. Loading 9mm or light loads in the .38 super, your per-unit cost of reloads would be less and you'd have to load less to break even. (Less cost, more savings, sooner payback.) If you were loading .38 Super Major, or .400 Cor-bon, .40 Super, .45 Super or .460 Rowland, your reloaded ammo cost would be greater, with a longer payback.

How long will it take you to shoot that much ammo? Not as long as you thought. With more ammo available, you'll shoot more. Instead of a range trip consisting of a box or two, perhaps 100 rounds, you'll find that a range trip easily turns into a 200-round session. Since it won't take weeks to reload that ammo, you can go to the range more often.

But the cost of ammunition is not just the expenditure of money for components, it is the time spent loading those components. Starting from clean brass, a reloading session with a progressive press will typically turn out 300 rounds the first hour. The time needed on a single stage press? If things go smoothly, your total production rate might be as slow as 25 to 35 rounds per hour or as fast as 50. An hour on

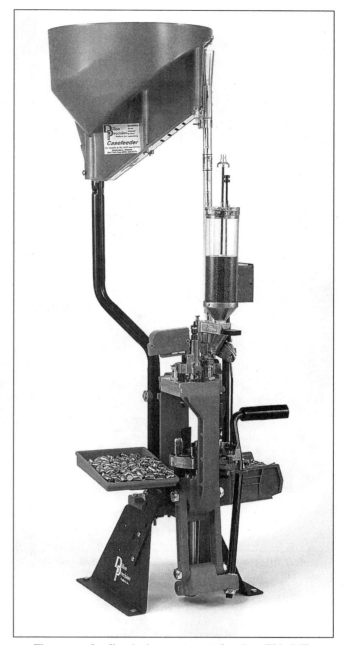

Time spent loading is time not spent shooting. This Dillon XL 650 will increase your output without breaking the bank. (Photo courtesy Dillon)

a progressive press can produce as much ammo as a week of evenings on a single-stage press. You should not discount the time factor. Modern life is hectic enough, and there are enough things vying for your time and attention. With a progressive reloading press, you can slip into the basement when your wife or girlfriend's favorite TV show comes on, and while she is watching, have loaded at least 100 rounds, maybe even 200. Or, get up a half an hour earlier in the morning, and before you go to work, you can load 100 rounds. Do it two times, and you're ready for a range trip.

Some shooters consider the time spent as part of the cost of their ammo, and figure a longer time to break even. Other shooters view the time spent loading as relaxation, and do not consider it a cost to charge against the press or ammo.

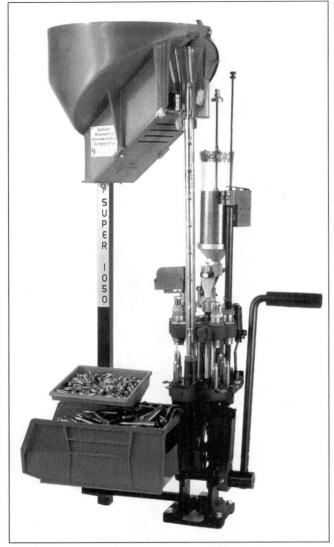

The 1050 turns out ammo almost faster than you can shoot it. (Photo courtesy Dillon)

While progressive presses are simple, you have to load on a regular basis so you remember how things work, and should keep detailed notes even if your memory is good. If you reload and shoot once a month, you'll stay in practice and pay off your investment in a year. After that, your ammo is dirt-cheap and loaded just the way you like it.

Serious competitors sometimes invest in more equipment, sometimes they don't. All the big name shooters have Dillon 1050's bolted to their reloading benches (Jerry Barnhart has three) because for a top shooter the greater production speed is a necessity. The 1050 is much more involved to use, and requires more than once-a-month familiarity. However, the top shooters will shoot 20,000, 30,000 or 40,000 rounds a year. They may keep 10,000 brass of a caliber in circulation. Over a weekend (the one spare one they have for a couple of months) they'll load all of those 10,000 empties, and then fire them in practice over the next couple of months.

Do you need that volume? If you do, the people at Dillon already have you on their mailing list. If not, there are progressive machines that don't cost nearly the money a 1050 does, but will still turn out buckets of ammo. And why so

The best balance between production, cost, complexity and ability to change calibers is undoubtedly the Dillon 550B. (Photo courtesy Dillon)

much ammo? Besides the mantra, "More is better", look at the ammo consumption matches call for. Local club practical matches can easily exceed 100 rounds for a monthly match. You'll need an absolute minimum of 175 rounds to shoot The Steel Challenge. A USPSA Nationals runs between 400 and 500 rounds before you start making up extra shots. You can fire that many at a bowling pin match depending on how many times you re-enter the Optionals. And the winner and still champion for ammunition consumption is the American Handgunner Shoot-Off. If you travel to Paul Miller's range in Montrose, Colorado, you had better take a 5-gallon bucket of ammo with you. It is common for shooters there to fire more than 1,000 rounds during the short week of the match. You bet all those shooters have progressives. (And most have 1911's.)

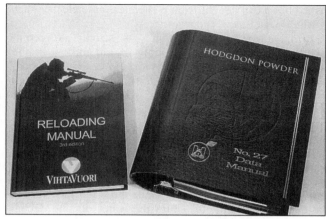

You must have reloading data, and for that you need manuals.

Before we plunge headlong into reloading details, we have to settle the questions of: Should you?

Broken down into its specific objections, "should you" means one or more of: Is it cost-effective (we've just covered that), is the ammo good enough to shoot, and is it safe?

How good is "good enough?" It is entirely possible to load ammunition just as accurate as the Match ammo produced by the commercial ammunition manufacturers. Bull's eye competitors had been doing it for decades before practical shooters started. When the practical shooters moved in, not only was the goal accurate ammo, but reliable ammo. There are no alibi strings in practical shooting. (Nor will there ever be any.) Ammunition must be reliable. As mentioned earlier, 85 percent of the competitors at the 2000 USPSA Limited Nationals used reloaded ammunition. The Open Nationals had an even higher percentage. All those shooters were depending on the reliability of their ammo, and very few were let down. In test-firing the 1911's for this book, I found that reloaded ammunition was often in the top three most-accurate loads for each pistol. Reloads can be accurate, depending on the person loading.

Is it safe? If you follow the data in loading manuals (I must stress plural manuals. By cross-checking you are unlikely to be blind-sided by a typographical error.) You will be safe. The 1911 has a large built-in safety margin. In 23 years of competition I've seen only three 1911s that blew out a case. (In those years, I've personally fired over 300,000 rounds, and probably observed 3 million rounds being fired. More than half were reloads.) Two of the blow-ups happened in the old days when we were still figuring out a lot of stuff. The third happened a few years ago, and it occurred because the loader insisted on using a powder that the manufacturer did not show data for in their book. He extrapolated the "correct" charge and blew the case on a 10mm. (The lesson? Powder manufacturers do not leave a powder out of a particular calibers data because they are lazy. If the powder maker doesn't list any loads with a particular powder for your caliber, they probably had a good reason.)

How traumatic were these events? Nearby shooters didn't know anything unfavorable had happened until they saw the involved shooter's reaction. There were no flames, no shrapnel, no shrieks of pain. (There wasn't any pain, thus no shrieks.) In these three incidents, there were three cases blown, two magazines trashed, one set of grips cracked and

Some manuals come from powder makers, and some from bullet makers. Buy both.

no harm done. The 10mm magazine was of the design where the baseplate came off for cleaning, and the parts of the magazine blew out of the gun. When the parts were all found, the magazine was reassembled and it worked fine. The .45 mags were older ones, before removable baseplates, and the jetting gas trashed them.

Pay attention to what you are doing, use published data, and you will not have any problems.

So, how do you reload, and what does the 1911 require that other pistols don't?

Let's start with empty brass picked up off the range. Your brass or the random brass that gets left behind by other shooters. To load, you must; in order: sort, clean, size, de-prime, re-prime, drop powder, seat the bullet and gauge. Some steps have additional details that have to be attended to.

Sort : Your brass is not all your brass, and may not all be your caliber. Unless you are shooting only on your property, no one else has shot there, and you have only the one caliber to feed, there will be other peoples' brass. There is always other brass. Most practical shooters sort the brass by caliber. While some shooters (Bull's eye primarily) are worried about getting all of, and only, their brass back, most high-volume shooters don't care. Some IPSC shooters who are using picky guns do care. Some of the guys I shoot with will only take back their particular type and even brand of brass back once they finish a stage. (More brass for me.) Sorting involves separating the 9mm's and .40's from the .45's, where they can nestle inside a case. If you shoot a Super, you want to sort the .38 Super from the .38 Super Comp and 9 Super Comp, 9X23, Largo and 38 TJ. If you are shooting .45 Super or .450 SMC, you want to keep those separate so you can safely load up to the power level of those cartridges. If you don't sort, and get some tired old .45 ACP cases into your Super/SMC loading, you can blow a case at your next shooting session.

Why are some shooters picky? The Bull's eye shooters want their brass for accuracy. They are shooting brass all from the same lot and same manufacturer. By using brass as identical as possible, they produce ammunition that is as accurate as possible. The difference is small, but in Bull's eye, points matter. They can matter a lot. The IPSC shooters who want only their own brass are doing so for reliability. A race gun can be a finicky beast. They may be using one of the rimless Supers, and don't want any of the rimmed .38 Super brass. Or they have a tight chamber and don't want other brass in their loading stream. They do their sorting at the range, while they pick up the brass. Me, I pick it all up and sort when I get home. As a result, I have small bins of everything. (And larger bins of some.)

Even if you don't reload them, keep the other brass separated from what you load. After all, you can always sell or trade them to other shooters in a similar situation, but opposite needs.

With the brass sorted down to the caliber you want, use the separator screen of your brass tumbler, or a plastic mesh bag, to clean the sand, dirt and grit off the brass. (Do this over a trash can, so you don't have to sweep up the dirt.) Drop the brass in, swirl it around, and dump the relatively clean brass into your dirty-storage bin. Grubby brass or tar-

nished brass can benefit from a chemical case cleaner such as Birchwood Casey's concentrate.

I mix the concentrate twice as strong as recommended, and store it in a couple of old milk jugs. To clean the brass, I sort out the nickeled cases (they contaminate the mix if dunked too long) and dump the brass in a plastic bucket. For the book, with the large amounts of brass generated, I used a 5-gallon bucket. Pour the mixture into the bucket until it covers the brass. Let sit for fifteen minutes, then decant the mix back into the milk jug/storage. Be careful not to pour the silt of washed-off dirt into your storage. Once decanted, I put the bucket in the laundry tub and turn on the hot water and let it rinse the bucket out. Once the water has washed the bucket for a minute, I turn the water off and decant the rinse water down the drain. Then, in the summer I

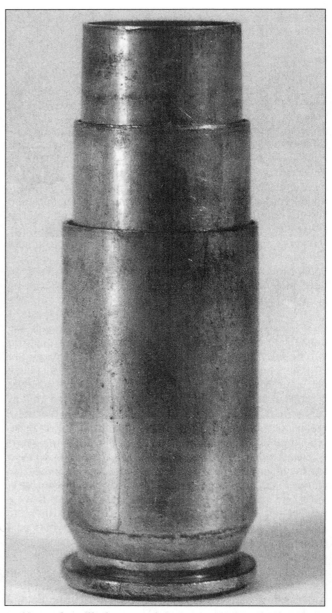

Not only will these nestled cases not get clean, run through the tumbler this way, they'll jam the auto case feed of a progressive press.

Some pistols would take all these, and some won't. You have to find out if your 1911 will, and sort brass accordingly.

These will all fit the shellholder, will all go through the sizing die, but will not all work in the same pistol. Sort, sort, sort.

If you have a large pile of brass, or very dirty brass, you'd be forever getting it clean with tumbling alone. The Birchwood Casey case cleaner concentrate will chemically clean buckets of brass before it is exhausted.

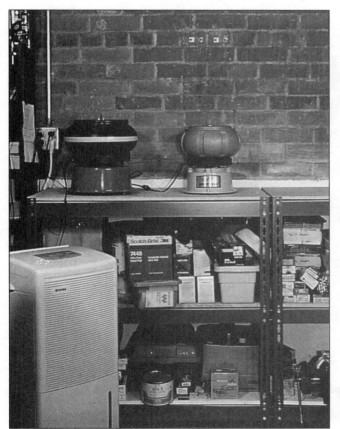

The brass tumblers/vibrators on the bench and the dehumidifier to the left. You must clean your brass before loading, but not everyone needs a dehumidifier.

spread an old beach towel in the sun on the deck and pour the brass out to dry. In the winter I pour the brass onto the same towel in my shop, turn the dehumidifier up, and leave it running overnight. Viola, dry brass.

I then pour them back into the storage bins awaiting their trip through the tumbler/vibrator. The tumbler is a noisy little beast that circulates the brass in a bin full of crushed walnut hulls or ground corncob. I prefer the corncob, mostly because a local feed store has 50-pound bags cheap as dirt. I call them tumblers out of habit, even though most vibrate the brass clean. Do not fill the tumbler, but leave room for the brass and media to circulate. Pour in a couple of capfuls of polishing media, let the media circulate for a minute, then dump in a load of brass. If you load it too full, the tumbler/vibrator can't circulate the load, and your brass won't get clean.

With clean media, a load of brass is clean in two hours. Once the media starts to get grubby, cleaning takes longer. When it takes four hours to clean brass, I dump the old media, wipe the bowl clean and put in fresh stuff. Dirty media still cleans brass, it just takes longer. I once ran out of media, and didn't get a chance to pick up more for a month. The media became so grubby I didn't want to touch it, and it took four to five hours each time to get the brass clean, but it came clean. That's when I started buying corncob in 50-pound bags.

Fish the clean brass out, or pour it through a strainer, to separate the brass from the media. Store your clean brass in a separate bin from the one that you stored the dirty/chemically washed brass in. Kept covered, cleaned brass will be ready to go through your press for years. I use Tupperware knock-offs as storage. The lids keep dust off, and the boxes

You have to sort, or you'll run into problems sizing. The 9mm Largo case on the right tried to fit into a sizing die for the .38 Super on the left. The trip was short and eventful.

can be stacked. I found that cardboard boxes became weak as they became worn, looked messy and rain and snow turned them into blobs. Old coffee cans were appealing for a while, but they are an inefficient method of storage. Cylinders take up a lot of shelf space, and only let you store 3/4 of the volume they take up. And they rust after they've been rained on.

Each bin is labeled with the brass, and if it is from a particular source or batch that I keep separate, then so marked.

From this point, loading depends on the press you are using. If you are using a progressive like a Dillon, and the dies are set, you feed components in, pull the handle, and produce ammo.

Using a single-stage press, or setting up a caliber on a progressive, is more involved.

The Steps

Size: The case expanded on firing. You have to squeeze it back down to spec. The first thing you have to keep in mind is Carbide. The second is any one of the modern plating fin-

You need dies to reload, including a taper crimp die if the regular die set doesn't include it. Dies last a long time, so don't be price-sensitive, buy the best.

ishes. Do not be cheap, buy a die that removes the need for case lubrication. The non-carbide dies will be a few dollars to $20 cheaper than the carbide or plated dies. Ignore them. For the hassle of lubing cases in order to size them, the few dollars saved are not worth it. I spent the first 10 years of my reloading using non-carbide dies. The first evening I loaded with carbide was enough to make me see the light. The next day I went out and replaced all my pistol-caliber sizing dies with carbide ones. If not carbide, then select some other miracle coating or compound, but do not for a moment consider steel dies and case lube.

On the bottleneck cases, you may be told you must use the old dies, for no one makes carbide bottleneck. Wrong. Tombstone Smokin' Deals makes carbide dies for bottleneck pistol calibers. Yes, they are pricey, but a few evenings spent using messy case lube to size and load, and they won't look so expensive.

Adjust your die just as the book says, with the sizing die coming into contact with the shell holder. You want the case sized down as far as possible. (Except the bottleneck cases, where you absolutely must have a case gauge. Adjust the sizing die until the sized case fits properly in the gauge.) The entry taper to the die mouth will keep you from sizing the case down to the extractor groove. Such is life.

Dies do not last forever, but you will be a long time wearing one out. You are more likely to need a new die from having gotten lazy and not cleaned your brass. A single piece of dirty brass with some grit on it can scratch your die, and make it useless. Clean your brass, use carbide, and start shopping for a new die somewhere around the 400,000 round mark.

Be sure you're using the correct powder, and the correct amount of it. Check, and check again.

De-prime: Most sizing dies also de-prime. The old primer has served its purpose and must be removed. The decapping pin squirms through the flash hole and snaps the old primer out. De-priming is messy. You'll end up with old primers on the floor. Sweep up when you're done and there is no harm. Reloaders of 9mm Parabellum, make sure you keep a supply of spare decapping pins on hand. If you load enough, you will sooner or later overlook a Berdan case when sorting. The Berdan case does not have a central flash hole, and your decapping pin will strain mightily to punch a new hole. It will bend or break in the process. If you don't have a spare on hand, your reloading press is shut down until you can get a spare.

Re-prime: On a single-stage press you can re-prime on the upstroke, or re-prime as a separate hand operation. On a progressive, re-priming is either on the upstroke, or the next station over. Old cases can have loose primer pockets. There is no way to deal with them on a progressive. You'll have to sort for the loose ones later. On a single-stage or when hand-priming you can feel how much force it takes to seat the primer, and reject those with loose pockets. An over-size pocket lets the primer drop out. It may or may not tie up the gun dropping out, but it sure isn't going to fire without a primer.

If you are worried that your brass may be too tired and the primer pockets could be worn, jostle your ammo before you gauge it. A large plastic jug, like a 2-gallon commercial mayonnaise jug, is the tool. Drop a couple of hundred rounds in and swirl them around, gently jostling them up and down a couple of times. Then, when you gauge your ammo, look at the primers. Loose pockets will often drop their primers during jostling, and you can set them aside. Pull the bullets for later use, or just deep-six the primerless cartridge.

Powder drop: In a single-stage press procedure, you have to bell the cases, then drop the powder charges. In a progressive, the powder drop station also does the belling. You have to bell the case in order to seat the bullet without damaging either of them. The bullet may be scarred, or the case crushed, if the bullet catches the lip of the case when seated in an unbelled case. When loading lead bullets, if the case isn't belled enough, you can scrape a small amount of bullet lube off of each round during seating, and the buildup in your seating die can gradually shorten the overall length of your loaded rounds.

How much is enough? It is hard to assign a figure. The amount of belling that happens depends on case length. Longer cases will get belled more than shorter ones in the same die. No one trims their pistol brass, absolutely no one. Rifle brass stretches enough to need trimming, but pistol brass doesn't. Lead bullets need more belling than jacketed ones. If you apply too much bell to your cases, the extra work will quickly crack them at the mouth. In extreme cases, a case can be belled so much the crimp doesn't squeeze down all the belling, and there is a "donut" behind the crimp. Setting the belling is a trial and error process that will take a few loading sessions. Once done, there is no need to make changes.

A straight-line bullet seating die reduces the amount of belling you have to do to your cases. The bell is there to be sure every bullet base stays inside the case when seated. The straight-line seater keeps the bullets under control, reducing the need for belling.

Not enough bell. The bullet base caught the case mouth and this was the end result.

A straight-line bullet seater improves accuracy and requires less belling of your cases.

Once belled, you need powder, in the correct amount, and a single portion of the desired powder then has to be put in each case. In a single-stage loading setup, you switch from the loading press to a powder measure and dropping machine called a powder thrower. It measures the correct volume of powder (which you have verified by weighing the

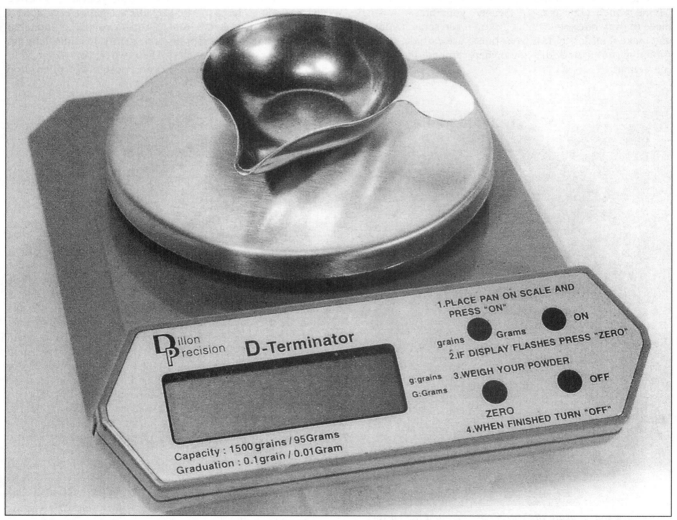

You must not guess about powder weight. Set your measure, weigh the charge, and adjust. "Close enough" isn't good enough.

powder on your scale as you have adjusted the thrower) on each cycle of the handle. With a single-stage loading process, you place the primed and belled cases in each of 50 holes in a loading block. You then hold each case against the bottom of the spout of the thrower and cycle the handle once. When you are done, stand under a light and look into each case to make sure they all have powder.

On a progressive, the powder drop station is also the belling station, and on a Dillon (and most other new designs) the case activates the powder drop. No case, no powder. On Dillon 650s and 1050s, where you have extra stations, you can install a powder check sensor, and make sure you have one powder charge, and not two or none.

Bullet seat: Once the case is ready, primed and charged, you need to seat a new bullet. Place a bullet of the desired weight, diameter and shape into the belled mount of the case, and pull the handle. The seating stem in the seating die will stop the bullet before the handle is done moving, and force the bullet into the case. For ammunition of the utmost accuracy, you can use a Redding Competition seating die. The Competition die uses a spring-loaded seating stem. The rising bullet contacts the stem, and then compresses the spring. While the bullet is compressing the spring, the stem is straightening any slightly mis-aligned bullet. Once the stem bottoms out, the bullet then gets seated.

Crimp: The belling in the case must be removed. In the old days, the only kind of crimp there available was called a rolled crimp. The edge of the case was rolled over, in a similar fashion to, although not as far as, the roll crimp on a shotgun slug. Roll crimp doesn't remove much belling, and is very sensitive to case length. When practical shooting competitors had to have accurate and reliable ammunition, the taper crimp became much more popular. The taper crimp die, rather than having a shoulder like the roll crimp die, has a section that is cone-shaped. The cone section evenly presses the case mouth into the bullet. Unlike the roll crimp, which only acts on the leading edge of the case, the taper crimp tapers in the first .030" of the case.

Ammo gauging: Once it is loaded, you have to gauge your ammunition to make sure it will fit the chamber. You don't have to gauge your practice ammo if you don't want to. But you might, as a result, spend some of your practice time dealing with clearing a wedged cartridge. You don't have to gauge if your brass is all your brass and there is no

chance someone else's empties snuck in. But if there is a chance, or if you are loading ammo for a match, gauge it.

The simplest gauge is the chamber of the barrel, out of the pistol. Strip the pistol and scrub the barrel and chamber clean. Then spend the time to drop each loaded cartridge into the chamber. What you are looking for is that each one drops fully into the chamber, and drops out cleanly when you turn the barrel over. If it sticks, or won't go in, or won't drop out, it is practice ammo. The barrel gauge method only works for the barrel in which you've tested the ammo. It will tell you nothing about how that ammo will react to a different barrel.

Bruce Britt is a serious bowling pin shooter here in Michigan. He decided some years back that he was not going to worry about ammo for the Main Event. Once he had developed an accurate, powerful load that broomed pins off the table the way he liked, he bought 1,000 empties of brand-new .45ACP. He loaded the new brass, inspected and gauged each one in his pin gun barrel, and stashed the ammo in metal ammo cans under his loading bench. He was now set for the Main Event for more than five years. Many serious competitors will only load brand-new brass for match use, and gauge it after loading, as Bruce did.

If you have several 1911's to feed, gauging the ammo in all their barrels can be a hassle. Rather than try to drop all your ammo into and out of all the chambers, use a case gauge. Made by Wilson, C.P. Bullets and many others, the gauge is simply a minimum-dimension chamber reamed in

Gauging and inspection will turn up these kinds of rounds before your 1911 vainly tried to feed them. The left one has a nicked case mouth, the right lacks neck tension.

You can eyeball taper crimp by holding two cartridges next to each other and use each as a straightedge for the other.

Gauge your ammo. If you don't, you may end up with a round such as this one trying to get into your chamber.

a stainless steel or aluminum block or cylinder. You use it instead of the chamber of your barrel. If you have several .45's to feed, here is how you check your new gauge. Gauge a batch of ammo, and set aside the ones that fail to pass the gauge. Now pull the barrels out of your pistols, and try the failed ammo in each chamber. Let's say that your batch of ammo produced 10 rounds that failed the gauge. You'll probably find that two or three of them will easily slip into the chambers of your pistols. One of the chambers may even take four or five of them. One chamber may reject seven of them.

Each time you gauge ammo, set the failed rounds in a bin by themselves. These are your practice rounds. Once the bin has accumulated enough ammo, take it to the range with the pistol that had the highest rate of rejection of the gauged rejects. You may find that your gauge is more strict than your tightest barrel, and all the ammo works fine. No problem, except that the overly-strict gauge has you rejecting otherwise suitable ammo.

In this case, use the reject bin as your practice ammo, and use the gauge-passed ammo for match use.

Part of the ammo testing process is to check velocity. A chronograph lets you know if your ammo is consistent and sufficiently powerful.

It may be that the gauge is less strict than one of your pistols' chambers. If so, the gauge will pass ammo that is too large for your chamber. How can this be? Barrel makers ream chambers on match barrels to the smallest possible working dimensions. Some shooters don't open the chamber to a working dimension, but leave the chamber tight. (It's supposed to help accuracy, but I've not seen it help.) The result is a pistol that won't take anything but factory-dimensioned brass. If you want a tight chamber, you are going to have to test gauges against your ammo until you find a gauge that agrees with your barrel. If a gauge is too large compared to your pistol's chamber, you have to sell or trade the gauge and try another. Otherwise, you will have a few rounds passing the gauge that will tie up your gun. We all know when you'll attempt to chamber that particular rounds, don't we? Yes, in the middle of a match.

A Solution?

One solution to the over-sized brass problem is the Image Industries Case Pro. Instead of sizing the brass by shoving it into a cylindrical die and pulling it out, the Case Pro uses two precision-ground plates. Each empty is dropped into a recess in the plates, and then the plates slide past each other to roll the case to size it. The rolling not only sizes the bulge right above the extractor slot, it irons out nicks and burrs on the rim. The reconditioning that the Case Pro does also has a tightening effect on loose or loosening primer pockets. Shooters who use the Case Pro report their brass lasts from a few to a whole lot more reloadings when run through the Case Pro.

Some high-volume commercial reloaders use a slightly different method to deal with swollen brass. Once the brass is cleaned and sorted, it goes through a case prep machine. The machine deprimes and sizes, and at the last station, there is a tapered hole or die under the shell plate. (The sizing, gauging and de-priming dies are all above the shell plate). At the last station the machine shoves the empty down away from the shell plate, out of the machine through the tapered die. The smallest diameter of the die is the correct diameter of the rim and base of the cartridge. Any bulge is ironed out as the whole case, rim and all passes through the die.

Why don't competition shooters do something like this? The machines are expensive, and it wouldn't work for .38 Super. The rim of the Super is larger than the case wall diameter, and ironing down the rims would not make for useable brass.

The rolling action of the Case Pro accommodates rims. You can size any case right down to the extractor groove, whether it has a rim or not. Competition shooters use gauges or the Image Industries Case Pro, or both.

Loading For The 1911

So, what is peculiar about the 1911, and what reloading tricks do we need to know? First, some background on the 1911 and its feeding stroke. When the slide moves back, the next cartridge rises to the feed lips of the magazine and waits its fraction of a second for the trip forward. That trip is not easy. The round sits low in the frame compared to more recent designs. When the slide hits the cartridge base, the nose of the bullet starts to dive down until it hits the feed ramp. (The nose drops because the slide is striking the rim only at the 12-o'clock position, and not on its full base.) The nose then gets shoved up the ramp while the rim stays trapped under the feed lips of the magazine. The bullet hits the top of the chamber, and the recently released rim slides up under the extractor as the case body pivots around the break-over line of the chamber/ramp juncture. The slide, with some energy dissipated, runs the cartridge forward. Once chambered, the round is done but the pistol isn't. The last bit of cartridge seating is done while the slide shoves the barrel forward, and cams it up over the slide stop to lock.

Whew. More recent designs place the cartridge in a higher position to the chamber. The Beretta M-92 is one such example. The round has such a straight shot to the chamber you wonder why they bothered with a feed ramp at all. The straight feed of the M-92 does not come without a cost. For despite being chambered in a smaller cartridge, it rolls as much in recoil as a .45 because the line of the bore is higher, giving it more leverage to your hand under recoil. If you want low recoil, a Commander 9mm pistol is soft to shoot.

The disadvantage, as we have seen, is that the cartridge gets worked hard in feeding. When Browning designed the 1911, he didn't care about that. All pistols back then shot full-metal-jacketed round nose ammo. That's what he designed it for, that's what the government wanted, and that's what the 1911 feeds best. Even military pistols with unmodified feed ramps gobble up hardball. (Although, in recent e-mail correspondence with Bill Wilson of Wilson Combat, he noted that he has seen the 200-grain lead semi-wadcutter bullet as being more reliable even than hardball.)

To get the pistol to feed other style bullets you have to widen the feed ramp, polish the break over line, and load correct ammo. Well, your gunsmith does the first two, and you do the last one.

The 1911 holds its rounds low to the chamber.

The Beretta M-92 gives the cartridge a straighter shot to the chamber.

From Top To Bottom

Overall length: The tip of the round nose on hardball is 1.250" to 1.270" from the base. If you load 230-grain round nose bullets, they must be within that spread. Longer and they won't fit the magazine. Shorter and feeding becomes "chunky". That is, you can feel the bullets going through each step.

Other bullets require different lengths. The length you need for each bullet takes some visualization. Imagine the bullet cross-section of 230-grain ball ammo. Now place the outline of your bullet on that cross-section. You want your bullet to be loaded to the length where its forward edges correspond to the outline of the 230 ball round. That way, when your bullet strikes the feed ramp, it will be doing so at the same location in space that the 230-grain bullet would have.

The best example of this in .45 is the 200-grain bullet now generically called the H&G 68. Hensley & Gibbs were mould makers several decades ago, and they developed a 200-grain lead bullet design that had its nose's leading edge right at the radius of the 230 ball bullet. As a near-perfect bullet design, it has a good length bearing surface, a long nose for feeding, room in the bearing surface for a good grease groove, and also room for a beveled base for ease of reloading. LaserCast tells me that their single largest sales volume item comes from that bullet alone. I wouldn't doubt it, as by far the most common bullet practical shooters use is that design.

An example of correct length being determined by the pistol is the .40 S&W. As factory-loaded, it is meant for 9mm-size pistols and is 1.15" at maximum length. Such a short cartridge will not feed in a full-length (front to back) 1911 magazine. To use 10mm magazines, you have to load the .40 to 1.200" or you'll be faced with many feeding malfunctions. You would be faced with the same problems if you were to try to use regular 9mm Parabellum rounds in a .38 Super magazine. What Colt did to correct the feeding problems when they chambered 1911s in 9mm was to put a spacer in the rear of the magazine to keep the cartridges under control. STI makes such a spacer for their magazines, for shooters who want to fire short .40s or 9mms out of a .40 or .38 Super magazine. It and its follower slide into the magazine during assembly, and can be removed later.

If the longer bullets feed better and are accurate, why do so many Bull's eye shooters still use short-nosed 185s? Habit and results. Their guns are tuned for the bullet, shoot it accurately and work, so why should they switch?

Crimp: The bullet must stay in place in the case, or feeding problems will ensue. If the bullet is not held in place, it may set back into the case when it is so rudely shoved against the feed ramp. A shortened round may fail to feed, but it won't fail to increase pressure. The set-back bullet decreases the size of the combustion chamber. It is easy to quickly exceed the strength of the brass. In testing done to solve the mystery of blown-up revolvers using wimpy .38 Special ammunition, the NRA found that setting the bullet back a short distance could easily double the chamber pressure when the round is fired. The .45 ACP has a top-end pressure under 18,000 PSI. The 10mm has a top end of 34,000. If you were to shove a bullet back in a .45 case and double the chamber pressure of that cartridge, you would be working at 10mm pressures with a case designed for half that.

The crimp holds the bullet in place. Too much crimp can harm accuracy, so if you find that your bullets are setting back even with a solid crimp, your belling stem is probably too large. The diameter of the belling stem/powder activator should be four thousandths smaller than the diameter of the bullets you are using. Thus, for a .45

ACP using .452" bullets, you want a belling stem with a shaft diameter of .448". In .38 Super, using bullets of .355" you want a stem diameter of .351". Your taper crimp should be three thousandths smaller than the nominal case diameter. For the .45 ACP, with a case diameter of .476", your taper crimp final spec should be around .473", and the Super, with a case diameter of .380", the taper crimp should end up around .377". Or so the book says. I've found the .45 to respond much better when the taper crimp is in the .467-.468" range, and the Super in the .375" area.

Case drag is another reason to be sure your taper crimp is correct. If your crimp doesn't remove the bell, the flared edges of the case will scrape the length of the chamber, creating drag. The larger diameter of the belled mouth also causes wedging of the case mouth in the chamber just as the cartridge is tipping over from its magazine feed angle to the centerline of the chamber. A typical result of insufficient taper crimp is a pistol that will not quite fully close, and where the slide has to be thumbed forward the last fraction of an inch to close and fire. The problems with too little crimp become worse as the pistol gets dirty and the chamber builds up powder residue.

Many shooters don't know the final diameter of their taper crimp because they have set the crimp by eye and test-firing. With patience and a few trips to the range, you can

The Laser-Cast from Oregon Trail Bullet Company is a modern H&G 68 bullet. We used a bunch in the book and it was quite often the most accurate bullet each 1911 shot.

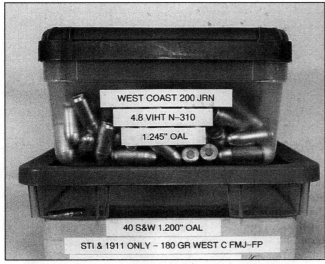

The top bin is .45ACP, and will work in any 1911. The bottom bin is .40S&W, and will only work in 1911's, and not in a pistol derived from a 9mm design.

The 200-grain LaserCast on the right is easier to get properly feeding than the old-style 185 on the left. But many shooters, not just Bull's eye shooters, stick with what works.

The matter of a case mouth stem diameter being .004" less than the bullet diameter is not a hard and fast rule. Also, the crimp sometimes is not best at .003" under standard mouth diameter. I measured my belling stems' diameters, and came up with the following:

9mm & .38 Super	.351"
40 S&W & 10mm	.397"
.45 ACP	.447"
.400 Cor-bon	.389"
.40 Super	.390"
.45 Super	.444"
.460 Rowland	.445"

The first three diameters are what you would expect. The .400 Cor-bon and .40 Super have relatively short case necks, and the extra tension keeps the bullets in place during feeding. Tension is needed for proper feeding of all four of the high-performance cartridges due to the need for heavy recoil springs. Without high neck tension, there would be a risk of bullet set-back during feeding. The tension also acts to create resistance to bullet movement, an important and necessary addition to ensure proper combustion of slow-burning powders.

If you find that your high-velocity loads are not consistent, and you are using a powder correctly (within the book specs) then your neck tension is probably insufficient to ensure proper combustion. Even in mild-recoiling calibers, neck tension can matter. For a while I was experimenting with 90- and 88-grain bullets in 9mm and .38 Super, in an attempt to come up with a Nine-pin load. The power factor needed for the Nine-pin event is only around 130, so all I had to do was get the little pills up in the high 1,400s fps. I found that I had to polish down a belling stem to .348" to get enough neck tension for proper burn. I eventually gave up and went back to 125-loads at 1050 fps, as the powder charges to get the needed velocity from the 90-grain bullets didn't help feed the compensator enough to be worth the effort.

In the .45 Super and .460 Rowland, there is plenty of gas to feed a comp, but without sufficient neck tension your velocities are all over the place.

have your crimp dialed in and properly set. To eyeball your crimp, hold two loaded cartridges side by side pointing in opposite directions. Slide them so their bullets are side by side. Look closely at the area of the taper crimp of each. If the crimp is not enough, you'll see a gap between the cases from the crimps still being belled too much. You can perform the same inspection with a steel straightedge. Also, a case that is not sufficiently crimped will feel sharp to the touch. Rub a fingertip across the crimp. You'll have a great advantage in setting your crimp if you shoot at a club with experienced reloaders who shoot practical matches. Ask the members in a squad to look at your ammo. If your crimp isn't enough, you'll be able to feel the difference between your crimp and theirs.

As an additional note, if you are loading the most popular bullet, the 200-grain lead semiwadcutter, the shoulder of the bullet must be ahead of the edge of the case. Not flush. The taper crimp has to have something to taper into, and adjusting the overall length so the shoulder of the bullet is flush will defeat the purpose of the crimp.

Case diameter: If your cases are swollen your pistol will object. Where do swollen cases come from? Cases get swollen either because the range brass you are using comes from someone's over-eager reloading, or their chamber is much larger than yours. High pressure loads are not much of a problem in .45 ACP, but you do see them. Usually someone is trying to load out on the edges of the useful ranges of the .45, like loading 155-grain bullets with slow powders to

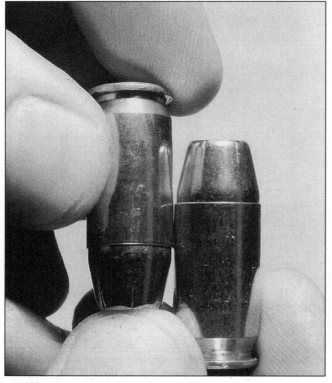

When the taper crimp is correct, you won't see or feel a sharp edge.

The shoulder goes forward of the case mouth, not flush with it.

feed a comp. More likely, it is a large chamber. Someone shooting a really old 1911, or a brand new Glock, can have a large chamber. While their pistol works fine, the oversized chamber can let the brass expand too much for your pistol.

Your sizing die can only size down so far along the case walls. Unless you are using the Image Industries Case Pro, the only way to be sure you don't have a problem is to gauge your ammo. Once you start a bin of gauge-rejected ammunition, you have to keep that ammo and brass separate from the rest of your brass. Use it for practice and leave it at the range, or use it for practice, keep it separate and run it through the Case Pro later.

If the swollen brass comes from you and not another shooter, you have two choices. Shoot lighter loads so you aren't bulging brass so much, or replace your barrel. A barrel with an oversized chamber can be fixed only by replacing the barrel. If the source is someone else, all you can do is gauge and sort.

Rim: If your extractor has a sharp edge on it, your case rims can quickly turn into a mass of burrs and gouges. The burrs can build up to the point that feeding becomes difficult. It was more of a problem in the old days, when fewer shooters and gunsmiths knew what a properly-polished extractor was supposed to look like. If you buy a brand-name part now, it will come already beveled, needing only a final polish (maybe) and tension adjusting (maybe) to work properly.

While the Case Pro will iron out the burrs to a certain extent, the best solution is to make sure your extractor is properly beveled and polished.

Primer: Your primers must be seated, either flush with the base of the brass, or slightly recessed. The 1911 does not have anything like the camming action of a bolt-action rifle. The base of the cartridge in a 1911 slides up the breechface, starting at an angle and then snapping flush. A high primer can create rim bind on the extractor. If your pistol is dirty, the chamber is caked with powder residue, or the crimp is not small enough, any of these and the high primer can take enough energy from the slide to keep it from going fully forward.

High primers come from a loose shell plate or the loader not paying attention to the proper press handle movement on primer seating.

Labels And A Log Book

There is one subject that doesn't get enough coverage in reloading manuals. Labels. Oh, they all have the brief bit of advice, "be sure and label your loads" but that isn't enough. What should go on those labels?

How much depends on how fussy and detailed you are, but at a minimum, you should mark each bin or box with: the caliber, what kind of brass it is loaded in, the brand of primer, the powder and its weight or measure setting (preferably both), the bullet weight, brand and style, and overall length. If it is a special load, then the label should also have that data. Why all this information? Because you'll forget. I started out loading in .38 Special (not in a 1911) and once I had two or three loads worked up I found I had run out of bullet styles to use as identifiers. I now have dies for over a dozen handgun cartridges. Some of them have half a dozen separate loads that I might use. Having loaded a special Nine-pin load in .45 or .38 Super, I want to make sure I don't get it mixed up with an IPSC load in that caliber.

Some of my .40 S&W ammo bins have additional notes. The rounds loaded short enough to fit my Glocks or EAA Witness pistols, are noted, and likewise the ones loaded long for the STI. The lead-bullet loads are clearly marked "No Glock!" and all my loads have an indication of the Power Factor to which they are loaded.

A very picky shooter (or one who is determined to produce the best ammo) might add more information such as the lot numbers of the powder, primer and bullets, the number of times that particular batch of brass has been loaded, and the loading date.

One kind of marker that you might not have to add is a color-code for use. When I lived near my two brothers, they could stop by and dip into my ammo stash when I wasn't around. (It was OK, I knew about it and they paid for the components.) To keep them from getting into trouble by using the wrong ammo, I used color tabs on the bins. The green labels indicated standard ammo, they

You can use a label maker, or write on masking tape, but you have to mark your production or your memory will fail you. Two calibers, two powders, four bullets, what is left out? The cases are random brand and number of times fired.

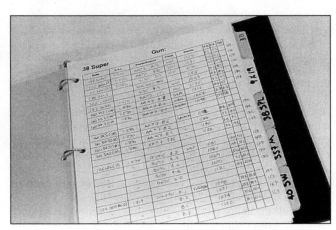

Write down what you load, how it performs and what 1911 you shot it in. Without notes, you'll have to re-invent your loads over and over again.

What powder was that again? Each bin should get a card listing the powder and its lot number. Work? Yes. But worth it when you want to duplicate a load.

You can't write down too much information, and you can't have too many reference manuals.

could use all they wanted. The blue labels were specialty ammo, and while it was safe they might not get the performance they expected. The orange labels were either my match ammo, or high-cost factory ammo or irreplaceable ammo, not to be opened until the apocalypse. Unless you are also feeding your relatives shooting habits, you needn't color-code your ammo. Unless you want to.

And all these are stored in plastic tubs with lids, to keep dust out. Some shooters like to use the ammo boxes with individual compartments for each round. I agree, for match ammo they are useful. For practice ammo I find them too fussy and inefficient. I long ago gave up on cardboard boxes and coffee cans. The cardboard doesn't stand up hard use, and coffee cans take up too much shelf space for the storage volume they offer.

The plastic bins are labeled using an adhesive label maker. I put the data I need to know on the bin. For ammunition that I load in high volume, like bowling pin or IPSC practice ammo, I make cards. Each card will have all the date, crimp diameter, performance specs and the like. With the card, I don't have to open my loading data books, I work off the card to load more ammo.

All of which leads to reloading/chronograph log books. You should keep a notebook that has all the standard settings for your loading, and the results of testing. It should include the measurements of the taper crimp diameter you are using, the bullet weight (actually, not just what the box says) accuracy and chronograph results, and which firearm was used to test with.

I also include such tidbits as the height of the dies above the die plate, so I can quickly re-set the dies in case I had to pull them out of a block to load another caliber.

The more specialized a firearm is, the more detailed the notes must be. This Modified international STI 2011 only sees one load, but that load is detailed down to the number of times its match brass has been fired.

The most common calibers, ones I reload regularly, stay in their blocks and are not removed. But the lower-volume cartridges have to take their turns through the other blocks, and it is easier to re-set the dies if I have the measurements noted.

Can you spend more time measuring and writing than loading? No, even though it may seem like it. But if something suddenly goes wrong with your reloads, you can't track down the change and correct it unless you have good notes.

CHAPTER TWELVE

.22 Conversions

The Colt Ace didn't show up until the 1911 was old enough to vote. (Photo courtesy Doug Turnbull)

A century ago, rimfire conversions of military rifles was a hot topic. Much energy was spent on conversion devices of the old Krag, and the new Springfield rifles, to allow soldiers to practice without needing the full-sized ranges that .30-caliber rifles required. Shooting clubs had indoor leagues in cities with .22 rimfire rifle matches. Every carnival and fair had shooting galleries, where for a few cents you could spend your time knocking over steel plates and ducks, and spinning weathervanes, trying to win a stuffed animal. John Browning had designed several rifles for Winchester to fill the market segment that gallery rifles and small game hunting required. He and Winchester made lots of money from those rifles. So you'd think it was natural that right away the newly-adopted 1911 would have a .22 conversion, right? Wrong.

Mechanically, the .22 long rifle has a big problem. It suffers from lack of horsepower. A standard velocity .22lr fires

a 40-grain bullet at around 1,000 fps. Less from a pistol, but at 1,000 fps the math is easy. It generates a Power Factor, which is a measurement of momentum, of 40. The standard .45 delivers a PF of around 185. The wimpiest 9mm load still delivers 115! So how is a .22 going to work the slide? By doing away with the locking lugs, and using the blow-back method. There are still problems with that approach, as the .22 still has half the PF of the .32 Auto, and has to push a slide of twice the weight of the Browning blowback pistols chambered in .32.

Colt didn't come out with a .22 conversion, or .22 model of the 1911 until 1931, with the introduction of the Ace. The Service Ace followed in 1935. Both were dropped with the start of war production for WWII. Some were assembled in 1947, no doubt from inventory left over from before the war. The pre-war Aces were made with slides milled thinner internally, and lighter than normal. They used a soft recoil

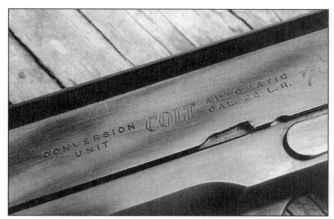

Later, Colt offered conversion uppers for existing 1911s.

When you take the Colt apart, the ejector drops off. Lose it, and your pistol is out of action.

The Colt conversion uses its own ejector, and the ejector is just a sheet metal stamping.

The Kimber conversion offers adjustable sights and pretty good accuracy on the Essex frame.

spring and a stack of leather washers to control slide travel. In 1935, Colt came out with a new .22 conversion called the Service Ace that worked differently. It used a floating chamber, like the floating piston of the M1 Carbine, (the 1911 variant obviously coming first) to give the slide enough oomph to cycle. The Service Ace, while still using a lightened slide, did not need the stack of leather washers, and more closely simulated the recoil of a standard .45. (That is, it came closer than the Ace but was still a wimpy thing to shoot.) The piston is prone to fouling with powder residue and lead shavings, and needs regular cleaning. They are also modestly accurate. While the conversions prior to 1948 were finished pistols, with serial numbers, the conversions afterwards were just that, conversion uppers without serial numbers. Colt made a new Ace pistol from 1978 to 1982, but by then they were making it for collectors and not users.

So, why did it take so long to make .22 caliber 1911s, and why were they not popular? Blame it on John Browning. You see, in 1915, Colt introduced the Woodsman. A .22 rimfire pistol, while it didn't look or work like the 1911, it was such a good .22 there was no need to make a less-satisfactory copy of it as a 1911 pistol. The Woodsman in one model or another, remained in the Colt line until 1977.

The idea of a .22 as a training pistol similar to the larger one has an appeal to many people. Even comparing new .22's (what else is there?) to reloaded .45's, the cost difference is readily apparent. Reloaded .45 ammo currently costs about $70 per 1,000 rounds, and you have to pull the handle

The floating piston/chamber of the Colt conversion kit.

of a reloading press to get the ammo. On the other hand, .22lr ammo can cost as little as $20 per thousand. It doesn't take a lot of shooting to pay for another pistol. Even less to pay for a conversion upper. But if the conversion upper isn't reliable or accurate (at least as reliable and as accurate at the original upper) there isn't much point to it.

Current conversions take two paths to solving the problem of the low power of the .22 cartridge. The Ciener, Wilson, Kimber and EAA conversions create a lighter slide by making the slide out of aluminum. The Marvel conversion uses an upper assembly shaped like the 1911, but has a fixed barrel and an aluminum breechblock that cycles underneath the barrel and its rear sight extension. Which method is better? That depends. The EAA, Wilson, Kimber and Ciener conversions are easier to install, and slide right from one pistol to another. To do so, they give up some accuracy, although they are more accurate than some .45's they might be installed on. The Marvel is accurate enough to be used as a target pistol, but has to be secured to a frame, and is best used on a frame dedicated to be just a .22.

The Kimber is neat. The slide is aluminum, as mentioned, and features a Kimber adjustable rear sight. The sight looks like a Bo-mar. The front is a Novak-style transverse dovetail, and is probably the Novak dimension. The barrel has its attachment block welded to the cylindrical barrel (no locking lugs) and the ejector is attached to the

barrel by staking it on. The Kimber does not (none of the conversions do) use the ejector on the frame. The magazines are machined from aluminum bar stock, with a removable baseplate for cleaning. The Kimber is available blued or white anodized, with adjustable sights. It fits Government model frames. One nice touch on the Kimber is that the magazines have a machined relief notch cut into the rear of the left-hand feed rail. The notch provides clearance for an extended ejector. There are cocking serrations front and rear. It is marked on the left side with the Kimber logo, and on the right with ".22LR Conversion". It comes in a plastic storage box with a magazine.

The Wilson follows the same pattern, is blued and has fixed sights. The front sight is an integral part of the slide, while the rear is the Wilson low-mount combat sight. In between the sights the slide is grooved, and it is an attractive feature. As with the Kimber, it has cocking serrations at the front and rear. Also as with the Kimber, it features a highly-polished anodized surface. The Wilson is marked on the left side with "Wilson Combat" in script, and on the right with ".22LR Conversion Unit". It comes in a plastic storage box with a magazine, and the magazine has a rubber bumper pad on it. The magazine has an ejector clearance notch like that of the Kimber. The Wilson is available as a Government Model unit and a Commander/Officer's

The Ciener conversion, with fixed sights and external extractor.

From the left side, the Ciener looks like any other 1911.

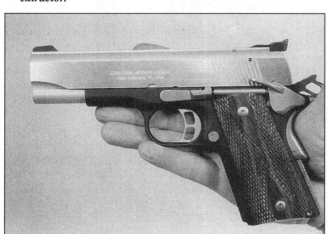

The Ciener Platinum Officer's/Commander on the Kimber Ultra CDP frame.

Once you find the ammo a .22 conversion likes, you get good accuracy and reliability.

While the conversions fit on the frame, you have to make sure the ejector clears the slide. The aluminum slide is so light, any binding will cause malfunctions.

Combine the conversion kit with an alloy frame, and you end up with a wispy-weight gun. The Ciener/Kimber combo only weighs 20.4 ounces.

Model unit. It also, unlike the other aluminum slide conversions, comes with an instruction sheet.

The EAA differs from the rest of the aluminum-slide conversions in several respects. The sights are not as large as the others, and use the EAA lo-mount adjustable rear. The front sight is an integral part of the slide, and shorter than the other units' front sights. However, several of the testers liked the EAA sights, which only goes to show that my tastes do not rule. The finish is not as highly-polished as the others, and would best be described as matte. It has

cocking serrations front and rear. The ejector on the EAA is a knob sticking up on the left-hand sidewall of the moulded plastic magazine. As a result, the EAA cannot use the magazines of the other conversions. The left side of the

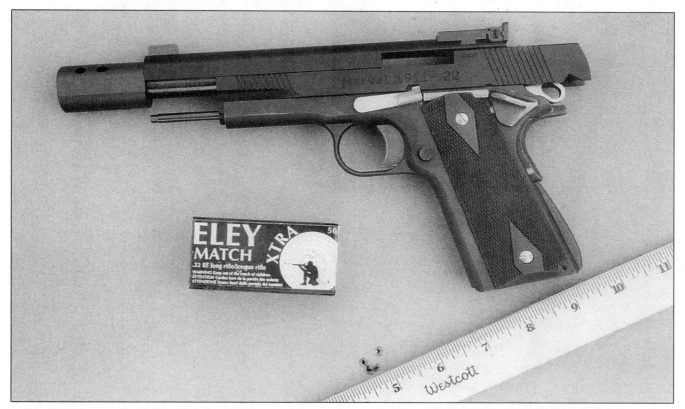

The Marvel conversion delivered stellar accuracy, and was much more forgiving of different ammo brands than the others.

EAA has "Warning: There is no automatic firing pin safety" and "EAA Cocoa, FL". The right side of the slide is marked "1911-22lr" and "FT-Made in Italy". The storage box (different than the others) contains the slide assembly, a magazine, spare recoil springs of two different weights and an owners manual/card.

The Ciener conversions offer a host of options. You can have your conversion in a couple of lengths, two colors, fixed or adjustable sights, and self-loading magazines. (Oops, that last part was only a wish on my part. .22's burn so much ammo you wish you could just toss the empty magazine into a bin of ammo and let it load itself.)

The Ciener comes in two lengths, Government and Commander/Officers. The colors are black and silver anodized. The sights are either fixed or the "Platinum Cup" which uses the Millett adjustable rear sight. The magazines are the new-pattern milled from aluminum bar stock design, rather than the old Colt conversion type. The ejector is staked to the barrel. The left side is marked "Jonathan Arthur Ciener Cape Canaveral FL". The right side is marked according to the model and length. The magazine is an aluminum assembly machined out of bar stock, with old magazines lacking the ejector clearance notch. Current production magazines have the notch. The Ciener units come in a plastic storage box with a magazine and parts list. Some of the units sent for testing had test-fire targets enclosed, others did not. The targets provided were impressive, usually with groups an inch or smaller.

To use any of the above conversions is simple. Remove the slide stop from your pistol and remove the slide assembly. You should store the slide in your range bag or at home, as you will only need the frame and slide stop. Wipe any powder residue off the frame and apply a drop of light oil on each rail. Slide the conversion kit onto the frame and press it back. Hold the slide and barrel in place and insert the slide stop as you normally would. The first time you go to install the conversion, leave the slide off and check the fit of the magazine. If the left-hand magazine feed lip stops against the bottom of the extended ejector, you may have to use a file to relieve the inside bottom corner of the ejector for clearance.

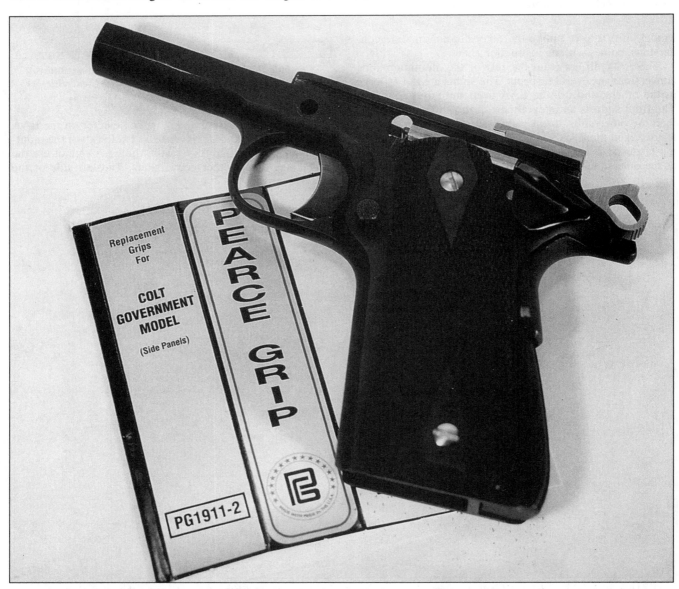

The Essex frame went together easily, and feels very comfortable with the Pearce grips in place.

Once the conversion is locked in place, load and shoot. None of the conversion kits lock the slide open when empty, something the Colt tried to do but often failed. The problem is that the slide stop needs as much lift as a .45 round offers (the width of the round, raising the magazine follower after the last shot) and the .22 simply isn't large enough. Count your shots, and stop when you're out.

The aluminum-slide conversions work only with high-velocity rimfire, and only the heavy-bullet high-velocity loads. If you use standard target velocity rimfire your conversion won't work. If you use the light-bullet hypervelocity loads, your conversion will be cranky. You are limited to standard weight high-velocity loads, but that is a small price to pay for low-cost shooting.

The magazines for the conversions feature thick-walled aluminum construction. the magazine well in the frame is proportioned for a .45 magazine. To fill the gap the .22 magazine has to be as wide, but the interior slot has to be .22lr proportion. You'll notice a notch in the feed lips of the magazines. That is the rim clearance. To load, place the rim of the cartridge in the notch, then press down and back. Repeat until you have filled the magazine, 10 rounds total. Be sure the top round is fully to the rear of the magazine, or it will not feed properly. The barrel has a small ramp on the bottom, to fill the gap between magazine and chamber. If the top round is forward, it may catch on the ramp.

The Marvel is something completely different. The first thing you notice is the weight. It is much heavier than the other units, but its reciprocating mass is lighter, simply by being smaller in size. The Marvel uses Colt conversion magazines that have the slide hold-open shelf on the follower removed. The breechblock is separate from the barrel and sights extension. Assembling the Marvel conversion is easy. Starting with the frame, slide the Marvel on and then insert the slide stop as usual. The Marvel offers greater accuracy than the others. The guide rod of the recoil spring guide rod is also set screw. Once the conversion is on, you can use the rod to tighten the fit between the barrel and slide stop pin, until there is no excess play.

The barrel, clamped firmly to the slide stop pin, is fixed in place, while the breechblock moves back and forth. Accurate and reliable in operation.

The upper half of the "slide" has an adjustable rear sight that looks remarkably like a Kimber. The front blade is a Clark dovetail front, where the dovetail runs in the same direction as the axis of the barrel, unlike the Novak which runs transversely. On top of the sight/barrel assembly are a pair of plug screws that fill the holes left when you aren't using the scope mount.

The barrel is quite massive, much larger in diameter than the other conversions, since the slide doesn't have to reciprocate while wrapped around the barrel. The ejector is secured to the barrel. On the muzzle end is a muzzle brake. The idea is not to tame the fierce recoil of the rimfire cartridge, but to strip the muzzle gases off as quickly as possible, reducing their opportunity to jostle the bullet and degrade accuracy. And does it work? I have not been able to test it enough to determine that, mostly because it is so accurate. More on that in a bit.

The Marvel uses Colt magazines. The Colt approach was to bend the sheetmetal of the magazine inwards to create an interior space appropriate for a .22, while keeping the exterior sized to fit the magazine well. One thing that always held back acceptance of .22 conversions was magazine cost. The Colt .22 magazines were always two to three times the cost of .45 magazines, and much more than surplus mags used to cost. The Colt mags are still almost twice the cost of the aluminum magazines, and there is no interchangeability. You can use the Ciener, Wilson and Kimber mags interchangeably, but the EAA must use its own, and the Marvel uses Colts with the slide stop shelf filed off.

Essex Arms

When I began this project, it became quickly apparent that I couldn't try all the conversions on all the pistols, at least not before the manuscript deadline, and not within any reasonable ammunition budget. I had to settle on a single frame to use as the test frame. But which one? In talking with manufacturers, I came across an old maker that I hadn't heard of for a few years. Essex has been making frames and slides for a number of years, and have recently converted to CNC machinery, increasing production and tightening tolerances. When they heard of this book, they eagerly sent me a frame as a test bed to put the conversions onto, and I assembled it as a basic pistol. The Essex took the reverse route of most makers of 1911s, starting out as a .22lr conversion, then later being built up as a .45.

The Ciener Platinum cup on the Essex frame.

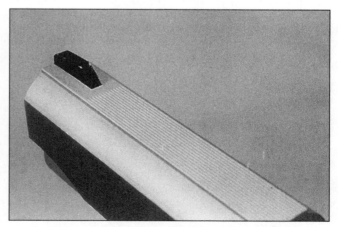

The Ciener and others with fixed front sights (machined out of the bar stock slide) would be difficult to change.

The frame Essex sent me was a blued standard Government Model. I dove into the parts bins and quickly had the frame assembled as a working pistol. Unlike some other frames I've worked on in the past, all the parts I assembled dropped right in and worked without my having to spend a lot of time filing and stoning. Once I had put the basic parts on it, I felt the need to improve the trigger pull and feel. I swapped the standard hammer and sear for a McCormick set, and put Pearce grips on it. Except for the finish being a little thin, and rubbing off from the abuse of being tossed into the range bag with all the other gear, the Essex has performed yeoman service, with the .22 conversion, a test afternoon with the Clark .460 Rowland conversion, and several top ends of .45 ACP.

Having a dedicated frame for testing all the units did not prevent me from trying a few combinations that showed some promise, like the Officer's conversions on an Officers frame or even the Kimber Ultra CDP frame.

With the Essex assembled I was ready to test-fire conversion units. The first problem I ran into was my lack of suitable ammo. The .22lr shelf contained mostly match accuracy ammo, which is all standard velocity. The Marvel conversion unit worked with them all, due to its lighter breechblock. The choices I had on hand were several types of Eley, Federal Gold Match, CCI Green Tag and some Remington Target. Of these, the Marvel worked spectacularly with the Eley Tenex and the Federal Gold Match. I could easily get 25 yard groups of an inch in size. Not as good as the test-fire target sent with the Marvel, but I'm sure with some lot-testing of ammunition and tweaking of the guide rod tightener I could improve on the 1-inch average. (I left the rod a little loose simply to ensure reliable function with all brands.) In the time available, it seemed that the muzzle brake improved accuracy, but I wasn't able to give it the thorough testing needed. The only way to find out would be to find at least three loads that the unit shot accurately and consistently. Then, test at least five, and better yet 10, five-shot groups both with and without the unit. Then it is a matter of statistics. My impression is that it is good for a few fractions of an inch improvement at 25 yards. Before you laugh, many shooters have worked very hard through the years for improvements no better, because in some competitions a point or two can make all the difference.

The aluminum-slide conversions didn't work at all with the standard velocity ammo. One peculiarity of .22lr firearms is that they can be quite sensitive to ammunition. Changing brands can have an effect on reliability and accuracy. I went out to the nearest "big-box" sporting goods store and bought some Remington High Velocity, and some

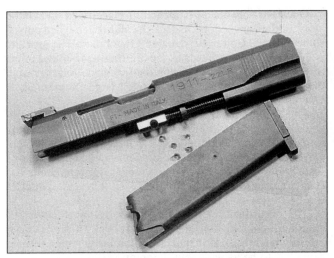

The EAA conversion and its plastic magazine.

Winchester "Expert" 36-grain hollow points. Using one or the other, I was able to get reliable function and good accuracy out of all of the units. Sometimes, the full-size conversion units didn't want to cycle with the 36-grain bullets, but they always worked with the Remington. The shorter units worked with the 36-grain hollow points, due to the lighter mass of the shorter slide.

The conclusion I came to was that for plinking and training, and used with the intention of getting used to the particular pistol, the standard conversion units are great. If you want to introduce someone to shooting, keep the cost and recoil down, and get them used to your 1911, then the Wilson, Kimber, EAA or Ciener units work great. Our club is building a falling plate rack designed for rimfire, and I think that I may have to hang on to one of these just to work the plates over.

If, on the other hand, you are going to try a more demanding shooting course, like Bull's eye or metallic silhouette, then the Marvel is what you want. With a speed hammer and match sear, and some tuning by a gunsmith, you can get your 1911 frame down to a 2-pound trigger pull. Coupled with the accuracy of the Marvel, you can stand shoulder-to-shoulder with dedicated .22 pistols and not have to give up any accuracy. The Marvel will not provide training that crosses over to a standard 1911 (the breechblock under the sight rail precludes most malfunction drills) but you will be able to shoot accurately.

Which one would I pick? In my usual response to such decisions, I'd take both, using one for training, and the other for competition.

CHAPTER THIRTEEN

Buying A Used 1911

Your search for an economical semi-custom 1911 need not go any farther than a factory pistol like this Entreprise Titleist 500.

There is no great trick to buying a new 1911. You can get either a factory pistol or a custom gun made to order by a gunsmith. You decide how much you're willing to spend, and then find the pistol that has the most features for the least money under the limit you've set.

But, sooner or later, you'll be tempted to buying a used pistol. Either a stock-looking one, or a custom one that has something you want on it. You must be careful.

But first, let me tell you about "The Ugly Gun." Over a decade ago, as the President of my gun club, it fell to me to organize and run the club's match for the State League Series. Things went well and the shooters had fun, and at the end of the match when the shooters had gone home one of the cleanup crew came to me with a pistol case. "Someone left this behind." "Who's is it?" I asked. "Don't know, and don't

want to know." He said as he hurriedly shoved the pistol case into my hands. Puzzled by this answer, I opened the case, and caught my breath. It was the ugliest pistol I had ever seen. While it had left the Colt factory as a blued pistol, now no two parts had the same finish. It had blued steel, nickel, stainless, hard chromed, painted, plastic and brazed parts, and some were rusty. The rear sight dovetail slot looked as if it had been hand-filed instead of milled. The rear sight was an old Micro rear, and stood a good half-inch above the slide. The front and rear sights had hammer marks on them, and marks on the slide around them from near misses. The front sight was as tall as the rear sight, and had clamp marks on it from where it had been straightened in a vise after installation. The ejection port had the side rail lowered with a hand-held grinder. The thumb safety had been enlarged by copper brazing a piece onto the original safety plate. The hammer spur had been slightly shortened by means of a bench grinder. Later, when I took it apart for cleaning, I found that the plastic magazine funnel had cracked, and was held on by superglue.

The grips were cracked, and held in place with duct tape. But the crowning glory, was the magazine release. As an impromptu extended button, someone had drilled a hole in the standard button and forced a flat-headed sheet metal screw into it.

While I didn't want it in my gun safe for fear it might infect my pistols, I was also intrigued. Someone had shot the match with this? I took it home, since the match was over and everyone had left. At my next practice session, I brought the ugly gun along and tried it with my regular ammo. It hit to the sights, and an offhand group at 25 yards was smaller than the "A" zone. As to its reliability, it fed flawlessly. In the next few weeks, I took it with me on each range trip, and used it to clean out my reloading mistakes box. You know, the stuff that is not dangerous to shoot, but the small mistakes you make when changing bullet weights or shapes. The ugly gun ate everything a pistol could be expected to eat. It worked 100 percent, and it kept everything in the A zone. When I got the phone call a couple of weeks after the match, I was relieved. I would not be faced with either accepting or rehabilitating this pistol. "Mr. Sweeney, I think I might have left my pistol at your range." "Describe it." "Well, it has this sheet metal screw..." "It's yours. Where do I send it?"

The point of all this is that while we all want a pistol to be cosmetically attractive, the real test is its performance. If you are careful in your selection, you can find a diamond in the rough, and spend a little time and or money cleaning it up. Or not. After all, if it looks ugly, but shoots straight, will your scores suffer? I only wish I had taken photos of The Ugly Gun, as mere descriptions hardly convey its looks.

Some might ask why does the 1911 require so much background when buying a used pistol? Wouldn't you be better off buying something that doesn't require such a close look? The answer to that is simple: I'd be looking just as closely, but at different things, were I to be buying a Glock, Sig, or Smith & Wesson. In buying used, you aren't suspicious of the pistol so much as you are suspicious of the previous owner.

Buying Your Used 1911

The first checks to make when inspecting a used 1911 are safety checks. The second checks you make are for potential repairs. When you go to handle a prospective 1911 purchase, ask the present owner if you can dry-fire it. Some people do not cotton to the idea of dry-firing, and even though it is perfectly safe in the 1911, it is after all their pistol for now. If they don't want you dry-firing their pistol, you will have to go through a bit more gymnastics to check it out.

First, make sure it isn't loaded. Yes, we all know they shouldn't be, but you have to be sure. There are times when it is normal and accepted that a pistol be loaded. What you have to do is make sure you know a particular pistol's state. Experienced practical shooters will always check a firearm each time they pick it up, even after they have seen other shooters check it moments earlier. One example was enough for Felicia. She had gone with me to Second Chance, and

was amazed at the ritual level of checking. "Eight guys sitting around a campfire, the last one has seen the other seven check to see it isn't loaded, and still he checks?" You bet, which is why we've never had an accident.

In another example, I regularly met with three other shooters from my club for camaraderie, Italian food and gunsmithing and/or reloading research. We were at Glenn Hibbert's house, in his work shop, when the question came up about some aspect of the firing grip. We all were avid competitors and carried pistols regularly, but for some reason none of us had a 1911 on us at the time. Nor was there a 1911 on the bench or in any of our gun bags. (A very curious state I have worked hard to avoid ever since, I might add.) Glenn went upstairs to get his house gun, and handed it to me. I checked it, and was not at all surprised to find it loaded. After all, he had just said it was his house gun.

I demonstrated the points I was illuminating, (keeping it pointed towards the concrete wall) and then put it down on the bench, pointing towards another wall. Glenn picked it up and checked it (he checked it, even though: He brought it down and knew it was loaded, and had just seen me check it, and I had not unloaded it) and he demonstrated his thoughts, and put it back down on the bench. Our third of the group, Paul, picked it up, checked it, hesitated for a moment, and then went about contributing to the discussion. Again, he used the concrete wall as an aiming point, made sure not to point it at any of us while picking it up, aiming it, or putting

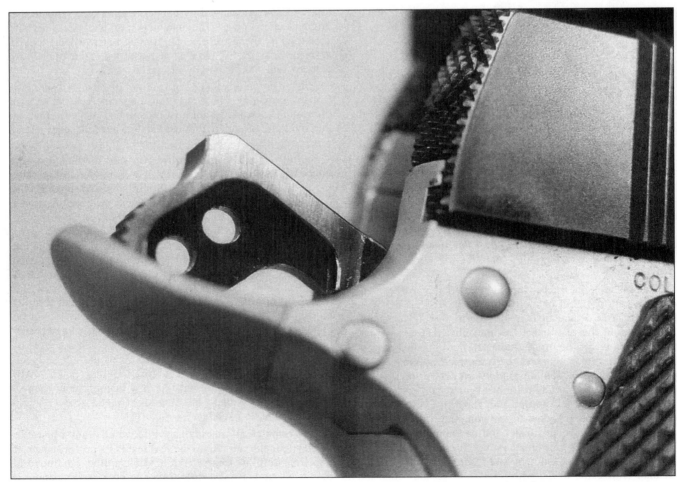

Some shooters think you can hurt a 1911 by dry-firing it. (No) Ask before you dry-fire someone else's firearm.

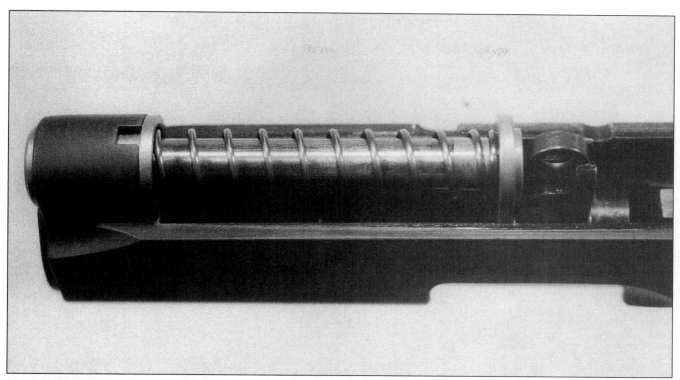

To check slide fit, you have to remove the slide. To remove the barrel, you may have to know a few more tricks. Save yourself some embarrassment, and ask before you go taking it apart.

it down. The fourth shooter picked up the 1911, and I guess when he barely swept my big toe (and nothing else) I must have momentarily grimaced. He froze. Pointing it at the wall, he checked. "It's loaded!" was his observation. Glenn said "It has been ever since I brought it down."

Now, before you assume that what I'm pointing out is that you can safely pass a loaded handgun around (You can, but that isn't the point I want to make) I want to point out that with the correct safety habits you can spend the rest of your life around firearms and never have a problem. Always check, never take someone's word for it, and never assume.

Three Origins

When checking a 1911 over for possible purchase, it comes from one of three categories. First, in the box new, from a dealer or fellow shooter. A fellow shooter selling a new pistol, what's up with that? Simple. At large competitions the prizes are often guns. After you've won a few, why not sell them? Brian Enos is a great guy, and was one of the most successful shooters of the 1980s and early 1990s. He spent much of the 1990s as an IPSC gypsy traveling the country shooting in area, regional and state championships. I had been running into him at shoots for almost 15 years when I saw him at a big match someplace in 1997 or so. (After a while, they all start to blur together.) He had a table in the exhibitors' tent, piled with firearms for sale. The rumor going around was that he was getting out of shooting, and selling all his stuff. I walked over to the table and looked at a brand-new Springfield Armory 1911 with a three-digit serial number. (The serial number sequence at Springfield had already passed a quarter million by then.) "Brian what's up?" I asked.

"Selling some spare stuff." He replied.

"Brian, I hear you're quitting, is that true?"

With almost an embarrassed grin, Brian looked at me and said "No, I have to sell something, I can't get the door to my spare bedroom closed."

It took me a moment to do the math. Over 15 years of national, area, regional and state championships, an average of more than a match every other week for 15 years, matches in which Brian was almost always in the loot. Rough figure, 500 to 600 firearms he could have won in that time period. Of course he had to sell stuff, who needs a couple dozen box-stock .45's? Did I buy any? No, I had my own closet stuffed with loot from matches.

The second category would be new guns straight from the gunsmith. Why would a gunsmith be selling a finished pistol? Usually because the customer who ordered it has bailed on the deal. In the time it takes to finish a full-house gun, many

Checking the thumb safety function. Yes, it works.

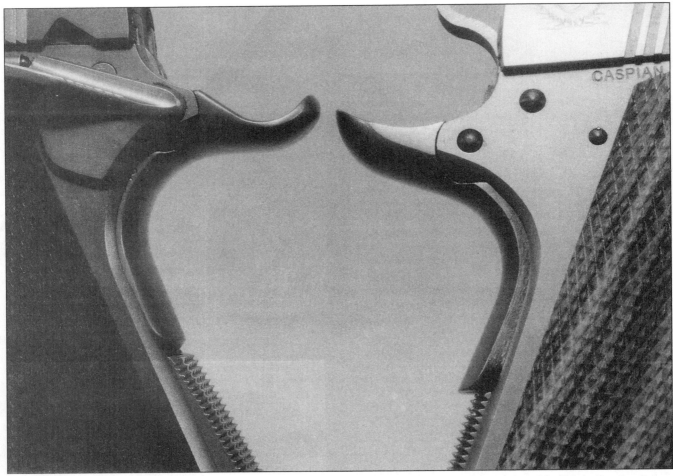

On the left, an old competition gun. The grip safety is pinned. Don't buy it unless the pin can be removed and the grip safety then works properly

things can change. Deaths, births, divorces or a burning desire to buy a convertible and move to Malibu all come to mind. The gunsmith, with a finished pistol, wants his or her money. He or she will gladly sell it to an interested shooter.

The third category is a used pistol, either from a dealer or a fellow shooter. While you have a little more of a safety net buying from the dealer, you still have to be careful with any pistol in the third category. A new pistol can be sent back to the factory if you find something wrong. The custom one can go back to the gunsmith for corrective action. The used one? The Latin phrase 'Caveat Emptor' applies in full. Buyer beware. Check it out thoroughly before you buy.

Small quirks or things that you don't like about a pistol in the first or second categories can be dealt with as part of the purchase. The dealer can have his gunsmith correct things, or send it back to the manufacturer for some warranty work. The custom gunsmith who made the pistol, he or she can certainly make changes for you. On a pistol in the third category, changes or corrections will almost certainly come out of your own pocket. Bargain hard so you'll have money left over in the budget to make those corrections. Some faults will be too expensive to warrant buying a pistol. Lets start the inspection.

Slide Function

With the checked-for-unloaded 1911 in hand and no magazine in it, work the slide slowly. Does it move smoothly back and forth? If the slide stays back at full stroke, it may be hanging up on the disconnector (possible with a very light recoil spring, and a light spring is a definite cause for inquiry), the slide may be wedging itself against the front of the rails, or you may have problems going on with the three-leaf spring binding the disconnector. Going forward, the slide may hesitate or have "hard" spots in its movement if the barrel is tightly fitted. The drag on the barrel from the slide may be slightly wedging the two, not a

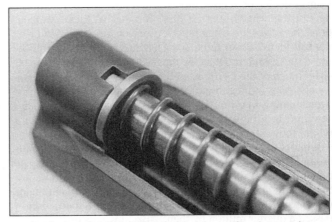

Replacing the Colt Officer's Model recoil spring retainer with a heavy-duty one is a sign of a serious pistolero. Doing it well is the sign of a good gunsmith.

You'd think this was an obvious problem, but the owner had no idea. When checking the chamber and ramp, look at other things, too.

The front lugs on this barrel are peened. A combination of soft barrel and improper fitting caused its demise.

cause for alarm. The bottom lug may bump as the barrel cams up, a sign that the bottom lug has not been properly contoured. All these are minor problems that any competent 1911 gunsmith can easily clean up.

If, however, the slide moves back and forth like it is running on ball bearings, and you can't feel any movement in the slide and barrel when closed, you're seeing the hallmarks of a well-fitted pistol.

What about the traditional "barrel test?" You know, pushing the barrel through the ejection port when the slide is closed? Go ahead, but it doesn't tell you much. The barrel may move and spring back. The barrel may move and not spring back. The barrel may not move. None of these three conditions tells you how the gun shoots. Do the check, because it is expected, but don't expect revelations because of it.

Safety Function

With the hammer cocked, push the safety on. Does it click into place? Push it down. Is it easier to put on or off? Or the same? Does it positively click in both directions? A properly-fitted safety will be positive in movement, and click into place. One not properly fitted is a red flag for the test that follows. Leave the safety off and dry-fire it. How does the trigger pull feel? Light, heavy, crisp, spongy? If the trigger pull feels good, you're ahead of the game.

Cock the hammer again and push the safety on. Pull the trigger. You don't have to lean into it, or use both hands. About 10 pounds of pressure is enough. Let go of the trigger and push the safety off. The hammer stayed back? Good. If it had fallen, it would mean that the thumb safety was not blocking the sear's movement, and is dangerous. In such a pistol you would be facing at least the cost of a new thumb safety and its fitting once you had bought it. Now dry-fire it. Does the trigger pull feel the same as it did before? While the hammer may have stayed cocked, the sear could have moved during your test. I once handled a National Guard property 1911A1 that had been worked on by a Guard Armorer. Whoever this person was had carefully fitted the safety so the sear partially moved during such a test. Once "set" (using the thumb safety as part of a set-trigger mechanism is dangerous, do not do this) the trigger pull was much lighter than the required regulations stipulated. As a means of gaining a few points in the slow-fire part of qualification it was dangerous and cheating.

The verification of a moving sear is an audible test. Cock the 1911, push the safety on and pull the trigger. Release the trigger and push the safety off. Bring the pistol up near your ear, and slowly thumb the hammer back with your other hand. If you hear a little "tink", what you heard is the sear tip snapping back into full engagement with the hammer hooks as the leaf spring pressure is relieved. Your safety is only partially effective.

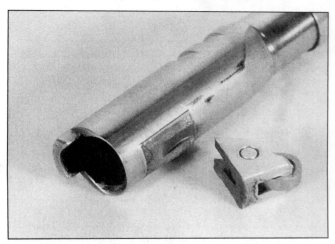

Yes, the owner knew something was up. First, accuracy went away. Then, it stopped working.

If you see something like this, immediately check the slide lugs for damage. Replacing barrels is moderately expensive, but replacing the slide is a third of the cost of the gun, or more.

If the pistol you are inspecting has a thumb safety that allows the sear to move, but not fall, the safety can be re-fitted to do its job properly and you will not have to buy another safety. Unless you want to.

The next safety check is the grip safety. Back in the old days (you know, when we used stone axes as a back-up to our 1911's) it was popular to pin down or otherwise deactivate the grip safety. The thinking went, Browning didn't put it on his original design, and it was only the fussy Cavalry who insisted on a grip safety. The follow-up design of the P-35, the Browning Hi-Power, didn't have one either. And some shooters with large but skinny hands using a high hold can't always be sure the grip safety will be pushed in far enough. Who needs one? We do. They leave the factory with one that works, and in this modern litigious society, removing a safety device is close to yelling "Fire" in a crowded theater.

If you run into an old competition pistol, you may find the grip safety doesn't work at all. If so, use the lack of function as a bargaining lever to bring the price down. And then get it fixed as soon as you have bought it. Many modern designs of grip safeties (the McCormick and Kimber designs come to mind) use a raised platform or swelling to make sure your hand presses the grip safety down.

To check, cock the pistol and leave the thumb safety off. Hold it so you do not depress the grip safety. Pull the trigger. From this point on, the checking you do is identical to the testing you did with the thumb safety, except you are testing the grip safety. Press the grip safety down and pull the trigger. Cock again, test again, and listen for the tink.

OK, you have a pistol that moves smoothly and all the safety devices work. What next? You have to field strip it. Ask the owner if you can take it apart.

You want to check the rails and the slide-to-rail fit. You want to check the condition of the feed ramp and the barrel-to-feed ramp fit. You want to inspect the barrel ramp and chamber. You want to inspect the locking lugs on top of the barrel and the seating lugs underneath. You want to inspect the locking lugs in the slide. And you want to inspect for cracks in the frame or slide.

Slide Fit

With the pistol disassembled, take a quick look at the frame rails. Do you see hammer marks, or peened sections fore and aft? If so, someone has worked hard to fit that slide

My lightweight Commander is cracked in the same spot, but it is easier to show a crack in a hard-chromed frame. Such a crack is no big deal, and the frame will last many thousands of rounds while cracked.

or another to the frame. Install the slide on the frame. Does the slide move back and forth smoothly? A binding slide is not good. It will have to be fitted or lapped to move smoothly. However, if the slide is so loose on the frame that it rattles around, you will have limited options for later custom work. Before a gunsmith will do more than basic work, he will insist on tightening such a loose fit. If you aren't looking for later custom work, then a loose fit is no problem.

Feed Ramp And Barrel Fit

For some reason, there are shooters who cannot leave a feed ramp alone. Regardless of how well a 1911 works, they have to have that ramp gleaming like a new dime. To start with, proper feeding depends on the ramp being at the correct angle, and the correct location between the magazine and chamber. A properly dimensioned ramp will feed even if it looks like it was carved with a chain saw. An improperly polished ramp turns a smooth-feeding pistol into an occasionally-feeding pistol. The top of the ramp must not be rounded over. There must be a small gap (1/32 of an inch) between the top of the frame ramp and the bottom of the barrel ramp. If they have been polished into a smooth line,

If you end up replacing parts with a Novak rear, custom hammer, and beavertail safety, your "bargain" 1911 may not be such a bargain.

you have a probably poorly-feeding pistol and an expensive repair. How expensive? The frame will have to be welded up, re-cut and polished. You might get lucky and not have to replace the barrel.

Barrel Ramp And Chamber

Along with over-polishing of the frame ramp, some shooters cannot leave the barrel alone. Look closely at the juncture between the barrel ramp and the chamber wall. Has the edge been rounded? Has it been rounded enough to turn the edge into just another curved surface? In the process of fitting a barrel and making it feed, a good gunsmith will break the edge enough to make the cartridges trip a smooth one. If the edge is rounded too much, the chamber cannot support the case on firing. An overly-rounded ramp, with hot loads, can lead to bulging brass. The bulged brass will cause feeding problems sooner or later, and may end up blowing out. The good news is that an overly-polished barrel can be fixed by replacing it, which is cheaper than fixing a overly-polished frame ramp.

Barrel Lugs And Link

The barrel lugs, top and bottom, work hard for a living. The bottom lug snaps back and forth over the slide stop pin, and gets slammed to a stop by the frame, slide stop pin or link. Look at the bottom lugs to see if it has been poorly fitted. Do you see file marks? Are the lugs peened? A poor fit job will reduce even a match barrel to mediocre accuracy. Peening is a sign that either the barrel is a low-quality and soft one, or a previous owner has fired hot loads in it. On the side of the lug you may see a stake mark from a center punch. This is a common method of keeping the link pin in its hole. One is fine, but if you see more, you have to wonder about the skill of the assembler.

The top lugs lock the barrel to the slide. Are the front corners clean and sharp? They must be. Tops lugs that are rounded, have their edges worn, or have been set back are a bad sign. A very bad sign. They indicate that the barrel is soft, poorly fitted, has been subjected to hot loads, or is in a slide with bad lugs. It could be some of each of the above. Repair is expensive. If the damaged barrel has not caused damage to the slide, then you'll need only a new barrel. One that is properly fitted. If the barrel has damaged the slide, or the slide has caused the barrel damage, you'll have to replace both. Buy such a 1911 only if you can get it for its value as an assembled frame. (And make sure the rails are good.)

Slide Lugs

Flip the slide over and look closely at the locking lugs. You need to see if the rear corners are sharp and clean. As with the top lugs of the barrel, rounded corners or set back lugs are bad news. A damaged slide will eat up and spit out any good barrel you put in it, so don't waste your money buying barrels for it. You can repair such a damaged slide only by replacing it, an expensive proposition. If you can get the gun at a low enough cost, it may be worth it. Otherwise, pass it up. One origin of soft slides that eat barrels is WWII production. With the war on, production meant more than durability decades later. Many manufacturers made slides that were good enough then, but which are too soft now. My first 1911A1 was an Ithaca-produced pistol that had a soft slide. Once the slide lugs went, and it had eaten the second barrel, I replaced the slide with a Caspian

and the barrel with a Bar-sto. No problems since. I did it because I already had the pistol, and replacing the parts was cheaper than buying a new pistol. However, if you are in the position of buying, it may not be cost-effective to buy one and immediately replace the slide and barrel. Be sure to inspect the lugs!

Crack Inspection

There are cracks that count, cracks that might count, and cracks that don't count. The cracks that don't count are the ones you see on the rear of the dust cover and the slide stop hole. The dust cover keeps the recoil spring in place. It is a long thin shell, and sometimes the rear of it cracks. My Lightweight Commander came to me used, and already cracked at the dust cover. Since then it has gone through Gunsite four times, has seen 5,000 rounds of various hard-ball and factory hollow points, daily carry for a decade, one auto accident and the crack has not gotten any larger.

The crack on the slide stop hole is so common that Colt decided to simply do away with that little web of steel, just to cut down on the complaints from customers. Both those cracks you leave alone. The much rarer cracks that might count are ones you see from a dropped pistol. Usually found at the rear corners of the magazine opening, they don't cause a problem unless the steel is bent enough to bind something. You repair those cracks by welding. I have not seen frames cracked elsewhere, but I'm sure it has happened. Anything on the frame can be welded and repaired if you want to.

The cracks that count are on the slide. A crack on a slide means immediate retirement. A cracked slide is a sign of too-hot loads, too-light a recoil spring or machine cuts made in the slide to make it lighter. With any of these you must retire the slide. You cannot repair a cracked slide by welding. Slides must be within a certain hardness range to work properly, and welding will change the hardness of the steel. If you see a crack, pass on it or offer the value of the assembled frame for the pistol.

What about the finish, the grips, the sights? Any finish can be stripped off and replaced. If you are going to do some work on the pistol, consider the cost of taking the old off and putting new on. Buying a hard-chromed pistol that has a standard grip safety and getting an Ed Brown grip safety installed can add $300 to $350 to the cost of the pistol, from stripping the old finish, fitting and re-plating. However, the same pistol in blue is no big deal. An epoxy finish can be touched-up in the altered area, without having to remove all the old finish.

It can be expensive to machine a slide for new sights, so consider the cost of new sights before buying a used pistol. You may get such a deal that the cost of machining for Novaks or a Bo-mar is not a problem. If you simply must have the new sights, consider them as part of the purchase price, and re-think the deal.

Ditto any extra parts that are "must-have" parts. If you'll be replacing the trigger with a McCormick, the sights with Novaks, the grip safety with a Wilson or Ed Brown, and the barrel with a Bar-sto, then your "bargain" pistol might end up not being such a bargain. Unless of course, you simply view the pistol as a platform for building on, and the extra costs would have been there anyway. (Curious how we can rationalize a new/used pistol, isn't it?)

CHAPTER FOURTEEN

Malfunction Clearance and Correction

When it comes to working properly, no firearm has the kind of schizophrenic reputation as the 1911. On the one hand, it is the pistol that works all the time, regardless of the conditions, weather or climate. Slopped with mud, caked with dust, underwater or on a mountaintop, the 1911 keeps working. Except that it is also the only handgun that has an entire industry built around taking this unreliable pistol and making it reliable. Ask any target shooter or revolver shooter, and they'll tell you that the 1911 is a jam waiting to happen, and unless you treat it with kid gloves and keep it scrupulously clean, it will jam on you.

How can this be? Two reasons, historical production and diverging uses. First, let's look at the 1911 compared to the Glock. The Glock, any model, has been produced only since 1984, and it has been produced in a single plant under the supervision of its designer and company owner, Gaston Glock. Designed and manufactured using modern methods, the idea that any part would vary from its specified dimension is ridiculous. The 1911? Starting in 1911, it has been produced through two world wars, on four continents, and in a dizzying number of variations. There are currently over three dozen manufacturers or importers in

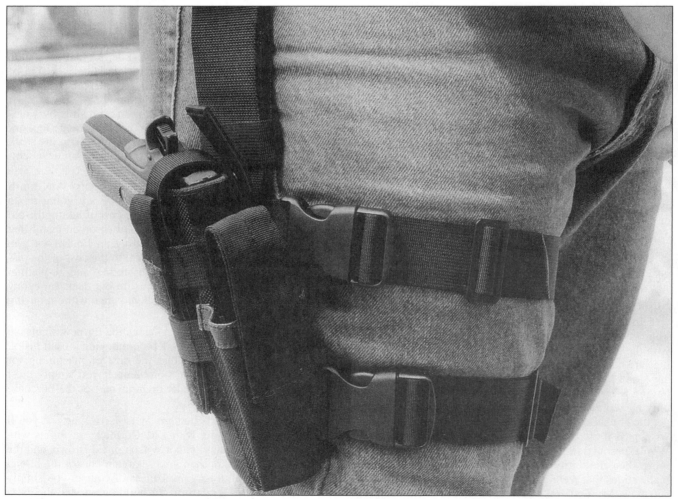

The interest in IPSC competition created the accurate and reliable 1911, and now it is becoming more and more popular in tactical holsters of SWAT and SpecOps teams.

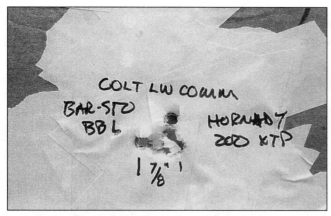

A lightweight carry gun that shoots like a Bull's eye gun and is reliable? You bet. A 25-yard group, and it hasn't failed in 10,000 rounds.

"Tap-rack-bang" solves most problems; even this one.

the United States. Is it any wonder that parts might not interchange? (Although, with the use of computerized design and machining equipment, the dimensions of 1911 parts are converging towards a standard, and it is already possible to readily interchange many manufacturers parts as drop-ins.)

So, there is your buddy, trying to use a pistol built up from gun show bargain parts, and wondering why it doesn't work 100 percent of the time.

The variety of parts sources set the stage, and diverging uses of the 1911 showed many shooters what they wanted to see. The shooters who wanted a dependable tool and a close-range weapon would use rattling 1911s, many of them "surplus" pistols from the war. While accuracy wasn't great by target standards, every single pistol would keep all of its shots between an opponents shirt pockets, and work all the time.

On the other end of the spectrum, target shooters would insist that their gunsmith build tight pistols. So tight that it would occasionally malfunction. On the range this was no problem, as each shooter could simply raise his hand and re-shoot the string as an "alibi" string. Anyone watching the match could plainly see that every alibi was being shot by a shooter with a 1911 and not a revolver, and simple logic would tell you that the 1911 was unreliable.

If you believe that, I have some land in Florida for sale.

The big change came about with the interest in "combat" shooting brought about by Jeff Cooper. In addition to not having static courses with the same targets and time limits for each match, no alibis were allowed. If your pistol jammed during a match, it was your problem, and your responsibility to fix in order to finish. Of course, at the start the wise shooters simply used those rattling old service 1911s, or revolvers. In time, gunsmiths had to adjust, because very soon shooters wanted accuracy, but it had to be reliable. Not all gunsmiths made the adjustment. When I started shooting, everyone knew there were certain gunsmiths in our area whom you went to for a target gun, and others you went to for a combat gun. Back then, if you wanted reliability even with a good gun, you used factory ammunition. Specifically, hardball. Not a problem then, as there was still large amounts available surplus. And, you treated your magazines as gently as possible, as reliable magazines were rare, and you never loaned one to anyone.

Flash forward from the late 1970s, when there were still shooters who were competitive with revolvers, to the 21st Century, where you can buy a blueprinted 1911, bulletproof magazines that you can't hurt with a car, and reloaded ammunition that is cheaper than and more accurate than factory ammo. Life is good. But the pistol will occasionally malfunction.

Two Steps

Clearing a malfunction is a two-step process. The first step is remedial correction, what you do at the range to get on with the match. The second step is identifying why it happened, and correcting or adjusting the system so it won't happen again. I say system because proper function is a process involving the pistol, magazine, ammunition and you. First we'll go through the range drills, then we'll go back and see about the likely sources and necessary fixes for those problems. In the early days, we assigned numbers, one, two, three and four, to the types of malfunctions, and worked on our drills, The idea was to identify exactly what the problem was and then apply the specific fix to it. Under the stress of competition, we ended up with two methods of correction, regardless of the malfunction.

The first correction is called "Tap, rack, bang." The pistol doesn't fire, so you slap the bottom of the magazine to re-seat it if needed and work the slide. The magazine may not have seated? Yes. It is possible for you to have inserted the magazine, but not have locked it in place. Riding lower than it should, the magazine of course would not feed a round. If, on the other hand, there was a round in the chamber, and it didn't go off, then you want to get rid of it, rather than try firing it again. Racking the slide ejects the dud/dead round and gives you a fresh one.

If the base of the round was oversized and the slide had not fully closed, racking the slide extracts the round and again presents a fresh one. If the problem was a bad round, why slap the magazine? Especially if it is already seated? Because it takes less time to automatically slap the magazine than it does to determine if you need to or not.

The second malfunction drill is applied if the first one doesn't do the job. Since the first one clears all the easy stuff, the second one will be more elaborate. Lock the slide open. Strip the current magazine out. (In a combat situation, if you have a limited supply of magazines, save the one you are pulling out, but keep it separate) Rack the slide several

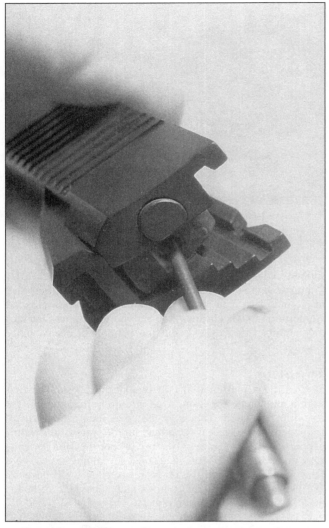

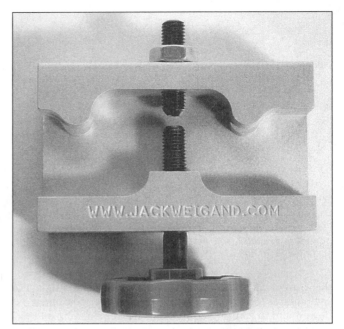

If your extractor lacks tension, the Jack Weigand tool will solve your problem.

If you are using reloads, be sure to clean your brass, size it properly, and gauge it after loading.

Extraction problems often require extractor tuning or replacement.

times, vigorously, insert a fresh magazine, work the slide one more time and get on with the task at hand.

What if the slide won't budge? You need carefully-applied force. Find a square edge. The corner of a post or wooden railing is perfect. Place the front of the slide against the edge so the barrel will clear it. Hold the slide with your left hand, and smack your right hand into the frame so you are vigorously grabbing it as you smack it. The force will snap the slide open. Clamp it with your left so it doesn't close again, and push the slide stop up with your right thumb to lock it open. Then proceed with clearing it.

If after all that it still doesn't work, you have two choices. In a match, quit. The Range Officer is going to step in when it becomes clear your pistol is not going to work. In real life, pull out a back-up gun, get one off of someone who has quit the fight, or stay behind someone else who is on your side. In the last case, keep working on your pistol to get that obstinate empty case out.

What about all the "traditional" malfunctions? Smoke-stacks? Double feeds? Wedged rounds, or noses smacked into hoods? Failure to close? Simple, in the conduct of a match or an altercation, you don't have to know the exact nature of the problem, just apply the fix.

During your practice sessions is a different matter entirely. In practice, if the pistol stops, stop and look at it. Identify exactly what went wrong. Make sure you keep track of which magazine you were using, and what batch or brand of ammunition was in it. If your problem is a bad magazine, then getting rid of it solves the problem. If your pistol doesn't like a particular brand or batch of ammo, don't use it any more. If you are reloading the ammo, then you want to identify the cause so you can improve your reloading process.

The Common Problems, And Their Typical Sources

Failure To Extract Or Eject: The "Stovepipe"

Empties not getting out are usually an extractor problem. Occasionally the load is too light or the spring is too heavy. Use 16- to 18-pound springs in a Government size pistol, and 18- to 20-pound springs in a Commander. In the old days, the advice was often to radically bump up spring power, to ensure function. The suggestion that a Government pistol needs a 22- or 24-pound recoil spring for standard ammo is nonsense. It beats the gun up and changes the feeding cycle, to the detriment of the extractor. That's right, a heavy spring doesn't save your extractor (supposedly by lowering the slide cycle velocity, and easing the extractor's yank on the brass) it actually harms it. (By going forward so fast it snaps the fed round ahead of the slide, where the extractor has to snap over the rim when it catches up, instead of sliding over as normally.)

Empties left behind that aren't a spring or power problem are due to extractor tension. With proper tension, the empties will be held against the breechface and pivoted out by the ejector. Without proper tension, the empty slips off the extractor and can't be pivoted by the ejector.

Adjust or replace your extractor.

In the rare event that you have proper extractor tension and still have smokestack, look to the chamber. A rough or tight chamber can increase the force needed to extract an empty. Also, overly hot reloads can increase extraction force. Look at the case. Do you see bright tool marks? If your load is normal, have a gunsmith ream or polish the chamber.

The next source manifests itself several different ways. An oversized cartridge base can keep the slide from fully closing. Once wedged, it may be tough to rack the slide to eject it. If the case is swollen enough to wedge, but not so

Unlike revolvers, you can't use shorter ammo in a pistol, not even a 1911. Left to right, a .40S&W round, a .40 fired in a 10mm chamber, and a 10mm.

large that it prevents full closure, it may not extract when fired. The empty wedged in the chamber prevents the next one from feeding.

Your problem is most likely in the reloading process, but you should check the chamber anyway.

When a round is fired, the pressure pushes the bullet out of the case, down the barrel and to (we hope) the target. The pressure also expands the case. Properly treated, a case will last quite a long time. I have some .45 brass in my bins that have been fired and reloaded so many time you can't read the headstamp. I have nickeled .38 Super brass that has lasted so long I'm wearing the nickel off. However, not all shooters are so kind to their brass. Or, they have an oversized chamber. Hot loads and a large chamber can over-expand brass. Your resizing die cannot resize all the way down to the extractor groove. Overly expanded brass that has been resized may still be at or over dimension between the extractor groove and the lower limit of sizing. Such brass will stick in your chamber.

To mis-quote Shakespeare, "the fault lies not with our pistols, but with our ammunition." Specifically, brass found at the range. There are two solutions to the problem (three if you count not picking up brass at the range as a "solution.") One, gauge all of your ammunition once you have loaded it, either in your chamber or in an ammo gauge. Two, use an Image Industries Case Pro to resize your brass right down to the shellplate.

The swollen cases can be a problem even if you think you have things under control, if you don't keep an eye on your situation. In 1992 I was shooting a single-stack .38 Super with 150-grain lead bullets. It was very clear that the future of IPSC competition was going to be towards higher capacity magazines and lighter-weight jacketed bullets. But, I had a reliable and accurate gun, a large supply of lead bullets, and I went off to the Nationals with them.

The weather was hot and humid. Through a quirk in the scheduling, I had no time to clean my pistol as I knew I

One malfunction no one likes to talk about is getting the wrong ammo in your 1911. The empty was a .40, (left) fired in a .45-caliber 1911. (Loaded 45 on right) They look close, but the results are messy.

should. On the last round of the last stage of Wednesday (with two days to go) the slide wouldn't go all the way forward. Luckily, I had finished the stage and the round was the one after the last one I needed to fire. Back at the hotel room I stripped the Super and found the chamber coated with a sheet of packed-down powder residue. The heat and humidity had been just right for the residue to collect and pack down, and I hadn't checked it for more than 200 rounds. I scraped the residue out, scrubbed the bore clean and then gauged all the ammo again.

Ever since, when I shoot lead bullets I check the chamber every 100 rounds or so to make sure the powder residue hasn't built up. Guess what? Since then, it hasn't.

Magazine Trouble

Bad magazines can cause just about every malfunction except loss of accuracy. And, it can have a small effect on accuracy if the rounds are being so poorly fed that the noses are chewed up bouncing off of edges and corners. A common magazine failure is nose-high wedging. Especially with lead bullets, if the nose comes to the chamber too high it can strike the hood. A jacketed bullet can bounce off (although marred in the process) but a lead bullet will dig in. The feed lips of the magazine have spread, usually because the rear clearance slot is cracked. Back when the clearance slot was broached as a square slot, the corners would crack. Cracked corners let the lips spread, and the cartridge would lift too high, or be released too soon in the feed cycle. In the old days we would try to weld them up and repair the crack. It was usually a waste of time then, it is a definite waste now.

If you have a magazine with cracked lip or lips, strip the bumper pad off, take the follower and spring out, and trash the tube. If you have a cracked high-capacity magazine, save the trashed tube as proof, and buy a replacement to build the magazine again.

The Pinned Cartridge

If you reload your ammo, or spend time fussing over springs and stuff, you'll sooner or later see a pinned cartridge. The pinned cartridge didn't make it into the chamber, and the rim is under the slide. The breech has the body of the case pressed against the feed ramp. The origins are several, and sometimes mixed. If you are shooting a .40 S&W, you could be using a standard-length cartridge (1.120" to 1.135") in a magazine intended for full-length (1.200") ammunition. Using short 40's in a 10mm magazine will do it, or using short .40's in an unblocked STI magazine will also do it. The short cartridge rattles back and forth in the mag, and its usual "porpoising" is made worse by the extra room. If the case rim is too low when the slide comes forward, the cartridge can't feed properly.

Another source could be springs. If your magazine spring is old and tired (it happens, nothing lasts forever) or you have installed a too-heavy recoil spring, you can get this malfunction. Again, the timing of the feed cycle is changed. In the case of a tired magazine spring, the round may not come up fast enough, or drag in the magazine tube can lift the cartridges unevenly. (Another sign of a weak magazine spring is nose-down failure to feed.) The too-heavy recoil spring can return the slide before the magazine spring has finished lifting the top cartridge tight to the feed lips.

If you have checked all the easy and obvious problems, and made the corrections needed, and your pistol still malfunctions, you need to hand it over to the expert. Determine the exact condition of the malfunction. Don't diagnose, describe. Hand the pistol and your description of the problem over to your gunsmith with the very magazine that was malfunctioning, and a box of the ammo you were using. He can then delve into the problem and apply the necessary fix.

If you are having regular malfunctions in a newly-purchased pistol, be sure to take or send it back to the maker. Include the description and magazine, but do not send the ammo unless they ask for it.

CHAPTER FIFTEEN

The Test Procedure and Crew

The Ransom Rest table, partway through the snowmelt.

This is only part of the cargo load each range trip required. (The table stayed at the range)

What good is a book that looks at a host of firearms without providing some hard data gathered through actual testing?

In the course of writing this book, I personally test-fired 29 pistols, and put more than 5,500 rounds through guns clamped in the Ransom Rest and over the chronograph. I know what you're thinking, how hard can that be? As it turned out, it was pretty difficult. Most of the chrono and Ransom work was done after we had a stormy month of snowfall that left some 3 feet of snow on the ground. Before I could shoot I had to shovel an opening in the snow for the Ransom table and brass tarp. Then my test-fire crew and I shot 20,000 rounds to test the pistols, which involved hauling all the pistols and ammunition to the range over a series of weekends. All told, I spent every weekend of four consecutive months hauling a literal ton of guns, ammo and gear to the range. The end result was our greater affinity for the 1911, and admiration for the genius of John Browning and skill of the modern manufacturer. And a 30-gallon drum full to overflowing with fired brass.

The last part of the test was to hold a match. After testing all the pistols, I selected the five pistols that had proved the most accurate, and absolutely reliable, and we used them in an IPSC match. Each pistol stayed at a stage, and every shooter in the match used that pistol on that stage with the remainder of the test ammo. (When it was all over there was a bit of ammo left, which the Range Officers promptly finished off.) Selecting them was not easy, as I had a dozen candidates for the five slots.

To start the testing for each pistol, once I had verified that the serial number on the paperwork was the same as that on the gun (you laugh, but mistakes happen) I performed the safety checks described in Chapter Thirteen. Then I disassembled each and had a look inside. When I was a full-time gunsmith I would always disassemble and inspect the internals of a 1911 that came in. If I was going to do custom work on a pistol I wanted to see what parts were already in it, and if anyone had been messing with them. And if it was just a disassembly and cleaning job I wanted to see if there was any wear or any broken parts.

As all the 1911 pistols for this book were new, or straight from the gunsmith's bench, I had no surprises.

Next, I measured the depth of each chamber with a dial caliper used as a depth gauge, checked the chamber with my Dave Manson headspace gauges, and measured the extractor tension with the Weigand gauge. I then reassembled them using Break Free or FP-10 as a light lube (I used whichever happened to be closest when I reached for a bottle of lube), Brian Enos' Slide Glide for the hard-working bearing points, and Chip McCormick's Trigger Job on the hammer hooks and sear tip. I then measured the trigger pull with my Brownells recording trigger pull gauge.

Why all the measuring? Properly done research requires that all variables be recorded, and this is an unparalleled opportunity to learn some juicy tidbits. One in particular is the tension of "proper" extractor tension. Every gunsmith out there who works on 1911's has an idea as to "proper" extractor tension, and how to set it. With all these pistols, I figured I could record their tension setting, and see what the acceptable range is, as determined by the pistols themselves. If, in the test-firing, it turned out that a particular pistol was not entirely reliable in extraction or ejection, I could compare its performance with the measured extractor tension, and viola, have a range of figures that works

In this regard my efforts were foiled. Despite recording extractor tensions from zero (yes, the gauge could not determine that there was any tension present) to 40 ounces, none of the pistols showed any reluctance to feed, extract and eject. I will still use my Weigand extractor tension

Good test results depend on proper ammo, and this isn't it. This factory ammo lacks neck tension, and the bullets set back into the case in feeding (right-hand round). Used in a revolver, the recoil pulls the bullet from the case (left-hand round).

adjusting fixture to set the extractor tension on all my future pistols at 20 to 25 ounces, but I won't be so maniacal about keeping them there as long as they are working properly.

The Ransom Rest, notebook, magazine, ammo, lube, water, and oh yes, a 1911.

We tested the pistols in small groups, to keep tabs on what ammo, what magazines and which pistols were being tested.

I only had enough of some ammo to check chronograph results and accuracy in a single pistol. These three high-performance rounds could only be checked for velocity, and they delivered.

Next, each pistol was treated to a trip to the Ransom Rest. Once it was settled in the inserts, I recorded the group sizes of four, five-shot groups with each brand or batch of ammunition. The pistols for which the Ransom folks do not make inserts I test-fired over my Outers Pistol Perch to check accuracy. The pistols that received a trip through the Ransom Rest will have their best groups listed and the group averages mentioned. Those pistols that I fired from the Pistol Perch will simply have their three favorite loads listed in order. There is no point in embarrassing the makers of the guns by listing the results of my efforts at shooting small groups with their pistols. Ditto the ammo makers.

In perusing the charts, you'll see the same names coming to the top time and again. You may think that the ammo that lags behind is "crummy surplus hardball" and you'd be wrong. All of the ammo shot well enough to compete with and do well in, or even win a match. One standard that I've heard used to judge a pistol or its ammo is "It does well enough you could get an 'E' Ticket at Gunsite with it." Every brand of ammo used will, out of almost every single pistol, keep all of its hits in the "A" zone of a USPSA/IPSC target at 50 yards. All the guns will keep every shot from any ammo tested in the "X" ring of the Option target used at Gunsite at 50 yards. You see, we get spoiled. After looking at groups 1 inch or smaller in size, when a 3-inch group

comes along we sneer at it. If you were to hold your pistol up, aimed at a 25 yard target, your front sight would appear (the technical term is "subtend") to be 4 inches wide. That means that "poor" 3-inch group is still smaller than the apparent width of your front sight. Be picky, but don't be a snob. I would be quite pleased to use any of the ammo tested in a match, or a class at Gunsite, or any other school for that matter.

After the measuring and accuracy testing, the test-fire crew and I spent several weekends putting all the ammo through all the guns to check function. My club is a small club, but we have sent shooters to every big match and every shooting school out there. We earned more than our fair share of loot and glory at the annual Second Chance Bowling Pin shoots. And we have done all that shooting 1911's. My instructions were simple. As each of them was handed his clipboard with the test-fire forms, I told them "Tell me the good and bad points. Tell me the sharp edges you find. If you have a malfunction, stop and show me." Rather than have 30 pistols with 70 magazines floating around, each pistol had a pair of magazines (usually those supplied by the manufacturer) tagged for its exclusive use. If the magazines proved troublesome, I had spare magazines of known reliability (100 percent, what else?) on hand to use instead. The back-up magazines were Chip McCormick Power Mags that Chip had sent when he heard about the book. And it was good that he did, for I needed to slide them into the rotation a couple of times. As a control and to cut down on the confusion I issued the pistols in batches, so there would only be half a dozen out at any time.

To no one's great surprise, the number of malfunctions was small. For some pistols, the entire process went by without a single malfunction of the slightest kind. One aspect I personally tested on each pistol was its ability to "live-eject." If you have a dud round, you have to cycle the slide to eject the loaded but unfired cartridge. If the nose of the cartridge strikes the ejection port and won't leave, then you can have a real problem. In the course of checking each pistol, I set aside a round of each sample ammunition. For testing, I simply sat down at the range one afternoon and loaded those rounds into a pair of magazines and cycled them through each pistol. At the end they were really beaten-up (A demonstration of why you should rotate fresh ammunition into your carry gun every few months) but when I was done they all fired and cycled the last test pistol. (Obviously the calibers other than .45 were only checked with their ammo.)

I also checked "slide-drop loading." Many trainers feel that when you shoot your gun to slide-lock (and you will, under enough stress) you should not be hunting for the small slide stop to close the slide after a reload. Instead, you should grab the slide, pull it back, and let it go forward. If you stack shock buffers in your gun, or build your own pistol and do not pay attention to the fitting, you may not be able to pull the slide back far enough to automatically depress the slide stop. I checked each one for the capability to whipsaw the slide to close it.

Some shooting was limited, due to ammo availability. In the hard-kicking calibers I tried to set enough ammunition aside so each of the ammo testers could try a magazine of each caliber. The .460 Rowland and .40 Super were particularly popular, at least for a few rounds. Every one had to try them, and having tried them, some declined the opportunity to fire more. However, as in any group, there were shooters in my crew who would fire all the ammunition supplied, and ask for more, regardless of how hard-kicking a caliber it was.

The Ammunition

The loads used were two types, factory and reloads. The factory ammunition was regular production ammunition, shipped to me from the various makers. The reloads I loaded on my Dillon 550B. While everything is chronographed, not all of the ammunition is Ransom-tested. I tried everything over the chronograph, using the Springfield Loaded pistol where possible, and the other caliber pistols where needed. If I did not have enough of a brand or load of ammunition to Ransom test it in all the pistols, I only chrono tested it. It wouldn't be fair to Ransom test a load in a pistol at random, not knowing if that pistol liked or disliked that load. As you will see looking over the chart, some guns prefer some loads, and you don't know which is which until you test.

The start of the handloading came when I mentioned the project to Bruce Gray of Oregon Trail bullets. He immediately shipped me a batch of 200-grain lead semi-wadcutter bullets. I had initially asked for their 230 LRN or 225 flatpoint bullets, but Bruce insisted that the 200-grain bullet was more accurate in their testing, and was by far the better-selling bullet. More accurate and more likely to be used, that was good enough for me. When the first Wilson pistol arrived, I looked at the test-fire target enclosed, and had my first load. The ragged single hole

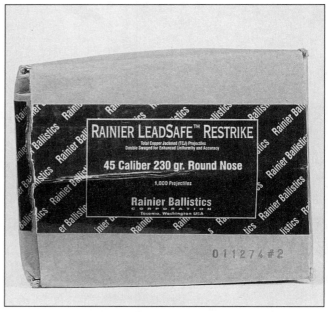

The Rainier Restrike bullets were absolutely reliable and gratifyingly accurate in my Gunsite ATP.

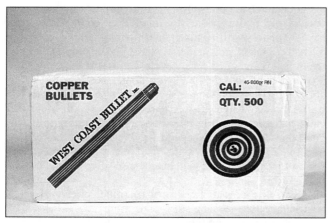

West Coast Bullet, of Nevada, makes excellent plated bullets.

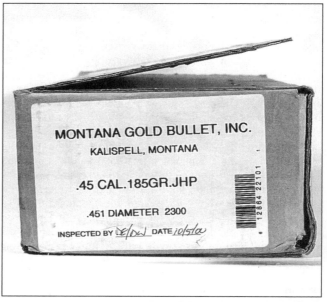

Accurate, and a large hollow point for taking pins off. The Montana Gold bullets are first-class.

Left to right, the Sierra 230 JHP, West Coast 200 JRN, Rainier 230 JRN, Oregon Trail 200 L-SWC, Montana Gold 185 JHP.

Left to right, the Sierra 230 JHP/Titegroup, West Coast Bullet 200/Vihtavuori, Rainier 230/Titegroup, Oregon Trail 200/Vihtavuori, Montana Gold 185/Titegroup.

Each 1911 required testing with factory ammo, too.

group was fired with a 200-grain L-SWC bullet and 4.5 grains of Vihtavuori N-310. The folks at Vihtavuori were kind enough to send me a supply of their N-310 for testing, and I am favorably impressed. It meters well and shoots clean. In my Stock Pin Gun, 4.6 grains of N-310 and the Oregon Trail 200-grain delivered an average of 869 fps, for a Power Factor of 173. Remember this load, you will see it often.

The second load was not as successful, and I can only blame myself for it. I have used West Coast bullets extensively, and shot their bullets at the World Shoot in the Philippines in 1999. Out of my IPSC Modified pistol in .40 S&W, their bullets are tack drivers. For this book I loaded their 200-grain jacketed round nose bullets over 4.7 grains of N-310. The load was 100 percent reliable, but struggled in the 3-inch range in almost every pistol. (Remember, 3 inches at 25 yards is 6 inches at 50 yards, and still in the "A" zone of a USPSA/IPSC target.) Had I not been distracted by the Herculean labors of this book, I could have fine-tuned the load to the accuracy levels I know West Coast delivers.

In talking with one of my club members who shot both IPSC and Cowboy Action, I heard nothing but praises for

Hodgden Titegroup. I called up Hodgden, and they sent me samples of Titegroup. And then another batch. I was afraid they'd keep sending more so I called and said enough was enough. I used the Titegroup with the Rainier 230 JRN's, the Sierra 230 JHP's, and the Montana Gold 185 JHP's. The ballistics engineers at Hodgden felt that my load for the Montana Gold bullet was a heavier charge than their tested ceiling was at. However, I loaded my ammunition to a longer overall length than they did, lowering the pressure in my load.

The Sierra and Montana Gold bullets turned in some impressive groups. The Rainier did not, and again I take the blame for that. I had time to work up chrono data, and check the accuracy of the Rainier load in my personal Stock gun. While it was "average" in the test guns, I can easily go 10 shots for 10 hits on our 100-yard gong with the Rainier load in my Stock gun. (A perfect example of the ammo selectivity of any firearm.) In my Stock gun (a Gunsite ATP with a Kart barrel) the Rainier load is a 1-inch grouping load. But my ATP is not one of the test guns. With some fine-tuning I'm sure their 230 would deliver the accuracy of other bullets.

For factory ammunition, I had an embarrassment of riches. Jeff Hoffman of Black Hills sent two loads, both 230 JRN bullets. He sent Black Hills blue-box, which are reloads, and he sent a bunch of Black Hills red box, which is ammunition loaded in brand-new cases. Both were solid performers, often in the hunt for best group or best load. Also sending primo ammunition was PMC. Ultra-reliable and dependably accurate, the PMC 230s duked it out for honors in the middle of the very competitive pack. The strugglers in hardball were the Magtech and PMP loads. I say struggle, because the competition was so fierce for top honors that one average group would knock a brand down. The Magtech comes from Brazil, and the PMP hails from South Africa. They are both good ammo, good enough to win a match or get an "E" Ticket at Gunsite. As a matter of fact, I won my clubs first USPSA/IPSC handgun match of the spring, using the Springfield Loaded pistol and Magtech ammo. It is hard to complain about a pistol that "only" shoots an average group of 2.25 inches at 25 yards. Yes, a 2.25-inch average knocked the PMP out of the standings in the search for "most accurate" in several guns. If that is "bad ammo" I'll buy all you have! I would not hesitate to use either one in a match or class. I won the overall in our first match of the season, against Open guns and Hi-cap Limited guns, shooting that uncomped Springfield and hardball. Practice, and you too can feel the force.

For non-hardball ammo I had two factory loads, Zero and Hornady. Zero is a commercial reloader from Alabama, with a stellar reputation in PPC circles. They sent me their reloaded 185-grain JHP. If I wasn't going to do any reloading any more, I would seriously consider simply shipping my brass to Alabama for them to reload. It proved absolutely reliable and was in serious contention for overall accuracy standings. The Hornady load is loaded with a 200-grain XTP bullet. In the course of testing, I found that my personal carry gun, a Colt LW Commander, shoots the Hornady ammo like it was a Bull's eye gun. (I had a spare half-hour at the range, ammo and my personal carry gun at hand. What else did you expect?) In addition to being very accurate, the XTP has a very good reputation for penetration and expansion.

For the non-Ransom testing, I had a bunch of ammo from Texas Ammo Co., both in the .45 Super and in other calibers as well. I ran the .45 Super through the Springfield V-16 for Ransom testing, and the other loads were shot over the chronograph. Cor-bon sent me a cross-section of their high-performance ammo, from 9mm and .357 Sig to .45 ACP+P. I did not have enough of any one to do Ransom Rest testing, so it all went over the chronograph. Georgia Arms Co. sent both .460 Rowland, which I chronoed and Ransom tested,

The Ransom base and the table have matching holes drilled through, and large lag bolts keep them tightly together

and their load of .357 Sig. Triton sent ammunition in .40 Super and .45 ACP+P. The .40 Super was Ransom tested, since there was only the one gun to try it in, and the +P was checked for velocity. The last gun to show up was the Casull, and its two loads were both checked in the Ransom Rest and over the chronograph. Once the formal testing was done, the test-fire crew took turns trying it out. Impressive performance with less recoil than you'd think.

At the spreading word of my book, I had no lack of volunteers for the "onerous chore of test-firing so many handguns" as one of my testers put it. Despite their eagerness for the project, I did manage to wear several of them out. A steady supply of hardball, interspersed with hard-kicking numbers like the .40 Super and .460 Rowland took the starch out of several at each session. In the end, we had a blast, and no one complained about recoil, except to ask for more ammo in the standard velocity range.

Ransom Rest

Getting accurate information while using a machine rest requires patience, repeatability, and good record keeping. First, the machine rest (Ransom or other) has to be secured and immobile. Ideally, you would want to mount your Ransom to a concrete pillar that extends down to bedrock. When I win the lottery, I will have a concrete pier cast on

The Ransom test table was built from solid lumber and a plywood top glued and screwed on. It doesn't move under recoil.

Tighten the knobs, make sure the frame is secure, and start firing settling groups.

The side lever fires the 1911. Once the pistol is secured, only touch the magazine button, and leave the rest of the pistol alone.

which to mount my Ransom Rest. Until then, I'll have to depend on the table. I built my table from a shipping pallet. While most shipping pallets are flimsy affairs, there are a few that are solidly made. I appropriated one that was made

Good record-keeping is essential to proper research. Without out records, your memory will play tricks on you.

of solid 4x8's on its skids, and 2x6's on its top. I then laminated half-inch plywood to the top, using a combination of construction adhesive (the table consumed an entire tube) and wood screws. I weighed the plywood down with boxes of bullets and ammunition to set the adhesive, a ton in all. It then received several coats of exterior latex paint, and I bolted 4x4 legs to it. Once assembled, I stiffened it with extra 2x4's. Once the warm weather arrives (much of the testing was done in bitter cold and 3 feet of snow) the support beams will also support a shelf.

I drilled four holes through the top, and matching holes in the Ransom base. In use, I run four bolts through the holes and bolt the Ransom unit to the table. The future shelf takes the ammo, gear bags and any extra weight I can locate on the range.

With the Ransom bolted down, the shooting ritual begins. To fit a pistol to the rest, remove the grips and slide the right-hand insert onto the bolts. Nestle the frame into the insert and slide the left-hand insert on. Use a screwdriver to depress the grip safety. Finger-tighten the knobs. You want the frame held securely, but not too tightly. (You can squeeze the frame tightly enough that the trigger cannot return.) Dry-fire the pistol a few times, and if the knobs are too tight, loosen them. With the pistol in place, adjust the front height screw until the sights are on your target frame.

My old insert is not cut to clear an ambidextrous safety. Due to the many guns equipped with such, I switched to the new inserts that the Ransom folks were kind enough to send me.

Hang a blank backer on the target frame, insert a loaded magazine and close the slide. Once the pistol is secure in the rest, you want to touch it as little as possible. When it is empty, drop the magazine by pushing the magazine button without touching the rest of the pistol. Close the slide by pushing down the slide release. Rotate the Ransom to get to the magazine by lifting the tab on the lower arm, not by pulling on the pistol itself. Shoot a group of five or more rounds to settle the pistol, and locate the point of impact. If the holes are near the center of the backer, you're set. If they aren't, adjust the vertical adjustment or move the target frame left or right. Shoot several groups, until you are getting groups that are uniform in size and shape. Use masking tape to cover the holes between shooting each group. As the frame settles into the inserts, it may move the point of impact or group size. The first few groups are not an indication of how the pistol does.

In the course of settling the pistols into the inserts and firing groups, I discovered how variable they can be. Some would walk the shots along the frame, then they would curl back and the groups finally settle down. Other pistols simply punched all the shots into the same area, and you could tell it was settled-in when the groups suddenly shrank in size. A couple didn't need any settling, shooting their best groups right from the start.

Once the pistol is settled into the inserts, you can begin testing for groups. As long as you stay with the same powder and bullet, you can simply shoot and record your groups. If you change anything, you may have to shoot re-settling groups. I discovered this little fact while testing my S&W M-41 .22lr for accuracy. When I used one super-accurate ammunition or another (my M-41 loves Eley and Green Tag) the groups were spectacular. (Less than two inches at 50 yards. Sometimes much less) If I switched back and forth, from one brand to another, the accuracy was lousy.

If you switch to a different weight powder charge, using the same powder and bullet, you will get a representative group. If you change bullet or powder, you may have to re-condition the bore to the new combination. The .45 ACP is much less likely to react to changes in loads than the .22lr is. I only had one pistol that showed a marked reaction to switching loads, and that was the Kimber Super Match. Considering how well it shot once you had fired a few groups, I would not feel cheated by this peculiarity. Other pistols had no such sensitivity. The AMT, for instance, shot

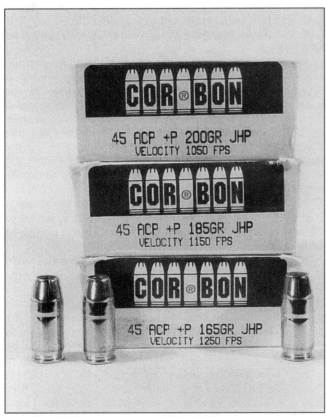

If you can't decide which defensive ammo to carry, testing them in the Ransom Rest can tell you which is more accurate. The difference may be small, but the peace of mind can be great

16 consecutive groups under 2 inches in size, going through four different brands and types of ammo.

You simply must experiment with your pistol to see if it is going to be touchy or phlegmatic in this regard.

While I'm shooting with the Ransom, I don't touch the table, and try to be as uniform as possible in the manner I handle the rest, magazines and trigger bar. I don't leave loose objects on the table, to rattle around and change the vibrations of the table and rest. Yes, these are little things, but the whole point of a rest is to isolate the accuracy of the pistol and its ammunition from all other variables. I will leave boxes of ammunition on the table. I've tested to see if they matter, and they don't. Rather than leave them on another table and walk a few feet, I'll be lazy and leave them on the table.

In the course of shooting the Ransom Rest testing, I fired four groups with each brand of ammo with each of the pistols. That, plus settling-in groups and re-shoots when I had brain fades. The target was 25 yards away, so I had to walk 50 yards with each group. In the course of testing for accuracy, I walked more than 30 miles to and from the target frame. No wonder I felt so tired after each range trip. Next time I'm bringing a golf cart.

What can the Ransom Rest tell you? Many things, my friend, many things. In addition to the size of a particular group, you can determine consistency over several groups, average number of rounds to decreased accuracy, and bad group habits of your pistol. One interesting phenomenon that pistols are sometimes prone to is the "first shot out" habit. The first round fired is chambered by the slide going forward from dropping off the slide stop, or pulled by hand. The slide can lock up differently to the barrel on that first round than it does when it cycles on its own. Some pistols, as a result, will shoot the first round away from the rest of the shot. Watching the shots and seeing where the first one goes will easily show you if a pistol does this. That is, if you're using a Ransom. By hand, it is a much more difficult thing to see.

None of the pistols tested showed the "first out" pattern. It is not a common trait. More common is the "4+1" or "3+2" habit. A pistol that shoots four shots into a tight group, but always throws a flyer, is trying to tell you something. Ditto a three-shot and pair pattern. What it is trying to tell you is either that the barrel is not always locking up the same way, or it doesn't like the ammo. A pistol that does it with all types of ammo needs to either have the barrel re-fitted, or a new barrel installed.

You can also see how much your pistol likes particular loads, or your reloads. I once had a client who wanted to know what ammo to carry in his defensive pistol. I told him "Whatever high-performance hollow point your pistol shoots most accurately, because it will be absolutely reliable once I'm done working on it." He then asked me to test those loads for accuracy. (Me and my big mouth.) It turned out that his Commander shot CCI Blazer 200-grain hollow points like it was a Bull's-eye gun. Out of the Ransom Rest, it shot groups around an inch at 25 yards. I saved a target for him, in case he ended up in an altercation and someone asked him why he was using that particular ammo.

My Ransom Rest told me that I was over-crimping my 9mm reloads, when I first started working up loads. I was getting occasional fliers, quite a distance from the rest of the group, but only with reloads. I backed off the crimp, and while the velocity extreme spread (a measure of consistency) increased, the fliers joined the rest of the group.

Accuracy over time can matter. For several years at the Second Chance bowling pin shoot, we shot an event called the Handgun Pop and Flop. We shot at steel bowling pin-shaped falling plates. The racks were at 45 and 55 yards, with a single pin at 90 yards. An afternoon's shooting could have you putting 300-400, maybe 500 rounds through your handgun. Despite the fact that I won a firearm each of the two years we shot the event, I determined that I should find out how often I should scrub the bore for best accuracy. My HGPF handgun was a Colt .38 Super with a Bar-sto barrel. The load was a 150-grain Durocast bullet over Accurate Arms #7 powder. I had 50,000 of the bullets on hand, so spending an afternoon practicing and trying the gun in the Ransom Rest was not going to use up my supply. I found that the gun didn't care how long I shot it, it was going to deliver accurate groups all day long. I gave up at the 600-round level, as I was running low on ammo and daylight. (And getting incredibly bored with the whole endeavor.)

Other Methods Of Accuracy

Can you accuracy-test a pistol without a Ransom Rest? Yes, but it will be hard work, and you can't be sure you are as reliable as the rest is. As you become tired at the range, your performance will suffer. While you might (as an example) shoot groups twice as large as the Ransom would at the start of your day, by the end of the range trip you might be shooting groups three times as large. That last group you shot, the ammunition might actually be performing better than the first batch did, but your performance will hide that fact.

While you can shoot a Ransom all day long and be sure it is delivering dependable information, you might be done for accuracy testing in 100 rounds. (Accuracy testing, done properly, is hard work.)

But if all you have is a regular shooting rest, here is how to get the most reliable information. Arrange your bench and shooting rest so you are in the most comfortable shooting position possible. Use folded towels as rests for your arms or elbows. Be as consistent as possible about where you place your arms, in how you grasp the pistol, and the pressure you apply to the pistol while it is in the rest.

Post a large target. By that, I mean a large black-on-white bull's-eye. A 1-foot target at 25 yards is not too large. If you are straining to see a little dot, you aren't going to be focused on shooting. Ignore the shift in impact center that some loads might have. Focus on keeping the front sight snugged up against the bottom of your bull's-eye, and put all your Zen concentration into the trigger. Watch the front sight, feel the trigger, and keep your sight and feel as consistent from shot to shot as you can.

You'll find on a good day you can occasionally shoot a group almost as good as if you were using the Ransom Rest can.

The Match

The five finalists were: The Wilson KZ-45, the STI The Edge, the Springfield Professional, the Kimber Super Match and the Nowlin Match Classic. To make the reloading easier in the match, and reduce the magazine-banging on the pistol, I temporarily installed a Clark magazine funnel on the Nowlin. As backup pistols, in case any of the main ones broke (an unthinkable problem, but I thought of it) I had on hand: the Caspian Race Ready, the Springfield Loaded and the Wilson CQB.

The turnout was quite impressive for a match early in the spring, with a possibility of snowfall, and the (nb. insert numbers) 66 shooters fired 7,500 rounds without a single malfunction.

SHOOTER'S MARKETPLACE

INTERESTING PRODUCT NEWS FOR THE ACTIVE SHOOTING SPORTSMAN

The companies represented on the following pages will be happy to provide additional information – feel free to contact them.

CUSTOM RESTORATION/CASE COLORING

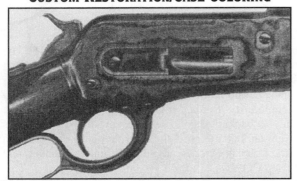

Doug Turnbull Restoration continues to offer bone charcoal case hardening work, matching the original case colors produced by Winchester, Colt, Marlin, Parker, L.C. Smith, Fox and other manufacturers. Also available is charcoal blue, known as Carbona or machine blue, a prewar finish used by most makers. "Specializing in the accurate recreation of historical metal finishes on period firearms, from polishing to final finishing. Including Bone Charcoal Color Case Hardening, Charcoal Bluing, Rust Blue, and Nitre Blue".

DOUG TURNBULL RESTORATION
P.O. Box 471, 6680 Rt 5&20, Dept SM2000
Bloomfield, New York 14469 • Phone/Fax: 716-657-6338
E-mail: turnbullrest@mindspring.com
Web: www.turnbullrestoration.com

An In-depth Look At Glock Pistols

The Gun Digest® Book of the Glock
by Patrick Sweeney

Examine the rich history and unique elements of the most important and influential firearms design of the past 50 years, the Glock autoloading pistol. This comprehensive review of the revolutionary pistol analyzes the performance of the various models and chamberings and features a complete guide to available accessories and little-known factory options. You'll see why it's the preferred pistol for law enforcement use and personal protection.

Softcover • 8½x11 • 336 pages • 500 b&w photos
Item# GDGLK • $27.99

 To order call **800-258-0929** Offer GNB3

Krause Publications, Offer GNB3
P.O. Box 5009, Iola WI 54945-5009 • www.krausebooks.com

Please add $4.00 for the first book and $2.25 each additional for shipping & handling to U.S. addresses. Non-U.S. addresses please add $20.95 for the first book and $5.95 each additional.
Residents of CA, IA, IL, KS, NJ, PA, SD, TN, WI please add appropriate sales tax.

This Book Could Save Your Life!

The Gun Digest® Book of Combat Handgunnery
5th Edition
by Massad Ayoob

Learn essential survival techniques to defend yourself, your loved ones, and your property with a handgun. All tactics and techniques are described in detail, including concealed carry. You'll be shown how to choose the right handgun and how to build and test the necessary handling skills, as well as where to find additional training. This reference will also help you avoid common mistakes and accidents.

Softcover • 8½x11 • 256 pages • 350 b&w photos
Item# COM5 • $22.95

To order call **800-258-0929** Offer DAB3

Krause Publications, Offer DAB3
P.O. Box 5009, Iola WI 54945-5009 • www.krausebooks.com

Please add $4.00 for shipping & handling to U.S. addresses.
Non-U.S. addresses please add $20.95.
Residents of CA, IA, IL, KS, NJ, PA, SD, TN, WI please add appropriate sales tax.

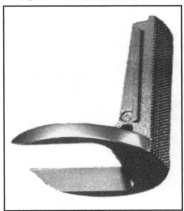
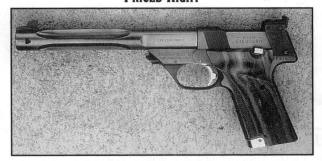

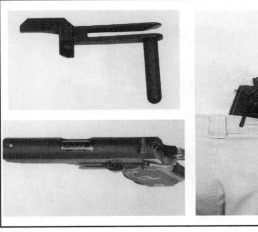

SHOOTER'S MARKETPLACE

XS SIGHTSYSTEMS

Uses proven Express Sight Principle with Big Dot Tritium or Standard Dot Tritium Front Sight with a vertical Tritium Bar within the Express Rear Sight. Ideal "flash sight alignment" stressed in defensive handgun courses. The tritium Express Rear enhances low-light sight alignment and acquisition. This improves a handgun for fastest sight picture in both normal and low light. Professional trainers rate it as the fastest acquisition sight under actual stress situations. Improves front sight acquisition for IDPA and IPSC shooting competition. Fits most handguns with factory dovetails; other models require dovetail front cuts. Also available in Adjustable Express Rear for Bomar, LPA, and Kimber.

Price: Pro Express Big Dot Tritium (or Standard Dot Tritium): $120.00

Price: Adjustable Pro Express Big Dot Tritium (or Standard Dot Tritium): $150.00

XS SIGHTSYSTEMS
2401 Ludelle, Fort Worth, TX 76105
Phone: 888-744-4880 or 817-536-0136 • Fax: 800-734-7939
Website: www.expresssights.com

For over 30 years D. Buehn Antique Arms has provided the Colt handgun collector market with an amazing array of handguns for sale. Buehn's inventory changes frequently, and a serious collector can provide a "wish list" for items needed to fulfill a collection. D. Buehn Antique Arms handle all the variations of 1911 and 1911A1 Government Models/U.S. Military, 1900, 1902 Sporting, 1902 Military, 1903 Pocket Hammer, 1903 & 1908 Hammerless, 1908 .25 Hammerless, Woodsman, National Match .45, Service Model & Ace .22. Also a large variety of U.S. military rifles and shotguns. Many U.S. martial holsters, belts, and other accoutrements. Other handguns include High Standards, and other discounted American pistols. A catalog is published 6-8 times per year ($10 subscription). Or check out their website.

D. BUEHN ANTIQUE ARMS
PhoneL 714-846-3666 • Fax: 714-846-6906
Email: dbcolts@aol.com • Website: www.colt455.com

MODULAR RUBBER GRIP SYSTEM

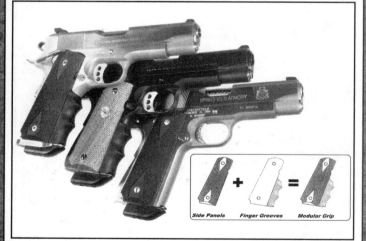

Side Panels + Finger Grooves = Modular Grip

Pearce Grip, Inc., originators of the popular ModularGrip™ for the full size Government Model 1911 style pistols, introduces the Officer's Model Series of this unique grip concept. These grips are a three-piece system which includes finger grooves and side panels. The finger grooves can also be used with other manufacturers exotic wood or other specialty side panel grips. The rubber side panels can be used independently of the finger grooves or combined as a complete set for an ultra slim wrap-around rubber grip.

PEARCE GRIP, INC.
P.O. Box 40367, Fort Worth, TX 76140
Phone: 800-390-9420 • Fax: 817-568-9707

Step-by-Step Takedown & Reassembly

Gun Digest Book of Firearms Assembly/Disassembly Part I: Automatic Pistols
2nd Edition
by J.B. Wood

Numerous clear photos and easy to follow instructions lead you through the steps to disassemble even the more complicated autoloading pistols among the 71 distinct models covered. Editor J.B. Wood, internationally recognized firearms engineering authority, updates this valuable book, adding 13 new autoloaders and nearly 100 additional pages to the first edition - plus revising and updating the entire text as necessary.

Softcover • 8¼x10¹¹⁄₁₆ • 592 pages
1,700 b&w photos
Item# AS1R2 • $24.95

To order call 800-258-0929 **Offer GNB3**

Krause Publications, Offer GNB3
P.O. Box 5009
Iola WI 54945-5009
kp www.krausebooks.com

Please add $4.00 for shipping & handling to U.S. addresses. Non-U.S. addresses please add $20.95.
Residents of CA, IA, IL, KS, NJ, PA, SD, TN, WI please add appropriate sales tax.

Semi-Custom
Pistol Tests

TESTING THE AMMO

Some pistols have definite ammo preferences (this Nowlin shot well with everything) and to properly test, you need more than one ammo source.

Proper testing requires large amounts of ammo. This 500-bullet box from Oregon Trail would be just enough to fire two full mags and a few extra rounds through each 1911 tested.

Proper testing requires more than just blasting bullets into a backstop. It is hard work, and it requires a lot of ammunition. But how much is "enough?" Compounding the problem I faced of "how much" ammunition was enough was the unknown of how many pistols I would be testing. The basic test of each pistol would require not less than 100 rounds, and usually more. Each brand-new pistol has to be fired with a couple of magazines of ammo to break it in and make sure it is working properly The Ransom rest testing consumes a minimum of 20 rounds for groups, plus some extra for spoiled groups, brain fade from not taping the previous group, and settling each pistol into the inserts. In order to get feedback from other shooters, at least a couple of magazines per tester add to the total. If I were the only tester, then several more magazines would be needed in order to get more data.

With the per pistol minimum now somewhere between 100 and 200 rounds, it is a matter of estimating how many pistols will be tested. At 10 1911's, the total becomes approximately 1,500 rounds. At 20 pistols we were looking at 3,000 rounds, and at 30 pistols the total reaches 4,500 rounds. Also a problem with depending on a single brand of ammunition is what if one or more of the pistols hate the ammo being used? Pistols, indeed all firearms, have preferences in ammunition, preferences in accuracy and reliability. Sometimes the preferences do not matter much, and sometimes they matter a lot. The problem of depending solely on one source of ammo came forcefully to the front of the line when initially testing the various brands of ammo sent me. I tried all of the ammo in one of the 1911s, for function and to chronograph them. One

brand of ammunition suffered from insufficient neck tension, coupled with undersized bullets, and the rounds suffered setback on feeding. Or rather, lack of feeding. I quickly tried that batch in all the pistols. Some of the pistols, like the Caspian, hated the ammo so much they refused to work. I could not get the Caspian to feed two consecutive rounds in testing it with the nameless ammo. Other pistols were more forgiving, and I could shoot for groups with a bit of hassle. But even the most-forgiving pistols produced one malfunction per magazine.

I attempted to contact the manufacturer to get the ammo replaced, to no avail. To inspect the ammo, I pulled a bullet and measured it. The diameter was .4495 inches. The case neck thickness was .009", sufficient for proper function. I cleaned a couple dozen cases, sized and reloaded them with a known reload out of my loading notes, and they worked fine. No set-back. Just on a lark, I tried the ammo in my S&W .45 ACP revolver. The bullets pulled forward on recoil. Each five shots fired lengthened the sixth round by .030". By putting the same round through several five-shot experiences, I had produced a cartridge too long to fit in a

The mystery ammo. On the right, once through the Caspian. On the left, several times through the revolver. Center, as sent.

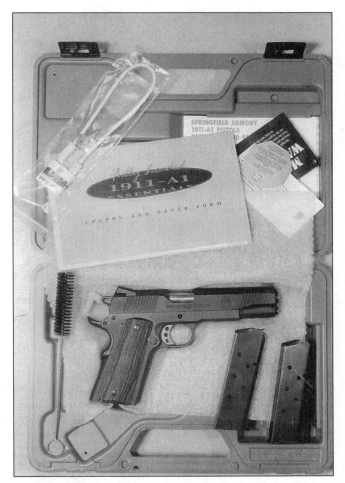

Springfield sent three pistols, the Professional, the V-16, and this Loaded model.

Some insist a lead semi-wadcutter of the H&G-68 is the most-reliable bullet shape, but if a pistol won't feed hardball, it should be handed to a competent gunsmith for work.

1911 magazine. What if I had been depending on this brand and batch of ammunition as my sole test-fire lot? I would have been up the creek without a paddle.

My acquisition process was simple; I contacted all the ammunition manufacturers, commercial reloaders and reloading component makers I knew of and could locate, and told them the project. I asked for 3,000 rounds each, or reloading components for 3,000 rounds. Those who could, sent as much of the 3,000 rounds as they could. And as it turned out, the nameless company sent 3,000 rounds, of which 2,500 are now a doorstop in my shop. I also contacted all the manufacturers of 1911s and asked them for a test pistol. I told them I would be checking function, accuracy and reliability, and putting as much ammo through each pistol as I could get for the book. Would they please send their most-accurate pistol, or their most popular model? When talking with some manufacturers, I requested a particular model. With Springfield, for instance, I specifically requested the Professional Model. I asked Para Ordnance for an LDA, and if possible, a single-stack version.

In both ammunition and handgun manufacturers, I had many who said they would ship product. I asked everyone, and left no-one out. Almost all promised to send something. If they all promised, then why are some missing from the list? I don't know why. There were some that I contacted repeatedly, who assured me they were building the gun they intended to send, who ended up not sending anything. Only one manufacturer declined to send a pistol. The un-named maker told me that they knew their pistols were good, and would be happy to sell me one. They do make good pistols, but since I already own several top-end 1911's (but not one of theirs), and they were offering it at the same price I could have bought it using my FFL, I declined.

Several of the ammunition makers declined to send samples, citing the end of the fiscal year and their depleted marketing budget. But those who responded, did so with an embarrassment of riches. The ammunition that was sent can be divided into the following categories: factory ammo, commercial reloads, reloading components, and specialty ammo.

Gun writers don't get free guns. We get loaned guns, some free ammo, and are left with the memories, notes and photographs. And the brass

Gun writers do not get free guns. When we are sent firearms for testing, we fire and test them, try not to scratch them too much, take pictures, and ship them back. Every now and then a firearm comes along that is too accurate to let slip through our fingers, and we wheedle the manufacturers for a discount. Some provide a discount, some don't. I've heard that back in the old days, manufacturers simply shipped guns off, and never asked for them back. I've also heard that some gun writers essentially blackmail manufacturers and custom gunsmiths for goods. Having been a gunsmith for many years, I can tell you that you don't get rich gunsmithing, and you sure don't get rich giving your products or services away.

Ammo, now that is a different story. Since ammunition is a consumable, the manufacturers can't expect to get any of it back. But, they don't give that much of it out. It isn't unusual for a request for ammunition for an article or chapter in a book to net a box or two. Or a box of each of three bullet weights. The ammo makers don't need to hire a semi to ship the test-fire ammo to gun writers, for they don't ship as much as you'd think. That is why I was so surprised that so many ammo makers, loaders and component manufacturers responded to my request. I really thought I was going to have to collect the ammo for the book by hitting up 20 or 30 makers for 500 rounds each.

Do the manufacturers keep a "special stock" of guns or ammo, for use only by gun writers? No. They don't have the time, storage room or energy to go to that much work. Usually, the marketing person that I talk to will simply walk down to the production line and grab the latest one that comes off and ship it to me. Or, walk to inventory and grab the first one that fits the needed requirements. Ammo

makers simply write a shipping order to the loading dock, and let the warehouse personnel grab what's on the shelf and ship it. "Gun Writer Select"? Please, I'll laugh so hard coffee will come out of my nose, and that hurts.

When you consider the economic constraints on loaners and freebies, the fact that so many manufacturers were so willing to send me stuff for the book is amazing. Based on the performance of the firearms, you won't find a bad deal in any of those I tested. Some 1911's will be more useful in certain situations than others, but none were lemons. That the ammo manufacturers, reloaders and component makers were so free with their product was a marvel. I can heartily endorse all the brands of ammo used in the book. They all worked, in some cases marvelously well, and I would not feel the least bit handicapped using any of them in a match. As with all things, I'd prefer some ammo to others for certain applications. My personal carry gun is not going to see anything but the remnants of the Hornady XTP ammo for a long while. And my revolver bowling pin gun is going to finish off the leftovers of the PMP, and maybe my 1911 pin gun too.

Please keep these manufacturers in mind when shopping for ammo, and thank them for their help. I will and did.

Triton sent a marvelous variety of ammo, from standard and +P .45 ACP, to the hot .40 Super. Good stuff, you can't go wrong.

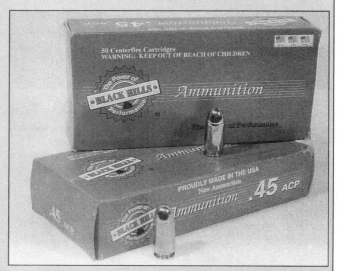

Black Hills Red and Black Hills Blue. (OK, so in a B&W photo it's hard to tell the difference.) They both shot like gold, and I would never hesitate to use either.

Hornady sent a generous supply of their excellent XTP 200-grain .45 ACP.

The Rainier bullet, loaded with Hodgden Titegroup. I should have spent some more time working up the proper load, but it was 100 percent reliable in all the pistols.

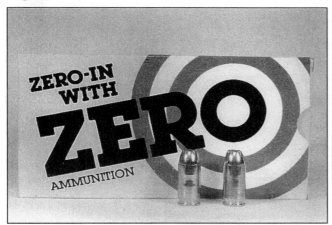

The Zero 185s shot reliably and accurately, and I can recommend them highly.

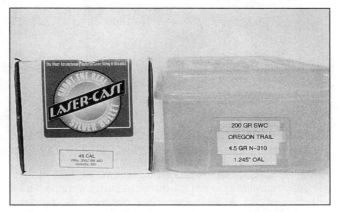

Oregon Trail and Vihtavuori, the most accurate load of the bunch.

Were I to depend solely on a jacketed reload, this would be it.

The factory ammo comprised the PMP, Magtech, PMC, Black Hills and Hornady. The Magtech and PMC were loaded with 230-grain round nose full metal jacket bullets. The PMP bullets are only 220-grains in weight, probably something to do with the metric system. The Hornady rounds were loaded with their excellent XTP bullet, 200 grains in weight. Black Hills sent two loads, one of their Red box, and one of their Blue box. The Red box ammo is loaded in new cases, and is factory ammo. The Blue box is reloaded in used cases, thus commercial reloads. Both were 230-grain RN-FMJ, with essentially identical velocities. Some of the test 1911s showed a preference for the Red, some for the Blue. Commercially reloaded ammo came from Zero, loaded with 185-grain jacketed hollow points, and loaded to a power factor that made Major. The reloaded ammo that I assembled used bullets from Rainier Bullet Co, Sierra, Oregon Trail, Montana Gold, and West Coast Bullet. The powders I used were Vihtavuori N-310 and Hodgden Titegroup. Primers were Remington Large pistol. I assembled all the reloaded test-fire ammunition on my Dillon 550B, changing only the overall length and powder charge between loads. The taper crimp on my press is set for .468" and has not been altered for many years. The Rainier bullets were 230-grain RN-FMJ, loaded over 4.7 grains of Titegroup. The Sierra 230-grain jacketed hollow points were also loaded over 4.7 grains of Titegroup. The Oregon Trail 200 grain lead semi-wadcutters used 4.5 grains of N-310. The Montana Gold 185 JHP's used a heavier charge of Titegroup than the heavier bullets, 5.9 grains. The West Coast Bullet 200-grain JRN's needed a bit more N-310 than the lead bullets, 4.7 grains.

The specialty ammo was mostly caliber-specific, but I was treated to some .45 ACP+P, for those who feel the 1911 needs a little more power but not a lot more. The specialty ammo came from Triton Cartridge, Georgia Arms, Texas

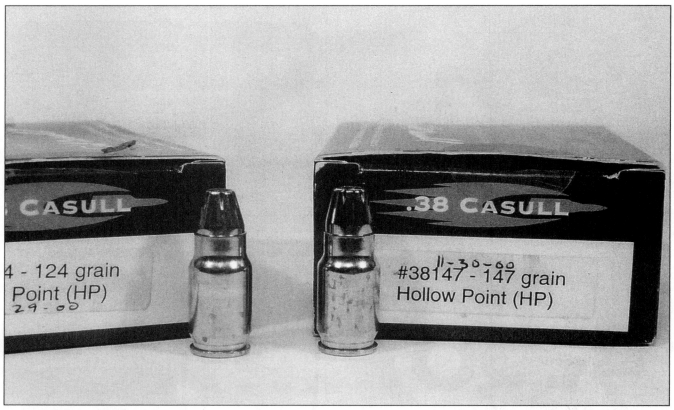

The hottest ammo was the Casull. No doubt about it, at 1,825 fps!.

Ammo, Cor-bon, and Casull. Triton sent me a bunch of their .40 Super ammunition in four different bullet weights, and a selection of .45 ACP+P. Georgia Arms sent the fantastic .460 Rowland and some .357 Sig. Texas Ammo sent .45 Super, .45 ACP+P, .40 S&W and some 9mm. Cor-bon sent .45 ACP+P and .357 Sig, and Casull sent the hottest stuff around, .38 Casull.

I had so much ammo I couldn't get to one of my shop benches. I was in hog heaven. My delivery driver spent several months with a big grin on his face, as he recognized the return addresses on the boxes. He did not appreciate the weight of the ammo, but my front door isn't that far from the street.

With the ammunition supply well in hand, the plan now switched to the test-fire program. I started out by taking the pistols to the range as they arrived. During the week, as each pistol showed up, I weighed it, measured trigger pull, extractor tension, chamber depth and headspace, checked the functionality of the safety controls, and generally fondled them. On the weekend, each week's crop of pistols went off to the range in my gun bag, along with a box of each ammunition per pistol for testing. There, I'd put the ammo through the newly-arrived pistols to see how they worked. I watched the ejected brass to see that it exited in generally the same direction and distance. I got a feel for the sights, to see if the pistol was zeroed. I checked magazine function; did they go in easily, drop free, lock open and feed reliably? The pistols started arriving in the winter, with much snow on the ground. To save the brass, I spread a tarp.

Once the snow had melted enough, I set up the Ransom rest bench and began testing for accuracy. Each pistol was tested with each load, and the group sizes were recorded and sometimes photographed. As each batch of pistols finished

Cor-bon sent ammo for chrono testing, including this .357 Sig ammo. Hot stuff.

Magtech sent three cases of their excellent 230 hardball.

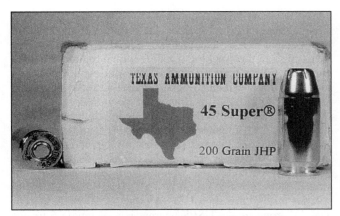

Texas Ammunition Company supplied all the .45 Super I needed for the test, and then some.

The .400 Cor-bon lost its velocity crown to the .40 Super, but still has many uses. I'm planning to build a pin gun in .400 Cor-bon.

As a hot number, the .40 Super (left) delivers weight and velocity. For recoil, the .460 Rowland (right) is the king. My testers fired a few rounds of each and then went back to the regular .45 ACP.

The testers were happy to consume the .45 ACP, and had to be encouraged to try the hot numbers.

its trip through the Ransom rest, I set it aside for the test-fire crew sessions. On a couple of weekends at the club, I had a small group of members of my gun club who were 1911 users come out and test-fire the pistols. Some were new, others were old hands at using a 1911. On the test-fire days each tester would fire three magazines through a pistol, then record his impressions of function, accuracy and any sharp edges found. The shooter would then go on to the next pistol, load the magazines and repeat the process. With two dozen pistols for the main testing, a dozen testers and an open range, the ammunition brought along for each session didn't last long. With the calibers that did not have enough ammo for all the testers to shoot some, I fired myself. Those who wanted to, fired a magazine or so of the other calibers, but I shot most of the .357 Sig, .38 Casull, .40 Super, .45 Super and .460 Rowland myself.

On looking at the testers reports after the sessions, I noticed several interesting correlations. Where more than one tester reported favorably on the accuracy of a pistol, the Ransom rest testing also showed small groups. Where they made no comment about accuracy other than the zero being off, accuracy in the Ransom rest was average. ("Average" in this bunch being 2 to 3 inches.) The testers who reported sharp edges were the ones to report sharp edges. Testers who didn't, didn't. That is, some of the testers were more prone to finding sharp edges than others. I noticed the same situation with magazines that failed to lock open. Where a

report sheet noted "magazine failed to lock" it was almost always from the same few testers.

I can only conclude that some of the common low-level malfunctions that we see from time to time are shooter-dependent. What if I had asked just one tester for help, and it happened to have been one of the testers who repeatedly reported magazines that failed to lock open? In reporting each pistol's results, if the failure to lock open came from one of the three who repeatedly had the problem, I left the notes out. While interesting, it isn't often enough to be statistically significant. I reported on the sharp edges, because it only takes one sharp edge to be significant if it is your hand being cut. I am lucky (or have had too much practice) and find that pistols like me. Even a pistol that doesn't lock open in some of the testers' hands will lock open for me. I rarely encounter sharp edges, and my grip is firm enough that even marginally reliable pistols will work fine when I shoot them. If you want to know if a pistol will malfunction, don't give it to me.

Once all the testing was done, the five top pistols were enlisted in the 1911 Match my club held. Each of the five was left at a stage, with a supply of ammunition (held out from the test-firing) and each shooter used the supplied pistol and ammunition under the direct supervision of the Range Officer who stayed at that stage all day long. I also kept a pair of 1911s on hand as spares, in case something happened. The courses of fire were relatively simple, and each shooter started with the pistol on the table in front of them. To quote the old saying, a good time was had by all.

Some calibers I had to use my own ammo. The .30 Luger is not often seen, which is a shame.

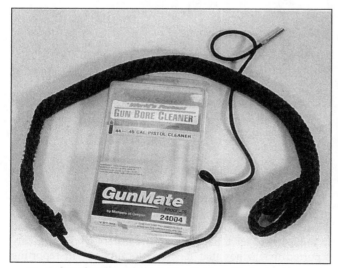

If you want a clean bore quickly, the Bore Snake is the way. One pull through and you're ready to go again.

And, the pistols worked flawlessly. There were a few occasions of shooter error, such as not getting the magazine in hard enough to lock it in place, or a double-feed caused by reloading and then racking the slide with a round still in the chamber. (Done briskly, racking the slide would not be a problem. But, hesitantly racking the slide only leaves the extracted round flopping around the ejection port, to get in the way as the next feeds in. Or tries to, anyway.) Collectively, the match consumed 7,500 rounds of ammunition.

There was one last test, one that my big mouth got me into. In talking about the pistols, the subject of accuracy came up. I defended one of the pistols that had demonstrated only "average" accuracy by saying that you could still get all "A" hits on a USPSA target at 50 yards with it. The "A" zone on the USPSA target is a rectangle 6 inches by 11 inches. One of the members commented on the pistol in question "It's a piece of "bleep" and you couldn't keep them all on the target that far out." (A new member, he didn't know that we old-timers plink at the 10-inch gong at 100 yards offhand.) The bet was made, but being stubborn he wouldn't just give me the good guns, I had to prove it with all of them. Since I was going to have to lie down in rollover prone and shoot two dozen guns over a sandbag, I figured I might as well include pictures in the book. (I bargained for the sandbag, he insisted that all the pistols be tested. I could have foregone the Match pistols, but I wanted the sandbags for insurance.) Except for the work of lying down and getting up a couple of dozen times, and walking a hundred yards for each gun, it was a piece of cake. (Add another mile and a half to the walking total I've done in testing for this book.) Luckily for me, I didn't have the hot numbers along on that trip. The Casull had gone back to Wyoming by then, and the .40 Super was on the bench getting some more fitting. But the .460 Rowland was in my gun bag. One of the onlookers asked about it, so it had to be added to the test. I plugged the Clark barrel into the Wilson CQB, and punched out a satisfying group that stayed in the A zone.

I've included the 50-yard group photo of each pistol in its test-fire chapter. Some will be good, some will be average, but they are all in the A zone. The test was enough work (and a good way to remember to keep my big mouth shut sometimes) doing a single group each. I sure don't want to be doing group averages shooting the pistols at 50 yards,

During the testing, the five best 1911's sent were enlisted in a match.

"We few, we happy few" got to run the guns.

For accurate long-range handgun shooting, it is hard to improve on the rollover prone. Here, Rob Gaffney demonstrates.

prone or from the Ransom rest. At least not until we build a little trolley to bring the targets back to the firing line.

In the test-firing program, I'd like to thank the following testers for their time, effort, input and eagerness to consume free ammo, in no particular order: Michael Sweeney, Dale Antila, Mel Campbell, Carl Provan, Rob Gaffney, Jim Hackenberg, Phil Kozlowski, Jeff Gerak, Bob Gerak, and Mike Clare.

.40 SUPER

For a parts gun, the .40 Super works great. I chalk it up to proper selection of the starting materials. Along with the rest, it needs Triton ammo and McCormick mags.

The .40 Super is a handful, but still comfortable to shoot.

The Bo-Mar tritium bar rear sight is very useful for low-light shooting.

The rear is a Bo-Mar.

My .40 Super is what many 1911 shooters call a "Frankenstein gun." (Those who have seen the movie Young Frankenstein pronounce it "Fronk-en-steen".) Not because it is ugly, but because it was assembled from parts with different origins. The three main parts, slide, frame and barrel, hailed from distant lands. (Well, disparate parts of the United States.) There is a Rock River Arms slide, a Caspian standard frame with a ramp cut for Para-Ordnance, and .40 Super barrel from KKM.

The slide and frame would not fit together, and the barrel was a gunsmith-fit, so I sent them off to Doug Jones for fitting. Once he had fitted the slide and frame, and then fitted the barrel, he finish-reamed the chamber to proper dimensions with a Dave Manson chamber reamer. As with the race-ready Caspian, the fit is bank-vault tight without binding.

The sights are a front blade with a Novak dovetail slot, and a Bo-Mar rear machined into the slide. The slide is brushed overall, with no attempt at polishing. For some time to come this pistol will stay in the white, so there was no need to polish it. It has cocking serrations front and rear. The barrel is coned at the muzzle, and ramped at the chamber. The 26-pound recoil spring is wrapped around a Clark Custom two-piece guide rod, and held in with an STI cylindrical reverse plug. I'm not usually a fan of shock buffers, but this gun has had one from the beginning, and will probably always have one when there is a .40 Super barrel installed.

The grip safety is the STI version of the Ed Brown highride safety. I installed a McCormick thumb safety, and ground the frame just enough to keep the edges from biting when I fired it. (I apologize for the rugged looks of some of the parts.)

The front a Novak.

The front is coned, not needing a bushing. The Clark two-piece guide rod controls the 26-pound spring.

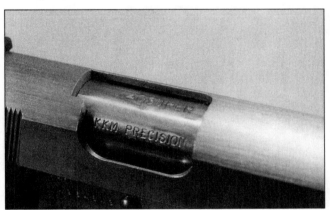

The KKM Precision barrel shoots great.

The scalloped STI grip safety, Ed Brown thumb safety, and tritium-bar Bo-mar rear sight.

OK, so it could qualify as a Frankenstein gun if you looked at it from some angles. I was not intending to make it ugly or pretty, but get it together in time to test-fire it for the book. Short-term, anyway, the important part is the caliber. If you don't want your gun to go through the ugly stage, you can simply buy an STI chambered in .40 Super and miss all the fun.

The .40 Super is from Triton Cartridge Corporation. Early testing involved necking the tough .45 Super down to .40 caliber. In order to increase velocity and keep the neck long enough for proper tension (we've seen earlier what insufficient neck tension can do) Triton lengthened the case from .45 ACP length (.898") to 10mm length (.992"). To control primer flow, the primer pocket specs were changed to small from large, allowing the use of small pistol magnum or small rifle primers. The operating pressure of the .40 Super is set at 37,000 PSI, just above the 9mm and 10mm ceiling.

To keep the cartridge from battering my pistol, or any pistol, it should be run with a 24- or 26-pound recoil spring.

Generally, bottlenecked cartridges feed better out of a 1911 single stack than blunt ones. A bottlenecked cartridge that is the same length as the cartridge it was initially designed for, the .45 ACP, should feed even better. I did not

have a single failure to feed during the testing. As for the ejection, at the pressures and velocities at which the cartridge is working, nothing could fail to eject. Indeed, the problem I had was chasing the empties up the side berm of the range.

One advantage the .40 Super has over the .400 Cor-bon is its ability to handle heavier bullets. In the .400, by the time you get up to 180- to 200-grain bullets, you aren't enough faster than what a .45 ACP+P could do to make it worth the effort. The .40 Super has enough case capacity to keep pushing the 200-grain bullets at high velocity. And what velocities and accuracy did we get?

The 135-grain Quik-Shok JHP proved to be very mild, and is the Triton tactical load in .40 Super. The reduced recoil is intended to reduce split times between shots, for competition and defensive use. The Quik-Shok is a hollow point bullet fabricated with a pre-segmented core. Upon impact, the three pieces of the core separate from the jacket and produce three different wound tracks. The idea is to increase the likelihood of damage to a vital function, such as clipping a vein or artery, puncturing the liver, etc. At only 1,224 fps, it makes Major for competition shooting. The bullet design, coupled with the soft recoil, ensures effectiveness on target. The 135 Hi-Vel JHP was another matter.

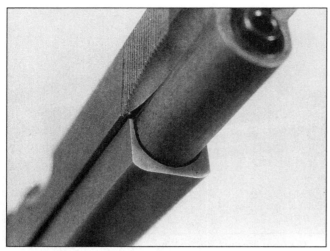

The Foster Industries/Caspian frame is boxy and slightly heavier than a standard frame in the dustcover.

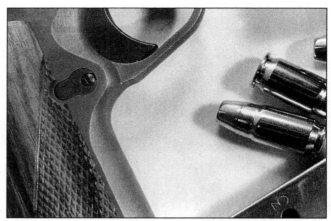

The Foster/Caspian frame is markedly radiused between the frontstrap and the trigger guard.

Once the tangs are radiused for the Ed Brown grip safety (left) they still need a lot of blending before they look like the frame on the right.

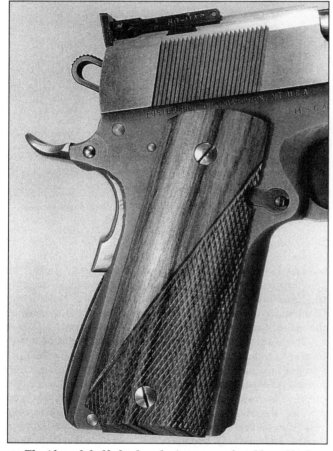

The Ahrends half-checkered grips are comfortable and look good.

Loading the .40 Super is easy, as it uses .45 ACP shell holders. Setting up an extra toolhead for my Dillon 550B is a piece of cake. The Redding dies make loading easy.

They screamed out of the muzzle at an average of 1,749 fps, posting a power factor of 236! The power was evident by the muzzle rise and felt recoil. The 5-inch barrel was lacking a compensator. If you built a hunting gun with a long slide or 6-inch barrel, and comped it, you'd be pushing on 1,800 fps, and the comp would keep the muzzle down.

The 155-grain Quik-Shok proved to be nearly as powerful as the 135 Hi-Vel. The 155s averaged 1,447 fps, for a PF of 224. The 165-grain Hi-Vel JHP generated the highest power factor of the .40 Super loads, going 1,579 fps and posting a 260 PF.

The 200-grain Hi-Vel JHP traveled 1,288 over the chronograph screens, for a PF of 258. I think for hunting using the .40 Super I would go with the 200s in a 6-inch comped barrel. You could easily get over 1,300 fps, perhaps even over 1,325 fps, and the compensator would keep things comfortable to shoot. For those of you who hunt with handguns in locales that require 500 foot-pounds at 100 yards, the 200-grain load has no problems delivering.

In recoil the most vigorous .40 Super ammo was much more punishing to shoot than the other high-velocity load, the .38 Casull. With as much velocity and more weight, the .40 Super came back hard. The only difference between the 165-grain Hi-Vel and the 200-grain load was the pitch of the muzzle blast.

In accuracy, the best load was the 155-grain Quik-Shok, which averaged an inch and a half. Close behind it was the 135 Hi-Vel, at 1.75 inches, and then the 200-grain Hi-Vel at 2 inches. Given the reputation of KKM barrels, this promises to be a very accurate caliber and pistol. As with the caveat of the Casull, the .40 Super is steaming along at a high enough velocity to damage steel plates. The gongs on our 100-yard range are beaten up, and we don't care. They are expected to expire and be replaced. But if you were to shoot someone's pepper poppers with the .40 Super, expect screaming and recriminations. You'll probably have to pay for the welding to repair the steel.

The .40 Super is a hot load, but the brass does not look at all abused.

.40 Super	
Trigger pull	4.25 lb
Extractor tension	22 oz
Chamber depth	N/A
.22 Conversion fit	
Kimber	N
EAA	Y*
Ciener	N
Wilson	N
Marvel	Y**
Bar-Sto .400 Cor-bon fit	N***
Clark .460 Rowland fit	Y***
Weight	41.0 oz
Barrel length	5"
Three favorite loads	
1- 155 gr Triton Q-S	
2- 135 Triton Hi-Vel	
3- 200 gr Triton Hi-Vel	
* The frame is ramped, the conversion is not ** The Marvel sometimes fed despite the ramp gap in the frame *** The unramped barrels would not feed despite fitting in the pistol	

.357 Sig

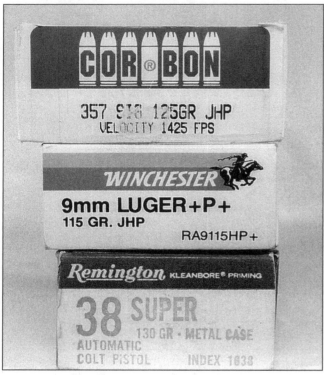

The .357 Sig exists to best the other pistol rounds, and match the .357 Magnum.

While the .40 case, necked down, was the design start, the .357 Sig case is longer. Don't make Sig cases from 40's!

The .357 Sig exists to match the performance of the .357 Magnum loaded with a 125-grain bullet. There are several methods of measuring stopping power, and one of them is the empirical method used by Evan Marshall and Ed Sanow. They simply looked at the end-result of all the shooting reports they could get their hands on, and looked to see which cartridges and loads performed well, and which ones didn't. (There is some argument about how precisely their ratings compare to real life, but rational men may disagree about many things.)

The cartridge and load that has ranked at the top of the lists, for years and years, has been the .357 Magnum loaded with a 125-grain jacketed hollow point. Its stopping power has been rated in the 90-plus percent range since Evan and Ed have been compiling their stats. While it does the job very well, there have always been problems with it. When Police officers all used revolvers, not all could qualify with the full magnum load. Not all departments offered or allowed the magnum option. The most popular .357 magnum revolvers in police service were the S&W K-frames, and in the K-frames, (The M-19, M-66, M-13 and M-65) the regular use of magnum loads would greatly diminish their

service life. Guns that were fed a steady diet of magnums quickly went out of time, forcing cones eroded, barrels cracked and the topstraps would get flame-cut. S&W had to design and build the L-frames (M-586, M-686) to solve the service life problems.

When police departments went wholesale to the pistol, they gave up the .357 Magnum option. The 9mm cannot deliver the velocity of the .357 Magnum, not even in the law-enforcement-only +P+ loads. "No problem" you say "Use a .38 Super or 9x23 Winchester load." But they bring a different problem. Cartridge length. You can't fit the Super or 9x23 into a double-stack magazine, install a double-action trigger mechanism, and expect everyone to be able to fit their hand around the gun. Yes, yes, you can say "Too

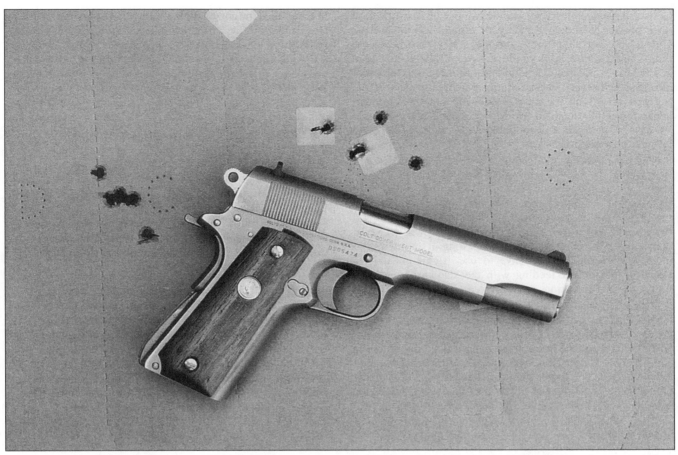

The Colt Delta Elite, with groups from the King's .40 barrel and the Ed Brown .357 Sig barrel. It takes less than a minute to switch from one to the other.

bad, let the short cops use a single-stack gun." And you as the Police Administrator would end up in court, explaining why you are discriminating against smaller officers.

Sig solved the problem by necking the .40 S&W down to 9mm, keeping the length within the 9mm magazine tube maximum, and loading to the maximum allowed pressure for the 40 case. (The .357 Sig does not actually use necked-down 40 cases, the Sig case is longer. But the design came from the 40. Only use cases marked ".357 Sig" to load your ammo.) There is some reloader in the back, asking why not load the lightest bullets in .40 caliber into the 40 case? Velocity. The .40 maxes out in the low to mid 1,300 fps range with a 135-grain bullet. A good load will deliver 1,325 to 1,350 fps. The .357 Sig adds at least 125 fps to that, with a slightly lighter bullet. I've had some lots of Cor-bon 125-grain bullets check out at 1,496 fps average.

The Sig duplicates the performance of the .357 Magnum, in a pistol. If you want velocity, it's the one. Some insist on

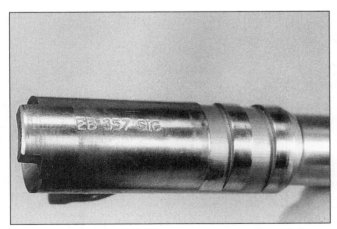

The Ed Brown .357 Sig barrel locked up tightly and shot accurately.

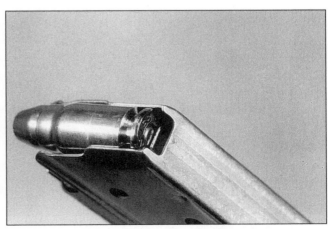

The .357 Sig requires magazines proportioned like the .40 S&W, so the Colt needs magazines with fillers in the back.

heavier bullets, and that leaves the Sig out of it, as the case does not have enough capacity to utilize heavier bullets. Unless you load them long, and use a 1911 instead of the 9mm-platform pistols. If you load long in a 1911, you have a .38 Casull Lite, and can add a bit more steam to the usual .357 Sig velocities. The reloading manuals insist that the Sig headspaces on the case mouth and not the shoulder, hence the requirement to use Sig cases and not re-formed .40 cases. But this is a pistol book, not a reloading book, so let's get down to pistols.

The base gun for this testing is a Colt Delta Elite, stainless 10mm. It was a prize gun from the Second Chance shoot, and to give you an idea of how loot-heavy the prize tables got at Second Chance, it was for third place. To convert it to .357 Sig was simplicity itself. I installed an Ed Brown .357 Sig barrel. With it, I used Ed Brown .40 S&W magazines. Were I to load the rounds long in an attempt to increase performance, I'd have to use 10mm magazines. However, for proper feeding with the standard-length Sig round, the .40 magazines are preferred.

The Ed Brown barrel has a slightly different point of impact than the Colt 10mm barrel, about an inch left and 2 inches low at 25 yards. The left to right is a normal change when going from one barrel to another, and simply plugging another Colt 10mm barrel into the pistol might create that much change. The lower point of impact is a result of the lighter bullets, getting out of the muzzle sooner before the pistol has recoiled enough to lift the muzzle.

The .357 Sig, being a bottlenecked case, you'd expect it to feed flawlessly. And you'd be right. In a lighter pistol, the hot Sig load might cause stiff recoil, but in the full-size Government frame of the Delta Elite, the recoil was no big deal. The hottest load was the 125-grain Cor-bon, with one lot producing an average velocity of 1,488 fps, and another producing 1,498 fps. The other loads were a tie in power, with the Cor-bon 115-grain bullets going 1,488 fps (a popular velocity that day) and the Georgia Arms 125 FMJ bullets going 1,458. When it came to accuracy, the winner was the Cor-bon 115-grain JHP, delivering 1-1/4-groups at 25 yards. It is a rare full metal jacket bullet that produces the accuracy of a good hollow point, and the Cor-bon delivered. The accuracy was good enough, and the trajectory flat enough, that to ring the 100-yard gong every time with the Cor-bon 115s, all I had to do was hold on the top edge of the plate. The rest was follow-through. The Georgia Arms and the 125 Cor-bon's both delivered averages under 2 inches, but the Colt and the Ed Brown barrel wanted the 115s.

So, what is it good for? Considering the accuracy, and the soft recoil you could get with mild reloads, it would make a very nice pistol/cartridge for the Handgunner Shoot-off. You would be hampered in using it in USPSA/IPSC competition, because as a bullet smaller in diameter than .400", you could only shoot it Minor. As a Minor cartridge, in Limited or Limited 10, it would work fine. You could use it in IDPA, and with a compensated barrel it would be a very efficient pin gun. The only drawback to some uses (Handgunner Shoot-off and bowling pins) is the expense of brass. At a big match you don't get your empties back. At the Shoot-off, that could be 1,000 empties.

CHRONOGRAPH
.45 SUPER RESULTS

Brand, Caliber, weight and style	Average	Stand Deviation	Extreme Spread.	PF.
.30 Luger				
Remington 93 gr. FMJ	1190	28.2	65.3	111
9X19 Parabellum				
PMC Starfire 124 JHP	1094	6.4	17.5	136
Rem Golden Saber 124 +P	1108	33.1	85.0	137
Black Hills 124 JHP	1164	15.1	34.6	144
Federal 115 JHP +P+	1273	14.7	36.1	146
Cor-bon 115 JHP +P	1342	6.3	15.1	154
Federal 147 Hydra Shok	945	6.9	17.3	139
W-W 115 JHP +P+ LE-Only	1348	12.0	30.8	155
Texas Ammunition Co. 115 JHP	1283	16.4	38.5	147
.38 Super				
W-W 130 FMJ	1156	17.3	40.6	150
Cor-bon, 115 JHP	1439	13.9	32.2	165
.38 Special				
Federal 148 WC Match	630	8.8	25.2	93
.357 Sig				
115 JHP Cor-bon	1488	5.6	12.1	171
125 JHP Cor-bon	1470	15.2	37.9	184
125 FMJ Georgia Arms	1458	18.8	45.1	182
125 JHP Federal	1393	14.1	34.3	173
.40 S&W				
W-W 180 FMJ White box	899	12.0	25.7	161
Remington Golden Saber 180 JHP	918	6.7	18.7	165
Cor-bon 180 JHP	1060	9.3	23.2	191
Cor-bon 165 JHP	1164	14.1	36.1	192
Cor-bon 135 JHP	1310	12.9	24.2	177
W-W Silvertip 155 JHP	1153	21.1	56.2	179
10MM				
W-W Silvertip 175 JHP	1242	13.7	28.0	217
Norma 170 JHP	1227	12.4	32.3	208
Hornady 180 XTP-JHP	1191	21.9	51.3	214
Cor-bon, 135 JHP	1467	15.5	33.3	198
Federal 155 JHP	1367	11.7	30.7	212
.38 Casull				
124 JHP	1824	14.1	33.8	226
147 JHP	1718	10.9	24.0	252

.40 Super

Triton 135 JHP Hi Vel	1749	16.6	44.2	236
Triton 135 JHP Quik-Shok	1224	30.6	77.5	165
Triton 155 JHP Quik-Shok	1447	19.3	49.9	224
Triton 165 JHP Hi Vel	1579	13.5	34.5	260
Triton 200 JHP Hi Vel	1288	7.4	18.9	258

.400 Cor-bon

135 JHP	1442	12.3	39.2	195
150 JHP	1362	16.1	44.5	204
155 FMJ	1226	9.2	21.4	190
165 JHP	1310	7.9	19.4	216

.45 ACP

Magtech, 230 JRN	781	22.2	49.6	179
PMP, 220 JRN	873	18.3	45.4	192
PMC, 230 JRN	809	7.6	19.6	186
Black Hills Blue, 230 JRN	809	12.7	35.5	186
Black Hills Red, 230 JRN	813	12.5	27.9	187
Zero, 185 JHP	891	17.2	33.9	165
West Coast, 200 JRN	844	13.7	32.5	169
Montana Gold, 185 JHP	948	11.3	28.5	175
Rainier, 230 JRN	747	13.9	37.4	172
Sierra, 230 JHP	781	15.1	35.2	179
Texas Ammo Co., 230 JRN	828	19.2	46.4	190
Texas Ammo Co., 185 JHP	953	11.8	28.8	176
Hornady 200 JHP-XTP	878	17.5	45.6	176
Oregon Trail 200 L-SWC	869	16.8	45.8	173

.45 ACP+P

Cor-bon, 165 JHP	1256	36.6	89.2	207
Cor-bon, 185 JHP	1157	24.0	51.6	214
Cor-bon, 200 JHP	1040	18.2	40.3	208
Cor-bon, 230 JHP	942	14.3	29.5	216
Triton, 185 JHP-Hi Vel	1086	27.8	53.4	201
Triton, 230 JHP-Hi Vel	921	5.2	11.2	212
Triton, 165 JHP-Quik-Shok	1202	13.9	34.9	198
Triton, 203 JHP-Quik-Shok	915	10.5	26.5	210
Texas Ammo Co. 185 JHP	952	9.9	26.3	176
Texas Ammo Co. 230 JHP	821	14.9	42.0	189

.45 Super

Texas Ammo Co. 185 JHP-XTP (Tactical load)	1174	15.6	39.9	217
Texas Ammo Co. 230 JHP-XTP (Tactical Load)	938	18.1	48.7	216
Texas Ammo Co. 200 JHP	1185	14.1	28.3	237
Texas Ammo Co. 230 JHP	1074	41.7	107.2	247
Texas Ammo Co. 230 JRN	1083	10.0	23.8	249
Texas Ammo Co. 230 JHP Express	1169	14.5	37.9	269
Texas Ammo Co. 230 JTC	1156	8.3	20.2	266

.460 Rowland

Georgia Arms 185 JHP-Defense	1362	14.6	32.2	251
Georgia Arms 185 Nosler JHP	1447	15.6	38.5	267
Georgia Arms 230 Gold Dot	1347	15.7	40.6	309

THE HARDBALLER

The Hardballer pistol was the most surprising one of the entire group. The original AMT pistols were made in southern California, and were famous for two things; being the first 1911 pistols made entirely of stainless steel, and a spotty record of reliability. If you have an original AMT that works, you've probably found it to be very reliable. Not all were.

The current 1911s are made in South Dakota by Galena Industries, who bought the AMT name and manufacturing tooling. (South Dakota has done a good job of luring manufacturing companies, particularly firearms and ammunition companies, from other states. Lower taxes and other business-friendly conditions have lured many companies out of less-friendly locales.) Having bought the name and tooling, Galena is now trying to overcome the reputation of the previous pistols. The 1911 we tested was a Government Model size pistol called the "Hardballer." It carried Millett sights, with an orange front blade and a plain black rear. The rear is adjustable, while the front blade is fixed in place by the Millett Dual-Crimp method. The Millett method is not compatible with the other systems, dovetail or staking. It is however, very secure, as I have never seen a Dual Crimp sight come off. The top of the slide has a rib running its length. The ejection port is lowered but not flared, but the empties did not have any problem exiting. The pistol live-ejects.

With a standard unramped barrel and a Gold Cup size hood manufactured by Galena the barrel uses a bushing to secure the muzzle end. The recoil spring is contained by a standard retaining plug with a smooth face. On the left side of the slide, it is marked "Cal .45 ACP -Hardballer- by

The Hardballer in its hard case, with magazine and instructions.

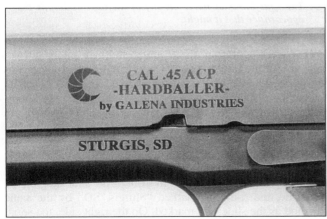

The new Hardballers come from Galena Industries, of Sturgis, S.D.

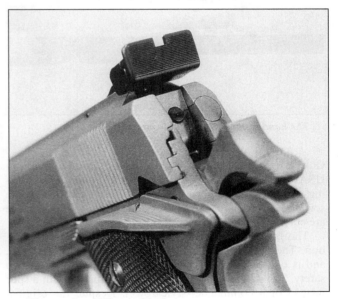

The rear is a Millett in black.

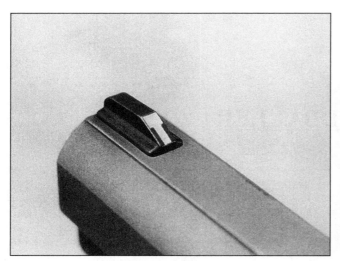

The front has an orange ramp.

The ejection port is lowered but not flared.

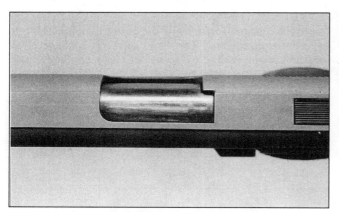

The hood is the narrow, Gold-Cup width.

The recoil spring plug is smooth.

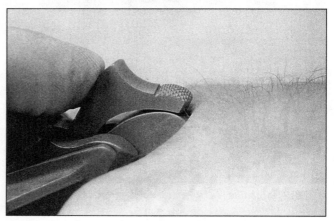

The spur hammer never bit any of the testers, despite the appearance that it might.

Galena Industries" and the right side has "Stainless made in USA" and a caution to read the owner's manual. The markings are not engraved or roll-marked, but appear to be some sort of etching that changes the color of the stainless. There are cocking serrations at the rear only.

The frame is a standard Government Model configuration. The grip safety is the original style, not a beavertail, and is one of only three pistols tested with this style grip safety. The hammer is a 1911A1 style hammer, with a spur instead of a commander-style rowel. Despite the original 1911A1 configuration, the hammer and grip safety did not bite any of the test shooters. The grip safety had large gaps between it and the frame, but worked properly. Despite expecting discomfort from the gaps, none of the test shooters reported any pinching from the grip safety gaps. Even the testers prone to reporting sharp edges turned in a clean report on the Hardballer.

The thumb safety is oversized, with a slight corner at the rear that promised to bite but never did. The slide stop is a standard unit with serrations. In front of the slide stop on the left side, the frame is marked "Sturgis, SD" by the same method as the slide was marked. On the right side, the serial number appears to be marked with an electric pencil in a

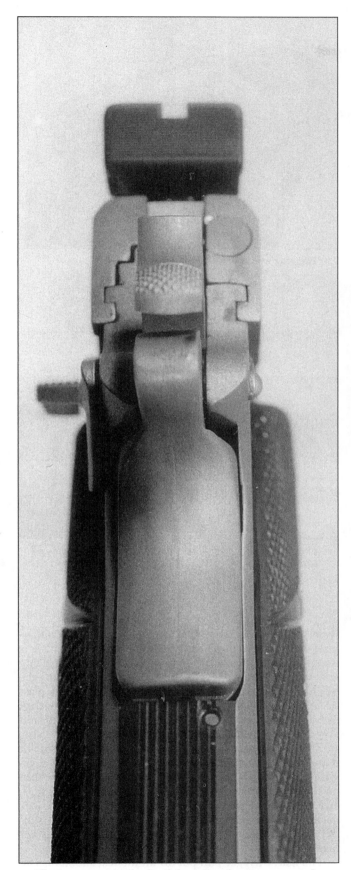

The large gaps in the fit of the grip safety never created a problem in testing.

Left side.

The serial number is punched into the frame.

The long trigger does not have an over-travel screw.

pantograph or CNC guiding unit. The trigger is extended, lacking a stop screw. The trigger also lacks the three holes commonly found on extended triggers. The trigger pull caused the most comment. It was so heavy I could not check it with my Brownells recording gauge. The gauge goes up to 6 pounds, and I can extrapolate to 7. In order to check the weight of the AMT, I had to use my trigger weights, and with the trigger holding all 5-1/4 pounds of dead weight, then add the tension from the gauge to drop the hammer. They were not enough. At an estimated 12-1/4 pounds, the hammer stayed cocked. I had to add another couple of pounds of pull to drop the hammer and complete the test. The grips are

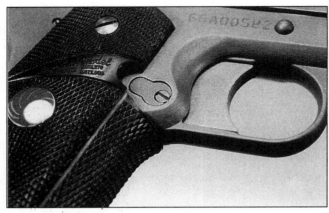

The mag catch and Pachmayr grips.

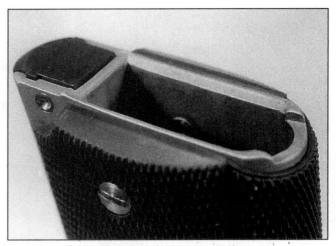

The mag well is bevelled for easy reloading.

The barrel lug machine cut which is found on all Hardballers.

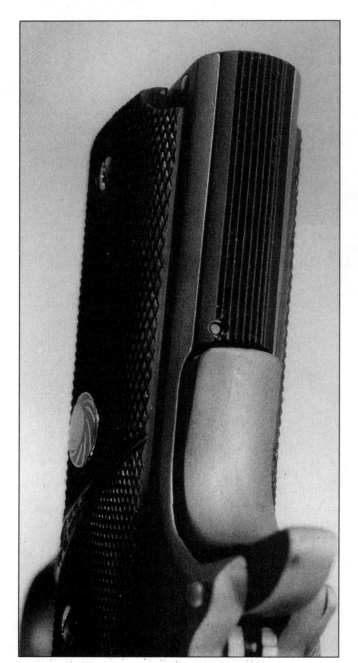

The mainspring housing is black plastic.

wraparound rubber grips that have AMT logo medallions inset on each side, made for AMT by Pachmayr. (Galena is using up the old stock of grips, and will be switching to a new style when the old ones are gone. Again, shedding the old AMT reputation.) The mainspring housing is black plastic. A plastic mainspring housing is an attractive choice for manufacturers, being lighter and cheaper than steel, and suitably durable. The magazine opening is beveled.

The finish is mostly matte, the original surface texture of the mould in which the slide and frame were cast of 17-4 stainless steel. The rails and top deck of the frame are then machined, as is the inside of the slide and its locking lugs, and then heat-treated. The frame still retains the curious machine cut of the original AMT, a tool cut meant to simplify the machining work of the recess for the barrel's lower lugs.

The heavy trigger pull put off all the test shooters. The pull was so heavy it made checking the zero of the sights difficult, as keeping the sights on the target while crushing the frame enough to drop the hammer was too much

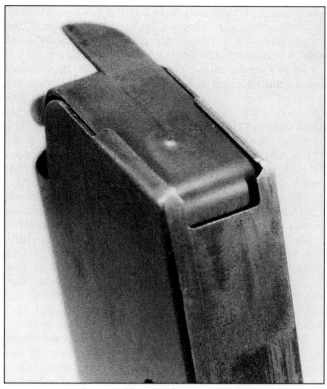

To take this one apart, depress the inner plate and slide the baseplate off.

While differing in details from the other magazines, the Hardballer mag worked 100 percent.

like work. The pistol worked 100 percent of the time. It never failed to feed, fire and eject, and it locked open when it was empty. The magazines dropped free when empty, and as best the shooters could tell, it was sighted in from the factory. It did not bite or pinch, and none of the apparently sharp edges cut, abraded or otherwise annoyed the shooters. While none of them were looking forward to shooting it, especially after word of the heavy trigger pull got around, they were all pleased that it functioned absolutely reliably. As far as the functionality was concerned, the Hardballer did not have to take a back seat to any other gun. And it helped our group start to shed their mind-set about AMT pistols.

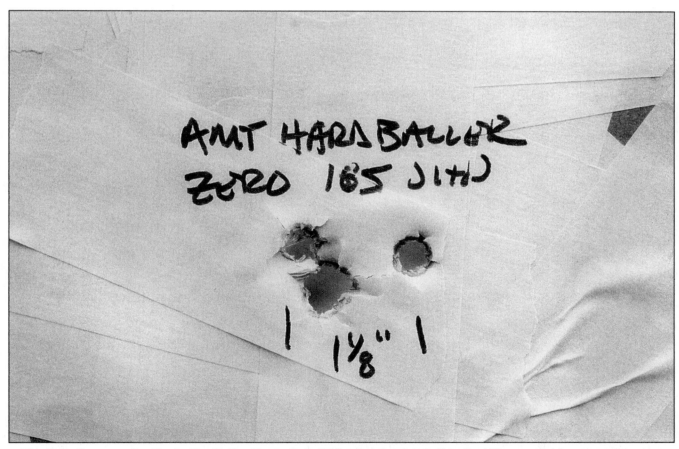

This is the first group fired by the Hardballer. Not the first after settling, but the absolute first. The rest were just as good.

I was not expecting anything more than average groups when I clamped it in the Ransom rest, and one of the testers even joked that I might have to staple a larger piece of cardboard up to mark the group size. After all, the table the Ransom rest is bolted to only weighs 250 pounds, and with that trigger pull... All joking stopped after the first group. Even the settling-in groups were better than average, and once I had fired four settling groups, the Hardballer did what no other pistol did; it fired a continual series of groups under 2 inches in size, with the first four types of ammo tested. Sixteen groups for record at the start, and every one of them under 2 inches in size. We stood with our jaws hanging open on every group fired.

I cannot say that every Hardballer will deliver like this one, but if this is any indication of the barrel quality and barrel fitting that they are doing in Sturgis, then the Hardballer shows promise, and lots of it. Of the things you might need done to a pistol, reliability work, accuracy work or trigger work, the least expensive to undertake is trigger work. Since this pistol already delivers on the first two, then a good trigger on it would vault it near the top of the heap. And for the suggested retail price, adding a trigger job would still make it a heck of a bargain.

During the test-firing of the pistols, I regularly talked with the representatives of each firm. At Galena I was talking to David Small, the president. When he heard of the trigger pull he was horrified. He asked that I send it back, as every Galena-manufactured pistol is covered under a lifetime warranty, and he would see to it that the trigger pull was adjusted to the correct weight, at no charge and immediately. He also said he would have done it for any customer, and not just a gun writer. It left here in a Next-Day Air box on a Monday, and returned on the following Friday. Upon its return, the trigger pull was a clean, crisp 5 pounds, certainly good enough to take advantage of the spectacular accuracy.

When I next contacted Galena, I found that the warranty repair gunsmith, and test-shooter was none other than the owner of Galena, Rick Filippi. He shoots them when they are made, and fixes those few returned. The Galena guns get fixed free, the old AMT-made guns are fixed (when they have the correct parts) at a fair hourly rate. I used to fix 1911s, and I charged more 10 years ago than Rick does today. If you've got a malfunctioning old AMT-made gun, send it in to see if he can fix it.

The most accurate load in the Hardballer was the Oregon Trail load, with an average of 1.31 inches. Coming in a close second was the Zero ammo, with 185-grain jacketed hollowpoints averaging 1.43 inches. Third was the Black Hills Blue, with 230-grain jacketed round nose bullets at 1.63 inches, and fourth was the Sierra 230 JHP load at 1.68 inches. Four different bullets designs in three weights, half factory and half reloads. Even the loads it "didn't" like grouped under 2-1/2 inches more often than they didn't. This pistol just doesn't care what you feed it, it wants to shoot.

When it came time to ship the guns back after the shooting was done, I thought long and hard about keeping this one. For a 1911 that sells for $500, you should too. When you consider the cost/performance ratio, it would be hard to beat the Hardballer as a beginning gun in the USPSA Limited 10 Division, or as a Stock gun for pins or falling plates. Just be sure you buy a Galena-made pistol. Check for a "G" in the serial number. If there is one, snap it up.

All the testers liked the Hardballer once the trigger pull problem was solved.

Hardballer	
Trigger pull	5.0 lb
Extractor tension	0 oz*
Chamber depth	.901
.22 Conversion fit	
Kimber	Y
EAA	Y
Ciener	N
Wilson	Y
Marvel	Y
Bar-Sto .400 Cor-bon fit	N**
Clark .460 Rowland fit	N**
Weight	35.5 oz
Barrel length	5"
Three favorite loads	
1-Oregon Tr/Viht	1.36"
2-Zero 185 JHP	1.43"
3-Black Hills Red	1.63"

* The extractor had no measurable tension, but never failed to work
** The Hardballer barrel has a Gold Cup dimension hood, and these barrels use a Government hood.

CASPIAN

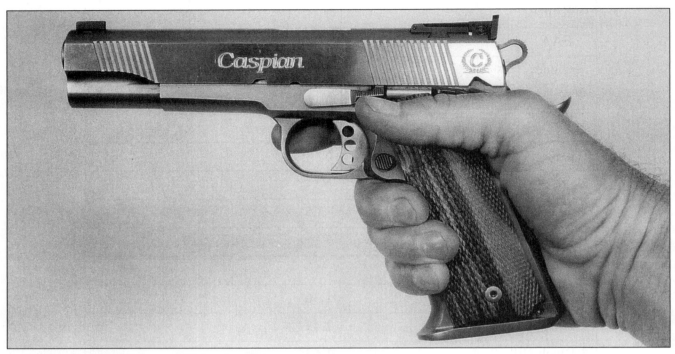

The Caspian Race-Ready, assembled and ready to go.

And the reason we get stainless is? Any other questions?

Caspian has been making 1911 components for themselves and other manufacturers for two decades now. You can count on three things from Caspian, the parts will be machined to the correct specs, they will be properly hard, and they will look good. You can order parts, or enough parts to put together a pistol (provided you have an FFL for the frame) and you can specify the details of those parts. You want a carbon steel commander slide with cocking serrations front and rear, and Novak sight cuts? They'll ask three questions: what caliber, how are you paying, and where do you want it shipped?

The 1911 we tested was a Race Ready frame kit. You do not have as many options in the kit. What Caspian has done is bundle all the most popular options, and those with a competitive advantage, into one box of parts. The kit included all parts except the thumb safety and the springs to get it running. Also, the barrel and the slide and frame rails were left oversize so they could be gunsmith fitted. I sent my kit off to Doug Jones for the fitting. (Yes, I know how to fit 1911 parts together. I've done it many times. But I can't fit and write, too. So off it went.) Doug has a hard-core following in Michigan, where he has many competitors (and those who carry 1911's for defensive work) who depend on him. Among the many satisfied customers here in Michigan is a fellow by the name of Jerry Barnhart. Jerry is quite happy with Doug's work, and I am in agreement. Doug's specialty is the Acc-U-Rail enhancement, where the rails of the slide and frame are machined to accommodate a section of drill rod. The hardened rod takes the wear and offers a larger bearing surface. In the event the frame and/or slide wear, the rod can be replaced with one a few thousandths larger to take up the slack.

Left rear of the Caspian. Note the rear sight, grip safety and Kim Ahrends Cocobolo grips.

The muzzle is coned, not needing a bushing, and has a captured recoil spring plug.

The front sight came too tall (they all do) and had to be trimmed at the range.

The ejection port is lowered and scalloped.

The advantages are that the slide and rail are more tightly fitted with a longer service life. The slide also moves very smoothly on the frame. The disadvantage is that once a pistol has the Acc-u-Rail, you can't go back. Despite the high volume of shooting I've done, I've never felt the need for rails. To be fair, I've never owned one with rails, and thus haven't had a chance to compare. I'll have to correct that one of these days.

Doug fitted the slide, frame and barrel together, and I installed the rest of the parts.

The Caspian did not get rails, being fitted in the usual method. Out of the box, the slide would not go onto the frame more than an inch, and the barrel didn't even come close to fitting in the slide. When Doug sent it back, the slide fit on the rails with no perceptible play, but would slide off of its own weight if the frame were tilted. The barrel locks up with a perceptible hesitation. If you ease the slide forward you can feel the barrel being picked up and going into lockup. If you move your hand forward slowly you can get the slide to hesitate just before final lockup, but when you let go of it the slide never fails to fully close. A textbook fit and lock job.

The Race Ready comes with all the machine cuts done. The sights are a Novak-dovetail front and an adjustable rear of the Bo-mar pattern but Caspian design and manufacture. The rear sight has the Caspian logo on it. The kit is shipped with two front sights and two rear blades. When you assemble, your choice of fronts is either the plain blade front, or a dual-post drilled front that holds a fluorescent fiber optic tube. The rear blades are either the standard notch or the ghost ring rear to use with the fiber optic front.

The stainless slide is finished in a brushed polish, with the sides a brighter polish. There are cocking serrations front and rear. The ejection port is lowered and scalloped, and live ejects. The rear of the slide is plain. On the left side of the slide, it is marked "Caspian" and has the Caspian logo behind the rear cocking serrations. On the right side, the only mark is the Caspian logo, again behind the rear cocking serrations.

The barrel is Caspian's Ultimatch Cal 450. It comes with a Para-pattern integral feed ramp and as-shipped the chamber is short to allow you or your gunsmith to ream it to final dimension. The muzzle is coned and has no need of a bushing. The recoil spring retainer is a bored circular one, rather than a shouldered one. The recoil spring guide rod is one-piece.

The frame is a standard Government Model pattern frame with a regular dust cover. It is marked with Caspian's name over the right grip, and the serial number is between the grip and the slide stop pin hole. If you order a frame from Caspian, you can specify what serial number you want. There are limits, however. It can't be more than 10 characters, and at least one of them has to be a number. Oh yes, it also has to be one they haven't used before. If you plan to have a special serial number on your pistol, it would pay to call and ask if someone has used your idea already, and have alternates ready. The number on this gun came as a surprise to me, I had no idea what it was until I opened the box.

The hammer is an oval commander hammer. The grip safety is a Wilson-pattern safety. I installed a McCormick thumb safety, partly because I had it on hand, and partly

You can have your Caspian with a custom serial number. I didn't ask for this, they just sent it.

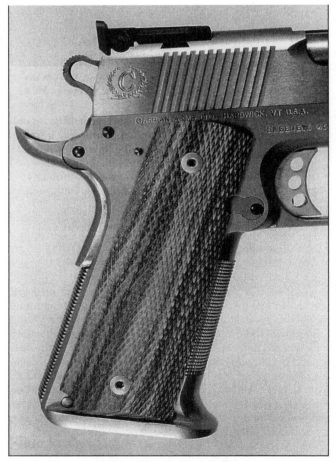

The right side. Note the mag funnel, Ahrends grips, the Caspian grip safety and tight frontstrap-to-trigger guard radius.

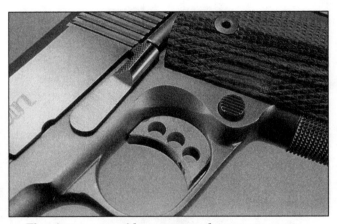

The trigger comes with an over-travel stop screw.

The huge mag funnel built into the Caspian Race frame.

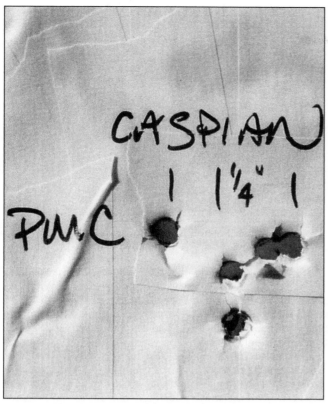

One of the better groups. The Caspian liked almost all I fed it.

because I wanted a low-profile safety that I knew would be comfortable. It is a standard and not an ambidextrous safety. The slide stop is a standard unit, checkered. The trigger is an aluminum extended one, with three holes and a stop screw installed. The supplied parts went together at 4-1/2 pounds of trigger pull, a little heavy for competition, but just fine for carry. And it can be lightened. The magazine catch is serrated, and the retainer a standard slotted pin. The radius between the frontstrap and the trigger guard is cut tighter and higher than normal. The frontstrap is checkered, but not the entire length. There are a few flat diamonds on the bottom row of checkering. The front of the frame is radiused enough that the curve of the frontstrap disappears under the leading edge of the grips. The effect is very comfortable. The mainspring housing is flat, stainless and checkered 20 lpi, the same as the frontstrap.

At the bottom of the frame we see the addition that really makes the Caspian stand out from the crowd. The magazine funnel is integral to the frame. The sides come up as high as the grips, and the front flares out to collect your little finger on the outside. Inside the funnel is smoothly radiused to the magazine tunnel. On the front of this frame, the funnel is notched to clear the front tab of the magazine. I have a large number of magazines that I have acquired over three decades of shooting, and some of them have oddly-shaped front tabs. To ensure they would all lock in place I had Doug re-cut the notch and radius it. I mentioned this to Gary Smith of Caspian and he told me that they have since

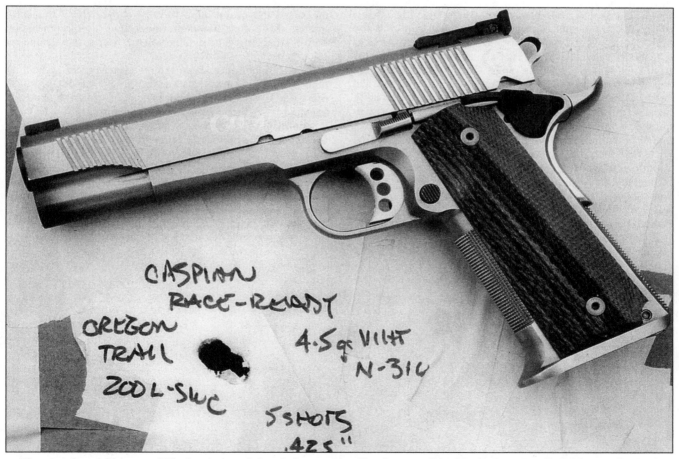

The winnah and Champeen! The best group of the whole test series. Yes, there are five shots in there. Yes I'm loading more of that combo, and no, you can't have this pistol.

The testers liked the Caspian, especially my brother, who thanked the folks at Caspian for making a .45 with "his" name in the serial number.

The 50-yard group from the Caspian. You shoot over 100 rounds prone and try to keep them all in tight little clusters.

changed the front interior of the funnel to a smooth curve that doesn't require a notch for clearance.

I installed a pair of Ahrends Cocobolo grips and tightened them down with the Allen-head grip screws that came in the kit. In all, it is a classy looking pistol that should earn you points on the range from looks alone.

In function it will get you more than that. The first couple of magazines had a few feeding stumbles, but you'd expect that with a freshly assembled pistol. By the time I had determined that the sights were centered but the front was too high, it was working perfectly. A high front sight creates low hits. I calculated the necessary amount to shorten the front sight and filed it at the range. Once it checked out and was working perfectly, I clamped it in the Ransom rest and got to work. It is a good thing Caspian put my name on it, because this pistol is not going back to them. The start was not auspicious, as I began with the factory ammunition that had to be withdrawn from the test. The bullets were setting back into the cases on feeding, and malfunctioning. The variations in velocity caused by the different seating depths of the bullets probably explained the large groups the pistol was shooting. The Caspian hated it worse than the other pistols, and I couldn't get it to work with the ammo for a long enough period of time to generate more than two groups.

I switched to PMP, which in the Caspian is a solid, if average, performer. Curiously enough, it didn't shoot much better with either the Zero load or the Sierra load, both of which performed well in many pistols. What the Caspian did like, it liked spectacularly. In third place for accuracy honors was the Hornady 200-grain XTP, averaging just under 2 inches. Not bad for a defense load. Second were the Montana Gold 185s, shooting into an average of just over 1-1/2 inches. The best load in the Caspian was the Oregon Trail load. It shot a group of 1-3/8 inches, two groups of 1-1/4 inches, and a spectacular group that was the best of all the range trips and Ransom testing. Center to center the smallest group ran .424 inches. I was so astounded by it I dug my dial calipers out of the bag and measured the group edge to edge (7/8 inches) and subtracted the bullet diameter, rather than simply measure with a steel rule. The average of the four groups came to 1.07 inches!

In all, it shot only seven groups larger than 2 inches, in nine loads of four groups each. While I cannot promise that your Caspian will shoot as well, you can depend on the quality of their components. The fitting is up to your gunsmith. The Race Ready they sent me would make a spectacular pistol for the Handgunner Shoot-off in San Juan, Colorado, a great USPSA/IPSC Limited 10 pistol, and if it holds its accuracy with powder-puff ammo, a killer steel gun for the Steel Challenge. Once this one is broken-in, and I fine-tune it for the ammo it likes (better than the Oregon Trails load?) it should be a consistent 1-inch gun at 25 yards. This one is not going back to Caspian. It stays with me, and I will keep it until I leave it to someone in my will.

Caspian Race Ready	
Trigger pull	3.75 lb
Extractor tension	19 oz
Chamber depth	.902"
.22 Conversion fit	
Kimber	Y
EAA	Y
Ciener	Y
Wilson	Y
Marvel	Y
Bar-Sto .400 Cor-bon fit	Y
Clark .460 Rowland fit	Y
Weight	38.8 oz
Barrel length	5"
Three favorite loads	
1-Oregon Tr/Viht	1.07"
2-Montana Gold/Titegroup	1.55"
3-Hornady 200 gr XTP	1.95"

.38 CASULL

In every subject, some people have to have the most, and shooters are no different. The .38 Casull fills that need, if what you want is velocity. And quality. Assembled in the Casull plant in Wyoming, the 3800 is composed of the best parts they can acquire, and those parts are assembled and fitted with only accuracy and power in mind. Dick Casull is a stickler for getting things right, and it shows.

Starting at the top, the Casull slide is a 6-inch slide. Actually, the barrel is 6 inches long, and the slide is long enough to match it. The sights are an adjustable rear that appears to be a Caspian sight, with a front blade in a Novak dovetail. The front sight has a small set screw to keep it in place, a good idea considering the performance the caliber delivers. There are cocking serrations only at the rear. On the left side under the rear sight is a screw head. The screw is the firing pin limiter, to keep the firing pin from exces-

The dovetailed front sight and its locking screw.

The Casull in its fitted case, with spare magazines, tools and room for ammo.

Left side, the etched logo and signature.

The rear sight, thumb safety and hammer.

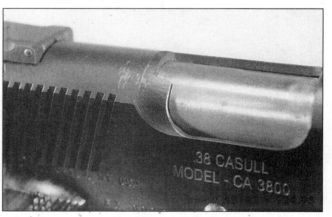

The lowered and scalloped ejection port, with some brassing evident.

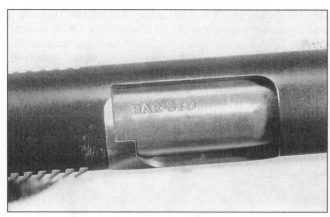

A Bar-sto barrel, it doesn't get better than this.

The firing pin limiter screw controls the firing pin's bounce during the cycle of the slide.

The muzzle, standard bushing, hollow recoil spring plug and two-piece guide rod.

The slide locked back.

sively bouncing around as the slide cycles. The slide is marked on the left with an engraved copy of Dick Casull's signature and the Casull Arms logo, and on the right with "38 Casull Model CA 3800". The ejection port is lowered, and has a flare at the rear that is different. Instead of simply being an angled machine cut, it is a scalloped and blended curve that is subtle and attractive. However, it does not live-eject. While annoying, the lack of live eject is not a big deal when you consider the likelihood of this pistol being used in a defensive situation. (Almost certainly zero.) Used as a hunting pistol, the non live-eject feature simply causes some extra fussing when unloading at the end of the day.

The recoil spring is stout. A specially-wound 30-pound spring, it is needed to keep the slide under control during recoil. Without its strength, the slide and frame would be battered during recoil, and the slide would not last long. Usually, such a heavy spring would hurl the firing pin forward upon closing, denting the primer, hence the firing pin limiter screw. The recoil spring guide rod is a full-length, two-piece unit, and the barrel uses a bushing. The Bar-sto barrel is tightly fitted, and ramped so as to provide as much support to the chambered cases as possible.

The frame is a standard single stack, with Ed Brown thumb and grip safeties. The hammer is a commander style. The trigger is extended, with three holes and a stop screw installed. The slide stop is standard, with checkering. The magazine catch is standard size, with checkering. On the pistol I have, the magazine catch is drilled and tapped for an oversize button, but there was no button installed. The mag catch retaining pin has an Allen-head socket, as do the grip screws, a nice touch like that of the Ed Brown 1911 and others, as well. The front of the grip strap is cut high under the trigger guard, and checkered 30 lpi. The mainspring housing is flat and checkered to match the frontstrap. The magazine opening is slightly beveled. The grips are figured but dark wood, checkered in the double diamond pattern.

The slide and frame, and all parts except the hammer and trigger are done in a matte polish blue.

The pistol comes in a case that puts all the others to the back of the line. A matte-black Zero Halliburton case, with fitted foam on the inside, and two Wilson magazines. The foam has cutouts for two boxes of ammunition, and the pistol rests under an illustrated and photograph-laden owner's manual. If you didn't know it was a gun case, you'd think it was an armored laptop computer case, or an undersized and pretentious attaché case.

The general impression is that of a stoutly and precisely-made pistol. And then you try to work the slide. Unless you are strong of grip, you will have trouble getting the slide back. Between the tight lockup and the 30-pound recoil spring, getting a round in the chamber is work. It is not a pistol for those who don't eat their famous breakfast cereal. Every shooter I handed it to initially tried to open the slide,

then stopped to check that the safety was not on. Then, they would put some muscle to it and it would open with a snap.

The .38 Casull is based on a .45 case (at least in the design stages) for two simple reasons: a necked-down .45 ACP case has the same capacity as a .357 Magnum, and there isn't a larger case available. Unlike the straight-wall .357 Magnum, the neck and shoulder of the Casull increase powder efficiency. The concept has been known for some time in the world of rifle shooting, where a short fat car-

The frontstrap is lifted and radiused. Note the Allen-head screws for grips and mag catch.

The case looks as good as the pistol.

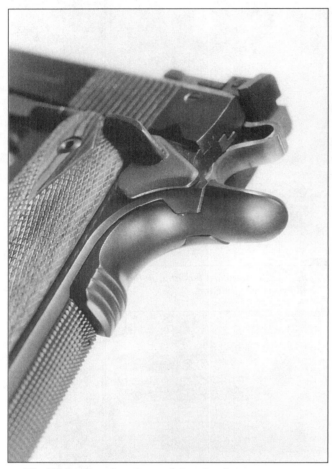

The Ed Brown grip safety and thumb safety.

The trigger, and mag catch drilled and tapped.

The Casull is a full-sized pistol, with a manly recoil spring.

It is nice to test a prototype, but at the end you have to send it back. There is no keeping the "Bond" gun.

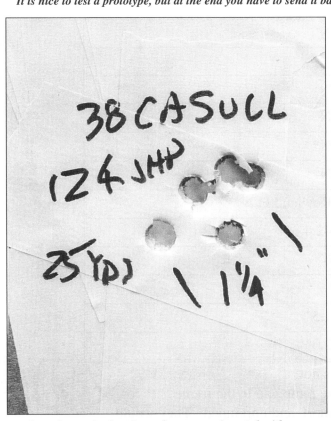

Once it was broken in and you experimented with some loads, I'm sure the Casull could improve on its already-good accuracy.

tridge is more efficient and often more accurate than a case with the same volume that is long and skinny. Current cases use a large pistol primer, but in the future new and improved cases will feature a small rifle primer. The smaller primer leaves more brass in the case, and ignites the powder as well or better than a large pistol primer.

Shooting the .38 Casull is a real hoot. The noise is impressive, and it isn't even a compensated pistol. On an overcast day of test-firing, there was a visible muzzle flash. Using the Ransom rest requires that I stand over and next to each pistol, and I received the full muzzle blast of the Casull each time I pressed the lever. While the recoil is heavy enough to bring the muzzle up quite a bit shooting offhand, the low weight of the bullets (124 and 147 grains) keeps it from being a sharp or harsh impact in your hands. The empties are tossed an impressive distance. I found the empty brass 25 feet behind me and slightly to the right. The brass went so far and so high I was afraid it would clear the berm and land on the range next to me. The 147-grain load tossed the brass farther than the 124-grain load did, and more behind than to the right. The accuracy was most impressive, but you'd expect accuracy from a tightly and correctly fitted Bar-sto barrel. The trajectory was so flat, and the accuracy so good that working over our gongs on 100-yard range was almost boring in its monotonous capability to hit each and every time.

The trigger pull is light and crisp, and makes hitting the selected target an easy task.

For jurisdictions that allow it, the Casull could be a most impressive hunting pistol. Where it may have some real promise is on the Long Range course at The Masters. If either load will reliably take down the 200 yard plates, the accuracy and flat trajectory could really be useful.

The ammunition choices were not nearly as extensive as that of the .45 pistols. Ammunition for now is loaded by Casull, and offered in two bullet weights, 124 grains and 147 grains. Of the two, the sample Casull liked the 124s better, shooting an average group size of 1-1/2 inches at 25 yards. The 147-grain bullets grouped into 2 inches. For all of its vigor, the ejection was quite consistent. Unlike many pistols that spray their empties over a large area, the Casull dropped the brass into two distinct locations, and each group of brass was spread over only a few feet of range. You had to walk to get to them, but once you arrived you could pick up all the empties without moving your feet.

One note about the Casull. Its velocity is high enough to crater steel plates. If you go to a club that has steel plates, ask before you shoot them with a .38 Casull. Otherwise, you may be faced with an impressive welding bill to fill and grind flush the craters.

I'm not sure what use I'd have had for this one, but I was sad to send it back. However, serial number EX 0007 had to get back to Wyoming.

Where the hunting regulations allowed it, the Casull could be a very good hunting round. For competition, I'm thinking The Masters.

.38 Casull	
Trigger pull	3.25 lb
Extractor tension	24 oz
Chamber depth	N/A
.22 Conversion fit	
Kimber	N
EAA	Y*
Ciener	N
Wilson	N
Marvel	N**
Bar-Sto .400 Cor-bon fit	N***
Clark .460 Rowland ift	Rowland fit N***
Weight	42.4 oz
Barrel length	6"
Favorite loads	
1-124 JHP	1.5"
2-147 JHP	2.0"
* The frame is ramped, the conversion is not	
** The Marvel sometimes fed despite the ramp gap in the frame	
** The barrels would not fit, being too short, and unramped. They would enter the slide	

 # CHARLES DALY

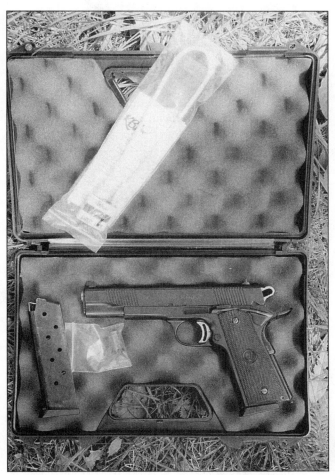

The Charles Daly in its hard case, with spare mag, lock and fired case.

A basic pistol with a few extras.

The rear sight, taller than a regular rear, but a bit thin.

The Charles Daly is one of the many firearms imported by KBI, Inc, of Harrisburg PA. In an era of near $1,000 "basic" .45's, they feel that there are shooters who will warm up to a plain and solid pistol for a plain and solid price.

The pistol Charles Daly sent for the test is a blued Government Model-size pistol. The sights are fixed, a front blade with a Novak dovetail with the blade ramped slightly. The rear is a fixed blade, but a blade that looks like it is too thin to stand up to much hard use. It appears to be a standard military-dimensioned blade that has been made tall enough to work with the Novak front sight, but not made thicker. (Easy enough to change a sight, after all.)

The slide has cocking serrations front and back. The ejection port is lowered slightly and flared, and live-ejects with an occasional hang up.

The slide is marked on the left side with "Charles Daly®" and on the right with "Cal.45 ACP". The barrel is a standard ramp and bushing barrel, with a tight lockup to the slide. The recoil spring, plunger and retainer is pure 1911, without the guide rod found on so many "improved" pistols. (Guide rods; I can take 'em or leave 'em.) The slide has side to side play, but does not rock when you wrestle with it.

The frame is a blued steel single stack. The hammer is a commander loop, and pivots back into the recess of an Ed Brown-shaped grip safety. The grip safety has a speed bump on the bottom. The thumb safety is an ambidextrous one, patterned on the King safety. Unlike safeties that use the right-hand grip to keep the thumb lever on the frame, the King uses an extended and notched sear pivot pin as a safety retainer. You can change grips without worrying about the thumb safety binding on the new grips.

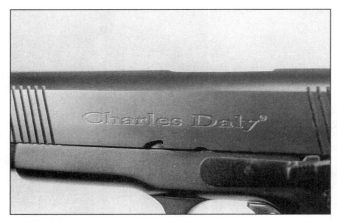

The left side.

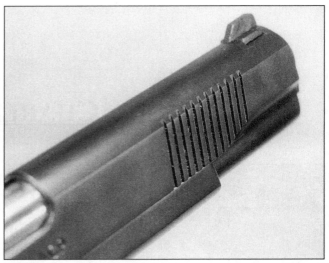

The forward cocking serrations, differently proportioned than any other pistol tested.

The ejection port, lowered and scalloped.

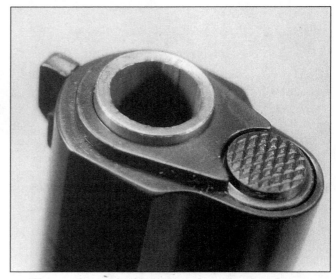

The muzzle, standard bushing and recoil spring plug.

The front sight, ramped but not serrated.

The slide stop is an extended one. I do not particularly like extended slide stop levers, as my right thumb usually rests on them and precludes the pistol from locking open when empty. And so it was for me with the Charles Daly. However, for all the testers who kept their thumbs down, it worked perfectly every time. The frame is marked on the right side with the serial number, between the slide stop pin and the grips. It is also marked on the underside of the dust cover "KBI-HBG,PA Philippines". The trigger is an extended steel trigger with an arc as a lightening cut, and

does not have an over-travel stop screw. The trigger pull is clean but a bit heavy. The magazine catch is serrated and standard size. The frontstrap is smooth, and the radius between the frontstrap and the trigger guard is the normal radius of a 1911. The mainspring housing is flat, serrated and steel. The magazine well is slightly beveled on the sides but not the back. The grips are plastic, with a "CD" logo cast as part of the pattern.

The finish is a semi-matte polish with a durable blue applied. At first glance it has the look of a modern casting, but there is obvious hand fitting that goes on in assembly.

The Charles Daly comes in a plastic storage case, with a lock and two magazines. The magazines are Mec-Gar, eight shots in capacity, and have a detachable baseplate for easier cleaning. Oh, and there is a fired case in a little plastic bag, for shipment to States with the silly fired-case requirement. One can only hope that in 10 years or so, when someone reports that not a single crime has been solved or materially aided by the storage of these empties, that the legislators

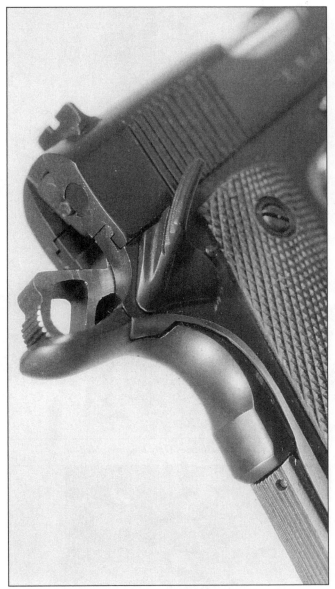

The right-hand lever of the ambidextrous safety is secured by an extra-long sear pin.

The slide stop is extended, and matches the thumb safety.

The trigger is slotted, the frontstrap has a standard curve, and the mag button is serrated.

Here's the beveled mag well.

who voted for it are held up to the public ridicule they deserve.

But back to the fun stuff. The testers did not report any sharp edges, nor any malfunctions. It fed all the ammo, locked open when empty and dropped the magazine cleanly once empty. By the time the Charles Daly hit the rotation, the crew was pretty tired, and it took longer than usual to go through the test ammo allotted it. Fast or slow, the Charles Daly ate it all. Several liked the ambidextrous safety, and one liked the slide stop and commented on it. In all, they were impressed with it as a solid and dependable pistol, even if it was plain compared to the exotica on the bench next to it. As a dependable beginners gun for competition, or a plain pistol as a defense gun, it got thumbs up from the crew.

In accuracy, it was solid if unspectacular. The favorite load of the Charles Daly was the Black Hills Red 230 FMJ. It managed to cozy five-shot groups into an average of just over 2-1/4 inches. Again, I have to remind you not to be jaded by what seems like pedestrian accuracy. Such a group

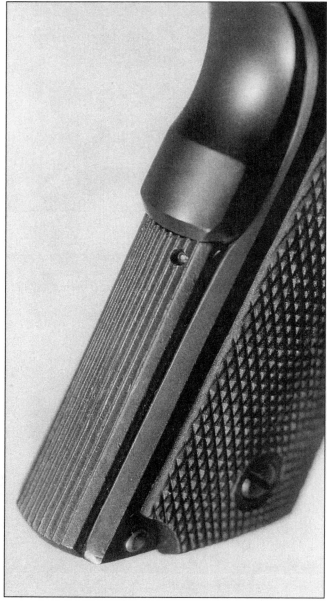

The Charles Daly, with flat mainspring housing, speed bump on grip safety, and plastic grips.

The grips have the Charles Daly logo moulded-in.

The Charles Daly comes with eight-shot Mec-Gar magazines.

at 25 yards equals 4-1/2 at 50, and 9 inches at 100. The pistol will keep every shot on our 100-yard gong, if the shooter is up to the task. The second load was the Oregon Trails 200-grain lead bullet at just over 2-1/2 inches on average. Third was the other Black Hills load, the Blue ammo 230 JRN, at just over 3 inches. The group averages were not distorted by overly large or small groups. Each load punched uniform patterns, and the groups were clustered around the average. If you were expecting tack-driving accuracy you'd be disappointed. If you were expecting a reliable pistol up to the task of winning a club match or keeping you safe when in harm's way, you've found a suitable candidate.

The Charles Daly would serve ably as a beginners gun for practical competition. Were I to set one up for a beginner, I would probably swap out the extended slide stop, and replace the skinny rear blade. In their places I'd put a standard slide stop, and install the McCormick rear sight that the Nowlin has. The accuracy is plenty good enough to start shooting, and even to work your way up in class once you became classified. As a defensive pistol I'd make the same changes, and be sure it worked 100 percent and hit to the sights with whatever is the favorite hollow-point load of the day.

The 50-yard group, prone over sandbags, for the Charles Daly.

Charles Daly	
Trigger pull	5.0 lb
Extractor tension	18 oz
Chamber depth	.909"
.22 Conversion fit	
Kimber	Y
EAA	Y
Ciener	Y
Wilson	Y
Marvel	Y
Bar-Sto .400 Cor-bon fit	N
Clark .460 Rowland fit	Rowland fit Y
Weight	35.6
Barrel length	5"
Three favorite loads	
1-Oregon Tr/Viht	2.30"
2-Black Hills Red	2.57"
3-Zero 185 JHP	3.05"

CLARK 50TH ANNIVERSARY

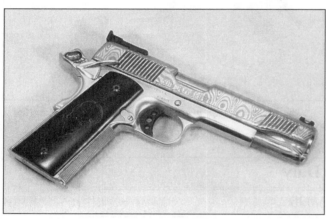

The Clark 50th Anniversary Gun is guaranteed to get noticed.

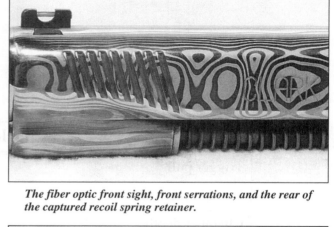

The fiber optic front sight, front serrations, and the rear of the captured recoil spring retainer.

The slide and hammer are Damascus. The rear sight is dehorned and can't hurt your hands.

The Clark Meltdown big bushing, to radically dehorn the front of the slide.

Jim Clark Sr. was one heck of a shooter. (Not that Jim Jr. isn't, but he not only has a big set of shoes to fill, Jim Sr. kept those shoes active for many years.) He set records in Bull's eye shooting back when it was all there was. He won just about every match he entered, and if that wasn't enough, he turned to gunsmithing. Back when a wadcutter gun was high-tech and expensive, he figured out how to convert a Colt .38 Super to work with .38 Special wadcutter ammo. For much less than a Colt (assuming you could find a Colt) wadcutter gun, you could have an accurate and reliable Clark conversion.

When IPSC came on the scene, it was a simple matter to shift his efforts into accurate, tough, reliable IPSC and pin guns. Jim Sr. was also a nice guy. I met him at the 1997 Three-Gun Nationals held at the Clark Custom range, and even though I was just another face and a struggling new gun writer, he talked to me like I had been in the business for decades.

Jim Clark Sr. is gone now, but to commemorate his 50 years of competition and gunsmithing, the crew at Clark Custom have come out with a pistol. And what a pistol it is!

The lowered, scalloped and melted ejection port.

The Clark barrel, left, is ramped. The center barrel is a Wilson ramp, and the right barrel an unramped one.

On the right, the extra machining needed to fit a ramped barrel to a frame.

The recoil spring retainer plug is shouldered and notched.

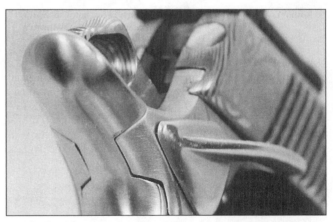

The hi-ride grip safety, blended to the frame, and the rear of the thumb safety, also melted.

The Clark 50th Anniversary is a standard-weight government-size pistol in .45 ACP. The basics are from Caspian. The slide is Damascus and the frame stainless, but that hardly begins to describe it. For those who remember their history in school (and for those whose schools still teach history) Damascus steel is a laminated and folded steel with at least two components. In the case of the slide of the Clark, it is two alloys of stainless steel, folded and laminated, then etched to bring out the character of the grain. The slide is tougher than a regular steel slide would be, and can be re-polished and etched if it gets scratched, so the Anniversary gun is not just some showpiece to be admired and pampered. It can be shot. (And boy did this one shoot.)

The slide is topped off with an adjustable rear sight of the Bo-mar pattern, and a fiber-optic front blade. The blade is notched so the fiber protruding through it can gather light and the rear face of it will glow. Even in dull conditions the sight is quite visible. In a match like the Handgunner Shoot-off, with its dark blue plates in the bright light of Colorado, the fiber optic front sight of the Clark would be a definite asset. The slide is a full-length government size with cocking serrations both front and back. The bushing is the Clark melted big bushing, that allows a smoothly curved front radius for easier carry and less wear and tear on holsters. The ejection port is lowered and scalloped, and live ejects. The left side of the slide is marked "Clark Custom" and the right side "50th Anniversary". The rear of the slide is smooth.

The barrel is a Clark Match barrel in .45 ACP, with an integral feed ramp. The lockup is bank-vault rigid. The recoil spring is wrapped around a Clark two-piece guide rod that passes through a reversed retaining plug that also protrudes to lock the bushing in place.

The stainless frame is a standard government frame. The hammer is made of Damascus steel, to match the slide. The safety is an ambidextrous one, with the off-side lever held in place by an extra-length sear pivot pin. The pin head rides in a slot milled on the back of the lever pad, completely hidden from view. Neat. The frame is marked on the right side with,

"Caspian Arms, Hardwick Vt. U.S.A." and the serial number. The serial number range for the Anniversary guns is CCG ("Clark Custom Guns") and the pistol number. The gang at Clark Custom sent me #001 to play with. When I spotted the number, I almost didn't lift the gun out of the box. I called and talked to Jim Clark Jr. and asked if it would be all right to shoot it. He said sure, they had shot it in testing and building it, and built it to be shot.

The grip safety is a hi-cut like the Ed Brown designs, with a speed bump that is checkered. The trigger is a long, three-hole trigger with over-travel stop screw installed. The trigger pull is clean and crisp. The radius of the frontstrap to trigger guard has been lifted and tightened, and the frontstrap is checkered. The mainspring housing is flat, and checkered to match the front.

The mag well is beveled. The grips are smooth ebony, with wire inlay on each panel. On the left side is "50th 1950 2000" and on the right the smiling face of Jim Clark Sr. The grip screws are Allen-headed, and engraved. The Anniversary gun has been treated to the Clark "Meltdown" where every edge that might cut your hand has been aggressively rounded and blended to the rest. The only part on the slide that has any sharp corners is the front sight, and only because it needs them. On the frame, the only sharp edges to be found are the diamonds of the checkering. The Anniversary comes in a plastic case with a Clark magazine. Clark

has begun manufacture of their own magazines, and if the one that came with this pistol is any indication, you will never have a problem with a Clark magazine.

In all, a solid and well-made 1911 that feels good in the hand.

I did not let the test-fire crew beat up the Anniversary gun. I reserved shooting it for myself. Once I had finished the inspection and measuring, I included it on a range trip

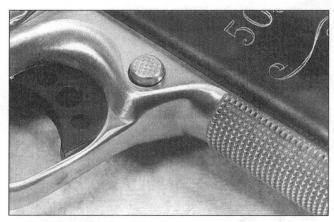

The arc of the frontstrap and trigger guard is raised and the edges blended in the Meltdown.

The first one off the bench.

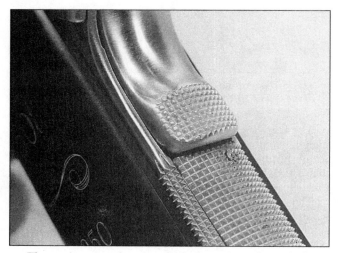

The mainspring housing and the grip safety of the Anniversary pistol are checkered.

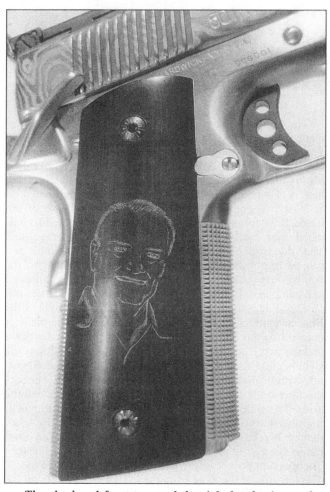

The checkered frontstrap and the right-hand grip panel with its portrait of Jim Sr.

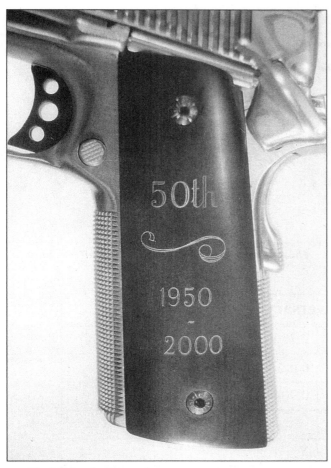

The left-hand grip panel.

Clark is now making their own magazines, and the Anniversary includes one of them.

for Ransom testing. I broke it in with a couple of magazines of each load, to make sure it was hitting to the sights and working 100 percent. It did both. Playtime over, I clamped it in and proceeded to see how it delivered. I was not at all surprised to see that the best accuracy came (as it did so many times in this test series) with the Oregon Trail load. The average of the groups was 1-1/2 inches. Coming in tied for second was Black Hills Blue ammo and the Sierra/Tite-group load, with the 230-grain jacketed round-nose bullets and the 230 gr JHP's both clustering into 1-3/4-inch groups. The third-place group came from the West Coast Bullets load, edging in just under 2 inches. Two inches out of the Ransom rest is still good enough for me to plink 10 hits out of 10 shots on our 100-yard gong after the test session.

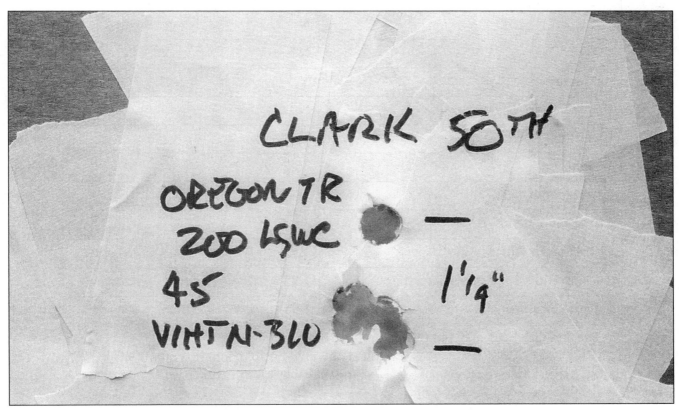

A typical group for the Anniversary and Oregon Trail.

The Clark showed no shifts in group zero, delivering all the shots to the same group center, without wandering as each load was introduced.

After the Ransom testing, I had some time left, but no energy for walking back and forth to the targets. After putting the rest of the gear away, I spent some time plinking on the 100-yard range, working over our gongs. The large plates were too easy, so I switched to the rifle pin rack at 75 yards. The rack has six pin-shaped steel plates, hinged to fall and is equipped with a cable re-set. Once I learned the hold (the top of sight at the top of pin) I was able to tip the pins over with scary regularity. The Clark Anniversary Gun #CCG 001 would have been a very useful 1911 to have had back when Second Chance was shooting the Handgun Pop and Flop. It is accurate, easy to shoot, and the grip fit brought the sights right back down to the rack after recoil. If you are at a gun show or the Clark Custom shop, admire number 001. It delivers as good as it looks, and I'm sure the rest of the series will, too.

The Anniversary #001 shot best with Oregon Trail bullets.

Clark Anniversary	
Trigger pull	2.75 lb
Extractor tension	6 oz
Chamber depth	0.904
.22 Conversion fit	
Kimber	Y
EAA	Y
Ciener	N*
Wilson	N*
Marvel	Y
Bar-Sto .400 Cor-bon fit	N
Clark .460 Rowland fit	Y
Weight	36.2 oz
Barrel length	5"
Three favorite loads	
1-Oregon Tr/Viht	1.5"
2-Black Hills Blue/Sierra-Titegroup	1.75"
3-West Coast Bullets-Viht	1.95"
* The slide fit the frame, but the ejector was binding	

ED BROWN
BOBTAIL

The Ed Brown Bobtail, a carry gun that shoots like a Bull's eye gun.

The Bobtail and its carry case.

The Ed Brown Bobtail is intended as a premium-quality carry gun. As such, it takes high marks in the testing as a carry gun that shot like a Bull's eye gun. Accurate? For both across-the-board results, and results with the ammo it liked best, the Ed Brown was a winner. The visually noticeable feature is the altered contour of the mainspring housing at the bottom of the frame. When you are carrying concealed (legally, safely, and prudently we hope) the hardest part to conceal is the butt of the gun. The bottom corner of the mainspring housing is particularly difficult to hide. The serrations or checkering on the housing can catch on the cloth of a jacket or shirt, and ride in the caught position. To anyone who is looking, it fairly screams "gun!" (That said, hardly anyone notices. I once went through a pistol class with John Farnam, and when it came time to go to lunch we drove off to the nearest fast-food emporium. When we went

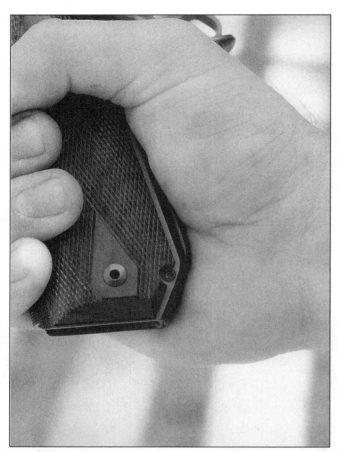

None of the testers had any problem with the missing bit of frame.

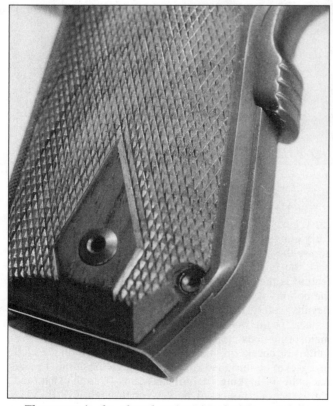

The secret is the altered mainspring housing, and the relocated pin.

The only slide markings are on the right side.

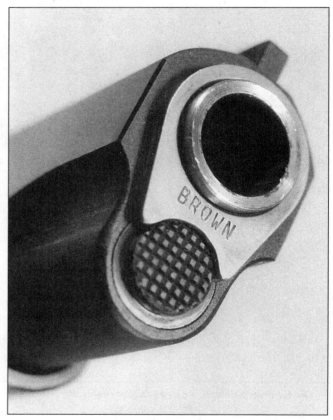

Ed Brown makes his own barrels, bushings and other small parts as well as slides and frames.

to exit the cars, we left our guns and magazines on, and simply pulled part of our shirttails over the gun. No one paid any attention. Everyone was legal, by the way, having either a badge or CCW.)

The Bobtail removes the problem by removing the corner. The changed radius is much less likely to catch, and since it is smooth the cloth won't snag on it.

The Bobtail came in an Ed Brown soft case with one magazine made by Metalform. The finish is blued. The slide, frame and barrel are all made by Ed Brown himself. Ed also designed and makes grip safeties, thumb safeties and a number of other small parts. He wasn't first in the parts business, but his designs were built on earlier ones and offer many improvements. His grip safety, for example, allows the highest and tightest grip of any grip safety extant. It requires some heavy-duty filing and polishing to install on a frame that is not yet ready for it, but once done is one of the best, if not the best, grip safety available.

On top, the sights are standard Novak front and rear. This particular pistol did not have night sights, but I'm sure they can be had as an option. The Commander-length slide has cocking serrations at the rear only. The top of the slide, the rear and the rear sight are all matted for a non-glare sight picture. The ejection port is lowered and scalloped. However, the brass seemed to be hitting the slide just above the scalloped portion, and the empties were thrown forward. If this proves objectionable, you can easily have the extractor and ejector tuning altered to throw the brass more to the side and back. The left side of the slide is bare of markings, and the right side only has "Custom by Ed Brown" on it. It live ejects.

The barrel is an Ed Brown barrel, and has a snug but not snapping lockup, as befits a carry gun. The recoil spring, plunger and retainer are all standard Commander design.

The grip safety is the Ed Brown pattern, which is higher and tighter than other designs. At the bottom it has a three-lump speed bump that ensures the grip safety is pressed fully in when you are shooting. The thumb safety is ambidextrous, in the Ed Brown low-profile contour. I find the Ed Brown thumb safety to be particularly comfortable, as the

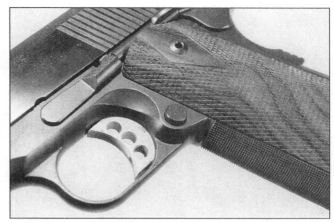

The radius between the frontstrap and trigger guard is a large part of what makes the Ed Brown pistols so comfortable.

The mag well is beveled.

The lowered and scalloped ejection port.

The grip safety has a speed bump with three grooves in it.

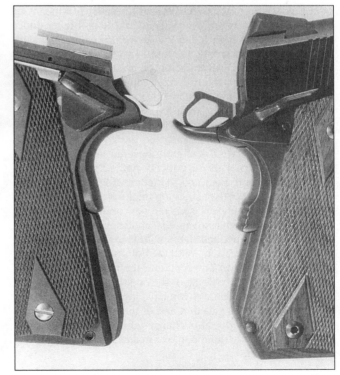

Comparing the Bobtail to a standard frame, you can easily see how the Bobtail is easier to carry.

The testers all reported favorably on the Ed Brown Bobtail.

bend in the lever comes where my thumb joint bends on the lever. The right side lever is slimmer than the left, to ease concealment and provide clearance for knuckles like mine.

The slide stop is standard in contour, but checkered on its lever and not just serrated. The head of the pin is radiused on the right side of the frame.

The trigger is a long aluminum one with three holes and a trigger stop screw. It connects to a large-loop Commander hammer and the trigger pull is a clean and crisp pull suitable for both carry and competition. The magazine catch is standard in size, checkered on its button, and has one of Ed's touches. The retaining screw/pin has an Allen-head socket head, to match the grip screws. It is a neat touch, but you do need a set of Allen wrenches to disassemble the gun.

The frontstrap is checkered, at what looks to be 40 lines per inch. The real secret of the Ed Brown and its comfortable grip is the top of the frontstrap where it meets the trigger guard. The steel of the frame has been cut up to the guard in a tighter radius than that of a standard frame. Your second finger, and thus your hand, can ride up higher under the trigger guard than it otherwise would. Combined with the Ed Brown grip safety, the gun locks to your grip tighter than others do. Despite being a commander, and thus slightly lighter than the full-sized guns, the Ed Brown was actually easier to shoot than others due to the improved frame contouring. (My wife has small hands, and the Ed Brown was the most comfortable in her hands of all the pistols.)

The magazine well is slightly beveled to ease magazine insertion. The grips are very nicely figured wood, and radiused to bring their front and rear edges down to the surface of the frame, rather than standing thick.

The point of the exercise is the new mainspring housing. The Bobtail design moves the mainspring housing pin higher on the frame, and the new housing also has its cross hole in a higher location. With the bottom of the mainspring housing thus freed of any function, the mainspring housing is radiused from the outside of the crosspin hole down to the magazine opening. Unless you have impossibly huge hands, your hand never touches that part of the mainspring housing anyway, so its loss does not change your grip. For concealed carry the changed frame contour makes carry and concealment a lot easier.

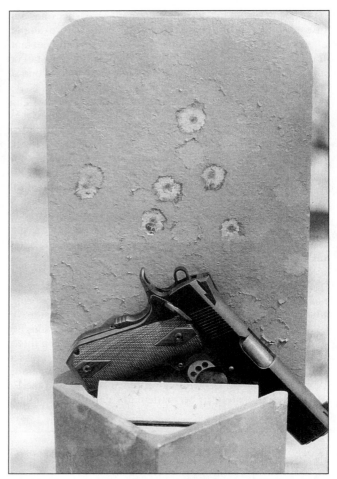

The 50-yard group shot with the Bobtail, and the start of the 50-yard test.

The Bobtail modification is available on your 1911, provided you have a steel-framed gun. Ed Brown doesn't do the Bobtail to aluminum frames, lacking the ability to anodize the aluminum after it has been cut. If you want your gun done, ring them up and find out the current time for turnaround. I don't think you'll be disappointed in the results.

The testers' comments were uniformly positive, and despite the appearance of not being de-horned no one found any sharp edges. The best comment was "The fit and finish are excellent, what you would expect from Ed Brown." There were no malfunctions of the pistol, and only a couple of times did it fail to lock open when empty. I rotated those magazines out and the failure to lock went away. Lesson learned: magazine springs get tired after a decade of hard use. For a pistol intended to be carried, the accuracy was very nice indeed. The most-accurate load was the Sierra 230 JHP and Titegroup, with an average of 1 inch. Yes, four, five-shot groups averaged an inch. Second were the Zero 185s, grouping at "only" 1-1/4 inches on average. Bringing up third place were the Montana Gold 185 JHP's at 1-3/4 inches. A solid pistol, accurate and reliable, and the rounded frame makes it easy to conceal. What more can you ask of a carry gun?

Ed Brown Bobtail	
Trigger pull	4.25 lb
Extractor tension	12 oz
Chamber depth	.907"
.22 Conversion fit	
Kimber	Y
EAA	Y
Ciener	Y
Wilson	Y
Marvel	Y
Bar-Sto .400 Cor-bon fit	N**
Clark .460 Rowland ift	Y**
Weight	33.6 oz
Barrel length	4.25"
Three favorite loads	
1-Sierra/Viht	1.0"
2-Zero 185 JHP	1.25"
3-Montana Gold/Titegroup	1.75"
** The barrels are gov't barrels, and should not be used in a Commander or shorter pistol	

ENTREPRISE
TITLEIST P500

The rear sight, much like the Kimber.

The front sight.

The Titleist 500 in its plastic case.

The Entreprise Titleist 500 is a hi-cap 1911 that uses magazines interchangeable with the Para Ordnance hi-caps. Based in California, Entreprise Arms mostly makes FN-FAL receivers and rifles. However, making rifles does not prove such a distraction as to keep them from making first-class pistols. While Para (there's that comparison again) makes pistols in a variety of calibers and sizes, from compact carry pistols to competition race guns, Entreprise concentrates on full-size competition and carry guns that fit the Limited or Stock category. The Titleist P500 we were sent is a very good example of the breed.

The sights are a Novak type front and an adjustable rear. The rear is a Bo-mar pattern sight, that looks very much like the Kimber rear sight. The edges of the rear sight are nicely rounded, and the corners of the rear blade knocked off. The slide has cocking serrations front and rear, and the rear of the slide is smooth. The slide is marked "Titleist P500" on the left side, and "Entreprise Arms" and their logo on the right. The ejection port is lowered and scalloped, and live ejects. The barrel is marked ".45 ACP" and is a standard unramped barrel. It uses a bushing at the front to lock up. The fit is snug without locking up hard. There is some spring in the chamber area, but the barrel moves back up

The right side.

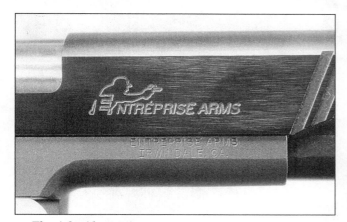

Left side of the slide.

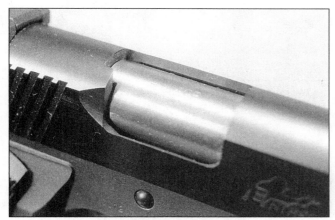

The lowered and scalloped ejection port.

Bushing and one-piece guide rod.

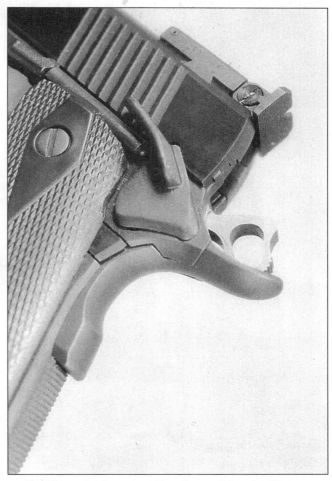

The Entreprise hammer, grip safety and thumb safety.

after you stop pushing on it. There is play between the frame and slide. The recoil spring is wrapped around a one-piece guide rod.

The hammer is a Commander rowel with an oval hole, and pivots back into the recess of an Ed Brown-pattern grip safety. The grip safety is nicely fitted and blended, without leaving any gaps or sharp edges, and has a speed bump at the bottom. The thumb safety is an ambidextrous one, with the left paddle large and the right one small. The thumb safety shape is very much like that of an Ed Brown safety.

The slide stop is a standard unit, with checkering. The plunger tube that rests between the safety and slide stop is an integral part of the frame. Unlike the standard 1911 frame, where the plunger tube is staked in place, on the Entreprise the tube is cast and machined as part of the frame.

The dust cover forward of the slide stop is larger in width than the frame at the slide stop, so there is a curved shoulder or step forward of the slide stop. The trigger is a long aluminum three-hole trigger with a stop screw installed. The trigger pull has a catch or step in the take-up, then proceeds to a clean but somewhat heavy-feeling release. The magazine catch is checkered and standard sized. The frontstrap is smooth, with the corners nicely rounded, a comforting touch for those with average sized hands. One of the potential problems of a hi-cap frame is the "2x4" feel. By rounding the corners Entreprise has made their frame more comfortable than it could have been. The mainspring housing is flat and checkered. The magazine well does not have any beveling around it, but it doesn't need it. Since the top of the magazine is tapered, you could consider the mag funnel to be on the magazine and not the frame.

The grips are plastic, held on with four large-headed flat screws that screw directly into the frame. The slot for the trigger bow is larger than the opening for the grip safety, so the grips have to have extensions to fill the gap. On this pistol the extensions weren't flush, and some testers felt the

The curve forward of the slide stop, indicating the increased thickness of the dust cover.

The rounded front of the frame reduces the potential "2x4" feel of a hi-cap pistol.

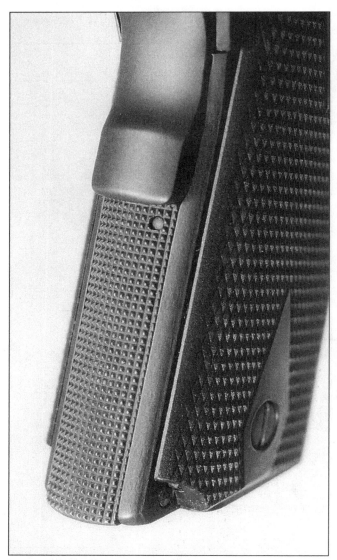

The mainspring housing, flat, checkered and steel.

The mag well is not beveled, but the magazines are.

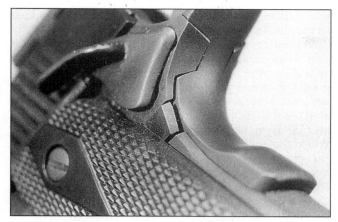

The grip filler in the trigger slot looked like it would bite, but it never did.

As a Stock gun, the Entreprise Titleist 500 is a good one, and if you can find hi-cap mags it would make a very nice USPSA Limited gun, too.

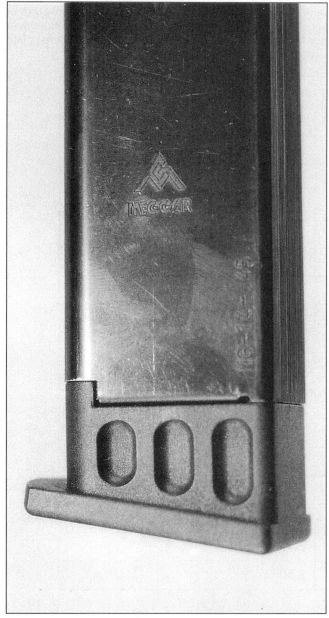

The plastic extension of the Mec-Gar magazine tube, to reduce capacity to 10 rounds.

The mags are double-stack, tapering down to a single feed. They were unfailingly reliable.

edges in their grip. It is a problem both with Paras and the Entreprise, and serious shooters fuss over their grips to eliminate the problem.

The Titleist is blued, with the slide polished to a medium polish while the frame is bead blasted to a matte finish. It comes in a plastic storage case, with a magazine and owner's manual. Entreprise sent two extra magazines along for testing. Due to the Crime Law of 1994, they have to supply newly-made 10-shot magazines. Theirs come from Mec-Gar, an Italian firm that makes high-quality magazines. (Pre-ban hi-cap Para mags will work just fine, if you feel the need for more shots.) The magazine construction uses plastic to avoid capacity increases. The steel tube extends just far enough to hold the follower, spring and 10 rounds. The plastic baseplate is shaped like the tube, and extends down out of the tube as if it were a full-sized magazine. As a technical method of keeping capacity down to 10, it is pretty clever. As a legal requirement it is pretty stupid.

In shooting, the Entreprise offered no surprises in terms of its function. It chugged right along, digesting all the ammo we had on hand to test it with. It fed fine, ejected positively and locked open when empty. The magazines fell free, and inserting a loaded magazine was no problem. It does exactly what Entreprise wants it to do, provide a reliable pistol for someone who wants to compete in Limited or Stock, without breaking the bank to do so.

The test shooters kept coming back to it, even after shooting the higher-priced pistols. The large frame offers a solid grip, and several of the testers found it more comfortable than the regular 1911 grip. As sent, it would be a fine Limited 10 pistol in IPSC. If you wanted to hunt down and acquire some hi-cap magazines for it, you could shoot in Limited with 14 to 16 rounds in each magazine. As your performance improved, you might want to have the Titleist fine-tuned. For the Handgunner Shoot-off or Steel Challenge you would probably want the trigger cleaned up and lightened. If you wanted to shoot the Bianchi Cup you'd want to have the fit tightened or the barrel replaced. At least on the pistol we tested.

In accuracy it was solid but unspectacular. The load it shot most accurately was the Rainier, but it struggled even then. With an average group size just over 2 inches, it only shot one group that was under 2. The next best ammo in accuracy was PMP, with a group average just under 2-1/2 inches. Third was the Magtech, with an average right at 2-1/2. The Titleist did love hardball. While the groups may seem less than accurate, I was encouraged by the consistency and closely-spaced results. A pistol that lacks promise shoots groups that are "4+1" or "3+2", that is, three or four shots in a tight cluster, and one out. Tightening the fit on a pistol that shoots such groups rarely brings the errant shot into the group. The Entreprise shot groups that were uniform, but not tight.

I think that with a little tightening of the slide-frame-barrel fit by a good 1911 gunsmith, this Entreprise could turn in some fine groups. Even so, the accuracy is much more than needed for USPSA/IPSC competition, bowling pins, plate shooting and casual Bull's eye or PPC.

Entreprise	
Trigger pull	5.5 lb
Extractor tension	7 oz
Chamber depth	.892"
.22 Conversion fit	
Kimber	Y
EAA	Y
Ciener	Y
Wilson	Y
Marvel	Y
Bar-Sto .400 Cor-bon fit	N
Clark .460 Rowland fit	Rowland fit N
Weight	38.3 oz
Barrel length	5"
Three favorite loads	
1-Rainier/Titegroup	2.05"
2-PMP 220 JRN	2.45"
3-Magtech	2.50"

FIRESTORM, GOVERNMENT AND COMPACT

The Firestorm Government in its box.

The Compact, box, instructions, one magazine.

The sights are shorter and thinner than what modern 1911 consumers have come to expect.

The importers of the Llama product line sent us two of their Firestorm pistols, one a full-size and one a Commander size. In basic layout, the Llamas differ from the U.S.-made 1911's in four respects, two of which are similar to pistols made here stateside. The Commander-sized pistol had a hard-chromed frame and high-gloss blued slide, while the Government size pistol was matte blue. For the most part, they are 1911s that originated in the old country, with a few twists.

From the top, they have fixed sights, both smaller and thinner than is customary in the U.S. The slides are marked, on the right "Fabrinor Vittoria (España)", and on the left with the Firestorm logo and either ".45 Compact" or ".45 Govt". The extractor is a pivoted external extractor, similar in design to the Wilson KZ-45 extractor. However, the ejection port on the Firestorms does not extend back far enough to uncover the tip of the extractor. The smaller ejection port does not hinder ejection, either of live ammo or fired empties. The firing pin works as usual, but with an internal firing pin block to prevent accidental firing when dropped.

The barrel is manufactured by Llama, proofed in Spain, and is a standard ramp and chambered barrel. The barrel crown is contained by a bushing and plunger, standard 1911 design. The slide and barrel both show play in fitting.

The frames are standard 1911 configuration, no extended dust covers, with single-stack magazines. The hammers on both are Commander hammers, with a modest but effective

The Government size is a solid pistol.

The Compact has the beautiful balance of the Commander-size 1911. As expected.

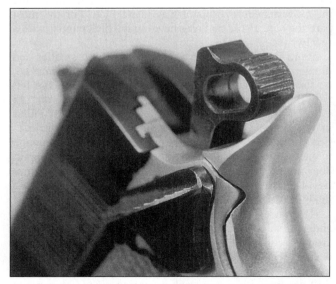

The grip safety fit is not bad, but could be better. The sharp corner on the thumb safety must be dealt with.

beavertail riding behind. The beavertail design on the Llamas is similar to that of early to mid-1980s custom designs, before we got so radical in grip safety design. The fit of the grip safety to the frame is not perfect, but effective. Where both could have used a little more design effort and fitting work was in the thumb safety. Both had sharp corners at the rear where they meet the grip safety, and several testers (and I) complained about the "owwie" we'd get if we shot the Llamas using a high thumb hold. Five minutes with a fine-cut file, stone and cold blue would solve that problem.

The slide stop is an extended affair on both. If you like it, fine. If not, it is easy enough to swap out. The triggers are extended, but lack an over-travel stop screw. The mag catch is in the standard location, and interchanges with regular 1911 mag catches.

The grips are rubber, and the mag well is not beveled. The grip safety of both Llamas lack a speed bump. The mainspring housing of both is a blend we used to modify back in the early 1980s, of flattening an arched mainspring housing. It is raised but flat.

The ejection port. Note the extractor pivot pin on top of the slide.

The slightly extended slide stop of the Firestorm is not as obtrusive as other extended stops.

The plunger tube is secured with a pair of screws. Note the lack of grip screw bushings.

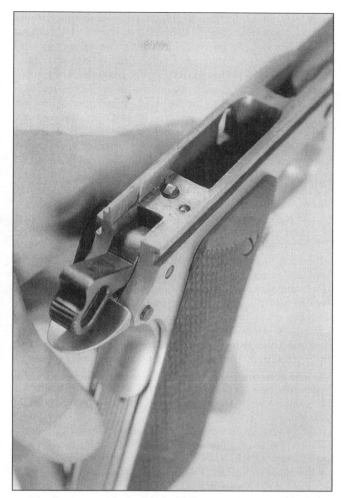

The firing pin safety is activated by the grip safety. No pressure on the grip safety, and the plunger stays down.

The differences between the Llamas and US-made 1911's are: 1) The external extractor, which worked fine on the test pistols. However, if your Llama goes awry, getting a new extractor (admittedly a rare occurrence) could be a hassle. 2) The thumb safety/slide stop plunger tube is secured to the frame with a pair of screws. Even in refinishing, it is not a part you typically remove. However, lose the screws and you're, well, you know. 3) The grips are held on by screws that fasten directly to the frame. There are no bushings. Lose a screw and you'll be hard-pressed to find a fine-thread metric screw. Strip the threads and you're even worse off. The last difference is the grip safety. 4) The Llamas, like the new Kimber Series II, use a firing pin safety block that is pushed out of the way by a plunger activated by the grip safety. I don't have any problem with it, but it does complicate later gunsmithing, if you have any done.

One question a tester posed to me was: Do other parts fit? What he meant was, what parts are interchangeable with standard 1911 parts? A spare Springfield Armory slide and barrel I had lying on the bench slid right onto both Llama frames. The Llama slide stop can be replaced with a regular 1911 unit. Regular single stack magazines worked in the two guns I tested. So, depending on the dimensional variances between manufacturers, parts should work. those that don't can be fitted by a competent gunsmith. Before you get bent out of shape over this, let me point out that you

Hold the grip safety down, and the plunger moves up and frees the firing pin.

couldn't interchange the barrels and slides between the Springfield Professional and the Nowlin Match Classic, just pick two at random and no one complains about that.

However, were you to install a new slide on the Llama frame, you'd have to figure out what to do about the firing pin safety linkage. Without clearance, the plunger couldn't rise from the frame. No rise, no trigger pull. I encountered just such a problem with the .22 conversions. They fit, but without clearance, couldn't be made to fire. I cannot recommend removal of a safety device, but milling the slide to install the firing pin plunger strikes me as going to a whole lot of trouble and effort. Let your conscience and wallet be your guide.

In testing, the two Llamas worked just fine. They ate everything, ejected all the empties, locked open when empty and dropped the mags free when the mag button was pushed. Other than biting some of the testers, there were no complaints about function. Some of the testers, used to larger sights, grumbled about the smaller sights of the Llamas. Even while they were grumbling, they were eagerly putting ammo downrange.

The Ransom rest testing was a bust. Without measuring the frames to death, I can't tell why, but the Llamas refused to settle down in the inserts. There is probably some slight difference in dimensions that keeps them from settling in tight, as I could not get groups to settle down even as small as I could shoot offhand, let alone over sandbags. (Perhaps the "high-flat" mainspring housings?) I had to settle for shooting them off the bench, and recording group sizes. Since the testing is not comparable to the Ransom rest, I'm not listing the groups sizes, just the relative accuracy with different ammo. However, both the Compact and the Government stayed inside the "A" zone in my 50-yard test, and both were able to ring the 100-yard gongs with regularity. They may not like the Ransom rest, but they both shot quite well indeed.

The Government pistol liked the Hornady 200-grain XTP load best of all, closely followed by the Magtech and the Rainier 230 JRN/Titegroup load. The Compact settled on the Sierra 230 JHP/Titegroup load as its favorite, with the Zero 185s close behind and the Oregon Trail 200 L-SWC/Vihtavuori load in third place.

So, where is their niche? Spanish pistols have a reputation to live down, and that is of soft steel. I know many modern-made pistols are plenty hard, but I don't know if I'd want to subject these to a steady diet of competition. A couple of weekends and 1,000 rounds each of ammo is not a sufficient durability test, but perhaps I can test them

for a longer period of time. However, as competition guns, the differing extractor and plunger tube design would make tuneups after a season of shooting a tough thing. They are reliable and accurate pistols, so a service life of house gun, car gun or shop gun would be an admirable station in life. Once zeroed and fired enough to make sure they worked 100 percent, they would serve you a lifetime waiting under the cash register, or on the top shelf of the safe. (Unless you are in the habit of letting

Top, the external extractor, bottom the standard mag catch.

The Compact acquitted itself well at the 50-yard line.

The mag well is not beveled.

children run loose, and I cannot help you there) I realize this marks me as an old-timer who grew up in a less gentle time, but what can I say besides it is better to have it and not need it than need it and not have it. For you, the decision comes down to the difference in money and the amount of shooting you'll do. The more you shoot, the more attractive the other pistols will be. After all, a competition shooters easily burns $500 to $1,000 a year in practice ammo. Add travel expenses, match entry fees and the cost of colorful T-shirts, and the cost difference between most of the pistols come to nothing. For the reader in a bad neighborhood, who will not shoot a box more than what is needed to test for accuracy and reliability, the Llamas look good. And they are good.

Right: The Government punched this very nice 3-1/2-inch group at 50 yards.

Firestorm Commander	
Trigger pull	3.5 lb
Extractor tension	12 oz
Chamber depth	.905"
.22 Conversion fit	
Kimber	Y*
EAA	Y*
Ciener	N1
Wilson	Y*
Marvel	Y*
Bar-Sto .400 Cor-bon fit	N
Clark .460 Rowland fit	N
Weight	36.0 oz
Barrel length	4.25"
Three favorite loads	
1-Sierra/Viht	
2-Zero 185 JHP	
3-Oregon Tr/Viht	

N1 The slide fit, but would not pass over the grip-safety activated firing pin plunger. Even so, it was too tight
* The grip-safety activated plunger fit under the slide, but could not move upwards when the pistol was gripped

Firestorm Government	
Trigger pull	7 lb
Extractor tension	20 oz
Chamber depth	.903"
.22 Conversion fit	
Kimber	Y*
EAA	Y*
Ciener	N1
Wilson	Y*
Marvel	Y*
Bar-Sto .400 Cor-bon fit	N
Clark .460 Rowland fit	Y
Weight	37.5 oz
Barrel length	5"
Three favorite loads	
1-Hornady 200 gr XTP	
2-Magtech 230 FMJ	
3-Rainier/Titegroup	

N1 The slide fit, but would not pass over the grip-safety activated firing pin plunger. Even so, it was too tight
* The grip-safety activated plunger fit under the slide, but could not move upwards when the pistol was gripped

GRIFFON

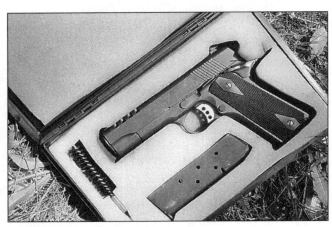

The Griffon in its foam-lined case.

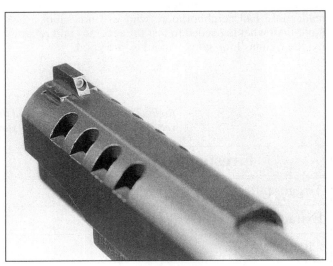

The front sight and the slots milled in the slide.

The left rear. Note the fixed rear night sight, beavertail grip safety and the extended slide stop.

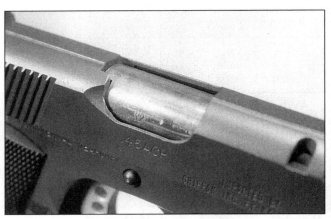

The ejection port is lowered and scalloped.

The Griffon is imported by Griffon Inc., of Ft. Worth Texas. It is made in South Africa. The sample sent was a blued Commander-sized pistol.

The slide has fixed night sights. The front is a Novak-style dovetail, and the rear looks similar to the Wilson fixed rear sight. The sights are of the "three-dot" pattern, with one tritium-filled cell in the front sight, and two others flanking the rear sight notch. There is a slight rib between the sights, but it is not matted or grooved. Between the front sight and the ejection port are eight holes. I guess they are cosmetic, as they aren't large enough to provide cooling, and a Commander slide doesn't have to be any lighter to "improve" its function. The ejection port is lowered slightly and scalloped. There are only rear cocking serrations. The slide is marked on the left with "Griffon 1911A1 Combat" and the Griffon logo. On the right, the slide is marked ".45 ACP" and "Imported by Griffon Inc., Ft. Worth Texas".

The barrel is made by Griffon, and has a proofmark over the chamber. It is a Commander length, with a bushing and regular feed ramp. The recoil spring plunger is a standard unit with a hole through it for a guide rod, but no guide rod installed. The lack of a guide rod is the apparent reason for the tinny-sounding recoil spring noise heard on hand cycling. When a commander-sized guide rod was installed, the weird spring noise went away. When closed, the barrel had some movement. The slide to frame fit had play.

The hammer is a large-oval commander rowel hammer that looks like it was copied directly from a McCormick hammer. The thumb safety is a moderately-sized extended safety, with a few sharp edges on it. The grip safety looks very much like a Caspian beavertail safety, but lacks a speed bump at the bottom. The slide stop lever is an oversized

The left-side markings.

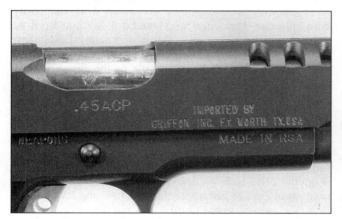

The right-side marking.

The Griffon's bushing and recoil spring retainer plug.

unit. Some shooters like them, I don't. My thumb is long enough that when I'm holding down the thumb safety my thumb also rests on the slide stop lever. Unless I shift my thumb, this pistol would never lock open when empty with me shooting it. (And it didn't.)

The frame is marked with the serial number on the left front end of the dust cover. On the right it has "Manufactured by Continental Weapons" over the grip panel, and "Made in RSA" on the right end of the dust cover.

The magazine release is checkered and of the standard size, while the trigger is an aluminum long trigger with three holes and a stop screw. The frontstrap is grooved vertically, while the mainspring housing is flat and grooved. The magazine opening is slightly beveled. The grips are Pearce rubber grips, with the surface between the grip screws dished in to create a subtle and comfortable curve for your hand.

The pistol comes in a plastic storage box lined with foam and cutout for the pistol and two magazines. The magazines are the least appealing parts of the package. They are tinny, with old-style tapered feed lips, and the baseplate is held on

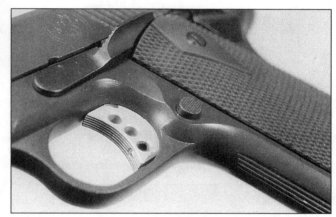

The extended slide stop, checkered mag button and long trigger with over-travel screw.

The mag well is beveled, but could use some more work.

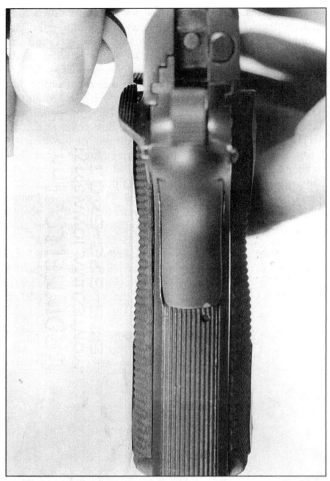

The Pearce grips gave a us comfortable hold on the Griffon.

with four tack or spot welds. We did not use the magazines in the test-firing, instead depending on the Chip McCormick Power Mags Chip was kind enough to send us. There were no malfunctions during the test-fire sessions.

The finish is interesting, as if it were polished and then given a light going-over with a very fine bead blasting, so it is a shiny matte surface, and blued. Call it a semi-gloss finish.

The overall impression is an uneven one. While the pistol is solidly made, and appears to have the right parts, details begin to stand out from the rest of the pistol. The fit is quite loose. It was the only pistol where we could move the slide and hear the movement, pushing from side to side to check fit.

With the somewhat odd appearance of the parts (the slide stop is a definite 1980s-era part) the testers were not too enthusiastic about the opportunity to shoot the Griffon. It turns out they were wrong. It proved to work faultlessly, with only one sharp edge found, and it didn't bite all of the shooters but only a couple. The thumb safety has a sharp edge on the outside of the paddle, as if the edge had not been broken after machining. Some of the shooters never noticed it, and others commented on it, but said it did not bother them. Two commented on the grips and how much they liked them.

The ammo hit to the sights, and accuracy was good enough in the test-firing that the Ransom testing was expected to show good results. The best ammo in the Griffon proved to be the Oregon Trail 200-grain lead bullet, shooting 2-1/2-inch groups. Behind it, and in the 3-inch range was Zero at just under three inches, and PMC at just over 3. However, as the Griffon was fed the ammo it didn't like, things were less encouraging. With some of the hardball loads it shot an occasional group in the four inch range, with one messy group running almost five inches.

At 50 yards, the Griffon came through.

So where does the Griffon fit? As a basic big-bore plinker, it would be a reliable pistol. Fed a surplus ammo it liked reasonably well, you can easily hit what you are shooting at within pistol distances. As a home defense gun, sitting on a nightstand when needed (and locked up other times) it would be a dependable pistol that didn't represent three house payments. If you decide to depend on a Griffon, test it thoroughly to make sure it likes the ammo you have to feed it, and use good magazines. It definitely works well when stoked with good magazines, as the McCormicks proved. I don't know how well it would have worked with the supplied magazines as I never tried them.

As a starter gun for competitive shooting, it will do, but don't expect a long service life from it. Not that I think it will quickly break or quit on you. When your skills improve and you want your pistol worked on, I think you might have to search for a gunsmith willing to undertake a rebuild. When that day comes, set the Griffon aside and begin the work on your new competition gun on another pistol. The Griffon will always be a dependable spare.

Griffon	
Trigger pull	6.5 lb
Extractor tension	9 oz
Chamber depth	.898"
.22 Conversion fit	
Kimber	Y
EAA	Y
Ciener	Y
Wilson	Y
Marvel	Y
Bar-Sto .400 Cor-bon fit	*
Clark .460 Rowland fit	**
Weight	33.5 oz
Barrel length	4.25"
Three favorite loads	
1-Oregon Tr/Viht	
2-Zero 185 JHP	
3-PMC	

* The barrel is a Gov't, and should not be used in a Commander pistol. It was too tight to fit.

** The barrel would enter the slide, but as a Gov't barrel must not be used in a Commander pistol

HIGH STANDARD
CAMP PERRY

The old High Standard company made rifles, shotguns and handguns for many years before going out of business while supplying firearms to Sears. Among their most popular models were the .22 target pistols they made. There are many High Standard target pistols still in use as plinkers and serious target guns on the line at matches across the country.

The new High Standard company started out by resurrecting the .22 pistols, and made them for several years before rolling up their sleeves and starting in on 1911s. The one they sent us is a basic pistol set up for target competition. For those who have been asleep for the last century, Camp Perry is the range where the National Championships are held, where men and women stand up and shoot handguns with one hand.

The Camp Perry model is a two-tone, blued and stainless single-stack Government Model. The slide has a tall staked front sight with a vertical white line on its face. The rear sight looks like a Mec-Gar adjustable sight, with a white outline around the rear notch. It has rear cocking serrations, a lowered and scalloped ejection port that live-ejects, and nicely polished flats. On the left side the slide is marked "High Standard" and on the right "Camp Perry Model". The extractor is stainless, contrasting the blued slide. The barrel is marked "45 ACP NM" in the same font as barrels marked by Olympic Arms. Olympic makes good barrels. The standard-ramped barrel is secured at the front with a bushing. The barrel lockup is solid, with no play in the chamber. The slide-to-frame fit has play, and can be moved side-to-side and rocked as well.

The hammer is a 1911A1 spur hammer, and the grip safety is a 1911 unit as well. This was one of three pistols tested with the old-style safety. As it is a spur safety it lacks

The Camp Perry Model in its hard case.

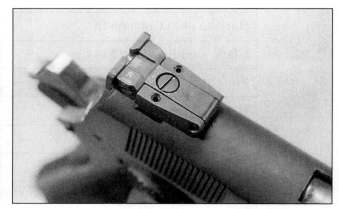

The rear is adjustable.

Two-tone, simple, solid.

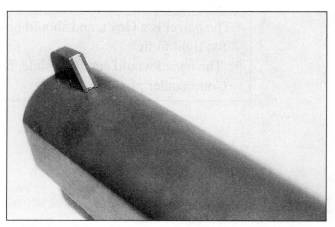

The front has a white stripe.

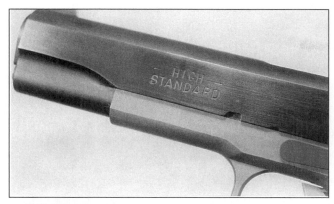

Left side.

Just as Browning invented it, bushing and standard recoil plug.

Right side.

The barrel locks up nicely.

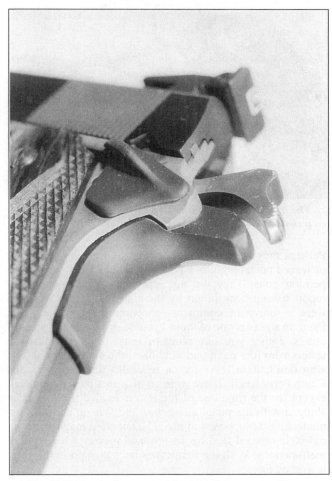

The 1911A1 spur hammer and grip safety, no speed bump.

a speed bump at the bottom. The thumb safety is a copy of the old Colt Series 70-era safeties. The slide stop is a standard, blued and checkered part. The stainless frame is marked on the right side only, with "Firearms International Inc., Hou Tex USA" above the grip, and the serial number forward of the slide stop pin. The trigger is an extended aluminum one, lacking lightening holes but having an overtravel screw installed. The trigger pull is clean if somewhat heavy. The magazine catch is standard and grooved. The frontstrap is smooth, and radiused in the old style under the trigger guard. The mainspring housing is flat, grooved and black plastic. The magazine opening is beveled on the outside but not the rear. The grips are double diamond, nicely figured and held on with standard screws.

The Camp Perry model comes in a plastic storage case with one magazine. The magazine sent was an old-style tapered-lip magazine. Rather than test both pistol and magazine, I used the Chip McCormick Power Mags he sent me, plus my old Wilson magazines. Well, we used those magazines except for one tester. The testers liked the Camp Perry.

The trigger has an over-travel screw. The slide stop is checkered, the mag button serrated.

The mag well is beveled, despite the High Standard's plain appearance.

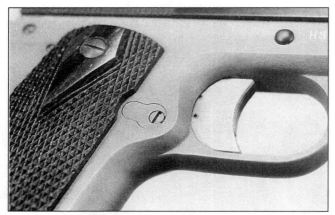

The frontstrap curve is standard, the mag catch button has a slotted head.

The stainless extractor in the blued slide. For those who like white-outline sights, the High Standard has them.

Perhaps they were overwhelmed by the tricked-out pistols, or waxed nostalgic over a pistol much like their early competition guns. They did not report any sharp edges, nor report having been bitten by the spur hammer. The sights were a source of comments concerning the white paint. Paint on sights is one of those "you do or you don't" sorts of things. Either you like paint or dots, or you don't. The testers who like paint and dots liked the sights. The testers who don't, didn't. As far as reliability is concerned, the Camp Perry has it. There were no malfunctions encountered except for the time one of the testers loaded the magazine shipped with the pistol along with the Wilson and McCormicks he was supposed to use. The supplied magazine is an old-style tapered feed lip design, and it caused a couple of malfunctions. With the magazines he was supposed to use, it worked fine.

In accuracy, the Camp Perry was the first pistol I clamped in the Ransom rest. No special reason, I had to start with one of them, and it was closest. I was not happy with the results. Unsure of the cause, I clamped one of my personal .45's in the Ransom rest, to see if the ammo, pistol or my technique was the fault. The Gunsite ATP with a Kart barrel shot an average of 1-1/2 inches with the first load tested.

I re-installed the Camp Perry and started over. It turns out the Camp Perry shows promise but needs tightening and tuning. The best load was the Oregon Trail, with an average

The testers were favorably impressed by the Camp Perry Model and gave it high marks.

of 2-1/2 inches. Second was a tie between the Sierra 230 JHP and the Montana Gold 185s, at 2-3/4 inches. Third goes to the West Coast 200-grain JRN's at 3 inches. As a basic gun, or a competition starter, the Camp Perry already has enough accuracy to be competitive for many shooters. It has the reliability. With a little tuning and some tightening, it could deliver cracking good accuracy along with its reliability. For someone who doesn't want a pistol festooned with the latest stylish parts, the looks of the Camp Perry are refreshing.

The 50-yard group ran just over 4 inches.

High Standard	
Trigger pull	7 lb
Extractor tension	40 oz
Chamber depth	0.899
.22 Conversion fit	
Kimber	Y
EAA	Y
Ciener	Y
Wilson	Y
Marvel	Y
Bar-Sto .400 Cor-bon fit	Y
Clark .460 Rowland fit	Rowland fit Y
Weight	36.3 oz.
Barrel length	5"
Three favorite loads	
1-Oregon Tr/Vihtavuori	2.5"
2-Sierra/Titegroup	2.75"
3-Montana Gold 185	3.0"

KAHR ARMS/
AUTO ORDNANCE

The Kahr is a close copy of the military-production 1911A1s of WWII.

The Kahr, with instructions, lock, fired case and desi-pack.

While lower than the original 1911's, the ejection port of the Kahr is not as low as is common practice today.

The old Auto Ordnance pistols had a reputation for being ugly pistols made of castings. When the Kahr Arms company bought the rights and parts, they spent a year programming their computer-aided machining centers to machine their new pistol to close tolerances, and to machine from forgings instead of the castings of the old pistol. The test pistol still had some cast parts on it (probably leftover inventory from the transition) but showed promise.

It is a plain Government Model pistol as much like the 1911A1 pattern contract guns built during World War II as possible. When I opened the case, I thought I was looking at my old Ithaca, made in 1943.

The sights are the old thumbnail-size front blade (and still an improvement over the 1911!) and the fixed rear to match. The front is only .094" high, and the rear is .140". Looking at sights like this, it isn't difficult to understand why point-shooting was held in such high regard in the old days. While the ejection port is not lowered and not scalloped, the empties get out just fine. It live-ejects, but you have to fiddle with it a bit to get a loaded round out. The slide is marked "Model 1911A1 U.S. Army" on the left side, and is unmarked on the right side. There are cocking serrations only at the rear.

The muzzle is standard, with a bushing and recoil plug.

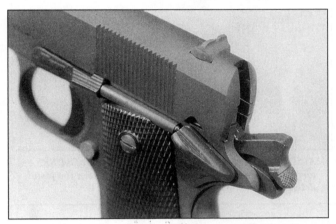

The Kahr has 1911-dimensioned hammer and grip safety, 1911A1 plastic grips and sights, and a post-war commercial thumb safety.

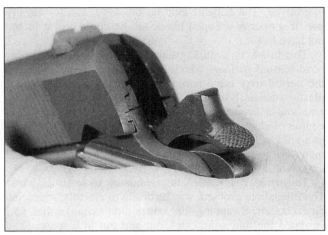

While the hammer threatened, it never bit.

The trigger is long, but does not have a trigger stop installed. The slide stop is the only cast part. Yours may be different.

The mag well is beveled, and the mainspring housing has a lanyard ring installed.

The barrel is their own, and fits snugly to the slide, even though the slide has some side to side movement on the frame. The ramp/chamber is standard, and not an integral ramp. It has a standard bushing and recoil plug, without a guide rod. The lockup does not have any extra feel or snap to it, the slide simply goes forward until it stops.

The hammer is a 1911 pattern hammer, with the widened spur. The grip safety is also the shorter 1911 pattern, and may bite those with fleshy hands. It did not bite any of the test-fire crew. The grip safety, being the old pattern, does not have a speed bump on the bottom. The thumb safety is the Colt teardrop pattern, and has a slightly better polish than the rest of the pistol. The slide stop is an obvious casting, with the mould mark still on the side of it. The trigger is not a 1911A1 military pattern trigger, being longer. While it looks like a competition trigger, it does not have an overtravel screw in it. It also has some sharp edges, from the machining or the mould. The trigger pull is light and clean, but feels just a tiny bit "spongy." While the more experienced testers noticed it when dry-firing, no one noticed it while shooting. Nor did it make any difference in the testers' performance.

From the trigger forward and downward the frame is a standard 1911A1 configuration, right to the brown plastic grips and the arched mainspring housing with lanyard loop on it. The frontstrap is smooth and the mainspring housing is grooved. The lanyard loop on the 1911 was for cavalry use. If a trooper dropped his pistol, he could reel it in and not have lost it.

The finish is a dark green Parkerizing over a heavy bead-blasted surface, which is quite durable and suited to the period they are attempting to recreate. It comes in a plastic storage box, with a gun lock, instructions, magazine and a fired case in a sealed envelope. (There are a couple of states that mandate a fired case from each handgun sold, a law passed by Legislators who have read too many crime novels.) Also included is a Metalform brand magazine, Parkerized.

Test-firing the Kahr/Auto Ordnance took some work. The immediate problem was its desire to eject the magazine on each shot. Swapping magazines didn't change that, so I swapped the magazine catch out and put in a spare. (You don't think I'd go to the range with 30+ pistols, and leave my spare parts and tools at the shop, do you?) The replacement magazine catch solved the problem, so all subsequent testing was done with the replacement catch in the frame. Once that problem was solved, the pistol cranked right through the test-fire ammo. We did not have any feeding problems, although it would occasionally fail to lock open when empty. The failure to lock never happened with the supplied magazine, so I'm inclined to ascribe it to weak springs in some of my magazines. As a test, I swapped the McCormick Power Mags that Chip had sent for the book into rotation with the Kahr, and they locked it open every time they emptied.

The testers were not bitten or gouged by any sharp edges, and except for the trigger, didn't feel any discomfort when shooting. There were no feeding malfunctions, even with the Hornady XTP hollow-points. Accuracy was good but not spectacular.

At 50 yards, all shots stayed within the "A" zone of a USPSA target. The small sights made it a tough job, but the pistol delivered.

Both the supplied mag and other test mags popped out with the factory mag catch. Changing the mag catch solved the dropping mag problem.

The load it shot most accurately was the Oregon Trail lead semi-wadcutter, but out of the Ransom rest it struggled to get its groups under 2-1/2 inches. In second place was the Rainier load, at just under 3 inches, and the Zero hollow-point right behind it. As I have mentioned before, we should be careful about becoming jaded with accuracy testing. Even with the loads it liked less than these, the Kahr can easily keep its hits inside the "A" zone of an IPSC target at 50 yards.

If you want a pistol that re-creates the look of a military WWII pistol, but is going to be more accurate (yes, more accurate) than a contract pistol of that time period, then the Kahr will do nicely. You may have to replace a few small parts to get an absolutely correct period look (the thumb safety is a Colt commercial one, and not correct for the time period of 1941-1945) or replace a casting, but otherwise it is a solid pistol. If you are looking for a beginning pistol for practical competition, the Kahr has some shortcomings. The sights will have to be changed, and any work you have done will present your gunsmith with a dilemma: No one makes aftermarket parts that are Parkerized. If the mis-match of finish with a Parkerized pistol and a stainless steel thumb safety (as an example) doesn't bother you, then start with a Kahr and spend the rest of your budget on practice ammo.

Kahr/Auto Ordnance	
Trigger pull	4.5 lb
Extractor tension	6 oz
Chamber depth	.904"
.22 Conversion fit	
Kimber	Y
EAA	N
Ciener	Y
Wilson	N
Marvel	Y
Bar-Sto .400 Cor-bon fit	Y
Clark .460 Rowland fit	Rowland fit Y
Weight	36.3 oz
Barrel length	5"
Three favorite loads	
1-Oregon Tr/Viht	2.45"
2-Rainier/Titegroup	2.95"
3-Zero 185 JHP	3.0"

 # KIMBER ULTRA CDP

The Ultra CDP is just about the smallest package you can launch a .45 ACP bullet from.

The Ultra CDP in hard case, with lock and NRA paperwork.

Once Kimber had gobbled up the market share that had previously belonged to Colt, they looked around to see what parts of the market they had overlooked. The compact, lightweight carry gun part of the market was one that Colt had never really addressed. Oh, Colt had made the Officer's Model and the LW Officer's Model, but they had made them as plain-Jane guns, and always with the reliability problems that Colt had in the last decade or so of the 20th century. (The problem? Some production batches worked flawlessly, others were plagued with malfunctions. You couldn't know until you tried a particular pistol which batch yours came from.)

When the Kimber pistols went into production, the CDP models were intended to be the best lightweight carry guns possible, and then some. CDP stands for Custom Defense Package, and Kimber is right on all three. Kimber makes the

CDP pistols in four sizes, full-size, Commander, Commander with short grip, and Officer's, or Ultra. The test gun for the book is the smallest model, the Ultra CDP. In the old days, it was considered the graduation exercise and ultimate show-off demonstration for a gunsmith to be able to chop a 1911 down to micro-size and still have it work and shoot accurately. It wasn't unheard-of for a gunsmith to charge nearly $2,000 (in 1980 dollars!) to perform such surgery. Now, you can buy it off the shelf for a suggested retail price of $1,142.

Based on an Officer's Model platform, the Ultra CDP uses shorter magazines, holding only seven rounds instead of eight. Longer magazines will work, but negate one of the advantages of the CDP, the ability to easily conceal the weapon. One option is to carry the holstered CDP with the short mag, and keep a full-sized magazine or magazines on your belt as your reloads.

The pistol we received is an Ultra CDP, with a two-tone finish. The slide is stainless steel, while the frame is machined from aluminum alloy and anodized matte black. The slide is 5-1/2 inches long, with cocking serrations only at the rear. The sights are a transverse-dovetailed front and Kimber/McCormick fixed rear, both with tritium inserts by Meprolight. On the left side the slide is marked "Custom Shop" with the Kimber logo in between. On the right side it is marked "Ultra CDP". The ejection port is lowered and scalloped, and has a slight radius on the front end to aid live-ejection. It live ejects, to no great surprise.

The barrel is 3.125" long, and is coned on the front to lock up to the slide. The barrel locks up firmly, but there is play between the slide and frame. The recoil spring assembly is a dual-spring dual-plunger arrangement, required in

You can use longer mags (like this 8-shot McCormick) but they make the pistol larger. Save the larger mags for your reloads.

The rear, with Meprolight inserts.

The front sight, dovetailed and with Meprolight insert.

The radically dehorned CDP, and the Custom Shop markings.

The lowered and scalloped ejection port, and it live ejects.

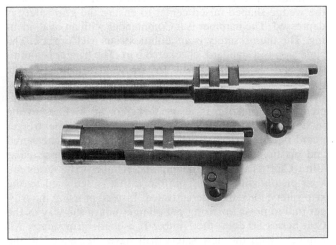

The Ultra CDP barrel is shorter than a Government Model barrel, and needs no bushing.

order to get enough spring behind the slide inside the radically-shortened dimensions of the pistol. The slide has noticeable play between it and the frame. In the old days, tightening the slide to an alloy frame was often a waste of time and money, as it wouldn't stay tight for long. I mentioned to Dwight Van Brunt of Kimber my reservations about the presently good accuracy of the Ultra CDP holding up over time. It turns out they machine the frame from a billet of 7075-T7, the hardest aluminum alloy out there. The fit will not wear any time soon. (As I will be hanging on to this pistol for long-term testing, we'll find out in a few years when it is time for *The Gun Digest Book of the 1911*, Vol. II.)

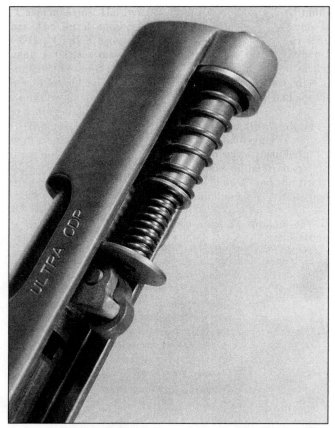

The telescoping dual spring recoil assembly of the Ultra CDP.

The slide moves nearly half the length of the barrel under recoil.

The frame as mentioned, is machined out of a billet of aluminum. The grip safety is a Kimber/McCormick, with the wedge-shaped raised center to ensure the grip safety is depressed. The hammer is a Commander with an oval opening. The thumb safety is an ambidextrous McCormick. The slide stop is a standard, checkered part. The trigger is aluminum, and skeletonized with two rectangles instead of the usual three holes. It has a trigger stop screw installed. The magazine catch is slightly longer than normal, and checkered. The frontstrap is also checkered, at 30 lines to the inch. The radius between the frontstrap and the trigger guard is raised. The mainspring housing is flat, checkered and plastic. The magazine well is beveled. This particular Ultra CDP is a pre-II model. The Kimber "II" series are their pistols with a firing pin block that is activated by the grip safety. Or rather, de-activated. Instead of using the trigger pull to press the firing pin plunger out of the way as the Colt Series 80 does, the Kimber II uses the grip safety. All Kimbers with the new safety will have "II" added to the model designation. The new models of this pistol will be known as "Ultra CDP II", and will be in production along with the regular Ultra CDP.

The grips are nicely figured double-diamond grips, a bit too round for my tastes, but several of the test-shooters particularly liked the grips. The grips screws are Allen-head screws, as is the magazine catch retaining pin.

The CDP comes in a plastic storage case, complete with owner's manual, lock, one magazine and an application to join the NRA (which you should fill out and send in.) This test pistol was shipped with three magazines, simply so your poor scribe would spend less time at the range stuffing the same magazine over and over again. All single-stack magazines will work in the Ultra CDP.

In contrast to the blued frame, the grip and thumb safeties, plunger tube, slide stop, magazine catch and mainspring housing are either stainless steel, silver-anodized aluminum, or gray plastic. In addition to the two-tone finish, the Ultra CDP has had an aggressive de-horning job performed on it. Every corner has been rounded as much as possible. Except for the places where you expect a sharp edge or corner, like the checkering on the magazine button or frontstrap, there is nothing to cut you. Every edge has been gone over so aggressively that the CDP has the "bar of soap" look about it.

The testers mostly raved about the CDP, although a few had reservations about such a light trigger on a carry gun. The factory specs call for a 4- to 4-1/2-pound trigger pull. this pistol's pull weighed out at 3-3/4 pounds, but was so clean and crisp it felt lighter. One tester came right out and said "the trigger is too light for a carry gun." (That particular tester carries a gun all day long within the borders of Detroit. I pay close attention to his opinions.) While another commented "I spent a whole lot of money to get my first Bull's eye gun's trigger this good." The highest compliment came from an experienced tester: "The only thing wrong with this gun is that it isn't mine."

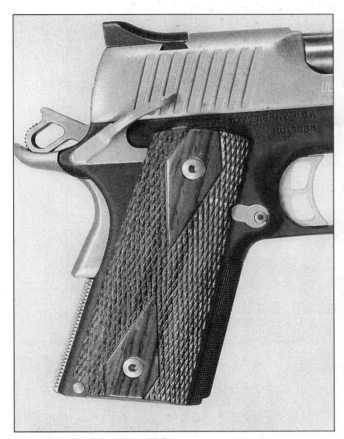

Right side of the Ultra CDP.

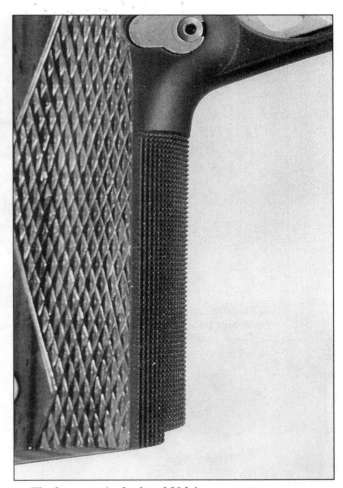

The frontstrap is checkered 30 lpi.

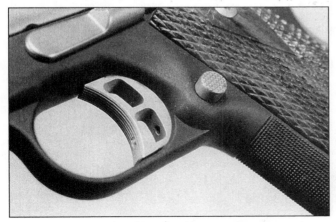

The stainless and white aluminum parts make a nice contrast to the black anodized frame.

The mag well is beveled, and nicely so.

In accuracy, the CDP proved to be capable, if not tack-driving. The best it could do with the Hornady 200-grain XTP's was a 2-inch average. Remember, this is a pistol with a short barrel that weighs only 23.1 ounces empty. To get a 2-inch group at 25 yards is damn good performance. Coming in second was the Zero 185 JHP load, at just under 2-1/4 inches. Third was the Oregon Trail/Vihtavuori load, just under 2-1/2 inches. At no time in the testing did the CDP malfunction. It always worked, always locked open when empty, and always dropped the empty magazine. It worked so well that one of my testers wanted to buy it. In felt recoil, despite its being such a light gun, no one felt pushed around

or abused by the recoil. Granted, the test crew was composed of "high-mileage" shooters who get in lots of range time, but they were eager to shoot the little Kimber.

As a competition gun, it would be right at home as an IDPA gun. For all other competitions its assets are diametrically opposed to a competition gun: It is too light, too short,

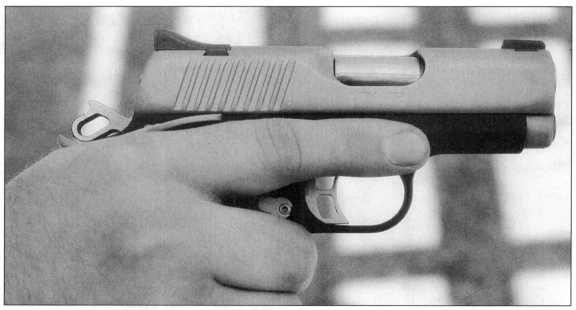

The Ultra CDP makes a compact, powerful and accurate carry pistol.

The extreme de-horning of the Ultra CDP, and the lack of a bushing, are both apparent from the muzzle end of things.

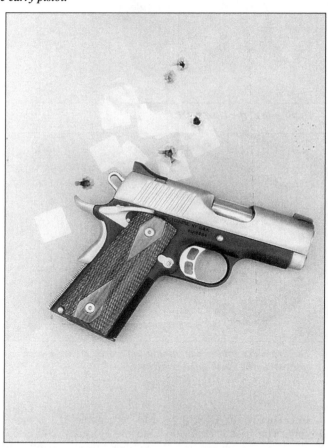

The Ultra CDP 50-yard test group. A 5-inch group at 50 yards from a .45 you can hide in a pocket? You bet.

All the testers liked the CDP, even though they hated digging empties out of the snow.

and doesn't hold enough ammo. Which makes it the perfect carry gun. And if the eight shots it holds (yes, the short little magazines hold seven rounds of .45 ACP!) aren't enough, you can quickly reload with eight or 10 more. If I didn't already have a Colt lightweight commander with a Bar-sto barrel I'd be carrying the Ultra CDP all day. I still might.

Kimber Ultra CDP	
Trigger pull	3.75 lb
Extractor tension	24 oz
Chamber depth	.902"
.22 Conversion fit	
Kimber	Y*
EAA	Y*
Ciener	N
Wilson	N
Marvel	N
Bar-Sto .400 Cor-bon fit	N**
Clark .460 Rowland fit	N**
Weight	23.1 oz
Barrel length	3.125"
Three favorite loads	
1-Hornady 200 gr XTP	2.0"
2-Zero 185 JHP	2.20"
3-Oregon Tr/Viht	2.40"

* The conversions fit, but the slide weight sometimes caused malfunctions. Use a shorter-slide conversion for reliable function
** The barrels are gov't barrels, and should not be used in a Commander or shorter pistol

KIMBER SUPER MATCH

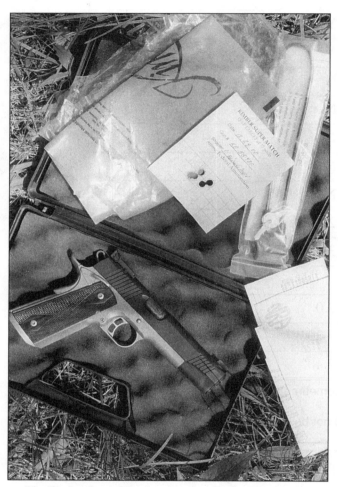

The Kimber Super Match, test target, lock, NRA material, and blue bag.

If anyone can be said to have put Colt out of business besides Colt, it would be Kimber. They did it by the simple process of offering a product the customer wanted, at the price a customer was willing to pay. And then ate up more market share by offering options previously unavailable. If you don't have a copy of the Kimber catalog, get one. If you like the 1911, there will be page after page of 1911s in a host of configurations. I've waited a long time for the line to expand to .38 Super/9mm, and it just happened before going to the printers. The Gold Match Special Edition is available in both .45 and .38 Super. The Kimber pistol used for this test was a full-sized 1911 in .45 ACP, the Kimber Super Match.

The Kimber Super Match comes out of the custom shop of the Kimber plant, where the already high quality Kimber parts receive extra attention. For those who know, the looks are obvi-ous, but for those who don't, the Kimber was designed by Kim-ber with guidance from Chip McCormick. Many of the parts are pure McCormick in design. Chip was a top-flight competi-tor in the early 1980s, and when it came time to do more, he sought a more exclusive path. Many top shooters make their living teaching, and use competition (and their success) to bur-nish their reputation and keep the clients coming. Chip, like Bill Wilson, went into manufacturing and marketing parts.

As with all of the all-steel Kimbers, the slide and frame are machined from forged parts. Early in a Kimber's manu-facturing, the slide and frame are matched and kept together. While some manufacturers might make slides and frames on separate lines, and then marry them in final assembly, Kim-ber matches the pair early and keeps them together through the final machining and assembly.

The slide is standard length, with adjustable rear sight in the Bo-mar pattern, and a front blade in a transverse dove-tail. There are beveled cocking serrations front and rear. The rear of the slide has the same matte finish as the rest of the slide. The barrel is a standard (unramped) design, with a bushing in front. The bushing is tight enough to require a bushing wrench to remove. The barrel locks up without any play, but does not lock hard. The recoil spring has a one-piece guide rod, with a standard retainer plug with a hole for the rod. On the left of the slide is the Kimber logo, flanked by "Custom" and "Shop". The right side has "Super Match" under the ejection port, which is lowered and scalloped.

The slide is stainless, finished in Kimber's Kimpro finish, a baked-on epoxy resin finish that protects the steel. The edges of the slide have been dehorned, and except for a couple of neces-sary edges on the sights, there is nothing on the slide that can cut you. The fit of the slide to the frame had no play in it.

The frame is a standard configuration Government Model frame, made of stainless steel and given a bead-blasted matte finish. The hammer is a McCormick-Locke oval commander hammer. The thumb safety is an ambidextrous unit, with both sides low enough in profile that you could use it as a carry gun. The grip safety is pure McCormick, using Chip's wedge speed bump to ensure your hand depresses the grip safety when you grasp it. The slide stop is a standard checkered part. The trigger is long, with a stop screw installed. It is the lone part that devi-ates from the McCormick parts in looks. It has two rectangular holes to lighten it, instead of the usual three circular holes. The trigger pull is clean and crisp. The magazine catch is standard size, checkered on the button, and uses an allen-socket retaining pin. The corner of the front strap where it joins the trigger guard has been radiused and brought higher, but not radically so.

The frontstrap is checkered 30 lines to the inch. The main-spring housing is checkered 20 lines to the inch. The magazine funnel is an S&A funnel, or a close copy. It is an integral part of the mainspring housing, with two arms that the bevel in the frame. If you miss a reload with this one, you have no one to

Left side of the Super Match.

The Kimber muzzle, with standard bushing and hollow recoil spring retainer.

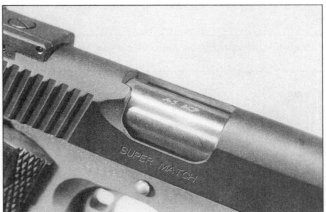

Ejection port lowered and scalloped, and the Super Match marking.

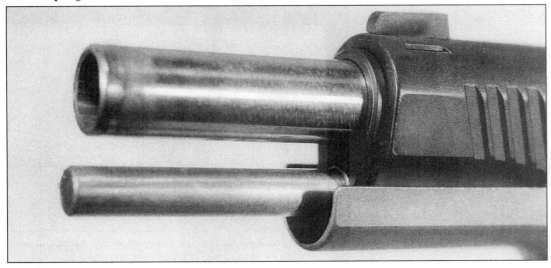

The slide locked back.

blame but yourself. However, for the money involved, you might expect a bit more fitting of the magazine funnel.

The grips are slightly figured reddish wood, checkered in a double diamond pattern. The checkering stops at small panels on the front and rear edges of the wood. The screws are Allen-socket screws.

The pistol comes in a lockable hard case with one magazine holding eight rounds. There is a vapor-phase inhibiting blue plastic bag to protect from rust, a bushing wrench, owner's manual, application to join the NRA (a good idea, by the way)

and the test-fire target. The target shows five shots into an inch, using un-specified Federal ammo at 25 yards. Promising.

What the accuracy testing uncovered was a phenomenon I had previously seen in .22lr handguns, but rarely in 1911s. When I first started shooting settling groups, it seemed that it needed more groups than usual to settle into the inserts. I usually get good groups by the third magazine, but the load I had started with was only producing groups 2-1/2 inches in size by then. I switched to another ammo, and almost fell

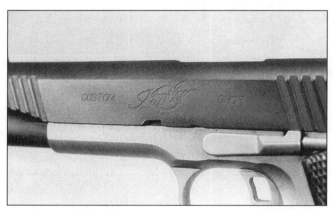

Left side, with the Kimber logo and Custom Shop marking.

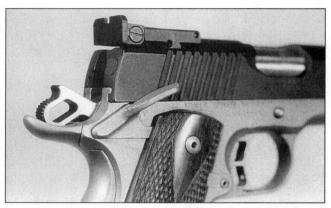

The Super Match rear sight, ambidextrous safety and hammer.

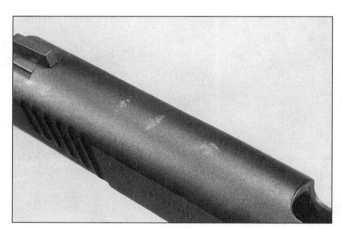

How tough is Kimpro? These are paint marks left from some barricade shooting in the testing.

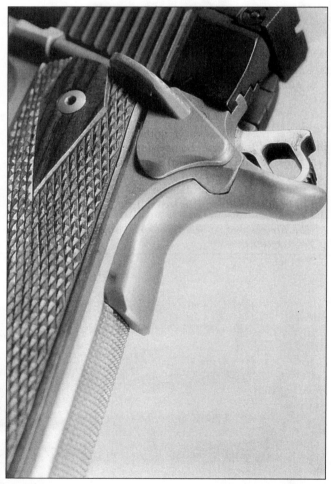

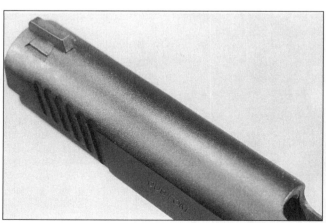

A little scrubbing with oil and steel wool, and the marks are gone.

The grip safety is not just equipped with a bump, but is raised down its spine for sure disengagement.

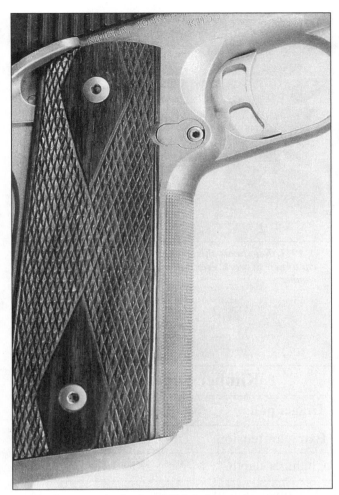

The frontstrap is checkered 30 lpi, the mag button uses an Allen head, and the trigger has two rectangular openings.

The mag funnel is large, and the grips come flush to meet it.

Once you find what this Kimber likes, stick with it. Other Kimbers have not been so fussy.

The Kimber rear sight is large, easy to see and nicely proportioned.

off my chair when the Kimber shot a 4-1/2 inch group. Then a 3-inch group, a 2-1/2-inch group, a 2-inch group. The secret was out. The Kimber was one of those rare pistols that was dogged in its insistence on being fed one type of ammo. If you switched ammo, it would take at least several groups to shoot well again.

I have concluded from previous test-firing sessions where I have seen this phenomena that it must be a product of bore fouling. With the bullet and powder material of the previous load in the bore, the next load would not shoot well. Once you had blown out enough of the old gunk with repeated groups, and replaced it with the residue of the new load, the Kimber would shoot well again.

The Oregon Trail load is a perfect example. Going to the Oregon Trail from a jacketed-bullet load, the first group was 2-1/4 inches, the second 2-3/4 inches, and the third 2-1/4 inches. An average of just under two and a half inches. Nice, but not what you would expect from a top-dollar pistol and a top-flight company. But, the more I shot it the better the groups got. The sixth, seventh and eighth groups averaged just over an 1-1/4 inches in size. (Now that's more like it.)

Were you to test the accuracy of this particular Kimber (and not all are like it, very few 1911s are) by the usual method, you'd conclude it was not accurate. Shooting a couple of groups of each type of ammo you might have on hand, one after the other, would get you a series of disap-

pointingly average groups. Only patience would uncover its true gem-like nature.

And gem it is. The test fire crew all had favorable impressions of the Kimber. Many of them own Kimbers, and found themselves right at home. One wrote "Accurate, reliable, nice trigger, just what you'd expect from a Kimber." There were no recorded failures to feed, fire or eject,

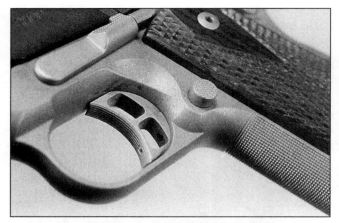

The clean, crisp trigger pull of the Kimber made it easy to shoot.

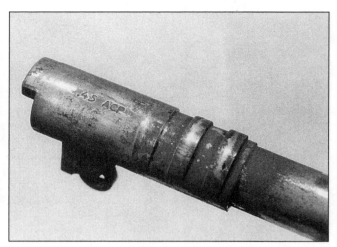

A 1911 that shoots this accurately, looks this good, and continues to work even when the barrel is grungy? A Kimber.

The Super Match 50-yard target, fired by yours truly. Under 4 inches, and I'm suspicious of me on that low shot, not the pistol.

Kimber Super Match	
Trigger pull	3.75 lb
Extractor tension	22 oz
Chamber depth	.900"
.22 Conversion fit	
Kimber	Y
EAA	Y
Ciener	Y
Wilson	Y
Marvel	Y
Bar-Sto .400 Cor-bon fit	N
Clark .460 Rowland fit	Y
Weight	37.9 oz
Barrel length	5.0"
Three favorite loads	
1-Oregon Trails/Viht	
2-Zero 185 JHP	
3-Hornady 200 XTP	

but a couple of shooters reported that a magazine wouldn't lock open. After a few boxes of ammo had disappeared downrange, that problem went away.

Its best load was the Oregon Trail/Vihtavuori load, where it averaged 1.33 inches. Second was the Zero 185 JHP's at 1.625 inches average. Third was the Hornady 200-grain XTP factory load, at 1.75 inches. If I ever give this pistol back, and Kimber turns around and sells it, my advice to the lucky future owner of #K055980, would be to lay in a supply of Oregon Trail bullets and experiment a bit.

The Kimber Super Match made the cut for the 1911 Match, and it spent the day on Range #4, going through ammo at the rate of 24 rounds per shooter. Around the 800-round mark, the shooter using it had to smack the back of the slide to get it to close on one round. One application of the Bore Snake, and a couple of drops of oil, and it was good for the rest of the match.

As a top-end carry and stock competition gun, the Kimber would be a very good choice. You could use the Kimber in an IDPA match, and (if legal) use it as your carry gun after the match. The checkering is first-rate, the trigger very nice, and it is utterly reliable. Once you found the load it liked, you could count on it delivering for you, in a match or on the street. A definite thumbs up.

LES BAER

HEAVYWEIGHT MONOLITH

The Les Baer is a real heavyweight, and the weight is out front and under the bore.

When it comes to competition shooting, the pistol I would want most to be using in a lot of matches would be the Les Baer. If you are on the line in a bowling pin match shooting in Stock, or at the Handgunner Shoot-off shooting Limited, and you see that the guy next to you has one of these, worry.

Les makes his own slides, frames and barrels, small parts and magazines and he offers a full line of single-stack pistols. The Heavyweight Monolith is the big bad boy of the bunch. It is the competition-crushing machine.

Shipped in a cardboard box with two Les Baer magazines, bushing wrench and catalogs, the Baer Monolith I received was swimming in oil. The heavy extended dust cover adds 3.5 ounces to the total weight. Available in .45, .400 Cor-bon, 40 S&W, 9mm and .38 Super, the Heavy-

The Les Baer Heavyweight Monolith in its shipping box, with spare mags, bushing wrench and catalog.

The dovetailed front sight, pinned in place, and the front cocking serrations.

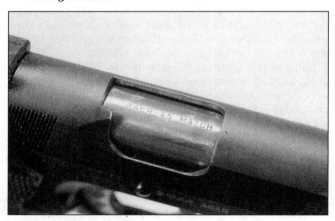

The Les Baer Match barrel, and its lowered and scalloped ejection port.

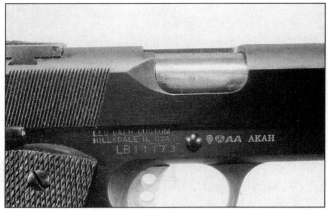

Yes, German proof marks. I guess someone in Germany isn't a hostage to H-K mania.

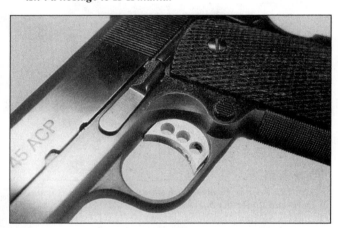

The dustcover doesn't "lift" forward of the trigger guard. The frontstrap is radiused where it meets the trigger guard.

The bushing is tight, the recoil spring standard, and the dustcover goes out to the muzzle.

weight Monolith also comes with a 3-inch group at 50-yard guarantee. As we found out, it delivers.

The slide has a Novak-dovetail front sight and a Bo-mar pattern rear sight with the Les Baer name and logo on it. There are cocking serrations front and back, of the fine-cut, angled serration style. The rear of the slide is smooth. The ejection port is lowered and flared, and it live ejects. On the left side, the slide is marked "45 ACP" and on the right side it has "Baer Custom." On the right side rear of this particular pistol is a German proof mark, as well as proof marks on the right side of the frame in front of the slide stop pin. This particular pistol had gone to Germany, and was back in the shop for I-don't-know-what. It couldn't have needed much work, as it never failed during our test fire sessions.

The barrel is a Les Baer, with the tightest lockup I have ever seen on a 1911. When I first went to cycle the slide, it wouldn't budge. I stopped to make sure the safety was off, and tried again. It opened with a snap. The lockup is not a bind or interference fit. No matter how close to closed you hold it, and even if you ease the slide forward, it will fully close. It just closes up tight. Really tight. The barrel is a standard one, no ramp, with a bushing up front. The bushing is tight enough that you need a solid wrench made of steel,

and not a flimsy little plastic one, to turn it. The recoil spring is standard, without a guide rod. The fit of the slide to frame had no play whatsoever. Just out of curiosity, I took it apart and tried the slide-to-frame fit. It still had no play. To say it is a nice fit is an understatement.

The frame has a Ed Brown pattern grip safety of Les' design and a speed bump a bit larger than most. The ambidextrous thumb safety has a large paddle on the left side and a slimmer one on the right. The hammer is another Les Baer product, commander style with an oval loop. The trigger is a long aluminum one, with three holes and a stop screw. The dustcover is full profile all the way to the end of the slide. Not only is it the full width of the frame and full length to the end of the slide, but the bottom edge of the dustcover does not rise from the line of the interior upper edge of the trigger guard. Most 1911 frames have the bottom edge of the dustcover lifted, the Heavyweight Monolith does not.

The radius of the frontstrap and trigger guard has been raised. The frontstrap is checkered at what appears to be 40 lines to the inch. The result of the long, heavy dustcover makes the Heavyweight Monolith 3 to 4 ounces heavier than most of the pistols. Some standard guns are an ounce or so heavier than usual, but the Les Baer is the fourth heaviest. Of the three ahead of it, two are the long-slide guns, and the third is the STI Edge. The Edge is heavier by 1/10 of an ounce, the others by 1-1/2 and 2 ounces. The extra weight is perfectly located to dampen felt recoil, below the bore and forward of your hands.

The mainspring housing is flat and serrated, and is completely normal. The magazine opening is slightly beveled. The grips are a dark wood, and are not relieved at the lower rear corner, hiding the mainspring housing retainer pin.

The frontstrap, very nicely checkered.

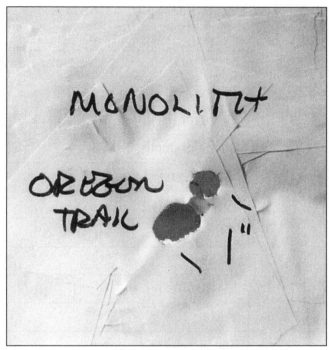

The weight dampens the recoil, and it shoots like this! You should be worried if the guy next to you has a Les Baer.

The mag funnel is beveled.

The Heavyweight Monolith and its 50-yard group. Under 3 inches, and I feel like I let it down.

With the Les Baer Heavyweight Monolith, you don't get a monogrammed carry case, or a sheaf of paperwork. What you get is a pistol, magazines to feed it, and a Les Baer catalog that is a Christmas wish list. The overall impression of the Monolith is that of a heavy, solid machine impervious to outside influence. From the moment you pick it up, you know that if anything doesn't go according to plan, it wasn't the pistol's fault. It live-ejects, but does not close by slide manipulation. Removing the installed shock buffer allows you to close it by whipsawing the slide, which I would do if it were mine. But, it is not and had to go back. Sigh.

In shooting, the weight of the dustcover dampened felt recoil, making even the hot PMP hardball feel softer in comparison. The test crew liked the Les Baer, a lot. The comments ranged from "very nice checkering" to "Like the weight and balance." One test shooter commented on a sharp edge he found on the thumb safety, but looking over the worksheets, it was made by a tester who found sharp edges on almost all the thumb safeties. The only bad com-ment made was that the Monolith needed a magazine fun-nel. Easy enough to fix.

Accuracy shooting proved the favorable impressions of the Monolith. The most accurate load was a tie between the Sierra 230 JHP and Titegroup ammunition, and the Oregon Trail and Vihtavouri load, at 1.41-inch average. Second went to the PMP hardball, with an average of 2 inches, closely followed by the Black Hills Red load at 2.1 inches. While the Monolith didn't post spectacularly tight groups as some of the pistols did, it was consistent to an amazing degree. (And the gun's "not spectacular" best groups were an even 1 inch in size.) The largest group it shot was a sole group of 3.5 inches in size. For 43 of its 44 groups, the larg-est was 3 inches. Other pistols shot better top-end groups, but if you fed them ammo they didn't like a string of 3- to 4-inch groups could result. The Monolith didn't care, and didn't do such a thing. Such dependability is highly valued in competition circles, and so is the Heavyweight Monolith.

Les Baer Heavyweight Monolith	
Trigger pull	4.75 lb
Extractor tension	22 oz
Chamber depth	.906"
.22 Conversion fit	
Kimber	Y
EAA	Y
Ciener	Y
Wilson	Y
Marvel	Y
Bar-Sto .400 Cor-bon fit	N
Clark .460 Rowland fit	Y
Weight	39.3
Barrel length	5"
Three favorite loads	
1-Sierra/Titegroup	1.41"
2-Oregon Tr/Viht	1.41"
3-PMP 220 JRN	2.0"

NOWLIN
MATCH CLASSIC

The Nowlin Match Classic in its case and with the factory test targets.

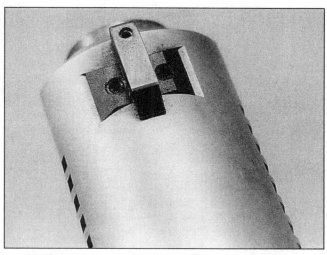

The Nowlin front sight, with its roll pin and set screw.

The Low Rider sight. Get one.

The Nowlin 1911 is possibly the most desirable pistol of the bunch, made more desirable by the fact that it sells for $1,000 less than the most-expensive pistols tested. And it performs better than many of them. While it doesn't have the snazzy appeal of having been adopted by the FBI as the Springfield Pro did (although the FBI would not have gone wrong had they selected the Nowlin) or the sheer power of the .45 Super, what it has is subtle and understated class. No, make that Class.

When I first saw it, and for some time after that, I thought the Match Classic was made of stainless steel. Later, I was filing paperwork, and saw on the invoice that it is listed as "chrome." It is the nicest chrome job I've ever seen. I'll have

to see if I can find out who does their chrome, and send some of my own guns there. It is a fixed-sight Government Model size pistol. At first glance nothing about it makes it stand out from the rest. Then you start noticing details. The sights are fixed, with a Novak-style front of Nowlin manufacture and a rear of Nowlin/McCormick design. The front sight is not only fastened into its dovetail, but there is a roll pin locating the blade to the slide centerline, and two set screws in the base. If anything knocks this front sight loose, the owner is not likely to survive the impact! The rear is called the "Low Rider" sight, and it is darned neat. Unlike the Novak rear sight design, which requires milling a large dovetail, the Low Rider uses the existing standard dovetail. The sight covers the dovetail, and clamps to an inner plate

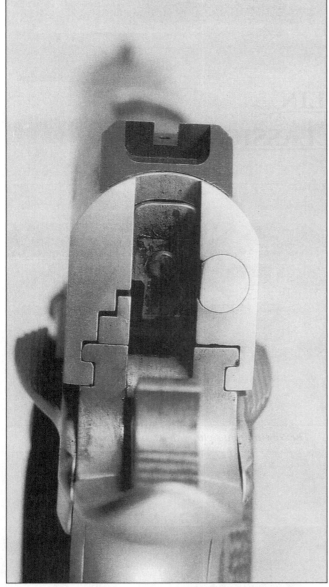

The rear of the slide is smooth, and the Low Rider sight offers a clean and crisp sight picture.

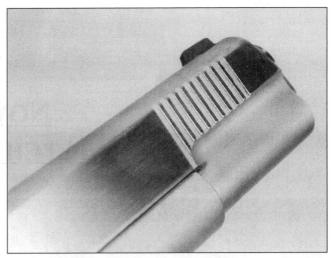

The front scallop is different and attractive.

Even as dirty as this barrel got (and is) it delivered the goods.

A standard front bushing, two-piece guide rod and very nice front cocking serrations.

that rests in the dovetail. The screw on top is your only clue as to how the sight is attached. The sight is compact, elegant, easy to see and use, and doesn't require extra machining of the slide. I think I'm going to use this sight for my future pistols.

The slide has cocking serrations front and back. The undercurve of the slide forward of the frame is machined with a smaller-radius ball end cutter than usual, and the tighter curve is attractive and distinctive. Except for the Nowlin logo on the right rear behind the cocking serrations, the sides of the slide are left bare of markings, and brushed to a brighter finish than the top, rear and bottom. The ejection port is lowered and scalloped, and live-ejects. The scallop is another different machine cut than usual, and is subtle and attractive.

The barrel is a Nowlin match barrel, and fits tightly. It locks shut with a definite click, but does not bind in its lockup. The barrel has no play in it when locked up. The

chamber is a standard ramp, and there is a bushing up front. The bushing is tight enough to require a wrench to remove. Remember when I said the Nowlin wasn't adopted by the FBI? Well, their barrel was. The Springfield Pro uses a Nowlin Match barrel. The recoil spring is wrapped around a two-piece guide rod.

The fit of the slide to the frame is marvelous. There is no perceptible play in the fit, and the slide moves so smoothly that it feels like there are ball bearings involved. Several of the test-fire crew spent a long time simply cycling the slide slowly back and forth, feeling the fit and lockup, before shooting it. When doing my initial inspection, I too felt the seductive smoothness of the slide-to-frame fit, and I took the barrel out and checked the slide to frame fit without the distraction of the barrel, and there was still no play.

The frame is a standard configuration Government-size frame. The hammer is a Commander style with an elongated

The left-hand side of the Nowlin.

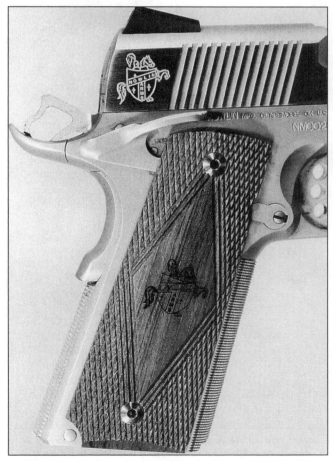

The right side. Note the fit of the grip safety and the Nowlin logos.

and sculpted oval. The grip safety is an Ed Brown pattern radius, cut for a high grip, with a speed bump on the bottom. The thumb safety is an ambidextrous one, appearing to be a Chip McCormick safety or close copy of it. The thumb safety clicked up and down with authority, and did not require undue force in either direction. The slide stop is a checkered standard unit. the trigger is an extended aluminum one, with three holes and a stop screw installed. The trigger pull is crisp and clean, with no perceptible overtravel, even though the trigger visibly moves when the hammer falls. So clean was the trigger pull that I had several testers ask how it was possible to get a 1911 trigger down under 2 pounds (it holds 3.5) and keep it safe. It is so clean in release it feels lighter than it actually is. The magazine catch is checkered and held in with a standard slotted retaining pin.

The Nowlin name and the pistol's serial number are on the right side of the frame, above the grip panel between the thumb safety and slide stop pin hole. The curve of the front strap to trigger guard is tighter than original specs, but not radically so. The frontstrap is checkered 30 lines to the inch and is perfect. Even a close inspection with a loupe could not uncover a single diamond that wasn't correct. The mainspring housing is flat, plastic and checkered 20 lines to the inch. Would I prefer a steel mainspring housing? Yes. Does the fact that the existing one is plastic matter as to fit, function or reliability? Not a bit. Would I change the mainspring

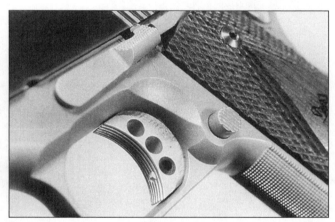

Trigger, slide stop, mag catch, grip screws, all beautifully fitted.

Name and serial number right where you'd expect them to be.

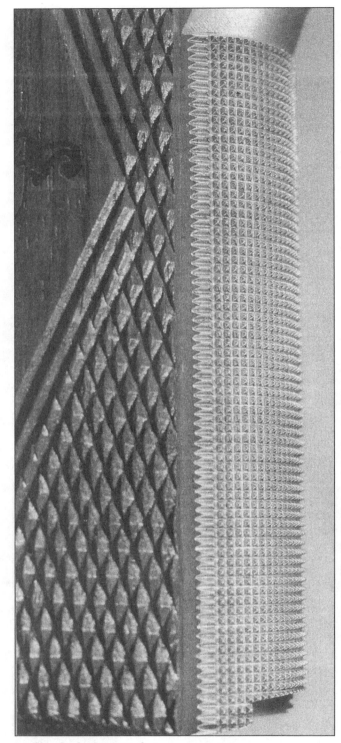

The checkering is perfect.

The mag well is beveled.

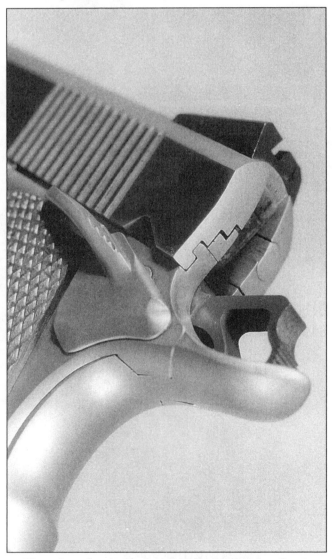

The grip safety is fitted very well, the thumb safety is obviously dehorned and the rest of it is dehorned even if it doesn't look it.

housing were this pistol mine? Probably not. The magazine opening is slightly beveled, with the bevel going into the radius of the front corner, not stopping short of the corner as others do.

The grips are exotic fruitwood, checkered in a single diamond pattern, with the Nowlin logo laser-engraved in the center of the diamond. The grip screws are stainless Allen-socket screws.

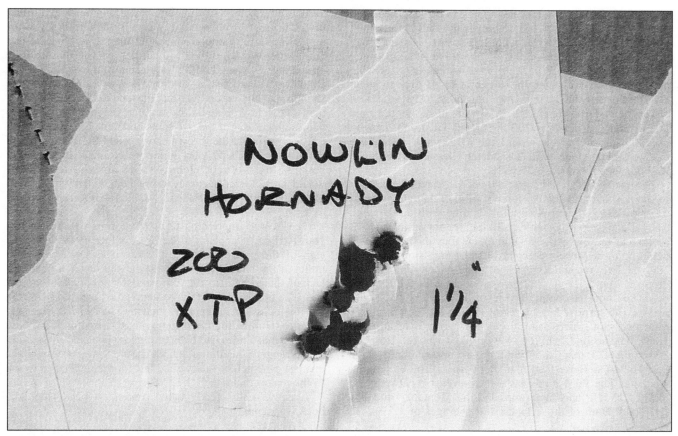

A typical and satisfactory 25-yard group.

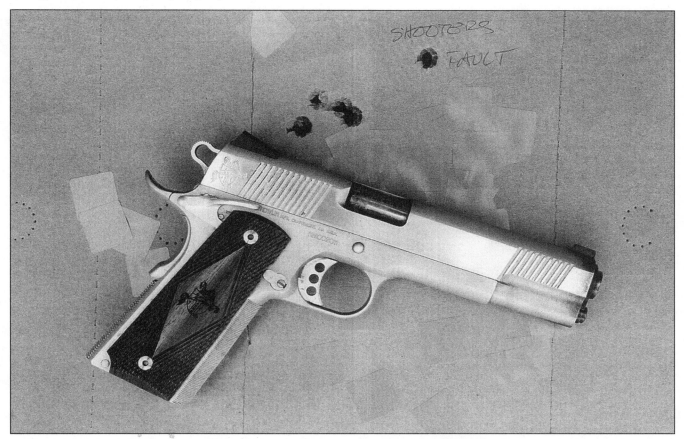

If only I hadn't mashed the trigger, this would be a real bragging 50-yard group. And this after 1,500 rounds of testing!

Overall, the Nowlin does not appear to be dehorned. You might think that with the slide polished as it is you would get cut, but you won't. The dehorning is done is such a way that it doesn't appear to be worn like a bar of soap, but it doesn't nip and bite you. The pistol comes in a lockable hard case with one magazine which at first I took to be an Ed Brown. It is Nowlin's own magazine. Also enclosed were a pair of test-fire targets. Both were under an inch, and one of them used a lead 200 SWC and Titegroup. Nowlin uses a grip-panel scope mount and a 7X scope to test-fire every pistol that they build. The Match Classic is guaranteed to shoot 1-inch groups at 25 yards.

With such a favorable appearance, the testers were eager to shoot it. Indeed, I had to force several of them to go on to other pistols and not spend all their time with the Nowlin. They did not report a single malfunction, nor an instance of a bite, cut or "owwie." The comments they did write down could be more closely described as lust than simply appreciative. The magazines locked open when empty, and dropped free when the button was pushed. In the Ransom rest it did not disappoint. The favorite load for the Nowlin was the (no surprise here) Oregon Trail load. The average of four, five-shot groups came in at just barely over an inch, 1.08". The second load the Nowlin liked was the Hornady 200-grain XTP load, shooting those groups into an average of 1.16"! A defense load that shoot like a Bull's eye gun, amazing. The third load was a dead-even tie between the Sierra 230 JHP and Titegroup, and the Montana Gold 185 JHP load. Both of those loads shot averages of 1.5" at 25 yards. Indeed, the Nowlin shot everything well, and you'd be hard-pressed to blame this pistol for any accuracy problems. It shot only one group larger than 2 inches, and that was a single group of the PMP hardball that went 3.25" The other three groups with PMP were an average of 1.5". When I did the 50-yard testing of the Nowlin, I called one of the shots out of the group, as I had mashed the trigger and saw the front sight wobble on the target as the gun went off. Too bad, because four of the five shots had gone into a group just over an inch, and the thrown shot opened the group up to 3 inches. A 1-inch 50-yard group would have been a real bragging-rights target! John Nowlin Jr. suggested that I would find greater accuracy using Federal 185-grain Gold Match. Unfortunately, Federal was not able to send me any to test.

The overall impression takes some time to sneak up on you. At first, it appears to be just another 1911. Then the sum of the parts begin to filter through. Once you start noticing the smooth fit of the slide, the clean trigger, the lack of sharp edges to cut your hands, you notice it for what it is: The best bargain of the top-end guns. It easily made the cut for inclusion in the 1911 match. The Nowlin went the distance, completing the match without a malfunction, even after the magazines had been dropped repeatedly in the sand of the range. Squad after squad, shooters would come back one last time before their squad left for the next stage to ask "Who makes that one?"

I really, really, really hated sending it back when the book was done.

Nowlin Match Classic	
Trigger pull	3.5 lb
Extractor tension	9 oz
Chamber depth	.900"
.22 Conversion fit	
Kimber	Y
EAA	Y
Ciener	Y
Wilson	Y
Marvel	Y
Bar-Sto .400 Cor-bon fit	Y, but tight
Clark .460 Rowland ift	Y
Weight	35.5 oz
Barrel length	5"
Three favorite loads	
1-Oregon Tr/Viht	1.08"
2-Hornady 200 gr XTP	1.16"
3-Sierra/Viht-Montana Gold/Titegroup (tie)	1.5"

* The conversions fit, but the slide weight sometimes caused malfunctions. Use a shorter-slide conversion for reliable function
** The barrels are gov't barrels, and should not be used in a Commander or shorter pistol

PARA-ORDNANCE LDA

The "LDA" stands for light double-action. Many shooters, and more who aren't shooters but carry guns, are put off by a cocked and locked 1911. As a result, many companies make pistols that have a safety that drops the hammer without firing the pistol. Some safeties stay on, others immediately push off, but the result is a pistol that trigger-cocks the first shot, then slide-cocks for the rest. Such pistols are known as "DA", or double-action, pistols. As an operational matter, law enforcement administrators love DA, as they feel it cuts down on accidents. (Actually, training cuts down on accidents, but it is easier to buy hardware than train.)

A pistol that does not slide-cock, but requires trigger-cocking for each shot, is known as a "Double-Action Only" or DAO pistol. (How something can be both double and only is beyond me, but no one asked me when it came time to name these things.) To add further to the confusion of categories, some DA and DAO pistols have a "second strike" capability, and others don't. A pistol with a second strike capability allows you to whack the primer again on a cartridge that failed to go off. Those that lack the second strike capability require you to rack the slide and eject the round in order to try again.

Once DA and later DAO became popular, the holy grail was to marry the 1911 to one of these systems. The Seecamp DA conversion of the 1911 was an early effort. Later, the Colt Double Eagle tried and failed. The problem was two-fold. One, the trigger pulls were heavy enough to have an effect on aim. And two, once cocked, the hammer could

The Para-Ordnance LDA 7.45 in its case, with manual, lock, fired case, and bushing wrench.

The Para-LDA solves the pesky "problem" some people have with cocked and locked pistols.

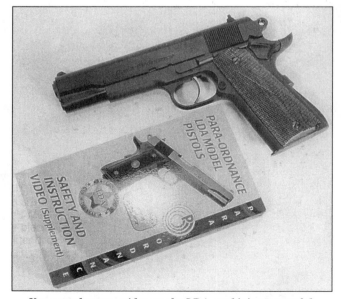

You can also get a video on the LDA, and it is very useful.

Except for the trigger, the Para looks like any other 1911A1 of the modern era.

Stroking the trigger cocks the hammer and fires the pistol.

be lowered only by thumbing the hammer while pulling the trigger.

The Para-LDA solves both problems. The trigger pull is light, very light, for a DA, and since it is DAO there is no need to de-cock the hammer when you are done. It has already done so itself. The LDA lacks a second strike capability. If it goes "click" instead of "bang" you will have to rack the slide just as you would with a regular 1911.

The LDA sent to us is a 7.45, meaning it is a Government Model size, single-stack .45 ACP pistol. The LDA lockwork is available in other frames with larger capacity magazines and different calibers, as well as the original Para-Ordnance single-action 1911 that is so popular with IPSC shooters.

The sights are fixed, a staked blade in front, and a standard blade in the rear. The sights have three white dots, to aid aiming. The slide has cocking serrations at the rear only, and the ejection port is lowered and flared. The slide is marked on the left with "Para-Ordnance" and on the right with "7.45 LDA." The barrel is an integral ramped barrel, of the Para-Ordnance pattern, with a bushing up front. The recoil spring assembly is pure 1911, lacking a guide rod. The barrel lockup has some spring to it, and the slide-to-frame fit has play. It is not the tightest pistol of the bunch, but not the loosest, either.

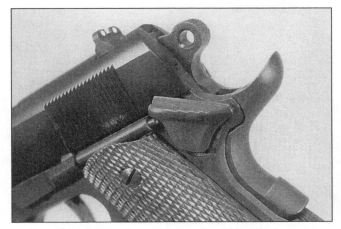

Something you won't see with any other 1911: The hammer is down and the safety is on. Only the Para can do this.

The ejection port is lowered and scalloped.

The hammer is a Commander-style hammer, swinging back into what looks like a Caspian grip safety. The grip safety has a speed bump at the bottom. The thumb safety is a Colt-pattern teardrop, the slide stop a standard serrated unit. The trigger is not like any other 1911 out there, having a pivot pin just under the slide stop lever, and no stop screw. The frame is marked on the right side only, with the serial number under the slide stop pin and in front of the trigger pivot pin. On the front end of the dust cover is "Para-Ordnance Inc Ft Lauderdale FL Made in Canada." The frontstrap is smooth, with a tight radius between the frontstrap and the trigger guard. The mainspring housing is arched, serrated, and steel. The magazine well opening is not beveled at all, one of three pistols tested that didn't have any work here. The grips are wood, reddish and nicely figured, held on with standard grip screws.

The finish is a blued two-tone. The slide is done in what appears to be a semi-gloss, baked-on finish, while the frame is a bead-blasted steel that is hot-dip blued. It is an attractive combination. The LDA comes in a Para-Ordnance plastic box, which is a neat display box but not as durable as the more-common Doskocil-type carrier. It comes with a magazine, lock, owner's manual/parts list, and a fired case in a small plastic bag. The magazine is an old-style, tapered-lip magazine that is not drilled or tapped for a bumper pad. Most of the test-firing was done with the Chip McCormick Power Mags that Chip so kindly sent us.

The LDA trigger in the "mechanism set" position, ready to fire if the safety is off.

The trigger back, in the fired and not re-set position.

So far, things appear more or less normal, if you overlook the trigger. The manual of arms, however, is quite a bit different. First of all, the grip safety is linked to the slide. If you do not have the grip safety depressed, you cannot cycle the slide. The mechanism is a single-strike trigger cocking mechanism. This means that in the case of a dud round you cannot simply stroke the trigger again. You must either thumb the hammer to re-set the mechanism, or cycle the slide to eject the round and re-set the mechanism.

To load and get ready, insert a loaded magazine. Gripping the Para so you depress the grip safety, cycle the slide to chamber a round. The hammer will follow the slide down as it normally does on the LDA. You can either leave the safety off, and depend on the DA trigger as your safety, or put the safety on. You can put the safety in the "On" position both when the mechanism is set and when it is not, so the safety is not an indication of readiness.

To fire, you draw, push the safety off, and then stroke through the trigger once your sights are on target. The pistol will fire, extract, eject, feed, and lock. The hammer will follow the slide forward, and the mechanism will re-set. To fire again, release the trigger and stroke through it again.

And what is the trigger like? Unlike anything you've shot before, unless you have fired a competition PPC revolver. The trigger pull is so light as a DA trigger, that if you couldn't see the hammer going back and forward, you'd doubt it happened. The initial trigger pull is very light, about 3 pounds, as you cock the hammer. Then the mechanism stops, or "stacks" and you have to exert another 3 pounds to finish cycling through the mechanism and drop the hammer. Once you get used to the long trigger movement, shooting the Para becomes like shooting any other 1911. The testers quickly got used to the trigger, and were downing the practice plates with ease.

The LDA trigger connects to a bar on the side of the frame above the grip. The bar pushes the hammer back to

The mag funnel is not beveled, a small and easy thing to correct.

cock and then release and fire. The lockwork is different than standard a 1911. When I was talking to Kerby Smith, head of marketing for Para-Ordnance, I mentioned that I was looking forward to taking it apart and seeing how it worked. Kerby, who has known me for 10 years and knows I was a professional gunsmith for 20, said "No." Taking the mechanism apart is easy, but unless you know a couple of specific tricks, putting it back together is not for the untrained. He offered to get me into the next armorer's class so I could learn the tricks, and I'll have to do that. However, there wasn't time before the book deadline, so I can only pass along the warning. If your Para-LDA starts to have problems, contact the factory. They will either have you send it back, or direct you to a factory-trained armorer in your area.

Do not let the warning about taking it apart put you off buying one. In function testing, the Para ate everything. It fed, functioned, and kicked out all the empties, both brass and magazine. It locked open every time it was empty. The testers did not report any sharp edges, cuts, or nicks from shooting it. For accuracy, the top load was the Sierra 230 JHP and Titegroup, which the Para put into an average group of just under 2-1/2-inches. The second load was the Black Hills Red, just over 2-1/2, and the West Coast Bullets load came in at just under 3. The groups were uniform and consistent, which bodes well for this pistol. With consistent groups, it would probably be fruitful to tighten the slide-to-frame and barrel-to-slide fit. Even without tightening, the accuracy is plenty good enough for competition and defense. If you've always wanted a 1911, but were put off by the cocked-and-locked design, the Para-LDA is for you.

The Para-LDA 7.45 and its 50-yard group. Given a little time, I'm sure I can improve on that, once I get used to the trigger. Very nice, though.

Para-Ordnance 7.45	
Trigger pull	6 lb*
Extractor tension	14 oz
Chamber depth	.905"
.22 Conversion fit	
Kimber	Y
EAA	Y
Ciener	N
Wilson	N
Marvel	Y
Bar-Sto .400 Cor-bon fit	N
Clark .460 Rowland fit	Y
Weight	36
Barrel length	5"
Three favorite loads	
1-Sierra/Viht	2.45"
2-Black Hills Red	2.60"
3-West Coast/Viht	2.90"
* Double Action trigger pull	

.460 ROWLAND

The Clark compensator is efficient, and tames the recoil of the Rowland quite nicely.

For some applications, the 1911 pistol has been viewed as inadequate. (I know, heresy, but what some people won't say to kick up a controversial subject for discussion.) Basically, for anything except use as a defensive cartridge, the .45 ACP lacks power. As an example, if you were going to hunt big game, or pack a handgun in bear country, it would be lacking. Yes, you could take a whitetail or feral hog with a .45 ACP (and many have done so) but you'd be starting out under-powered. The 10mm made up for the perceived lack of power, but it still fell short of the .44 Magnum, which is the gold standard in handgun hunting. The 10mm pushes a 200-grain bullet 1,200 fps (the original Norma load) for a 240PF, which is quite a bit less than the standard .44 Magnum load of 240 at 1,250, for a 300PF. Many .44 Magnum loads greatly exceed a 300PF, but for over-the-counter ammo, the 240/1,250 equation is the standard.

Then Johnny Rowland got into the act. An experimenter and TV host down in Louisiana, Johnny worked out the dimensions of really tough brass that would feed through a 1911, and could be pumped up to enough pressure to match

The Clark conversion of the .460 Rowland, installed in the Wilson CQB.

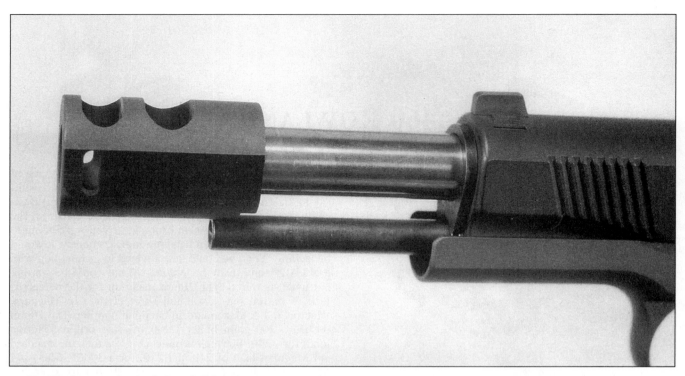

The Clark conversion includes a full-length, two-piece guide rod.

the .44 Magnum. Loaded ammunition is available from Georgia Arms, and from Triton. Loading data comes from Georgia Arms right now, but several of the powder manufacturers are working on reloading data for the .460 Rowland. (If you invent a new cartridge, you get to name it.) If you lack loading data for the Rowland, you can use .45 Super loading data as a starting point in your Rowland cases. (Never, NEVER use standard .45 ACP cases, or .45 ACP+P cases, to load either the Super or Rowland loads. You have been warned.)

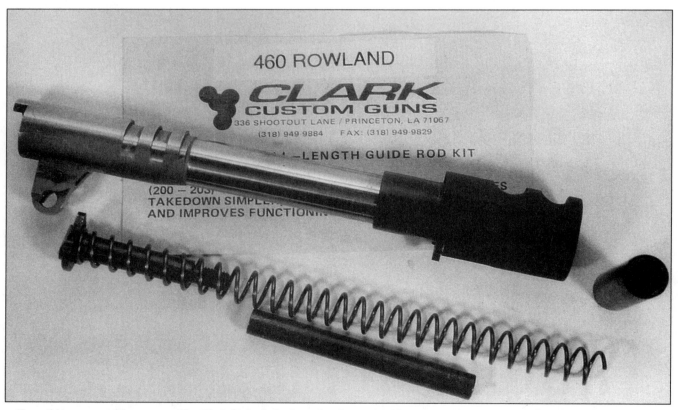

Everything you need but ammo. The Clark kit includes barrel and comp, guide rod, recoil spring and recoil spring retainer.

Basically, the .460 Rowland case is a lengthened .45 ACP, with tougher and thicker brass. Despite the longer brass, the overall length of the loaded cartridge is the same as that of the standard .45 ACP. By using longer brass, the Rowland won't chamber in a standard .45, and, by keeping it the same overall length, you can rebuild a suitable .45 to .460 Rowland. The .45 Win Mag required longer pistol frames and magazines, and ended up too large for many shooters' hands.

The rebuilding for the book involved installing a Clark conversion barrel into one of the test pistols. The Clark barrel is a standard Government-length barrel, with a Clark compensator on the end. The comp is not just an accessory, you need the forward push of the comp to keep the recoil under control and prevent battering of your pistol with the .460 Rowland ammo. When the Clark barrel arrived, I looked it over and then set it aside until all the pistols had arrived. The conversion comes with a comped barrel, two-piece guide rod, recoil spring retainer, and 24-pound recoil spring. Once the pistols had arrived, I tried the Clark for fit in all of them. There were a couple where the fit was snug, almost a force-fit, and a couple where I could feel some play, but in most it felt fine. The Clark drop-in is a standard ramp, so while I checked it for fit and lockup in the STI, Entreprise, Caspian, and .40 Super pistols (it fit), it obviously could not be used in them, due to their frames having been machined for integral ramp barrels. Ditto the Ed Brown, Kimber Ultra CDP, Griffon, and Firestorm Compact, which are too short. With the Springfield V-16 and Casull, the long slide obviously made fitting impossible. Clark makes an integral-ramp barrel in .460 Rowland, for the Para ramp cut. However, due to the variations of ramp cuts in different brand frames, they have to fit the ramped barrels. The standard is a drop-in, and it fits. It fits nicely, as all Clark barrels I've tried do.

When it came time to do the chrono testing, the closest pistol on the bench to the Clark conversion was the Wilson CQB. I tried a few shots to check impact to the sights, then ran the ammo over the chronograph. It worked flawlessly, so I used the Wilson CQB for all subsequent testing of the Clark/Rowland conversion. After several hundred rounds of this hot ammo, the CQB didn't show any signs of stress or wear. It is one tough gun. And the .460 is all it is advertised. Whether it is all it can be or not, I don't know, but it is already "enough." The softest load is the Georgia Arms defensive load, using a 185-grain JHP. It posted a velocity of "only" 1,362 fps, with a power factor of 251. (Please note, the downloaded "soft" load already exceeds 10mm power.) The velocity sounds very high, and you'd expect the recoil to be nasty. The load is nicely tuned for the comp, and the felt recoil and muzzle rise are almost normal. If you were to shoot it, and guess the velocity from the felt recoil, you'd likely guess a couple of hundred feet per second too low. The gun and load would make a stellar pin load. Any

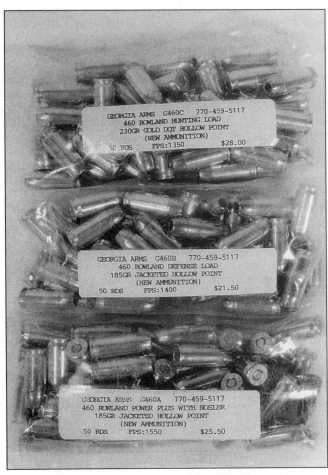

Georgia Arms offers loaded ammo, and it delivers the velocities printed on the label.

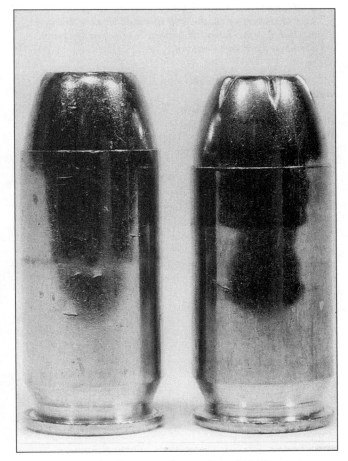

The .460 Rowland cases are longer than .45 ACP cases, so they won't chamber in regular 1911s not built to handle the hotter load.

While you probably won't get it mixed up with your .45 ACP brass very often, the .460 Rowland brass is clearly marked. Use this brass, and only this brass, in any barrel chambered for .460 Rowland.

hit would broom a pin off, and the comp would keep the sights under control.

The next load up in power is the 185-grain Nosler JHP Power Plus. They left the muzzle at an average of 1,447 fps, for a power factor of 267. The load is slightly heavier in recoil than the defensive load, but again, the comp keeps things under control.

The top-end load is the 230-grain Gold Dot JHP, at a recorded velocity of 1,347 fps, and a power factor of 309. When shooting it, you know there is power at work. The gun comes back at you, the muzzle rises, the empties exit briskly. And you survive the experience. While the testers were eager to shoot the two 185-grain loads, they were not so eager to shoot the 230s. That left more for me, and the bullets make a satisfying smack when they hit our 100-yard gongs.

For accuracy, the best load in this gun (the accuracy order can change by plugging the Clark barrel into another pistol; I didn't have enough time or ammo to try others) was the 185 Nosler in first place, with an average of just over 2 inches. The average was spoiled by a single group over 3 inches. The 230 Gold Dots were second, with an average just under 3 inches. the 185-grain defense load averaged just over 3 inches. Both the Gold Dot and defense loads had "4+1" groups, often clustering four shots into an inch or 1-1/2, and tossing the fifth shot out of the group. I simply must try the barrel in a few other guns to see if I can make that problem go away.

So, what is all this for? As a hunting round, it is stellar. If a state allows big-game handgun hunting, they won't have any objections to the .460 Rowland. It exceeds the .40 Super in power and matches it in energy. It matches the .44 Magnum in both power and energy. It is a straight-wall case, so a state that disallows bottlenecked cases would still allow the Rowland. For big-game hunting, I think I'd stick with Georgia Arms ammo, or reloaded equivalents using the Gold Dot 230-grain bullet. It has weight and velocity, and the Gold Dot will hold together while creating a through-and-through wound channel in a whitetail. If I were carrying a handgun in bear country (and this means leaving my .458 Win Mag rifle behind!) I'd use a 230-grain jacketed truncated cone bullet, loaded to the same velocity as the Gold Dot. On bear, any handgun is marginal, and expansion pointless. I'd want the penetration the JTC bullet delivers, and hope I never had to use it. One of the members of my gun club built a .460 Rowland to go pig hunting. So far he hasn't recovered a bullet, as they all exit the far side and disappear into the Tennessee landscape.

With a minor adjustment of your crimp die, you can load the .460 Rowland on your .45 ACP dies. The case uses common components, large pistol primers and .451" to .452" diameter bullets. You can load your ammo as soft as .45 ACP, or as hot as .44 Magnum, and get soft-recoil practice and still have lots of power for hunting. What you can't do is shoot .45 ACP ammo in your Rowland barrel. The extra length of the chamber creates excessive headspace, and you'll pierce primers and blow cases. I don't have to try it to know, I've seen .40 S&W ammo fired in a 10mm pistol. If you want to shoot .45 ACP-cased ammo, put your .45 ACP barrel back in.

Did I like it? The barrel sits on the shelf next to the ammo and brass, and I have a Dillon 550 tool head set up with dies, marked "460 Rowland." You bet I like it.

SPRINGFIELD LOADED

The Loaded model is Springfield's successful attempt at offering a basic and affordable pistol with the features most-desired by shooters. As such, and with the performance this one delivered, it was the best bargain of the bunch.

The Loaded is a standard 1911-A1 with some semi-custom and custom features. The one sent to me was a Parkerized model, but they can be had blued and stainless. It comes in a Springfield blue fitted hard case, with two magazines. The magazines are the only drawback to the pistol, and minor ones at that. The baseplates are drilled (and tapped!) for installing a bumper pad. The tubes are welded on the center of the spine. The slide cut has a tight radius at the corners, and the lips are a combination of controlled-feed and old-style taper. From my experience with 1911 magazines, I would estimate they will stand up to a couple of years of hard use, then crack at the rear of the lips. When

they start to give you problems, toss them and shed no tears over them. Even with all that, the two magazines fed 100 percent during the testing, snapped in place without extra effort, locked the slide open when empty, and dropped free when empty. Go ahead and use them. (I have some of identical configuration in my magazine case, and they have worked fine for years. Perhaps I'm being too harsh on these.)

From the top, the sights are a Novak low-mount rear and a plain ramped front blade. The Novak is set in the standard machined dovetail, and is without dots, night sights, or additional colors. The front sight is staked in place. While many shooters opt for a dovetail front sight installation, a staked sight will stay in place. Those that don't stay usually leave

The Novak rear.

The Springfield Loaded with hard case, magazines, instruction book, lock, and cleaning brush.

Staked front, ramped and serrated.

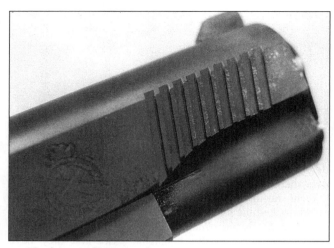

The front cocking serrations.

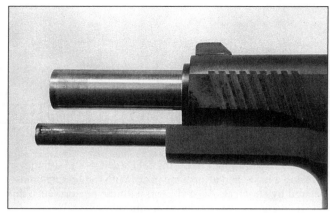

Bushing and two-piece guide rod.

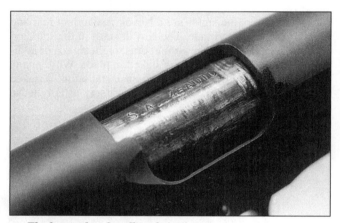

The lowered and scalloped ejection port.

Springfield commander hammer and grip safety.

Speed bump on the safety.

the slide within the first few hundred rounds. After 2,200 rounds this sight is still on, so I'm not worried.

For a basic pistol, the Loaded has some nice features. The slide has cocking serrations front and back. The ejection port is lowered and scalloped, and it live-ejects. The rear of the slide is smooth. The left side of the slide bears "Model 1911-A1" and underneath it "CAL .45." The barrel is a Springfield. Some Springfield barrels in the past have been two-piece, with the rifled tube high-temperature soldered to, and sleeved in, the locking lug section. Some object to two-piece barrels, but I don't have any problem with them except for pistols that need the utmost in performance. The barrel in this Loaded is a one-piece barrel, and as testing proved, it delivered the goods. The lockup is firm but not so tight you get the impression of the barrel and slide locking in place with a hard snap that the tightest pistols give. The bushing is loose enough to be disassembled by finger pressure, but does not have any perceptible wobble. The recoil spring guide rod (on a basic pistol, no less) is a two-piece design, requiring an Allen wrench to unscrew.

The grip safety is the standard Springfield model, of the Wilson pattern and with a speed bump. The hammer is the SA Commander with the Springfield Armory triangular loop. The thumb safety is not ambidextrous and clicks up and down smoothly. The safety lever is the Swensen design. The slide stop lever is a standard 1911-A1 design,

with grooves, and the end of the pin is radiused and raises over the right side surface of the frame as usual for a 1911.

The trigger is a long aluminum trigger with three holes and no stop screw installed. The lack of a stop screw did not preclude Springfield from tuning the trigger pull to a clean and crisp pull suitable for both competition and carry. The magazine catch is an utterly stock unit with serrations and a standard-weight spring. The mainspring housing is a serrated flat housing. The front-strap is smooth and bare. The front radius of the frame is the slightly thicker and squarer contour that has appeared from time to time on various manufacturers frames over the last few decades. Some shooters find the slightly squarer contour noticeable, but I don't.

The magazine opening is beveled, but there is no extra funnel to make it wider. On a competition gun you'd want the extra opening of a bolt-on magazine funnel. As a carry gun the beveling present is more than good enough. Fast reloads come from practice, not big funnels. For a standard-configuration 1911-A1, the Loaded came in on the heavy end of the curve. While other standard guns weighed 35 to 36 ounces, the Loaded tipped the scales at 38.5 ounces.

The grips on the Loaded were the same reddish brown kind of wood grips that were on the Professional. How-ever, the ones on the Loaded had more figure than the Pro did. I guess which grips go on which pistol are a matter of luck.

There were no sharp edges to be found, at least none that were sharp enough to cause the test shooters any problems or comments. Function was flawless once a couple of magazines had gone through to break it in. The testers liked the Loaded, commenting "A solidly built

gun" and "Good basic stock gun." One commented about short creep in the trigger, but I didn't feel it. As far as accuracy was concerned, the Springfield Loaded we tested loves Montana Gold 185s. It shot an average group size of 1-1/2 inches. Coming in a close second was the Sierra 230 JHP load, which averaged 1-3/4. The Oregon Trail bullets grouped just over two inches on average, which is a very nice average indeed. Even the ammuni-tion the Loaded didn't "like" it shot well. The Magtech, both Black Hills loads, the Hornady XTP, and the Zero loads all averaged under 2-1/2 inches.

The Loaded pistol turned in such a good performance that it was listed as a backup for the main guns in the 1911 match, and it stepped to the fore when needed. One of the pistols that started the match broke a sight pin, and

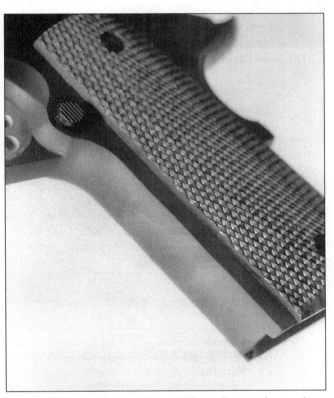

The frontstrap is smooth, and the radius at the top is standard.

The thumb safety on this one is not ambidextrous, but you can get it with one.

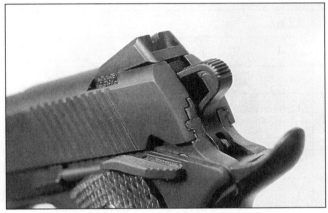

The trigger is an aluminum three-hole with stop screw, the slide stop and mag button are serrated.

The mag well is beveled. Note the squarer front radius on the Springfield Loaded than on other 1911s.

the Springfield Loaded was brought up as its replacement.

If someone offers you a Springfield Loaded for a good price, you should not pass it up.

The Loaded during the testing, with its magazines ready to go.

The Loaded and its 50-yard group.

Springfield Loaded	
Trigger pull	5.5 lb
Extractor tension	22 oz
Chamber depth	.894"
.22 Conversion fit	
Kimber	Y
EAA	Y
Ciener	Y
Wilson	Y
Marvel	Y
Bar-Sto .400 Cor-bon fit	Y
Clark .460 Rowland fit	Y
Weight	38.5
Barrel length	5"
Three favorite loads	
1-Montana Gold/Titegroup	1.5"
2-Sierra/Titegroup	1.75"
3-Oregon Tr/Viht	2.05"

SPRINGFIELD PROFESSIONAL

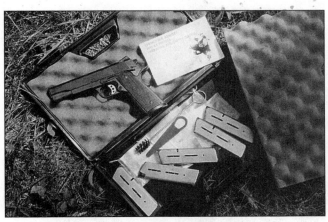

The Springfield Professional and its hard case, with mags, brush, instructions, and bushing wrench.

Nowlin guns may not have made the FBI contract, but their barrels did.

The Springfield Professional used to be known as the "Bureau Model." The FBI wanted a new pistol for their SWAT teams, and opened the field to manufacturers and custom gunsmiths. Along with a list of required features, the prospective pistol had to deliver the goods as far as accuracy was concerned. The initial testing of the pistols had to produce groups under 1-1/2 inches at 25 yards with Remington Golden Saber 230 JHP. Then, after the pistols had

The Professional may seem simple, but in the details it would have made a gunsmith of 20 years ago green with envy.

The Pro slide stop lever has the right end shaved down to prevent...

the shooter's finger from popping it out and tying up the gun, as in this Colt.

The Novak sights have Tritium inserts, rear and front.

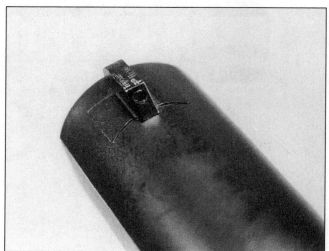

The front sight is blended with the slide so well as to make the rest of us envious.

fired a dumpster full of ammunition, they still had to deliver tight groups, but not quite as tight.

When I first read of the specifications and the features the FBI wanted, I was not impressed. It appeared that they were re-inventing the IPSC pistol, circa 1982. (And spending a lot of money, time, and taxpayer-funded ammunition doing it.) As the saying goes, the devil is in the details. What they wanted met the specs for the gun I shot the 1984 USPSA Nationals with. What they got was much more. Were you to travel back in time to 1982 and drop this particular pistol on the bench of a gunsmith, he would turn green with envy.

First, it is one of the tightest-locking pistols I have handled. Only the Monolith and Casull were harder in locking, and the Casull has a 30-pound recoil spring. And the accuracy was everything you would expect from a pistol with this pedigree. The accuracy came with no loss in reliability, as it gobbled up everything that I had to feed it. I don't know if the tight lockup would make it uncertain in function if fed powder-puff ammo like factory target wadcutter loads, or a 9-pin load. Since it wasn't made for those kinds of loads, I didn't test it with any. (And besides, with all these guns, and the ammo I do have to test, adding more ammunition to the pile would have been gilding the lily.)

The Professional comes in a hard case with five Wilson eight-shot magazines. Starting at the top, it has a set of Novak night sights with Trijicon inserts installed. The front sight base, instead of being left squared-off as so many

sights are, has the base blended to match the contour of the slide. (The first of many nice touches.) The slide only has cocking serrations at the rear, with none up front. The rear of the slide is smooth, without checkering or stippling. The

The Springfield Custom Shop makes the Pro model.

ejection port is lowered and scalloped to allow the empty brass to clear. It live-ejects.

The left side of the slide is marked "Professional" with "CAL 45" underneath it. On the right side is the Springfield logo, "Springfield Armory," and the Springfield Custom logo. The serial number is in the regular place, on the frame underneath the ejection port. The major parts are marked with the serial number.

The barrel is a Nowlin barrel, with the muzzle end centerless ground or lathe-turned to be a precise fit to the bush-

ing. The bushing fit is tight enough to require a bushing wrench for disassembly. There is no recoil spring guide rod other than the standard 1911-A1. No doubt the lack of a rod is to allow one-handed malfunction manipulation by pressing the slide against an object. The recoil spring feels like a standard 18.5-pound spring.

Things get even more interesting on the frame. On the rear, it has a Wilson-pattern grip safety with speed bump. I like the design, and it hits my hand just right to depress the grip safety every time. If this design doesn't work for you, then the McCormick design grip safety is the one for you. The hammer is a Commander-style hammer of Springfield's own spur design. The thumb safety is an ambidextrous one, and an exact copy of the Swenson design that started the trend to ambidextrous safeties so long ago. The slide stop lever has been trimmed down on the left side to be unobtrusive but still useful. The lever doesn't stick out any farther than it needs to in order to be useful, and is less likely to be in the way when carried concealed. On the other side of the frame, the slide stop pin has been shortened so it is flush with the frame. Why? When you (properly) have your finger out of the trigger guard, it can rest on the slide stop pin. Men with strong grips have been known to push the slide stop out of the frame enough to tie up the gun. To preclude this, the FBI wanted the stop flush. The slide stop hole is beveled so you can disassemble it without too much hassle.

The trigger is an aluminum trigger, long with three holes in it. There is a trigger stop screw installed, and the trigger pull is clean and crisp if somewhat heavy by competition standards. In other words, perfect for a carry gun. As befit-

The slide stop is subdued in size and serves well.

ting a carry gun, the magazine button is no larger than the standard size, with the normal serrations across its top and the standard-weight spring.

The lower frame is checkered on the frontstrap at 30 lines to the inch. The mainspring housing is a flat S&A magazine funnel housing, checkered to match the frontstrap. The edges of the magazine funnel and the frame have been blended to make a smooth curve into the magazine tunnel.

As you would expect from such a pistol, and the Wilson magazines, each magazine locked the slide back, and cleanly ejected when the magazine button was pressed.

The whole pistol, except for the trigger, has been finished with a flat black baked-on coating that leaves it smooth to the touch and gives a business-like appearance. The nicely figured reddish wooden grips make an attractive contrast to the finish. My only quibble, a minor one at that, concerns the magazines. It would be nice to have them numbered so you can keep track of rotating them and cleaning them. Getting them numbered is a small thing, and you could probably have someone do it for you at the next big match you go to. The MTM case the Professional comes in is an oversized one, containing the pistol, five magazines each in its own plastic bag, owner's manual, and cleaning brush. Also, the case has a hook inside and a loop cast into the case so you can hang the case up and hide it between clothing in the closet.

In the test-firing sessions, one of my testers paid the Professional the highest compliment. In a crowd that uses 1911s in competition and carry, and each of whom had built at least one themselves, one of my testers came back from the line with the Professional saying "The only thing wrong with this pistol is that I don't own it."

Oh, the name. When Springfield won the contract, they began offering an identical model to the FBI-spec contract guns to their regular customers, listing it as the "Bureau Model." The FBI raised an objection. I'm not a copyright attorney (and I don't play one on TV) and I don't think the FBI had a leg to stand on. But rather than annoy their biggest single customer, Springfield changed the name. If you have an older one that is "Bureau" marked, it is a rarity and will be a collector's item some day.

When it came to accuracy, the Professional delivered. The ammo it liked best was the Sierra 230 JHP which it shot into an average of 1.6". The second ammo was Zero 185 JHPs and they came in at 1.75". A close third was the Black Hills Red, 230 JRNs grouping at an average of 1.75". I broke the tie between the Zero and Black Hills in favor of the Zero simply because the Black Hills shot its largest group 1/4 inch larger than that of the Zero. Regardless of the ammo I fed it, it refused to shoot a group larger than 2-3/4 inches. No, it didn't deliver on the FBI specs of 1-1/2 inches, but I didn't have any Golden Saber to shoot through it.

The Professional handily made it into the group of pistols used in the 1911 Match, where we came across its sole drawback. The Wilson magazines it came with have the black plastic Wilson extended pads. The pads are a bit too short for the mag funnel. For experienced shooters who briskly whack a magazine into place, it never fails. For newer shooters, or those less-experienced with a 1911, the

The Springfield Pro at the test sessions, patiently waiting its turn. It will not disappoint the shooters.

The Mag funnel is blended to the frame before they are both finished with a black baked-on epoxy resin.

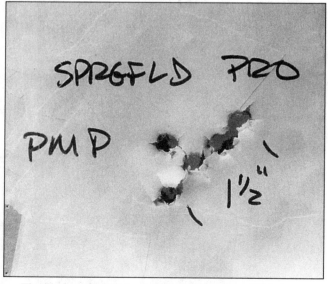

The Professional and one of its good groups. I'd have no problem using the PMP in a match, or for real.

The 50-yard group. I'd like to take the credit, but the Professional did most of the work.

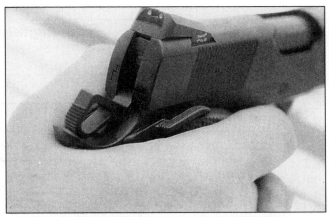

One fault I alone had, was the corner of the off side of the ambidextrous safety banged my knuckle. Were it mine, I'd be tempted to blend that spot, but when you're loaned an expensive pistol you don't go using a file and stones on it.

magazines sometimes failed to lock in place simply because they weren't inserted forcefully enough. Were the Professional to stay with me I'd invest in some larger magazine pads to replace the ones it came with. Bill Wilson himself makes larger ones, and they would be my first choice.

Except for the magazines, we didn't have a problem with the Professional in the match until the end of the day. After dozens of shooters dropping mags into the sand of the range, the magazines started getting too gritty to be loaded. Since we had to take a break to clean the mags, we also gave the Pro quick strip and lube, which it didn't really need, and finished the day without a problem.

Springfield Professional	
Trigger pull	5 lb
Extractor tension	13 oz
Chamber depth	.901"
.22 Conversion fit	
Kimber	Y
EAA	Y
Ciener	N
Wilson	N
Marvel	Y
Bar-Sto .400 Cor-bon fit	N
Clark .460 Rowland fit	Y
Weight	37.7
Barrel length	5"
Three favorite loads	
1-Sierra/Titegroup	1.6"
2-Zero 185 JHP	1.75"
3-Black Hills Red	1.75"

SPRINGFIELD V-16
.45 SUPER

The V-16 is a long-slide, with a 6-inch barrel.

The Springfield V-16 in its hard plastic blue case, with spare mags, instructions, lock and cleaning brush.

The Springfield V-16 is a long-slide ported hunting pistol, set up to take .45 Super ammunition. For hunting with a pistol, it offers many advantages. First, the ammo. The .45 Super is the same overall size as .45 ACP, but with tougher brass and loaded to a higher pressure. Here in Michigan, if you want to hunt deer with a handgun in the lower half of the lower peninsula, you have to use a straight-wall case. The idea is to keep guys from running through farm country using T/C Contenders chambered in .30-30. (Not that there is anything wrong with that combo.)

The .45 Super comes out of Texas (surprise there, big state, big calibers) and the main source of loaded ammunition is Texas Ammunition Co. The ballistics of the .45 Super offer a big step up from those of the regular .45 ACP, or even that of the .45 ACP+P.

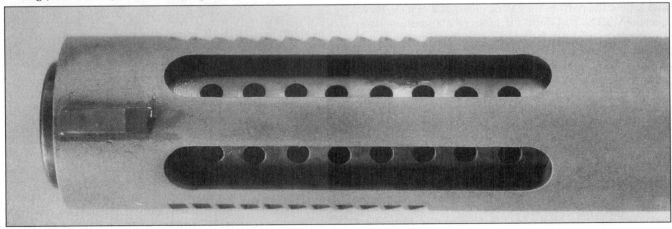

The exhaust ports of the barrel jet through a slot in the slide.

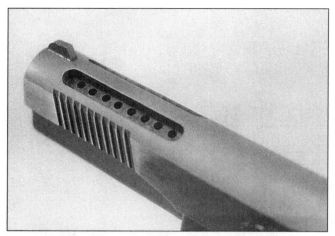

The slots are behind and to either side of the staked front sight.

The extractor is a different shade of white than the slide.

The Bo-mar pattern rear sight and commander hammer. Note the non-ambidextrous thumb safety.

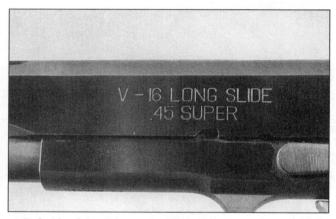

Left side of the slide.

The exhaust port warning on the chamber.

The slide of the Springfield houses a 6-inch barrel, and is 8-1/2 inches long. The sights are an adjustable rear of the Bo-mar pattern, marked with the Springfield logo, and a front blade that is staked in. Immediately behind the front sight, and to either side of the centerline, are two oval slots milled through the slide. The slots are 1-7/8 inches long, and expose the ports in the barrel, all 16 of them. (V-16, any questions?) The ports vent the gases of combustion, dampening muzzle rise and felt recoil. As a test, I installed a 24-pound recoil spring in an unported pistol and fired a few rounds of .45 Super. I was not surprised to find that the V-16 ports work.

The slide is heavily bead-blasted on the top arc, and polished on the flats. The rear of the slide received the same bead blasting treatment. The extractor appears to be a different material, and is a lighter white than the frame and slide. It may be a different stainless alloy, or it may be hard-chromed carbon steel. The slide has cocking serrations front and back. On the left side of the slide it is marked "V-16 Long Slide .45 Super" and on the right "Springfield Armory" and the Springfield logo. The roll markings and logo are clean and sharp-edged, indicating that the final polishing/machining of the slide was done after the roll marks

were applied. The ejection port is lowered and scalloped, and live ejects.

The barrel is a Springfield barrel, 6 inches long with the aforementioned ports. The muzzle is a cone lockup, and the barrel is fitted well, with a slight amount of vertical give in the rear. The chamber is marked "S.A. .45 Auto" and "Danger Exhaust Ports Read Manual." The barrel is a two-piece assembly, but Springfield has proven the method produces accurate and durable barrels. It has a full-length recoil spring guide rod and a reverse plug. Despite being chambered in the .45 Super, the chamber is a standard ramp, not an integral-ramp barrel. There is no play in the fit between the slide and frame.

The frame is a standard 1911-A1 frame. The hammer is Springfield's ovaled Commander loop. The grip safety is a Wilson pattern safety with a speed bump at the bottom. The grip safety has the same white cast that the extractor does, and again may be a different stainless alloy or hard-chromed carbon steel. The thumb safety is not ambidextrous and is Springfield's interpretation of the Swensen design. The slide stop is a standard unit. The trigger is an extended aluminum unit with three holes, lacking a stop screw. The trigger pull was clean and crisp. The magazine catch is standard size and serrated. The serial number and Springfield name are punched on the right side above the trigger.

The corner where the frontstrap joins the trigger guard is a tighter radius than the original 1911 or A1, but not as tight

The grip safety has a speed bump to ensure proper function.

The right side of the frame. Note the trigger (no over-travel screw), the standard frontstrap radius, and the serial number. I once owned #1270, and Springfield has been busy since then.

The beveled magazine well, and silver-color plastic mainspring housing.

The V-16 uses a cone lockup, and has no need for a bushing.

The grip safety shows a slight gap in its fit to the frame, but nothing objectionable.

The .45 Super has horsepower, and the Express load is the top-end load in the Super.

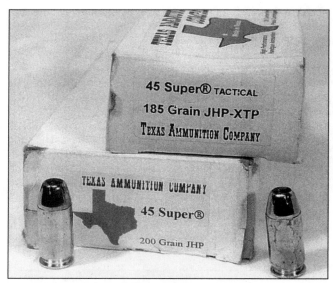

The Tactical load is on par with a .45 ACP+P load, the Super is hotter, and the Express hottest of all the loads with a ".45 Super" headstamp.

The V-16 and its 50-yard group. Noise, flash, recoil, and dust from firing it prone, and they all stayed in the "A" zone.

as the modern interpretation of Ed Brown and others. The frontstrap is smooth but heavily bead blasted like the top of the slide. The curve of the frontstrap is the slightly larger radius, and thus slightly squared edges that some pistols have today. The mainspring housing is flat, plastic, and serrated. In an attempt at matching the stainless color of the rest, it is a silver color. It doesn't come very close, but it is close enough. The magazine opening is slightly beveled. The grips are wood, checkered, and with good figure. All of this adds up to making the Springfield V-16 the second-heaviest pistol in the test. The only pistol heavier was the Casull, and I think the difference is the slots cut for the V-16's ports. Fill the slots and the V-16's 40.8 ounces would be bumped up to that of the Casull's 42.4.

The two-tone stainless look, with the top and bottom of the slide dark, and the front and rear of the frame dark, is attractive. While the V-16 may lack features seen on some of the other pistols, like checkering or ambidextrous safeties, it delivers what it promises, power.

The pistol comes in Springfield's blue plastic case, with moulded insides to fit all models of the 1911. It has a lock, cleaning brush, owner's manual, and two magazines. The magazines were the same kind as that of the Springfield Loaded, blued with a weld up the spine. They are also drilled and tapped for bumper pads. I tested the magazines just to be sure they would work, then did all my test-firing

with my own Wilson eight-shot and McCormick 10-shot magazines. As for the lock, I can understand its inclusion, given the current political climate, but were I to keep the V-16 the lock would get tossed in a box with all the other locks. I can afford to be casual about gun locks, as all my handguns are in a locked safe, which is in a concrete room with a steel door, which is inside a brick building. But the case is durable and convenient, and one I would keep. (I wonder if Springfield sells them? I'll have to ask.)

The point of the V-16 is horsepower, and the .45 Super delivers. With 185-grain bullets at 1,240 fps, and 230s at

.45 Super brass

Out of curiosity, I fished a few fistfulls of brass out of the 5-gallon buckets we were using, and sorted out a few headstamps. When I got back to the shop I weighed them and averaged the weights, to see what was up. While the .45 Super brass was among the heavyweights, it wasn't the heaviest brass. What makes the .45 Super brass tougher is its being whacked when made. The headstamp on brass is created when the brass is firmly held over a post and hit with what is called a bunting die. The impact of the die impresses the headstamp and work-hardens the brass. The .45 Super brass is worked to be harder than regular brass. Does regular .45 brass sometimes weigh as much as .45 Super brass, or more? It sure does. But just because a particular batch of brass weighs as much or more than .45 Super brass does not mean it is suitable for use in loading .45 Super ammunition.

Only use brass headstamped as .45 Super to create Super-level loads! If you were to be cheap and load the powerful prescription into regular brass, you risk blowing out a case, trashing a magazine, and splattering oil, powder residue, and bits of brass all over your face and shooting glasses. You have been warned.

The Starline-made brass is marked "45 Super" and you should use it for your hot loads. Ammo loaded to standard .45 ACP specs can be loaded in regular ACP brass.

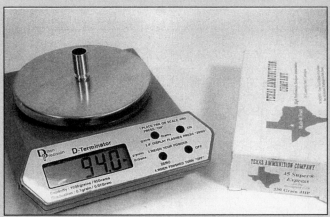

The .45 Super brass is as heavy as the heaviest .45 ACP brass.

1,074, you've got plenty of power. If the regular .45 Super ammunition is not enough, then you can use the special .45 Super Express load. Some states that allow handguns for hunting require that the handgun cartridge involved be able to muster a minimum of 500 foot-pounds at 100 yards. (Michigan is not one of them. You can legally hunt deer with a Walther PPK in .380, but you can't use a bottle-necked handgun cartridge like the .400 Cor-bon. At least not in the lower half of the lower peninsula.) The Express loads deliver 525 calculated foot-pounds of energy at 100 yards. The extra weight, and the ports, dampen even the Express load to comfortable recoil levels. The brass is ejected briskly and cleanly, but not as far as some other loads hurled theirs.

There were no malfunctions with .45 Super ammunition. The Texas Ammunition Super loads worked without a fault. While the testers all lined up to shoot a magazine or two out of it, only a couple stayed with it for more than that. The recoil wasn't oppressive, but with so many toys to play with, the recoil was enough to have them eyeing the other guns. I won't say I had to flog them into shooting it, and they wanted to shoot it more than the heavier calibers, but there was .45 Super ammo left over. One question that came up every time the V-16 came out of the case was: Will it cycle with regular .45 ACP ammo? The question is a qualified yes. It cycled for me, using the 230 hardball ammo I had to test. The brass did not eject very far. I have quite a rigid grip, and can get a 1911 to cycle with ridiculously soft loads. The rest of the testers could also get it to cycle with the hot hardball. We had some failures to eject with the softer reloads, but only in the hands of the testers who have softer grips, and thus let the frame move more on recoil. Whether it works 100 percent for you or not with .45 ACP ammo will depend on how soft your ammo is, and how strong your grip is.

The V-16 tested showed a definite preference for the Express loadings, and even if I didn't need the power to meet a hunting regulation I would use the express load in this pistol.

For accuracy, the favorite load for this pistol was 230-grain Express load, with an average group size just over 2 inches. The second load was the 185-grain .45 Super load, at just under 2-1/4 inches. Third was the 230-grain JHP Super load, at three inches.

Springfield V-16	
Trigger pull	5.5 lb
Extractor tension	32 oz
Chamber depth	.896"
.22 Conversion fit	
Kimber	Y
EAA	Y
Ciener	Y
Wilson	Y
Marvel	Y
Bar-Sto .400 Cor-bon fit	N/A*
Clark .460 Rowland fit	N/A*
Weight	40.8
Barrel length	6"
Three favorite loads	
1-230 gr Texas Ammo Express	2.10"
2-185 gr Texas Ammo Super	2.20"
3-230 gr Texas Ammo Super	3.0"
* The slide is longer than these barrels, 6" vs. 5"	

STI - THE EDGE

The STI frame came about because of the perceived need for capacity. In competition, more is better. (Some would say that Competition is Life, and others would say that Life is Competition.) In the late 1980s, the Para Ordnance frame came out, and anyone who didn't have more than the usual number of rounds was suddenly in trouble in a match. A standard 1911-A1 could hold nine rounds of .45 ACP, or 11 rounds of .38 Super. The Para held 15 rounds of .45, and about 20 rounds of .38 Super. (This was before extended magazines.)

In a field course in IPSC, with reloading a must, higher capacity meant fewer reloads and more choices as to when to do them. But the Para had some drawbacks. The metal frame, combined with grips to clad it, made a bulky package. Some shooters left the grips off, knocked the sharp edges off the frame and applied skateboard tape. Others couldn't bring themselves to do that, or even then the frame was too large. STI took a different route. The STI frame uses steel rails to guide the slide and hold the internals, and has a plastic grip portion bolted to the rails unit. Without external grips, the STI is slightly smaller than the Para frame. Some shooters even apply a belt sander to the plastic, to make it better fit their hands.

In short order competition guns were all high-capacity guns. When the USPSA added Limited as a competitive division, serious shooters built hi-cap Limited guns on the same model frame upon which their Open guns were built.

The Edge sent for testing is a high-capacity frame Limited Division gun chambered in .45 ACP. While many competitors would opt for the same gun in .40 S&W for competition (more rounds, even if only a few, can be comforting), I tested one in .45 to keep all the guns on a level playing field. And, getting additional calibers would only make things completely crazy in test-firing.

The STI, "the Edge," in its padded case with magazine.

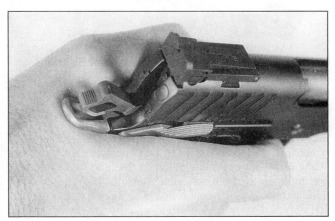

The ambidextrous safety is nicely shaved on the far side, to clear your trigger finger knuckle.

While it is a handful, the STI frame is not a big, blocky thing to grasp.

The dovetailed front sight is pinned in place.

The lowered and scalloped ejection port.

The STI uses a cone-barrel lockup and full-length guide rod.

The dust cover goes all the way to the muzzle.

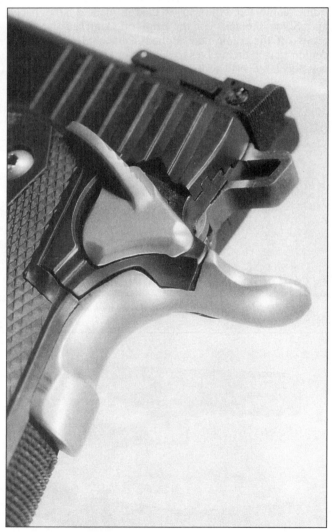

The grip safety of the STI. Note the scallops on the beavertail, and the beveled edges of the thumb safety.

The Edge comes in a plastic case with one 10-round magazine. I know, I said it is a hi-cap gun, but high-capacity magazines are too expensive to ship one with each gun. One of the drawbacks to a hi-cap gun is that you have to go out and hunt down the magazines yourself. They are easy to find, and this gun is worth it. It is also known as the "Model 2011" (yes, I know it isn't 2011 yet, but...) in recognition of the century of improvements to the basic gun, and in recognition of the yeoman's service the old design provided for us. Yes, STI makes single-stack guns too.

From the top; the front sight is a Novak-style blade, pinned in place with a roll pin to keep it from moving. The rear is a Bo-Mar pattern adjustable sight with the STI logo on it. The blued slide has STI-pattern cocking serrations front and back. The STI serrations are wider and on a wider spacing than regular serrations, and the cuts are rectangular in cross-section. The ejection port is lowered and flared. The rear of the slide is smooth. The slide, rather than being scalloped on the front underneath the front sight, is full profile all the way to the muzzle, to match the frame. On the left side of the slide is "STI The Edge .45" and on the right side are the initials STI inside an outline of the State of Texas. The slide live-ejects.

The barrel is an STI, with an integral feed ramp and a cone lockup. It locks tightly without snapping in place, and does not have play once closed. The reverse plug is a circular one. The recoil spring guide rod is a single piece rod.

The slide travel allows for slide manipulation to lower the slide after a reload. There is no perceptible play in the slide-to-frame fit.

The frame has an Ed Brown pattern stainless grip safety on it with the STI scallops on the sides for greater comfort. The scallops provide clearance for those shooters whose thumb joint rides right at the edge of the grip safety. The hammer is a square-loop, Commander-type hammer of Chip McCormick design. The safety is a stainless ambidextrous unit of McCormick design, with the levers slim enough to be unobtrusive but large enough you won't miss them. The slide stop is a standard 1911-A1 pattern part.

The long, heavy dust cover adds weight forward and underneath.

The frame contour of the dust cover is what sets the Edge apart from a standard 1911-A1. The frame has been widened on its exterior, and the width of the frame has been maintained all the way to the end of the slide. Underneath, the usual scallop up from the trigger guard is not present, and the bottom edge of the dust cover (the name of the part of the frame we're discussing) is a continuation of the line of the inside top of the trigger opening.

Called a "Wide, heavy dust cover," this feature puts more weight into the gun forward of the hands and under the axis of the bore. The additional weight out there is more useful in dampening felt recoil than extra weight between the hands would be.

The look is similar to that of the old Model 1900s by Colt. In order to accommodate the extra steel, the slide stop is in its own recess. (That way STI can use standard slide stops, and not have to use custom-made ones.) On the right side of the frame where the slide stop pokes out, the hole is beveled so you can push the slide stop out for disassembly.

Now the real trickery begins. The screws that look like grip screws? The top ones bolt the plastic to the rail unit. The bottom ones are fakes. The third one in front of the trigger secures the front of the trigger guard to the rail unit. Due to the width of the frame at the magazine catch level, the magazine catch is a new part nearly twice as long as the old one. The plastic frame holds the mag catch and a trigger with a wide bow to accommodate the wide magazine tubes. It also provides a place for you to hold, and secures the mainspring housing. What more does a frame need to do?

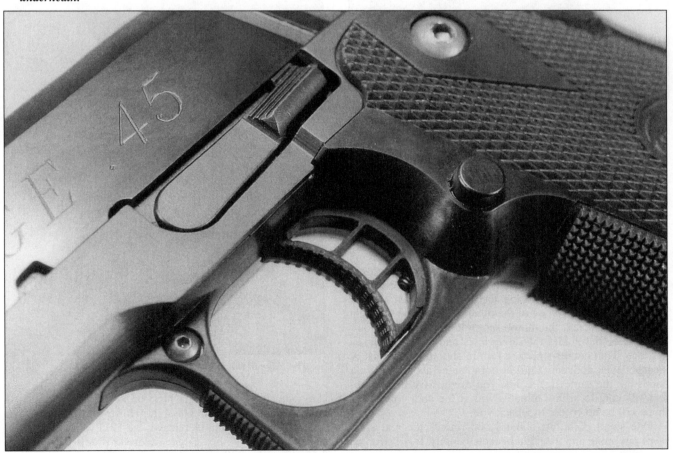

The screws you see are what hold the plastic to the steel. Leave them alone.

The checkering you see, and what looks like grips, are moulded into the plastic lower half of the frame.

With a magazine funnel like this, if you miss it is entirely your own fault.

The 50-yard group. Not bad work for accuracy shooting at the end of the day.

Dave Skinner at the World Shoot in Cebu, The Philippines, 1999. If you're going to show the guns, you might as well get some shooting in.

The Edge in the match.

On the bottom is a magazine funnel large enough to stick your fist into. Well, if you have small hands. It is large enough that if you miss it you really have no one to blame but yourself. In weight, the Edge comes in third, with both guns ahead of it being the long-slides.

The magazines are high-capacity tubes that have been crimped and slit to create 10-shot magazines. If you remove the crimp the magazine will fall apart. If you want more rounds than 10 for competition or plinking, simply go out and buy an existing high-capacity magazine or three.

In the course of test-firing the Edge, one test shooter found a sharp edge. None of the others did. It is on the right side, where beneath the thumb safety lever there is a shoulder of steel that guides the safety lever and locks the plastic in place. That corner whacked him in shooting. The rest of us never even noticed it until he complained about it. If your hands are the same size as his, you might have this "problem." If you do, a few minutes with a file and stones, and there will be no corner to whack you.

One small point. At about 2,000 rounds the rear sight pivot pin broke and the sight became wobbly. It still worked as a sight, and the point of impact didn't change all that much, but I figured there was no point in abusing the sight.

Any adjustable sight might have broken this way, and it is nothing inherent to the STI sight. However, the broken pin did keep the STI from its place in the 1911 Match.

In accuracy, the Edge favored Black Hills Red, launching the 230-grain jacketed round nose bullets into clusters just over 1-1/4 inches in size. Second was the

The Edge preferred Black Hills Red 230-grain jacketed round nose.

Oregon Trail load of 200-grain semi wadcutters, running just under 1-1/2 inches. Filling out the top three was the PMP, the hottest of the hardball loads. With the PMP posting groups just under 2 inches, and a power factor of 192, I would be very happy stepping to the line at a bowling pin match using the Edge and PMP. And with its accuracy using the other loads, happy to use it in an IPSC match.

STI The Edge	
Trigger pull	3.5 lb
Extractor tension	32 oz
Chamber depth	.907"
.22 Conversion fit	
Kimber	Y*
EAA	Y*
Ciener	N
Wilson	N
Marvel	Y*
Bar-Sto .400 Cor-bon fit	N**
Clark .460 Rowland fit	N**
Weight	39.4 oz
Barrel length	5"
Three favorite loads	
1-Black Hills Red	1.30"
2-Oregon Tr/Viht	1.40"
3-PMP 220 FMJ	1.90"

* The STI barrel is ramped, the conversions are not. The conversion magazines are single-stack, the STI frame a hi-cap
** The barrels fit, but are not ramped, and would not feed if installed.

WILSON CQB

The Wilson CQB with magazines, case, and test-fire target. Damn fine target, too.

Bill Wilson was an early gunsmith in IPSC, and an early maker of re-designed parts intended for competition. As his parts inventory grew, the idea of making frames and slides became more attractive. One of the problems with being a custom gunsmith was making the disparate accessory parts supplied by customers fit onto every frame that showed up. (I know, I've done my share of head scratching over "how is this going to fit?" on guns that were out of spec.) The easiest way was to make your own frames and slides, ones that were built to the blueprints. Then the other parts would fit properly.

Once you're making all the parts, it is a relatively simple matter to offer assembled custom guns.

The CQB is a mid-level custom gun built entirely of Wilson parts. It has a bunch of the desirable custom features that shooters want, but is not a full-house custom gun with the full-house price tag. It comes in a soft case with two

The CQB is a very nicely fitted 1911, which you would not be disappointed in owning.

The right side, showing the Wilson laminated grips, grip safety, and frontstrap radius.

The Wilson sight is marvelously compact, durable, and useable.

Left side, the thumb safety is large enough and yet smooth and out of the way.

Wilson magazines. The case has pockets for extra magazines, tools, and a test-fire target. Seeing the test-fire target, I immediately knew what one of my test-fire handloads would be. I almost broke down and bought the gun right then and there. The test-fire target is a 15-yard group that is less than an inch center-to-center. Fired by "scrawled initials illegible" on 10-16-00, it impressed me enough to call Vihtavuori and order a bunch of N-310 powder.

The sights are Novak-dovetailed front and rear sights with tritium night-sight inserts. The rear sight is the Wilson's Tactical Combat sighting system with the "Combat Pyramid™." While the rear uses a Novak dovetail, it is Bill Wilson's interpretation of what a sight should be. Instead of

The rear of the slide, showing the night sights.

The engraved/etched "CQB" on the right side.

Simple and tasteful. The trigger has an over-travel screw, the mag catch is checkered, and the slide stop grooved.

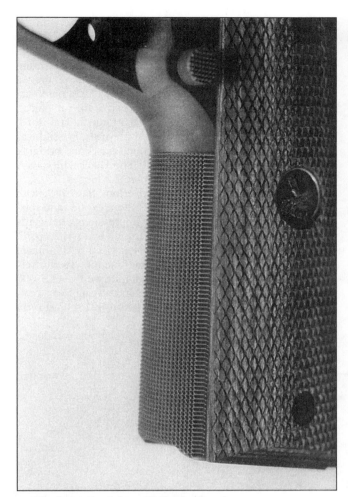

The frontstrap is beautifully checkered.

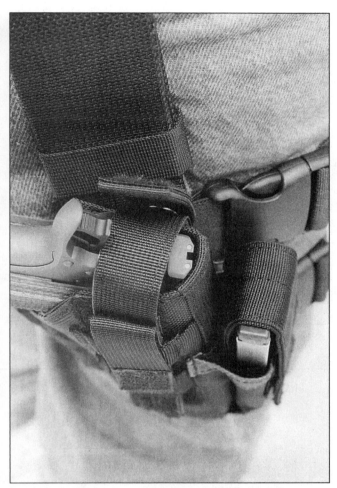

The CQB where it may spend much time, a tactical holster from Blackhawk. If you have to go through doorways for a living, this setup would be first-class.

being composed of angled flat surfaces, the front and rear of the sight are gentle arcs. The slide has cocking serrations front and back, of the Colt Gold Cup size and spacing. The rear of the slide is smooth, and all the sharp edges are rounded, in a very nice de-horning job. The barrel is a (guess what?) Wilson, standard with a bushing at the front. The lockup is tight, without the hard snap of a Bull's-eye-fitted gun. The bushing is a tight finger fit. If you're strong you can move it. Otherwise you'll need a bushing wrench. The recoil spring does not use a guide rod. The left side of the slide is etched or machined with "Wilson Combat" while the right side simply has "CQB" on it.

The frame has a Wilson grip safety at the rear, with a speed bump on the bottom. The hammer is also Wilson, of the commander style. The thumb safety is the Wilson interpretation of the Swensen, without the swoop of the curve and without the sharp edges so many Swensen-style safeties have. It is not an ambidextrous safety, but that is an option. The slide stop is a standard design. The trigger is blackened aluminum, with three holes and a trigger stop. The magazine catch is standard size, and checkered. The frontstrap radius at the trigger guard has been raised to a contour that feels good and looks good, without coming to the sharp-edged looking cut that the Ed Brown has.

The frontstrap of the CQB has possibly the nicest checkering of the whole bunch, and is 30 lines to the inch. To be fair, some of the guns I have for the book may well be "professional loaners" that get sent to gun writers for inspection, and their checkering might have been worn down a bit. The CQB was sent first to me (and if Wilson sells it if I return it, then some lucky owner is going to get a hell of a gun), so the checkering is right from the checkering cradle. The mainspring housing is flat and checkered to match the frontstrap. The magazine opening is beveled to make reloading easier.

The finish is Wilson's Armor-Tuff™. A tough synthetic finish of the type that is becoming so popular, the CQB is done in a two-tone combination. The slide and its parts are done in a matte black, while the frame and its parts are done in an OD green. In the frame, the hammer and trigger are black. Armor-Tuff™ is a baked-on phenolic resin that contains molybdenum disulfide. If you do have to run the gun dry (that is, without lubricant) the finish will provide some lubricity. However, you should oil the bearing surfaces. The finish can stand up to greater heat or cold, or stronger solvents, acids or bases, than you can. And, the finish is less than .001" thick. So thin, in fact, it doesn't fill the lettering on the slide or the checkering on the frame.

The CQB with one of its groups. A Wilson pistol and Black Hills ammo, good enough to ride the river with.

The grips are black and brown laminated wood with the Wilson logo medallion inset. The CQB comes in a soft case with a spare magazine made by, no surprise, Wilson, the test-fire target, owner's manual, and spare recoil spring plunger with installed shock buff. The test-fire target drew a number of comments from my test-fire crew. Most marveled at the group size, while a few wondered what the job paid.

For accuracy, the CQB preferred the Oregon Trail load, shooting an average of 1-1/2 inches at 25 yards. Second was the Black Hills Blue 230 jacketed round-nose, and bringing up a close third was PMC hardball. The Black Hills averaged 1.9 inches while the PMC average 2.1 inches.

It was easy for the test crew to overlook the CQB, with the sometimes flashy and sometimes more exotic other pistols arrayed before them. And their impressions afterwards were similarly muted. I made them try all, and write up all. On looking over the results sheets I noticed a significant fact. There was not a single noted malfunction. Two different teams on two different weekends put well over 1,000 rounds downrange through the CQB, and no one had a malfunction, reported a sharp edge, or had a bad thing to say about it.

It may not have been flashy, but it sure got the job done.

The mag funnel is beveled, and makes reloads easy.

My 50-yard group. Right to the point of aim, smaller than the "A" zone.

Wilson CQB	
Trigger pull	4 lb
Extractor tension	8 oz
Chamber depth	.896"
.22 Conversion fit	
Kimber	Y
EAA	Y
Ciener	N
Wilson	Y
Marvel	Y
Bar-Sto .400 Cor-bon fit	Y
Clark .460 Rowland fit	Rowland fit Y
Weight	35.9
Barrel length	5"
Three favorite loads	
1-Oregon Tr. Viht	
2-Black Hills Blue	
3-PMC	

The Wilson KZ-45 with mag, case and test-fire target.

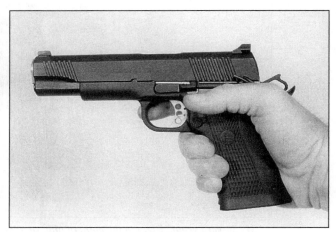

in a smaller hand the KZ is still fine, the advantage of the mid-cap frame.

In a large hand, the KZ is fine...

Back in 1994, the passage of the Crime Bill caused many changes in the firearms landscape. One of the changes was the limitation on magazine capacity. Manufacturers could no longer make new high-capacity magazines. Magazine capacity was limited to 10 shots. Suddenly, previously high-capacity firearms started showing up with crimped magazines that only held 10 rounds. Or shooters began showing up at matches with single-stack guns with extended, 10-shot magazines. Why not use a single-stack and 10-shot magazines? Sure, if you have one. And the rules allow it. If you don't already have one, or the rules don't allow it (IDPA comes to mind) then how to get 10 shots? Especially if your hands don't feel comfortable around a hi-cap frame?

Bill Wilson thought differently. He worked on a magazine of the standard length that would hold 10 rounds, and would fit in a frame that did not have a fat high-cap grip. It took a couple of years to finish the magazine (always the most difficult part of a new design) but the unveiling in 1999 was met with enthusiasm. (Bill held up the introduction of the new pistol until all the bugs had been worked out of the new magazine.)

The KZ-45 slide appears normal, for a moment. There are cocking serrations front and back, and the sights are the Wilson fixed pattern. The first big change is the extractor. Since he was changing so much, Bill Wilson had a look at the extractor. While a standard Browning extractor works, and works well, it is not easy to manufacture. It can be a hassle to fit to some slides. To make the job easier, Bill Wilson changed the extractor to a spring-loaded hook that runs along the outside of the slide. Pivoting around the pin that holds it in place, the extractor doesn't have to be bent to adjust its tension. The spring at its rear takes care of that. The extractor is left bright. The slide is finished in Wilson's black Armor-Tuff™, with a heavy matte finish.

The left side of the slide is marked "Wilson Combat" while the right side has "KZ-45" marked forward of the ejection port. The cocking serrations are round-bottomed grooves milled into the slide. The ejection port is lowered and scalloped, and live ejects. The barrel is a Wilson, and locks up snugly without a hard snap as it closes. The slide has no side-to-side play in its fit on the frame, but I can feel a little bit of play when I attempt to rock it from side to side, clockwise, or counterclockwise. The external contours of the slide are normal, and the recoil spring and retainer are standard 1911. But there are more surprises in store.

The frame is a steel insert that contains all the bearing surfaces and pin holes for the slide and internal parts. The slide moves on steel, and the hammer, sear, and both safeties pivot on steel. The insert is honeycombed on its lower part, so the polymer portion of the frame is securely bonded to the steel when moulded onto the steel. The polymer has

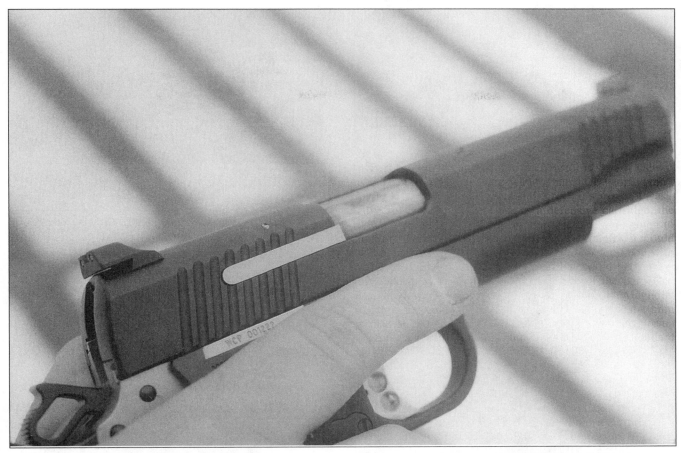

The Wilson KZ-45, and the external extractor.

Fiberglas and kevlar fibers mixed in for greater strength. The stainless insert is left bright, while the polymer of the frame is black. The frame has moulded-in checkering of 18 lines per inch, and the flat mainspring housing is also checkered 18 lpi. The serial number is on the exposed portion of the stainless insert on the right side, and just underneath it, cast into the frame, is "Wilson Combat Berryville.AR.USA."

The grip safety is a Wilson, as is the non-ambidextrous thumb safety. An ambidextrous safety is an option. The slide stop is standard. The magazine release is not a standard unit, as it has to be longer than usual to span the width of the magazine. The magazine catch can be swapped to the other side for left-handed shooters. The mainspring housing is flat, and the location of the mainspring housing pin is different on the KZ-45 than on a standard 1911s. You cannot use a different housing than the Wilson KZ housing. The result of the change in frame design and construction is a frame that doesn't feel any wider than a standard 1911 frame, and weighs 7 ounces less than a steel-framed 1911.

By making the frame of polymer, and by carefully designing the magazine, the size of the grip area of the frame is no larger than that of a standard 1911. While it feels slightly blockier, it is not wider nor longer front to back.

The polymer lower is moulded to the stainless steel insert. You can't get them apart without destroying the frame.

The Wilson KZ-45 comes with a Wilson barrel, of course.

The rear, showing the tight fit of slide to frame, and the Wilson night sights.

The slide stop sits in a slight recess. The mag catch is reversible.

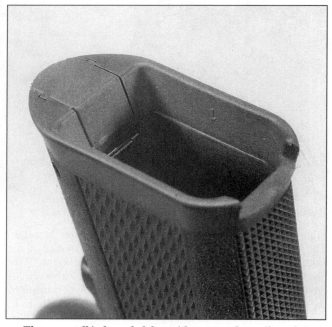

The mag well is funneled, but with a tapered mag it needn't be. Bill Wilson thinks of everything.

The magazines are tapered to the top, and hold 10 shots each. The bottom is a polymer baseplate that is removable for cleaning and tending to the spring and follower.

To strip and clean the magazine, unload it. Then gently pry down the center catch on the rear of the baseplate and slide the baseplate forward. As you expose the spring, contain it so it doesn't shoot across the room. Pull the spring and follower out. Wipe everything down, spray the interior of the magazine with Krunch Products spray lube, and reassemble.

The KZ-45 comes in a Wilson soft case with a magazine, spare recoil spring, guide rod, test fire target, and letter from Bill Wilson with recommended loads. The test target was with the same load used in the CQB, fired by test shooter "initials illegible" and puts all the shots into a tight cluster from 15 yards. On the page listing recommended loads, Bill once again reminds those who haven't been paying attention that the most reliable load is a properly hand-loaded 200-grain lead semiwadcutter of the H&G 68 design.

The Wilson front night sight.

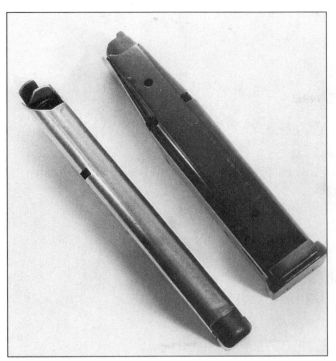

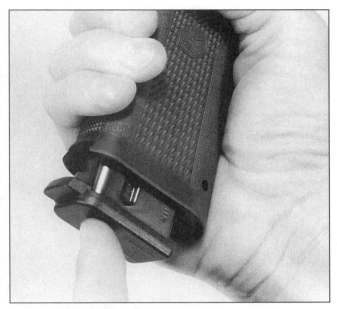

The KZ-45 mag going home.

The Wilson mid-cap is 10 rounds, and shorter than a standard seven- or eight-shot magazine.

The Wilson KZ-45 and its 50-yard group. Could I do that again? Not on a bet. Could the Wilson? I wouldn't bet against it.

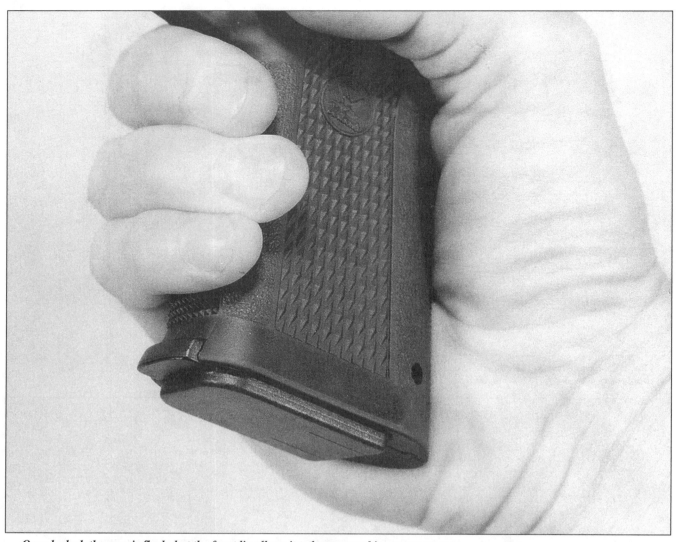

Once locked, the mag is flush, but the front lip allows it to be extracted in an emergency.

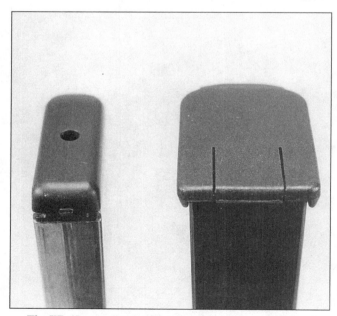

The KZ-45 magazine is wider than a standard mag, but not so wide it makes the frame feel like a 2x4.

In the shooting tests, we had a few failures to feed when breaking it in, but after the first few magazines that went away. As with other polymer-framed pistols, the KZ-45 seemed softer in recoil due to the flex of the polymer fame. The mid-cap magazines were easy to load, and went in to and out of the pistol smoothly. When it came time to check accuracy, I found one of the drawbacks to a new pistol. There aren't any Ransom inserts for the Wilson mid-cap frame yet. I had to check accuracy by shooting off the bench, either over sandbags or off the Outers Pistol Perch. Since I can't shoot as well as the Ransom rest, I won't compare group sizes of the KZ-45 with other pistols. It wouldn't be fair to Bill and this pistol to compare my shooting abilities and those of the Ransom rest, to the detriment of the KZ-45.

The smallest groups were with the Sierra load, followed closely by the Magtech and then the Black Hills Blue. Another 1911 that favors hardball, imagine that. For me, the sights were perfectly adjusted and the groups were dead on the aiming point.

The KZ-45 is a great bargain at the suggested retail price of $995. The magazines are not that expensive, at $39.95 each, for which you get 10 shots and Wilson reliability.

Wilson KZ-45	
Trigger pull	5.0 lb
Extractor tension	0 oz*
Chamber depth	.896"
.22 Conversion fit	
Kimber	Y
EAA	Y
Ciener	N
Wilson	Y
Marvel	Y
Bar-Sto .400 Cor-bon fit	N
Clark .460 Rowland fit	N
Weight	28.3 oz
Barrel length	5"
Three favorite loads	
1-Sierra/Viht	
2-Magtech 230 JRN	
3-Black Hills Blue	

* Despite no measurable extractor tension (perhaps due to the unique design), the KZ-45 never failed to extract and eject

SUPPLIERS

Accurate Plating & Weaponry
940 Harbor Lake Dr.
Safety Harbor, FL. 34695
(727)-796-5583
www.apwcogan.com

Ace Custom 45's
1880-1/2 Upper Turtle Creek
Kerrville, TX. 78028
(830)-257-4290
(830)-257-5724-Fax
www.acecustom45.com

Ajax
9130 Viscount Row
P.O. Box 560129
Dallas, TX. 75247
214-630-8893
214-630-4942-Fax
www.ajaxgrips.com

Aristocrat Products Co.
405 Agostino Rd.
P.O. Box 523
San Gabriel, CA. 91778
(626)-287-4110
(626)-287-3527-Fax

Baer Custom
29601 34th Ave.
Hillsdale, IL. 61257
(309)-658-2716
(309)-658-2610-Fax
www.lesbaer.com

Jerry Barnhart
Tactical Shooting Technology
P.O. Box 426
Oxford, MI. 48371
(248)-628-6301
(248)-628-6029-Fax
http://ic.net/~burner

Bar-sto Precision Machine
73377 Sullivan Rd.
P.O. Box 1838
Twentynine Palms, CA. 92277
760-367-2747
760-367-2407-Fax
www.barsto.com

Birchwood Casey
7900 Fuller Rd.
Eden Prairie, MN. 55344
(952)-937-7933
(952)-937-7979-Fax
www.birchwoodcasey.com

Blackhawk Industries, Inc.
1133 Executive Blvd.
Chesapeake, VA. 23320
757-436-3101
757-436-3088-Fax
www.blackhawkindustries.com

Black Hills Ammunition
P.O. Box 3090
Rapid City, SD. 57709
605-348-5150
605-348-9827-Fax
www.black-hills.com

Ed Brown Products
43825 Muldrew Tr.
Perry, MO. 63462
573-565-3261
573-565-2791-Fax
www.edbrown.com

Brownells, Inc.
200 south Front St.
Montezuma, IA. 50171-1000
641-623-5401
641-623-3896-Fax
www.brownells.com

Caspian Arms Ltd.
P.O. Box 465
Hardwick, VT. 05843
802-472-6454
802-472-6709-Fax
www.caspianarmsltd.8m.com

Casull Arms Corp.
P.O. Box 1629
Afton, WY. 83110
307-886-0200
307-886-0300-Fax
www.casullarms.com

Charles Daly (KBI)
P.O. Box 6625
Harrisburg, PA. 17112
717-540-8518
717-540-8567-Fax
www.charlesdaly.com

Chip McCormick Corp
P.O. Box 1560
Manchaca, TX. 78652
512-280-4280
www.chipmccormickcorp.com

Jonathan Ceiner, Inc.
8700 Commerce St.
Cape Canaveral, FL. 32920
321-868-2200
321-868-2201
www.22lrconversions.com

Clark Custom Guns
336 Shootout Lane
Princeton, LA. 71607
318-949-9884
318-949-9829-Fax
www.clarkcustomguns.com

Cor-bon
1311 Industry Rd.
Sturgis, SD. 57785
800-626-7266
800-923-2666-Fax
www.cor-bon.com

Dawson Precision
3585 CR 272
Suite 300
Leander, TX. 78641
512-260-2011
512-260-2211-Fax
www.dawsonprecision.com

Dillon Precision
8009 E. Dillons Way
Scottsdale, AZ. 85260
480-948-8009
480-998-2786
www.dillonprecision.com

EAA
P.O. Box 1299
Sharpes, FL. 32959
321-639-4842
321-639-7006-Fax
www.eaacorp.com

EGW
4050 Skyron Dr.
Doylestown, PA. 18901

Entreprise Arms
15861 Business Dr.
Irwindale, CA. 91706
626-962-8712
626-962-4692-Fax
www.entreprise.com

Essex Arms
Box 959
Hardwick, VT. 05843
802-472-3215
www.essex-arms.com

John Farnam
DTI. Inc.
749 S. Lemay
Suite A3-337
Ft Collins, CO. 80524
970-482-2520
www.defense-training.com

FTI, Inc.
8 Vreeland Rd.
Florham Park, NJ. 07932
973-443-0004
www.tetraproducts.com

Galena Ind.
3551 Mayer Ave.
Sturgis, SD. 57785
605-423-4105
www.galenaindustries.com

Griffon USA
2513 East Loop
820 North
Fort Worth, TX. 76118
817-284-7474
817-284-7528
www.texn.com/griffon.htm

Gunsite
2900 W. Gunsite Rd.
Paulden, AZ. 86334
520-636-4104
520-636-1236
www.gunsite.net

High Standard Mfg. Co.
10606 Hempstead Hwy.
Suite 116
Houston, TX. 77092
713-462-4200
www.highstandard.com

Hodgdon Powder Co. Inc.
6231 Robinson
Shwanee Mission, KS. 66202
913-362-9455
913-362-1307-Fax
www.hodgdon.com

Hogue, Inc.
P.O. Box 1138
Paso Robles, CA. 93447
800-438-4747
805-239-2553-Fax
www.getgrip.com

Hornady Manufacturing Co.
P.O. Boc 1848
Grand Island, NE. 68802
308-382-1390
308-382-5761-Fax
www.hornady.com

IDPA
P.O. Box 639
Berryville, AR. 72616
870-545-3886
www.idpa.com

Image Industries Inc.
382 Balm Court
Wood Dale, IL. 60191
630-766-7373

ISMI
P.O. Box 204
Carthage, IN. 46115
765-565-6108
765-565-7143-Fax
www.ismi-gunsprings.com

Kahr Arms
P.O. Box 220
630 Route 303
Blauvelt, NY. 10913
914-353-5996
914-353-7833-Fax
www.kahr.com

Kimber of America, Inc.
1 Lawton St.
Yonkers, NY. 10705
914-964-0771
406-758-2223-Fax
www.kimberamerica.com

King's Gun Works
1837 West Glen Oaks Blvd.
Glendale, CA. 91201
818-956-6010
818-548-8606
www.kingsgunworks.com

KKM Precision
26 Affonso #101
Carson Ctiy, NV. 89706
775-246-5444
775-246-9182
www.kkmprecision.com

LFI-Mas Ayoob
P.O. Box 122
Concord, NH. 03301
603-224-6814
www.ayoob.com

Mag na Port Int.
41502 Exectutive Dr.
Harrison Twsp. MI. 48045
810-469-6727
810-469-0425-Fax
www.magnaport.com

Magtech Ammunition Co. Inc.
837 Boston Post Rd.
#12
Madison, CT. 06443
800-466-7191
203-245-2883-Fax
www.magtechammunition.com

Dave Manson Reamers
8200 Embury Rd.
Grand Blanc, MI. 48439
810-953-0732
810-953-0735-Fax
www.mansonreamers.com

Marvel Products
245 84th
#215
Lincoln, NE. 68510
402-826-3013
www.marvelprod.com

Paul Miller-San Juan Range
19878 Dave Wood Road
Montrose, CO. 81401
970-249-4227
www.sanjuanrange.com

Millett
7275 Murdy Circle
Huntington Beach, CA. 92648
www.millettsights.com

Miniature Machine Co.
2513 East Loop
820 North
Ft. Worth, TX. 76118
817-595-0404
817-595-3074-Fax
www.mmcsight.com

Montana Gold Bullet Inc.
400 18th Street East
P.O. Box 8074
Kalispell, MT. 59901
406-755-2717
406-755-5454-Fax
www.montanagoldbullet.com

Nowlin Mfg. Co.
20622 S. 4092 Rd.
Claremore, OK. 74017
918-342-0689
918-342-0642-Fax
www.nowlinguns.com

Novak's Inc.
1206-1/2 30th Street
Parkersburg, WV. 26101
304-485-9295
304-428-6722-Fax
www.colt380.com/novaks.htm

Oregon Trail Bullet Co.
Box 529
Baker City, OR. 97814
800-811-0548
www.laser-cast.com

Para Ordnance
980 Tapscott Rd
Scarborough, Ont. CA. M1X 1E7
416-297-7855
416-297-1289-Fax
www.paraord.com

PMC-Eldorado Cartridge Corp
P.O. Box 62508
12801 US Hwy 95 S
Boulder City, NV. 89005
702-294-0025
702-294-0121-Fax
www.pmcammo.com

Rainier Ballistics
4500 15th Street East
Tacoma, WA. 98424
800-638-8722
206-922-7854-Fax
www.rainierballistics.com

Ransom Int. Corp.
1027 Spirie Dr.
Prescott, AZ. 86302
520-778-7899
520-778-7993-Fax
www.ransom-intl.com

Redding Reloading Equipment
1089 Starr Rd.
Cortland, NY. 13045
607-753-3331
607-756-8445-Fax
www.redding-reloading.com

Remington Arms Co.
870 Remington Drive
P.O. Box 700
Madison, NC. 27025
336-548-8578
336-548-7778-Fax
www.remington.com

The Robar Companies
21438 N. 7th Avenue
Suite B
Phoenix, AZ. 85027
602-581-2648
602-582-0059-Fax
www.robarguns.com

SGS Imports (Firestorm)
1750 Brielle Ave.
Unit B-1
Wnamassa, NJ. 07712
732-493-0302
732-493-0301-Fax
www.firestorm-sgs.com

Sierra
1400 West Henry Street
Sedalia, MO. 65301
660-827-6300
660-827-4999-Fax
www.sierrabullets.com

Spradlins
457 Shannon Rd.
Texas Creek, CO. 81223
719-275-7105
719-275-3852-Fax
www.spradlins.net

Springfield Armory
420 W. Main
Geneseo, IL. 61254
309-944-5631
309-944-3676-Fax
www.springfield-armory.com

Starline
1300 West Henry St.
P.O. Box 833
Sedalia, MO. 65301
800-280-6660
660-827-6650-Fax
www.starlinebrass.com

STI 114 Halmar Cove
Georgetown, TX. 78628
512-819-0656
512-819-0465-Fax
www.sti-guns.com

Texas Ammunition Co.
P.O. Box 248
Ballinger, TX. 76821
915-365-4077
915-365-5765-Fax
www.texas-ammo.com

Thunder Ranch
HCR 1
P.O. Box 53
Mt. Home, TX. 78508
830-640-3138
830-640-3183-Fax
www.thunderranchinc.com

Triton Ammunition
P.O. Box 50
Wappingers Falls, NY. 12590
800-861-3362
800-421-6391-Fax
www.tritonammo.com

Uncle Mikes/Michaels of Oregon
P.O. Box 1690
Oregon City, OR. 97045
503-655-7964
503-655-7546-Fax
www.michaels-oregon.com

USPSA
P.O. Box 811
Sedro Wooley, WA. 98284
360-855-2245
360-855-0380-Fax
www.uspsa.org

Vihtavuori Oy
Kaltron-Pettibone
1241 Ellis Street
Bensenville, IL. 60106
630-350-1116
630-350-1606-Fax
www.vihtavuori.fi

Weigand Combat
685 South Main Road
Mountain Top, PA. 18707
570-868-8358
www.jackweigand.com

West Coast Bullets
P.O. Box 2270
Dayton, NV. 89403
800-482-2103
206-282-4578-Fax
www.westcoastbullet.com

Wilson Combat
2234 CR 719
Berryville, Ar. 72616
870-545-3618
870-545-3310
www.wilsoncombat.com

Zero Ammunition
P.O. Box 1188
Cullman, AL. 35056
800-204-1526
256-739-4683-Fax
zerobulletco@aol.com

THE ARMS LIBRARY

FOR COLLECTOR ◆ HUNTER ◆ SHOOTER ◆ OUTDOORSMAN

IMPORTANT NOTICE TO BOOK BUYERS

Books listed here may be bought from Ray Riling Arms Books Co., 6844 Gorsten St., P.O. Box 18925, Philadelphia, PA 19119, Phone 215/438-2456; FAX: 215-438-5395. E-Mail: sales@rayrilingarms-books.com. Joe Riling is the researcher and compiler of "The Arms Library" and a seller of gun books for over 32 years. The Riling stock includes books classic and modern, many hard-to-find items, and many not obtainable elsewhere. These pages list a portion of the current stock. They offer prompt, complete service, with delayed shipments occurring only on out-of-print or out-of-stock books.

Visit our web site at **www.rayrilingarmsbooks.com** and order all of your favorite titles on line from our secure site.

NOTICE FOR ALL CUSTOMERS: Remittance in U.S. funds must accompany all orders. For your convenience we now accept VISA, Master-Card & American Express. For shipments in the U.S. add $7.00 for the 1st book and $2.00 for each additional book for postage and insurance. Mini-mum order $10.00. International Orders add $13.00 for the 1st book and $5.00 for each additional book. All International orders are shipped at the buyer's risk unless an additional $5 for insurance is included. USPS does not offer insurance to all countries unless shipped Air-Mail please e-mail or call for pricing.

Payments in excess of order or for "Backorders" are credited or fully re-funded at request. Books "As-Ordered" are not returnable except by permis-sion and a handling charge on these of 10% or $2.00 per book which ever is greater is deducted from refund or credit. Only Pennsylvania customers must include current sales tax.

A full variety of arms books also available from Rutgers Book Center, 127 Raritan Ave., Highland Park, NJ 08904/908-545-4344; FAX: 908-545-6686 or I.D.S.A. Books, 1324 Stratford Drive, Piqua, OH 45356/937-773-4203; FAX: 937-778-1922.

BALLISTICS AND HANDLOADING

ABC's of Reloading, 6th Edition, by C. Rodney James and the editors of Hand-loader's Digest, DBI Books, a division of Krause Publications, Iola, WI, 1997. 288 pp., illus. Paper covers. $21.95
The definitive guide to every facet of cartridge and shotshell reloading.

Accurate Arms Loading Guide Number 2, by Accurate Arms. McEwen, TN: Accu-rate Arms Company, Inc., 2000. Paper Covers. $18.95
Includes new data on smokeless powders XMR4064 and XMP5744 as well as a special section on Cowboy Action Shooting. The new manual includes 50 new pages of data. An appendix includes nominal rotor charge weights, bullet diameters.

The American Cartridge, by Charles Suydam, Borden Publishing Co. Alhambra, CA, 1986. 184 pp., illus. $24.95
An illustrated study of the rimfire cartridge in the United States.

Ammo and Ballistics, by Robert W. Forker, Safari Press, Inc., Huntington Beach, CA., 1999. 252 pp., illustrated. Paper covers. $18.95
Ballistic data on 125 calibers and 1,400 loads out to 500 yards.

Ammunition: Grenades and Projectile Munitions, by Ian V. Hogg, Stackpole Books, Mechanicsburg, PA, 1998. 144 pp., illus. $22.95
Concise guide to modern ammunition. International coverage with detailed specifications and illustrations.

Barnes Reloading Manual #2, Barnes Bullets, American Fork, UT, 1999. 668 pp., illus. $24.95
Features data and trajectories on the new weight X, XBT and Solids in calibers from .22 to .50 BMG.

Big Bore Rifles And Cartridges, Wolfe Publishing Co., Prescott, AZ, 1991. Paper covers. $26.00
This book covers cartridges from 8mm to .600 Nitro with loading tables.

Black Powder Guide, 2nd Edition, by George C. Nonte, Jr., Stoeger Publishing Co., So. Hackensack, NJ, 1991. 288 pp., illus. $14.95
How-to instructions for selection, repair and maintenance of muzzleloaders, making your own bullets, restoring and refinishing, shooting techniques.

Blackpowder Loading Manual, 3rd Edition, by Sam Fadala, DBI Books, a division of Krause Publications, Iola, WI, 1995. 368 pp., illus. Paper covers. $20.95
Revised and expanded edition of this landmark blackpowder loading book. Covers hundreds of loads for most of the popular blackpowder rifles, handguns and shotguns.

Cartridges of the World, 9th Edition, by Frank Barnes, Krause Publications, Iola, WI, 2000. 512 pp., illus. Paper covers. $27.95
Completely revised edition of the general purpose reference work for which collectors, police, scientists and laymen reach first for answers to cartridge identification questions.

Cartridge Reloading Tools of the Past, by R.H. Chamberlain and Tom Quigley, Tom Quigley, Castle Rock, WA, 1998. 167 pp., illustrated. Paper covers. $25.00
A detailed treatment of the extensive Winchester and Ideal line of handloading tools and bullet molds, plus Remington, Marlin, Ballard, Browning, Maynard, and many others.

Cast Bullets for the Black Powder Rifle, by Paul A. Matthews, Wolfe Publishing Co., Prescott, AZ, 1996. 133 pp., illus. Paper covers. $22.50
The tools and techniques used to make your cast bullet shooting a success.

Complete Blackpowder Handbook, 3rd Edition, by Sam Fadala, DBI Books, a di-vision of Krause Publications, Iola, WI, 1997. 400 pp., illus. Paper covers. $21.95
Expanded and completely rewritten edition of the definitive book on the subject of blackpowder.

Complete Reloading Guide, by Robert & John Traister, Stoeger Publishing Co., Wayne, NJ, 1997. 608 pp., illus. Paper covers. $34.95
Perhaps the finest, most comprehensive work ever published on the subject of reloading.

Complete Reloading Manual, One Book / One Caliber. California: Load Books USA, 2000. $7.95 Each
Containing unabridged information from U. S. Bullet and Powder Makers. With thousands of proven and tested loads, plus dozens of various bullet designs and different powders. Spiral bound. Available in all Calibers.

Early Loading Tools & Bullet Molds, Pioneer Press, 1988. 88 pages, illustrated. Softcover. $7.50

European Sporting Cartridges: Volume 1, by Brad Dixon, Seattle, WA: Armory Publications, 1997. 1st edition. 250 pp., Illus. $60.00
Photographs and drawings of over 550 centerfire cartridge case types in 1,300 illustrations produced in Germany and Austria from 1875-1995.

European Sporting Cartridges: Volume 2, by Brad Dixon, Seattle, WA: Armory Publications, 2000. 1st edition. 240 pages. $60.00
An illustrated history of centerfire hunting and target cartridges produced in Czechoslovakia, Switzerland, Norway, Sweden, Finland, Russia, Italy, Denmark, Belguim from 1875 to 1998. Adds 50 specimens to volume 1, Germany-Austria. Also, illustrates 40 small arms magazine experiments during the late 19th Century, and includes the English-Language export ammunition catalogue of Kovo (Povazske Strojarne), Prague, Czeck. from the 1930's.

Game Loads and Practical Ballistics for the American Hunter, by Bob Hagel, Wolfe Publishing Co., Prescott, AZ, 1992. 310 pp., illus. $27.90
Hagel's knowledge gained as a hunter, guide and gun enthusiast is gathered in this informative text.

German 7.9MM Military Ammunition 1888-1945, by Daniel Kent, Ann Arbor, MI: Kent, 1990. 153 pp., plus appendix. illus., b&w photos. $35.00

Handbook for Shooters and Reloaders, by P.O. Ackley, Salt Lake City, UT, 1998, (Vol. I), 567 pp., illus. Includes a separate exterior ballistics chart. $21.95
(Vol. II), a new printing with specific new material. 495 pp., illus. $20.95

Handgun Muzzle Flash Tests: How Police Cartridges Compare, by Robert Olsen, Paladin Press, Boulder, CO.Fully illustrated. 133 pages. Softcover. $20.00
Tests dozens of pistols and revolvers for the brightness of muzzle flash, a critical factor in the safety of law enforcement personnel.

Handgun Stopping Power; The Definitive Study, by Marshall & Sandow. Boulder, CO: Paladin Press, 1992. 240 pages. $45.00
Offers accurate predictions of the stopping power of specific loads in calibers from .380 Auto to .45 ACP, as well as such specialty rounds as the Glaser Safety Slug, Federal Hydra-Shok, MagSafe, etc. This is the definitive methodology for predicting the stopping power of handgun loads, the first to take into account what really happens when a bullet meets a man.

Handloader's Digest, 17th Edition, edited by Bob Bell. DBI Books, a division of Krause Publications, Iola, WI, 1997. 480 pp., illustrated. Paper covers. $27.95
Top writers in the field contribute helpful information on techniques and components. Greatly expanded and fully indexed catalog of all currently available tools, accessories and components for metallic, blackpowder cartridge, shotgun reloading and swaging.

Handloader's Manual of Cartridge Conversions, by John J. Donnelly, Stoeger Publishing Co., So. Hackensack, NJ, 1986. Unpaginated. $39.95
From 14 Jones to 70-150 Winchester in English and American cartridges, and from 4.85 U.K. to 15.2x28R Gevelot in metric cartridges. Over 900 cartridges described in detail.

Hatcher's Notebook, by S. Julian Hatcher, Stackpole Books, Harrisburg, PA, 1992. 488 pp., illus. $39.95
A reference work for shooters, gunsmiths, ballisticians, historians, hunters and collectors.

THE ARMS LIBRARY

History and Development of Small Arms Ammunition; Volume 2 Centerfire: Primitive, and Martial Long Arms. by George A. Hoyem. Oceanside, CA: Armory Publications, 1991. 303 pages, illustrated. $60.00

Covers the blackpowder military centerfire rifle, carbine, machine gun and volley gun ammunition used in 28 nations and dominions, together with the firearms that chambered them.

History and Development of Small Arms Ammunition; Volume 4, American Military Rifle Cartridges. Oceanside, CA: Armory Publications, 1998. 244pp., illus. $60.00

Carries on what Vol. 2 began with American military rifle cartridges. Now the sporting rifle cartridges are at last organized by their originators-235 individual case types designed by eight makers of single shot rifles and four of magazine rifles from .50-140 Winchester Express to .22-15-60 Stevens. plus experimentals from .70-150 to .32-80. American Civil War enthusiasts and European collectors will find over 150 primitives in Appendix A to add to those in Volumes One and Two. There are 16 pages in full color of 54 box labels for Sharps, Remington and Ballard cartridges. There are large photographs with descriptions of 15 Maynard, Sharps, Winchester, Browning, Freund, Remington-Hepburn, Farrow and other single shot rifles, some of them rare one of a kind specimens.

Hodgdon Powder Data Manual #27, Hodgdon Powder Co., Shawnee Mission, KS, 1999. 800 pp. $27.95

Reloading data for rifle and pistol loads.

Hodgdon Shotshell Data Manual, Hodgdon Powder Co., Shawnee Mission, KS, 1999. 208 pp. $19.95

Contains hundreds of loads for lead shot, buck shot, slugs, bismuth shot and steel shot plus articles on ballistics, patterning, special reloads and much more.

Home Guide to Cartridge Conversions, by Maj. George C. Nonte Jr., The Gun Room Press, Highland Park, NJ, 1976. 404 pp., illus. $24.95

Revised and updated version of Nonte's definitive work on the alteration of cartridge cases for use in guns for which they were not intended.

Hornady Handbook of Cartridge Reloading, 5th Edition, Vol. I and II, Edited by Larry Steadman, Hornady Mfg. Co., Grand Island, NE, 2000., illus. $49.95

2 Volumes; Volume 1, 773 pp.; Volume 2, 717 pp. New edition of this famous reloading handbook covers rifle and handgun reloading data and ballistic tables. Latest loads, ballistic information, etc.

How-To's for the Black Powder Cartridge Rifle Shooter, by Paul A. Matthews, Wolfe Publishing Co., Prescott, AZ, 1995. 45 pp. Paper covers. $22.50

Covers lube recipes, good bore cleaners and over-powder wads. Tips include compressing powder charges, combating wind resistance, improving ignition and much more.

The Illustrated Reference of Cartridge Dimensions, edited by Dave Scovill, Wolfe Publishing Co., Prescott, AZ, 1994. 343 pp., illus. Paper covers. $19.00

A comprehensive volume with over 300 cartridges. Standard and metric dimensions have been taken from SAAMI drawings and/or fired cartridges.

Kynock, by Dale J. Hedlund, Armory Publications, Seattle, WA, 2000. 130 pages, illus. 9" x 12" with four color dust jacket. $59.95

A comprehensive review of Kynoch shotgun cartridges covering over 50 brand names and case types, and over 250 Kynoch shotgun cartridge headstamps. Additional information on Kynoch metallic ammunition including the identity of the mysterious .434 Seelun.

Lee Modern Reloading, by Richard Lee, 350 pp. of charts and data and 85 illustrations. 512 pp. $24.95

Bullet casting, lubricating and author's formula for calculating proper charges for cast bullets. Includes virtually all current load data published by the powder suppliers. Exclusive source of volume measured loads.

Loading the Black Powder Rifle Cartridge, by Paul A Matthews, Wolfe Publishing Co., Prescott, AZ, 1993. 121 pp., illus. Paper covers. $22.50

Author Matthews brings the blackpowder cartridge shooter valuable information on the basics, including cartridge care, lubes and moulds, powder charges and developing and testing loads in his usual authoritative style.

Loading the Peacemaker—Colt's Model P, by Dave Scovill, Wolfe Publishing Co., Prescott, AZ, 1996. 227 pp., illus. $24.95

A comprehensive work about the history, maintenance and repair of the most famous revolver ever made, including the most extensive load data ever published.

Lyman Cast Bullet Handbook, 3rd Edition, edited by C. Kenneth Ramage, Lyman Publications, Middlefield, CT, 1980. 416 pp., illus. Paper covers. $19.95

Information on more than 5000 tested cast bullet loads and 19 pages of trajectory and wind drift tables for cast bullets.

Lyman Black Powder Handbook, edited by C. Kenneth Ramage, Lyman Products for Shooters, Middlefield, CT, 1975. 239 pp., illus. Paper covers. $14.95

Comprehensive load information for the modern blackpowder shooter.

Lyman Pistol & Revolver Handbook, 2nd Edition, edited by Thomas J. Griffin, Lyman Products Co., Middlefield, CT, 1996. 287 pp., illus. Paper covers. $18.95

The most up-to-date loading data available including the hottest new calibers, like 40 S&W, 9x21, 9mm Makarov, 9x25 Dillon and 454 Casull.

Lyman Reloading Handbook No. 47, edited by Edward A. Matunas, Lyman Publications, Middlefield, CT, 1992. 480 pp., illus. Paper covers. $24.95

A comprehensive reloading manual complete with "How to Reload" information. Expanded data section with all the newest rifle and pistol calibers.

Lyman Shotshell Handbook, 4th Edition, edited by Edward A. Matunas, Lyman Products Co., Middlefield, CT, 1996. 330 pp., illus. Paper covers. $24.95

Has 9000 loads, including slugs and buckshot, plus feature articles and a full color I.D. section.

Lyman's Guide to Big Game Cartridges & Rifles, by Edward Matunas, Lyman Publishing Corporation, Middlefield, CT, 1994. 287 pp., illus. Paper covers. $17.95

A selection guide to cartridges and rifles for big game—antelope to elephant.

Making Loading Dies and Bullet Molds, by Harold Hoffman, H & P Publishing, San Angelo, TX, 1993. 230 pp., illus. Paper covers. $24.95

A good book for learning tool and die making.

Metallic Cartridge Reloading, 3rd Edition, by M.L. McPherson, DBI Books, a division of Krause Publications, Iola, WI., 1996. 352 pp., illus. Paper covers. $21.95

A true reloading manual with over 10,000 loads for all popular metallic cartridges and a wealth of invaluable technical data provided by a recognized expert.

Military Rifle and Machine Gun Cartridges, by Jean Huon, Alexandria, VA: Ironside International, 1995. 1st edition. 378 pages, over 1,000 photos. $34.95

Superb reference text.

Modern Combat Ammunition, by Duncan Long, Paladin Press, Boulder, CO, 1997, soft cover, photos, illus., 216 pp. $34.00

Now, Paladin's leading weapons author presents his exhaustive evaluation of the stopping power of modern rifle, pistol, shotgun and machine gun rounds based on actual case studies of shooting incidents. He looks at the hot new cartridges that promise to dominate well into the next century .40 S&W, 10mm auto, sub-sonic 9mm's - as well as the trusted standbys. Find out how to make your own exotic tracers, fléchette and sabot rounds, caseless ammo and fragmenting bullets.

Modern Exterior Ballistics, by Robert L. McCoy, Schiffer Publishing Co., Atglen, PA, 1999. 128 pp. $95.00

Advanced students of exterior ballistics and flight dynamics will find this comprehensive textbook on the subject a useful addition to their libraries.

Modern Handloading, by Maj. Geo. C. Nonte, Winchester Press, Piscataway, NJ, 1972. 416 pp., illus. $15.00

Covers all aspects of metallic and shotshell ammunition loading, plus more loads than any book in print.

Modern Reloading, by Richard Lee, Inland Press, 1996. 510 pp., illus. $24.98

The how-to's of rifle, pistol and shotgun reloading plus load data for rifle and pistol calibers.

Modern Sporting Rifle Cartridges, by Wayne van Zwoll, Stoeger Publishing Co., Wayne, NJ, 1998. 310 pp., illustrated. Paper covers. $21.95

Illustrated with hundreds of photos and backed up by dozens of tables and schematic drawings, this four-part book tells the story of how rifle bullets and cartridges were developed and, in some cases, discarded.

Modern Practical Ballistics, by Art Pejsa, Pejsa Ballistics, Minneapolis, MN, 1990. 150 pp., illus. $29.95

Covers all aspects of ballistics and new, simplified methods. Clear examples illustrate new, easy but very accurate formulas.

Mr. Single Shot's Cartridge Handbook, by Frank de Haas, Mark de Haas, Orange City, IA, 1996. 116 pp., illus. Paper covers. $21.50

This book covers most of the cartridges, both commercial and wildcat, that the author has known and used.

Nick Harvey's Practical Reloading Manual, by Nick Harvey, Australian Print Group, Maryborough, Victoria, Australia, 1995. 235 pp., illus. Paper covers. $24.95

Contains data for rifle and handgun including many popular wildcat and improved cartridges. Tools, powders, components and techniques for assembling optimum reloads with particular application to North America.

Nosler Reloading Manual #4, edited by Gail Root, Nosler Bullets, Inc., Bend, OR, 1996. 516 pp., illus. $26.99

Combines information on their Ballistic Tip, Partition and Handgun bullets with traditional powders and new powders never before used, plus trajectory information from 100 to 500 yards.

The Paper Jacket, by Paul Matthews, Wolfe Publishing Co., Prescott, AZ, 1991. Paper covers. $13.50

Up-to-date and accurate information about paper-patched bullets.

Reloading Tools, Sights and Telescopes for S/S Rifles, by Gerald O. Kelver, Brighton, CO, 1982. 163 pp., illus. Softcover. $15.00

A listing of most of the famous makers of reloading tools, sights and telescopes with a brief description of the products they manufactured.

Reloading for Shotgunners, 4th Edition, by Kurt D. Fackler and M.L. McPherson, DBI Books, a division of Krause Publications, Iola, WI, 1997. 320 pp., illus. Paper covers. $19.95

Expanded reloading tables with over 11,000 loads. Bushing charts for every major press and component maker. All new presentation on all aspects of shotshell reloading by two of the top experts in the field.

The Rimfire Cartridge in the United States and Canada, Illustrated history of rimfire cartridges, manufacturers, and the products made from 1857-1984. by John L. Barber, Thomas Publications, Gettysburg, PA 2000. 1st edition. Profusely illustrated. 221 pages. $50.00

The author has written an encyclopedia of rimfire cartridges from the .22 to the massive 1.00 in. Gatling. Fourteen chapters, six appendices and an excellent bibliography make up a reference volume that all cartridge collectors should aquire.

Sierra 50th Anniversary, 4th Edition Rifle Manual, edited by Ken Ramage, Sierra Bullets, Santa Fe Springs, CA, 1997. 800 pp., illus. $26.99

New cartridge introductions, etc.

Sierra 50th Anniversary, 4th Edition Handgun Manual, edited by Ken Ramage, Sierra Bullets, Santa Fe, CA, 1997. 700 pp., illus. $21.99

Histories, reloading recommendations, bullets, powders and sections on the reloading process, etc.

THE ARMS LIBRARY

Sixgun Cartridges and Loads, by Elmer Keith, The Gun Room Press, Highland Park, NJ, 1986. 151 pp., illus. $24.95

A manual covering the selection, uses and loading of the most suitable and popular revolver cartridges. Originally published in 1936. Reprint.

Speer Reloading Manual No. 13, edited by members of the Speer research staff, Omark Industries, Lewiston, ID, 1999. 621 pp., illustrated. $24.95

With thirteen new sections containing the latest technical information and reloading trends for both novice and expert in this latest edition. More than 9,300 loads are listed, including new propellant powders from Accurate Arms, Alliant, Hodgdon and Vihtavuori.

Street Stoppers, The Latest Handgun Stopping Power Street Results, by Marshall & Lanow. Boulder, CO, Paladin Press, 1996. 374 pages, illus. Softcover. $42.95

Street Stoppers is the long-awaited sequel to Handgun Stopping Power. It provides the latest results of real-life shootings in all of the major handgun calibers, plus more than 25 thought-provoking chapters that are vital to anyone interested in firearms, would ballistics, and combat shooting. This book also covers the street results of the hottest new caliber to hit the shooting world in years, the .40 Smith & Wesson. Updated street results of the latest exotic ammunition including Remington Golden Saber and CCI-Speer Gold Dot, plus the venerable offerings from MagSafe, Glaser, Cor-Bon and others. A fascinating look at the development of Hydra-Shok ammunition is included.

Understanding Ballistics, Revised 2nd Edition by Robert A. Rinker, Mulberry House Publishing Co., Corydon, IN, 2000. 430 pp., illus Paper covers. New, Revised and Expanded. 2nd Edition. $24.95

Explains basic to advanced firearm ballistics in understandable terms.

Why Not Load Your Own?, by Col. T. Whelen, Gun Room Press, Highland Park, NJ 1996, 4th ed., rev. 237 pp., illus. $20.00

A basic reference on handloading, describing each step, materials and equipment. Includes loads for popular cartridges.

Wildcat Cartridges Volumes 1 & 2 Combination, by the editors of Handloaders magazine, Wolfe Publishing Co., Prescott, AZ, 1997. 350 pp., illus. Paper covers. $39.95

A profile of the most popular information on wildcat cartridges that appeared in the Handloader magazine.

COLLECTORS

A Glossary of the Construction, Decoration and Use of Arms and Armor in All Countries and in All Times. By George Cameron Stone., Dover Publishing, New York 1999. Softcover. $39.95

An exhaustive study of arms and armor in all countries through recorded history - from the stone age up to the second world war. With over 4500 Black & White Illustrations. This Dover edition is an unabridged republication of the work originally published in 1934 by the Southworth Press, Portland MA. A new Introduction has been specially prepared for this edition.

Accoutrements of the United States Infantry, Riflemen, and Dragoons 1834-1839. by R.T. Huntington, Historical Arms Series No. 20. Canada: Museum Restoration. 58 pp. illus. Softcover. $8.95

Although the 1841 edition of the U.S. Ordnance Manual provides ample information on the equipment that was in use during the 1840s, it is evident that the patterns of equipment that it describes were not introduced until 1838 or 1839. This guide is intended to fill this gap in our knowledge by providing an overview of what we now know about the accoutrements that were issued to the regular infantryman, rifleman, and dragoon, in the 1830's with excursions into earlier and later years.

Age of the Gunfighter; Men and Weapons on the Frontier 1840-1900, by Joseph G. Rosa, University of Oklahoma Press, Norman, OK, 1999. 192 pp., illustrated. Paper covers. $21.95

Stories of gunfighters and their encounters and detailed descriptions of virtually every firearm used in the old West.

Air Guns, by Eldon G. Wolff, Duckett's Publishing Co., Tempe, AZ, 1997. 204 pp., illus Paper covers. $35.00

Historical reference covering many makers, European and American guns, canes and more.

Allied and Enemy Aircraft: May 1918; Not to be Taken from the Front Lines, Historical Arms Series No. 27. Canada: Museum Restoration. Softcover. $8.95

The basis for this title is a very rare identification manual published by the French government in 1918 that illustrated 60 aircraft with three or more views: French, English American, German, Italian, and Belgian, which might have been seen over the trenches ofFrance. Each is describe in a text translated from the original French. This is probably the most complete collection of illustrations of WW1 aircraft which has survived.

American Beauty; The Prewar Colt National Match Government Model Pistol, by Timothy J. Mullin, Collector Grade Publications, Cobourg, Ontario, Canada. 72 pp., illustrated. $34.95

Includes over 150 serial numbers, and 20 spectacular color photos of factory engraved guns and other authenticated upgrades, including rare "double-carved" ivory grips.

The American Military Saddle, 1776-1945, by R. Stephen Dorsey & Kenneth L. McPheeters, Collector's Library, Eugene, OR, 1999. 400 pp., illustrated. $59.95

The most complete coverage of the subject ever writeen on the American Military Saddle. Nearly 1000 actual photos and official drawings, from the major public and private collections in the U.S. and Great Britain.

American Police Collectibles; Dark Lanterns and Other Curious Devices, by Matthew G. Forte, Turn of the Century Publishers, Upper Montclair, NJ, 1999. 248 pp., illustrated. $24.95

For collectors of police memorabilia (handcuffs, police dark lanterns, mechanical and chain nippers, rattles, billy clubs and nightsticks) and police historians.

Ammunition; Small Arms, Grenades, and Projected Munitions, by Greenhill Publishing. 144 pp., Illustrated. $22.95 The best concise guide to modern ammunition available today. Covers ammo for small arms, grenades, and projected munitions. 144 pp., Illustrated. As NEW – Hardcover.

Antique Guns, the Collector's Guide, 2nd Edition, edited by John Traister, Stoeger Publishing Co., So. Hackensack, NJ, 1994. 320 pp., illus. Paper covers. $19.95

Covers a vast spectrum of pre-1900 firearms: those manufactured by U.S. gunmakers as well as Canadian, French, German, Belgian, Spanish and other foreign firms.

Arming the Glorious Cause; Weapons of the Second War for Independence, by James B. Whisker, Daniel D. Hartzler and Larry W. Tantz, Old Bedford Village Press, Bedford, PA., 1998. 175 pp., illustrated. $45.00

A photographic study of Confederate weapons.

Arms & Accoutrements of the Mounted Police 1873-1973, by Roger F. Phillips and Donald J. Klancher, Museum Restoration Service, Ont., Canada, 1982. 224 pp., illus. $49.50

A definitive history of the revolvers, rifles, machine guns, cannons, ammunition, swords, etc. used by the NWMP, the RNWMP and the RCMP during the first 100 years of the Force.

Arms and Armor In Antiquity and The Middle Ages. By Charles Boutell, Combined Books Inc., PA 1996. 296 pp., w/ b/w illus. Also a descriptive Notice of Modern Weapons. Translated from the French of M.P. Lacombe, and with a preface, notes, and one additional chapter on Arms and Armour in England. $14.95

Arms and Armor in the Art Institute of Chicago. By Waltler J. Karcheski, Bulfinch, New York 1999. 128 pp., 103 color photos, 12 black & white illustrations. $50.00

The George F. Harding Collection of arms and armor is the most visited installation at the Art Institute of Chicago - a testament to the enduring appeal of swords, muskets and the other paraphernalia of medieval and early modern war. Organized both chronologically and by type of weapon, this book captures the best of this astonishing collection in 115 striking photographs - most in color - accompanied by illuminating text. Here are intricately filigreed breastplates and ivory-handled crossbows, samurai katana and Toledo-steel scimitars, elaborately decorated maces and beautifully carved flintlocks - a treat for anyone who has ever been beguiled by arms, armor and the age of chivalry.

Arms and Armor in Colonial America 1526-1783. by Harold Peterson, Dover Publishing, New York, 2000. 350 pages with over 300 illustrations, index, bibliography & appendix. Softcover. $29.95

Over 200 years of firearms, ammunition, equipment & edged weapons.

Arms and Armor: The Cleveland Museum of Art. By Stephen N. Fliegel, Abrams, New York, 1998. 172 color photos, 17 halftones. 181 pages. $49.50

Intense look at the culture of the warrior and hunter, with an intriguing discussion of the decorative arts found on weapons and armor, set against the background of political and social history. Also provides information on the evolution of armor, together with manufacture and decoration, and weapons as technology and art.

Arms and Equipment of the Civil War, by Jack Coggins, Barnes & Noble, Rockleight, N.J., 1999. 160 pp., illustrated. $12.98

This unique encyclopedia provides a new perspective on the war. It provides lively explanations of how ingenious new weapons spelled victory or defeat for both sides. Aided by more than 500 illustrations and on-the-scene comments by Union and Confederate soldiers.

Arms Makers of Colonial America, by James B. Whisker, Selinsgrove, PA:, 1992: Susquehanna University Press. 1st edition. 217 pages, illustrated. $45.00

A comprehensively documented historial survey of the broad spectrum of arms makers in America who were active before 1783.

Arms Makers of Maryland, by Daniel D. Hartzler, George Shumway, York, PA, 1975. 200 pp., illus. $50.00

A thorough study of the gunsmiths of Maryland who worked during the late 18th and early 19th centuries.

Arms Makers of Pennsylvania, by James B. Whisker, Selinsgrove, PA, Susquehanna Univ. Press, 1990. 1st edition. 218 pages, illustrated in black and white and color. $45.00

Concentrates primarily on the cottage industry gunsmiths & gun makers who worked in the Keystone State from it's early years through 1900.

Arms Makers of Western Pennsylvania, by James B. Whisker, Old Bedford Village Press. 1st edition. This deluxe hard bound edition has 176 pages, $45.00

Printed on fine coated paper, with many large photographs, and detailed text describing the period, lives, tools, and artistry of the Arms Makers of Western Pennsylvania.

Arsenal Of Freedom: The Springfield Armory 1890-1948, by Lt. Col. William Brophy, Andrew Mowbray, Inc., Lincoln, RI,1997. 20 pgs. of photos. 400 pages. As new - Softcover. $29.95

A year by year account drawn from offical records. Packed with reports, charts, tables, line drawings, and 20 page photo section.

Artistic Ingredients of the Longrifle, by George Shumway Publisher, 1989 102 pp., with 94 illus. $20.00

After a brief review of Pennsylvania-German folk art and architecture, to establish the artistic enviroment in which the longrifle was made, the author demonstrates that the sophisticated rococo decoration on the many of the finer longrifles is comparable to the best rococo work of Philadelphia cabinet makers and silversmiths.

The Art of Gun Engraving, by Claude Gaier and Pietro Sabatti, Knickerbocker Press, N.Y., 1999. 160 pp., illustrated. $34.95

The richness and detail lavished on early firearms represents a craftmanship nearly vanished. Beginning with crossbows in the 100's, hunting scenes, portraits, or mythological themes are intricately depicted within a few square inches of etched metal. The full-color photos contained herein recaptures this lost art with exquisite detail.

Astra Automatic Pistols, by Leonardo M. Antaris, FIRAC Publishing Co., Sterling, CO, 1989. 248 pp., illus. $55.00

Charts, tables, serial ranges, etc. The definitive work on Astra pistols.

Basic Documents on U.S. Martial Arms, commentary by Col. B. R. Lewis, reissue by Ray Riling, Phila., PA, 1956 and 1960. *Rifle Musket Model 1855.*

The first issue rifle of musket caliber, a muzzle loader equipped with the Maynard Primer, 32 pp. *Rifle Musket Model 1863.* The typical Union muzzle-loader of the Civil War, 26 pp. *Breech-Loading Rifle Musket Model 1866.* The first of our 50-caliber breechloading rifles, 12 pp. *Remington Navy Rifle Model 1870.* A commercial type breech-loader made at Springfield, 16 pp. *Lee Straight Pull Navy Rifle Model 1895.* A magazine cartridge arm of 6mm caliber. 23 pp. *Breech-Loading Arms (five models)* 27 pp. *Ward-Burton Rifle Musket 1871*-16 pp. Each $10.00.

Battle Weapons of the American Revolution, by George C. Neuman, Scurlock Publishing Co., Texarkana, TX, 2001. 400 pp. Illus. Softcovers. $34.95

The most extensive photographic collection of Revolutionary War weapons ever in one volume. More than 1,600 photos of over 500 muskets, rifles, swords, bayonets, knives and other arms used by both sides in America's War for Independence.

The Bedford County Rifle and Its Makers, by George Shumway. 40pp. illustrated, Softcover. $10.00

The authors study of the graceful and distinctive muzzle-loading rifles made in Bedford County, Pennsylvania. Stands as a milestone on the long path to the understanding of America's longrifles.

Behold the Longrifle Again, by James B. Whisker, Old Bedford Village Press, Bedford, PA, 1997. 176 pp., illus. $45.00

Excellent reference work for the collector profusely illustrated with photographs of some of the finest Kentucky rifles showing front and back profiles and overall view.

The Belgian Rattlesnake; The Lewis Automatic Machine Gun, by William M. Easterly, Collector Grade Publications, Cobourg, Ontario, Canada, 1998. 584 pp., illustrated. $79.95

The most complete account ever published on the life and times of Colonel Isaac Newton Lewis and his crowning invention, the Lewis Automatic machine gun.

Beretta Automatic Pistols, by J.B. Wood, Stackpole Books, Harrisburg, PA, 1985. 192 pp., illus. $24.95

Only English-language book devoted to the Beretta line. Includes all important models.

The Big Guns, Civil War Siege, Seacoast, and Naval Cannon, by Edwin Olmstead, Wayne E. Stark, and Spencer C. Tucker, Museum Restoration Service, Bloomfield, Ontario, Canada, 1997. 360 pp., illustrated. $80.00

This book is designed to identify and record the heavy guns available to both sides by the end of the Civil War.

Birmingham Gunmakers, by Douglas Tate, Safari Press, Inc., Huntington Beach, CA, 1997. 300 pp., illus. $50.00

An invaluable work for anybody interested in the fine sporting arms crafted in this famous British gunmakers' city.

Blue Book of Gun Values, 22nd Edition, edited by S.P. Fjestad, Blue Book Publications, Inc. Minneapolis, MN 2001. $34.95

This new 22nd Edition simply contains more firearms values and information than any other single publication. Expanded to over 1,600 pages featuring over 100,000 firearms prices, the new Blue Book of Gun Values also contains over million words of text – no other book is even close! Most of the information contained in this publication is simply not available anywhere else, for any price!

Blue Book of Modern Black Powder Values, by Dennis Adler, Blue Book Publications, Inc. Minneapolis, MN 2000. 200 pp., illustrated. 41 color photos. Softcover. $14.50

This new title contains more up-to-date black powder values and related information than any other single publication. With 120 pages, this new book will keep you up to date on modern black powder models and prices, including most makes & models available this year! .

The Blunderbuss 1500-1900, by James D. Forman, Historical Arms Series No. 32. Canada: Museum Restoration, 1994. An excellent and authoritative booklet giving tons of information on the Blunderbuss, a very neglected subject. 40 pages, illustrated. Softcover. $8.95

Boarders Away I: With Steel-Edged Weapons & Polearms, by William Gilkerson, Andrew Mowbray, Inc. Publishers, Lincoln, RI, 1993. 331 pages. $48.00

Contains the essential 24 page chapter 'War at Sea' which sets the historical and practical context for the arms discussed. Includeds chapters on, Early Naval Weapons, Boarding Axes, Cutlasses, Officers Fighting Swords and Dirks, and weapons at hand of Random Mayhem.

Boarders Away, Volume II: Firearms of the Age of Fighting Sail, by William Gilkerson, Andrew Mowbray, Inc. Publishers, Lincoln, RI, 1993. 331 pp., illus. $65.00

Covers the pistols, muskets, combustibles and small cannon used aboard American and European fighting ships, 1626-1826.

The Book of Colt Firearms, by R. L. Wilson, Blue Book Publications, Inc, Minneapolis, MN, 1993. 616 pp., illus. $158.00

A complete Colt library in a single volume. In over 1,250.000 words, over 1,250 black and white and 67 color photographs, this mammoth work tells the Colt story from 1832 throught the present.

Boothroyd's Revised Directory Of British Gunmakers, by Geoffrey Boothroyd, Long Beach, CA: Safari Press, 2000. Revised edition. 412pp, photos. $39.95

Over a 30 year period Geoffrey Boothroyd has accumulated information on just about every sporting gun maker that ever has existed in the British Isles from 1850 onward. In this magnificent reference work he has placed all the gun makers he has found over the years (over 1000 entries) in an alphabetical listing with as much information as he has been able to unearth. One of the best reference sources on all British makers (including Wales, Scotland and Ireland) in which you can find data on the most obscure as well as the most famous. Contains starting date of the business, addresses, proprietors, what they made and how long they operated with other interesting details for the collector of fine British guns.

Boston's Gun Bible, by Boston T. Party, Ignacio, CO: Javelin Press, August 2000. Expanded Edition.Softcover. $28.00

This mammoth guide for gun owners everywhere is a completely updated and expanded edition (more than 500 new pages!) of Boston T. Party's classic Boston on Guns and Courage. Pulling no punches, Boston gives new advice on which shoulder weapons and handguns to buy and why before exploring such topics as why you should consider not getting a concealed carry permit, what guns and gear will likely be outlawed next, how to spend within your budget, why you should go to a quality defensive shooting academy now, which guns and gadgets are inferior and why, how to stay off illegal government gun registration lists, how to spot an undercover agent trying to entrap law-abiding gun owners and much more.

Breech-Loading Carbines of the United States Civil War Period, by Brig. Gen. John Pitman, Armory Publications, Tacoma, WA, 1987. 94 pp., illus. $29.95

The first in a series of previously unpublished manuscripts originated by the late Brigadier General John Putnam. Exploded drawings showing parts actual size follow each sectioned illustration.

The Breech-Loading Single-Shot Rifle, by Major Ned H. Roberts and Kenneth L. Waters, Wolfe Publishing Co., Prescott, AZ, 1995. 333 pp., illus. $28.50

A comprehensive and complete history of the evolution of the Schutzen and single-shot rifle.

The Bren Gun Saga, by Thomas B. Dugelby, Collector Grade Publications, Cobourg, Ontario, Canada, 1999, revised and expanded edition. 406 pp., illustrated. $65.95

A modern, definitive book on the Bren in this revised expanded edition, which in terms of numbers of pages and illustrations is nearly twice the size of the original.

British Board of Ordnance Small Arms Contractors 1689-1840, by De Witt Bailey, Rhyl, England: W. S. Curtis, 2000. 150 pp. $18.00

Thirty years of research in the Archives of the Ordnance Board in London has identified more than 600 of these suppliers. The names of many can be found marking the regulation firearms of the period. In the study, the contractors are identified both alphabetically and under a combination of their date period together with their specialist trade.

The British Enfield Rifles, Volume 1, The SMLE Mk I and Mk III Rifles, by Charles R. Stratton, North Cape Pub. Tustin, CA, 1997. 150 pp., illus. Paper covers. $16.95

A systematic and thorough examination on a part-by-part basis of the famous British battle rifle that endured for nearly 70 years as the British Army's number one battle rifle.

British Enfield Rifles, Volume 2, No.4 and No.5 Rifles, by Charles R. Stratton, North Cape Publications, Tustin, CA, 1999. 150 pp., illustrated. Paper covers. $16.95

The historical background for the development of both rifles describing each variation and an explanation of all the "marks", "numbers" and codes found on most parts.

British Enfield Rifles, Volume 4, The Pattern 1914 and U. S. Model 1917 Rifles, by Charles R. Stratton, North Cape Publications, Tustin, CA, 2000. Paper covers. $16.95

One of the lease know American and British collectible military rifles is analyzed on a part by part basis. All markings and codes, refurbishment procedures and WW 2 upgrade are included as are the varios sniper rifle versions.

The British Falling Block Breechloading Rifle from 1865, by Jonathan Kirton, Tom Rowe Books, Maynardsville, TN, 2nd edition, 1997. 380 pp., illus. $70.00

Expanded 2nd edition of a comprehensive work on the British falling block rifle.

British Gun Engraving, by Douglas Tate, Safari Press, Inc., Huntington Beach, CA, 1999. 240 pp., illustrated. Limited, signed and numbered edition, in a slipcase. $80.00

A historic and photographic record of the last two centuries.

British Service Rifles and Carbines 1888-1900, by Alan M. Petrillo, Excalibur Publications, Latham, NY, 1994. 72 pp., illus, Paper covers. $11.95

A complete review of the Lee-Metford and Lee-Enfield rifles and carbines.

British Single Shot Rifles, Volume 1, Alexander Henry, by Wal Winfer, Tom Rowe, Maynardsville, TN, 1998, 200 pp., illus. $50.00

Detailed Study of the single shot rifles made by Henry. Illustrated with hundreds of photographs and drawings.

British Single Shot Rifles Volume 2, George Gibbs, by Wal Winfer, Tom Rowe, Maynardsville, TN, 1998. 177 pp., illus. $50.00

Detailed study of the Farquharson as made by Gibbs. Hundreds of photos.

British Single Shot Rifles, Volume 3, Jeffery, by Wal Winfer, Rowe Publications, Rochester, N.Y., 1999. 260 pp., illustrated. $60.00

The Farquharsen as made by Jeffery and his competitors, Holland & Holland, Bland, Westley, Manton, etc. Large section on the development of nitro cartridges including the .600.

British Single Shot Rifles, Vol. 4; Westley Richards, by Wal Winfer, Rowe Publications, Rochester, N.Y., 2000. 265 pages, illustrated, photos. $60.00

In his 4th volume Winfer covers a detailed study of the Westley Richards single shot rifles, including Monkey Tails, Improved Martini, 1872,1873, 1878,1881, 1897 Falling Blocks. He also covers Westley Richards Cartridges, History and Reloading information.

British Small Arms Ammunition, 1864-1938 (Other than .303 inch), by Peter Labbett, Armory Publications, Seattle, WA. 1993, 358 pages, illus. Four-color dust jacket. $79.00

A study of British military rifle, handgun, machine gun, and aiming tube ammunition through 1 inch from 1864 to 1938. Photo-illustrated including the firearms that chambered the cartridges.

The British Soldier's Firearms from Smoothbore to Rifled Arms, 1850-1864, by Dr. C.H. Roads, R&R Books, Livonia, NY, 1994. 332 pp., illus. $49.00

A reprint of the classic text covering the development of British military hand and shoulder firearms in the crucial years between 1850 and 1864.

British Sporting Guns & Rifles, compiled by George Hoyem, Armory Publications, Coeur d'Alene, ID, 1997. 1024 pp., illus. In two volumes. $250.00

Eighteen old sporting firearms trade catalogs and a rare book reproduced with their color covers in a limited, signed and numbered edition.

Browning Dates of Manufacture, compiled by George Madis, Art and Reference House, Brownsboro, TX, 1989. 48 pp. $10.00

Gives the date codes and product codes for all models from 1824 to the present.

Browning Sporting Arms of Distinction 1903-1992, by Matt Eastman, Matt Eastman Publications, Fitzgerald, GA, 1995. 450 pp., illus. $49.95

The most recognized publication on Browning sporting arms; covers all models.

Buffalo Bill's Wild West: An American Legend, by R.L. Wilson and Greg Martine, Random House, N.Y., 1999. 3,167 pp., illustrated. $60.00

Over 225 color plates and 160 black-and-white illustrations, with in-depth text and captions, the colorful arms, posters, photos, costumes, saddles, accoutrement are brought to life.

Bullard Arms, by G. Scott Jamieson, The Boston Mills Press, Ontario, Canada, 1989. 244 pp., illus. $35.00

The story of a mechanical genius whose rifles and cartridges were the equal to any made in America in the 1880s.

Burning Powder, compiled by Major D.B. Wesson, Wolfe Publishing Company, Prescott, AZ, 1992. 110 pp. Soft cover. $10.95

A rare booklet from 1932 for Smith & Wesson collectors.

The Burnside Breech Loading Carbines, by Edward A. Hull, Andrew Mowbray, Inc., Lincoln, RI, 1986. 95 pp., illus. $16.00

No. 1 in the "Man at Arms Monograph Series." A model-by-model historical/technical examination of one of the most widely used cavalry weapons of the American Civil War based upon important and previously unpublished research.

Camouflage Uniforms of European and NATO Armies; 1945 to the Present, by J. F. Borsarello, Atglen, PA: Schiffer Publications. Over 290 color and b/w photographs, 120 pages. Softcover. $29.95

This full-color book covers nearly all of the NATO, and other European armies' camouflaged uniforms, and not only shows and explains the many patterns, but also their efficacy of design. Described and illustrated are the variety of materials tested in over forty different armies, and includes the history of obsolete trial tests from 1945 to the present time. More than two hundred patterns have been manufactured since World War II using various landscapes and seasonal colors for their look. The Vietnam and Gulf Wars, African or South American events, as well as recent Yugoslavian independence wars have been used as experimental terrains to test a variety of patterns. This book provides a superb reference for the historian, reenactor, designer, and modeler.

Camouflage Uniforms of the Waffen-SS A Photographic Reference, by Michael Beaver, Schiffer Publishing, Atglen, PA. Over 1,000 color and b/w photographs and illustrations, 296 pages. $69.95

Finally a book that unveils the shroud of mystery surrounding Waffen-SS camouflage clothing. Illustrated here, both in full color and in contemporary black and white photographs, this unparalleled look at Waffen-SS combat troops and their camouflage clothing will benefit both the historian and collector.

Canadian Gunsmiths from 1608: A Checklist of Tradesmen, by John Belton, Historical Arms Series No. 29. Canada: Museum Restoration, 1992. 40 pp., 17 illustrations. Softcover. $8.95

This Checklist is a greatly expanded version of HAS No. 14, listing the names, occupation, location, and dates of more than 1,500 men and women who worked as gunmakers, gunsmiths, armorers, gun merchants, gun patent holders, and a few other gun related trades. A collection of contemporary gunsmiths' letterhead have been provided to add color and depth to the study.

Cap Guns, by James Dundas, Schiffer Publishing, Atglen, PA, 1996. 160 pp., illus. Paper covers. $29.95

Over 600 full-color photos of cap guns and gun accessories with a current value guide.

Carbines of the Civil War, by John D. McAulay, Pioneer Press, Union City, TN, 1981. 123 pp., illus. Paper covers. $12.95

A guide for the student and collector of the colorful arms used by the Federal cavalry.

Carbines of the U.S. Cavalry 1861-1905, by John D. McAulay, Andrew Mowbray Publishers, Lincoln, RI, 1996. $35.00

Covers the crucial use of carbines from the beginning of the Civil War to the end of the cavalry carbine era in 1905.

Cartridge Carbines of the British Army, by Alan M. Petrillo, Excalibur Publications, Latham, NY, 1998. 72 pp., illustrated. Paper covers. $11.95

Begins with the Snider-Enfield which was the first regulation cartridge carbine introduced in 1866 and ends with the .303 caliber No.5, Mark 1 Enfield.

Cartridge Catalogues, compiled by George Hoyem, Armory Publications, Coeur d'Alene, ID., 1997. 504 pp., illus. $125.00

Fourteen old ammunition makers' and designers' catalogs reproduced with their color covers in a limited, signed and numbered edition. Completely revised edition of the general purpose reference work for which collectors, police, scientists and laymen reach first for answers to cartridge identification questions. Available October, 1996.

Cartridge Reloading Tools of the Past, by R.H. Chamberlain and Tom Quigley, Tom Quigley, Castle Rock, WA, 1998. 167 pp., illustrated. Paper covers. $25.00

A detailed treatment of the extensive Winchester and Ideal lines of handloading tools and bulletmolds plus Remington, Marlin, Ballard, Browning and many others.

Cartridges for Collectors, by Fred Datig, Pioneer Press, Union City, TN, 1999. In three volumes of 176 pp. each. Vol.1 (Centerfire); Vol.2 (Rimfire and Misc.) types; Vol.3 (Additional Rimfire, Centerfire, and Plastic.). All illustrations are shown in full-scale drawings. Volume 1, softcover only, $19.95. Volumes 2 & 3, Hardcover $19.95

Civil War Arms Makers and Their Contracts, edited by Stuart C. Mowbray and Jennifer Heroux, Andrew Mowbray Publishing, Lincoln, RI, 1998. 595 pp $39.50

A facsimile reprint of the Report by the Commissioner of Ordnance and Ordnance Stores, 1862.

Civil War Arms Purchases and Deliveries, edited by Stuart C. Mowbray, Andrew Mowbray Publishing, Lincoln, RI, 1998. 300pp., illus. $39.50

A facsimile reprint of the master list of Civil War weapons purchases and deliveries including Small Arms, Cannon, Ordnance and Projectiles.

Civil War Breech Loading Rifles, by John D. McAulay, Andrew Mowbray, Inc., Lincoln, RI, 1991. 144 pp., illus. Paper covers. $15.00

All the major breech-loading rifles of the Civil War and most, if not all, of the obscure types are detailed, illustrated and set in their historical context.

Civil War Cartridge Boxes of the Union Infantryman, by Paul Johnson, Andrew Mowbray, Inc., Lincoln, RI, 1998. 352 pp., illustrated. $45.00

There were four patterns of infantry cartridge boxes used by Union forces during the Civil War. The author describes the development and subsequent pattern changes to these cartridge boxes.

Civil War Commanders, by Dean Thomas, Thomas Publications, Gettysburg, PA. 1998. 72 pages, illustrated, photos. Paper Covers. $9.95

138 photographs and capsule biographies of Union and Confederate officers. A convenient personalities reference guide.

Civil War Firearms, by Joseph G. Bilby, Combined Books, Conshohocken, PA, 1996. 252 pp., illus. $34.95

A unique work combining background data on each firearm including its battlefield use, and a guide to collecting and firing surviving relics and modern reproductions.

Civil War Guns, by William B. Edwards, Thomas Publications, Gettysburg, PA, 1997. 444 pp., illus. $40.00

The complete story of Federal and Confederate small arms; design, manufacture, identifications, procurement issue, employment, effectiveness, and postwar disposal by the recognized expert.

Civil War Infantryman: In Camp, On the March, And in Battle, by Dean Thomas, Thomas Publications, Gettysburg, PA. 1998. 72 pages, illustrated, Softcovers. $12.95

Uses first-hand accounts to shed some light on the "common soldier" of the Civil War from enlistment to muster-out, including camp, marching, rations, equipment, fighting, and more.

Civil War Pistols, by John D. McAulay, Andrew Mowbray Inc., Lincoln, RI, 1992. 166 pp., illus. $38.50

A survey of the handguns used during the American Civil War.

Civil War Sharps Carbines and Rifles, by Earl J. Coates and John D. McAulay, Thomas Publications, Gettysburg, PA, 1996. 108 pp., illus. Paper covers. $12.95

Traces the history and development of the firearms including short histories of specific serial numbers and the soldiers who received them.

Civil War Small Arms of the U.S. Navy and Marine Corps, by John D. McAulay, Mowbray Publishing, Lincoln, RI, 1999. 186 pp., illustrated. $39.00

The first reliable and comprehensive guide to the firearms and edged weapons of the Civil War Navy and Marine Corps.

The W.F. Cody Buffalo Bill Collector's Guide with Values, by James W. Wojtowicz, Collector Books, Paducah, KY, 1998. 271 pp., illustrated. $24.95

A profusion of colorful collectibles including lithographs, programs, photographs, books, medals, sheet music, guns, etc. and today's values.

Col. Burton's Spiller & Burr Revolver, by Matthew W. Norman, Mercer University Press, Macon, GA, 1997. 152 pp., illus. $22.95

A remarkable archival research project on the arm together with a comprehensive story of the establishment and running of the factory.

Collector's Guide to Colt .45 Service Pistols Models of 1911 and 1911A1, Enlarged and revised edition. Clawson Publications, Fort Wayne, IN, 1998. 130 pp., illustrated. $45.00

From 1911 to the end of production in 1945 with complete military identification including all contractors.

A Collector's Guide to United States Combat Shotguns, by Bruce N. Canfield, Andrew Mowbray Inc., Lincoln, RI, 1992. 184 pp., illus. Paper covers. $24.00
This book provides full coverage of combat shotguns, from the earliest examples right up to the Gulf War and beyond.

A Collector's Guide to Winchester in the Service, by Bruce N. Canfield, Andrew Mowbray, Inc., Lincoln, RI, 1991. 192 pp., illus. Paper covers. $22.00
The firearms produced by Winchester for the national defense. From Hotchkiss to the M14, each firearm is examined and illustrated.

A Collector's Guide to the '03 Springfield, by Bruce N. Canfield, Andrew Mowbray Inc., Lincoln, RI, 1989. 160 pp., illus. Paper covers. $22.00
A comprehensive guide follows the '03 through its unparalleled tenure of service. Covers all of the interesting variations, modifications and accessories of this highly collectible military rifle.

Collector's Illustrated Encyclopedia of the American Revolution, by George C. Neumann and Frank J. Kravic, Rebel Publishing Co., Inc., Texarkana, TX, 1989. 286 pp., illus. $36.95
A showcase of more than 2,300 artifacts made, worn, and used by those who fought in the War for Independence.

Colonial Frontier Guns, by T.M. Hamilton, Pioneer Press, Union City, TN, 1988. 176 pp., illus. Paper covers. $17.50
A complete study of early flint muskets of this country.

Colt: An American Legend, by R.L. Wilson, Artabras, New York, 1997. 406 pages, fully illustrated, most in color. $60.00
A reprint of the commemorative album celebrates 150 years of the guns of Samuel Colt and the manufacturing empire he built, with expert discussion of every model ever produced, the innovations of each model and variants, updated model and serial number charts and magnificent photographic showcases of the weapons.

The Colt Armory, by Ellsworth Grant, Man-at-Arms Bookshelf, Lincoln, RI, 1996. 232 pp., illus. $35.00
A history of Colt's Manufacturing Company.

Colt Blackpowder Reproductions & Replica: A Collector's and Shooter's Guide, by Dennis Miller, Blue Book Publications, Minneapolis, MN, 1999. 288 pp., illustrated. Paper covers. $29.95
The first book on this important subject, and a must for the investor, collector, and shooter.

Colt Heritage, by R.L. Wilson, Simon & Schuster, 1979. 358 pp., illus. $75.00
The official history of Colt firearms 1836 to the present.

Colt Memorabilia Price Guide, by John Ogle, Krause Publications, Iola, WI, 1998. 256 pp., illus. Paper covers. $29.95
The first book ever compiled about the vast array of non-gun merchandise produced by Sam Colt's companies, and other companies using the Colt name.

The Colt Model 1905 Automatic Pistol, by John Potocki, Andrew Mowbray Publishing, Lincoln, RI, 1998. 191 pp., illus. $28.00
Covers all aspects of the Colt Model 1905 Automatic Pistol, from its invention by the legendary John Browning to its numerous production variations.

Colt Peacemaker British Model, by Keith Cochran, Cochran Publishing Co., Rapid City, SD, 1989. 160 pp., illus. $58.00
Covers those revolvers Colt squeezed in while completing a large order of revolvers for the U.S. Cavalry in early 1874, to those magnificent cased target revolvers used in the pistol competitions at Bisley Commons in the 1890s.

Colt Peacemaker Encyclopedia, by Keith Cochran, Keith Cochran, Rapid City, SD, 1986. 434 pp., illus. $65.00
A must book for the Peacemaker collector.

Colt Peacemaker Encyclopedia, Volume 2, by Keith Cochran, Cochran Publishing Co., SD, 1992. 416 pp., illus. $60.00
Included in this volume are extensive notes on engraved, inscribed, historical and noted revolvers, as well as those revolvers used by outlaws, lawmen, movie and television stars.

Colt Percussion Accoutrements 1834-1873, by Robin Rapley, Robin Rapley, Newport Beach, CA, 1994. 432 pp., illus. Paper covers. $39.95
The complete collector's guide to the identification of Colt percussion accoutrements; including Colt conversions and their values.

Colt Pocket Hammerless Pistols, by Dr. John W. Brunner, Phillips Publications, Williamstown, NJ, 1998. 212 pp., illustrated. $59.95
You will never again have to question a .25, .32 or .380 with this well illustrated, definitive reference guide at hand.

Colt Revolvers and the Tower of London, by Joseph G. Rosa, Royal Armouries of the Tower of London, London, England, 1988. 72 pp., illus. Soft covers. $15.00
Details the story of Colt in London through the early cartridge period.

Colt Rifles and Muskets from 1847-1870, by Herbert Houze, Krause Publications, Iola, WI, 1996. 192 pp., illus. $34.95
Discover previously unknown Colt models along with an extensive list of production figures for all models.

Colt's SAA Post War Models, by George Garton, The Gun Room Press, Highland Park, NJ, 1995. 166 pp., illus. $39.95
Complete facts on the post-war Single Action Army revolvers. Information on calibers, production numbers and variations taken from factory records.

Colt Single Action Army Revolvers: The Legend, the Romance and the Rivals, by "Doc" O'Meara, Krause Publications, Iola, WI, 2000. 160 pp., illustrated with 250 photos in b&w and a 16 page color section. $34.95
Production figures, serial numbers by year, and rarities.

Colt Single Action Army Revolvers and Alterations, by C. Kenneth Moore, Mowbray Publishers, Lincoln, RI, 1999. 112 pp., illustrated. $35.00
A comprehensive history of the revolvers that collectors call "Artillery Models." These are the most historical of all S.A.A. Colts, and this new book covers all the details.

Colt Single Action Army Revolvers and the London Agency, by C. Kenneth Moore, Andrew Mowbray Publishers, Lincoln, RI, 1990. 144 pp., illus. $35.00
Drawing on vast documentary sources, this work chronicles the relationship between the London Agency and the Hartford home office.

The Colt U.S. General Officers' Pistols, by Horace Greeley IV, Andrew Mowbray Inc., Lincoln, RI, 1990. 199 pp., illus. $38.00
These unique weapons, issued as a badge of rank to General Officers in the U.S. Army from WWII onward, remain highly personal artifacts of the military leaders who carried them. Includes serial numbers and dates of issue.

Colts from the William M. Locke Collection, by Frank Sellers, Andrew Mowbray Publishers, Lincoln, RI, 1996. 192 pp., illus. $55.00
This important book illustrates all of the famous Locke Colts, with captions by arms authority Frank Sellers.

Colt's Dates of Manufacture 1837-1978, by R.L. Wilson, published by Maurie Albert, Coburg, Australia; N.A. distributor I.D.S.A. Books, Hamilton, OH, 1983. 61 pp. $6.00
An invaluable pocket guide to the dates of manufacture of Colt firearms up to 1978.

Colt's 100th Anniversary Firearms Manual 1836-1936: A Century of Achievement, Wolfe Publishing Co., Prescott, AZ, 1992. 100 pp., illus. Paper covers. $12.95
Originally published by the Colt Patent Firearms Co., this booklet covers the history, manufacturing procedures and the guns of the first 100 years of the genius of Samuel Colt.

Colt's Pocket '49: Its Evolution Including the Baby Dragoon and Wells Fargo, by Robert Jordan and Darrow Watt, privately printed, Loma Mar, CA 2000. 304 pages, with 984 color photos, illus. Beautifully bound in a deep blue leather like case. $125.00
Detailed information on all models and covers engaving, cases, accoutrements, holsters, fakes, and much more. Included is a summary booklet containing information such as serial numbers, production ranges & identifing photos. This book is a masterpiece on its subject.

Complete Guide to all United States Military Medals 1939 to Present, by Colonel Frank C. Foster, Medals of America Press, Fountain Inn, SC, 2000. 121 pp., illustrated, photos. $29.95
Complete criteria for every Army, Navy, Marines, Air Force, Coast Guard, and Merchant Marine awards since 1939. All decorations, service medals, and ribbons shown in full-color and accompanied by dates and campaigns as well as detailed descriptions on proper wear and display.

Complete Guide to the M1 Garand and the M1 Carbine, by Bruce N. Canfield, 2nd printing, Andrew Mowbray Inc., Lincoln, RI, 1999. 296 pp., illus. $39.50
Expanded and updated coverage of both the M1 Garand and the M1 Carbine, with more than twice as much information as the author's previous book on this topic.

The Complete Guide to U.S. Infantry Weapons of the First War, by Bruce Canfield, Andrew Mowbray, Publisher, Lincoln, RI, 2000. 304 pp., illus. $39.95
The definitive study of the U.S. Infantry weapons used in WW1.

The Complete Guide to U.S. Infantry Weapons of World War Two, by Bruce Canfield, Andrew Mowbray, Publisher, Lincoln, RI, 1995. 303 pp., illus. $39.95
A definitive work on the weapons used by the United States Armed Forces in WWII.

A Concise Guide to the Artillery at Gettysburg, by Gregory Coco, Thomas Publications, Gettysburg, PA, 1998. 96 pp., illus. Paper Covers. $10.00
Coco's tenth book on Gettysburg is a beginner's guide to artillery and its use at the battle. It covers the artillery batteries describing the types of cannons, shells, fuses, etc.using interesting narrative and human interest stories.

Cooey Firearms, Made in Canada 1919-1979, by John A. Belton, Museum Restoration, Canada, 1998. 36pp., with 46 illus. Paper Covers. $8.95
More than 6 million rifles and at least 67 models, were made by this small Canadian riflemaker. They have been identified from the first 'Cooey Canuck' through the last variations made by the 'Winchester-Cooey'. Each is desribed and most are illustrated in this first book on The Cooey.

Cowboy Collectibles and Western Memorabilia, by Bob Bell and Edward Vebell, Schiffer Publishing, Atglen, PA, 1992. 160 pp., illus. Paper covers. $29.95
The exciting era of the cowboy and the wild west collectibles including rifles, pistols, gun rigs, etc.

Cowboy Culture: The Last Frontier of American Antiques, by Michael Friedman, Schiffer Publishing, Ltd., West Chester, PA, 1992. 300 pp., illustrated.
Covers the artful aspects of the old west, the antiques and collectibles. Illustrated with clear color plates of over 1,000 items such as spurs, boots, guns, saddles etc.

Cowboy and Gunfighter Collectible, by Bill Mackin, Mountain Press Publishing Co., Missoula, MT, 1995. 178 pp., illus. Paper covers. $25.00
A photographic encyclopedia with price guide and makers' index.

Cowboys and the Trappings of the Old West, by William Manns and Elizabeth Clair Flood, Zon International Publishing Co., Santa Fe, NM, 1997, 1st edition. 224 pp., illustrated. $45.00
A pictorial celebration of the cowboys dress and trappings.

THE ARMS LIBRARY

Cowboy Hero Cap Pistols, by Rudy D'Angelo, Antique Trader Books, Dubuque, IA, 1998. 196 pp., illus. Paper covers. $34.95
Aimed at collectors of cap pistols created and named for famous film and television cowboy heros, this in-depth guide hits all the marks. Current values are given.

Custom Firearms Engraving, by Tom Turpin, Krause Publications, Iola, WI, 1999. 208 pp., illustrated. $49.95
Over 200 four-color photos with more than 75 master engravers profiled. Engravers Directory with addresses in the U.S. and abroad.

The Decorations, Medals, Ribbons, Badges and Insignia of the United States Army; World War 2 to Present, by Col. Frank C. Foster, Medals of America Press, Fountain Inn, SC. 2001. 145 pages, illustrated. $29.95
The most complete guide to United States Army medals, ribbons, rank, insignia nad patches from WWII to the present day. Each medal and insignia shown in full color. Includes listing of respective criteria and campaigns.

The Decorations, Medals, Ribbons, Badges and Insignia of the United States Navy; World War 2 to Present, by James G. Thompson, Medals of America Press, Fountain Inn, SC. 2000. 123 pages, illustrated. $29.95
The most complete guide to United States Army medals, ribbons, rank, insignia nad patches from WWII to the present day. Each medal and insignia shown in full color. Includes listing of respective criteria and campaigns.

The Derringer in America, Volume 1, The Percussion Period, by R.L. Wilson and L.D. Eberhart, Andrew Mowbray Inc., Lincoln, RI, 1985. 271 pp., illus. $48.00
A long awaited book on the American percussion deringer.

The Derringer in America, Volume 2, The Cartridge Period, by L.D. Eberhart and R.L. Wilson, Andrew Mowbray Inc., Publishers, Lincoln, RI, 1993. 284 pp., illus. $65.00
Comprehensive coverage of cartridge deringers organized alphabetically by maker. Includes all types of deringers known by the authors to have been offered to the American market.

The Devil's Paintbrush: Sir Hiram Maxim's Gun, by Dolf Goldsmith, 3rd Edition, expanded and revised, Collector Grade Publications, Toronto, Canada, 2000. 384 pp., illus. $79.95
The classic work on the world's first true automatic machine gun.

Dr. Josephus Requa Civil War Dentist and the Billinghurst-Requa Volley Gun, by John M. Hyson, Jr., & Margaret Requa DeFrancisco, Museum Restoration Service, Bloomfield, Ont., Canada, 1999. 36 pp., illus. Paper covers. $8.95
The story of the inventor of the first practical rapid-fire gun to be used during the American Civil War.

The Duck Stamp Story, by Eric Jay Dolin and Bob Dumaine, Krause Publications, Iola, WI, 2000. 208 pp., illustrated with color throughout. Paper covers. $29.95; Hardbound. $49.95.
Detailed information on the value and rarity of every federal duck stamp. Outstanding art and illustrations.

The Dutch Luger (Parabellum) A Complete History, by Bas J. Martens and Guus de Vries, Ironside International Publishers, Inc., Alexandria, VA, 1995. 268 pp., illus. $49.95.
The history of the Luger in the Netherlands. An extensive description of the Dutch pistol and trials and the different models of the Luger in the Dutch service.

The Eagle on U.S. Firearms, by John W. Jordan, Pioneer Press, Union City, TN, 1992. 140 pp., illus. Paper covers. $17.50.
Stylized eagles have been stamped on government owned or manufactured firearms in the U.S. since the beginning of our country. This book lists and illustrates these various eagles in an informative and refreshing manner.

Encyclopedia of Rifles & Handguns; A Comprehensive Guide to Firearms, edited by Sean Connolly, Chartwell Books, Inc., Edison, NJ., 1996. 160 pp., illustrated. $26.00.
A lavishly illustrated book providing a comprehensive history of military and civilian personal firepower.

Eprouvettes: A Comprehensive Study of Early Devices for the Testing of Gunpowder, by R.T.W. Kempers, Royal Armouries Museum, Leeds, England, 1999. 352 pp., illustrated with 240 black & white and 28 color plates. $125.00.
The first comprehensive study of eprouvettes ever attempted in a single volume.

European Firearms in Swedish Castles, by Kaa Wennberg, Bohuslaningens Boktryckeri AB, Uddevalla, Sweden, 1986. 156 pp., illus. $50.00.
The famous collection of Count Keller, the Ettersburg Castle collection, and others. English text.

European Sporting Cartridges, Part 1, by W.B. Dixon, Armory Publications, Inc., Coeur d'Alene, ID, 1997. 250 pp., illus. $63.00
Photographs and drawings of over 550 centerfire cartridge case types in 1,300 illustrations produced in German and Austria from 1875 to 1995.

European Sporting Cartridges, Part 2, by W.B. Dixon, Armory Publications, Inc., Coeur d'Alene, ID, 2000. 240 pp., illus. $63.00.
An illustrated history of centerfire hunting and target cartridges produced in Czechoslovakia, Switzerland, Norway, Sweden, Finland, Russia, Italy, Denmark, Belguim from 1875 to 1998. Adds 50 specimens to volume 1 (Germany-Austria). Also, illustrates 40 small arms magazine experiments during the late 19th Century, and includes the English-Language export ammunition catalogue of Kovo (Povazske Strojarne), Prague, Czeck. from the, 1930's.

Fifteen Years in the Hawken Lode, by John D. Baird, The Gun Room Press, Highland Park, NJ, 1976. 120 pp., illus. $24.95.
A collection of thoughts and observations gained from many years of intensive study of the guns from the shop of the Hawken brothers.

'51 Colt Navies, by Nathan L. Swayze, The Gun Room Press, Highland Park, NJ, 1993. 243 pp., illus. $59.95.
The Model 1851 Colt Navy, its variations and markings.

Fighting Iron, by Art Gogan, Andrew Mowbray, Inc., Lincoln, R.I., 1999. 176 pp., illustrated. $28.00.
It doesn't matter whether you collect guns, swords, bayonets or accountrement—sooner or later you realize that it all comes down to the metal. If you don't understand the metal you don't understand your collection.

Fine Colts, The Dr. Joseph A. Murphy Collection, by R.L. Wilson, Sheffield Marketing Associates, Inc., Doylestown, PA, 1999. 258 pp., illustrated. Limited edition signed and numbered. $99.00.
This lavish new work covers exquisite, deluxe and rare Colt arms from Paterson and other percussion revolvers to the cartridge period and up through modern times.

Firearms, by Derek Avery, Desert Publications, El Dorado, AR, 1999. 95 pp., illustrated. $9.95.
The firearms included in this book are by necessity only a selection, but nevertheless one that represents the best and most famous weapons seen since the Second World War.

Firearms and Tackle Memorabilia, by John Delph, Schiffer Publishing, Ltd., West Chester, PA, 1991. 124 pp., illus. $39.95.
A collector's guide to signs and posters, calendars, trade cards, boxes, envelopes, and other highly sought after memorabilia. With a value guide.

Firearms of the American West 1803-1865, Volume 1, by Louis A. Garavaglia and Charles Worman, University of Colorado Press, Niwot, CO, 1998. 402 pp., illustrated. $59.95.
Traces the development and uses of firearms on the frontier during this period.

Firearms of the American West 1866-1894, by Louis A. Garavaglia and Charles G. Worman, University of Colorado Press, Niwot, CO, 1998. 416 pp., illus. $59.95.
A monumental work that offers both technical information on all of the important firearms used in the West during this period and a highly entertaining history of how they were used, who used them, and why.

Firearms from Europe, by David Noe, Larry W. Yantz, Dr. James B. Whisker, Rowe Publications, Rochester, N.Y., 1999. 192 pp., illustrated. $45.00.
A history and description of firearms imported during the American Civil War by the United States of America and the Confederate States of America.

Firepower from Abroad, by Wiley Sword, Andrew Mowbray Publishing, Lincoln, R.I., 2000. 120 pp., illustrated. $23.00.
The Confederate Enfield and the LeMat revolver and how they reached the Confederate market.

Flayderman's Guide to Antique American Firearms and Their Values, 7th Edition, edited by Norm Flayderman, DBI books, a division of Krause Publications, Iola, WI, 1998. 656 pp., illus. Paper covers. $32.95.
A completely updated and new edition with more than 3,600 models and variants extensively described with all marks and specifications necessary for quick identification.

The FN-FAL Rifle, et al, by Duncan Long, Paladin Press, Boulder, CO, 1999. 144 pp., illustrated. Paper covers. $18.95.
Detailed descriptions of the basic models produced by Fabrique Nationale and the myriad variants that evolved as a result of the firearms universal acceptance.

The .45-70 Springfield, by Joe Poyer and Craig Riesch, North Cape Publications, Tustin, CA, 1996. 150 pp., illus. Paper covers. $16.95.
A revised and expanded second edition of a best-selling reference work organized by serial number and date of production to aid the collector in identifying popular "Trapdoor" rifles and carbines.

The French 1935 Pistols, by Eugene Medlin and Colin Doane, Eugene Medlin, El Paso, TX, 1995. 172 pp., illus. Paper covers. $25.95.
The development and identification of successive models, fakes and variants, holsters and accessories, and serial numbers by dates of production.

Freund & Bro. Pioneer Gunmakers to the West, by F.J. Pablo Balentine, Graphic Publishers, Newport Beach, CA, 1997. 380 pp., illustrated $69.95.
The story of Frank W. and George Freund, skilled German gunsmiths who plied their trade on the Western American frontier during the final three decades of the nineteenth century.

From the Kingdom of Lilliput: The Miniature Firearms of David Kucer, by K. Corey Keeble and **The Making of Miniatures,** by David Kucer, Museum Restoration Service, Ontario, Canada, 1994. 51 pp., illus. $25.00.
An overview of the subject of miniatures in general combined with an outline by the artist himself on the way he makes a miniature firearm.

Frontier Pistols and Revolvers, by Dominique Venner, Book Sales Inc., Edison, N.J., 1998. 144 pp., illus. $19.95.
Colt, Smith & Wesson, Remington and other early-brand revolvers which tamed the American frontier are shown amid vintage photographs, etchings and paintings to evoke the wild West.

The Fusil de Tulole in New France, 1691-1741, by Russel Bouchard, Museum Restorations Service, Bloomfield, Ontario, Canada, 1997. 36 pp., illus. Paper covers. $8.95
The development of the company and the identification of their arms.

Game Guns & Rifles: Percussion to Hammerless Ejector in Britain, by Richard Akehurst, Trafalgar Square, N. Pomfret, VT, 1993. 192 pp., illus. $39.95.
Long considered a classic this important reprint covers the period of British gunmaking between 1830-1900.

The Gas Trap Garand, by Billy Pyle, Collector Grade Publications, Cobourg, Ontario, Canada, 1999 316 pp., illustrated. $59.95.
The in-depth story of the rarest Garands of them all, the initial 80 Model Shop rifles made under the personal supervision of John Garand himself in 1934 and

1935, and the first 50,000 plus production "gas trap" M1's manufactured at Springfield Armory between August, 1937 and August, 1940.

George Schreyer, Sr. and Jr., Gunmakers of Hanover, Pennsylvania, by George Shumway, George Shumway Publishers, York, PA, 1990. 160pp., illus. $50.00.
This monograph is a detailed photographic study of almost all known surviving long rifles and smoothbore guns made by highly regarded gunsmiths George Schreyer, Sr. and Jr.

The German Assault Rifle 1935-1945, by Peter R. Senich, Paladin Press, Boulder, CO, 1987. 328 pp., illus. $60.00.
A complete review of machine carbines, machine pistols and assault rifles employed by Hitler's Wehrmacht during WWII.

The German K98k Rifle, 1934-1945: The Backbone of the Wehrmacht, by Richard D. Law, Collector Grade Publications, Toronto, Canada, 1993. 336 pp., illus. $69.95.
The most comprehensive study ever published on the 14,000,000 bolt-action K98k rifles produced in Germany between 1934 and 1945.

German Machine Guns, by Daniel D. Musgrave, revised edition, Ironside International Publishers, Inc. Alexandria, VA, 1992. 586 pp., 650 illus. $49.95.
The most definitive book ever written on German machineguns. Covers the introduction and development of machineguns in Germany from 1899 to the rearmament period after WWII.

German Military Rifles and Machine Pistols, 1871-1945, by Hans Dieter Gotz, Schiffer Publishing Co., West Chester, PA, 1990. 245 pp., illus. $35.00.
This book portrays in words and pictures the development of the modern German weapons and their ammunition including the scarcely known experimental types.

The German MP40 Maschinenpistole, by Frank Iannamico, Moose Lake Publishing, Harmony, ME, 1999. 185 pp., illustrated. Paper covers. $19.95.
The history, development and use of this famous gun of World War 2.

German 7.9mm Military Ammunition, by Daniel W. Kent, Daniel W. Kent, Ann Arbor, MI, 1991. 244 pp., illus. $35.00.
The long-awaited revised edition of a classic among books devoted to ammunition.

The Golden Age of Remington, by Robert W.D. Ball, Krause publications, Iola, WI, 1995. 194 pp., illus. $29.95.
For Remington collectors or firearms historians, this book provides a pictorial history of Remington through World War I. Includes value guide.

The Government Models, by William H.D. Goddard, Andrew Mowbray Publishing, Lincoln, RI, 1998. 296 pp., illustrated. $58.50.
The most authoritative source on the development of the Colt model of 1911.

Grasshoppers and Butterflies, by Adrian B. Caruana, Museum Restoration Service, Alexandria, Bay, N.Y., 1999. 32 pp., illustrated. Paper covers. $8.95.
No.39 in the Historical Arms Series. The light 3 pounders of Pattison and Townsend.

The Greener Story, by Graham Greener, Quiller Press, London, England, 2000. 256 pp., illustrated with 32 pages of color photos. $64.50.
W.W. Greener, his family history, inventions, guns, patents, and more.

A Guide to American Trade Catalogs 1744-1900, by Lawrence B. Romaine, Dover Publications, New York, NY. 422 pp., illus. Paper covers. $12.95

A Guide to Ballard Breechloaders, by George J. Layman, Pioneer Press, Union City, TN, 1997. 261 pp., illus. Paper covers. $19.95
Documents the saga of this rifle from the first models made by Ball & Williams of Worchester, to its production by the Marlin Firearms Co, to the cessation of 19th century manufacture in 1891, and finally to the modern reproductions made in the 1990's.

A Guide to the Maynard Breechloader, by George J. Layman, George J. Layman, Ayer, MA, 1993. 125 pp., illus. Paper covers. $11.95.
The first book dedicated entirely to the Maynard family of breech-loading firearms. Coverage of the arms is given from the 1850s through the 1880s.

A Guide to U. S. Army Dress Helmets 1872-1904, by Kasal and Moore, North Cape Publications, 2000. 88 pp., illus. Paper covers. $15.95
This thorough study provides a complete description of the Model 1872 & 1881 dress helmets worn by the U.S. Army. Including all componets from bodies to plates to plumes & shoulder cords and tells how to differentiate the originals from reproductions. Extensively illustrated with photographs, '8 pages in full color' of complete helmets and their components.

Gun Collecting, by Geoffrey Boothroyd, Sportsman's Press, London, 1989. 208 pp., illus. $29.95.
The most comprehensive list of 19th century British gunmakers and gunsmiths ever published.

Gunmakers of London 1350-1850, by Howard L. Blackmore, George Shumway Publisher, York, PA, 1986. 222 pp., illus. $35.00.
A listing of all the known workmen of gun making in the first 500 years, plus a history of the guilds, cutlers, armourers, founders, blacksmiths, etc. 260 gunmarks are illustrated.

Gunmakers of London Supplement 1350-1850, by Howard L. Blackmore, Museum Restoration Service, Alexandria Bay, NY, 1999. 156 pp., illustrated. $60.00.
Begins with an introductory chapter on "foreighn" gunmakers followed by records of all the new information found about previously unidentified armourers, gunmakers and gunsmiths.

The Guns that Won the West: Firearms of the American Frontier, 1865-1898, by John Walter, Stackpole Books, Inc., Mechanicsburg, PA.,1999. 256 pp., illustrated. $34.95.
Here is the story of the wide range of firearms from pistols to rifles used by plainsmen and settlers, gamblers, native Americans and the U.S. Army.

Gunsmiths of Illinois, by Curtis L. Johnson, George Shumway Publishers, York, PA, 1995. 160 pp., illus. $50.00.
Genealogical information is provided for nearly one thousand gunsmiths. Contains hundreds of illustrations of rifles and other guns, of handmade origin, from Illinois.

The Gunsmiths of Manhattan, 1625-1900: A Checklist of Tradesmen, by Michael H. Lewis, Museum Restoration Service, Bloomfield, Ont., Canada, 1991. 40 pp., illus. Paper covers. $8.95.
This listing of more than 700 men in the arms trade in New York City prior to about the end of the 19th century will provide a guide for identification and further research.

The Guns of Dagenham: Lanchester, Patchett, Sterling, by Peter Laidler and David Howroyd, Collector Grade Publications, Inc., Cobourg, Ont., Canada, 1995. 310 pp., illus. $39.95.
An in-depth history of the small arms made by the Sterling Company of Dagenham, Essex, England, from 1940 until Sterling was purchased by British Aerospace in 1989 and closed.

Guns of the Western Indian War, by R. Stephen Dorsey, Collector's Library, Eugene, OR, 1997. 220 pp., illus. Paper covers. $30.00.
The full story of the guns and ammunition that made western history in the turbulent period of 1865-1890.

Gun Powder Cans & Kegs, by Ted & David Bacyk and Tom Rowe, Rowe Publications, Rochester, NY, 1999. 150 pp., illus. $65.00.
The first book devoted to powder tins and kegs. All cans and kegs in full color. With a price guide and rarity scale.

The Guns of Remington: Historic Firearms Spanning Two Centuries, compiled by Howard M. Madaus, Biplane Productions, Publisher, in cooperation with Buffalo Bill Historical Center, Cody, WY, 1998. 352 pp., illustrated with over 800 color photos. $79.95.
A complete catalog of the firearms in the exhibition, "It Never Failed Me: The Arms & Art of Remington Arms Company" at the Buffalo Bill Historical Center, Cody, Wyoming.

Gun Tools, Their History and Identification by James B. Shaffer, Lee A. Rutledge and R. Stephen Dorsey, Collector's Library, Eugene, OR, 1992. 375 pp., illus. $30.00.
Written history of foreign and domestic gun tools from the flintlock period to WWII.

Gun Tools, Their History and Identifications, Volume 2, by Stephen Dorsey and James B. Shaffer, Collectors' Library, Eugene, OR, 1997. 396 pp., illus. Paper covers. $30.00.
Gun tools from the Royal Armouries Museum in England, Pattern Room, Royal Ordnance Reference Collection in Nottingham and from major private collections.

Gunsmiths of the Carolinas 1660-1870, by Daniel D. Hartzler and James B. Whisker, Old Bedford Village Press, Bedford, PA, 1998. 176 pp., illustrated. $40.00.
This deluxe hard bound edition of 176 pages is printed on fine coated paper, with about 90 pages of large photographs of fine longrifles from the Carolinas, and about 90 pages of detailed research on the gunsmiths who created the highly prized and highly collectable longrifles. Dedicated to serious students of original Kentucky rifles, who may seldom encounter fine longrifles from the Carolinas.

Gunsmiths of Maryland, by Daniel D. Hartzler and James B. Whisker, Old Bedford Village Press, Bedford, PA, 1998. 208 pp., illustrated. $45.00.
Covers firelock Colonial period through the breech-loading patent models. Featuring longrifles.

Gunsmiths of Virginia, by Daniel D. Hartzler and James B. Whisker, Old Bedford Village Press, Bedford, PA, 1992. 206 pp., illustrated. $45.00.
A photographic study of American longrifles.

Gunsmiths of West Virginia, by Daniel D. Hartzler and James B. Whisker, Old Bedford Village Press, Bedford, PA, 1998. 176 pp., illustrated. $40.00.
A photographic study of American longrifles.

Gunsmiths of York County, Pennsylvania, by Daniel D. Hartzler and James B. Whisker, Old Bedford Village Press, Bedford, PA, 1998. 160 pp., illustrated. $40.00.
160 pages of photographs and research notes on the longrifles and gunsmiths of York County, Pennsylvania. Many longrifle collectors and gun builders have noticed that York County style rifles tend to be more formal in artistic decoration than some other schools of style. Patriotic themes, and folk art were popular design elements.

Hall's Military Breechloaders, by Peter A. Schmidt, Andrew Mowbray Publishers, Lincoln, RI, 1996. 232 pp., illus. $55.00.
The whole story behind these bold and innovative firearms.

The Handgun, by Geoffrey Boothroyd, David and Charles, North Pomfret, VT, 1989. 566 pp., illus. $60.00.
Every chapter deals with an important period in handgun history from the 14th century to the present.

Handgun of Military Rifle Marks 1866-1950, by Richard A. Hoffman and Noel P. Schott, Mapleleaf Militaria Publishing, St. Louis, MO, 1999, second edition. 60 pp., illustrated. Paper covers. $20.00.
An illustrated guide to identifying military rifle and marks.

Handguns & Rifles: The Finest Weapons from Around the World, by Ian Hogg, Random House Value Publishing, Inc., N.Y., 1999. 128 pp., illustrated. $18.98.
The serious gun collector will welcome this fully illustrated examination of international handguns and rifles. Each entry covers the history of the weapon, what purpose it serves, and its advantages and disadvantages.

THE ARMS LIBRARY

The Hawken Rifle: Its Place in History, by Charles E. Hanson, Jr., The Fur Press, Chadron, NE, 1979. 104 pp., illus. Paper covers. $15.00.
A definitive work on this famous rifle.

Hawken Rifles, The Mountain Man's Choice, by John D. Baird, The Gun Room Press, Highland Park, NJ, 1976. 95 pp., illus. $29.95.
Covers the rifles developed for the Western fur trade. Numerous specimens are described and shown in photographs.

High Standard: A Collector's Guide to the Hamden & Hartford Target Pistols, by Tom Dance, Andrew Mowbray, Inc., Lincoln, RI, 1991. 192 pp., illus. Paper covers. $24.00.
From Citation to Supermatic, all of the production models and specials made from 1951 to 1984 are covered according to model number or series.

Historic Pistols: The American Martial Flintlock 1760-1845, by Samuel E. Smith & Edwin W. Bitter, The Gun Room Press, Highland Park, NJ, 1986. 353 pp., illus. $45.00.
Covers over 70 makers and 163 models of American martial arms.

Historical Hartford Hardware, by William W. Dalrymple, Colt Collector Press, Rapid City, SD, 1976. 42 pp., illus. Paper covers. $10.00.
Historically associated Colt revolvers.

The History and Development of Small Arms Ammunition, Volume 2, by George A. Hoyem, Armory Publications, Oceanside, CA, 1991. 303 pp., illus. $65.00.
Covers the blackpowder military centerfire rifle, carbine, machine gun and volley gun ammunition used in 28 nations and dominions, together with the firearms that chambered them.

The History and Development of Small Arms Ammunition, Volume 4, by George A. Hoyem, Armory Publications, Seattle, WA, 1998. 200 pp., illustrated $65.00.
A comprehensive book on American black powder and early smokeless rifle cartridges.

The History of Colt Firearms, by Dean Boorman, Lyons Press, New York, NY, 2001. 144 pp., illus. $29.95.
Discover the fascinating story of the world's most famous revolver, complete with more than 150 stunning full-color photographs.

History of Modern U.S. Military Small Arms Ammunition. Volume 1, 1880-1939, revised by F.W. Hackley, W.H. Woodin and E.L. Scranton, Thomas Publications, Gettysburg, PA, 1998. 328 pp., illus. $49.95.
This revised edition incorporates all publicly available information concerning military small arms ammunition for the period 1880 through 1939 in a single volume.

History of Modern U.S. Military Small Arms Ammunition. Volume 2, 1940-1945 by F.W. Hackley, W.H. Woodin and E.L. Scranton. Gun Room Press, Highland Park, NJ. 300 + pages, illustrated. $39.95
Based on decades of original research conducted at the National Archives, numerous military, public and private museums and libraries, as well as individual collections, this edition incorporates all publicly available information concerning military small arms ammunition for the period 1940 through 1945.

The History of Winchester Rifles, by Dean Boorman, Lyons Press, New York, NY, 2001. 144 pp., illus. $29.95.
A captivating and wonderfully photographed history of one of the most legendary names in gun lore. 150 full-color photos.

The History of Winchester Firearms 1866-1992, sixth edition, updated, expanded, and revised by Thomas Henshaw, New Win Publishing, Clinton, NJ, 1993. 280 pp., illus. $27.95.
This classic is the standard reference for all collectors and others seeking the facts about any Winchester firearm, old or new.

History of Winchester Repeating Arms Company, by Herbert G. Houze, Krause Publications, Iola, WI, 1994. 800 pp., illus. $50.00.
The complete Winchester history from 1856-1981.

Honour Bound: The Chauchat Machine Rifle, by Gerard Demaison and Yves Buffetaut, Collector Grade Publications, Inc., Cobourg, Ont., Canada, 1995. $39.95.
The story of the CSRG (Chauchat) machine rifle, the most manufactured automatic weapon of World War One.

Hopkins & Allen Revolvers & Pistols, by Charles E. Carder, Avil Onze Publishing, Delphos, OH, 1998, illustrated. Paper covers. $24.95.
Covers over 165 photos, graphics and patent drawings.

How to Buy and Sell Used Guns, by John Traister, Stoeger Publishing Co., So. Hackensack, NJ, 1984. 192 pp., illus. Paper covers. $10.95.
A new guide to buying and selling guns.

Hunting Weapons From the Middle Ages to the Twentieth Century, by Howard L. Blackmore, Dover Publications, Meneola, NY, 2000. 480 pp., illustrated. Paper covers. $16.95.
Dealing mainly with the different classes of weapons used in sport—swords, spears, crossbows, guns, and rifles—from the Middle Ages until the present day.

Identification Manual on the .303 British Service Cartridge, No. 1-Ball Ammunition, by B.A. Temple, I.D.S.A. Books, Piqua, OH, 1986. 84 pp., illus. $12.50

Identification Manual on the .303 British Service Cartridge, No. 2-Blank Ammunition, by B.A. Temple, I.D.S.A. Books, Piqua, OH, 1986. 95 pp., 59 illus. $12.50

Identification Manual on the .303 British Service Cartridge, No. 3-Special Purpose Ammunition, by B.A. Temple, I.D.S.A. Books, Piqua, OH, 1987. 82 pp., 49 illus. $12.50

Identification Manual on the .303 British Service Cartridge, No. 4-Dummy Cartridges Henry 1869-c.1900, by B.A. Temple, I.D.S.A. Books, Piqua, OH, 1988. 84 pp., 70 illus. $12.50

Identification Manual on the .303 British Service Cartridge, No. 5-Dummy Cartridges (2), by B.A. Temple, I.D.S.A. Books, Piqua, OH, 1994. 78 pp. $12.50

The Illustrated Book of Guns, by David Miller, Salamander Books, N.Y., N.Y., 2000. 304 pp., illustrated in color. $34.95.
An illustrated directory of over 1,000 military and sporting firearms.

The Illustrated Encyclopedia of Civil War Collectibles, by Chuck Lawliss, Henry Holt and Co., New York, NY, 1997. 316 pp., illus. Paper covers. $22.95.
A comprehensive guide to Union and Confederate arms, equipment, uniforms, and other memorabilia.

Illustrations of United States Military Arms 1776-1903 and Their Inspector's Marks, compiled by Turner Kirkland, Pioneer Press, Union City, TN, 1988. 37 pp., illus. Paper covers. $7.00.
Reprinted from the 1949 Bannerman catalog. Valuable information for both the advanced and beginning collector.

Indian War Cartridge Pouches, Boxes and Carbine Boots, by R. Stephen Dorsey, Collector's Library, Eugene, OR, 1993. 156 pp., illus. Paper Covers. $20.00.
The key reference work to the cartridge pouches, boxes, carbine sockets and boots of the Indian War period 1865-1890.

An Introduction to the Civil War Small Arms, by Earl J. Coates and Dean S. Thomas, Thomas Publishing Co., Gettysburg, PA, 1990. 96 pp., illus. Paper covers. $10.00.
The small arms carried by the individual soldier during the Civil War.

Japanese Rifles of World War Two, by Duncan O. McCollum, Excalibur Publications, Latham, NY, 1996. 64 pp., illus. Paper covers. $18.95.
A sweeping view of the rifles and carbines that made up Japan's arsenal during the conflict.

Kalashnikov Arms, compiled by Alexei Nedelin, Design Military Parade, Ltd., Moscow, Russia, 1997. 240 pp., illus. $49.95.
Weapons versions stored in the St. Petersburg Military Historical Museum of Artillery, Engineer Troops and Communications and in the Izhmash JSC.

Kalashnikov "Machine Pistols, Assault Rifles, and Machine Guns, 1945 to the Present", by John Walter, Paladin Press, Boulder, CO, 1999, hardcover, photos, illus., 146 pp. $22.95
This exhaustive work published by Greenhill Military Manuals features a gun-by-gun directory of Kalashnikov variants. Technical specifications and illustrations are provided throughout, along with details of sights, bayonets, markings and ammunition. A must for the serious collector and historian.

The Kentucky Pistol, by Roy Chandler and James Whisker, Old Bedford Village Press, Bedford, PA, 1997. 225 pp., illus. $60.00.
A photographic study of Kentucky pistols from famous collections.

The Kentucky Rifle, by Captain John G.W. Dillin, George Shumway Publisher, York, PA, 1993. 221 pp., illus. $50.00.
This well-known book was the first attempt to tell the story of the American longrifle. This edition retains the original text and illustrations with supplemental footnotes provided by Dr. George Shumway.

Know Your Broomhandle Mausers, by R.J. Berger, Blacksmith Corp., Southport, CT, 1985. 96 pp., illus. Paper covers. $12.95.
An interesting story on the big Mauser pistol and its variations.

Krag Rifles, by William S. Brophy, The Gun Room Press, Highland Park, NJ, 1980. 200 pp., illus. $35.00.
The first comprehensive work detailing the evolution and various models, both military and civilian.

The Krieghoff Parabellum, by Randall Gibson, Midland, TX, 1988. 279 pp., illus. $40.00.
A comprehensive text pertaining to the Lugers manufactured by H. Krieghoff Waffenfabrik.

Las Pistolas Espanolas Tipo "Mauser," by Artemio Mortera Perez, Quiron Ediciones, Valladolid, Spain, 1998. 71 pp., illustrated. Paper covers. $34.95.
This book covers in detail Spanish machine pistols and C96 copies made in Spain. Covers all Astra "Mauser" pistol series and the complete line of Beistegui C96 type pistols. Spanish text.

Law Enforcement Memorabilia Price and Identification Guide, by Monty McCord, DBI Books a division of Krause Publications, Inc. Iola, WI, 1999. 208 pp., illustrated. Paper covers. $19.95.
An invaluable reference to the growing wave of law enforcement collectors. Hundreds of items are covered from miniature vehicles to clothes, patches, and restraints.

Legendary Sporting Guns, by Eric Joly, Abbeville Press, New York, N.Y., 1999. 228 pp., illustrated. $65.00.
A survey of hunting through the ages and relates how many different types of firearms were created and refined for use afield.

Legends and Reality of the AK, by Val Shilin and Charlie Cutshaw, Paladen Press, Boulder, CO, 2000. 192 pp., illustrated. Paper covers. $35.00.
A behind-the-scenes look at history, design and impact of the Kalashnikov family of weapons.

LeMat, the Man, the Gun, by Valmore J. Forgett and Alain F. and Marie-Antoinette Serpette, Navy Arms Co., Ridgefield, NJ, 1996. 218 pp., illus. $49.95.
The first definitive study of the Confederate revolvers invention, development and delivery by Francois Alexandre LeMat.

Les Pistolets Automatiques Francaise 1890-1990, by Jean Huon, Combined Books, Inc., Conshohocken, PA, 1997. 160 pp., illus. French text. $34.95
French automatic pistols from the earliest experiments through the World Wars and Indo-China to modern security forces.

Levine's Guide to Knives And Their Values, 4th Edition, by Bernard Levine, DBI Books, a division of Krause Publications, Iola, WI, 1997. 512 pp., illus. Paper covers. $27.95
All the basic tools for identifying, valuing and collecting folding and fixed blade knives.

REFERENCE

The Light 6-Pounder Battalion Gun of 1776, by Adrian Caruana, Museum Restoration Service, Bloomfield, Ontario, Canada, 2001. 76 pp., illus. Paper covers. $8.95

The London Gun Trade, 1850-1920, by Joyce E. Gooding, Museum Restoration Service, Bloomfield, Ontario, Canada, 2001. 48 pp., illus. Paper covers. $8.95
Names, dates and locations of London gunmakers working between 1850 and 1920 are listed. Compiled from the original Kelly's Post Office Directories of the City of London.

The London Gunmakers and the English Duelling Pistol, 1770-1830, by Keith R. Dill, Museum Restoration Service, Bloomfield, Ontario, Canada, 1997. 36 pp., illus. Paper covers. $8.95
Ten gunmakers made London one of the major gunmaking centers of the world. This book examines how the design and construction of their pistols contributed to that reputation and how these characteristics may be used to date flintlock arms.

Longrifles of North Carolina, by John Bivens, George Shumway Publisher, York, PA, 1988. 256 pp., illus. $50.00.
Covers art and evolution of the rifle, immigration and trade movements. Committee of Safety gunsmiths, characteristics of the North Carolina rifle.

Longrifles of Pennsylvania, Volume 1, Jefferson, Clarion & Elk Counties, by Russel H. Harringer, George Shumway Publisher, York, PA, 1984. 200 pp., illus. $50.00.
First in series that will treat in great detail the longrifles and gunsmiths of Pennsylvania.

The Luger Handbook, by Aarron Davis, Krause Publications, Iola, WI, 1997. 112 pp., illus. Paper covers. $9.95.
Quick reference to classify Luger models and variations with complete details including proofmarks.

Lugers at Random, by Charles Kenyon, Jr., Handgun Press, Glenview, IL, 1990. 420 pp., illus. $59.95.
A new printing of this classic, comprehensive reference for all Luger collectors.

The Luger Story, by John Walter, Stackpole Books, Mechanicsburg, PA, 2001. 256 pp., illus. Paper Covers $29.95.
The standard history of the world's most famous handgun.

M1 Carbine, by Larry Ruth, Gun room Press, Highland Park, NJ, 1987. 291 pp., illus. Paper $19.95.
The origin, development, manufacture and use of this famous carbine of World War II.

The M1 Carbine: Owner's Guide, by Scott A. Duff, Scott A. Duff, Export, PA, 1997. 126 pp., illus. Paper covers. $19.95.
This book answers the questions M1 owners most often ask concerning maintenance activities not encounted by military users.

The M1 Garand: Owner's Guide, by Scott A. Duff, Scott A. Duff, Export, PA, 1998. 132 pp., illus. Paper covers. $19.95.
This book answers the questions M1 owners most often ask concerning maintenance activities not encounted by military users.

The M1 Garand Serial Numbers and Data Sheets, by Scott A. Duff, Export, PA, 1995. 101 pp., illus. Paper covers. $11.95.
Provides the reader with serial numbers related to dates of manufacture and a large sampling of data sheets to aid in identification or restoration.

The M1 Garand 1936 to 1957, by Joe Poyer and Craig Riesch, North Cape Publications, Tustin, CA, 1996. 216 pp., illus. Paper covers. $19.95.
Describes the entire range of M1 Garand production in text and quick-scan charts.

The M1 Garand: Post World War, by Scott A. Duff, Scott A. Duff, Export, PA, 1990. 139 pp., illus. Soft covers. $19.95.
A detailed account of the activities at Springfield Armory through this period. International Harvester, H&R, Korean War production and quantities delivered. Serial numbers.

The M1 Garand: World War 2, by Scott A. Duff, Scott A. Duff, Export, PA, 1993. 210 pp., illus. $39.95.
The most comprehensive study available to the collector and historian on the M1 Garand of World War II.

Maine Made Guns and Their Makers, by Dwight B. Demeritt Jr., Maine State Museum, Augusta, ME, 1998. 209 pp., illustrated. $55.00.
An authoritative, biographical study of Maine gunsmiths.

Marlin Firearms: A History of the Guns and the Company That Made Them, by Lt. Col. William S. Brophy, USAR, Ret., Stackpole Books, Harrisburg, PA, 1989. 672 pp., illus. $75.00.
The definitive book on the Marlin Firearms Co. and their products.

Martini-Henry .450 Rifles & Carbines, by Dennis Lewis, Excalibur Publications, Latham, NY, 1996. 72 pp., illus. Paper covers. $11.95.
The stories of the rifles and carbines that were the mainstay of the British soldier through the Victorian wars.

Mauser Bolt Rifles, by Ludwig Olson, F. Brownell & Son, Inc., Montezuma, IA, 1999. 364 pp., illus. $59.95.
The most complete, detailed, authoritative and comprehensive work ever done on Mauser bolt rifles. Completely revised deluxe 3rd edition.

Mauser Military Rifles of the World, 2nd Edition, by Robert Ball, Krause Publications, Iola, WI, 2000. 304 pp., illustrated with 1,000 b&w photos and a 48 page color section. $44.95.
This 2nd edition brings more than 100 new photos of these historic rifles and the wars in which they were carried.

Mauser Smallbores Sporting, Target and Training Rifles, by Jon Speed, Collector Grade Publications, Cobourg, Ontario, Canada 1998. 349 pp., illustrated. $67.50.
A history of all the smallbore sporting, target and training rifles produced by the legendary Mauser-Werke of Obendorf Am Neckar.

Military Holsters of World War 2, by Eugene J. Bender, Rowe Publications, Rochester, NY, 1998. 200 pp., illustrated. $45.00.
A revised edition with a new price guide of the most definitive book on this subject.

Military Pistols of Japan, by Fred L. Honeycutt, Jr., Julin Books, Palm Beach Gardens, FL, 1997. 168 pp., illus. $42.00.
Covers every aspect of military pistol production in Japan through WWII.

The Military Remington Rolling Block Rifle, by George Layman, Pioneer Press, TN, 1998. 146 pp., illus. Paper covers. $24.95.
A standard reference for those with an interest in the Remington rolling block family of firearms.

Military Rifles of Japan, 5th Edition, by F.L. Honeycutt, Julin Books, Lake Park, FL, 1999. 208 pp., illus. $42.00.
A new revised and updated edition. Includes the early Murata-period markings, etc.

Military Small Arms Data Book, by Ian V. Hogg, Stackpole Books, Mechanicsburg, PA, 1999. $44.95. 336 pp., illustrated.
Data on more than 1,500 weapons. Covers a vast range of weapons from pistols to anti-tank rifles. Essential data, 1870-2000, in one volume.

Modern Beretta Firearms, by Gene Gangarosa, Jr., Stoeger Publishing Co., So. Hackensack, NJ, 1994. 288 pp., illus. Paper covers. $16.95.
Traces all models of modern Beretta pistols, rifles, machine guns and combat shotguns.

Modern Gun Values, The Gun Digest Book of, 10th Edition, by the Editors of Gun Digest, DBI Books, a division of Krause Publications, Iola, WI., 1996. 560 pp. illus. Paper covers. $21.95.
Greatly updated and expanded edition describing and valuing over 7,000 firearms manufactured from 1900 to 1996. The standard for valuing modern firearms.

Modern Gun Identification & Value Guide, 13th Edition, by Russell and Steve Quertermous, Collector Books, Paducah, KY, 1998. 504 pp., illus. Paper covers. $14.95.
Features current values for over 2,500 models of rifles, shotguns and handguns, with over 1,800 illustrations.

More Single Shot Rifles, by James C. Grant, The Gun Room Press, Highland Park, NJ, 1976. 324 pp., illus. $35.00.
Details the guns made by Frank Wesson, Milt Farrow, Holden, Borchardt, Stevens, Remington, Winchester, Ballard and Peabody-Martini.

Mortimer, the Gunmakers, 1753-1923, by H. Lee Munson, Andrew Mowbray Inc., Lincoln, RI, 1992. 320 pp., illus. $65.00.
Seen through a single, dominant, English gunmaking dynasty this fascinating study provides a window into the classical era of firearms artistry.

The Mosin-Nagant Rifle, by Terence W. Lapin, North Cape Publications, Tustin, CA, 1998. 30 pp., illustrated. Paper covers. $19.95.
The first ever complete book on the Mosin-Nagant rifle written in English. Covers every variation.

The Navy Luger, by Joachim Gortz and John Walter, Handgun Press, Glenview, IL, 1988. 128 pp., illus. $24.95.
The 9mm Pistole 1904 and the Imperial German Navy. A concise illustrated history.

The New World of Russian Small Arms and Ammunition, by Charlie Cutshaw, Paladin Press, Boulder, CO, 1998. 160 pp., illustrated. $42.95.
Detailed descriptions, specifications and first-class illustrations of the AN-94, PSS silent pistol, Bizon SMG, Saifa-12 tactical shotgun, the GP-25 grenade launcher and more cutting edge Russian weapons.

The Number 5 Jungle Carbine, by Alan M. Petrillo, Excalibur Publications, Latham, NY, 1994. 32 pp., illus. Paper covers. $7.95.
A comprehensive treatment of the rifle that collectors have come to call the "Jungle Carbine"—the Lee-Enfield Number 5, Mark 1.

The '03 Era: When Smokeless Revolutionized U.S. Riflery, by Clark S. Campbell, Collector Grade Publications, Inc., Ontario, Canada, 1994. 334 pp., illus. $44.50.
A much-expanded version of Campbell's *The '03 Springfields*, representing forty years of in-depth research into "all things '03.'

Observations on Colt's Second Contract, November 2, 1847, by G. Maxwell Longfield and David T. Basnett, Museum Restoration Service, Bloomfield, Ontario, Canada, 1997. 36 pp., illus. Paper covers. $6.95.
This study traces the history and the construction of the Second Model Colt Dragoon supplied in 1848 to the U.S. Cavalry.

Official Guide to Gunmarks, 3rd Edition, by Robert H. Balderson, House of Collectibles, New York, NY, 1996. 367 pp., illus. Paper covers. $15.00.
Identifies manufacturers' marks that appear on American and foreign pistols, rifles and shotguns.

Official Price Guide to Gun Collecting, by R.L. Wilson, Ballantine/House of Collectibles, New York, NY, 1998. 450 pp., illus. Paper covers. $21.50.
Covers more than 30,000 prices from Colt revolvers to Winchester rifles and shotguns to German Lugers and British sporting rifles and game guns.

Official Price Guide to Military Collectibles, 6th Edition, by Richard J. Austin, Random House, Inc., New York, NY, 1998. 200 pp., illus. Paper cover. $20.00.
Covers weapons and other collectibles from wars of the distant and recent past. More than 4,000 prices are listed. Illustrated with 400 black & white photos plus a full-color insert.

The Official Soviet SVD Manual, by Major James F. Gebhardt (Ret.) Paladin Press, Boulder, CO, 1999. 112 pp., illustrated. Paper covers. $15.00.

Operating instructions for the 7.62mm Dragunov, the first Russian rifle developed from scratch specifically for sniping.

Old Gunsights: A Collector's Guide, 1850 to 2000, by Nicholas Stroebel, Krause Publications, Iola, WI, 1998. 320 pp., illus. Paper covers. $29.95

An in-depth and comprehensive examination of old gunsights and the rifles on which they were used to get accurate feel for prices in this expanding market.

Old Rifle scopes, by Nicholas Stroebel, Krause Publications, Iola, WI, 2000. 400 pp., illustrated. Paper covers. $31.95.

This comprehensive collector's guide takes aim at more than 120 scope makers and 60 mount makers and features photos and current market values for 300 scopes and mounts manufactured from 1950-1985.

The P-08 Parabellum Luger Automatic Pistol, edited by J. David McFarland, Desert Publications, Cornville, AZ, 1982. 20 pp., illus. Paper covers. $11.95.

Covers every facet of the Luger, plus a listing of all known Luger models.

Packing Iron, by Richard C. Rattenbury, Zon International Publishing, Millwood, NY, 1993. 216 pp., illus. $45.00.

The best book yet produced on pistol holsters and rifle scabbards. Over 300 variations of holster and scabbards are illustrated in large, clear plates.

Parabellum: A Technical History of Swiss Lugers, by Vittorio Bobba, Priuli & Verlucca, Editori, Torino, Italy, 1996. Italian and English text. Illustrated. $100.00.

Patents for Inventions, Class 119 (Small Arms), 1855-1930. British Patent Office, Armory Publications, Oceanside, CA, 1993. 7 volume set. $250.00.

Contains 7980 abridged patent descriptions and their sectioned line drawings, plus a 37-page alphabetical index of the patentees.

Pattern Dates for British Ordnance Small Arms, 1718-1783, by DeWitt Bailey, Thomas Publications, Gettysburg, PA, 1997. 116 pp., illus. Paper covers. $20.00.

The weapons discussed in this work are those carried by troops sent to North America between 1737 and 1783, or shipped to them as replacement arms while in America.

The Pitman Notes on U.S. Martial Small Arms and Ammunition, 1776-1933, Volume 2, Revolvers and Automatic Pistols, by Brig. Gen. John Pitman, Thomas Publications, Gettysburg, PA, 1990. 192 pp., illus. $29.95.

A most important primary source of information on United States military small arms and ammunition.

The Plains Rifle, by Charles Hanson, Gun Room Press, Highland Park, NJ, 1989. 169 pp., illus. $35.00.

All rifles that were made with the plainsman in mind, including pistols.

Powder and Ball Small Arms, by Martin Pegler, Windrow & Green, London, 1998. 128 pp., illus. $39.95.

Part of the new "Live Firing Classic Weapons" series featuring full color photos of experienced shooters dressed in authentic costumes handling, loading and firing historic weapons.

The Powder Flask Book, by Ray Riling, R&R Books, Livonia, NY, 1993. 514 pp., illus. $69.95.

The complete book on flasks of the 19th century. Exactly scaled pictures of 1,600 flasks are illustrated.

Proud Promise: French Autoloading Rifles, 1898-1979, by Jean Huon, Collector Grade Publications, Inc., Cobourg, Ont., Canada, 1995. 216 pp., illus. $39.95.

The author has finally set the record straight about the importance of French contributions to modern arms design.

E. C. Prudhomme's Gun Engraving Review, by E. C. Prudhomme, R&R Books, Livonia, NY, 1994. 164 pp., illus. $60.00.

As a source for engravers and collectors, this book is an indispensable guide to styles and techniques of the world's foremost engravers.

Purdey Gun and Rifle Makers: The Definitive History, by Donald Dallas, Quiller Press, London, 2000. 245 pp., illus. Color throughout. $100.00

A limited edition of 3,000 copies. Signed and Numbered. With a PURDEY book plate.

Reloading Tools, Sights and Telescopes for Single Shot Rifles, by Gerald O. Kelver, Brighton, CO, 1982. 163 pp., illus. Paper covers. $13.95.

A listing of most of the famous makers of reloading tools, sights and telescopes with a brief description of the products they manufactured.

The Remington-Lee Rifle, by Eugene F. Myszkowski, Excalibur Publications, Latham, NY, 1995. 100 pp., illus. Paper covers. $22.50.

Features detailed descriptions, including serial number ranges, of each model from the first Lee Magazine Rifle produced for the U.S. Navy to the last Remington-Lee Small Bores shipped to the Cuban Rural Guard.

Revolvers of the British Services 1854-1954, by W.H.J. Chamberlain and A.W.F. Taylerson, Museum Restoration Service, Ottawa, Canada, 1989. 80 pp., illus. $27.50.

Covers the types issued among many of the United Kingdom's naval, land or air services.

Rhode Island Arms Makers & Gunsmiths, by William O. Archibald, Andrew Mowbray, Inc., Lincoln, RI, 1990. 108 pp., illus. $16.50.

A serious and informative study of an important area of American arms making.

Rifles of the World, by Oliver Achard, Chartwell Books, Inc., Edison, NJ, 141 pp., illus. $24.95.

A unique insight into the world of long guns, not just rifles, but also shotguns, carbines and all the usual multi-barreled guns that once were so popular with European hunters, especially in Germany and Austria.

The Rock Island '03, by C.S. Ferris, C.S. Ferris, Arvada, CO, 1993. 58 pp., illus. Paper covers. $12.50.

A monograph of interest to the collector or historian concentrating on the U.S. M1903 rifle made by the less publicized of our two producing facilities.

Round Ball to Rimfire, Vol. 1, by Dean Thomas, Thomas Publications, Gettysburg, PA, 1997. 144 pp., illus. $40.00.

The first of a two-volume set of the most complete history and guide for all small arms ammunition used in the Civil War. The information includes data from research and development to the arsenals that created it.

Ruger and his Guns, by R.L. Wilson, Simon & Schuster, New York, NY, 1996. 358 pp., illus. $65.00.

A history of the man, the company and their firearms.

Russell M. Catron and His Pistols, by Warren H. Buxton, Ucross Books, Los Alamos, NM, 1998. 224 pp., illustrated. Paper covers. $49.50.

An unknown American firearms inventor and manufacturer of the mid twentieth century. Military, commerical, ammunition.

The SAFN-49 and The FAL, by Joe Poyer and Dr. Richard Feirman, North Cape Publications, Tustin, CA, 1998. 160 pp., illus. Paper covers. $14.95.

The first complete overview of the SAFN-49 battle rifle, from its pre-World War 2 beginnings to its military service in countries as diverse as the Belgian Congo and Argentina. The FAL was "light" version of the SAFN-49 and it became the Free World's most adopted battle rifle.

Sam Colt's Own Record 1847, by John Parsons, Wolfe Publishing Co., Prescott, AZ, 1992. 167 pp., illus. $24.50.

Chronologically presented, the correspondence published here completes the account of the manufacture, in 1847, of the Walker Model Colt revolver.

J. P. Sauer & Sohn, Sauer "Dein Waffenkamerad" Volume 2, by Cate & Krause, Walsworth Publishing, Chattanooga, TN, 2000. 440 pp., illus. $79.00.

A historical study of Sauer automatic pistols. This new volume includes a great deal of new knowledge that has surfaced about the firm J.P. Sauer. You will find new photos, documentation, serial number ranges and historial facts which will expand the knowledge and interest in the oldest and best of the German firearms companies.

Scottish Firearms, by Claude Blair and Robert Woosnam-Savage, Museum Restoration Service, Bloomfield, Ont., Canada, 1995. 52 pp., illus. Paper covers. $8.95.

This revision of the first book devoted entirely to Scottish firearms is supplemented by a register of surviving Scottish long guns.

The Scottish Pistol, by Martin Kelvin. Fairleigh Dickinson University Press, Dist. By Associated University Presses, Cranbury, NJ, 1997. 256 pp., illus. $49.50.

The Scottish pistol, its history, manufacture and design.

Sharps Firearms, by Frank Seller, Frank M. Seller, Denver, CO, 1998. 358 pp., illus. $55.00.

Traces the development of Sharps firearms with full range of guns made including all martial variations.

Simeon North: First Official Pistol Maker of the United States, by S. North and R. North, The Gun Room Press, Highland Park, NJ, 1972. 207 pp., illus. $15.95.

Reprint of the rare first edition.

The SKS Carbine, by Steve Kehaya and Joe Poyer, North Cape Publications, Tustin, CA, 1997. 150 pp., illus. Paper covers. $16.95.

The first comprehensive examination of a major historical firearm used through the Vietnam conflict to the diamond fields of Angola.

The SKS Type 45 Carbines, by Duncan Long, Desert Publications, El Dorado, AZ, 1992. 110 pp., illus. Paper covers. $19.95

Covers the history and practical aspects of operating, maintaining and modifying this abundantly available rifle.

Smith & Wesson 1857-1945, by Robert J. Neal and Roy G. Jinks, R&R Books, Livonia, NY, 1996. 434 pp., illus. $50.00.

The bible for all existing and aspiring Smith & Wesson collectors.

Sniper Variations of the German K98k Rifle, by Richard D. Law, Collector Grade Publications, Ontario, Canada, 1997. 240 pp., illus. $47.50.

Volume 2 of "Backbone of the Wehrmacht" the author's in-depth study of the German K98k rifle. This volume concentrates on the telescopic-sighted rifle of choice for most German snipers during World War 2.

Southern Derringers of the Mississippi Valley, by Turner Kirkland, Pioneer Press, Tenn., 1971. 80 pp., illus., paper covers. $4.00.

A guide for the collector, and a much-needed study.

Soviet Russian Postwar Military Pistols and Cartridges, by Fred A. Datig, Handgun Press, Glenview, IL, 1988. 152 pp., illus. $29.95.

Thoroughly researched, this definitive sourcebook covers the development and adoption of the Makarov, Stechkin and the new PSM pistols. Also included in this source book is coverage on Russian clandestine weapons and pistol cartridges.

Soviet Russian Tokarev "TT" Pistols and Cartridges 1929-1953, by Fred Datig, Graphic Publishers, Santa Ana, CA, 1993. 168 pp., illus. $39.95.

Details of rare arms and their accessories are shown in hundreds of photos. It also contains a complete bibliography and index.

Soviet Small-Arms and Ammunition, by David Bolotin, Handgun Press, Glenview, IL, 1996. 264 pp., illus. $49.95.

An authoritative and complete book on Soviet small arms.

Sporting Collectibles, by Jim and Vivian Karsnitz, Schiffer Publishing Ltd., West Chester, PA, 1992. 160 pp., illus. Paper covers. $29.95.

The fascinating world of hunting related collectibles presented in an informative text.

The Springfield 1903 Rifles, by Lt. Col. William S. Brophy, USAR, Ret., Stackpole Books Inc., Harrisburg, PA, 1985. 608 pp., illus. $75.00.

The illustrated, documented story of the design, development, and production of all the models, appendages, and accessories.

THE ARMS LIBRARY

Springfield Armory Shoulder Weapons 1795-1968, by Robert W.D. Ball, Antique Trader Books, Dubuque, IA, 1998. 264 pp., illus. $34.95.
This book documents the 255 basic models of rifles, including test and trial rifles, produced by the Springfield Armory. It features the entire history of rifles and carbines manufactured at the Armory, the development of each weapon with specific operating characteristics and procedures.

Springfield Model 1903 Service Rifle Production and Alteration, 1905-1910, by C.S. Ferris and John Beard, Arvada, CO, 1995. 66 pp., illus. Paper covers. $12.50.
A highly recommended work for any serious student of the Springfield Model 1903 rifle.

Springfield Shoulder Arms 1795-1865, by Claud E. Fuller, S. & S. Firearms, Glendale, NY, 1996. 76 pp., illus. Paper covers. $17.95.
Exact reprint of the scarce 1930 edition of one of the most definitive works on Springfield flintlock and percussion muskets ever published.

Standard Catalog of Firearms, 11th Edition, by Ned Schwing, Krause Publications, Iola, WI, 2001.1328 Pages, illustrated. 6,000+ b&w photos plus a 16-page color section. Paper covers. $32.95.
This is the largest, most comprehensive and best-selling firearm book of all time! And this year's edition is a blockbuster for both shooters and firearm collectors. More than 12,000 firearms are listed and priced in up to six grades of condition. That's almost 80,000 prices! Gun enthusiasts will love the new full-color section of photos highlighting the finest firearms sold at auction this past year –including the new record for an American historical firearm: $684,000!

Standard Catalog of Winchester, 1st Edition, edited by David D. Kowalski, Krause Publications, Iola, WI, 2000. 704 pp., illustrated with 2,000 B&W photos and 75 color photos. Paper covers. $39.95.
This book identifies and values more than 5,000 collectibles, including firearms, cartridges shotshells, fishing tackle, sporting goods and tools manufactured by Winchester Repeating Arms Co.

Steel Canvas: The Art of American Arms, by R.L. Wilson, Random House, NY, 1995, 384 pp., illus. $65.00.
Presented here for the first time is the breathtaking panorama of America's extraordinary engravers and embellishers of arms, from the 1700s to modern times.

Stevens Pistols & Pocket Rifles, by K.L. Cope, Museum Restoration Service, Alexandria Bay, NY, 1992. 114 pp., illus. $24.50.
This is the story of the guns and the man who designed them and the company which he founded to make them.

A Study of Colt Conversions and Other Percussion Revolvers, by R. Bruce McDowell, Krause Publications, Iola, WI, 1997. 464 pp., illus. $39.95.
The ultimate reference detailing Colt revolvers that have been converted from percussion to cartridge.

The Sumptuous Flaske, by Herbert G. Houze, Andrew Mowbray, Inc., Lincoln, RI, 1989. 158 pp., illus. Soft covers. $35.00.
Catalog of a recent show at the Buffalo Bill Historical Center bringing together some of the finest European and American powder flasks of the 16th to 19th centuries.

The Swedish Mauser Rifles, by Steve Kehaya and Joe Poyer, North Cape Publications, Tustin, CA, 1999. 267 pp., illustrated. Paper covers. $19.95.
Every known variation of the Swedish Mauser carbine and rifle is described including all match and target rifles and all sniper fersions. Includes serial number and production data.

Televisions Cowboys, Gunfighters & Cap Pistols, by Rudy A. D'Angelo, Antique Trader Books, Norfolk, VA, 1999. 287 pp., illustrated in color and black and white. Paper covers. $31.95.
Over 850 beautifully photographed color and black and white images of cap guns, actors, and the characters they portrayed in the "Golden Age of TV Westerns." With accurate descriptions and current values.

Thompson: The American Legend, by Tracie L. Hill, Collector Grade Publications, Ontario, Canada, 1996. 584 pp., illus. $85.00.
The story of the first American submachine gun. All models are featured and discussed.

Toys That Shoot and Other Neat Stuff, by James Dundas, Schiffer Books, Atglen, PA, 1999. 112 pp., illustrated. Paper covers. $24.95.
Shooting toys from the twentieth century, especially 1920's to 1960's, in over 420 color photographs of BB guns, cap shooters, marble shooters, squirt guns and more. Complete with a price guide.

The Trapdoor Springfield, by M.D. Waite and B.D. Ernst, The Gun Room Press, Highland Park, NJ, 1983. 250 pp., illus. $39.95.
The first comprehensive book on the famous standard military rifle of the 1873-92 period.

Treasures of the Moscow Kremlin: Arsenal of the Russian Tsars, A Royal Armories and the Moscow Kremlin exhibition. HM Tower of London 13, June 1998 to 11 September, 1998. BAS Printers, Over Wallop, Hampshire, England. xxii plus 192 pp. over 180 color illustrations. Text in English and Russian. $65.00.
For this exhibition catalog each of the 94 objects on display are photographed and described in detail to provide a most informative record of this important exhibition.

U.S. Breech-Loading Rifles and Carbines, Cal. 45, by Gen. John Pitman, Thomas Publications, Gettysburg, PA, 1992. 192 pp., illus. $29.95.
The third volume in the Pitman Notes on U.S. Martial Small Arms and Ammunition, 1776-1933. This book centers on the "Trapdoor Springfield" models.

U.S. Handguns of World War 2: The Secondary Pistols and Revolvers, by Charles W. Pate, Andrew Mowbray, Inc., Lincoln, RI, 1998. 515 pp., illus. $39.00.
This indispensable new book covers all of the American military handguns of World War 2 except for the M1911A1 Colt automatic.

United States Martial Flintlocks, by Robert M. Reilly, Mowbray Publishing Co., Lincoln, RI, 1997. 264 pp., illus. $40.00.
A comprehensive history of American flintlock longarms and handguns (mostly military) c. 1775 to c. 1840.

U.S. Martial Single Shot Pistols, by Daniel D. Hartzler and James B. Whisker, Old Bedford Village Pess, Bedford, PA, 1998. 128 pp., illus. $45.00.
A photographic chronicle of military and semi-martial pistols supplied to the U.S. Government and the several States.

U.S. Military Arms Dates of Manufacture from 1795, by George Madis, David Madis, Dallas, TX, 1989. 64 pp. Soft covers. $6.00.
Lists all U.S. military arms of collector interest alphabetically, covering about 250 models.

U.S. Military Small Arms 1816-1865, by Robert M. Reilly, The Gun Room Press, Highland Park, NJ, 1983. 270 pp., illus. $39.95.
Covers every known type of primary and secondary martial firearms used by Federal forces.

U.S. M1 Carbines: Wartime Production, by Craig Riesch, North Cape Publications, Tustin, CA, 1994. 72 pp., illus. Paper covers. $16.95.
Presents only verifiable and accurate information. Each part of the M1 Carbine is discussed fully in its own section; including markings and finishes.

U.S. Naval Handguns, 1808-1911, by Fredrick R. Winter, Andrew Mowbray Publishers, Lincoln, RI, 1990. 128 pp., illus. $26.00.
The story of U.S. Naval Handguns spans an entire century—included are sections on each of the important naval handguns within the period.

Walther: A German Legend, by Manfred Kersten, Safari Press, Inc., Huntington Beach, CA, 2000. 400 pp., illustrated. $85.00.
This comprehensive book covers, in rich detail, all aspects of the company and its guns, including an illustrious and rich history, the WW2 years, all the pistols (models 1 through 9), the P-38, P-88, the long guns, .22 rifles, centerfires, Wehrmacht guns, and even a gun that could shoot around a corner.

Walther Pistols: Models 1 Through P99, Factory Variations and Copies, by Dieter H. Marschall, Ucross Books, Los Alamos, NM. 2000. 140 pages, with 140 b & w illustrations, index. Paper Covers. $19.95.
This is the English translation, revised and updated, of the highly successful and widely acclaimed German language edition. This book provides the collector with a reference guide and overview of the entire line of the Walther military, police, and self-defense pistols from the very first to the very latest. Models 1-9, PP, PPK, MP, AP, HP, P.38, P1, P4, P38K, P5, P88, P99 and the Manurhin models. Variations, where issued, serial ranges, calibers, marks, proofs, logos, and design aspects in an astonishing quantity and variety are crammed into this very well researched and highly regarded work.

The Walther Handgun Story: A Collector's and Shooter's Guide, by Gene Gangarosa, Steiger Publications, 1999. 300., illustrated. Paper covers. $21.95.
Covers the entire history of the Walther empire. Illustrated with over 250 photos.

Walther P-38 Pistol, by Maj. George Nonte, Desert Publications, Cornville, AZ, 1982. 100 pp., illus. Paper covers. $11.95.
Complete volume on one of the most famous handguns to come out of WWII. All models covered.

Walther Models PP & PPK, 1929-1945 – Volume 1, by James L. Rankin, Coral Gables, FL, 1974. 142 pp., illus. $40.00
Complete coverage on the subject as to finish, proofmarks and Nazi Party inscriptions.

Walther Volume II, Engraved, Presentation and Standard Models, by James L. Rankin, J.L. Rankin, Coral Gables, FL, 1977. 112 pp., illus. $40.00.
The new Walther book on embellished versions and standard models. Has 88 photographs, including many color plates.

Walther, Volume III, 1908-1980, by James L. Rankin, Coral Gables, FL, 1981. 226 pp., illus. $40.00.
Covers all models of Walther handguns from 1908 to date, includes holsters, grips and magazines.

Winchester: An American Legend, by R.L. Wilson, Random House, New York, NY, 1991. 403 pp., illus. $65.00.
The official history of Winchester firearms from 1849 to the present.

Winchester Bolt Action Military & Sporting Rifles 1877 to 1937, by Herbert G. Houze, Andrew Mowbray Publishing, Lincoln, RI, 1998. 295 pp., illus. $45.00.
Winchester was the first American arms maker to commercially manufacture a bolt action repeating rifle, and this book tells the exciting story of these Winchester bolt actions.

The Winchester Book, by George Madis, David Madis Gun Book Distributor, Dallas, TX, 1986. 650 pp., illus. $49.50.
A new, revised 25th anniversary edition of this classic book on Winchester firearms. Complete serial ranges have been added.

Winchester Dates of Manufacture 1849-1984, by George Madis, Art & Reference House, Brownsboro, TX, 1984. 59 pp. $9.95.
A most useful work, compiled from records of the Winchester factory.

Winchester Engraving, by R.L. Wilson, Beinfeld Books, Springs, CA, 1989. 500 pp., illus. $135.00.
A classic reference work of value to all arms collectors.

The Winchester Handbook, by George Madis, Art & Reference House, Lancaster, TX, 1982. 287 pp., illus. $24.95.
The complete line of Winchester guns, with dates of manufacture, serial numbers, etc.

THE ARMS LIBRARY

The Winchester-Lee Rifle, by Eugene Myszkowski, Excalibur Publications, Tucson, AZ 2000. 96 pp., illustrated. Paper Covers. $22.95
 The development of the Lee Straight Pull, the cartridge and the approval for military use. Covers details of the inventor and memorabilia of Winchester-Lee related material.

Winchester Lever Action Repeating Firearms, Vol. 1, The Models of 1866, 1873 and 1876, by Arthur Pirkle, North Cape Publications, Tustin, CA, 1995. 112 pp., illus. Paper covers. $19.95.
 Complete, part-by-part description, including dimensions, finishes, markings and variations throughout the production run of these fine, collectible guns.

Winchester Lever Action Repeating Rifles, Vol. 2, The Models of 1886 and 1892, by Arthur Pirkle, North Cape Publications, Tustin, CA, 1996. 150 pp., illus. Paper covers. $19.95.
 Describes each model on a part-by-part basis by serial number range complete with finishes, markings and changes.

Winchester Lever Action Repeating Rifles, Volume 3, The Model of 1894, by Arthur Pirkle, North Cape Publications, Tustin, CA, 1998. 150 pp., illus. Paper covers. $19.95.
 The first book ever to provide a detailed description of the Model 1894 rifle and carbine.

The Winchester Lever Legacy, by Clyde "Snooky" Williamson, Buffalo Press, Zachary, LA, 1988. 664 pp., illustrated. $75.00
 A book on reloading for the different calibers of the Winchester lever action rifle.

The Winchester Model 94: The First 100 Years, by Robert C. Renneberg, Krause Publications, Iola, WI, 1991. 208 pp., illus. $34.95
 Covers the design and evolution from the early years up to the many different editions that exist today.

Winchester Rarities, by Webster, Krause Publications, Iola, WI, 2000. 208 pp., with over 800 color photos, illus. $49.95.
 This book details the rarest of the rare; the one-of-a-kind items and the advertising pieces from years gone by. With nearly 800 full color photos and detailed pricing provided by experts in the field, this book gives collectors and enthusiasts everything they need.

Winchester Shotguns and Shotshells, by Ronald W. Stadt, Krause Publications, Iola, WI, 1995. 256 pp., illus. $34.95.
 The definitive book on collectible Winchester shotguns and shotshells manufactured through 1961.

The Winchester Single-Shot- Volume 1; A History and Analysis, by John Campbell, Andrew Mowbray, Inc., Lincoln RI, 1995. 272 pp., illus. $55.00.
 Covers every important aspect of this highly-collectible firearm.

The Winchester Single-Shot- Volume 2; Old Secrets and New Discoveries, by John Campbell, Andrew Mowbray, Inc., Lincoln RI, 2000. 280 pp., illus. $55.00.
 An exciting follow-up to the classic first volume.

Winchester Slide-Action Rifles, Volume 1: Model 1890 & 1906, by Ned Schwing, Krause Publications, Iola, WI, 1992. 352 pp., illus. $39.95.
 First book length treatment of models 1890 & 1906 with over 50 charts and tables showing significant new information about caliber style and rarity.

Winchester Slide-Action Rifles, Volume 2: Model 61 & Model 62, by Ned Schwing, Krause Publications, Iola, WI, 1993. 256 pp., illus. $34.95.
 A complete historic look into the Model 61 and the Model 62. These favorite slide-action guns receive a thorough presentation which takes you to the factory to explore receivers, barrels, markings, stocks, stampings and engraving in complete detail.

Winchester's North West Mounted Police Carbines and other Model 1876 Data, by Lewis E. Yearout, The author, Great Falls, MT, 1999. 224 pp., illustrated. Paper covers. $38.00
 An impressive accumulation of the facts on the Model 1876, with particular empasis on those purchased for the North West Mounted Police.

Worldwide Webley and the Harrington and Richardson Connection, by Stephen Cuthbertson, Ballista Publishing and Distributing Ltd., Gabriola Island, Canada, 1999. 259 pp., illus. $50.00
 A masterpiece of scholarship. Over 350 photographs plus 75 original documents, patent drawings, and advertisements accompany the text.

GENERAL

Action Shooting: Cowboy Style, by John Taffin, Krause Publications, Iola, WI, 1999. 320 pp., illustrated. $39.95.
 Details on the guns and ammunition. Explanations of the rules used for many events. The essential cowboy wardrobe.

Advanced Muzzleloader's Guide, by Toby Bridges, Stoeger Publishing Co., So. Hackensack, NJ, 1985. 256 pp., illus. Paper covers. $14.95.
 The complete guide to muzzle-loading rifles, pistols and shotguns—flintlock and percussion.

Aids to Musketry for Officers & NCOs, by Capt. B.J. Friend, Excalibur Publications, Latham, NY, 1996. 40 pp., illus. Paper covers. $7.95.
 A facsimile edition of a pre-WWI British manual filled with useful information for training the common soldier.

Air Gun Digest, 3rd Edition, by J.I. Galan, DBI Books, a division of Krause Publications, Iola, WI, 1995. 258 pp., illus. Paper covers. $19.95
 Everything from A to Z on air gun history, trends and technology.

American and Imported Arms, Ammunition and Shooting Accessories, Catalog No. 18 of the Shooter's Bible, Stoeger, Inc., reprinted by Fayette Arsenal, Fayetteville, NC, 1988. 142 pp., illus. Paper covers. $10.95.
 A facsimile reprint of the 1932 Stoeger's Shooter's Bible.

America's Great Gunmakers, by Wayne van Zwoll, Stoeger Publishing Co., So. Hackensack, NJ, 1992. 288 pp., illus. Paper covers. $16.95.
 This book traces in great detail the evolution of guns and ammunition in America and the men who formed the companies that produced them.

Ammunition: Small Arms, Grenades and Projected Munitions, by Ian V. Hogg, Greenhill Books, London, England, 1998. 144 pp., illustrated. $22.95.
 The best concise guide to modern ammunition. Wide-ranging and international coverage. Detailed specifications and illustrations.

Armed and Female, by Paxton Quigley, E.P. Dutton, New York, NY, 1989. 237 pp., illus. $16.95.
 The first complete book on one of the hottest subjects in the media today, the arming of the American woman.

Arming the Glorious Cause: Weapons of the Second War for Independence, by James B. Whisker, Daniel D. Hartzler and Larry W. Yantz, R & R Books, Livonia, NY, 1998. 175 pp., illustrated. $45.00.
 A photographic study of Confederate weapons.

Arms and Armour in Antiquity and the Middle Ages, by Charles Boutell, Stackpole Books, Mechanicsburg, PA, 1996. 352 pp., illus. $22.95.
 Detailed descriptions of arms and armor, the development of tactics and the outcome of specific battles.

Arms & Armor in the Art Institute of Chicago, by Walter J. Karcheski, Jr., Bulfinch Press, Boston, MA, 1995. 128 pp., illus. $35.00.
 Now, for the first time, the Art Institute of Chicago's arms and armor collection is presented in the visual delight of 103 color illustrations.

Arms for the Nation: Springfield Longarms, edited by David C. Clark, Scott A. Duff, Export, PA, 1994. 73 pp., illus. Paper covers. $9.95.
 A brief history of the Springfield Armory and the arms made there.

Arsenal of Freedom, The Springfield Armory, 1890-1948: A Year-by-Year Account Drawn from Official Records, compiled and edited by Lt. Col. William S. Brophy, USAR Ret., Andrew Mowbray, Inc., Lincoln, RI, 1991. 400 pp., illus. Soft covers. $29.95.
 A "must buy" for all students of American military weapons, equipment and accoutrements.

Assault Pistols, Rifles and Submachine Guns, by Duncan Long, Paladin Press, Boulder, CO, 1997, 8 1/2 x 11, soft cover, photos, illus. 152 pp. $21.95
 This book offers up-to-date, practical information on how to operate and field-strip modern military, police and civilian combat weapons. Covers new developments and trends such as the use of fiber optics, liquid-recoil systems and lessening of barrel length are covered. Troubleshooting procedures, ballistic tables and a list of manufacturers and distributors are also included.

Assault Weapons, 5th Edition, The Gun Digest Book of, edited by Jack Lewis and David E. Steele, DBI Books, a division of Krause Publications, Iola, WI, 2000. 256 pp., illustrated. Paper covers. $21.95.
 This is the latest word on true assault weaponry in use today by international military and law enforcement organizations.

The Belgian Rattlesnake: The Lewis Automatic Machine Gun, by William M. Easterly, Collector Grade Publications, Inc., Cobourg, Ont. Canada, 1998. 542 pp., illus. $79.95.
 A social and technical biography of the Lewis automatic machine gun and its inventors.

The Big Guns: Civil War Siege, Seacoast, and Naval Cannon, by Edwin Olmstead, Wayne E. Stark and Spencer C. Tucker, Museum Restoration Service, Bloomfield, Ontario, Canada, 1997. 360 pp., illus. $80.00.
 This book is designed to identify and record the heavy guns available to both sides during the Civil War.

Blackpowder Loading Manual, 3rd Edition, by Sam Fadala, DBI Books, a division of Krause Publications, Iola, WI, 1995. 368 pp., illus. Paper covers. $20.95.
 Revised and expanded edition of this landmark blackpowder loading book. Covers hundreds of loads for most of the popular blackpowder rifles, handguns and shotguns.

Bolt Action Rifles, 3rd Edition, by Frank de Haas, DBI Books, a division of Krause Publications, Iola, WI, 1995. 528 pp., illus. Paper covers. $24.95.
 A revised edition of the most definitive work on all major bolt-action rifle designs.

The Book of the Crossbow, by Sir Ralph Payne-Gallwey, Dover Publications, Mineola, NY, 1996. 416 pp., illus. Paper covers. $14.95.
 Unabridged republication of the scarce 1907 London edition of the book on one of the most devastating hand weapons of the Middle Ages.

Bows and Arrows of the Native Americans, by Jim Hamm, Lyons & Burford Publishers, New York, NY, 1991. 156 pp., illus. $19.95.
 A complete step-by-step guide to wooden bows, sinew-backed bows, composite bows, strings, arrows and quivers.

British Small Arms of World War 2, by Ian D. Skennerton, I.D.S.A. Books, Piqua, OH, 1988. 110 pp., 37 illus. $25.00.

"Carbine," the Story of David Marshall Williams, by Ross E. Beard, Jr. Phillips Publications, Williamstown, NJ, 1999. 225 pp., illus. $29.95.
 The story of the firearms genius, David Marshall "Carbine" Williams. From prison to the pinnacles of fame, the tale of this North Carolinian is inspiring. The author details many of Williams' firearms inventions and developments.

Combat Handgunnery, 4th Edition, The Gun Digest Book of, by Chuck Taylor, DBI Books, a division of Krause Publications, Iola, WI, 1997. 256 pp., illus. Paper covers. $18.95.
 This edition looks at real world combat handgunnery from three different perspectives—military, police and civilian.

REFERENCE

The Complete Blackpowder Handbook, 3rd Edition, by Sam Fadala, DBI Books, a division of Krause Publications, Iola, WI, 1997. 400 pp., illus. Paper covers. $21.95.

Expanded and completely rewritten edition of the definitive book on the subject of blackpowder.

The Complete Guide to Game Care and Cookery, 3rd Edition, by Sam Fadala, DBI Books, a division of Krause Publications, Iola, WI, 1994. 320 pp., illus. Paper covers. $18.95.

Over 500 photos illustrating the care of wild game in the field and at home with a separate recipe section providing over 400 tested recipes.

The Complete .50-caliber Sniper Course, by Dean Michaelis, Paladin Press, Boulder, CO, 2000. 576 pp, illustrated. $60.00

The history from German Mauser T-Gewehr of World War 1 to the Soviet PTRD and beyond. Includes the author's Program of Instruction for Special Operations Hard-Target Interdiction Course.

Complete Guide to Guns & Shooting, by John Malloy, DBI Books, a division of Krause Publications, Iola, WI, 1995. 256 pp., illus. Paper covers. $18.95.

What every shooter and gun owner should know about firearms, ammunition, shooting techniques, safety, collecting and much more.

Cowboy Action Shooting, by Charly Gullett, Wolfe Publishing Co., Prescott, AZ, 1995. 400 pp., illus. Paper covers. $24.50.

The fast growing of the shooting sports is comprehensively covered in this text— the guns, loads, tactics and the fun and flavor of this Old West era competition.

Crossbows, edited by Roger Combs, DBI Books, a division of Krause Publications, Iola, WI, 1986. 192 pp., illus. Paper covers. $15.95.

Complete, up-to-date coverage of the hottest bow going—and the most controversial.

Custom Firearms Engraving, by Tom Turpin, Krause Publications, Iola, WI, 1999. 208 pp., illustrated. $49.95.

Provides a broad and comprehensive look at the world of firearms engraving. The exquisite styles of more than 75 master engravers are shown on beautiful examples of handguns, rifles, shotguns, and other firearms, as well as knives.

Dead On, by Tony Noblitt and Warren Gabrilska, Paladin Press, Boulder, CO, 1998. 176 pp., illustrated. Paper covers. $22.00

The long-range marksman's guide to extreme accuracy.

Death from Above: The German FG42 Paratrooper Rifle, by Thomas B. Dugelby and R. Blake Stevens, Collector Grade Publications, Toronto, Canada, 1990. 147 pp., illus. $39.95.

The first comprehensive study of all seven models of the FG42.

Early American Flintlocks, by Daniel D. Hartzler and James B. Whisker, Bedford Valley Press, Bedford, PA 2000. 192 pp., Illustrated.

Covers early Colonial Guns, New England Guns, Pennsylvania Guns and Souther Guns.

Encyclopedia of Modern Firearms, Vol. 1, compiled and publ. by Bob Brownell, Montezuma, IA, 1959. 1057 pp. plus index, illus. $70.00. Dist. By Bob Brownell, Montezuma, IA 50171.

Massive accumulation of basic information of nearly all modern arms pertaining to "parts and assembly." Replete with arms photographs, exploded drawings, manufacturers' lists of parts, etc.

Encyclopedia of Native American Bows, Arrows and Quivers, by Steve Allely and Jim Hamm, The Lyons Press, N.Y., 1999. 160 pp., illustrated. $29.95.

A landmark book for anyone interested in archery history, or Native Americans.

The Exercise of Armes, by Jacob de Gheyn, edited and with an introduction by Bas Kist, Dover Publications, Inc., Mineola, NY, 1999. 144 pp., illustrated. Paper covers. $12.95.

Republications of all 117 engravings from the 1607 classic military manual. A meticulously accurate portrait of uniforms and weapons of the 17th century Netherlands.

Exploded Long Gun Drawings, The Gun Digest Book of, edited by Harold A. Murtz, DBI Books, a division of Krause Publications, Iola, WI, 512 pp., illus. Paper covers. $20.95.

Containing almost 500 rifle and shotgun exploded drawings.

Fighting Iron; A Metals Handbook for Arms Collectors, by Art Gogan, Mowbray Publishers, Inc., Lincoln, RI, 1999. 176 pp., illustrated. $28.00.

A guide that is easy to use, explains things in simple English and covers all of the different historical periods that we are interested in.

The Fighting Submachine Gun, Machine Pistol, and Shotgun, a Hands-On Evaluation, by Timothy J. Mullin, Paladin Press, Boulder, CO, 1999. 224 pp., illustrated. Paper covers. $35.00.

An invaluable reference for military, police and civilian shooters who may someday need to know how a specific weapon actually performs when the targets are shooting back and the margin of errors is measured in lives lost.

Fireworks: A Gunsight Anthology, by Jeff Cooper, Paladin Press, Boulder, CO, 1998. 192 pp., illus. Paper cover. $27.00

A collection of wild, hilarious, shocking and always meaningful tales from the remarkable life of an American firearms legend.

Frank Pachmayr: The Story of America's Master Gunsmith and his Guns, by John Lachuk, Safari Press, Huntington Beach, CA, 1996. 254 pp., illus. First edition, limited, signed and slipcased. $85.00; Second printing trade edition. $50.00.

The colorful and historically significant biography of Frank A. Pachmayr, America's own gunsmith emeritus.

From a Stranger's Doorstep to the Kremlin Gate, by Mikhail Kalashnikov, Ironside International Publishers, Inc., Alexandria, VA, 1999. 460 pp., illustrated. $34.95.

A biography of the most influential rifle designer of the 20th century. His AK-47 assault rifle has become the most widely used (and copied) assault rifle of this century.

The Frontier Rifleman, by H.B. LaCrosse Jr., Pioneer Press, Union City, TN, 1989. 183 pp., illus. Soft covers. $17.50.

The Frontier rifleman's clothing and equipment during the era of the American Revolution, 1760-1800.

The Gatling Gun: 19th Century Machine Gun to 21st Century Vulcan, by Joseph Berk, Paladin Press, Boulder, CO, 1991. 136 pp., illus. $34.95.

Here is the fascinating on-going story of a truly timeless weapon, from its beginnings during the Civil War to its current role as a state-of-the-art modern combat system.

German Artillery of World War Two, by Ian V. Hogg, Stackpole Books, Mechanicsburg, PA, 1997. 304 pp., illus. $44.95.

Complete details of German artillery use in WWII.

Grand Old Lady of No Man's Land: The Vickers Machine Gun, by Dolf L. Goldsmith, Collector Grade Publications, Cobourg, Canada, 1994. 600 pp., illus. $79.95.

Goldsmith brings his years of experience as a U.S. Army armourer, machine gun collector and shooter to bear on the Vickers, in a book sure to become a classic in its field.

The Grenade Recognition Manual, Volume 1, U.S. Grenades & Accessories, by Darryl W. Lynn, Service Publications, Ottawa, Canada, 1998. 112 pp., illus. Paper covers. $29.95.

This new book examines the hand grenades of the United States beginning with the hand grenades of the U.S. Civil War and continues through to the present.

The Grenade Recognition Manual, Vol. 2, British and Commonwealth Grenades and Accessories, by Darryl W. Lynn, Printed by the Author, Ottawa, Canada, 2001. 201 pp., illustrated with over 200 photos and drawings. Paper covers. $29.95.

Covers British, Australian, and Canadian Grenades. It has the complete British Numbered series, most of the L series as well as the Australian and Canadian grenades in use. Also covers Launchers, fuzes and lighters, launching cartridges, fillings, and markings.

Gun Digest Treasury, 7th Edition, edited by Harold A. Murtz, DBI Books, a division of Krause Publications, Iola, WI, 1994. 320 pp., illus. Paper covers. $17.95.

A collection of some of the most interesting articles which have appeared in Gun Digest over its first 45 years.

Gun Digest 2002, 56th Edition, edited by Ken Ramage, DBI Books a division of Krause Publications, Iola, WI, 2001. 544 pp., illustrated. Paper covers. $24.95.

This all new 56th edition continues the editorial excellence, quality, content and comprehensive cataloguing that firearms enthusiasts have come to know and expect. The most kept gun book in the world for the last half century.

Gun Engraving, by C. Austyn, Safari Press Publication, Huntington Beach, CA, 1998. 128 pp., plus 24 pages of color photos. $50.00.

A well-illustrated book on fine English and European gun engravers. Includes a fantastic pictorial section that lists types of engravings and prices.

Gun Notes, Volume 1, by Elmer Keith, Safari Press, Huntington Beach, CA, 1995. 219 pp., illustrated Limited Edition, Slipcased. $75.00

A collection of Elmer Keith's most interesting columns and feature stories that appeared in "Guns & Ammo" magazine from 1961 to the late 1970's.

Gun Notes, Volume 2, by Elmer Keith, Safari Press, Huntington Beach, CA, 1997. 292 pp., illus. Limited 1st edition, numbered and signed by Keith's son. Slipcased. $75.00. Trade edition. $35.00.

Covers articles from Keith's monthly column in "Guns & Ammo" magazine during the period from 1971 through Keith's passing in 1982.

Gun Talk, edited by Dave Moreton, Winchester Press, Piscataway, NJ, 1973. 256 pp., illus. $9.95.

A treasury of original writing by the top gun writers and editors in America. Practical advice about every aspect of the shooting sports.

The Gun That Made the Twenties Roar, by Wm. J. Helmer, rev. and enlarged by George C. Nonte, Jr., The Gun Room Press, Highland Park, NJ, 1977. Over 300 pp., illus. $24.95.

Historical account of John T. Thompson and his invention, the infamous "Tommy Gun."

Gun Trader's Guide, 23rd Edition, published by Stoeger Publishing Co., Wayne, NJ, 1999. 592 pp., illus. Paper covers. $23.95.

Complete specifications and current prices for used guns. Prices of over 5,000 handguns, rifles and shotguns both foreign and domestic.

Gun Writers of Yesteryear, compiled by James Foral, Wolfe Publishing Co., Prescott, AZ, 1993. 449 pp. $35.00.

Here, from the pre-American rifleman days of 1898-1920, are collected some 80 articles by 34 writers from eight magazines.

The Gunfighter, Man or Myth? by Joseph G. Rosa, Oklahoma Press, Norman, OK, 1969. 229 pp., illus. (including weapons). Paper covers. $14.95.

A well-documented work on gunfights and gunfighters of the West and elsewhere. Great treat for all gunfighter buffs.

Gunfitting: The Quest for Perfection, by Michael Yardley, Safari Press, Huntington Beach, CA, 1995. 128 pp., illus. $24.95.

The author, a very experienced shooting instructor, examines gun stocks and gunfitting in depth.

THE ARMS LIBRARY

Guns Illustrated 2002, 3rd Edition, edited by Ken Ramage, DBI Books a division of Krause Publications, Iola, WI, 1999. 352 pp., illustrated. Paper covers. $22.95.

Highly informative, technical articles on a wide range of shooting topics by some of the top writers in the industry. A catalog section lists more than 3,000 firearms currently manufactured in or imported to the U.S.

Guns & Shooting: A Selected Bibliography, by Ray Riling, Ray Riling Arms Books Co., Phila., PA, 1982. 434 pp., illus. Limited, numbered edition. $75.

A limited edition of this superb bibliographical work, the only modern listing of books devoted to guns and shooting.

Guns, Bullets, and Gunfighters, by Jim Cirillo, Paladin Press, Boulder, CO, 1996. 119 pp., illus. Paper covers. $16.00.

Lessons and tales from a modern-day gunfighter.

Guns, Loads, and Hunting Tips, by Bob Hagel, Wolfe Publishing Co., Prescott, AZ, 1986. 509 pp., illus. $19.95.

A large hardcover book packed with shooting, hunting and handloading wisdom.

Handgun Digest, 3rd Edition, edited by Chris Christian, DBI Books, a division of Krause Publications, Iola, WI, 1995. 256 pp., illus. Paper covers. $16.95.

Full coverage of all aspects of handguns and handgunning from a highly readable and knowledgeable author.

Hidden in Plain Sight, "A Practical Guide to Concealed Handgun Carry" (Revised 2nd Edition), by Trey Bloodworth and Mike Raley, Paladin Press, Boulder, CO, 1997, 5 1/2 x 8 1/2, softcover, photos, 176 pp. $20.00

Concerned with how to comfortably, discreetly and safely exercise the privileges granted by a CCW permit? This invaluable guide offers the latest advice on what to look for when choosing a CCW, how to dress for comfortable, effective concealed carry, traditional and more unconventional carry modes, accessory holsters, customized clothing and accessories, accessibility data based on draw-time comparisons and new holsters on the market. Includes 40 new manufacturer listings.

HK Assault Rifle Systems, by Duncan Long, Paladin Press, Boulder, CO, 1995. 110 pp., illus. Paper covers. $27.95.

The little known history behind this fascinating family of weapons tracing its beginnings from the ashes of World War Two to the present time.

The Hunter's Table, by Terry Libby/Recipes of Chef Richard Blondin, Countrysport Press, Selma, AL, 1999. 230 pp. $30.00.

The Countrysport book of wild game guisine.

I Remember Skeeter, compiled by Sally Jim Skelton, Wolfe Publishing Co., Prescott, AZ, 1998. 401 pp., illus. Paper covers. $19.95.

A collection of some of the beloved storyteller's famous works interspersed with anecdotes and tales from the people who knew best.

In The Line of Fire, "A Working Cop's Guide to Pistol Craft", by Michael E. Conti, Paladin Press, Boulder, CO, 1997, soft cover, photos, illus., 184 pp. $30.00

As a working cop, you want to end your patrol in the same condition you began: alive and uninjured. Improve your odds by reading and mastering the information in this book on pistol selection, stopping power, combat reloading, stoppages, carrying devices, stances, grips and Conti's "secrets" to accurate shooting.

Joe Rychertinik Reflects on Guns, Hunting, and Days Gone By, by Joe Rychertinik, Precision Shooting, Inc., Manchester, CT, 1999. 281 pp., illustrated. Paper covers. $16.95.

Thirty articles by a master story-teller.

Kill or Get Killed, by Col. Rex Applegate, Paladin Press, Boulder, CO, 1996. 400 pp., illus. $39.95.

The best and longest-selling book on close combat in history.

Larrey: Surgeon to Napoleon's Imperial Guard, by Robert G. Richardson, Quiller Press, London, 2000. 269 pp., illus. B & W photos, maps and drawings. $23.95

Not a book for the squeamish, but one full of interest, splendidly researched, bringing both the character of the Napoleonic wars and Larrey himself vividly to life. Authenticity of detail is preserved throughout.

The Long-Range War: Sniping in Vietnam, by Peter R. Senich, Paladin Press, Boulder, CO, 1994. 280 pp., illus. $49.95.

The most complete report on Vietnam-era sniping ever documented.

Manual for H&R Reising Submachine Gun and Semi-Auto Rifle, edited by George P. Dillman, Desert Publications, El Dorado, AZ, 1994. 81 pp., illus. Paper covers. $12.95.

A reprint of the Harrington & Richardson 1943 factory manual and the rare military manual on the H&R submachine gun and semi-auto rifle.

The Manufacture of Gunflints, by Sydney B.J. Skertchly, facsimile reprint with new introduction by Seymour de Lotbiniere, Museum Restoration Service, Ontario, Canada, 1984. 90 pp., illus. $24.50.

Limited edition reprinting of the very scarce London edition of 1879.

Master Tips, by J. Winokur, Potshot Press, Pacific Palisades, CA, 1985. 96 pp., illus. Paper covers. $11.95.

Basics of practical shooting.

The Military and Police Sniper, by Mike R. Lau, Precision Shooting, Inc., Manchester, CT, 1998. 352 pp., illustrated. Paper covers. $44.95.

Advanced precision shooting for combat and law enforcement.

Military Rifle & Machine Gun Cartridges, by Jean Huon, Paladin Press, Boulder, CO, 1990. 392 pp., illus. $34.95.

Describes the primary types of military cartridges and their principal loadings, as well as their characteristics, origin and use.

Military Small Arms of the 20th Century, 7th Edition, by Ian V. Hogg and John Weeks, DBI Books, a division of Krause Publications, Iola, WI, 2000. 416 pp., illustrated. Paper covers. $24.95.

Cover small arms of 46 countries. Over 800 photographs and illustrations.

Modern Custom Guns, Walnut, Steel, and Uncommon Artistry, by Tom Turpin, Krause Publications, Iola, WI, 1997. 206 pp., illus. $49.95.

From exquisite engraving to breathtaking exotic woods, the mystique of today's custom guns is expertly detailed in word and awe-inspiring color photos of rifles, shotguns and handguns.

Modern Guns Identification & Values, 13th Edition, by Russell & Steve Quertermous, Collector Books, Paducah, KY, 1999. 516 pp., illus. Paper covers. $12.95.

A standard reference for over 20 years. Over 1,800 illustrations of over 2,500 models with their current values.

Modern Law Enforcement Weapons & Tactics, 2nd Edition, by Tom Ferguson, DBI Books, a division of Krause Publications, Iola, WI, 1991. 256 pp., illus. Paper covers. $18.95.

An in-depth look at the weapons and equipment used by law enforcement agencies of today.

Modern Machine Guns, by John Walter, Stackpole Books, Inc. Mechanicsburg, PA, 2000. 144 pp., with 146 illustrations. $22.95.

A compact and authoritative guide to post-war machine-guns. A gun-by-gun directory identifying individual variants and types including detailed evaluations and technical data.

Modern Sporting Guns, by Christopher Austyn, Safari Press, Huntington Beach, CA, 1994. 128 pp., illus. $40.00.

A discussion of the "best" English guns; round action, over-and-under, boxlocks, hammer guns, bolt action and double rifles as well as accessories.

The More Complete Cannoneer, by M.C. Switlik, Museum & Collectors Specialties Co., Monroe, MI, 1990. 199 pp., illus. $19.95.

Compiled agreeably to the regulations for the U.S. War Department, 1861, and containing current observations on the use of antique cannons.

The MP-40 Machine Gun, Desert Publications, El Dorado, AZ, 1995. 32 pp., illus. Paper covers. $11.95.

A reprint of the hard-to-find operating and maintenance manual for one of the most famous machine guns of World War II.

Naval Percussion Locks and Primers, by Lt. J. A. Dahlgren, Museum Restoration Service, Bloomfield, Canada, 1996. 140 pp., illus. $35.00

First published as an Ordnance Memoranda in 1853, this is the finest existing study of percussion locks and primers origin and development.

The Official Soviet AKM Manual, translated by Maj. James F. Gebhardt (Ret.), Paladin Press, Boulder, CO, 1999. 120 pp., illustrated. Paper covers. $18.00.

This official military manual, available in English for the first time, was originally published by the Soviet Ministry of Defence. Covers the history, function, maintenance, assembly and disassembly, etc. of the 7.62mm AKM assault rifle.

The One-Round War: U.S.M.C. Scout-Snipers in Vietnam, by Peter Senich, Paladin Press, Boulder, CO, 1996. 384 pp., illus. Paper covers $59.95.

Sniping in Vietnam focusing specifically on the Marine Corps program.

Pin Shooting: A Complete Guide, by Mitchell A. Ota, Wolfe Publishing Co., Prescott, AZ, 1992. 145 pp., illus. Paper covers. $14.95.

Traces the sport from its humble origins to today's thoroughly enjoyable social event, including the mammoth eight-day Second Chance Pin Shoot in Michigan.

Powder and Ball Small Arms, by Martin Pegler, Windrow & Greene Publishing, London, 1998. 128 pp., illustrated with 200 color photos. $39.95.

Part of the new "Live Firing Classic Weapons" series. Full-color photos of experienced shooters dressed in authentic costumes handling, loading and firing historic weapons.

Principles of Personal Defense, by Jeff Cooper, Paladin Press, Boulder, CO, 1999. 56 pp., illustrated. Paper covers. $14.00.

This revised edition of Jeff Cooper's classic on personal defense offers great new illustrations and a new preface while retaining the timeliness theory of individual defense behavior presented in the original book.

E.C. Prudhomme, Master Gun Engraver, A Retrospective Exhibition: 1946-1973, intro. by John T. Amber, The R. W. Norton Art Gallery, Shreveport, LA, 1973. 32 pp., illus. Paper covers. $9.95.

Examples of master gun engravings by Jack Prudhomme.

The Quotable Hunter, edited by Jay Cassell and Peter Fiduccia, The lyons Press, N.Y., 1999. 224 pp., illustrated. $20.00.

This collection of more than three hundred memorable quotes from hunters through the ages captures the essence of the sport, with all its joys idiosyncrasies, and challenges.

A Rifleman Went to War, by H. W. McBride, Lancer Militaria, Mt. Ida, AR, 1987. 398 pp., illus. $29.95.

The classic account of practical marksmanship on the battlefields of World War I.

Sharpshooting for Sport and War, by W.W. Greener, Wolfe Publishing Co., Prescott, AZ, 1995. 192 pp., illus. $30.00.

This classic reprint explores the *first* expanding bullet; service rifles; shooting positions; trajectories; recoil; external ballistics; and other valuable information.

The Shooter's Bible 2002, No. 93, edited by William S. Jarrett, Stoeger Publishing Co., Wayne, NJ, 2001. 576 pp., illustrated. Paper covers. $23.95.

Over 3,000 firearms currently offered by major American and foreign gunmakers. Represented are handguns, rifles, shotguns and black powder arms with complete specifications and retail prices.

Shooting To Live, by Capt. W. E. Fairbairn & Capt. E. A. Sykes, Paladin Press, Boulder, CO, 1997, 4 1/2 x 7, soft cover, illus., 112 pp. $14.00

Shooting to Live is the product of Fairbairn's and Sykes' practical experience with the handgun. Hundreds of incidents provided the basis for the first true book on life-or-death shootouts with the pistol. Shooting to Live teaches all concepts, considerations and applications of combat pistol craft.

REFERENCE

THE ARMS LIBRARY

Shooting Sixguns of the Old West, by Mike Venturino, MLV Enterprises, Livingston, MT, 1997. 221 pp., illus. Paper covers. $26.50.
A comprehensive look at the guns of the early West: Colts, Smith & Wesson and Remingtons, plus blackpowder and reloading specs.

Sniper Training, FM 23-10, Reprint of the U.S. Army field manual of August, 1994, Paladin Press, Boulder, CO, 1995. 352pp., illus. Paper covers. $30.00
The most up-to-date U.S. military sniping information and doctrine.

Sniping in France, by Major H. Hesketh-Prichard, Lancer Militaria, Mt. Ida, AR, 1993. 224 pp., illus. $24.95.
The author was a well-known British adventurer and big game hunter. He was called upon in the early days of "The Great War" to develop a program to offset an initial German advantage in sniping. How the British forces came to overcome this advantage.

Special Warfare: Special Weapons, by Kevin Dockery, Emperor's Press, Chicago, IL, 1997. 192 pp., illus. $29.95.
The arms and equipment of the UDT and SEALS from 1943 to the present.

Sporting Collectibles, by Dr. Stephen R. Irwin, Stoeger Publishing Co., Wayne, NJ, 1997. 256 pp., illus. Paper covers. $19.95.
A must book for serious collectors and admirers of sporting collectibles.

The Sporting Craftsmen: A Complete Guide to Contemporary Makers of Custom-Built Sporting Equipment, by Art Carter, Countrysport Press, Traverse City, MI, 1994. 240 pp., illus. $35.00.
Profiles leading makers of centerfire rifles; muzzleloading rifles; bamboo fly rods; fly reels; flies; waterfowl calls; decoys; handmade knives; and traditional longbows and recurves.

Sporting Rifle Takedown & Reassembly Guide, 2nd Edition, by J.B. Wood, DBI Books, a division of Krause Publications, Iola, WI, 1997. 480 pp., illus. $19.95.
An updated edition of the reference guide for anyone who wants to properly care for their sporting rifle. (Available September 1997)

2001 Standard Catalog of Firearms, the Collector's Price & Reference Guide, 11th Edition, by Ned Schwing, Krause Publications, Iola, WI, 2000. 1,248 pp., illus. Paper covers. $32.95.
Packed with more than 80,000 real world prices with more than 5,000 photos. Easy to use master index listing every firearm model.

The Street Smart Gun Book, by John Farnam, Police Bookshelf, Concord, NH, 1986. 45 pp., illus. Paper covers. $11.95.
Weapon selection, defensive shooting techniques, and gunfight-winning tactics from one of the world's leading authorities.

Stress Fire, Vol. 1: Stress Fighting for Police, by Massad Ayoob, Police Bookshelf, Concord, NH, 1984. 149 pp., illus. Paper covers. $9.95.
Gunfighting for police, advanced tactics and techniques.

Survival Guns, by Mel Tappan, Desert Publications, El Dorado, AZ, 1993. 456 pp., illus. Paper covers. $21.95.
Discusses in a frank and forthright manner which handguns, rifles and shotguns to buy for personal defense and securing food, and the ones to avoid.

The Tactical Advantage, by Gabriel Suarez, Paladin Press, Boulder, CO, 1998. 216 pp., illustrated. Paper covers. $22.00.
Learn combat tactics that have been tested in the world's toughest schools.

Tactical Marksman, by Dave M. Lauch, Paladin Press, Boulder, CO, 1996. 165 pp., illus. Paper covers. $35.00.
A complete training manual for police and practical shooters.

Thompson Guns 1921-1945, Anubis Press, Houston, TX, 1980. 215 pp., illus. Paper covers. $15.95.
Facsimile reprinting of five complete manuals on the Thompson submachine gun.

To Ride, Shoot Straight, and Speak the Truth, by Jeff Cooper, Paladin Press, Boulder, CO, 1997, 5 1/2 x 8 1/2, soft-cover, illus., 384 pp. $32.00
Combat mind-set, proper sighting, tactical residential architecture, nuclear war - these are some of the many subjects explored by Jeff Cooper in this illustrated anthology. The author discusses various arms, fighting skills and the importance of knowing how to defend oneself, and one's honor, in our rapidly changing world.

Trailriders Guide to Cowboy Action Shooting, by James W. Barnard, Pioneer Press, Union City, TN, 1998. 134 pp., plus 91 photos, drawings and charts. Paper covers. $24.95.
Covers the complete spectrum of this shooting discipline, from how to dress to authentic leather goods, which guns are legal, calibers, loads and ballistics.

The Ultimate Sniper, by Major John L. Plaster, Paladin Press, Boulder, CO, 1994. 464 pp., illus. Paper covers. $42.95.
An advanced training manual for military and police snipers.

Unrepentant Sinner, by Col. Charles Askins, Paladin Press, Boulder, CO, 2000. 322 pp., illustrated. $29.95.
The autobiography of Colonel Charles Askins.

U.S. Marine Corp Rifle and Pistol Marksmanship, 1935, reprinting of a government publication, Lancer Militaria, Mt. Ida, AR, 1991. 99 pp., illus. Paper covers. $11.95.
The old corps method of precision shooting.

U.S. Marine Corps Scout/Sniper Training Manual, Lancer Militaria, Mt. Ida, AR, 1989. Soft covers. $19.95.
Reprint of the original sniper training manual used by the Marksmanship Training Unit of the Marine Corps Development and Education Command in Quantico, Virginia.

U.S. Marine Corps Scout-Sniper, World War II and Korea, by Peter R. Senich, Paladin Press, Boulder, CO, 1994. 236 pp., illus. $44.95.
The most thorough and accurate account ever printed on the training, equipment and combat experiences of the U.S. Marine Corps Scout-Snipers.

U.S. Marine Corps Sniping, Lancer Militaria, Mt. Ida, AR, 1989. Irregular pagination. Soft covers. $17.95.
A reprint of the official Marine Corps FMFM1-3B.

Weapons of the Waffen-SS, by Bruce Quarrie, Sterling Publishing Co., Inc., 1991. 168 pp., illus. $24.95.
An in-depth look at the weapons that made Hitler's Waffen-SS the fearsome fighting machine it was.

Weatherby: The Man, The Gun, The Legend, by Grits and Tom Gresham, Cane River Publishing Co., Natchitoches, LA, 1992. 290 pp., illus. $24.95.
A fascinating look at the life of the man who changed the course of firearms development in America.

The Winchester Era, by David Madis, Art & Reference House, Brownsville, TX, 1984. 100 pp., illus. $19.95.
Story of the Winchester company, management, employees, etc.

Winchester Repeating Arms Company by Herbert Houze, Krause Publications, Iola, WI. 512 pp., illus. $50.00.

With British Snipers to the Reich, by Capt. C. Shore, Lander Militaria, Mt. Ida, AR, 1988. 420 pp., illus. $29.95.
One of the greatest books ever written on the art of combat sniping.

The World's Machine Pistols and Submachine Guns - Vol. 2a 1964 to 1980, by Nelson & Musgrave, Ironside International, Alexandria, VA, 2000. 673 pages, illustrated. $59.95
Containing data, history and photographs of over 200 weapons. With a special section covering shoulder stocked automatic pistols, 100 additional photos.

The World's Submachine Guns - Vol. 1 1918 to 1963, by Nelson & Musgrave, Ironside International, Alexandria, VA, 2001. 673 pages, illustrated. $59.95.
A revised edition covering much new material that has come to light since the book was originally printed in 1963.

The World's Sniping Rifles, by Ian V. Hogg, Paladin Press, Boulder, CO, 1998. 144 pp., illustrated. $22.95.
A detailed manual with descriptions and illustrations of more than 50 high-precision rifles from 14 countries and a complete analysis of sights and systems.

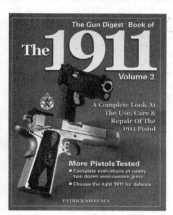

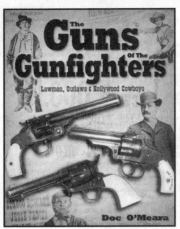

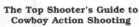

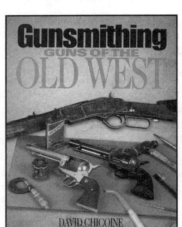